7-97

Barry Goldwater

Robert Alan Goldberg

Yale University Press   New Haven and London

Barry Goldwater

Title page photo: Barry Goldwater in the 1980s. (Courtesy of Joanne Goldwater)

Designed by James J. Johnson and set in Caledonia Roman by Marathon Typography Services, Inc., Durham, North Carolina.
Printed in the United States of America by R. R. Donnelley & Sons, Harrisonburg, Virginia.

A catalogue record for this book is available from the British Library.

The paper in this book meets the guidelines for permanence and durability of the Committee on Production Guidelines for Book Longevity of the Council on Library Resources.

10 9 8 7 6 5 4 3 2 1

Library of Congress Cataloging-in-Publication Data

Goldberg, Robert Alan, 1949–
    Barry Goldwater / Robert Alan Goldberg.
        p. cm.
    Includes bibliographical references and index.
    ISBN 0-300-06261-3

    1. Goldwater, Barry M. (Barry Morris), 1909–   . 2. Conservatism—United States—History—20th century. 3. Legislators—United States—Biography. 4. United States. Congress. Senate—Biography. 5. United States—Politics and government—1945–1989.
I. Title.
E748.G64G65   1995
973.92'092—dc20
[B]   94-46848

For my father and mother

Contents

Part III: From Martyrdom to Canonization

Preface

As public opinion polls show, America's allegiance to its leaders is quick-silver, changing from week to week. And leaders, once out of office, do not easily retain honor. Like prophets in their own land, they not only see their constituency withdraw but also often become embarrassing relics out of place and time. Such has been the inheritance of such presidents as Woodrow Wilson, Calvin Coolidge, Harry Truman, Lyndon Johnson, Gerald Ford, and perhaps Ronald Reagan. Even the martyred John Kennedy elicits ambivalent reactions, his record ignored as conspiracy theorists, tabloid reporters, and a new generation of politicians cast lots for his memory. A worse fate awaits political failures. The American people did more than reject Alton Parker, John Davis, Alf Landon, Thomas Dewey, and Michael Dukakis. They forgot them.

Arizona Senator Barry Goldwater also failed politically, suffering an overwhelming defeat in the 1964 presidential election. Yet Americans did not consign Goldwater to the wasteland. His stature with both commenta-tors and the public has grown, and his words, years after his retirement, still garner front-page headlines. This continuing influence is, in part, a result of Goldwater's personality. Blunt and colorful, he differs from other politicians as a man who speaks his mind without hesitation or hedging. It is, as well, a matter of contrast. Unlike Lyndon Johnson and Richard Nixon, he lacks a dark side and casts the image of a citizen-politician. A sense of service, not power or material gain, animated his public career. He can boast of leaving the political arena financially poorer than when he entered.

More important, however, is an awareness that Barry Goldwater is a prophetic figure linked to two related trends that have shaped modern America: the rise of the postwar conservative movement and the emergence of the West in the twentieth century. As the political mainstream shifted to the right in the 1970s and 1980s, Americans reassessed Goldwater. They remembered that his books, speeches, and example had aroused conservatives in the 1950s against big government, deficit spending, high taxes, and social programs. In the aftermath of McCarthyism the right had found a new standard-bearer. Goldwater empowered the right wing during the 1960s and planted the seeds for the future growth of conservative agitation and the eventual political success of Ronald Reagan and George Bush. In program, organization, and constituency, he built the bridge between the old and new rights. He was, said Pat Buchanan, "our John the Baptist" (*Salt Lake Tribune,* September 12, 1991). Goldwater and his supporters did more than change the ideological complexion of the Republican Party. Under his tutelage, Republicans broke their financial and demographic ties to the North and East for new moorings in the South and West.

It is hard to conceive of Goldwater's appeal or the persistence of his influence without reference to his western roots. Americans have always looked west for their future; no other region has held such promise in the popular imagination. Americans have also mythologized westerners as a breed apart. In *The Mythic West*, historian Robert Athearn writes, "The ordeal in the wilderness created the American, we believe: free thinking, open, tough, optimistic, self reliant—the litany goes on and on. The western hero has embodied these virtues and this message. He is us, only a little bigger, tougher, braver." Goldwater was born in territorial Arizona and steeped in western mores and style. He preaches the frontier values of rugged individualism and tough-mindedness. To his supporters and to a wider audience he epitomizes the western man, the American frontier hero. Goldwater did more than draw energy and credence from the emergence of the West. He assisted its ascent from a frontier society to a technologically advanced outpost vying for political and cultural leadership.

Barry Goldwater, then, is far more than his defeat in 1964. He is inseparable from trends that shaped him, and, in turn, those that he helped to direct. If Goldwater stands in the foreground, he assumes definition against a backdrop painted in conservative and western hues. It was his opportunity to fashion a viable right-wing challenge while cultivating the enthusiasm that would link West and South into a stable conservative coalition housed in the Republican Party.

He occupied the center stage of American politics between June 1963 and November 1964. It was the only time in his career that he lost control of his public persona. Goldwater had, from his political beginnings, reflected the editorial views of the most powerful Arizona newspapers, and they provided him strong support. Later, national correspondents, warmed by his philosophy or personality, worked to shape positive perceptions. Seven book-length Goldwater biographies, all written before 1965, have appeared. Supporters or staff members wrote five of these, with each feeding off the previous volumes. He has had the last word, twice, publishing two autobiographies, *With No Apologies* in 1979 and *Goldwater* in 1988.

Two images emerge from the sources. In 1963 and 1964 an unmerciful press, shrewd Republican opponents, and opportunistic Democratic strategists scared the American people with a politically inept and irresponsible Goldwater eager to destroy the Social Security system and itching to trigger nuclear war. Compliments offered in a backhanded fashion heightened concern: Goldwater had integrity and the courage of his convictions, but his simplistic answers to difficult problems only enhanced the risks of military conflict, racial strife, and financial setback. Nor is the packaged "legend" much help in focusing Goldwater. Here, the rough-hewn citizen-statesman Goldwater disregards personal ambition and partisan advantage to battle for the public good. The West Point motto "Duty, Honor, Country" is his sole guide. Capturing the theme is his 1964 campaign slogan "In your heart, you know he's right."

Neither image truly informs. Neither caricature brings us closer to an understanding of Goldwater the man—his drives, needs, and dreams. To approach him is to study the legacy of his Jewish immigrant grandfather, a man who died before Barry Goldwater was born. It demands a return to small-town Phoenix and a family of privilege. It means discerning the impact of the Great Depression and World War II. These formative experiences shaped Goldwater's worldview. They also created a man of competing loyalties and conflicting roles. Goldwater is a naturalist in love with Arizona and, at the same time, a businessman boosting development. He is an opponent of big government and a westerner who acquiesces to massive federal aid in order to guarantee his region's economic well-being. He believes in military superiority, but he shuns the commitment of American troops to distant battlefields. Goldwater is sensitive to the plight of minorities, yet he is often unable to look beyond the individual and the immediate. Sometimes his words and deeds have acted to appease bigotry. While primed to matters of conscience, he is pressed by allegiance to friends and party. Thus, the Watergate scandal did not tar him, but personal loyalties and partisanship caused him to let down his guard. Reagan administration policy in Central America would cause similar conflicts. Nor could Goldwater reconcile the sacrifice of family with the demands of driving ambition. This, then, is the complexity of character beneath the caricatures. The private man casts a shadow on the public figure, demanding a portrait of diverse colors and shades.

Many of those I have interviewed for this biography asked me two questions before they consented to talk. "Did Barry authorize you to write this book?" No, but he and his family are cooperating with me. "Are you a Republican or a Democrat?" My answer to this simple question was more lengthy. The first political books I read were Barry Goldwater's *The Conscience of a Conservative* and *Why Not Victory?* My brother and I were the only students in our New York City high school to campaign for Goldwater for president. I still treasure the convention scorecard tallying the Goldwater vote. In 1964, when I was fifteen, my mother let me cast her ballot for Barry Goldwater against Lyndon Johnson. She did warn me, however, that if he won by one vote I should not come home. In 1965 my family moved to Scottsdale, Arizona. I rarely missed the sight of Goldwater's large ham radio antennae. During the 1960s, however, the struggle for civil rights and the war in Vietnam caused me to reexamine my views. I moved to the left politically and remain there today. This political background combined with my historical training enable me to be sympathetic to Barry Goldwater yet capable of critical analysis. Both, I believe, are vital in the writing of biography.

This book would not have been possible without the cooperation of Barry Goldwater and his family. Senator Goldwater made himself available for interviews and responded in writing to follow-up questions. He opened his educational, military, and personal records for my research. Access was denied only to his Federal Bureau of Investigation files. Joanne Goldwater shared generously of her time and knowledge and facilitated my contacts with other family members and the review of Goldwater materials. Michael Goldwater, Peggy Goldwater Clay, and Milton Friedman graciously permitted me to search their personal collections for information. Russell Kirk and General William Quinn provided their unpublished memoirs. Many took time from busy schedules to be interviewed for the book. I am particularly grateful to Barry Goldwater, Jr., Denison Kitchel, Ray Johnson, J. Terry Emerson, Roy Elson, Bill Schulz, William Scranton, John Tower, Ronald Reagan, Benjamin Bradlee, William F. Buckley, Jr., George McGovern, Stewart Udall, Orren Beaty, Patrick Leahy, Stephen Boyden, Ellen Thrasher, Jack Williams, Judy Rooney Eisenhower, Daniel Patrick Moynihan, and Jonathan Marshall. William Saufley not only talked with me for hours about his friend Barry Goldwater but also provided a garageful of materials accumulated over fifty years.

This book is the work of many minds, hands, and hearts. I have accumulated heavy debts, both personal and academic, in its research and writing.

Evelyn Cooper, Susan Sato, Maria Hernandez, Marlene Ware, and Kris Darnall of the Arizona Historical Foundation gave to the limit professionally. Walter Jones of Special Collections and the members of the Interlibrary Loan Department of the Marriott Library, University of Utah, went above and beyond the call in meeting my needs. Trudy Croes and John Wheat of the Barker Texas History Center and Byron Parham, William Joyner, and Paul Guite of the Nixon Presidential Materials Project greatly aided my work in their collections. Dr. Donald A. Ritchie, associate historian of the U.S. Senate, generously shared transcripts of oral histories with me. Dee Reigel of the *Arizona Republic–Phoenix Gazette* library department diligently tracked down hard-to-find facts. I very much appreciate the efforts of Catherine Goldberg of President Ronald Reagan's staff and of Senator Patrick Leahy aide Kevin McDonald in securing interview time. I am grateful to the archivists at the Carter, Ford, Hoover, Johnson, and Kennedy presidential libraries for their assistance. The determined editing efforts of Heidi Downey of Yale University Press are visible on every page and have made this a better book.

I learned much from my friends and colleagues. F. Alan Coombs meticulously read the draft, keeping me from errors in fact and style. The incisive yet gently tendered insights of L. Ray Gunn, Greg Thompson, and Dean and Cheryll May suggested weaknesses in the early drafts, many of which I hope have been remedied. Jennifer Rigby, Kurt Wall, and Leslie Bates proved to be more than research assistants. Their enthusiasm, diligence, hard work, and occasional touches of sarcasm were integral to the research process. For their patience in listening to me drone on for years about Barry Goldwater, I thank Lindsay Adams, Peggy Adams, John Bennett, Jim Clayton, Ron Coleman, Alan Fogel, Marc Fuller, Abby Grayzel, David Green, John Henkels, Jess Hurtado, Mike Jones, Michael Kottler, Jeff Kraus, Tom Lund, David Mack, Duane Shrontz, Cheryl Sneddon, Dick Tompson, Alison Van Frank, Cliff White, and Mike Zuhl. The Charles Redd Center for Western Studies at Brigham Young University, the Dirksen Congressional Center, and the University of Utah's College of Humanities and Research Committee all provided grants of time or money to assist my research. Wadsworth Publishing Company has permitted me to use materials from my book *Grassroots Resistance*.

My rock is my family. The encouragement and support of my father, brother, sister, nephew, and nieces never slackened. My eldest son, Dave, listened to or read most of the manuscript, helping me comb for inconsistencies and errors. Josh, in junior high school, took it upon himself to offer psychological advice. At one point he diagnosed me as "obsessed with the

Barry book." In fact, he noted that the problem was contagious; he had begun writing "Josh Goldwater" on the top of his math tests. My wife, Susan, makes possible all that I accomplish. Despite her own career, she took the time to listen, edit, and ease the soul-searching. Her love is overwhelming and underwrites this labor.

Part I The Making of a Conservative

1

Legacy

We grow strong against the pressure of a difficulty, and ingenious by solving problems. Individuality and character are developed by challenge. We tend to admire trees, as well as men who bear the stamp of their successful struggles with a certain amount of adversity.

—JOSEPH WOOD KRUTCH
The Voice of the Desert

Perseverance . . . that's been the story of my family.

—BARRY GOLDWATER

"No country that I have yet visited," wrote the sometime promoter, sometime adventurer J. Ross Browne, "presents so many striking anomalies as Arizona." Browne entered the Arizona territory at Fort Yuma on Christmas Day 1863 after a hard twelve-day journey from Los Angeles. Guarded against Apache attack by military escort, he accompanied his old friend Charles D. Poston, President Abraham Lincoln's recently appointed superintendent of Arizona Indian affairs. Poston, politically ambitious and seeking to advance his career, had persuaded Browne to serve as publicist during a tour of territorial reservations and of his mining properties. But it was the "anomalies" of the Arizona territory and not Poston's exploits that fixed Browne's attention. What Browne encountered was a region besieged by Apache warriors and Confederate troops: "With millions of acres of the finest arable lands, there was not at the time of our visit a single farm under cultivation in the Territory; . . . with forts innumerable, there is scarcely any protection of life and property; with extensive pastures, there is little or no stock. . . . There are Indians the most docile in North America, yet travelers are murdered daily by Indians the most barbarous on earth. . . . Mines without miners and forts without soldiers are common. Politicians without policy, traders without trade, storekeepers without stores, teamsters without teams, and all without means, form the mass of the white population."[1]

They rode east to Maricopa Wells, traveling through "vast deserts dotted with mesquite, sage, and grease-wood," marking their distance by the "watering-places" of the Yuma, Papago, and Pima tribes or by the few isolated ranchos. Turning south, the Poston party headed for Tucson, the territory's largest settlement. Browne was not impressed with what he saw: "A city of mud-boxes, dingy and dilapidated, cracked and baked into a composite of dust and filth: littered about with broken corrals, sheds, bake-ovens, carcasses of dead animals, and broken pottery . . . grimly desolate in the glare of a southern sun." Contemptuous of the inhabitants and their "greaser style," he wrote, "If the world were searched over I suppose there could not be found so degraded a set of villains as then formed the principle [sic] society of Tucson." Browne's observations received wide circulation and influenced eastern audiences hungry for news of the West. *Harper's Monthly* would serialize Browne's journal, which later appeared in book form as *Adventures in the Apache Country: A Tour Through Arizona and Sonora, 1864.* Perhaps Senator Benjamin Yates of Ohio had been right when he quipped during consideration of the Arizona territory bill: "O yes, I have heard of that country—it is like hell. All it lacks is water and good society."[2]

Arizona made nineteenth-century Americans uncomfortable. This was unfamiliar country. Neither the wilderness described in their Bibles nor travel through the sodded "desert" of the Great Plains had prepared them. The Arizona territory was land scraped raw, with rock and bare, baked ground exposed. Immense desert valleys, flat bottoms of vanished seas, rose to jagged foothills and then to naked mountain peaks devoid of the softening green of grasses and trees. The country offered no comfort or amenity. Hostile to change, the desert pressed existence to its margin. It was not the desert's beauty but its hegemony that awed settlers. The sun, sky, and land humbled and overwhelmed the individual. Distances isolated physically and psychologically—an isolation felt even more profoundly because travel was slow and often uncertain.[3]

The inescapable aridity and heat enveloped all life. This is the country of little rain or flowing water. New England enjoys forty inches of rain annually, and east Tennessee, fifty inches; the desert clouds over central and southern Arizona yield less than ten inches—in some places but three or four. The dry washes, or arroyos, offered water, and danger, only in flood time. The Salt, Verde, and Gila Rivers, which would be considered streams anywhere other than in Arizona, are unpredictable and thus undependable. And the powerful Colorado River, which frames Arizona on the west and north, offered no relief. Its waters were inaccessible to all but a few in the nineteenth century. Even those on its banks cursed the river as "too thick to drink and too thin to plow."[4] Exacerbating the dryness is the intense heat that drives summer temperatures to 120 degrees. The heat saps energy and slows life. "Everything dries," wrote J. Ross Browne. "Wagons dry; men dry; chickens dry; there is no juice left in any thing living or dead by the close of summer."[5]

The desert creates survivors. In this environment of permanent heat and drought the plant or animal that can find water and conserve it, survives. Plants in the desert are cisterns, growing long taproots or developing root systems that lattice the soil. Their leaves are small and thick and covered with resin to reduce evaporation. The Palo Verde tree adapted by having no leaves at all, and photosynthesis is performed in its bark. Similarly, the rattlesnake, scorpion, and Gila monster have learned the moods of the desert and accept its majesty. Americans have been more stubborn. In the nineteenth century survival required a grudging acceptance of limits. The twentieth century and its technology have spawned the will to conquer.[6]

The Arizona territory offered up another danger. Beginning in the early 1860s settlers and Apaches locked in intermittent but bloody warfare. Only with the capture and exile of Geronimo in 1886 and the confinement of Apache bands to reservations did the killing end. Perhaps it was more than the Apaches' fierceness in battle that frightened settlers. The outnumbered and outgunned Apaches appeared omnipresent and omnipotent because they had conformed to the desert's dictates. Having made the land their ally, they seemed to have harnessed its power.[7]

For most, Arizona was just a way station, a country to pass through as quickly as possible. They may have heard the booster's assurance that "where the mesquite grows, you can make fence posts bloom if you bring water," but few would believe it.[8] They could not imagine a garden in the desert. Arizona promised a hard and an austere life, but California or Oregon appeared as lands at the end of the rainbow. Better to go farther west than risk all. Arizona seemed only to mock those who dreamed of taming it. Thus, Apache wars, heat, and drought deterred prospective settlers, and in the 1860s the territory could boast fewer than five thousand men and women, the large majority of them Hispanic. Yet those who did take up the desert's challenge and triumphed did more than raise themselves. They bequeathed to their heirs an empowering legacy.[9]

Arizona, however, could lure men and women back into even the most hostile of worlds. In the late 1850s the Butterfield Stage carried news to Los Angeles of a gold strike twenty miles east of Fort Yuma along the lower Gila River. California forty-niners, Mexicans from Sonora, Papago Indians, and others rushed to the site to stake their claims. Gila City, thrown helter-skelter like so many boom camps before and since, quickly boasted a population of more than a thousand.[10]

The strike created an instant and captive market for food, clothing, and shelter, among other things. With quickened demand guaranteeing exorbitant prices and high profits, a second gold rush, this time of merchants, followed in the miners' wake. These merchants were hardly well established. Selling under tents or from their wagons, they, like the miners, were determined men who persevered for a new beginning. But they were more practical. As businessmen, they set their sights modestly and would not place their stake directly in the uncertainties of the gold fields.

Barry Goldwater's grandfather, Michel Goldwater, was one of the merchants who looked to Arizona for a second chance. He hitched four mules to a peddler's wagon and left Los Angeles for the Gila City diggings in 1860. California had not been Michel Goldwater's promised land. A few months before his departure a state court had declared him bankrupt, accepting his claim of owning property valued at just one hundred dollars against substantial debts. Goldwater was a troubled man. With a wife and five children to support, he had to find in Arizona the success that had eluded him in his adopted country. As he drove his mules to Arizona, perhaps he took courage from an old Yiddish proverb: "Change of place, change of luck."

Born in 1821 in Konin, a Jewish shtetl in Russian Poland, Michel was one of twenty-two children of innkeepers Elizabeth and Hirsch Goldwasser. The Goldwassers were observant Jews, and Michel, like most Jewish boys, attended synagogue and the local *kheyder*, or Hebrew school. In these one-room schools, the *malamed*, or teacher, drilled the boys to read Hebrew in preparation for prayer and participation in Jewish ceremony and ritual. Hirsch Goldwasser also considered his son's financial future. Well aware of the tsarist restrictions on economic opportunities, he apprenticed Michel to a tailor, so he could learn a trade that was open to Jews. Apprenticeship meant servitude, a life that was particularly hard when the master was himself of small means.[11]

If family and community held Michel in the Konin shtetl, other factors pushed him to leave. The tsars considered the Jews a "foreign" menace within their land. To dissolve the threat they offered inducements to Jews who sought assimilation and levied sanctions on those who clung to their beliefs. The Jewish population would be winnowed through departure, conversion, and death so that an empire of one faith, one culture, and one people would emerge. Thus, the tsars restricted Jewish rights and made the practice of Judaism more difficult. They confined Jewish residence to the Pale of Settlement, consisting of the fifteen western provinces of Russia. Jews were denied access to other parts of the empire unless they had special permission. Particularly onerous was an 1827 imperial edict requiring that all Jewish males ages eighteen to twenty-five serve twenty-five years as soldiers of the tsar. Removed from the support of family and community, many would die or be converted to Christianity. Sometimes boys as young as eight or nine were caught in the conscription net.[12]

Russia offered Michel a stunted future with no hope that tomorrow would be any different from today or yesterday. He left Poland in 1835 at the age of fourteen, journeying across Germany to Paris, where he found work as a tailor. He remained there until the revolution of 1848 forced him to move to London. Michel Goldwasser adjusted quickly to his new home. He anglicized his name to Goldwater, learned English, became a part of the Jewish community, and married, all within two years. Sarah Nathan, his bride, was a twenty-four-year-old Englishwoman, the daughter of a prominent Jewish furrier. Her father's death, when Sarah was sixteen years old, had led to a decline in the family's fortunes, and she went to work as a dressmaker. Although only a "greener," or recent immigrant, Goldwater was an attractive choice for a husband. Six feet tall, fair, and clean-shaven except for a mustache, he was a handsome man. His Parisian manners and tailor's sense of fashion put him in step with sophisticated London. They married in 1850 in the Great Synagogue of London with its chief rabbi presiding, perhaps a reflection of the Nathan family's former standing.[13]

The couple settled, briefly, into domesticity. Two children, Caroline and Morris, were born to the Goldwaters within two years. Michel's tailoring business expanded. But events in the California gold fields beckoned Michel as they had so many others from around the world. Prompted by Joseph Goldwater—his younger brother, recently arrived from Poland—Michel convinced Sarah of the fortune to be made in America, and she agreed to let him go. Wasting little time, the Goldwater brothers chose the cheapest route to California. They bought steerage tickets to New York City. From there they traveled to Grey Town in Nicaragua, crossed the 212-mile-wide isthmus by mule and on foot, and then sailed up the coast to San Francisco. They left England in August 1852, and in three months they disembarked in California.[14]

The Goldwater brothers, who had no mining experience, never had any intention of digging for gold. They hoped to make their strike as merchants, filling the needs of the miners. Having arrived years after the 1849 rush, however, they found San Francisco economically inhospitable. They could not match merchants who were now well established and commanded substantial resources. Better to go into the California hinterland, closer to the diggings, and operate a business within their means. For advice and support the brothers turned to fellow Jews. With religion and Yiddish as common bonds, they joined an informal Jewish business network that acted to advance the mutual prospects of its members.[15] Jewish merchants staked the Goldwaters to several hundred dollars and suggested Sonora, a gold camp of four thousand people about one hundred miles east in the Sierra Nevada foothills, as a potential business site.[16]

The Sonoran Jews who welcomed the Goldwaters, however, had disappointing news. The brothers had entered the market too late with too little, for Sonora was overstocked in dry goods, and general merchandising was beyond their modest budget. Refusing to admit defeat or return to San Francisco, the Goldwaters decided to fill another business niche: quenching the thirsts of the miners. The brothers opened a saloon in a room beneath a brothel, an ideal business location. Set-up costs were minimal: rent, chairs, tables, liquor, and beer. They were soon doing a thriving business.[17]

In fifteen months, Michel Goldwater had accumulated enough money to pay passage for Sarah, their two children, and Sarah's sister; they arrived from England in July 1854. The move to Sonora tested the marriage. Sarah Goldwater had lived her entire life in London and was unaccustomed not only to America but also to the rough-and-tumble of a boomtown. And she was concerned about raising her young children in so primitive and crude a place. Adding to her pain, their rented house was small and crowded, a situation exacerbated in 1855 with the birth of the Goldwaters' third child. Sarah endured Sonora for three years. In 1857, again pregnant, she finally prevailed upon Michel to allow her and the children to live in relatively refined San Francisco. Michel would remain in Sonora to operate the saloon and travel to San Francisco to visit his family. Over the next three decades of their marriage, Michel and Sarah would be apart for months and sometimes years, a pattern that would recur in future Goldwater family relationships.[18]

Maintaining two homes, supporting a growing family (a fifth child was born in 1858), and taking time away from work strained the saloon. Michel could no longer depend on his brother, who had left Sonora for Los Angeles. Other factors were beyond Michel's control. The "color had played out" in Sonora, meaning that the miners had depleted the surface gold deposits. The flush times were over, customers disappeared, and the town retrenched. Michel Goldwater recognized the obvious at the end of 1858. To buy time in order to pay mounting debts, he assigned his remaining business assets to creditors and closed the saloon. This bought him a little more than a year. A Los Angeles court declared him an "insolvent debtor" on March 19, 1860.[19]

Michel Goldwater was in Los Angeles, where the family went to regroup, when he heard of the Arizona gold strike at Gila City. J. Ross Browne described the scene in his journal: "At one time over a thousand hardy adventurers were prospecting the gulches and cañons in this vicinity. The earth was turned inside out. Rumors of extraordinary discoveries flew on the wings of the wind in every direction. Enterprising men hurried to the spot with barrels of whiskey and billiard-tables; Jews came with ready-made clothing and fancy wares; traders crowded in with wagon-loads of pork and beans; gamblers with cards and monte tables."[20]

Michel conferred with his brother about this latest opportunity and borrowed money from him to buy a wagon and team and an assortment of goods to peddle to the miners. Despite the competition, Goldwater sold out his wagon at a profit and returned to Los Angeles to restock. Because of Michel's credit history, Joseph fronted for him and obtained merchandise with payment due at some future date. Bernard Cohen, a Jewish Polish immigrant and business associate of the Goldwaters', offered additional financial backing. Sales remained brisk in the goldfields, and Michel continued making trips into 1862.[21]

The brothers' success came to an abrupt halt in late 1862. Joseph had overextended his credit and was unable to make repayment. Two days after Christmas 1862 the Los Angeles county sheriff auctioned the Goldwaters' assets to satisfy creditors. The brothers lost everything, including Michel's wagon and team of mules. Once more, Michel was penniless. Adding to the burden was the birth of Sarah and Michel's sixth child. Goldwater was now without the means to make a living, and the California economy was in decline. Drought followed by flood devastated cattle raising and agriculture, and Confederate Navy gunboats disrupted trade with eastern and northern markets.[22]

It is hardly surprising, then, that Michel Goldwater grabbed the opportunity to return to Arizona. Cohen, who had left Los Angeles to open a general merchandise store in La Paz, asked Michel to clerk for him. Prospects in La Paz, seventy miles north of Fort Yuma and the site of the most recent Arizona gold rush, appeared even greater than in Gila City. "Ho, For The Colorado!" headlined the Los Angeles *Star*. "Gold is fast flowing into our city merchants and traders, and the gold fields of the Colorado are now among the richest of the California placers."[23] Promised gold had kindled another boom market, with rising prices holding instant reward for the entrepreneur. Reports circulated that the three thousand inhabitants of La Paz and the surrounding diggings were clamoring for supplies. According to La Paz merchant Isaac Goldberg, "People had little to eat besides mesquite beans and river fish."[24] They bid the price of flour up to twenty-five dollars a hundredweight, and a pound of coffee and a gallon keg of water each fetched a dollar. La Paz seemed to have a future. Located on the Colorado River, it had a landing to off-load steamboats that carried supplies upstream from the Gulf of California and was the terminus of the Bradshaw Road from San Bernardino. La Paz boosters envisioned their town as the outfitting and supply center for miners and settlers pushing into Arizona's interior. Michel Goldwater was already clerking in the Cohen store by January 1863.[25]

La Paz was heat, dust, and mosquitos surrounded by desert. Built without plan or even forethought, it was a jumble of tents and log huts fronting a dirt street. There was, however, another La Paz beyond the physical reality. For those like Michel Goldwater, who lived as much in the future as the present, La Paz was the opening that would enable the industrious, and the lucky, to pass to a better life. The inconveniences of the desert and the separation from loved ones were nothing compared to the tomorrow before them. Goldwater made the most of La Paz's promise. Jovial, fluent in six languages—including Spanish and German—and fair in business dealings, he catered to his clientele and earned their gold. He was "Big Mike" to the miners—a reference to his six-foot, 200-pound frame; he was one of them. Goldwater's industriousness impressed Cohen, who delegated more responsibility to him and gradually became a stranger in his own store. Perhaps afraid that Goldwater would strike out on his own and become a competitor, Cohen soon made him a partner.[26]

As more prospectors and settlers filtered into Arizona through La Paz, Goldwater decided to diversify. He began supplying traveling peddlers with cash advances and goods, a financial ground-breaking that would prove quite profitable for him. The Arizona territorial census gives a measure of his progress by spring 1864. In the year and a half since arriving in La Paz, Goldwater had accumulated a stake of fifteen thousand dollars. The self-made man, beaten in California, had prospered in the Arizona wilderness because he never surrendered to his fears. He never lost the courage to persevere to eventual success. His history became hallowed, a patrimony passed from Goldwater generation to generation.[27]

Anti-Semitism did not bar Mike Goldwater's advance in La Paz. Nor did it hamper the activities of Bernard Cohen, Isaac Goldberg, or the town's ten other Jewish businessmen. Jews throughout the territory enjoyed an environment devoid of overt prejudice and discrimination. Jews opened businesses in Tucson, Yuma, Prescott, Isaacson (Nogales), Clifton, Solomonville, St. Johns, Phoenix, and nearly every other settlement during the territorial period. Merchant families like the Drachmans, Solomons, Zeckendorfs, Goldbergs, and Steinfelds exerted, along with the Goldwaters, a powerful influence not only within their communities but on Arizona's history and economy.[28]

Christians welcomed Jews because they offered Arizona so much. Foremost, Jewish business underwrote existence in the desert by bringing goods at reasonable prices to miners and townspeople. Jewish minds and money would later play key roles in developing Arizona mining, smelting, farming, ranching, and banking. The Jewish businessmen of Arizona and the larger Southwest, concludes geographer D. W. Meinig, were "catalytic agents" who were "the principal architects in the formation of a functioning regional society from an array of disparate parts."[29] Arizonans also turned to Jews for leadership. Educated, service-minded, and determined to maintain a climate attractive to business, they entered politics and won election to town councils, to the territorial legislature, and as mayors. Jews helped organize and sometimes led fraternal orders, literary clubs, social groups, militia units, and volunteer fire companies.[30]

Because Jews were few in number and scattered across the territory, they posed little threat to Christian dominance. Their very decision to go west reflected attitudes and values that dampened resentment. Many were entrepreneurs first and Jews second. Less traditional and more assimilated, they had voluntarily distanced themselves from Jewish communities and their institutions. Such Jews, with at least an American veneer, may have elicited caricature but not fear. Finally, Jews possessed white skins, valuable tokens of acceptance in American society. With large populations of Native Americans and Hispanics nearby, the ethnic and religious lines dividing Anglos blurred. White Christians counted Jews as allies in the face of more powerful enemies. As Arizona became more "civilized" in the years after statehood, however, the tolerance of the territorial days faded, and anti-Semitism joined racism to mark social and economic relationships.[31]

Mike Goldwater held to his faith. He was the founding vice president of Congregation B'nai B'rith in Los Angeles in 1862. There were no synagogues in territorial Arizona, so he maintained membership in San Francisco's Congregation Sherith Israel. Goldwater timed his buying trips to coincide with synagogue ceremonies so that he would not miss High Holiday services. The Goldwaters sent their sons to Hebrew school in California, where they studied Judaism and prepared for bar mitzvah, the passage from childhood to adult responsibilities. In business, too, Mike Goldwater remained conscious of his Jewish roots. It was more than convenience or profit that motivated Goldwater. Religious commitment and personal experience outlined responsibility and shaped action. He remained involved with the Jewish merchants' network that had helped him make a start in California. In Arizona he forged new links in this business chain. As Bernard Cohen had employed him, Big Mike hired Solomon Barth and Harris Cohen to work in the La Paz store. Goldwater assisted both when they went out on their own. Looking back in 1898 as president of the First Hebrew Benevolent Society of San Francisco, Goldwater remembered: "Quite a large number of able-bodied heads of families I have furnished with horse and wagon where with they have been placed in a position to earn a livelihood. Others were furnished with tools or wares."[32] When they came of age, Big Mike would bring his sons into the network, sending Morris to work for Pincus Berwin's hat and cap company as an apprentice clerk, Ben to B. Blumenthal's glove-making company, and Henry to the Prager clothing store.[33]

The supply lines that linked Goldwater to businessmen like Barth and Cohen expanded as Arizona's interior mining camps evolved into towns. Maintaining the store in La Paz, Goldwater assumed a middleman's role, contracting with California suppliers for Arizona distributors. This meant more than stockpiling goods for sale to retailers. Goldwater also had to ensure delivery of merchandise, a task that he took on himself. Hitching oxen or mules to freight wagons coupled into a train, he rode the "cobweb of trails" that fanned out into the desert toward Prescott, Wickenburg, and the smaller settlements of north and central Arizona.[34] These were not short hauls. Goldwater spent weeks on round trips covering hundreds of miles of backcountry, carrying everything from hats and boots to shovels and black powder.[35]

His reasons for leaving the comfort of the store are unknown. Perhaps he sought adventure and time away from the routine of La Paz. He was in his mid-forties, and it may have been an attempt to recapture the vigor of younger days. He surely looked to the future. Brother Joseph had joined him in Arizona, as had Julius and Simon, brothers newly arrived from Poland. His business also had to absorb sons coming of age, and this diversification promised resources and places for the next generation. Similarly, the birth in 1866 of Baron, the last of his eight children, further impressed on him the financial needs of family. Goldwater's expansion of the wholesaling side of the business accelerated when he transferred operations from La Paz to Ehrenberg, six miles south. The capricious Colorado River had anointed Ehrenberg the new center of supply when it shifted course and left the La Paz landing stranded several miles from water. Quickly adjusting to yet another business reversal, Big Mike opened a new store and built a warehouse to stow his inventory.[36]

Miner and settler demand alone was not yet sufficient to persuade Goldwater to look beyond La Paz. Although the territory's population had nearly doubled to about ten thousand men and women in 1870, a highly competitive business environment made financial security precarious. Arizona was overstocked with competitors, with more than one trader for every ten inhabitants. But as Mike Goldwater and every other Arizona business operator knew, the federal government was the moving force in the economic life of the territory. Federal troops had combed Arizona for potential railroad and wagon routes as early as 1851. Military explorers doubling as prospectors

had mapped the territory during subsequent decades. In addition to surveying Arizona, the government allocated monies to build wagon roads, dig
wells, subsidize mail service, and fund Secretary of War Jefferson Davis'
experiment in bringing camels to Arizona for transportation. The federal
government also subsidized railroad construction, transferring title to millions of acres of Arizona land to rail entrepreneurs.[37]

Particularly important to Arizona and Goldwater was the government's
more permanent military presence in the territory. Arizona was an important
theater of operations for the U.S. Army after the Civil War. Citizens had
demanded early on that the federal government dispatch troops to subdue
the Apaches and guard reservations. The response was the establishment of
Fort Whipple near Prescott, Fort McDowell in the Salt River Valley, Fort
Defiance in Navajo country, and fifteen other military outposts in the territory. In 1867 an army report described Arizona as a "vortex into which the
greater portion of the available military material on the Pacific Coast disap-
pears."[38] If Arizonans were beholden to the army as their defender, they
never lost sight of the army as their most important customer. In the six
years after 1867 Congress appropriated $15 million to fund the war against
the Apaches. This sum, notes historian Howard Lamar, "virtually sustained
the economy of the territory."[39] According to General E. O. C. Ord in 1870:
"Hostilities in Arizona are kept up with a view of protecting inhabitants,
most of whom are supported by the hostilities."[40] Military spending would
continue at high levels into the 1880s, when 20 percent of the U.S. Army was
stationed in Arizona.[41]

In war and peace, the army traveled on its stomach. To provision soldiers
and feed livestock the federal government contracted with businessmen to
supply food and fodder and transport equipment. The competition for government contracts was stiff, for payment was sure, if slow. In time of truce
government expenditures continued to maintain military outposts and support Native Americans confined to reservations. Big Mike Goldwater was
often a successful bidder for government work. He landed contracts to carry
freight and troops to Fort McDowell and grain to Camps Hualpai and Verde.
In addition, he contracted with the federal government to deliver the mail to
the Salt River Valley. Military outposts also stimulated local economies. To
reduce long-distance freighting costs, the army awarded contracts to
encourage nearby production of hay, grain, and food. Towns, moreover, welcomed soldiers and their wives, who spent their pay in local markets. Goldwater and other middlemen, in turn, responded to the growing demand
from these interior markets for their services. Federal money thus rippled
through the territorial economy and fueled growth in population, transportation, farming, and trade.[42]

Government contracting, army policy encouraging local production, the increasing population, and the exhaustion of gold-placer deposits along the Colorado River pressed the Goldwaters to seek a business outlet in Arizona's interior. Most promising was Phoenix, a new farming settlement near Fort McDowell. Because of its central location, it had the potential to become a supply depot for the entire territory. Settled in 1867 to raise crops for sale to army posts and mining camps, Phoenix claimed 235 people in 1870. The town had taken root at the junction of the Salt and Gila Rivers amid ancient ruins and the remains of the extensive canal system of the prehistoric Hohokam, "the people who had gone." Clearing out some of the more than two hundred miles of abandoned canals, farmers irrigated the desert and put fifteen hundred acres under the plow. Like the mythical bird that burned itself on a pyre and rose from the ashes to live again, Phoenix rose from its Hohokam past to begin its American incarnation.[43]

The Goldwaters opened their store in December 1872 at First and Jefferson streets, in the heart of the settlement. Mike chose his eldest son, Morris, to manage operations. Morris Goldwater had received a Jewish education in California, but he was less devout than his father and thoroughly assimilated. He had clerked in the La Paz store in 1866 when he was fourteen and went on to work for Big Mike's business associates in California. At age twenty he stood behind the counter of the Phoenix store selling a grab bag of general merchandise that ranged from hair nets and garters to harnesses, shovels, and plows. The Goldwaters also tried to corner the local grain trade, advertising the highest prices to farmers for their crops. The federal government remained an important source of funds for the Goldwaters, with the army accepting their bid to supply food to three posts in 1873.[44]

Phoenix disappointed the Goldwaters. Despite their resources and contacts, they were forced to close the store after just two and a half years. Morris Goldwater could not break his neighbors' allegiance to the six already-existing general merchandise stores in Phoenix, nor could he secure an adequate share of the grain business. This failure was no reflection on Morris' ability. The business climate in Phoenix remained unstable for decades, with a high rate of failure and low business persistence. The Goldwaters abandoned Phoenix in 1875 and would not return to stay for twenty-one years.[45]

The Phoenix venture set the family back financially, but it did not chill their desire to relocate from the Colorado River. The Goldwaters, always tuned to California happenings, were certainly aware of the Southern Pacific Railroad's plans to build east toward Arizona. The railroad would bind the territory to a national market and sharply reduce transportation costs and shipment time. Savings and accessible markets would, in turn, spur growth in mining, lumbering, agriculture, and cattle raising as they encouraged immigration. Ehrenberg and the Colorado River trade promised to be early victims of the railroad. Promoters boasted that freight transported from San Francisco to Yuma by rail would arrive within forty hours; the steamer time was fourteen to eighteen days. Nor was it hard to read the future of the over-land freighting business. When feeder railroads eventually tied Arizona towns into the east-west transcontinental route, traders would be confined to the backcountry. Good business sense reinforced the need to change sites and even orientation. So, too, did a freighting accident that shattered Big Mike Goldwater's knee and limited his mobility.[46]

As Southern Pacific Railroad crews began working their way across the desert to the Colorado River and Yuma, the Goldwaters opened for business in Prescott in October 1876. Prescott, one hundred fifty miles east of Ehren-berg, was the largest town in the territory after Tucson. Feeding on nearby gold and silver mines, forests, and Fort Whipple, its population had grown to 668 people, almost triple that of Phoenix. Prescott traders also developed wagon routes that allowed them to dominate the economy of central Arizona. In early 1877, Anglo Prescott became the territorial capital, relieving Hispanic Tucson not only of the honor but of revenue and political clout. For the Goldwaters this was no temporary stopping place. Here they would put down deep roots.[47]

The Goldwaters felt at home immediately in Prescott. They quickly built a loyal clientele whose patronage prompted them to move to larger quarters in 1880. Sales were so good that Big Mike slowly phased out his more dangerous and risky freighting operations. He also put his sons Henry and Sam to work in the store beside himself and Morris. As their neighbors soon realized, the Goldwaters' attachment to Prescott went beyond money-making. The family felt a sense of community and common fate. Building on their reputation for honest dealing and integrity in business, they earned the respect and trust that enabled them to influence Prescott's political and social worlds.[48]

This was especially true of Morris Goldwater, who emerged as the family's leader. Blunt and unassuming, Morris was a slight, short man with a face dominated by a thick walrus moustache. He fancied wool suits even in summer and was accustomed to drinking shots of bourbon throughout the day. He held strong political convictions, standing as a Jeffersonian Demo-crat suspicious of the powerful and committed to government limited in authority and close to the people. Community problems, Goldwater believed, demanded local solutions for which individuals first, and then elected leaders, took responsibility. Morris had so impressed townspeople that they elected him mayor just two years after his arrival in Prescott. Governing least and thus, in Mayor Goldwater's eyes, best, he gave Prescott a clean, efficient, and low-cost administration. In a period of American and Arizona history notorious for official corruption and bribery, this was no small feat. "An honest politician," he would later tell his nephew Barry, "would never make money. . . . A man can't butter his bread on both sides. If he doesn't respect honesty, he shouldn't go into politics."[49] Uncle Morris was Barry Goldwater's model of the public man. "He has always been," wrote Barry in 1972, "my example of integrity, of honesty, and of fair play."[50]

Morris Goldwater followed his first term as mayor with election to the city council. In 1882 he represented Yavapai County in the upper house of the territorial legislature. He would serve as Prescott's mayor for nine non-consecutive terms, his last ending in 1927; as city council member from 1898 to 1901; as Yavapai County supervisor from 1890 to 1894; as vice president of the Arizona Constitutional Convention in 1910; and as president of the state senate during its second legislative session (1914–16). In addition to his political activities, he organized the Prescott Rifles militia company and a volunteer fire brigade. He joined the Masonic lodge and eventually rose to become the grand master of the Arizona lodge. Working with town boosters, Morris established a bank in Prescott and lobbied for a feeder railroad to connect his community to a transcontinental line.[51]

With his son so active in community affairs, Big Mike spent most of his time tending the store. Only once did politics draw him from behind the counter. Citing Prescott's need for such civic improvements as sidewalks, street lighting, and wooden crossings at corners, he ran and won election as mayor in 1886. Controversy, however, marred his term, for store owners and residents balked at proposed spending and higher taxes. Unwilling to compromise, Mayor Goldwater resigned and left office after serving less than eight months of his term. His frustration may have invited self-reflection. Politics offered no outlet for his energies, and the store was doing well in his sons' capable hands. In 1886 he celebrated his sixty-fifth birthday. After a quarter-century in Arizona, Mike Goldwater decided to return to Sarah and California. He spent the seventeen years of his retirement serving the San Francisco Jewish community in religious, charitable, and Zionist organizations. He never went back to Arizona. Big Mike Goldwater died in 1903, six years before the birth of his grandson Barry.[52]

As the eldest son, Morris Goldwater claimed a birthright that gave him controlling interest in the store and paternal acknowledgment of his ascendancy in the family. It also gave him responsibility for Baron, the youngest brother. In 1882, sixteen-year-old Baron came to work in the store. Baron had spent his childhood with Sarah in Los Angeles and San Francisco, seeing his father and older brother only during their infrequent visits. Sarah, charged with the task of educating the last of her children, enrolled him in both public and religious schools. At age thirteen Baron was a bar mitzvah and assumed his adult religious obligations. Perhaps at Sarah's insistence, he maintained a commitment to the synagogue after coming of age and served as vice president of the young people's Sabbath worship program at Congregation Sherith Israel. Baron, like all of the Goldwater brothers, was apprenticed after he completed his education, working for a San Francisco jeweler in 1881.[53]

Life in San Francisco and away from his father had shaped Baron. He was, remembers his son Barry, "a town man, I'd call him a dude."[54] Impeccably dressed with hair slicked, perfumed, and parted in the middle, Baron enjoyed the indoor life, playing cards and, when older, drinking with friends. He was slight of body, standing five feet, six inches, and he shunned all sports except boxing, which he loved to watch. Lacking manual dexterity and mechanical ability, Baron was also uncomfortable at the work bench. "My father couldn't drive a nail, he couldn't screw a screw. . . . He had one splendid motto: 'Don't do anything you can pay some one else to do.'"[55] Though Baron had much to learn, his contribution would reshape the business and make the Goldwaters the leading mercantile family in Arizona.[56]

Baron worked his way up from the bottom. He unloaded wagons, hauled barrels, unpacked boxes, ran errands, swept floors, and made deliveries. He shelved according to the custom of the country store, stacking dry goods along the right wall, groceries, tobacco, and patent medicine on the left, and whiskey, farm implements, and tools in the rear. Hard work and obedient service eventually brought him to the counter, where he developed merchandising skills and rapport with customers. Over time, Morris delegated greater responsibility to Baron, sending him on buying trips to California. Baron, more dedicated than older brothers Henry and Sam, emerged as Morris' heir.[57]

Morris Goldwater was less successful in strengthening Baron's religious inheritance. Morris took pride in Judaism, but his religiosity was more form and identity than content. Thus, he tacked a tin mezuzah with a Hebrew prayer to his doorpost, contributed to Jewish charities, and closed the store on Jewish holidays. He also rejected Royal Arch Masonry because it required him to renounce all faiths but Protestantism. But as Morris admitted to Baron, he was "not well versed in Jewish theology."[58] Baron, without familial or institutional supports, would drift away from his faith. On his own later in Phoenix, he did not join the Jewish congregation, affiliate with Jewish organizations, or close the store on holy days. While many of his friends were born Jews, some had married Christians and converted, and others felt no attachment to the Jewish community. Even before marrying out of the faith, Baron occasionally attended the local Episcopal church.[59]

Prescott's time on center stage proved brief. In November 1878 Southern Pacific Railroad crews headed east from Yuma, laying an average of one and a half miles of track per day. They reached Tucson in March 1880 and the New Mexico border six months later. In the north, the Atlantic and Pacific Railroad, later acquired by the Atchison, Topeka, and Santa Fe, spanned Arizona with a second transcontinental line by the mid-1880s. Dependable, fast, and economical transportation gave access to national markets, luring large corporations to exploit the mineral resources in Arizona. The expanding need for telegraph and electrical wire created a particular demand for Arizona copper. Extensive copper districts developed far to the south and east of Prescott, in the Clifton-Morenci, Globe-Miami-Superior, and Bisbee-Douglas areas. Economic growth lured people, and the population of the territory increased by almost 120 percent from 40,440 in 1880 to 88,243 in 1890. By 1900 the number of Arizonans had risen to 122,931. Growing national and local markets prompted expansion of irrigation canal networks and agricultural acreage and the first experiments with winter vegetables and citrus.[60]

Merchants in Phoenix and the Salt River Valley moved aggressively to take advantage of a changing Arizona. Private companies and individuals, in response to new demand, accelerated the renovation of the Hohokam canals and the digging of new ones to provide water to reclaim the desert. The Arizona Canal, completed in 1885, would carry as much water as the Erie Canal, Phoenix boosters said.[61] In the early 1890s Salt River Valley farmers were irrigating 120,000 acres, and Phoenix proudly advertised itself as the "garden city of Arizona."[62] Phoenix had also by 1895 linked to both transcontinental rail lines, becoming the territory's transportation hub. Surrounded by the territory's largest irrigable area, connected by railroads, and with easy access to the copper districts, the town was the focal point of Arizona collection and distribution. Location, economic progress, business initiative enhanced the appeal of Phoenix to newcomers, and the population rose from 1,708 men and women in 1880 to 5,554 in 1900. Recognizing that Prescott was being left behind, Arizona legislators voted in 1889 to make Phoenix the new territorial capital.[63]

Despite their setback two decades before, the Goldwaters could not resist the opportunities that Phoenix offered. Morris chose thirty-year-old Baron over older brother Henry to manage the store they opened in March 1896. The Phoenix operation was unlike any previous Goldwater store. For inspiration Baron looked to the East and to California, where the merchandising concept of the department store had taken hold. In place of simply stacking goods, department stores employed the art of commercial display. In R. H. Macy's and Gimbel's in New York City, Filene's in Boston, Marshall Field's in Chicago, and Emporium in San Francisco, buying became drama played on a stage set with furniture props, mannequins, and backdrop murals. Fashion shows and interior sets shaped tastes and fixed fashions as they advertised products and promoted a culture of consumption in an environment of glamour, comfort, and elegance. Gone were the general store's disparate menu of goods and bulk purchasing from bins and barrels. New trends brought a specialization of offerings, departmentalized stock, and fixed prices that discouraged bargaining. With items for sale in a range of prices, department store managers catered across class lines, from the shawl to the carriage trade.[64]

While Phoenix was too small to support a Macy's or Filene's, a scaled-down version in the form of a Goldwater's could fill an unoccupied commercial niche. From its opening, Baron distanced the store from competitors and sought to establish it as the leader of Phoenix fashion. He assured customers that all of his merchandise was "known to be new from the eastern markets,"[65] and he guaranteed them their money back if they were not completely satisfied. Goldwater's flattered buyers with appeals to fine taste and high quality: "We won't sell you cotton for wool, or jute for flax. The meaner sort of merchandise we have no time to bother with. Neither have you, if we judge our trading public right." And, "clean, honest, reliable stuff at the lowest prices is what intelligent buyers are looking for. We want none other."[66] Like the larger department stores, Goldwater's specialized in women's fashions and furnishings, offering a large assortment of suits, gloves, shirtwaists, corsets, and parasols. The left, right, and rear divisions of the dry goods store had no place in the new Goldwater's. Instead, Baron created separate departments for housewares, notions, toilet articles, and neckwear. He also installed a telephone, one of the first in Phoenix, to ensure the most prompt and modern customer service. Goldwater's caused a sensation in small-town Phoenix. Many, like the newspaper reporter covering the store's opening, were impressed by the "quality of goods, the newness of ideas; in completeness of assortment; in everything that tends to make a store a 'thing of beauty.'"[67] Baron Goldwater had set high standards. Using the slogan pioneered by brother Morris, he promised Phoenicians "The Best Always."

The business was an immediate success, and Goldwater's moved to larger quarters in 1899. Baron, clearly in step with eastern stores' architectural design, installed a theaterlike balcony and mezzanine in the rear of the building, a skylight, and more than a hundred incandescent lights for nighttime shopping. For Phoenix and a growing out-of-town clientele, Goldwater's had transformed buying from the mere purchase of goods into a grand act pitched to dreams and self-identity. Baron had succeed where the family had failed, and in a business environment known for its unpredictability and hostility to newcomers. He had also enhanced the stature of the Goldwater name. To a reputation for honesty and quality, Baron had added the role of trendsetter. Baron Goldwater would claim membership in the elite of Phoenix not only because of his financial standing, but also because of his position as arbiter of style and fashion.[68]

Phoenix boomed in the 1890s, untouched by the national depression, but even the most heady boosters hedged their bets when predicting the community's future. Phoenix remained a backwater, a small-town capital of a desert territory. Local conditions, moreover, threatened continued development and dimmed dreams of city status. As everywhere in Arizona, the problem was water. The Salt River, the main irrigation source for Phoenix and surrounding Maricopa County, flowed erratically, with water supply significant only one year in three. Years of good flow often brought floods that washed out diversion dams and cropland. Phoenix experienced both precipitation extremes during the 1890s, with floods bracketing drought years that forced abandonment of thousands of cultivated acres. Without a dependable water supply to bolster an important segment of the economy, the community would stay small and slow paced.[69]

Convinced that control of the Salt River was beyond local resources and expertise, Phoenicians joined thirsty citizens of other western states in lobbying for federal action. The result, despite denunciations of socialism and government interference with natural economic law, was the National Reclamation Act of 1902. To encourage settlement in the arid West, the law authorized the government to fund and build dams and supplementary water projects. Congress required repayment of construction costs but subsidized water users by levying no interest; allowing a generous time period with liberal extensions for repayment; and, in the end, creating a relatively inexpensive supply of water.[70]

The Roosevelt Dam on the Salt River was the first multipurpose federal reclamation project. Begun in 1905 and completed six years later, the dam stored the seasonal runoff of the wet years for use during dry seasons. The project was enormous by existing standards, and it energized the boosters, who noted that the reservoir held water "capable of floating the combined Atlantic and Pacific fleets."[71] In subsequent years other federally sponsored dams on the Salt and Verde Rivers, along with canal system improvements, would enlarge storage and delivery facilities and provide hydroelectric power. The federal government would grant Salt River Project users several repayment extensions, and the $10 million cost of the Roosevelt Dam was not retired until 1955. Similar federal dams and water projects would dot the West, shaping the economies of such states as California, New Mexico, Utah, Colorado, and Idaho.[72]

The effect of the Roosevelt Dam project was felt immediately. Federal funds quickened the local economy, creating business and jobs, which in turned spurred an influx of residents. The population of Phoenix doubled between 1900 and 1910 to 11,134 inhabitants, and Maricopa County experienced a 68 percent increase to 34,448 people. A heightened self-confidence infused the business community, and merchants expanded their stock and looked for larger quarters. Baron Goldwater, anticipating the dam's completion, opened a larger store—a "Palace of Feminine Finery"—on December 31, 1910. The Roosevelt Dam had the greatest impact on farmers, of course. A dependable water supply combined with the Arizona climate produced a 365-day growing season. With the dam capable of watering 240,000 acres, farmers increased agricultural land by 400 percent between 1910 and 1920. The Salt River Valley had become, said area promoters, an "agricultural paradise" where farmers continuously harvested vegetables, grains, and fruits.[73] In 1912 farmers planted the area's first commercial crop of cotton. Five years later, under the stimulus of war demand, it became Arizona's leading crop. Maricopa County dairy farmers and cattle ranchers similarly increased their herds and reached for growing markets. The money that farmers earned from local and national consumers was recycled in Phoenix for goods and services, accelerating the tempo of business activity. Roosevelt Dam and the continuing development of water resources would underwrite Phoenix and Maricopa County growth for three decades.[74]

Arizona had proved a promised land for entrepreneurs like Michel, Morris, and Baron Goldwater. It would also mean deliverance for another type of Arizona pioneer: those in poor health. By the turn of the century Arizona was known throughout the United States as a "lungers' mecca," its dry, clean air prescribed as a cure for respiratory disease. Phoenix promoters added this reputation to their arsenal, inviting the sick and the weak to "the healthiest city in the known world."[75]

It was this desire to "chase the cure" that brought Josephine Williams, Barry Goldwater's mother, to the Arizona territory. JoJo Williams, the youngest of six children, was born in March 1875 on a farm near the small town of Bowen, Illinois. The family took pride in a lineage that reached to America's beginnings and specifically to freethinker and dissenter Roger Williams of Rhode Island. Nineteenth-century Williamses were staunch Republicans and similarly determined in the defense of their beliefs. In 1883 the family sold its farm and moved west to take up land near Omaha.

Life in Nebraska was primitive and farming a struggle. "I started with nothing," remembered JoJo Williams. "My people were poor."[76] Early on, JoJo showed a "fierce independence" and a resolve not to abide by convention or be bound by poverty.[77] She defied gender prescriptions, learning with her brothers to ride, shoot, hunt, and fish. Most of her life JoJo would sleep with a loaded revolver under her pillow. She was the only girl on the local baseball team. At age sixteen, JoJo received a certificate to teach, seeking to rise in one of the few professions open to women. She taught for two years and then shifted direction, enrolling at the Illinois Training School for Nurses in Chicago. After earning her nursing certificate, JoJo went to work in a city hospital. By her early twenties she was emancipated from her family, unmarried, and self-sufficient.[78]

In 1903, illness set back JoJo Williams' rise. The doctor's diagnosis of "lung fever" carried a poor prognosis. JoJo refused to accept her fate, however. "The doctor told me I had six months to live, but I never had any idea of dying. I liked living too well."[79] With the Arizona climate the only possible cure, Williams boarded a train, informing her family only that she was accompanying a patient to the territory. She had booked passage to Phoenix but found herself stranded in Ash Fork, Arizona, a railroad stop 125 miles north of her destination. Without money but refusing to accept defeat, she began walking south along the tracks. A freight train eventually stopped, picked her up, and carried her to Phoenix. For months JoJo lived with other "lungers" in an army tent several miles north of town. Her health gradually improved, and she began working as a special-duty nurse in a Phoenix hospital.[80]

JoJo Williams met Baron Goldwater in 1906 while shopping at his store. During their courtship she did not disguise her self-reliant, confident, and assertive nature. When Baron offered to furnish her with clothing from the store without charge, she indignantly replied: "'Until I'm Mrs. Goldwater, I'll pay my own bills and buy my own clothes where I choose.' . . . He respected my independence."[81] She would purchase her wedding dress from a rival merchant. Mother Sarah Goldwater's death in 1905 had removed all parental pressure for Baron to marry within his faith. Following brother Morris, who the year before had married in a Protestant service, Baron and JoJo were married on New Year's Day 1907, at St. Luke's Episcopal Church in Prescott. Their first child, Barry Morris Goldwater, was born at home in the fashionable section of Phoenix exactly two years later—on January 1, 1909.[82]

Six decades later, in a speech titled "The West That Was," Barry Goldwater declared, "People—not stereotypes, but individuals—inhabited the West that proved to be a land of opportunity for my immigrant grandfather, my uncles, and father. . . . There was a future for the bold."[83] Their struggle in the desert was an important lesson for Goldwater. Throughout his life he returned to it in body and mind to draw inspiration. From a hard land, men and women had reaped the promise of America. Success had not come easily, and it was all the more dear because they had begun with so little and the desert foe had been so unyielding. The federal government may have been a prime mover in their history, yet it is the deeds of individuals that fill his memory. The immigrant peddler Michel Goldwater was the core of family legend. Morris, Baron, and JoJo were the living embodiments of the self-made. In them, the next generation would discover its role models. "We don't find people like that today," said Barry Goldwater. "People want it handed out to them, they don't want to work. Even people on relief don't want to work. There was no such a thing in those days. You either worked or you starved. People who lived then were a different breed."[84] In a land without tradition and of only recent experience, the family's history became Barry's lodestar. With his forebears' legacy he found himself and the means to understand the world.

2 Coming of Age

You grew up in the West with a sense of change, of growth and improvement that even a kid could see and feel. . . . The future seemed as wide as the horizon.
                                                                    —ERIC SEVAREID
                                        "They're Closing on the Great Open Spaces"

Barry comes from the old bare-knuckles frontier conservatism, not the hellfire and brimstone type.
                                                                    —JOHN TOWER

Arizona, at Barry Goldwater's birth in 1909, was a territory approaching statehood. The next year, census takers bolstered Arizona's bid, reporting a 66 percent increase in population from 1900, up from 122,931 men and women to 204,354. The territory took pride in Tucson, with 16,060 inhabitants, and Phoenix, whose more than 11,000 people anticipated economic take-off with the completion of the Roosevelt Dam. Phoenix and Maricopa County remained Arizona's bread and fruit basket, accounting for one-half of the value of the territory's crops. Arizonans also trumpeted their industrial base. Eight smelting and refining establishments, employing one-half the territory's industrial work force, produced the copper vital to American economic development.[1]

Still, critics derided Arizona as a primitive frontier. More than two-thirds of the territory's population lived outside incorporated towns. Phoenix was a capital in name only. It encompassed just 3.2 square miles, and paving of downtown streets did not begin until 1910. Hitching posts for horses still stood before homes and stores. Travel through the valley was difficult, for no vehicle bridge connected the north and south banks of the Salt River. Because major railroads did not stop in Phoenix, the town continued to feed off branch lines. With only 304 industrial wage earners, manufacturing was insignificant, and masons, bakers, and ice makers serviced only a local market. In a reminder of frontier days, on February 17, 1909, just over a month after Barry Goldwater was born, Geronimo died in confinement at Fort Sill, Oklahoma.[2]

Opponents of statehood also pointed to Arizona's proposed constitution as evidence of its "cowboy" recklessness. In tune with national progressive movements, delegates to the constitutional convention had approved a range of reforms, including the initiative, referendum, recall, direct primary, and short terms of office for elected leaders. The constitution also authorized an eight-hour workday and workers' compensation. Blacklists were forbidden in Arizona, and child labor was confined to after-school hours. President William Howard Taft, complaining about Arizona's "crank constitution," refused to approve statehood until the recall of judges provision was removed from the document.[3] Only then—after recognizing the economic progress and population growth of the territory—did Congress and Taft support its entrance into the union. It became the forty-eighth state in 1912. Afterward, Arizonans would defiantly vote to reinstate the recall of judges provision into their constitution.[4]

The futures of Barry Goldwater and Arizona were entwined from the beginning. One of Barry's first memories was of his mother taking down the American flag that hung on the pole in front of their Phoenix house to sew on a new star. "My mother was very religious in seeing that this was carried out."[5] At age three, he was the ring bearer in the first wedding performed in Arizona after it gained statehood.[6]

The transition to statehood in no way diminished Goldwater influence. Morris Goldwater, still esteemed by residents of Prescott, had been an active participant in the proceedings of the constitutional convention. Baron Goldwater was the leading businessman in Phoenix, absorbed in the store and a principal stockholder in the fledgling Valley National Bank. His spare time was spent with friends or in playing cards or billiards in the Arizona Club and Phoenix Country Club. Socially prominent and financially secure, the Goldwaters were one of a dozen families who formed the tight-knit leadership circle in Phoenix. Befitting their status, Jewish-born Baron and Presbyterian JoJo attended the Trinity Episcopal Church.[7]

Perhaps because of social convention, concern about the store's future, or desire to secure some sort of immortality, Baron Goldwater had reluctantly married and begun a family. "I got married when I was forty-two," he told Barry, "and that was eight years too soon."[8] The telling comment still stirred his son three-quarters of a century later. "It's frightening how that stayed with me."[9] Like his own father, Baron was emotionally removed from his family. He was self-centered and unwilling to suffer inconvenience or disruption to his routine. The children came quickly—Barry in 1909, Bob in 1910, and Carolyn in 1912—but the home would move to his needs and rhythm. Rigid, faultfinding, and impatient, he would parent from a distance, leaving discipline and day-to-day responsibility for the children to his wife.

Appearances and propriety were important to Baron, and his high expectations for the children's behavior were difficult to fulfull. "My father," recalls Barry, "was a very private man, almost solitary. . . . My mother said he wanted children but never knew quite how to cope with us."[10] Baron's relationships with his children came on his terms, for he refused to involve himself in their concerns. This meant playing cards or chess with their father or catering to his interest in "the boxing thing. . . . We all had to learn how to box."[11] Bob and Carolyn proved compliant and willing to accept their father, but Barry was less accommodating. His playmates steered clear of Barry's father. Harry Rosenzweig, Barry's best friend, found Baron Goldwater cold and undemonstrative. Jack Williams, who would later become Arizona governor, described Baron as "stolid, stodgy, and sober."[12] "We were always very careful," remembered future Arizona governor and senator Paul Fannin, "not to do anything that would irritate his father."[13]

Baron, mirroring Big Mike Goldwater, was away from his wife and children for long periods. He went on buying trips for the store that took him out of Phoenix for almost four months of the year. The family also spent summers apart. As was the custom of the Phoenix wealthy, Baron sent JoJo and the children to the northern mountains of Arizona or to the California beaches to escape the heat while he remained at work. Baron rarely joined his family on their frequent outings into the Arizona outback. Even when in Phoenix, Baron insulated himself from the family, passing free hours at his clubs with business associates and friends. Baron and JoJo usually ate separately from the children, and family gatherings were not regular occurrences. Lack of intimacy made time together stressful. Few stories about Baron, whether true or imagined, have passed to the next generation of Goldwaters or to family friends. One that has, offers insight into the Goldwater dynamic. During one family dinner, Baron, without outward sign, became angry because a milk bottle had been placed on the table. Upset by this breach of etiquette, he picked up the bottle and smashed it against the wall. He offered no explanation for his behavior and continued eating in silence. Writes Barry Goldwater: "I never really knew him. What I knew about him I learned from my mother and my Uncle Morris."[14]

Acting as patriarch, Baron Goldwater had resolved the question of his children's religious training before they were born. He was already estranged from his faith, and to JoJo's questions about Judaism, which she described as a "beautiful religion," Baron pleaded ignorance.[15] So even though there was a Hebrew school in Phoenix, Barry, Bob, and Carolyn were baptized in the Episcopal church.[16] It is not surprising, then, that another of Barry's earliest memories recalls Christmas, a decorated tree, presents, and a Jewish-born Aaron Goldberg portraying Santa Claus. Baron rarely attended church, entrusting his wife with the children's religious upbringing. Barry served his church as an acolyte and was later confirmed. Baron's alienation from Judaism was so profound that when second son Bob was asked about his father's religious background, he replied: "Did Dad have a bar mitzvah? I don't even know."[17] Barry Goldwater heard no references to Judaism or Jewish customs when he was growing up. "Here I am a half-Jew," he complained, "and I don't know a damn thing about what I'm supposed to know."[18] But ignorance insulated Goldwater. Despite his Jewish roots and occasional experiences with anti-Semitism, he never felt an outsider and was never on the defensive in Christian America.[19]

Barry developed no interest in any religious theology or doctrine, and he felt no strong attachment to institutionalized religion. Later in life, when elected a lay delegate to an Episcopal synod, he asked his adviser Stephen Shadegg, "What does this mean and what do I do?"[20] Religion to Barry Goldwater was an ethical commitment, "an inner conviction and an inspiration to a better life."[21] Barry's mother was his role model, and he quoted her as saying: "You can find God walking through the desert, or walking through the forest, or climbing the mountains just as easily as you can find God in a church."[22] In this vein, Goldwater remarked, "I'm a very religious man. I don't go to church every Sunday."[23]

Compensating for his lack of attentiveness, Baron indulged the family. A cook, an "around the clock" maid, a nurse, and a chauffeur staffed the spacious house on North Central Avenue.[24] He showered gifts on the children, with Barry receiving sporting equipment and expensive model train and crystal radio sets. Baron also converted the top of the garage into a gymnasium, complete with boxing ring and punching bags. Dubbing it the North Central Athletic Club, the boys made it the headquarters of their Center Street Gang. There was even space on the property for a miniature golf course. "I guess I was a spoiled well-off kid," Barry would later joke. "I've often told people that I was born in a log cabin equipped with a golf course, a pool table, and a swimming pool."[25] On the vacant lot next door the children created a racetrack for their bicycles. Just inside the back door of their home, the Goldwaters kept a well-stocked icebox, "and the neighborhood kids would wander in and help themselves."[26] Baron's financial interest in a Phoenix theater allowed the children to attend movies for free. Given these attractions and Barry's gregarious nature, the Goldwater home became a gathering place.[27]

Even as a youth, Barry Goldwater was given to impulsive acts of generosity. Money became for Barry a means to the good life rather than a driving goal. With the Goldwaters well known in their community and Baron's financial standing unquestioned, Barry carried no money, signing his name to all purchases. This became a lifelong habit that was not even broken by the easy accessibility of credit cards or checking accounts.[28]

In Baron's absence, the children turned to their mother. Bob and Carolyn called her "Mungie," a combination of mother and Angie, the name of a Goldwater maid. "They loved her dearly and saw her more than they did me," explained JoJo.[29] Barry alone called her "Mun." Like her husband, JoJo was not given to displays of affection. She had a "tremendous bark,"[30] and "her space went way out there."[31] She also was involved with her friends and own interests. Entrusted with primary responsibility for the children, however, she was determined to teach them what their father either could or would not. She encouraged Barry's mechanical abilities and skill in working with his hands. Afraid only of lightning and tornados (a midwestern legacy), she packed provisions and her shotgun and went alone with the children into the Arizona backcountry. They took these trips at a time when there were few paved or marked roads in Arizona. Their fragile automobile was pressed to negotiate rutted trails and sandy washes. The excursions doubled as learning sessions, with JoJo schooling her children in camping, hunting, and fishing. In 1916, when Barry was seven years old, they visited Old Orabi on the Hopi Tribe's Third Mesa, kindling in him an appreciation for Native American customs and art. In his teens, he traded for the first of what would become a collection of more than four hundred Hopi Kachina dolls. Other outings brought the family to Navajo country, the border towns, mining areas, and mountain regions. On one of these trips Barry took his first pictures with his mother's box camera. Carolyn and Bob would tire of "roughing it" and, like their father, grow to feel more comfortable with room service and luxury accommodations.[32] For Barry, these trips with mother shaped his identity and interests.[33]

Barry was receptive to his mother's learning-by-doing method. Books did not stimulate him, and he showed little interest in intellectual pursuits. According to sister Carolyn: "I don't think he ever read a book growing up."[34] As an adult Barry Goldwater would read more, but even then most of his time was consumed by the "little two-bit Westerns you buy. In fact, I usually have a briefcase with Mickey Spillane and all of those things."[35] He preferred, whether in business or politics, the memorandum that could distill issues into the space of a single page. Even though Barry's IQ was within the range of average intelligence at 103, his parents placed little stock in his abilities.[36] "I was tickled to death," said JoJo, "that I got him through the first grade school."[37] They thus did little to prepare him academically and fostered in their son instead "a born instinct" that his place would be in the store.[38] Still, Goldwater was curious and an avid learner, absorbing information primarily through personal contact and hands-on activity. "The education I've had has been from people, talking with people, living with people, getting advice from people, catching hell from people. I'd have to say it's a pretty good education."[39]

Following Baron's lead, JoJo never physically punished her children; she "spoiled us rotten," Barry later wrote.[40] Yet she expected much from her children. She preached a tough-minded independence and self-sufficiency, instilling a belief in the power of the individual to effect change. As her own life had proved, opportunities beckoned those who worked hard and desired to better themselves. Self-reliance and the will to succeed, she reminded them, offered solutions to any problem, personal or social. Barry internalized these teachings, often finding inspiration in the poem *Invictus*: "I am the master of my fate; / I am the captain of my soul."[41] Family history reinforced maternal instruction: the Goldwaters were just one generation removed from their self-made, immigrant origins. Growing up in the Goldwater home gave daily proof of the rewards America offered those who strived for their goals. Thus, he would declare, "I've seen what people standing on their own two feet and working for themselves can do when they're [of] a mind to do it—one case after another of personal success through personal effort."[42]

The Goldwaters were conservative, but they were neither prudish nor ascetic. Their style evoked the relaxed manner of the West rather than the moralistic tone of the small town and church. When Arizona citizens adopted Prohibition in the 1914 elections, the Goldwaters refused to abandon their taste for whiskey and beer. Baron bought the bar and brass rail of his favorite saloon and installed them in the basement of the house. Nor did the national Prohibition amendment change their habits. "The country went dry, but that bar was always wet."[43] For less formal occasions, the Goldwaters kept bottles of liquor on the sideboard of their dining room so that friends passing by could come in and help themselves. When their supply ran low, they bought from bootleggers and made beer. Carolyn remembers, "We would go to sleep with the popping of beer caps going off in the cellar."[44] JoJo carried a flask and smoked in public, and both she and Baron could be heard to curse. These behaviors, when combined with the Goldwaters' tolerant attitudes toward religion, were hardly the milk of zealotry. Barry memorized what his mother taught him: "The other person may have the right to feel the way he or she does. Hear them out. You may learn something. They'll respect you for taking the time and are more likely to listen to your side."[45]

Goldwater family socialization produced more than self-centered, rugged individualists. JoJo Goldwater instructed her son in a sense of social responsibility. "Mom drilled us: . . . all of us have to pay rent for the space we occupy on this earth."[46] In a poem, he wrote:

> Those of us who walk in light
> must help the ones in darkness up
> for that's what life is all about.
>
> . . . .

Those of us that turned out sound
should look across our shoulders once
and help the weak ones to their feet.
It only takes an outstretched hand,
and how few, how few people know that.[47]

As members of an elite Phoenix and Arizona family and heirs to a heritage of community service, the Goldwater children were trained to assume leadership roles in social, civic, and economic affairs. Parental lessons about self-reliance and individual initiative fostered such participation. Successful local problem-solving would, in turn, heighten feelings of personal effectiveness. What was learned in the community seemed to offer solutions to more complex issues in wider contexts. With duty to serve came commitment to America. Patriotism—simple love of country and flag—imbued JoJo Goldwater, and she made certain that the same faith animated her children. Her most powerful means of teaching were repeated ritual observances. Thus, as the children were growing up, she drove them three miles every evening to the Phoenix Indian School to stand and salute as the flag was lowered. Barry, Bob, and Carolyn were impressed for a lifetime with this devotion.[48]

Her patriotism was absolute, and so was her standard of integrity. JoJo would tolerate no dishonesty in her children. Her strict code became the highest commandment. "I don't care what you do," she would say again and again, "but don't ever lie."[49] Barry used just three words to describe his mother and the house she ran: "open, direct, and honest."[50] Even keeping secrets might break the rule, and it is telling that Barry remembers the only time that he kept something from his mother—when he learned to fly at age twenty-one. The prime directive instilled in the children great respect for truth and honor. Yet establishing absolutes of right and wrong and good and bad shaded nuances and blurred subtleties. With such a compass, misunderstandings and mistakes in judgment might degenerate into issues of honor, personalized and colored by the implication of dishonesty in an adversary. Societal problems became conflicts between individuals divorced from institutional and abstract causes. Compromise, too, would be difficult, for give-and-take did not fit so rigid a code. Clashes in these terms produced, on the one hand, anger and feelings of betrayal, and, on the other, an exaggerated sense of loyalty to supporters. This overweening trust could become self-defeating when it denied evidence of failure and guilt. A friend of Barry Goldwater's observed, "His mind is closed to weaknesses in people, and maybe that's his weakness."[51]

"He was the first," JoJo said about Barry, "so we tried to make him perfect."[52] Many of their expectations were clear, and Barry summarized his parents' legacy: "honesty, loyalty to America, respect for our flag, understanding the responsibilities of citizenship."[53] These he passed on to his children just as succinctly. To youngest son Mike, he wrote: "Tell the truth, be honest, stay out of trouble, use your head, and get a good education."[54] He pressed upon Barry Jr. the necessity of "honest conviction and honest action."[55] As Barry's parents had taught him through word and example, the power to shape personal destiny was in the hands of the individual acting by and for himself. Individuals working in concert were the legitimate agents of community change. Past and present in Arizona confirmed in Barry's mind the primacy of individual initiative and local control. "We didn't know the federal government. Everything that was done, we did it ourselves. That is the backbone of my philosophy."[56] Noblesse oblige might temper his rugged individualism, but social and economic amelioration remained the responsibility of the private sector, not the public. As Barry Goldwater puts it, "I grew up among conservative people."[57]

Barry received other messages from his parents as well. Both expected obedience and achievement befitting the family status. "Barry had something to prove in the sense of his heritage," says longtime friend General William Quinn. "He couldn't let the Goldwater name down."[58] If JoJo and Baron had given their son a mission, they did not arm him with feelings of adequacy or self-worth. Barry's father was absent or absorbed in business and friends, making the family a secondary concern. Baron shared neither time nor interests with his son. There was no dialogue, no closeness. While Barry may have worked hard to gain his father's approval, it was not forthcoming, and paternal expectations continually climbed beyond his grasp. His mother was physically present but emotionally detached. Barry imitated her interests and accepted her strict honor code. Like her, he was stubborn, hot-tempered, impatient, blunt, and, on occasion, profane. Still, he could not breach the wall that separated them. Insecurity and feelings of inadequacy may have ignited ambition, but they took a toll on the boy and, later, on the man.[59]

What emerged was a Barry Goldwater whose public persona was very different from his private one. To the world, Barry was an outgoing, decisive individual secure in his role and eager to assume leadership and exercise authority. Campaign manager Stephen Shadegg called him an "arrogant man. He was always a winner. He was a baronial character."[60] Although he was competitive, ambitious, and determined, even his enemies would never accuse him of hungering for the trappings of power or seeking it for its own sake. Goldwater appeared tough and without weakness. When under pressure, he seemed in control, nonchalant, and relaxed. Said his son, "He never lets you see him sweat."[61] His open manner and blunt talk suggested that nothing was left hidden.[62]

Beneath this mask there was another Barry Goldwater. This Goldwater was shy and vulnerable, "like a little boy."[63] Harry Rosenzweig, who knew him best, described his friend "as kind of a loner."[64] Goldwater found security in the company of his few close friends but never was able to shed the feeling that he was somehow unworthy of love or admiration. William Miller, Barry Goldwater's vice presidential running mate in 1964, maintained, "I've never seen anyone more susceptible to a pat on the back than Barry Goldwater. He responded to all manner of flattery. Dick Nixon, when he was president, would take Barry to Burning Tree for a round of golf and Barry would be in his hip pocket for another six months."[65] Goldwater was surprised by the adulation he received. "The guy is so humble," remarked Phyllis Thompson of his Senate office staff, "he didn't think he had any influence."[66] His son concludes, "He's a man of great contradiction."[67]

Early on, Barry rejected his father as a role model. Unlike Baron, Barry loved the outdoors, "the broad expanses where there is nothing but the Lord and the wind."[68] He excelled in athletics, becoming a fine swimmer and playing football and golf. He even distanced himself from his father in appearance. Baron was stylish and fashion-conscious, and Barry defiantly was the "worst dresser in Phoenix," and he carried his taste for outrageous outfits into adulthood.[69] To replace his father, Barry sought out male mentors who would give him guidance and support. Uncle Morris was the first, and Barry claims him as an important influence on his life. Contrasting Baron's mechanical ineptitude, Barry built identity and confidence through his mastery of gadgets. Though he didn't enjoy reading books, he never missed an issue of *Popular Mechanics*. Barry constructed model airplanes and radio transmitters and receivers, pastimes that became lifelong hobbies. He attached to Earl Nielsen and worked in his radio shop after school for no pay, sweeping the floors and helping assemble wireless sets. In 1922, at age thirteen, Barry assisted in setting up the first commercial radio transmitter in Arizona. KFDA was only the thirty-sixth station licensed in the United States, and it was operating less than two years after KDKA in Pittsburgh made the first nongovernmental broadcast in the United States. While still a teenager he filled a radio announcer's slot, broadcasting with Jack Williams and Howard Pyle, both of whom would also play important roles in Arizona politics.[70]

Carolyn probably referred only to herself and to her brother Bob when she observed, "We were obedient. They were the authorities and we didn't mind."[71] As the youngest child and only daughter, Carolyn was her father's pet.[72] Bob Goldwater was a superior student who skipped a grade to catch up with his brother. Barry was different. Perhaps in seeking attention or searching for independence in rebellion, "he was always getting into trouble."[73] There are many stories of Barry's pranks and misbehavior. To the amusement of his brother and sister, Barry flipped pats of butter onto the kitchen ceiling and defied his mother when ordered to clean up the mess. Talking back to his mother was a constant problem, and as Rosenzweig recalled, Barry "had a bad mouth."[74] The Center Street Gang, at Barry's suggestion, packed their mud balls with rocks before aiming at members of rival cliques. He took friends' bicycles, disassembled them, and hid the parts. During World War I he and Bob worked for a day picking cotton for the war effort. Barry was caught putting rocks in his bag to inflate the five-cent-per-pound payment. Once, needing money for a date, he pawned his brother's saxophone. In 1924 fifteen-year-old Barry hosted a party at the Phoenix Country Club. When things became dull, he used lipstick to draw a circle on the wall and led the adolescents in throwing ice picks at the target. Mrs. Goldwater paid to repair the damage. This behavior did nothing to bring Barry closer to his father. "Dad may have liked cards, but not wild ones."[75]

Even more problematic was Barry Goldwater's performance in school. Although he had a quick mind and was adept at topics that interested him, he posted a poor record. Schoolwork bored him, and he did not study. He also became a discipline problem, disrupting classes and fighting with schoolmates. "My father just wanted me to succeed. When I was in school my grades were never good enough, and they weren't, and my decorum was never up to par."[76] Barry graduated from grade school and junior high school but stalled in his first year at Phoenix Union High School. Though he was always popular, and his classmates elected him freshman class president, he failed algebra and ancient history and barely passed English. The school principal summoned the Goldwaters at the end of the year and recommended that because of his grades and behavior Barry not return in the fall. Goldwater never sugarcoated the experience: "Hell, I got kicked out of Phoenix Union."[77]

Baron Goldwater's solution for his problem child was military school. He selected Staunton Military Academy in Virginia's Shenandoah Valley, perhaps after scanning the boarding schools listed in the back pages of the "Fashion-Society" section of the *New York Times*. Baron, who was on his way to New York City, accompanied Barry on the five-day train trip to Staunton. He had little awareness of how his son felt: "I kept getting smaller, weaker, and more frightened."[78] On arriving at their destination, Baron handed Barry five dollars and said: "Son, you find out how to get to the school, get there, and report in and keep in touch with me."[79] Barry walked the two miles to the school alone. In the four years that Barry attended Staunton, he saw his father during visits to Arizona or when Baron went east on buying trips.

During one such encounter in New York City, Baron grew angry because Barry had violated fashion rules by not wearing a hat. He told his son never to visit him again unless he dressed more conventionally. His son's reaction was predictable: "I didn't go back."[80]

Staunton Military Academy promised to teach discipline and provide direction. The school routine rarely varied from a regimen that began with 5:30 A.M. calisthenics and was filled by drill, schoolwork, athletic practice, and study. The "rat" system operating at the academy required all first-year students to shine the shoes, clean the rifles, and make the beds of upperclassmen. In his first two years at Staunton, Barry chafed at these demands and resisted school rules. Infractions meant demerits, and Barry earned the nickname the "Beat King" for his punishment time. He was destructive, and bills for breakage gathered in Baron Goldwater's store safe. His schoolwork did show improvement. He repeated ninth grade and received C's in English, Latin, and algebra, and a D in history. His progress was more uneven as a sophomore. Although Barry was able to maintain his English grade and raise his history score to a C, he earned a D in algebra and failed Latin. His best subject was military science.[81]

Another nickname suggests that Barry's transition to military school was harder than that of the other students. Classmates called him "Goldberg" because of his "Jewish ancestry," even though "he didn't look it."[82] As one of the students explained, "You know how it is, they call you 'kike' if you were a Jew and 'dago' if you were Italian."[83] Such slurs stung Barry, who had never experienced prejudice. "I had to go back east and leave Arizona before I found out that Jews were somehow different from other Americans."[84] Resistance to school authorities, the common enemies, may have offered him a means to gain his peers' acceptance and to rejoin the majority. Thus, Barry's confrontation with prejudice did not sensitize him or bring insight or spur action. Throughout his life he would accommodate the bigotry of others while personally distancing himself from it.

In his junior year Barry came under the influence of Major Alexander "Sandy" Patch. Patch, in charge of military instruction at Staunton, was born in Fort Huachuca, Arizona, in 1889 and graduated from West Point in 1913. Six feet tall, trim, and possessed of a military bearing, Patch was a career army officer who offered students a strong role model. His authority came less from rank or fear than from a presence that commanded confidence and respect. "The thing that marked him as a man and an officer," wrote Barry, "was his personal discipline. He wasn't tough or mean. He was calm. He never lost his temper, no matter what."[85] Barry admired Major Patch and adopted him as a mentor. This helped him to end his rebellion and accept Staunton and its aims. The years at Staunton, Barry believes, "were like a compass for me."[86] The academy reinforced his patriotism and sense of service and instilled a personal discipline and respect for authority. It also cultivated a devotion to the military—its rituals, traditions, and needs.[87]

Barry, now committed to his school, went off report, receiving his last demerits after Christmas vacation of his third year. He plunged into athletics, becoming captain of the swim team and the center on the football team while participating in varsity basketball and track. Barry joined the school's social clubs and worked as the circulation and business manager of the year book. In his senior year, Barry was class treasurer and captain of "C" Company. He won the confidence and admiration of his classmates, who elected him to chair the student honor committee that oversaw the academy's ideals of "truth, honor, and duty" and meted out punishment to violators. Even his grades improved. Barry earned a few B's in his junior and senior years and received no grade lower than a C. The change impressed his teachers. In a confidential report one wrote, "An excellent boy. Full of fun. Capable of real work. A good mixer." Another described Barry as "quite affable, loyal and trustworthy. Splendid moral outlook." The reports also sounded a cautionary note: "Will have to work hard in college."[88] It was the combination of leadership, athletics, and academic improvement that won him—even though he graduated 46th of 101 students—the faculty-bestowed Kable Legion of Honor Award as Staunton's best all-around cadet. The award assured Barry an appointment to West Point, which his instructors encouraged him to accept. But with Baron Goldwater in declining health, JoJo insisted that Barry be close to home. He returned to Arizona and enrolled at the university in Tucson. Barry would regret the decision not to attend West Point his entire life.[89]

Eighteen-year-old Barry Goldwater came home to an Arizona on the rise. The 1920s were years of strong population growth and economic activity in the nation's youngest state. Although it could not match the 63 percent growth it saw between 1910 and 1920, the state attracted more than 100,000 men and women in the twenties, marking a 30 percent gain by 1930. Economic development, following a World War I–generated boom, also quickened during the decade. Wartime demand had pushed up the prices of cotton, copper, and beef and stimulated production. Although they were halted by a sharp but brief national depression in the early 1920s, Arizona producers recouped their losses and continued to advance until the 1930s. Copper smelting and refining still dominated the state's manufacturing sector, contributing more than two-thirds of the total value of Arizona industrial products. Agricultural acreage, expanding because of new irrigation projects, climbed 400 percent between 1909 and 1919. During the 1920s Arizona farmers aggressively plowed up the desert or converted it to pasture, increasing their holdings 80 percent, to more than 10.5 million acres by 1930. Cotton cultivation led this expansion. In 1909 Arizona growers planted nineteen acres in cotton; in 1919, 106,283 acres; and in 1930, 211,178 acres. Still, the extreme heat, with no technology to tame it, surely deterred an even heavier migration and dampened more significant economic activity.[90]

In contrast to the summer heat, Arizona's winter climate had spawned tourism, a new service industry. Arizona remodeled itself from mecca for health seekers to Grand Canyon state, a wintertime escape with attractions for the entire family. An expanding automobile industry prompted road-building projects that enabled men and women to take to their Model T Fords in search of America. In the automobile's wake came resorts, motels, service stations, repair shops, restaurants, and the other roadside businesses that catered to tourists. The first campground with cabins had opened in 1913 in Douglas, Arizona. Road building and the tourist trade would be hard pressed to keep up with car-borne demand.[91]

The federal government maintained its high profile in Arizona even though the importance of military spending had declined since the end of the Indian wars. Washington was the state's largest landowner, and its bureaus exercised great power over natural resources and their uses. In the 1920s federal payments to Arizona amounted to more than 15 percent of the total annual gross state product. Of particular benefit to the state was federal spending for Native Americans, agriculture, ranching, reclamation, vocational education, health services, and highway construction.[92]

Phoenix and Maricopa County spearheaded the Arizona boom. Phoenix surpassed Tucson in population in 1920 with its 29,000 people, a 161 percent increase since 1910. More than 48,000 men and women had arrived by 1930, up 66 percent from ten years before. To these totals, Maricopa County added 60,523 residents in 1920 and almost 103,000 in 1930. Phoenix had emerged as the largest community between El Paso and Los Angeles. Phoenix had other claims to city status. In 1926 it connected directly to the Southern Pacific railroad, ending dependence on feeder lines. This link solidified the city's position as trade depot for agricultural and manufactured products from Arizona and the central southwest. So too did three more U.S. Corps of Engineers and Bureau of Reclamation dams built in the 1920s on the Salt River, which increased water storage facilities and electric power supplies. Supplementing railroad and highway links was the Phoenix airport, which announced scheduled airline service in 1927. Phoenicians could also look to a skyline with buildings of seven, ten, eleven, and sixteen stories, several of which were experimenting with air cooling. Automobiles quickly replaced horses and pedestrian traffic, and by 1929 one in every three resi-

dents was driving. Said a city official, "The people in this town have forgotten how to walk."[93] Along with these signs of the modern life, Phoenix
developed a sophisticated air. "We are not only getting rich," boasted a
Phoenix resident, "but we are keeping sane. Do you know that we have a
Harvard Club here? . . . I'll bet you you can hardly throw a stone in Phoenix
without hitting a house where they read *The Atlantic Monthly* or *Literary
Digest*; in some cases both."[94] Meanwhile, manufacturing continued to play
only an insignificant part in the local economy.[95]

During the 1920s boosters aggressively pitched Phoenix to America in
hope of attracting new residents and tourists. Local leaders were "determined, God willing or not, to have a population of 100,000 by 1930, and Los
Angeles be damned."[96] Promotional literature beckoned easterners to
"Winter Among the Roses," reminding them that "Here Roses Grow When
You Have Snow."[97] Particularly innovative and effective in drawing national
attention were golf tournaments; in 1932 the first Phoenix Open was held. It
was hard to resist the siren call of a promoter like M. E. Bemis, who summed
up the appeal of Phoenix:

> With the wonderful production of the soil plus the climate, this little oasis in
> the desert is each season attracting a desirable class of people from all parts
> of the United States who . . . seek here that calm and contentment which
> comes in the country with an ideal climate, with paved roads that lead to
> markets and modern towns, to schools that are unexcelled, to churches, and
> to places of entertainment. Country life in this valley offers all the attractions
> of the city without the noise and drawbacks that belong with the city. . . .
> Downtown Phoenix is busy and bustling. . . . To sum it all up, Phoenix is
> a truly progressive city of the West.[98]

Supporting this pitch to the outside world were local campaigns to expand
transportation facilities, plant trees, and remove rubbish and weeds. "Let's
do away with the Desert," Phoenicians proclaimed as they supported "anti-
knocker" campaigns to stifle those blind to the city's greatness.[99]

The community's hand was not extended to everyone. Advertising in the
Phoenix City Directory in 1920, the Chamber of Commerce announced that
"Phoenix is a modern town of forty thousand people, and the best kind of
people too. A very small percentage of Mexicans, negroes, or foreigners."[100]
Mayor Frank Jeffers, seven years later, assured those worried about racial
mixing that "Phoenix is . . . segregated into three districts, those of white,
negro, and Mexican residents."[101] The U.S. Census Bureau substantiated the
mayor's claims. Of the twenty-nine precincts in Phoenix, fourteen contained
no blacks and seven more counted fewer than ten black residents each.
While residential covenants kept blacks and Hispanics from Anglo neighborhoods, de facto segregation separated the races in hospitals, pools, parks,

hotels, restaurants, and theaters. De jure segregation, meanwhile, confined black children to segregated schools at every level of the Phoenix educational system. Custom, class, and law had combined to hold people of color to an inferior status in Phoenix. Racial injustice did not preoccupy community leaders, and inequality remained the status quo, unquestioned and acceptable. Restricted to the poorest sections of the city and to the lowest paying jobs, the 7,293 Hispanics and 2,366 blacks in Phoenix had no influence on community decision-making.[102]

These issues were far from Barry Goldwater's mind when he entered the University of Arizona in the fall of 1928. The atmosphere at the university was more relaxed than at structured Staunton, an environment that had brought forth his best efforts. Nor could the university kindle in him, as West Point might have, a commitment to serious work. Barry's priority, from the beginning, was extracurricular activity. "My idea was to have a good time in college and then enter the family business."[103] What a friend remembered of Barry Goldwater during his college days were "a big Chrysler, lots of money, clothes, and lots of girls."[104] Barry pledged Sigma Chi, the most prestigious fraternity on campus. He remained there even though his friend Harry Rosenzweig was denied admission because of fraternity restrictions against Jewish members.[105] Barry joined the football and swim teams, and he played sax, clarinet, and trombone. In the second semester his peers elected him freshman class president. Barry was less motivated in his schoolwork than he was in extracurricular activity. During the first semester he enrolled in courses in economics, mathematics, English, Spanish, and physical education. He received an A in general gymnastics but only C's and D's in his other courses. Grades improved in the second term, with a B in both philosophy and economics, a C in English, and a D in elementary statistics. Still, the school penalized him a unit of credit for his frequent absences.[106]

Barry Goldwater chose to leave college soon after the death of his father at age sixty-two in March 1929.[107] His decision resulted from his lackluster academic performance rather than family need. "If I'd been after a degree, I'd still be in the university," Goldwater candidly noted more than three decades after his year in college. "I was somewhat slow. I finished my freshman year but not with flying colors."[108] Baron Goldwater had left to his family stocks, securities, and insurance valued at almost $300,000. In the late 1920s the store generated sales of $400,000 annually. And there was no vacuum in store management. On Baron's death, business leadership at the store shifted to Sam Wilson, who had served the store since 1909. The Great Depression, moreover, had not yet touched Phoenix, and business at Goldwater's stayed at near-record levels through 1930. While Barry returned to his mother's home, brother Bob remained at Stanford University. After graduating in 1931, Bob worked briefly in the store before moving over to the Valley National Bank, the state's largest, to represent Goldwater interests on its board of directors.[109]

Wilson took charge of Barry's education, just as Michel had done with young Baron's. He made Barry a junior clerk with a starting salary of fifteen dollars per week and rotated him through each of the store's departments. Barry excelled behind the counter. His personality and charm sparked a talent for merchandising, and he set a store record of two hundred sales in a single day. When Barry had learned piece goods and ready-to-wear clothing, Wilson promoted him to office management. Barry was less successful here, never developing the financial and managerial abilities to match his skills in marketing. Along with this practical knowledge, Barry absorbed the store's philosophy. In a 1932 memorandum to Bob titled "Be Yourself," twenty-three-year-old Barry wrote:

> Why have we been so successful as merchants, and when I say "we" I mean the store and not ourselves . . . ? I say that it was chiefly because Goldwaters has always been Goldwaters and not a small town edition of a larger store. We have our own envirement [sic], our own reputation, our own service, our own standards, and our own methods. . . . We have been and will continue to be outstanding as long as we boast individuality. . . .
>
> Let's Be Goldwaters. Let us be the leaders of the city and not the trailers.[110]

In later years, after completing his apprenticeship in the store, Barry followed his father's path east on buying trips. He reflected humbly, "There was nothing I did that made me a success. You might say I was a success by being born into a successful family."[111]

It was under Wilson's experienced management that the store weathered the hardest years of the 1930s. The depression rippled through Arizona in the spring and summer of 1931; it was first felt in rapidly falling copper and cotton prices. By 1932 Phoenicians had recorded a significant decline in the winter tourist trade. Two of the six banks in Phoenix and two of the city's five building and loan associations failed. Retail trade was down by almost two-thirds between 1929 and 1933. To meet the store's financial emergency, Wilson directed cost-cutting, slashing inventory and reducing advertising and delivery services. Shrinking sales dictated that everyone take a pay cut, but Goldwater's was always proud that no employee was ever let go. It was not until the end of 1936, after the worst of the depression was over, that Sam Wilson retired and Barry and Bob assumed chief responsibility for the family business.[112]

While working his way up in the store Barry Goldwater was active in a range of community and social activities. He began to assume his father's civic responsibilities at age twenty-one, serving as a director of the Phoenix Chamber of Commerce. Fraternal ties cemented business associations when he joined the Masons, Shriners, and Elks, among other lodges. Barry mixed business and pleasure, playing basketball in a corporate league during the 1932–33 season. In 1934 he claimed a share of the winner's trophy in the Phoenix pro-am golf tournament. Especially important to Barry's emergence as a leader was time spent at the exclusive Phoenix Country Club. The club was the local elite's gathering spot and the city's informal center of power. On the golf links, in the locker room, and over drinks the personable Goldwater networked with such men as Walter Bimson of the Valley National Bank, builder Del Webb, and recent Harvard Law School graduate Denison Kitchel, the head of Phelps Dodge Corporation's labor relations division. Friendships that developed here solidified business relationships and ensured cooperation in community affairs. Also nurtured by such interactions were the elite vision and conservative perspective that parental example and instruction had instilled. Barry's identity and interests thus matured in an environment of reinforcing messages. With peer guidance and support, Barry became a leader without ever having to confront determined challenges to his values or beliefs.[113]

Barry did not allow business and social duties to absorb all of his time and energy. He applied for a commission as a second lieutenant in the officers reserve corps in 1928 and assumed the rank in 1930. During the summers of 1930 and 1931 he spent several weeks on active duty as a platoon commander at Arizona's Camp Stephen Little. Efficiency reports indicate that his superiors were impressed, giving him high marks for his military bearing, attention to duty, handling of men, and athletic ability. In 1933 he was promoted to first lieutenant in the infantry reserve, a rank he would not hold during the rest of the decade because the army placed him on inactive status. Barry's interest in Arizona and its people, cultivated when he was a child, matured on his frequent trips into the backcountry. Developing his photographic skills, he patiently framed the raw power of desert and sky in landscapes and the dignity of Navajo and Hopi in sensitive portraits. In 1935 he exhibited his photographs in what would be the first of many showings. As the number of photographs grew, so did his Kachina doll collection; it became one of Arizona's foremost holdings of Native American art. Barry was also involved in historical preservation, gathering an impressive body of Arizoniana, maps and documents that detailed the history of Anglo settlement. Later he would help found the Arizona Historical Foundation to safeguard these treasures. Spare moments remaining in Barry Goldwater's day were consumed with radio transmitting, model building, and tinkering with gadgets.[114]

Of all of his hobbies, flying was Barry's greatest passion. He learned to fly in 1930, soloing after only ten hours of instruction. Flights around Phoenix and Arizona quickly lengthened, and Barry made his first cross-country trip, to Los Angeles, in 1931. He would, over his lifetime, clock twelve thousand hours of flight time in 165 different types of aircraft, including helicopters and gliders. For Goldwater, flying was an experience that confirmed the majesty of God and realized the "ultimate extension of individual freedom."[115] The interface of pilot and machine, moreover, convinced him of technology's power to solve human problems. "My faith in the future rests squarely on the belief that man, if he doesn't destroy himself, will find new answers in the universe, new technologies, new disciplines, which will contribute to a vastly different and better world in the twenty-first century."[116] Flying proved more than a leisure-time pursuit. During the severe winter of 1936 Goldwater helped organize relief flights that dumped hay and feed to save stranded Navajo livestock. On other occasions he delivered medicines to Native American reservations and flew the sick to hospitals.[117]

Yet most intense of all his pursuits during this time was Peggy Johnson. Her acceptance of him would lead the *Arizona Republic* to headline, "Engagement of Social Import Links Old Arizona Family with Aristocracy of Indiana."[118] Peggy Johnson, while not royalty, was born in 1909 to a family of wealth and position. Her father was Ray Prescott Johnson, Sr., the president of multimillion-dollar Warner Gear Company, a maker of automobile equipment and accessories. Later he served as the executive vice president of giant Borg-Warner, the result of a merger of his company and another firm. Peggy grew up in small-town Muncie, a homogeneous community that counted few foreign-born residents or African-Americans among its more than thirty thousand people. Her childhood diaries describe an insulated, upper-class life of comfort and privilege. In them she reveals few anxieties, writing in meticulous detail of movies, parties, and outings with friends. Often her parents took her traveling, only occasionally leaving her in the care of the family's six servants. The family's wealth made Peggy neither arrogant nor selfish. Like many adolescents, she was self-conscious about her appearance and dress, attuned to fads, athletic, and aware of boys. If popular, she was also shy, reserved, and lacking in self-confidence. Peggy did not challenge convention. Patient, proper, nurturing, and even self-effacing, she readily aspired to the supporting roles of wife and mother.[119]

Peggy's parents enrolled her, at age thirteen, in Elmhurst, a boarding school for girls. After two years she transferred to Mount Vernon Academy in Washington, D.C., where she completed her high school education and two years of college. Mount Vernon was far more than a finishing school. She took courses in English, science, and mathematics while playing on the hockey and basketball teams. After graduation in 1929 Peggy entered the Grand Central Art School in New York City, and in 1932 she worked for the David Crystal Company, a dress manufacturing firm. She left her job and New York City when her father suffered a stroke in 1933.[120]

Peggy had met Barry in December 1930, when her family was vacationing in Phoenix. Her mother had taken her to Goldwater's to introduce her to Barry and, through him, to the Phoenix social set. Barry was immediately drawn to the attractive and stylish Peggy, and she, in turn, liked his gregarious nature and good looks. Barry pursued Peggy during her stay in Phoenix and later visited her in New York City and Muncie. In 1933 she returned to Phoenix to care for her ailing father, and her relationship with Barry grew more serious. Her father's death that year brought Peggy a sizable inheritance of money and stock. That summer, Barry proposed marriage, but she rejected him. Peggy never acted impulsively, hesitating, as well, because of the Johnson family's concern about her suitor's Jewish heritage. Barry persisted, however, and Peggy soon weakened, attracted to a man who was generous, financially secure, and convivial and who shared her interest in fashion. She accepted his proposal in December 1933, just two days before embarking on a round-the-world cruise. Perhaps Peggy's mother hoped that the lengthy trip would chill the relationship and cause her daughter to reconsider. They married nine months later in an Episcopal service in Muncie and returned to Phoenix to live. Marriage for Peggy meant absolute dedication and commitment to her husband. According to close friend and sister-in-law Alice Johnson McGreavy, "If Barry said he'd crawl across the Sahara Desert, Peggy would do it with him."[121] Peggy Jr. says of her mother, "Her life was Dad."[122] After briefly renting an apartment, they built a luxurious home just off the third fairway at the Phoenix Country Club. JoJo, brother Bob, and sister Carolyn would eventually occupy homes nearby, forming what their neighbors called the Goldwater compound. In January 1936, Joanne, their first child, was born.[123]

The year 1936 marked twenty-seven-year-old Barry Goldwater's coming of age. The retirement of Sam Wilson made Barry and his brother the store's highest authorities. It was now their business to direct or change as they saw fit. Barry had married, moved into his own home, and become a father. His apprenticeship had been an extended one. Role models, their power reinforced by compatible messages from the surrounding environment, had shaped Barry and his frame of reference. His parents, military school, and the business and country club communities had cast deep imprints on his mind and identity. Standing on Baron's shoulders and maturing under Wilson's grooming, he had joined the economic and civic leadership of

Phoenix. Barry was hardly passive in his rise. Through his multifaceted activities he had emerged as his own person. This empowering self-awareness, combined with personal magnetism and a sense of service, enabled him not only to command attention but to exert influence. Marriage to Peggy had only reinforced his assets and accelerated his emergence. Still, 1936 was only the beginning. As yet, politics held no interest for him. If he had absorbed a conservative perspective, his opinions had not jelled into reasoned, articulated principles. Consciousness-raising would occur under the impact of events, both at home and abroad, of the 1930s and 1940s. With his instincts and inherited beliefs stimulated, Barry Goldwater would complete his education as a conservative.

3

The Consciousness of a Conservative

I suggest to you that government never did a thing for us. Government didn't think up the branding iron or antsie pants, nor did it open the Scottsdale shop or the Prescott shop.
                                                                    —BARRY GOLDWATER

Perhaps my commitment . . . to maintaining weapons systems superior to any potential enemy is only the natural outcome of my frustrations and disappointments in this period just prior to World War II.
                                                                    —BARRY GOLDWATER
                                                                    With No Apologies

The Great Depression of the 1930s was more than an economic event. It was a blow to the American psyche. Dreams of opportunity and mobility turned to dross. In a world where desperate farmers dumped milk in ditches and hungry veterans marched on the nation's capital, events seemed out of control. Expectations that had guided lives and framed futures lost their relevance. Rugged individualism was a cruel irony to those standing before locked factory gates or in breadlines that snaked through city streets. Men in their three-piece suits hawking apples on street corners inadvertently mocked basic beliefs in personal initiative and optimism. Many lost hope, turning inward in silent acceptance of their defeat. Others, usually heading west, sought escape on the road or rails in a last rush to survive. The disillusionment of some was so profound that they found their faith in revolution.

Arizona did not escape the depression's path. Initially, Arizonans perceived the economic downturn as an eastern problem with little effect on their lives. State newspapers, in tune with their readers, gave only passing notice to the stock market crash in October 1929. Depression-related news received more coverage in 1930, but reporters still portrayed events as remote. Perceptions changed during the spring and summer of 1931, when the depression shook the pillars of the Arizona economy. The copper industry reeled before the weakening demand, which sent prices down sharply from 18.1 cents per pound in 1929 to a low of 5.6 cents in 1932. In response, all Arizona copper mines either shut down or employed only skeleton crews. Along with the copper miners, cotton growers suffered a "severe beating."[1] Farmers who had received 11 cents per pound for their crop in 1929 watched prices fall to 4 cents in 1932. Cattlemen had earned 9 cents per pound for beef in 1929 but could count on just 3 cents in 1933. Arizona retailers were not immune, and their ledger books recorded a 160 percent decline in net sales. The state tourism industry was gutted as well, for the depression curtailed vacation plans and forced Americans to stay home. Reacting to the economic fallout, more than 50,000 people abandoned the state between 1930 and 1933. In December 1932, 55,700 Arizonans were on the dole.[2]

The situation in Phoenix and Maricopa County was no better. The winter of 1931–32 exhausted the resources of private welfare agencies, and local leaders warned of an impending crisis. Delinquent taxes in Maricopa County totaled more than the 1932 budget, and officials were forced to use scrip to meet obligations. As economic conditions deteriorated, more men and women were thrown out of work. By December 1933, 9,898 Phoenicians, or 20 percent of the population, were receiving public assistance. Those still employed, while thankful to have a job, suffered severe wage cuts, and individual income was down an average of 51 percent. Precipitous declines in the prices of food, clothing, and consumer goods, however, did much to brake a free-fall in living standards.[3]

Beleaguered by the depression's assault, Arizonans joined other Americans in seeking out a scapegoat and a savior. President Herbert Hoover and New York Governor Franklin Delano Roosevelt assumed their respective roles in the 1932 election, which proved as much a contest for power as a morality play. Real fear for the present and future rallied Americans to Roosevelt and his vague pledges of relief, recovery, and reform. In overwhelming numbers they lined up at the polls to crush Hoover and end twelve years of Republican Party rule. Hoover carried only six states, none west of the Appalachian mountains.

In his first hundred days, President Roosevelt launched the New Deal and produced a fundamental shift in economic and political power to Washington, D.C. What emerged in the 1930s was an activist federal government determined to secure economic stability and take new responsibility for the welfare of Americans. In expanding federal regulatory power and founding the welfare state, the New Deal extended the government's hand into the local community and the daily life of citizens.

New Deal legislation created an array of federal agencies designed to cope with the economic emergency. Congress authorized $500 million for the Federal Emergency Relief Administration (FERA) to combat hunger and distress. The Civilian Conservation Corps (CCC) "primed the pump" by providing work relief. The Tennessee Valley Authority (TVA) was a government-owned hydroelectric and flood control system eventually consisting of twenty-five dams and encompassing forty-one thousand square miles in seven states. More comprehensive were the National Industrial Recovery Act (NIRA) and the Agricultural Adjustment Act (AAA). The NIRA, under its Blue Eagle symbol, sought to steady American business with codes of "fair" competitive practice. Codes in each industry, argued NIRA framers, would keep surviving businesses solvent by setting prices and assigning production levels. The law also made provision for the Public Works Administration (PWA), a relief program creating jobs building highways, airports, schools, and other public structures. The AAA confronted the problems of overproduction and low prices that had plagued farmers through repeated cycles of boom and bust. Under the provisions of this law, the government promised to pay farmers if they curtailed production of crops and livestock. These laws were supplemented later in the decade by the Works Progress Administration (WPA), the unemployment and old-age insurance programs of Social Security, and the Wagner Act, which guaranteed the rights of labor unions to organize and bargain collectively.

New Deal money flowed to the West in disproportionate amounts. Federal per capita expenditures were higher in the West than anywhere else in the country, and the region received assistance at a rate three times the national average. Emergency aid from FERA, AAA, PWA, and WPA relieved acute economic distress, saved homes, and put government checks into westerners' hands. Providing more longterm benefit, the federal government initiated extensive capital investment regionwide. Washington spent enormous sums developing the West's infrastructure of roads, bridges, power lines, and especially waterworks. In the 1930s the Bureau of Reclamation had nineteen major water projects under construction in the West, including Boulder (Hoover) Dam, the Central Valley Project in California, and Grand Coulee Dam on the Columbia River.[4] In subsidizing hydroelectric power, flood control systems, irrigation projects, and highway construction, the federal government became the region's prime contractor. While the West remained an economic colony of the East, supplying raw materials and importing industrial goods, Washington had laid the foundation for future regional development.[5]

Arizonans did not miss their opportunity at the public trough. Fifty federal agencies established offices in the state and were primed to aid in the recovery. As early as June 1, 1933, five CCC camps were in operation with their four hundred men working on reforestation, soil erosion, and flood control projects. The federal government would eventually establish forty CCC camps, enrolling more than 15,000 Arizonans and spending nearly $44 million. In July FERA provided relief assistance to more than 100,000 people. Arizona expenditures from FERA would reach $17.5 million by 1936. Benefits provided by AAA in 1934 led state farmers to shift 64,000 acres of cotton, wheat, and corn to soil-building crops and conservation use. Beginning in 1936 the WPA employed 16,000 men and women in grading and surfacing Phoenix streets, building parks and schools, and expanding Sky Harbor Airport facilities. New Deal funds were also allocated for construction of the Gila River Project and Bartlett Dam, renovation of Horse Mesa, Mormon Flat, and Roosevelt Dams, and expansion of Phoenix waterlines. This created jobs for Arizona's unemployed, supported local merchants, and opened new agricultural lands. It generated, as well, cheap electrical power to fuel industrial development.[6]

The federal government, although a longtime player in the Arizona economy, expanded its role significantly in the 1930s. New Deal agencies collectively provided Arizona with more than $342 million in assistance. At the same time, the federal government collected less than $16 million in taxes from the state. The New Deal made Washington the largest employer and consumer in Phoenix and Maricopa County. According to builder Del Webb, Phoenix construction was "no longer a private enterprise but rather a subsidiary of the federal government."[7] With Washington's help, Arizona and Phoenix began to sense recovery as early as 1934 and certainly by 1935. Area merchants reported fewer bankruptcies, bank deposits returned to pre-depression levels, and copper and cotton prices were again on the rise. By 1936 the number of Arizona families on relief had been cut in half. Like a sudden desert rainstorm, the depression had only briefly clouded Arizona before passing.[8]

From the first, Franklin D. Roosevelt had not impressed Barry Goldwater. Following his mother's lead, Barry registered to vote as a Republican in 1930. He did this despite Uncle Morris' standing among Arizona Democrats and the party's lopsided seven-to-one voter advantage. Such an overwhelming majority meant that Arizona was a one-party state where the general elections had less relevance to victory than did the outcome of the Democratic primaries. Goldwater explains: "The Democratic Party had ruled Arizona with an arrogance that offended me. My decision to register as a Republican was an act of defiance."[9] So, too, was his vote for Herbert Hoover in 1932, for Arizonans gave Roosevelt a landslide victory.[10]

Goldwater's upbringing made him suspicious of the new administration, but he believed that patriotism demanded support for President Roosevelt. He approved of the New Deal's western reclamation policies and efforts to reform the stock market and the nation's banking system. The Goldwater's store, promising "We Do Our Part," participated in the NIRA and displayed the Blue Eagle emblem in its store window and newspaper advertising. Barry did not deny the impact of the New Deal on his city's depressed economy. He wrote in 1940, "Another factor that has been of extreme importance to retailing in all its branches has been the huge expenditures of public moneys in this area. Arizona ranks near the top in per capita money received from the New Deal."[11]

The honeymoon, however, was short. The Blue Eagle disappeared from the store and its advertising copy as early as April 1934. Barry Goldwater criticized the NIRA for enabling Washington "to impose its will on private business."[12] More specifically, store management targeted as offensive NIRA codes that prescribed prices, wages, and employee hours. Further, Goldwater argued that federal spending was counterproductive because, "if it continues, it will be at the expense of business and is . . . robbing Peter to pay Paul."[13] The expansion of federal control, deficit spending, and business regulation countered Goldwater's conservative instincts. He believed that relief programs were potentially dangerous threats to the nation, for they inhibited self-reliance and fostered dependency. New Deal agencies, in siphoning power from the states and cities, also undermined authorities at the grassroots. Direction, Goldwater believed, should come from men and women in the private sector who understood the needs and people of the local community better than bureaucrats in distant Washington. "The progress of mankind . . . ," he later declared, "is measured in the acts of man-to-man charity and person-to-person justice performed on an individual basis, motivated by the desire of the free individual to serve his God and to love his fellow man."[14] Only a minority, however, shared his views of the New Deal. In 1936 Arizonans joined the majority of Americans to reelect Franklin Roosevelt and render a strong endorsement of his policies.[15]

The New Deal danger, as Goldwater saw it, went beyond business regulations and encroachments on individual and community freedom. The rise of organized labor under federal government auspices—or, as friend Denison Kitchel described it, "This NIRA-labor business"—also alarmed Barry Goldwater.[16] The NIRA and later the Wagner Act, with their guarantees of workers' rights, encouraged union activists to organize. Telling men and women that "the President wants you to join the union," organizers enrolled hundreds of thousands of new members in the American Federation of Labor (AFL) and the recently created Congress of Industrial Organizations (CIO). Federal law breathed new life into the Arizona labor movement as well. Arizona unionists organized agricultural workers, miners, and government employees, among others. Phoenix alone counted forty-five union locals that a community leader noted were "becoming more and more powerful."[17] Local AFL and CIO organizers moved jointly to translate their economic strength into political leverage. In the late 1930s they established the Arizona League for Better Government, a political vehicle that would marshal union votes and resources for candidates friendly to labor's aims. The arrival of labor at the political and economic bargaining table could only portend a lessening of the power of business and Republican Party players.[18]

The 1930s tested Goldwater and proved formative. "I think the foundations of my political philosophy were rooted in my resentment against the New Deal," he wrote.[19] Goldwater's opposition to the New Deal and organized labor was more than simply a small-town businessman's knee-jerk reaction. His family history and conservative upbringing taught him the virtues of self-reliance, local initiative, and private-sector action. Service in the leadership cadre of Phoenix buttressed these beliefs and endowed him with a vested interest in the status quo. Similarly, a westerner's sense of isolation and distance from the national government kindled apprehension and then resistance to Washington's edicts. The depression, moreover, did not force Goldwater to reassess his conservative outlook. Phoenix had emerged rapidly and relatively unscathed from the depression when compared with eastern industrial cities. Financially insulated from the ravages of depression, Barry Goldwater and his family had suffered neither displacement nor distress. Complementing these attitudes was Barry's newborn loyalty to the Republican Party. Fed by his competitive nature, political partisanship conditioned him to resist the recovery program of the Democratic Party.

Stoking both this anti–New Deal perspective and his identity as a Republican was Barry Goldwater's admiration for Herbert Hoover. In early 1933 Paul Sexson, Barry's brother-in-law and a Hoover family staff member, arranged for Goldwater to meet the defeated president. With this meeting began a relationship that, while never warm, would be especially meaningful to Goldwater. Unlike Barry's other mentors, Hoover inspired him philosophically. To Goldwater, Hoover was a fighter for an America submerged in New Deal bureaucracy and red ink. Rather than representing a failed past, Hoover offered inspiration for the restoration of time-honored American values. Goldwater collected all of Hoover's books and described him to a friend as "one of the greatest Americans who has ever lived."[20] As Goldwater rose in Republican Party ranks, their relationship became less one-sided and more reciprocal, and the pace of their correspondence and visits increased.[21]

Barry did not keep his political opinions to himself or his friends at the Phoenix Country Club. On June 23, 1938, he made his first public pronouncement in a *Phoenix Gazette* guest editorial titled "A Fireside Chat with Mr. Roosevelt." In the editorial Goldwater took Roosevelt to task for the "queer antics of those in Washington." In five years, Goldwater asked, what have you "done that would be of any value to me as a business man and a citizen[?]" He criticized the president for raising taxes and increasing government spending. While conceding that working hours were shorter and wages higher, he deplored a recent economic downturn that had reversed gains made since 1933 and ballooned the ranks of the unemployed. Goldwater was especially incensed about the federal government's support of labor unions. "The worst thing about your labor plan has been that you have turned over to the racketeering practices of ill-organized unions the future of the working man. Witness the chaos they are creating in eastern cities. Witness the men thrown out of work, the riots, the bloodshed, and the ill feeling between labor and capitol [*sic*] and then decide if that plan worked." Goldwater further condemned Roosevelt and the New Deal for alienating businessmen "who distrust you and fear your every utterance" and using relief funds "to prime a few votes." He concluded: "I would like to know just where you are leading us. Are you going further into the morass that you have led us into or are you going to go back to the good old American way of doing things where business is trusted, where labor earns more, where we take care of our unemployed, and where a man is elected to public office because he is a good man for the job and not because he commands your good will and a few dollars of taxpayers' money."[22] A few days after it appeared in print, Barry Goldwater sent a clipping of the editorial to Herbert Hoover.[23]

His resistance was not limited to this single volley; it was in motion even before the appearance of the editorial. He realized that the depression had exposed real problems that he could not ignore or deny. Nor could he leave unchallenged a liberal remedy that rejected everything that he believed. Instinctively, Goldwater staked out an alternative. It would not be, in light of Goldwater's training and skills, a philosophical response. He confronted the New Deal in the second half of the thirties with actions that championed the cause of individual and local self-determination. In two arenas—the store and the Phoenix community—Goldwater offered a role model for conservatives. In such counterattacks would opponents of liberalism find the means to recapture public favor and achieve a new influence.

A simple motto, said Barry, governed labor relations at the store: "Treat people right and they will treat you right."[24] With the store in their hands after 1936, Barry and brother Bob made their business a showcase for welfare capitalism. Paternalism, enlightened self-interest, and anti-unionism alone are insufficient to explain store policy. The Goldwater brothers also acted from a sense of fairness, a desire to do the right thing for those economically dependent on their decisions. Thus, employees worked a five-day, forty-hour week and were offered wages higher than the national retail-store average. The store assumed the full cost of employees' health, accident, and life insurance. Baron Goldwater's informal pension arrangements with employees, which the store subsidized when individual funds proved inadequate, gave way to structured and secure retirement plans. In later years Goldwater's instituted paid sick leave, created a profit-sharing plan, and hired a store psychologist. The store was one of the first in Phoenix to hire blacks. They were not, however, employed in sales positions except during the Christmas season rush.[25]

More unusual was the store's purchase in 1942 of a twenty-five-acre farm eight miles from Phoenix. Run by an elected committee of employees, the farm offered men and women the opportunity to raise vegetables on garden plots and to obtain meat, milk, and eggs against wartime shortages. A picnic area, clubhouse, swimming pool, and outdoor dance floor were available for recreation. During the summer months, when school was not in session, a bus picked up the children of working parents and took them to the farm for day care. The store also owned a cabin near Prescott that it made available without charge to vacationing employees. To boost morale, Goldwater's promoted its own acting company, with plays staged by employees. Through the Flying G Club store personnel could learn to fly. The store bought an airplane and hired an instructor, leaving the student only the expense of paying for flight time. The Goldwaters' impulsive acts of generosity further enhanced loyalty. It was not uncommon for the brothers to help employees by paying overdue bills, providing paid vacations, and even assuming home mortgages.[26]

Fringe benefits did not by themselves keep morale high. The Goldwaters gained respect and trust by sharing information, soliciting employee input, and working hard to maintain access. "When we embarked on a new store policy," remembers Barry, "we explained just why we do [it] and how it will benefit everyone in the company by increasing our profits. And anyone, no matter what his job, is entitled to examine the company books to find out if we are telling the truth."[27] A monthly newsletter and breakfast supplemented daily informal interactions. Employees also elected an advisory committee to meet with store managers on policy and grievances. The result was an employee record of lengthy store service and worker rejection of two unionization attempts. In a letter to Barry, Jackie Hedges spoke for many of her fellow employees: "Although I like to feel that I have earned a definite and worthwhile place in your organization, I realize full well that it is in most part due to your unusual policy of live and let live. If I have made good it is because working with you has always been a proposition of 33⅓% cooperation from you, 33⅓% confidence from you and the other 33⅓% friendship from you."[28]

Outside the store Barry Goldwater set for himself a frenzied pace of civic activities. Sure that economic development and growth translated into individual opportunity and mobility, he avidly boosted Phoenix to draw tourist dollars and business investment. He was convinced that the "challenge of attracting industry" was his generation's primary charge; if met, it could counter the need for federal action.[29] But the determined entrepreneur could not counter federal encroachment alone. Goldwater was thus convinced that local problems demanded the collective action of neighbors helping neighbors. Unemployment, health care, and poverty were amenable to solution, as they had been in the past, through "a spirit of community" service that galvanized business, professional, religious, and social organizations into a commitment to act.[30]

Goldwater's civic activism took many forms. He joined the Chamber of Commerce's Royal Order of Thunderbirds "to work for the glorious future of Phoenix."[31] He taught a "tourist information" class to area merchants. He was president of the Chamber of Commerce and the Community Chest and was the general chairman of the Community Chest drive in 1937. In addition, Barry served on the board of directors of the Heard Museum, the Civic Center Association, the Young Men's Christian Association, and the Boys' Club of Phoenix. St. Joseph and St. Luke hospitals appointed him to their advisory boards, and he networked in numerous fraternal orders. Goldwater also had time to join Prescott's Smoki Clan, a group of Arizona professional and business people who performed Native American dances in full regalia to publicize and boost the community.[32]

Peggy Goldwater, while occupied with the care of daughter Joanne and, after 1938, with Barry Jr., also participated in community affairs. Her main interest was the Birth Control Federation of America, later renamed Planned Parenthood. Birth control, by the 1930s, had discarded its image as a radical movement of feminists and anticapitalists and become "fashionable."[33] Advocating birth control as America's means to cope with the unfit and foreign-born, the movement promised, according to historian David Kennedy, "a conservative program for social control."[34] This message attracted a national membership composed primarily of Protestant, native-born, upper-middle-class, Republican women. In Phoenix, women like Peggy Goldwater, Florence Bimson, and Margaret Kober organized in 1937 the Mothers' Health Clinic, which targeted Mexican-American women for assistance. They proposed birth control to raise health standards, produce only "wanted" children, lessen the city's relief burden, and weed out the mentally and physically deficient. Approving of his wife's work, Barry wrote letters seeking financial support for Planned Parenthood.[35]

From his work in the store and community, Barry Goldwater gained an authority to which he had previously laid claim only by inheritance. He had shown both that the individual alone and individuals united could make a difference. The store was a model of successful labor-management relations and still able to turn a profit. Barry had worked hard at local problem-solving. Phoenix organizations and ad hoc coalitions of citizens animated with the spirit of community could address area needs and help pull their city from the ashes of the depression.

Still unresolved, however, were questions that addressed the limits of individual and community self-determination. Was individual role-modeling sufficient to bring change, or did it permit existing abuses to continue while quieting activism? Would local groups unite without the stimulus of crisis and make sustained efforts against stubborn problems of class, race, and gender? Do white power brokers, acting on their own, undercut minority claims to influence? If an individual or community rejected national norms and values, what would compel them toward social or economic redress? How was the private sector's contribution to economic growth to be assessed in light of the expanding role of the federal government in the American and Arizona economy? If not foremost in Goldwater's mind in the 1930s, these questions would demand his attention in later decades.

New achievements raised Goldwater's already high profile. His interest in photography had evolved, by the late 1930s, from a hobby into a serious pursuit. In 1939 he sold his first photographs to *Arizona Highways*. Eventually, almost two hundred of his pictures appeared in the magazine. He published *Arizona Portraits*, the first volume appearing in 1940 and the second in 1946. For the books, he chose from his five thousand negatives to create a montage of photographs that vividly contrasted Arizona's wide vistas with intimate portraits of native peoples. The Royal Photographic Society of London was impressed with his work and elected him to membership.[36]

He also enhanced his reputation as an outdoorsman. In 1940 Barry made plans to join the Norman Nevills party on a trip down the Colorado River. Nevills had warned him, "The Colorado is just as tough[,] rough[,] and dangerous as it was when our forerunners Powell, Stone, Stanton, and others took it."[37] Peggy Goldwater, pregnant with her third child, was distraught about Barry's decision and "dissolve[d] in tears at the thought of his going."[38] Despite "every kind of pressure known to womankind and mankind," Barry would not be denied.[39] "I have wanted to take this trip for so long that the very thought of it gives me the willies."[40] His only concession to Peggy was a change in itinerary that shortened his time away. Barry met the expedition at Green River, Utah, and for forty-two days ran the rapids in a plywood boat. The river and the Grand Canyon awed him: "At this sunset hour the canyon walls are indescribably beautiful, and I fear the magic of photography can never record what I see now. The tall spires near the canyon's top and the walls of the canyon up there look as if God had reached out and swiped a brush of golden paint across them, gilding these rocks in the bright glow of the setting sun."[41]

His naturalist instincts were aroused: "We are on the Colorado . . . that means something more to me than thoughts of electrical power or a harnessed river."[42] At least temporarily then, the river had quieted any conflict he felt between wilderness preservation and economic growth and development. On reaching Lake Mead, he became only the seventy-first known person to travel the Colorado River's length. Barry kept a journal of the trip and published privately *An Odyssey of the Green and Colorado Rivers* soon after his return. Edited by *Phoenix Gazette* columnist and friend Bert Fireman, *Odyssey* is an informative and entertaining blend of geology, geography, history, river lore, and rapid-running techniques. More important to his future, Barry recorded the trip on film.[43]

Business success, meanwhile, brought him national recognition and enhanced his prestige locally. If budgets and bookkeeping were not his style, design and merchandising were. Barry created and nationally marketed the "branding iron" design, hand-printed cattle brands on white broadcloth. The idea was quite popular, and Goldwater's sold six thousand branding-iron summer frocks in 1938 alone. Branding irons soon appeared on towels, glassware, bookmarks, wrapping paper, and other assorted items the store marketed. Barry created a national fad with "antsy pants," men's underwear printed with large red ants. "You'll rant and dance with ants in your pants," the ads promised.[44] He also fashioned blue denim dresses, desert colors for women's wear, and Goldwater cologne. Only one of his ideas, Native American motifs on fine china, lost money. His success drew the attention of *Women's Wear Daily*, which in 1939 described him as a "creative merchandising dynamo."[45] By 1941 the three Goldwater's stores in the Phoenix area and the one in Prescott were doing $1 million in annual business.[46]

The store did not consume the Goldwater brothers. According to a retailing competitor, "Neither Barry nor his brother Bob was ever a damn bit interested in the store. As a result, it never made much money. Barry was interested in everything else, and Bob was interested in golf. The store was just a place to hang their hats."[47] Barry and Bob turned over to Bill Saufley, who replaced Sam Wilson, the implementation of their labor relations and retirement plans and most of the store's day-to-day operations. This allowed Barry time for merchandising creativity and his hobbies. Bob, who was "not too tied down," spent his days at the Phoenix Country Club.[48] Barry's purchase of a second home in La Jolla, California, in 1940 made his infrequent appearances in the store during the summer months even more rare. While the store was profitable under Saufley's direction, it could not support expansion, employee benefits, and the extravagant Goldwater brothers' lifestyles. Continuously overspending their store income, Barry and Peggy had to use the interest generated by her trust fund accounts to balance their budget.[49]

The store failed to fulfill Barry. Moneymaking had never been an end in itself, and storekeeping did not give him a sense of purpose. Despite his success with antsy pants, he later wrote, work "left me empty."[50] Business responsibility was also stressful. The opening of a new store in Prescott in 1937 was especially difficult. In preparation, Barry worked for five days and nights without sleep. Tired and anxious, he became short-tempered and "just blew my stack."[51] Peggy, however, was quite shaken. Years later, she described her husband as having suffered a "nervous breakdown": "His nerves broke completely. He couldn't sleep nights. He was very nervous."[52] In 1938, according to a sympathetic biography, Barry "crack[ed] again" under business-induced strain.[53] Dr. Leslie Kober, Barry's physician, did not share the laymen's opinions and rendered his diagnosis without qualification: "I tell you flatly Barry Goldwater never suffered any nervous breakdown in 1937, 1939 or at any other time. . . . To my knowledge, he has never had to take a tranquilizer."[54] Brief vacations after each incident refreshed Goldwater and quieted concern. Never again would Barry's well-known quick temper threaten to turn into something more serious. Yet rumors of the "breakdowns" persisted and would surface to haunt Goldwater later.[55]

He did suffer from "periods of depression."[56] The whirl of civic activity and business stress sometimes overwhelmed him. Public attention and acclaim had not eased his sense of inadequacy or raised feelings of low self-esteem. Temporary relief came through escape, and he would disappear into the desert for days exploring and taking photographs. These trips recharged Barry and bolstered him for another cycle of activities. More troubling, and perhaps related to his depression, Goldwater was a heavy drinker with a taste for bourbon and tequila. A note that he wrote while running the Colorado River is only superficially amusing and reveals much: "Bob has gone on the wagon—he must be ill mentally or the heat has gotten him. The wagon is a fine thing, though, says one who has spent three weeks lolling on it. The lining is now back in my stomach and I sweat water instead of Old Taylor."[57] Barry never denied his problem. When asked during John Tower's confirmation hearings in 1989 about allegations of his friend's drinking, he remarked, "You start counting noses on that and we're all dead. You can say that about anyone, starting with me."[58]

As merchant, civic activist, socialite, photographer, and adventurer, Goldwater had made an impression in Phoenix. And a changing economic climate had by 1940 revised the political forecast. The depression lost much of its salience in Arizona and Phoenix as the new decade began and growth replaced stagnation. Arizona had rebounded from its depression-caused population decline to post a gain of almost 15 percent by 1940. Phoenix, while growing more slowly than it had in previous decades, showed a 36 percent increase to nearly 65,500 people. In designating for the first time a "Phoenix metropolitan area," census takers announced the coming of age of Phoenix and Maricopa County. Economic indicators also pointed to a community on the mend. By the decade's end construction in Phoenix was rivaling that of the boom years of the 1920s. Similarly, merchants matched their 1929 sales highs in 1940. Boosters busily turned out literature promoting Phoenix and its environs as the "valley of the sun" and claiming that "the desert has been converted into California. The dream of Arizona's visionary prophets has indeed come true."[59] Technological advances made the boosters' pleas more believable. As larger and more efficient models replaced makeshift cooling units, Phoenix began to proclaim itself the "air conditioning capital of the world."[60] Offices and stores eagerly converted, making Phoenix a year-round community. Thirty-five thousand tourists visited the city in the 1939–40 winter season alone and breathed new life into local business. Barry Goldwater noted the upturn: "The stimulus from the injection of these tourist dollars into the veins of our economy have been felt by every person doing business in this area. The farmer has sold more produce. The hotels have filled more rooms. The merchants have sold more goods. It is easy to see, therefore, why businessmen are so unanimously enthusiastic about the continuance and enlargement of a proper advertising program."[61]

The passing of hard times made men and women more receptive to criticism of Franklin Roosevelt and the New Deal. They were tired after eight years of relief and reform, and they questioned the government's ability to bring recovery when 7.5 million people remained unemployed nationally. The president, too, had exposed himself to attack because of his Supreme Court packing plan, the recession of 1937–38, and the launching of a campaign for an unprecedented third term. Despite the flow of New Deal dollars, critics raised dissenting voices throughout the West. Senator Pat McCarran of Nevada, Idaho Governor C. Ben Ross, and Montana Senator Burton Wheeler condemned the president and his programs, and their condemnations were echoed in Oregon, California, Colorado, and Arizona.[62]

If not yet fully prepared for or even aware of his ultimate destination, Barry Goldwater edged toward politics in 1940. He had begun to develop confidence and a public speaking style by lecturing to Phoenix audiences about his photographic slides of Arizona and Native Americans. Barry, hardly glib or polished, impressed audiences with his historical and geographical knowledge and artistic skills. His use of simple, colorful language, delivered in a conversational tone without pretention or written notes, fixed his listeners' attention. Handsome, personable, and framed by his powerful slides, Barry's face and image remained in people's minds. By February 1940 he was making two slide presentations a week. Barry continued showing his slides while he expanded the range of his lecture topics. More self-assured, he appeared on the Rotary Club, Lions' Club, and PTA speaking circuit to talk about "Retailing," "Kachina Dolls," and "Arizona's National Monuments."[63]

Even greater exposure came through the showing of his film of the Colorado River trip. Barry screened the movie before civic organizations and packed audiences in a rented Phoenix movie theater. Success in Phoenix led him to take the movie on the road, and he exhibited it throughout the state. He wrote Norman Nevills in January 1941 that more than eight thousand people had attended film screenings, and he estimated that as many as fifteen thousand more would see it by the end of the year. Barry underestimated the film's draw. "I got to showing that damn thing as often as five times a day."[64] By April 1941 audiences had surpassed nineteen thousand people. Those who attended the showings took in more than rapids-running and Grand Canyon scenery. Before them on film and in person was Barry Goldwater, the rugged individualist and courageous outdoorsman living the strenuous life of their dreams. To ten-year-old Jim Byrkit, who attended a showing in 1940 in Jerome, Arizona, Barry appeared as a "bronze god who had just beaten the river."[65] Athletic, six feet tall, the grandson of an Arizona pioneer, and a successful businessman, Barry only enhanced the mystique by flying his plane to movie exhibitions. He was more than a temporary sensation. In communities throughout Arizona, Barry sowed political seeds, making personal contacts with men and women who would not forget him. The movie "gave me access to so damn many Arizonans that it was just a natural step for me to go into politics."[66]

The foundation for a political career was now in place, but its weight strained the Goldwater family. Civic and business obligations, hobbies, and now speaking engagements took Barry away from Peggy and their children, Joanne, Barry Jr., and newly born Michael. Peggy bowed to her husband's ambitions and offered little resistance. The children, however, were more sensitive to their father's remoteness and less forgiving. Joanne would later describe the increasing time her father spent away as "abandonment."[67] Nor was Peggy temperamentally suited to fill the void in her children's lives. Barry was her focus, and she kept the children at a distance, delegating to the servants much responsibility for their upbringing. Even when caring for the children, Peggy insulated herself. Nephew Paul Sexson remembers Peggy's inattention when, during a particularly rambunctious play time, one of the children was injured: "She just sat in the middle of it all, quiet and placid, absorbed with the knitting on her knee."[68] His mother, says Barry Jr., "was passive, subservient; a caretaker. She wasn't a strong influence. I never really knew my mother."[69] Early on, their father's absence and mother's isolation had opened in the children's psyches what Barry Jr. calls "a common wound."[70] They had received the same wordless message that Baron and JoJo had sent to Barry.

Events thousands of miles from home would postpone his political plans and further strain family relations. Goldwater's focus during the 1930s had been on Arizona's people and places, but this did not blur for him the European situation. The rise of Adolf Hitler and the Nazi campaign against the Jews had stirred thoughts of grandfather Michel and his exodus from Poland. Barry was sufficiently alarmed to read Hitler's *Mein Kampf*. He watched German armies advance and the dominos fall in Austria, Czechoslovakia, Poland, Denmark, Norway, the Low Countries, and finally France. Like many of his generation, he read into history the lessons of military weakness and lack of will before aggressors. If only the western powers had preserved their military might, united, and drawn the line against Hitler, the world would have been spared war. "Perhaps," he later wrote, "my commitment through the years to maintaining weapon systems superior to any potential enemy is only the natural outcome of my frustrations and disappointments in this period just prior to World War II."[71] Though he was disgusted with Hitler and a proponent of a strong military, Goldwater rejected President Roosevelt's plan to aid Great Britain against the Nazi threat. Until this became an "American" war affecting the nation's vital interests, he adhered to a hands-off policy. His distrust of Roosevelt certainly played a role. Like Herbert Hoover, Barry supported the platform of the America First Committee and opposed intervention in European affairs.[72]

In 1941 Goldwater sensed that America could not long remain isolated from war. He continued on inactive duty with the army reserves, but patriotic fervor made him eager to serve. Recalling flag ceremonies at the Phoenix Indian School and his mother's teachings about country, he said, "The little boy never quite forgot."[73] Three children, age, bad knees, and astigmatism meant deferment, however, and they were barriers that would be difficult to overcome. His opportunity to serve would come through civic activities. Barry had agreed to chair the Phoenix Chamber of Commerce's Military Affairs committee, with the charge to facilitate the arrival of the American army in the Valley of the Sun. The Army Air Corps had chosen the area because of its excellent flying weather and because the land had been donated by the city. With the establishment of Luke and Williams Air Bases and Falcon and Thunderbird Fields, Phoenix emerged as a prime Air Corps training site, and Goldwater's assignment grew in importance. In July, as part of his duties, Goldwater approached Luke's commanding officer, Colonel Ennis Whitehead, with offers of city service and support. The colonel wanted, instead, an officer who "knew his way around Arizona."[74] Never one to hesitate and not waiting to discuss the matter with Peggy, Barry volunteered on the spot. He immediately applied for a transfer from the infantry reserves and to active duty. To overcome his obstacles, Barry enlisted the help of Arizona senators Carl Hayden and Ernest McFarland, who intervened to speed paperwork. Within four weeks First Lieutenant Barry Goldwater was in uniform and assigned as public relations officer of the base. He was later authorized to coordinate the base's supply system. To his startled employees, Barry explained: "Then came this trouble with the little moustached so-and-so who infests parts of Europe. With it came a realization that this country of ours would play an increasingly important role in the ultimate outcome and with that realization came the desire to help. I was ready to go when the opportunity came!"[75] Barry had another reason for joining: "If I could get on duty, I could quit showing that God-damn movie."[76]

On December 7, 1941, Goldwater was playing golf with his mother at the Phoenix Country Club. Like most Americans, his attention had been fixed on Europe and especially the North Atlantic, where American and German forces were locked in undeclared naval war. Already, American warships had been torpedoed and 126 sailors had died. The news of the Japanese attack on Pearl Harbor both shocked and energized him. Said JoJo, "He just dropped his clubs and ran."[77] Despite his enthusiasm, the declaration of war the next day still left Goldwater far from combat. Age and poor eyesight disqualified him as an Air Corps pilot, and he reluctantly filled logistical and training slots. In July 1942, after a year at Luke, the Air Corps transferred now Captain Goldwater to Yuma, Arizona, where he oversaw construction and requisitioned supplies for an advanced flying school for combat pilots. Staying on at the school, Goldwater served as an aerial gunnery instructor and helped to perfect a technique that dramatically increased accuracy and the number of successful candidates. For this his commanding officer recommended him for a commendation ribbon. He also participated in training programs for Chiang Kai-shek's nationalist Chinese pilots. Yet after eighteen months of war Barry remained confined to Arizona, fighting vicariously through his trainees. He would not be denied, however. In hope of a change in policy, he had unofficially accumulated two hundred hours of flight experience even before the war began by offering to take photographs of newly graduated fliers in exchange for stick time. His efforts to see action would soon bear fruit.[78]

The Air Corps' desperate need for pilots gave Barry his chance to fly and relief from stateside duty. To ferry aircraft and fly supplies the long distances to the war theaters, the army created a service-pilot rating open to civilians and combat-disqualified fliers who had sufficient flight experience with large aircraft. Goldwater qualified and transferred, in May 1943, to the 27th Ferry Squadron of the Air Transport Command (ATC), headquartered in New Castle, Delaware. He won his regular army wings later that year. Wearing his "go-to-hell hat," Barry had joined the "pony-express run" and the war.[79] Despite appearances, there was nothing glamorous about the duty. Flying cargo over vast distances was boring, tedious, and exhausting. Without warning, potentially deadly crises could interrupt the routine. Captain Goldwater would never engage a single enemy plane in combat, but his support missions and those of the ATC would prove critical to the outcome of the conflict.[80]

"Living like dogs and flying like fiends," the pilots of the ATC carried the tools of war to the front along three major supply routes.[81] The SNOWBALL run brought military aircraft, equipment, and personnel to the United Kingdom. Goldwater flew one of his early missions on SNOWBALL, volunteering to pilot a P-47 Thunderbolt fighter over the North Atlantic. His commanding officer recommended him for an air medal because engine failure would have resulted "in almost certain death in the freezing waters."[82] He also piloted B-26s, B-25s, and C-86s to war zones. Through 1943 Captain Goldwater primarily drew his assignments on the CRESCENT and FIREBALL routes. CRESCENT followed a line of flight southeast from the United States through the Azores, across North Africa and the Middle East to India. The destination of FIREBALL was also the China, Burma, and India theater of operation, but its crews flew farther south, through central Africa.[83]

In February 1944 Goldwater was stationed in India and assigned to "fly the Hump," the last leg of both the FIREBALL and CRESCENT ten-thousand-mile runs. The Japanese army's closing of the Burma Road in 1942 had cut off supplies to Chiang Kai-shek's army and General Claire Chennault's 14th Air Force. To sustain them and pin down a million and a half Japanese soldiers, allied military planners initiated an around-the-clock airlift of war material from India over the Himalayas to Chinese air fields.[84]

If the five-hundred-mile Hump air routes were easy to plot on maps, terrain and weather made them among the war's most difficult and dangerous. "The weather over the Hump," wrote General William Tunner, "changed from minute to minute, from mile to mile. One end was set down in the low, steamy jungles of India, the other in the mile-high plateau of western China. And between the two lies the Rockpile, a law unto itself."[85] Pilots took off from India's hot and humid Assam Valley and climbed quickly to an altitude of seventeen thousand feet to clear the massive ridges and high peaks of the Himalayan range. They descended rapidly off the mountains into China, landing on gravel airstrips at Kunming. From there they shuttled supplies to Dinjan, Tezpur, and Moran. Monsoons lasted from mid-May to mid-October, bringing two hundred inches of rain, thunderstorms, clouds, fog, low visibility, and icing conditions as low as twelve thousand feet. In bad weather pilots had to push their planes up to twenty-five thousand feet or more. The mountains made flying the rest of the year no less dangerous. The towering Himalayas not only forced pilots to altitudes that strained their aircraft but also created updrafts and downdrafts that cause planes to "drop at the rate of five thousand feet a minute then suddenly be whisked upward at the same speed."[86] Compared to these hazards, Japanese Zeros were less threatening.[87]

Flight crews worried about more than the elements. The pilots did not place great confidence in their C-46 Commando aircraft, the workhorse of the airlift. "Ol' Dumbo," or less affectionately, the "flying coffin," carried up to four tons of supplies but was prone to mechanical trouble. Gas line blocks and breaks, carburetor icing, and vapor lock caused engine failure and forced planes down. Because the jungle and mountain terrain made most safe emergency landings impossible, mechanical problems were fatal to men and machines. Pilot error added to casualty rolls. The airlift ran twenty-four hours a day, with take-offs occurring every two and a quarter minutes. Working sixteen-hour shifts and flying the Hump three or four times daily, flight crews remained on the ground only long enough to unload and refuel. The pace fatigued the fliers, and many became "Hump happy" and unable to continue. In 1944, when Barry Goldwater began flying the Hump, accidents claimed three American lives for every one thousand tons of supplies delivered. So many had gone down along one route that it was dubbed the "aluminum trail" because of the wreckage from crashed planes. By operation's end in 1945, the airlift had delivered three-quarters of a million tons of supplies to the Chinese. America paid a heavy price for its success. In all, more than 1,300 fliers had died, 345 were missing, and nearly 600 planes had been lost. Sacrifice and success would bring a presidential citation, the first time in American military history that a unit not directly engaged in combat achieved this honor.[88]

Barry Goldwater was a valuable cog in the airlift over the Hump. Despite flight hazards, the loss of squadron members, and primitive living conditions, he performed his duties with distinction. Goldwater earned "superior" ratings in fitness reports and won promotion to major and then lieutenant colonel. In August 1944, after six months of duty in the China-Burma-India theater of operations, he was rotated stateside to a training unit in California.[89]

Years later, when one of his grandsons asked him, "What did you do in the war?" Barry replied tersely, "Not much."[90] Goldwater's memoirs recount the war years only briefly and without emotion. Friends and family noticed no change in Barry's values or beliefs on his return. There is little to indicate that the wartime experience affected him in any significant way. Barry, in his mid-thirties, was older than most of his comrades, who went to war at more impressionable ages. As an aviator in a support role, he was always several steps removed from the battlefield and untouched by the horrors of ground war. Surely, in light of his high hopes for combat duty, his assignments had proved disappointing. Goldwater had performed his job and served honorably. He never believed that his service was extraordinary or beyond what was expected of any other American soldier. Unlike many in public life, he would not be tempted to inflate or exploit his deeds to build a hero's reputation.

As an ATC pilot, Barry was able to arrange leave and go home during the war. Thus, Peggy Jr., the Goldwaters' fourth child, was born in 1944. Long letters to Peggy and the children helped to maintain contact during absences. Parenting by mail, Barry offered his children direction and advice. He composed parables with animal characters illustrating the Golden Rule and, more concretely, the importance of studying hard, arising early, and obeying their mother. To Joanne, he wrote, "Think right[,] . . . believe in God and your family and your country."[91] He praised perseverance and prayer: "If we hide the disappointment in our hearts and buckle down and wish and work twice as hard and ask God to pitch in and help too[,] then . . . we have what we want."[92] He cautioned Joanne and Barry Jr. about racial prejudice: "There is one thing that I want you both to learn if you don't already know it. You will hear a lot of children call colored people . . . 'Nigger.' Well, don't ever do that. They are . . . people just like you are."[93] Echoing the words of JoJo and exemplifying his own philosophy, he advised four-year-old Mike: "Pay attention to your own affairs and don't stick your head into other peoples [sic] unless they ask you."[94] Mixed in with these thoughts were stories of Big Mike Goldwater and the peoples, customs, and places he had seen in wartime.[95]

The letters also reflect Peggy's difficulties in raising the children alone. Barry repeatedly conjured up an angry bird, a picture of which he drew on the envelopes, who reported the children's misdeeds to him. The bird informed him that "some little girls and little boys who received a certain allowance and who were suppose [sic] to spend most of it for War Stamps [were] buying things like candy."[96] Another time, the bird had "the darnest disgusted look on his face" because the children were "so ornery to their mother."[97] The bird's knowledge of events proved so vivid that the children were convinced that their father was not only omnipotent but omnipresent. The children were watchful, as well, of a "gremlin" their father had trained to "stand out on our driveway and every time one of you three even thinks of going out in the street he will come up and kick you right in the neck so hard your teeth will rattle."[98] Despite his efforts to remain close to them, time away had eroded relationships. "When I came home, the children actually didn't know me," Barry wrote.[99]

Unforeseen, the letters initiated a style of family communication that continued after the war's end. In writing, Barry reached out to the children; he was clearly concerned about their lives, and he offered encouragement and love. He could not, however, express similar thoughts and emotions in person. "He's incapable of showing his love," Joanne said.[100] Barry Jr. recalled, "The only fatherly advice I ever really got has been through letters."[101] The letters, all of which the children have kept and continue to cherish, were one-way communications. They did not create the necessary dialogue between parent and child that builds rapport, nurtures intimacy, and fosters mutual respect. According to his eldest son, "My father didn't even appear human." The letters never bridged the growing void. Barry Jr. continued: "I did achieve, I did excel, I was successful. But he wasn't around to say, 'Good job!' It must not have been that good, or I'm sure he would have patted me on the back."[102] On another occasion, he remembered, "I was in trouble, and the worst thing was that Dad was never really physically there when I needed him most."[103] Outside the context of a warm and close father-child relationship, the letters became "preachings and pronouncements," regardless of the intention.[104] In meeting their father's expectations, the children neglected their own needs. "I can speak for my brother and sisters," offered Michael, "when I say that whenever any one of us endeavors to do something we do our best with the thought in mind that it is not primarily to build our own egos, but to make our parents proud."[105] Sister Peggy later concurred, "Dad did have a visual image of how he wanted us all to look. He wanted us all to be beautiful children—on the exterior. He needed to work more on the interior."[106]

Lieutenant Colonel Goldwater was mustered out of the Army Air Corps in November 1945, three months after VJ Day. He returned immediately to Phoenix and reassumed his place in the store and community. Friends noticed his changed appearance; his black hair had turned gray. Also apparent was Barry's restlessness with business and civic routines. In part, his impatience was a carryover from the prewar period. It came, too, from his war experiences and readjustment to civilian life. And it was a response to the energized atmosphere of boomtown Phoenix. The federal government, first through the New Deal and then more decisively with World War

II spending, had triggered in Phoenix and Arizona significant economic expansion and diversification. Military bases and defense contractors fueled job and local business growth. Older economic sectors were not neglected, and the government's golden touch had extended to mining and agriculture. Not since territorial days had Arizona been so dependent on Potomac decision-makers.

In tune with the new momentum and ignoring the paradox, Barry Goldwater praised the free-enterprising entrepreneur who thrived in what had become a federally charged atmosphere. Success in peace and war made Goldwater blink Washington's role to see only the handiwork of the individual and local community. Crisis may have made the New Deal necessary, but now the private sector was ready to lead. Hitler had convincingly demonstrated the folly of military weakness, and wartime experience had made Barry an air force disciple and advocate of air power. In a dangerous world, he argued, defense spending was essential. It was also constitutionally sound. Thus, he applauded not only the rise of the military establishment but also its collateral power to fuel the domestic economy. Events had joined with family tradition, community networks, and business concerns to raise Barry Goldwater's conservative consciousness.

If the store had left Barry empty, he now had a conservative message that gave him meaning. He had, moreover, built the platform that would allow him to deliver it. Goldwater's was in responsible hands and would not miss his attention. His business and civic credentials were in order, and the Colorado River film had provided him skills, exposure, and a base. Military service and a lieutenant colonel's rank were political assets in postwar America. To these he added a pioneer's name and an intimate knowledge of Arizona and its resources. A head of gray hair created a look of maturity that accentuated the handsome and athletic appearance of the thirty-seven-year-old. Barry had also set his family priorities behind other interests. Like Phoenix, he was poised for flight.

Part II   A Conservative in the
Age of Liberalism

4

Take-Off

Although chance must play a role in shaping history as well as our lives, in the main men control events just as they do their personal destinies.

— F. CLIFTON WHITE
Suite 3505

It ain't for life, and it may be fun.

— BARRY GOLDWATER
Goldwater

Ironically, Franklin Roosevelt and the Democratic Party structured the environment that facilitated the emergence of Barry Goldwater and the transformation of the West into a Republican stronghold. During World War II the American West became a proving ground for what Peter Wiley and Robert Gottlieb call "Washington-funded military Keynesianism."[1] Federal spending lifted the region from depression to prosperity. Yet this was not simply a temporary adrenaline fix. As world war evolved into cold war competition and then into conflict in Southeast Asia, Washington continuously primed the pump, flooding the western states with federal dollars. These funds did more than stimulate traditional industries like mining, oil production, agriculture, and cattle raising. They also accelerated the rise of the service sector and sponsored manufacturing and research in electronics, aerospace, and military hardware. Community entrepreneurs played their critical role by exploiting federally spawned opportunities, shaping them according to local needs and tastes. In wartime America and in the postwar era, the economic lure of the West would again create a rush of people, this time to fill slots in the new service and manufacturing bureaucracies. These men and women formed a new middle class and became the foot soldiers of modern American conservatism. Economic and political power had begun to ebb from the East and flow toward the West.

World War II significantly deepened the federal imprint on the region. Military installations and defense-related industries brought $70 billion in federal funds to the western states between 1941 and 1945, with California absorbing half the total. Steel, synthetic rubber, chemical, aircraft manufacturing, ship-building, and military-related-electronics facilities mushroomed in wartime California, creating two million new jobs. Los Angeles emerged from the war with half a million new residents and as the second largest manufacturing center in the nation. At the same time, San Diego had increased its population by 147 percent. The northwestern states sheltered aluminum, fabricating, and aircraft-manufacturing plants. Portland almost doubled in population during the war while Seattle, holder of $5.6 billion in military contracts, expanded from 368,000 people in 1940 to 530,000 just four years later. In the Rocky Mountain states, Utah acquired 49,000 jobs and ten military bases. Denver became a regional center for defense-related aeronautics and electronics production. New Mexico, meanwhile, grappled with its new tasks in atomic energy research and development. In all of these states, the federal impact was not limited to direct expenditure, wage payments, grants, and subsidies. In letting contracts, creating jobs, and making purchases, Washington indirectly fostered expansion in retail, banking, real estate, construction, food, health care, and education sectors.[2]

Arizona also made impressive gains. Although holding fast to its frontier image, the state eagerly plunged into the modern era, a transition made easier by $360 million in federal funds and contracts. Military installations circled Phoenix, and Tucson claimed Davis-Monthan Air Force Base. Smaller Arizona communities, such as Yuma and Mesa, would similarly cut into the defense pie. Choosing Phoenix as their site, Goodyear Aircraft, Consolidated Aircraft, and AiResearch built plants in which to manufacture airplane parts while Alcoa constructed an aluminum extrusion facility. Several dozen subcontractors, making components for tanks and planes, grew in their shadow. Jobs attracted new residents and Arizona's population increased by 100,000, with Phoenix and Tucson nearly doubling in size. Arizona had entered the war with an economy based on the four "C's"—cotton, copper, climate, and cattle. It would emerge with the four C's stable and prosperous but with a new formula for economic growth. In the fast-developing service and manufacturing sectors, Arizona saw its future.[3]

If the future was visible, it was not inevitable. Peace threatened to still the wartime engine of Arizona's economic diversification and good times. Some, echoing national opinion-makers, predicted slower growth and even a return to depression. Declining war orders closed Phoenix's AiResearch plant in 1946, giving credence to such fears. Even more basic was the danger posed by a rapidly developing but water-poor California. The future, as it had been for every generation of Arizonans, was premised on the availability of water, for there could be no manufacturing, agriculture, tourism, or even settlement without it. If California's encroachments on southwestern water resources were not blocked, Arizona's potential was stillborn. Barry Goldwater, with other Arizona leaders, took up these challenges. Having tasted prosperity, they were unwilling to give up gained ground nor halt the advance. Together they moved to create the climate that made the desert attractive to businesses, tourists, and new residents. Their achievements would position Phoenix and Arizona as outposts in an emerging Sunbelt.[4]

Barry Goldwater was ready for an expanded role. His restlessness in the store, felt before the war, returned with greater intensity in peacetime. "My mind," he complained, "could no longer focus on merchandising."[5] Resentment of federal price and wage controls imposed during the war also chilled his enthusiasm for business. "We had seven employees who did nothing, but . . . keep my brother out of jail, by keeping up on all the regulations that he was suppose to abide by."[6] Nor would the store miss Barry. His absence had made him superfluous in store operations. Bob Goldwater had replaced his brother with a merchandising department, and now "there wasn't a lot for him to do."[7] With the store in capable hands and no longer dependent on his energies, Barry could pursue other interests without looking back.

In light of his concerns about organized labor, the newly mobilized right-to-work campaign was a natural choice for commitment. Labor had become an important contender for both economic and political power in Arizona during the 1930s. Strikes and collective bargaining agreements had built up union locals and membership while enabling labor to command influence within the state Democratic Party. With federal support, union activists had expanded labor's base during World War II, launching membership drives in defense industries. A union card often became the prerequisite for employment. By 1946 the Arizona labor movement claimed between thirty-five thousand and forty thousand men and women in 125 farm worker, retail, mining, transportation, and public employee locals. Employers, especially farm owners, mobilized to block union efforts. Supplementing their resistance in the fields and on the shop floor, employers had proposed right-to-work legislation making it illegal to require union membership as a condition for employment. The public and the Democratic Party resisted such bills, which were then defeated, despite lobbying from employer, civic, and business groups.[8]

Arizonans revised their interpretation of right-to-work legislation in the war's aftermath. Veterans returning to the state encountered a saturated labor market, the closed shop, and union members who were first in line for job openings. Operating on a seniority system, unions even rejected applications until current members had been placed. Frustrated job seekers organized the Veterans Right to Work Committee in 1945 and the following year filed an initiative petition to place on the ballot a measure that would, in the words of one proponent, "make sure that a man does not have to join a union to get or hold a job."[9] In Arizona, the right to work became more than an economic issue. It was a debt America owed its veterans and a matter of patriotism. The old coalition of employers, farm owners, mine operators, and conservatives was quick to adapt to the changing environment, equating union leaders with America's enemies. As one radio ad declared: "It's almost as if we were living in pre-war Germany. We just can't let that sort of thing happen here! These despotic little labor racketeers, the would-be Hitlers, must be crushed now—once and for all—before it's too late."[10]

Barry Goldwater volunteered for the right-to-work campaign for several reasons. The measure reflected his beliefs in individual freedom and self-initiative and against concentrations of private power. As a veteran, he sympathized with those who had sacrificed for their country while defense workers, who remained on the home front, had advanced economically and tightened their grip on available jobs. As an employer, he had pursued an enlightened labor policy in his store, partly to thwart unionization, which threatened to restrict his authority. The issue, moreover, aroused his partisan senses, for labor was a key element of the Democratic Party coalition, helping to bankroll election campaigns and ferrying the faithful to the polls. At the same time, a right-to-work law would make Phoenix and Arizona more attractive to out-of-state industrialists drawn to communities without strong unions and high labor costs. Without hesitation, Goldwater agreed to head the retailers' wing of the right-to-work campaign. He wrote letters to fellow merchants soliciting their assistance and funds. He also spoke publicly in support of the effort, portraying the initiative as a reform aimed at corrupt and power-hungry labor racketeers and not at unions or their members.[11]

Goldwater's words and the thrust of the campaign drew meaning less from Arizona examples than national events. Demobilization and reconversion from war to peace had stressed the American economy with shortages, high prices, and labor unrest. In the year following VJ Day five million men and women went on strike, creating the greatest work stoppage in American history. Newspaper headlines in 1945 and 1946 announced major strikes in the automobile, electrical, steel, shipping, and transportation industries. Just a few days before the 1946 elections, President Harry Truman ordered a federal takeover of the mines to quell strike activity in the coal fields. Inflation and inconvenience made Americans receptive to charges of union abuses, and a Gallup Poll recorded a majority in favor of legislation to curb labor's power. In addition, cold war tensions encouraged politicians and employers to voice their fears of communist infiltration of the American labor movement.[12]

Arizona's unions never moved from their defensive positions. The public accepted the right-to-work indictment and dismissed as a scare tactic labor's claim that if the legislation passed "Arizona's progress and development will be set back 50 years. Wage scales will collapse. The earner will be impover-ished. There will be no money above subsistence in the pockets of the masses."[13] With Democrats divided between liberal and conservative wings, organized labor held little hope for success, and the initiative passed, cap-turing 55 percent of the vote. By 1948 thirteen other states had approved similar right-to-work measures.[14]

The Arizona right-to-work effort did more than add an amendment to the state constitution. The campaign acted as a transitional vehicle for con-servative Democrats who bridled at their party's liberal thrust. Through the right-to-work movement they had tasted success, and for some it was the first opportunity to work closely with Republicans like Barry Goldwater. Once the Arizona Republican Party matured and became a viable alterna-tive, allegiance would be less a break with the past than the completion of a process under way. Further, the right-to-work effort accelerated the rise to influence of a new breed of Arizona Republicans who had not reconciled themselves to the status of permanent political outsiders. The campaign attracted Barry Goldwater, Phelps-Dodge's Denison Kitchel, and John Rhodes, a Harvard Law School graduate who had settled in Arizona after wartime service. Together they enhanced their organizational skills and developed the mutual respect that framed close personal and working rela-tionships. This would prepare them well for future battles.[15]

Goldwater did not retreat after the campaign. In 1947, to prevent a labor counterattack, he joined Arizona business leaders in an association to pro-mote legislation "that is advantageous to and in the best interests of the employer." The group's initial task was the passage of enabling legislation "to put teeth" into the right-to-work initiative.[16] Barry, meanwhile, pursued other means to a pro-business environment. Responding to a call for "new industries, with the accompanying pay envelopes," he joined the Chamber of Commerce's Thunderbirds.[17] The Thunderbirds, each attired like a Hopi medicine man in a high-necked jacket of blue velvet with a necklace of silver beads from which dangled a huge turquoise and silver bird, entertained out-of-state entrepreneurs to lure their business to Phoenix. To Goldwater, selling Phoenix also meant creating the proper community environment. In a December 1946 letter to Chamber of Commerce director Norman Hull he complained that during his wartime absence Phoenix had "retrogressed morally and I might say spiritually. This is a community in which vice is ram-pant, in which squalor exists where there was formerly beauty, and there is very evidently more interest in the almighty dollar than the almighty man."[18] Barry responded by challenging his neighbors and business associates to become involved in public affairs and resolve problems. He backed his words with service in Community Chest drives and campaigns to raise money to build a hospital and civic center. In addition, he lobbied Arizona legislators to send the right message by cracking down on gambling and passing laws regulating horse and dog racing. Success reinforced boosterism. Phoenix received a major stimulus in 1948 when Motorola established its military electronics division in the community. The move encouraged smaller firms to relocate and others to organize there. Once begun, this seedbed process was its own selling point.[19]

Also in 1946 Barry accepted appointment to Arizona's important Colorado River Commission, later renamed the Interstate Stream Commission. The commission's task was formidable: to secure Arizona's claim to Colorado River water from an ever-demanding California. Geography had locked Arizona and California in competition, and each looked to the Colorado River for its salvation. They were not the river's only claimants, for other states demanded access to the Colorado's waters.[20]

The dispute over water rights had begun decades before, but Barry Goldwater and most Arizonans were familiar with its history. Partial resolution of the conflict had occurred in 1922 at a conference in Santa Fe, New Mexico. Setting the river's flow at 17.5 million acre-feet per year, an arbitrary estimate of its capacity, representatives drew up a compact that allocated 8.5 million acre-feet to the lower basin states of Arizona, California, and Nevada.[21] The agreement went into effect even though the Arizona legislature refused to ratify the compact without the safeguard of a specific division of water. Arizonans, unable to compete with California's population growth and political clout in Congress, saw the Colorado's water slipping away from them.[22]

Congress reified Arizona's fears in 1928. It authorized construction of Boulder Dam on the Colorado River to provide hydroelectric power, ensure flood control in California's Imperial Valley, and augment the water supply of Los Angeles. "Now that means," declared a bitter Arizonan, "that the construction profit goes to Las Vegas; the franchise goes to Nevada; the power goes to Los Angeles; the water goes to Mexico; and Arizona goes to hell."[23] To gain passage of the legislation, California had agreed to set a limit on its annual diversion of Colorado River water. Arizona was not consoled, for this "paper guarantee" failed to protect its supply, and Californians siphoned whatever quantity they desired.[24] California, now primed for further growth, would be in a stronger position in the future to press its need to tap even more Colorado River water.[25]

Realizing, finally, that it could no longer afford to ignore water realities, Arizona changed course in 1944 and went on the offensive to defend its claims on the river. The state legislature ratified the 1922 compact and endorsed the visionary Central Arizona Project (CAP), appropriating $200,000 to survey a canal route to carry water from the Colorado River to Phoenix and the Salt River Valley. What had seemed a mirage now took shape on engineers' drafting tables. Arizonans predicted technological advances that would soon allow them to pump Colorado water high over mountain ranges through hundreds of miles of aqueducts and canals to irrigate the central desert. While boasting of the CAP's feasibility, few Arizonans worried about the costs of creation. As they had so many times in the past, Arizonans would call upon the federal government for support. Arizona Senator Carl Hayden made the request official, introducing a bill in Congress seeking CAP authorization.[26]

Arizona's Colorado River Commissioner, Barry Goldwater, took his assignment to lobby for the CAP quite seriously. With California already using more than its prescribed share of the river and Arizona depleting its groundwater, he surely felt an urgency to act. He wrote to the eastern suppliers of his department store, asking them to appeal to their congressional representatives in support of Arizona's plan.[27] In a note to California customers Barry explained that Arizona must have a fair share of the Colorado River "or die." He stressed the economic ties that bound the two states and condemned the "small group with specialized interests [that] is dominating the situation and strangling the life from California-Arizona trade relations."[28] To heighten the commitment of Arizonans he predicted in a newspaper interview that water shortages "would wipe out many, many businesses whose relationship to farming is not evident to the unpracticed eye. It would mean ruining one third of an agricultural empire. . . . It would mean destroying that much of our real property tax base. It would mean the ruin of more than 4,000 farms." Barry concluded, "We are in dire peril when our agriculture is in peril."[29] While Goldwater's warnings of the danger were overstated, California's needs clearly limited Arizona's growth.

He also assumed personal responsibility for answering Arizona's critics. When former New Dealer-turned-conservative-commentator Raymond Moley questioned the cost of the CAP, Barry wondered how he had been "so glibly taken in by California propaganda." He asked Moley to reconsider the CAP case: "If we go on arguing about the cost of these projects *that must be built,* we will reach a point some day where we will have starving people and land not producing food for these people."[30] As part of his duties, Barry testified before Congress. The Central Arizona Project, he argued, was not a luxury but a basic necessity for maintaining life in the desert. "I know of my own observation that Central Arizona needs water from the Colorado River for a supplemental supply to irrigate lands now under cultivation, not to bring in new lands but to keep land now under cultivation from going back to the desert."[31] The initial CAP bill was buried under opposition from

California, and Arizona's claim would not be recognized for more than two decades.[32]

In the rush to exploit the river an important fact escaped Barry Goldwater and his fellow westerners. Few realized that the Colorado was a "deficit river" unable to satisfy all the demands made on it.[33] The estimate of an annual flow of 17.5 million acre-feet was highly optimistic; a flow of 13 million acre-feet was a more realistic assessment of the river's capacity. If this discrepancy gave no one pause in the 1940s, it would pose a more dangerous problem for the "hydraulic" societies that covered the desert by the end of the twentieth century. Also unquestioned was the wisdom of programming a desert landscape for water-intensive agriculture.[34]

As a CAP proponent, Goldwater also personified, in the most direct way, an inherent contradiction between principle and practice. He championed a philosophy of free enterprise and laissez-faire. The image of his grandfather and Arizona pioneers as rugged individualists animated him and offered identity and meaning. Yet these men and women had realized early on that they lacked the resources to deal successfully with the harsh environment. To settle, develop, and diversify they required the support of the federal government. Without it their communities would have remained backwaters. Goldwater, like his western neighbors, opted for a pragmatic solution to this irony. Deciding that the end justified the means, they adopted a flexible approach without following logic to its conclusions in philosophy. Thus they scoffed at those who described reclamation as a "paternalistic rainbow"[35] and applauded as the Army Corps of Engineers and the Bureau of Reclamation devoted billions of dollars to western development, damming rivers and carrying water and electricity to consumers.[36]

Goldwater was not blind to his inconsistencies and was uncomfortable advocating federal spending and intervention. Throughout the long fight for the CAP, Barry remained in the background, and he played only a peripheral role in its success. He defended reclamation projects like the CAP as within the legitimate realm of federal power, for the Constitution allowed government "to do things that we cannot well do for ourselves."[37] Barry countered opponents of the CAP by describing it as a "loan project," with 85 percent of the costs to be repaid with interest.[38] Thus Goldwater differentiated the CAP from other federal projects, like the Tennessee Valley Authority. Critics balked at that distinction and continually heckled him, calling his reasoning hypocritical and expedient. They would find more ammunition as CAP expenses escalated significantly and repayment was postponed far into the future. Barry was aware also of the political cost of opposition to CAP. When asked if an Arizona senator could dare oppose the project, he responded, "Well, if he didn't mind staying home."[39]

The right-to-work campaign, promoting Phoenix, and protecting the Arizona claim on the Colorado River did not absorb all of Goldwater's time and energy. Immediately upon his return from the war he accepted an assignment from Governor Sidney Osborn to create the Arizona Air National Guard. Goldwater, who resigned his commission as a lieutenant colonel in the U.S. Air Force Reserve and was reduced in rank to captain, engaged in the sometimes exhilarating and more often tedious task of building an organization from scratch. Not only did he supervise the recruitment and training of pilots and personnel, construction of facilities, and the stockpiling of aircraft and supplies, he set unit regulations and procedures. It was under Goldwater's direction that the Arizona wing became the first air national guard unit to open ranks to African-Americans. He accomplished this in typical Goldwater fashion: "I didn't issue an order. I just did it."[40] The federal government also called on Goldwater to serve. His relationships with Arizona Native Americans, cultivated over the years through photographic trips, air missions of aid, and ownership of a trading post at Navajo Mountain, prompted his appointment to the Department of Interior's Advisory Commission on Indian Affairs. Goldwater, at his own expense, continued making mercy flights, bringing food to men and women in flooded Sonora, Mexico, and medical supplies to isolated Arizona communities. He shuttled stranded Arizona servicemen home from California in time for Christmas. During the same period Barry looked for business opportunities outside of Goldwater's, investing in an appliance store, a pharmacy, and a Mexican cattle ranch.[41]

Other activities reflected political ambitions just below the surface. Barry returned to the Kiwanis–Chamber of Commerce luncheon lecture circuit with a wider range of topics. In addition to talks on the people and places of Arizona, he spoke about "Indian Problems," "City and State Government," and "Socialism and Communism."[42] His Colorado River-running movie remained popular, and he showed it to packed houses throughout Arizona. Meanwhile, local commentators kept Barry's name before the public, trumpeting on radio and in the newspapers the store's progressive labor record and Barry's civic efforts and relief missions.[43]

Despite his accomplishments, some questioned Barry's commitment and qualities for leadership, even calling him a playboy.[44] Phoenix Mayor Nicholas Udall described him as a "young merchant prince who liked to get his picture taken and fly airplanes."[45] In part, this image was a reflection of his lifestyle. Unlike business associates and friends, Barry suffered few economic or social restraints in his pursuit of happiness. The Goldwaters lived well and continued to "drain that store."[46] Barry's income, supplemented by Peggy's inheritance, provided a summer home in California, automobiles, and an airplane. Yet it was more than wealth and leisure that forged the image. Not given to serious reading or furthering his education, Goldwater was prone to one-liners and appeared unable to discuss issues in depth.[47] Critics disparaged him for seemingly frittering away time in hobbies. They did not see the insecure, private man behind the assertive, public persona, tinkering with gadgets, taking photographs, and operating his ham radio to build self-esteem and reduce stress. Barry also had a reputation as a practical joker. His most notorious trick was a device rigged to the guest bathroom at home. Sitting down tripped a tape recording of Barry's voice asking from the bottom of the bowl: "Hi, honey, how ya doin'? Can I be of any help?"[48] More important was a drinking problem that could surface in public and suggested a lack of personal discipline.[49]

Another outlet opened that would dampen the playboy image and prove more consistent with Goldwater's political ambitions. In late 1947 Phoenix Mayor Ray Busey appointed Barry and thirty-nine other leading citizens to a committee to study city government and suggest charter revisions and reforms. Phoenix had, in 1913, chosen a hybrid form of administration that combined mayor-commission with city-manager government in an attempt to enhance efficiency, eliminate corruption, and reduce expenditures. Instead, administrative instability plagued Phoenix, with thirty-one city managers appointed in thirty-five years. Nonpartisan government had become politicized, and cronyism was the rule in letting contracts and hiring. Factionalism, mediocrity, and low morale paralyzed city government. Reformers, who were first heard from in 1923, called for the removal of "politics" from government and the return of professionalism to municipal administration. Those backing revision of the Phoenix charter, however, made little headway while the city's sights remained low and its vision insular.[50]

Their words echoed more loudly in the 1940s. Driving for a greater Phoenix, community leaders supported a growth-oriented, businesslike administration and a government attuned to modern needs. It was time, believed the Chamber of Commerce, to change "our horse and buggy charter."[51] City officials, remembers Barry, were not dishonest but "incapable people. The government was not the type of government that a fast-growing community like Phoenix should have."[52] Margaret Kober, Goldwater's friend and a prominent Phoenician, agreed: "They just weren't big people."[53] If these issues stirred Phoenix leaders, they were less significant to average citizens. Of greater urgency to them were more sensational allegations. During the war, military authorities had temporally placed Phoenix off-limits to personnel because of soaring venereal disease rates and assorted vice problems.

Brothels and betting parlors operated with little concealment and suggested official collusion. Moreover, as one merchant declared, "the army's payrolls constitute one of the community's largest sources of revenue."[54] A flurry of raids and arrests did little to restore public confidence in city officials, and the situation continued to arouse concern after the war. The image of a wide-open town was hardly one that Phoenix wanted to project to the outside world.[55]

The Phoenix Charter Revision Committee announced its findings in 1948. To enhance stability and improve administration, it recommended the appointment of a professional city manager, who would be immune from political pressure and have expanded appointment and managerial powers. It proposed to eliminate petty graft with a separate finance department to oversee tax collections and disbursement. Further, the committee suggested replacing the city commission with a council, the members of which, along with the mayor, would be selected every two years in citywide, nonpartisan elections. These revisions drew broad support, and in a special election in November 1948, Phoenicians approved the changes by a two-to-one margin. The election, however, did not bring change, for holdover city officials balked at reform and ignored the intent of the revisions. In response, reformers reconvened in July 1949 and reorganized themselves as the nonpartisan Charter Government Committee to contest the November municipal elections.[56]

Barry Goldwater plunged into the effort with even greater intensity than he had given to civic and philanthropic work. He and his longtime friend Harry Rosenzweig, a jeweler and fellow Thunderbird, took charge of the Charter Government candidate selection committee and drew up a slate for the coming elections. Looking to the city's socially and economically prominent, they approached Margaret Kober—a member of the Phoenix Junior League and Planned Parenthood and the wife of Barry's physician—and businessmen and Chamber of Commerce members Hohen Foster and Frank Murphy. The committee also endorsed incumbent Mayor Nicholas Udall and city council member Charles Walters, both supporters of the charter revisions. That left two slots open on the ticket. While draining what Rosenzweig called "the biggest bottle of Old Crow that I could find," they made their choice. Barry and Harry decided to run. As Barry recalls: "'Pick anybody,' I said. 'I have,' Harry replied, 'you and I.'"[57] In a letter to his brother and Bill Saufley, Barry explained:

> You both will probably think me seven kinds of a dirty bastard when you hear that I have decided to run for councilman with Harry. . . . I don't think a man can live with himself when he asks others to do his dirty work for him. I couldn't criticize the government of this city if I myself refused to help. . . .

> There have always been one, and sometimes two, Goldwaters damned
> fools enough to get into politics, and they always did it with service in their
> minds. . . .
>
> The city needs help more than any of our governments. Maybe we can
> give it to them. Maybe we will suffer in doing it, but in our minds we will
> be doing what Americans should always be doing: helping each other.
>
> Don't cuss me too much. It ain't for life, and it may be fun.[58]

Again, Barry had not consulted with Peggy about an important decision in
the family's life. He surely knew that Peggy would disapprove, for "everything that I did that took me away from the store, she didn't like." But, like
volunteering for World War II service, this was an opportunity for which he
yearned and would not be denied. As always, Peggy "accepted those
things."[59]

The selection committee announced the Charter Government slate on
September 8, 1949, and it immediately assumed the front-runner position.
Its members were the business and civic leaders of Phoenix, the majority of
them native Arizonans able to lay claim to the pioneer heritage. The slate
included a woman, and although no people of color were named, it did strive
for religious balance, with representation accorded to Episcopalians,
Methodists, Presbyterians, Catholics, Mormons, and Jews. Other candidates
could not match the Charter Government's ticket in reputation or appeal.
The slate's main opposition was so intimidated that it did not complete its
candidate selection until just three weeks before the election.[60]

Not surprisingly, the Charter Government slate drew support from
Valley National banker Walter Bimson, lawyers Frank Snell and Paul Roca,
and other members of the Phoenix elite. The Phoenix Ministerial Association and the Chamber of Commerce also enlisted on the ticket's side. Even
more important, Eugene Pulliam, the owner of the daily newspapers in
Phoenix—the *Arizona Republic* and the *Phoenix Gazette*—backed the
slate.[61] Pulliam, the editor of the *Indianapolis Star* and a winter visitor to
Phoenix, bought the newspapers in 1946 for reasons that went beyond money-
making. Determined to turn Arizona public opinion to his conservative,
Republican views, he personally dictated a political agenda that spilled over
from the editorial pages into the reporting of news. The *Arizona Republic*
and *Phoenix Gazette*, often without even the pretense of objectivity, targeted
opponents, slinging mud and slanting coverage and content to trivialize and
marginalize their positions. If the Charter Government activists welcomed
Pulliam to their cause, they also feared him. "The *Arizona Republic* could be
merciful or unmerciful," said Margaret Kober. "I was always glad it was on
our side. Pulliam struck at anybody he didn't like. . . . He was a rough-and-
tumble guy."[62] Phoenix School Board president and movement supporter

Jack Williams concurred: "He had just a bit of the brute in him."[63] Barry Goldwater was more charitable. "That old Pulliam, when he called you on the phone and he said, 'I think we ought to do this,' you knew goddamn well we were going to do it. Wonderful man."[64]

Less visible but vital was Gus Greenbaum's work on behalf of the ticket. Greenbaum, an associate of organized crime figures Meyer Lansky and Benjamin "Bugsy" Siegel, ran a gambling syndicate in Phoenix. He and his brother Sam had been investigated by local authorities and found wanting. Said state Attorney General John Sullivan: "The Greenbaums must leave Arizona. Phoenix will not become a rendezvous for the type of gangsterism prevailing in Chicago as long as I am attorney general."[65] Gus Greenbaum was also a friend of Harry and Barry's. When Harry Rosenzweig approached him for "support," Greenbaum handed over a package of money and said, "You'll get this every week till the election." These funds would make up a significant portion of the nearly $18,000 the slate spent during the campaign. Because of their friendship, and to avoid embarrassing Harry and Barry, Greenbaum let Rosenzweig know that when the Charter Government ticket won in November he would "wrap up" his gambling operations and "take it all back to Vegas."[66] Goldwater was aware of Greenbaum's contributions but denied knowledge of his criminal activities. "He was a generous person," Barry remarked. "I'm not a gambler, I didn't know about that."[67] Years later Gus Greenbaum was murdered in a gangland-style execution in Phoenix. Then-Senator Barry Goldwater was an honorary pallbearer at his friend's funeral.[68]

Goldwater and the other members of the slate hammered away at government incompetence and inefficiency. They promised, as a first priority, to hire an experienced city manager who would bring professionalism to city hall. Victory, Barry pledged, would deliver an administration dedicated to lowering taxes and providing better services and an end to "boss-controlled government."[69] Boosterism was an integral part of the message, and Charter Government candidates echoed the Chamber of Commerce slogan of "More jobs for more people in Phoenix."[70] According to mayoral candidate Nicholas Udall, "Peace and quiet in city hall will encourage industrial development in Phoenix."[71] Barry similarly encouraged citizens to look forward to the expansion of Sky Harbor Airport and its positive impact on commerce and tourism. In this vein, the Charter Government team urged Phoenicians to promote economic growth by supporting two ballot measures mandating the repeal of the city's "nuisance" tax on manufacturers' inventories and the reduction of tax levies on manufacturers' machinery and equipment. The Phoenix newspapers, throughout the campaign, beat their drums in support of the ticket. With favorable commentary and page one editorials and cartoons, they set the terms of debate according to Charter Government claims.[72]

More cynically, Charter Government candidates catered to public fears about the moral climate of Phoenix. Prodded by the *Arizona Republic*, they accused their opponents of corruption and of having ties to the criminal underworld. "As a mother," Margaret Kober declared at a campaign stop, "I am vitally interested in a clean city for my children. Vice is a menace to the health and morals of the community."[73] The *Arizona Republic* spotlighted her charges: "The good women of Phoenix have been horrified and aroused by . . . the link between vice, crime, and the low order of politics being practiced in and around City Hall."[74] Privately, Charter Government candidates acknowledged the hollowness of their allegations. "Down to real brass tacks," said Charles Walters, "I don't believe there was any [gambling or prostitution] to speak of. It was not a problem." Barry noted similarly, "There was no connection with organized crime." In line with these views, none of the allegations was ever substantiated, and no Phoenix official was charged with a crime.[75]

Opponents offered few alternatives to this campaign for change. Unable to defend their record, they belittled the Charter Government candidates as "blue bloods and little Lord Fauntleroys."[76] Some lashed out at Eugene Pulliam, charging that "the *Republic* and *Gazette* monopoly is controlled by out-of-state professional politicians who have resorted to propaganda and half-truths in an effort to put their man in city hall as manager."[77] These allegations mustered little public enthusiasm, and election day brought victory to all Charter Government candidates. Barry Goldwater led the pack, receiving 16,408 votes of the total of 22,353 cast, winning every city precinct, and running 1,500 votes ahead of second-place Harry Rosenzweig. Voters also approved both pro-business tax measures, testifying to the city's willingness to adapt to the needs of manufacturers.[78]

At the age of forty, Barry Goldwater had claimed his first election victory and public office. His pride of accomplishment, however, came from more than a sense of personal achievement. Despite its nonpartisan nature, the campaign built on the right-to-work effort and solidified "the nucleus of the Republican Party."[79] Election work furthered the political education of young Republicans like Paul Fannin, Jack Williams, Harry Rosenzweig, and Barry Goldwater. In a real election battle, they sharpened their skills in fund-raising, precinct organizing, and stump speaking. Victory had energized feelings of efficacy and thickened bonds of loyalty. The election, moreover, was an educational experience for the voters, for they became more familiar with Republican names and faces and continued a conditioning that would shape new political identities. The campaign had also whetted

Eugene Pulliam's appetite for change and convinced him that his newspapers could play a key role in the transformation of Arizona politics. Finally, success in the municipal elections had left Goldwater well positioned for the future. As a Phoenix city council member, he was the leading Republican officeholder in the state.[80]

Mayor Nicholas Udall swore the new council in to office on January 3, 1950, declaring, "This day will be regarded as the beginning of better government in Phoenix after 35 years of difficult administration."[81] The new council was determined to prove the mayor right and proceeded immediately to fulfill its campaign agenda. Under the leadership of Barry Goldwater, their choice as vice-mayor, the council members moved to streamline government, improve services, reduce spending, and cut taxes. They worked well with the newly hired city manager and attacked administrative duplication by reorganizing finance, public works, and police organizations, and shearing the number of city departments from twenty-seven to twelve. Members revamped city budgetary procedures, initiating more accurate accounting practices and requiring competitive bidding on municipal contracts. Setting the annexation of unincorporated land as another priority, they authorized studies of future municipal transportation and water needs. Through Chamber of Commerce members on the council, city government joined with business groups in an expanded campaign to sell Phoenix to manufacturers and tourists. The council, remembers Goldwater, was "always a group of business people, with business interests. Getting things done by them was no problem."[82] Enhancing the city's image while meeting citizens' needs, the council allocated additional funds for parks and recreational facilities. In a sign of the times, the council required all city employees to sign oaths of loyalty to the United States.[83]

Guided by beliefs in fiscal responsibility and limited government, Goldwater made himself a strong presence on the city council. The minutes show him to be a frequent questioner during meetings, raising issues of cost and excessive regulation. Outside the public eye, he did his homework, immersing himself in the minutia of city administration. He became expert in easements, bidding, zoning, business license applications, and road repair. Barry frequently made on-site inspections to learn the facts in a case. On several occasions he worked late into the night with the city manager reviewing the budget item by item for waste. With the same thoroughness, Goldwater scrutinized citizens' requests for municipal expenditures, always preferring a private solution to a public one. Thus, when downtown merchants asked the city to build municipal parking lots to ease congestion, Barry spearheaded the opposition and persuaded the council to let them "do it for themselves."[84]

Council votes were usually unanimous, but Barry's strict insistence that government not interfere in people's lives sometimes made him a minority of one. He was the only council member to oppose Federal Housing Authority efforts to gain land by eminent domain. "I am not voting against the idea of housing," said Goldwater. "I am voting against the almost Gestapo methods that you have employed."[85] Barry also stood alone when neighborhood and church groups opposed a merchant's request for a license to sell beer and wine. Here he fused his parents' moral lessons with a belief in free enterprise to reject government intrusions. According to Goldwater, "I have walked by such places when I could hardly walk and I don't think it did me any harm. . . . When a man wants to open a business, he has a right to."[86] In a similar case, he placed responsibility for morality beyond the domain of government authorities and directly on parents and religious leaders, declaring, "I don't think the argument is too strong . . . that beer and wine sold in a grocery store is contributing to the delinquency of minors. They have to get that beer. Nobody is going to pour it down their throats. I think the churches that protest and the homes that protest . . . should look to their children."[87]

After a year in office, the council pointed with pride to tangible evidence of its success. Cost cutting, efficient management, and consolidation had produced a budget surplus of more than a quarter of a million dollars. Phoenix had annexed seventeen square miles of unincorporated land and extended services to new residents. In regard to gambling and prostitution, the American Social Hygiene Association reported, "Phoenix, Arizona is a changed city. It is no longer a vice center."[88] These accomplishments led the National Municipal League to name Phoenix to its "All American" team of cities because of the great improvement in municipal administration. The U.S. Census Bureau also gave city leaders reason to cheer. In 1950 the population of Phoenix reached 106,818 persons, a 63 percent increase over the 1940 figure. Rival Tucson, meanwhile, had faded, claiming only 45,454 inhabitants. During the same period the Phoenix metropolitan area had grown 78 percent and counted 331,770 people. Within the Valley of the Sun lived nearly half of Arizona's population. These census figures attracted the attention of Barry Goldwater, the city official and businessman. As a politician, too, he would see opportunities in Arizona's changing population pattern.[89]

Hard work on the council had enhanced Barry's reputation and dampened his playboy image. His high-profile activities in city government, described and praised in the Pulliam press, created a following for Goldwater throughout the Phoenix metropolitan area. It seemed only natural for him to contemplate advancing to a higher political rung. The revived Republican Party, which had only recently, in Barry's words, "been worse than

Barry's grandfather,
Michel Goldwater.
(Arizona Historical
Foundation)

Barry's uncle, Morris Goldwater.
(Arizona Historical Foundation)

Baron Goldwater, Barry's father. (Arizona Historical Foundation)

From left: brother Robert, Barry,
sister Carolyn, and mother
Josephine. (Arizona Historical
Foundation)

Barry—the teenage years.
(Arizona Historical Foundation)

Cadet Goldwater at Staunton Military Academy, late 1920s.
(Arizona Historical Foundation)

Peggy Johnson Goldwater. (Arizona Historical Foundation)

Goldwater in the Army Air Corps, early 1940s.
(Courtesy of Peggy Goldwater Clay)

Barry on leave with the children, from left, Michael, Joanne, Peggy Jr., and Barry Jr., during World War II. (Courtesy of Peggy Goldwater Clay)

MIKE, JOANNE, PEGGY JR, BARRY JR.

Goldwater children pictured for a Christmas card during the 1940s.
(Courtesy of Joanne Goldwater)

Another pose at
Christmas. Note the
results of Barry's
electrical tinkering
in the foreground.
(Courtesy of Joanne
Goldwater)

defunct," also encouraged his ambitions.[90] Long denied access to power in Democratic Arizona, the Republicans boasted popular candidates and heightened activity at the grassroots. In addition, the party benefited from the postwar influx of men and women who carried Republican loyalties to their adopted state. "There was a time," remarked Democratic politician and later Arizona governor Sam Goddard, "when you could have had a meeting of the Republicans in a telephone booth. We got shipped East Texas, North Chicago, and Orange County. And they came in here in droves. It altered the whole demography of the place."[91] Migration combined with Republican mobilization had whittled the Democratic advantage in voter registration to four-to-one. Even this was not absolutely daunting to the Republicans, for they counted on the support of "pinto" Democrats, conservatives who would cross party lines to vote for an attractive candidate. In 1950, for the first time in a generation, the Republicans of Arizona could look forward to an election campaign.[92]

Goldwater and Arizona Republicans drew strength, as well, from national political trends. The 1946 elections had signaled the end of the New Deal era. Asking voters, "Got enough inflation? . . . got enough debt? . . . got enough strikes? . . . got enough communism?" Republicans won majorities in both houses of Congress for the first time since 1928.[93] This identification of undesirable social changes with treason brought the conservative critique out of the political wilderness where it had been consigned as radical and the property of the privileged. Harnessing domestic liberalism to internal subversion diverted the mainstream and offered conservatives enhanced respectability and legitimacy. The election thus raised a bumper crop of new Senate conservatives, including John Bricker, Richard Nixon, and Joseph McCarthy.[94]

Harry Truman's upset victory in the 1948 presidential election had blunted the Republican comeback, but events in 1949 and 1950 gave new life to the GOP's charges and chances. In August 1949 China was "lost" to Communism, another free world defeat in a line of dominos that stretched back to the Soviet advance in Eastern Europe at the close of World War II. The following month the Russians ended America's atomic monopoly by exploding their own bomb. To many Americans the cause of their country's decline was obvious: the United States had been betrayed, its secrets exposed to the enemy. As Wisconsin Senator Joseph McCarthy declared in February 1950, America was losing the struggle with "communistic atheism . . . not because our only powerful potential enemy has sent men to invade our shores, but rather because of the traitorous actions of those who have been treated so well by this Nation." In his hand McCarthy claimed to hold a list of names "that were made known to the Secretary of State as being members of the Communist party and who nevertheless are still working and shaping policy in the State Department."[95] The Alger Hiss case and the arrests of Klaus Fuchs and Julius and Ethel Rosenberg as atomic spies appeared to validate Republican accusations. In June 1950 the Republicans added the communist invasion of South Korea to their indictment; an another example, they said, of Democratic bungling and Russian perfidy.

It was in this context of heightened Republican opportunities that Barry Goldwater met with Howard Pyle to plan for the 1950 elections. Pyle was well known in Arizona. The son of a Baptist preacher, he was the most popular radio personality in the state. Like his second cousin Ernie Pyle, he had been a war correspondent and had broadcast interviews with Arizona soldiers to the home front. Many Arizonans remembered him also as the correspondent who covered the Japanese surrender on board the U.S.S. *Missouri* in August 1945. Although Pyle had no political experience, Republicans considered him a rising star. If, as he admitted, "I knew absolutely nothing about politics," he was hardly alone in the party.[96] Barry, no longer interested in the Phoenix city council, wanted Pyle's support in a run for the governorship. In turn, Barry offered to endorse Pyle for the U.S. Senate race in 1952. Events and Pyle's ambition overtook their agreement. On May 20, 1950, in a keynote address to the Arizona Young Republican convention, Pyle offered himself to the delegates, volunteering for any service they thought he might perform. Pyle's friends were ready and stampeded the convention into drafting him for the governor's race. As the spearhead of the party, the Young Republicans' endorsement carried much weight and was sufficient to garner the regular organization's nod. Although "trumped," Goldwater's partisan loyalties ruled, and he graciously consented to be Howard Pyle's campaign manager.[97]

Despite the long drought for Republicans in Arizona, Goldwater was optimistic about Pyle's chances. Pyle had high name recognition and the support of the *Arizona Republic* and *Phoenix Gazette*. In addition, he was an excellent public speaker and a master in the use of the radio. The campaign, moreover, would suffer no shortage of funds. Equally significant, Pyle's opponent, Ana Frohmiller, was vulnerable to attack. Frohmiller was Arizona's first woman state auditor, winning election in 1926 and holding that office for twenty-four years. Although a proven vote-getter, her run for the governor's chair was marred by a fractured Democratic Party that had failed to coalesce behind her after a bitter primary election. Political observers also doubted whether Arizonans could conquer their prejudices and vote a woman into the governor's mansion.[98]

Goldwater's political activities in 1950 suggest that he had more in mind than the election of Howard Pyle. Arizona, like most of the western states, had candidate-oriented campaigns and weak party organizations. With party structure undeveloped and discipline conditional, it was "every candidate for himself."[99] Even longtime Arizona Senator Carl Hayden kept the party at "arm's length," preferring to build a personal organization down to the precinct level.[100] To give the reborn Republican Party a present and future, Goldwater acted to fuse personal politics to a stable party machinery. He did this by working to field a Republican ticket that contested all state offices. Thus, he called Mesa lawyer John Rhodes and said, "I'm drafting you to run for attorney general." When Rhodes demurred and indicated that he did not feel qualified, Goldwater replied, "Don't worry, you haven't a chance in hell of winning."[101] Men and women responded to the Goldwater style and attached to him a powerful charisma. Attorney Richard Kleindienst would later write: "When Goldwater thrusts out that square jaw, looks at you with those piercing eyes, and tells you to do something, your only response is assent."[102]

The Pyle campaign was a six-month hands-on effort for Goldwater. In addition to overseeing scheduling, fund-raising, and speech-making, Goldwater crisscrossed Arizona with Pyle, flying him twenty-five thousand miles in a single-engine airplane. Pyle stood squarely on the Arizona Republican Party platform, advocating the right to work, tax incentives for business, reclamation, states' rights, and the passage of legislation to protect local utilities and factories from communist saboteurs. Taking his cue from the Phoenix municipal elections, Pyle accused Frohmiller of being a member of the boss-ridden Democratic statehouse machine. In a thinly disguised reference to gender, he pleaded with voters not to elect the "voiceless stooge" of the back-room boys.[103] Frohmiller made things easier for Pyle by running an "unorthodox campaign."[104] Democratic voter registration figures made her supremely confident, and she opened no headquarters, erected no billboards, raised no funds, and acted as her own campaign manager. In all, she spent $875 in her effort. This combination of Republican assets and Democratic liabilities produced a narrow 3,000-vote edge for Pyle from the more than 195,000 ballots cast. The election marked only the third time since Arizona statehood that a Republican had won the governorship. Democrats, meanwhile, captured all other state offices by two-to-one margins.[105]

Barry basked in the glow of Pyle's triumph. As the strategist of the only Republican statewide victory, he now owned a reputation for success that brought recognition and respect from outside of Phoenix. Yeoman service in a hard-fought campaign raised his standing with the party faithful. Pyle's break of the Democratic lock on state offices also refuted those who dismissed a vote for a Republican as wasted. The sun was rising for Republicans, and Goldwater's prospects grew brighter. Finally, victory galvanized Republicans and accelerated the building of what was becoming a formidable support network. Goldwater, who "had the name and the color," could only be pleased by this evolving blend of personal and organizational politics.[106]

Despite Goldwater's prestige in the party, or perhaps because of it, Governor Pyle found no place for him in the administration. In fact, Pyle never again consulted Barry about state politics or policy. Goldwater took such matters personally but gave no public sign of a breach. Rather than souring Goldwater on politics, the rejection only heightened his ambitions and desire to serve the party. Although the governorship was in Republican hands, all the other state offices had yet to be wrestled from the Democrats. With state elections nearly two years away, he would have ample time to weigh options and await opportunities to firm his future.[107]

He returned to the Phoenix city council in 1951 and added to his commendable public service record. Development remained a central goal for Goldwater and his fellow council members, and they pressed forward even though some citizens were reluctant. "I have never known," said Barry, "a town that sits backs and squawks about annexation as much as Phoenix does."[108] The council moved to incorporate surrounding land and to expand waterworks and airline service while offering businesses incentives to come to Phoenix. When combined with the Valley of the Sun's weak unions, comparatively low wage scale, and growing pool of skilled and professional workers, such efforts encouraged growth. AiResearch and the Goodyear Aircraft Corporation returned to the community in 1951. By 1960 almost three hundred new manufacturing firms had located in Phoenix; they included General Electric, Sperry Rand, and Kaiser Aircraft and Electronics. Not only did these defense-related companies double the number of Phoenix men and women engaged in manufacturing, they also stimulated all sectors of the local economy. These changes and Barry's fiscal conservatism and watchdogging of city administrators garnered high praise from the Pulliam papers. At the same time, the favorable press coverage kept Goldwater's name and face before the voters in the state's most populous urban center. In November 1951 he and the rest of the Charter Government ticket stood for reelection. They campaigned on the city's promise and against the old regime's "gangsterism" and its "boodle, bossism, and balderdash."[109] But the opposition was token, and the slate achieved an overwhelming victory. Barry, again, out-polled every other candidate.[110]

Even before the council campaign began, Goldwater had planned to run for higher office. National and international events, not Arizona affairs, shaped his decision. President Harry Truman, elected in his own right in 1948, attempted to extend Franklin Roosevelt's New Deal with his own Fair Deal program. He pushed through Congress legislation that raised the minimum wage, brought more Americans under Social Security, and authorized the construction of public housing. But opponents stalled his requests for a civil rights bill, for federal aid to education, and for national health insurance, among other agenda items. Truman's Fair Deal incensed Goldwater, whose conservative critique had been seasoned by Friedrich von Hayek's best-selling *Road to Serfdom*, published in 1944. Goldwater believed, like Hayek, that an impulse to "collectivism" animated the New Deal and Fair Deal as it did socialism, communism, and fascism. The liberals' agenda of centralized planning and government intervention in the economy, no matter how noble in purpose, weakened America from within by eroding property rights and free enterprise. Government control of economic life would, in turn, infect the political sphere, curtailing individual rights and speeding America toward totalitarianism and a modern serfdom. Barry sounded the alarm in an ad for Goldwater's department store on July 4, 1950, warning his neighbors of the "dark clouds of socialism forming on the horizon . . . [that] may roll across the American scene. . . . It's later than you think."[111] Goldwater pressed this theme hard in speeches throughout Arizona in 1951. He told a Nogales audienÁe that the socialists had been "boring" into the federal government for almost twenty years and had "gotten so far I hate to think what will happen in 1952 if we don't get busy. We are not fighting Democrats, we are fighting Socialism."[112] In Tucson he was more intemperate, cautioning the members of the Pima County Republican Women's Club that unless Truman was defeated in 1952, "it probably is the last election the American people will ever have."[113]

Equally distressing to him was the crisis in Korea. The United Nations' counterattack in 1950 had pushed the North Koreans back across the border and north toward China. On November 25, 1950, the tide of battle turned as Chinese infantry poured into Korea and forced American troops into full retreat. The front stabilized in 1951, roughly along the thirty-eighth parallel, and the two sides settled into a war of attrition. Reluctant to wade into a major ground war on the Asian mainland, the Truman administration abandoned liberation of the north for the more limited goal of defending the south. General Douglas MacArthur, however, insisted that "there is no substitute for victory" and proposed to widen the war by bombing Manchuria and blockading Chinese ports.[114] Seeing his policies and the principle of civilian control of the military undermined by the general's insubordination, Truman removed MacArthur from command on April 11, 1951. This ignited a firestorm of protest in the United States fueled by the general's popularity and the public's dissatisfaction with the "no-win" policy of the president.

Goldwater eagerly joined the chorus of Truman critics. He introduced a resolution before the city council inviting General MacArthur to visit

Phoenix "and make it his home."[115] It passed unanimously. Despite the obvious risks, Goldwater was convinced that MacArthur's strategy would have ended the Korean war. He wrote: "We could have taken all of Korea and reunited this divided country. The politicians fearful of provoking a full-scale conflict with the Red Chinese and Russia, refused to let MacArthur pursue victory." MacArthur was relieved, he alleged, not for insubordination or in defense of the principle of civilian control of the military. Rather, Truman had embraced "appeasement," the same policy that had encouraged Adolf Hitler and led to World War II. "Was it the result of poor judgement," Goldwater asked darkly, "or was it by design?"[116] Ideology and partisanship alone do not explain Goldwater's stance. Asian events had also touched him personally. Among the Chinese nationalists who fled to Taiwan in 1949 before the communist advance were pilots he had trained in Arizona during World War II and with whom he had maintained contact. Despite his objections to Truman's decisions, Goldwater applied for active duty with the Air Force. Arizona National Guard units were dispatched to Korea, but he was not activated.[117]

For Barry Goldwater, time was running out for America. "I was fed up with President Franklin D. Roosevelt's New Deal, especially the ballooning federal government and its increasing invasion of our lives, and President Harry Truman's no-win policy in Korea."[118] Illinois Republican Senator Everett Dirksen, during a trip to Phoenix in 1951, called Barry aside and suggested a run for the U.S. Senate in 1952. The suggestion was not a surprise to knowledgeable observers. Even before his chat with Dirksen, Goldwater had begun clipping news articles about Senator Ernest McFarland in preparation for the race.[119]

Although he had hoped to focus on the coming Senate campaign, Barry found that city business demanded his attention. Postwar Supreme Court decisions and presidential rhetoric defining racial equality as simple justice stirred Phoenicians, as it did men and women across America. A strict color line scarred Phoenix, dividing black and white worlds socially, economically, and residentially. While discrimination was mainly of a de facto nature, it proved as restrictive and humiliating to blacks as the system existing in the South. African-American businessman Lincoln Ragsdale remembers the Phoenix of the 1950s as "just like Mississippi."[120] Goldwater's butler, Otis Burns, noted that the community "wasn't any better than a southern town."[121] Unlike southern states, Arizona granted blacks the vote, but whites tested this right on occasion. In one instance, Phoenix attorney and Young Republican William Rehnquist was ordered away from a polling place when he demanded that African-Americans read from the Constitution before being allowed to mark their ballots.[122]

In 1951 the Greater Phoenix Council for Civic Unity and the local chapters of the National Association for the Advancement of Colored People and the Urban League joined in support of a law suit challenging de jure school segregation. Goldwater seemed a natural ally in the cause. He was one of the first Phoenix merchants to employ blacks, and he had integrated the Arizona Air National Guard. Barry was also a member of the Tucson chapter of the NAACP, a tie that made him "suspect" in conservative Arizona.[123] As one of the most influential citizens of Phoenix, his endorsement could bolster the movement while helping to silence resistance and speed acceptance of racial change. Though he was never a key player, Goldwater endorsed the drive. At a meeting called to raise funds to finance the lawsuit, he took a public stand, contributing $400 to the cause. "I don't like segregation," he later stated, "in any form, any place, amongst any people."[124]

Yet there were limits to his activism. Goldwater's involvement in the civil rights struggle was minimal and intermittent because he believed that issues of discrimination and prejudice were inconsequential in Phoenix. "Well, to be honest with you," he contended, "there never was a lot of it. . . . [I]t was never a problem as far as I was concerned."[125] Having lived in a segregated community his entire life, Barry, while free of bigotry, was conditioned to ignore inequality or to understand it as an individual failing. He was not unusual, suggests civil rights proponent and attorney Ruth Finn, because, "like everybody around, with a few exceptions, he was blind . . . [he] didn't pay attention."[126] Thus, insensitivity, not racism, defined the Goldwater's department store practice of giving a wristwatch to the top graduate of every Phoenix high school but black George Washington Carver. When informed of this double standard, an embarrassed Goldwater immediately rectified the oversight, explaining that it "just escaped me."[127]

Closer to home, Barry seemed oblivious to anti-Semitism. The leading hotels and resorts in Phoenix, except for the Biltmore, carried such statements as "restricted to Gentile guests" or "selected clientele" in their advertising brochures.[128] Most notorious in the eyes of local Jews was the Camelback Inn, which was almost in the shadow of the mountain site Goldwater had chosen for his dream house. The Phoenix Country Club, while founded by men who were Jewish born, similarly restricted Jews and other minorities. Despite his background and Jewish friends, Goldwater did not hesitate to visit any of the restricted establishments. If he believed that discrimination was morally wrong, his conservative instincts opposed the disruption of property rights and the infringement of freedom of association. As Goldwater would later argue: "Our aim, as I understand it, is neither to establish a segregated society nor to establish an integrated society as such. It is to preserve freedom."[129]

Political considerations also fixed the level of his commitment. In its early years, Goldwater was an important financial contributor to the Phoenix Urban League. Urban League president William Bowman credits Goldwater with twice providing the assistance necessary "to keep the doors open." While Barry was a "true friend," he declined to serve on the League's board of directors, and he kept his association with the black organization from the public.[130] Rather than maintaining a formal and open relationship, he asked friend Mary Jo Pritzlaff to act "in his name" on the board, and she became the League's "major individual donor."[131] The political Goldwater pragmatically bowed to Arizona opinion and never exposed these private tracks. "A lot of times," recalls Bowman, "I would hear him talk and it didn't seem like it was the same person. Being absolutely honest will not get you the votes."[132]

This inattention and inaction contradicted Goldwater's own prescription for reform. Barry opposed outside interference in local affairs. He would later say, "I am unalterably opposed to . . . discrimination, but I know that [the federal] government can provide no lasting solution. No law can make one person like another if he doesn't want to. . . . The ultimate solution lies in the hearts of men."[133] Goldwater assigned primary responsibility for community problem-solving to neighbors acting in concert. Moral suasion was their tool to effect redress. Despite his influence and opportunities, Goldwater refused to take up the roles of opinion maker and educator. He had offered no explanation or public announcement when he integrated the Arizona Air National Guard. Rather than lighting a spark that may have ignited a chain reaction of change, the move had no impact on the wider society. In the campaign against Phoenix school segregation, Goldwater's participation was confined to a single donation. Similarly, his concealed relationship with the Urban League did nothing to raise the level of white tolerance. Nor did he conceive his position on the city council as an opportunity to advocate or advance the cause of religious and racial tolerance. "I think I had an intimate involvement with the fight here for civil rights," remarked Herb Finn, the attorney who argued the case for Phoenix school desegregation, "and Goldwater was just no where there."[134] Ragsdale concurred: "He was never out front. He didn't carry a banner."[135] Moreover, his frequenting of establishments that shunned minorities legitimized their discriminatory practices.[136]

An inability to conceptualize prejudice and discrimination beyond the individual experience to institutional or societal conditions inhibited Goldwater as well. Thus, his unprejudiced and generous nature led him to intervene on behalf of friends or in response to personal requests without acknowledging larger issues. Accordingly, Lincoln Ragsdale found him cooperative when approached but concluded, "Goldwater liked individuals.

I don't know if he liked the black race or not."[137] Barry's actions while president of the Phoenix Country Club in 1949–50 are especially revealing. Club directors refused membership to Harry Rosenzweig because he was Jewish. Goldwater forced them to admit his friend: "Either you take him or I will blackball every name you put in."[138] Yet he did not press the board to end its restrictive policy, and no other Jew was admitted for another decade. Blacks and Hispanics would have to wait even longer.[139]

The usually activist Phoenix city council was reluctant to intervene in racial matters, but it was forced to act following an incident on September 17, 1952. Herb and Ruth Finn and black band leader Louis Jordan were refused service at the Sky Chef restaurant at the municipal airport. The following day, Herb Finn went before the council and asked for a prohibition against discrimination in the city-leased facility. Mayor Hohen Foster and Jack Williams, who had replaced Harry Rosenzweig on the city council, took the lead and persuaded members to order the restaurant to admit people without regard to color. When the restaurant ignored the order, the council met in emergency session and directed the city attorney to revoke the lease unless the owners complied, which they did a few days later. Barry played no part in these deliberations. Politics dictated his absence. On the day the council went on record against discrimination, Goldwater stood on the steps of the Yavapai County Courthouse in Prescott delivering the speech that launched his campaign for the U.S. Senate.[140]

Barry Goldwater had matured in these years after World War II. On a reputation for business success and wartime experience, he had built a strong record of community service. Goldwater's efforts in the right-to-work campaign, the Colorado River Commission, the Republican Party, and Phoenix city government had inspired public confidence and respect. Service had seasoned Goldwater. His focus had become tighter, his aim more steady. As he secured a Phoenix base, Barry made his name and face familiar throughout Arizona. Confidently, in a time more amenable to his conservative beliefs, he prepared to continue his climb.

5
In the "Land of Oz"

I was personally very fond of Senator Goldwater. He worked extremely hard, was tough, had a sense of humor. He played politics to the hilt and sometimes slightly beyond. He could cut you to ribbons, slit your throat, but always in such a pleasant manner that you would have to like him.

—ROBERT F. KENNEDY
The Enemy Within

Barry Goldwater had taken on a formidable challenge in running for the U.S. Senate. His opponent, Ernest McFarland, was a two-term senator, one of the authors of the GI Bill, and the Senate's Democratic majority leader. McFarland laid claim to incumbency, a national reputation, a political record that extended back to 1923, and voter registration figures that bulged in his party's favor. Goldwater was surely the underdog, but his bid was far from quixotic. Nationally, and in Arizona, there was widespread dissatisfaction with President Harry Truman and the Democratic Party. Twenty years of Democratic rule heightened the pressure for change made urgent by Truman administration scandals, the Korean Conflict, and fears of communist infiltration of American government. Truman's decision not to seek reelection and the Democratic Party's nomination of Illinois Governor Adlai Stevenson did not change Republican campaign rhetoric. In General Dwight Eisenhower the Republicans believed they had found a candidate who could shake the Democratic hold on the White House and reassert party power. Across America they campaigned on the slogan "K_1C_2"— Korea, corruption, and communism. The choice, Republican candidates told voters, was "Liberty or Socialism."[1]

To close the gap between himself and McFarland, Goldwater began campaigning early in the spring of 1952. With his usual energy he paced the state, tarring McFarland with Truman, whom he condemned as "that architect of socialism."[2] Goldwater could count on the support of the influential *Arizona Republic* and *Phoenix Gazette*. He had also won the endorsement of the *Arizona Daily Star*, Tucson's largest newspaper. Barry recruited Stephen Shadegg to be his campaign manager. Shadegg was the experienced and shrewd publicist who had guided Senator Carl Hayden to reelection in 1950. Goldwater stood at the head of a united Republican Party. Unlike its counterparts in other states, the Arizona party had avoided the acrimonious struggle between supporters of Ohio Senator Robert Taft and General Eisenhower at the national convention. Goldwater, although a "Taft man," had quelled intraparty conflict by engineering a compromise at the Arizona convention that gave the Eisenhower faction representation on the state delegation to the national gathering.[3] Having won the appreciation of all party wings, he faced only token opposition in the Republican primary, allowing him to focus all of his resources against McFarland.[4]

In a gesture to Big Mike and Uncle Morris, Barry formally opened his campaign for the U.S. Senate on September 18, 1952, in Prescott, the family's ancestral Arizona home. With the pioneer past still so close and celebrated, the location was a powerful reminder of Barry's deep Arizona roots. The enthusiastic hometown crowd of seven hundred welcomed Goldwater as a local hero. Shadegg ensured that his candidate's message went beyond the small community, arranging television and radio hookups that broadcast the address throughout the state.[5]

With a flat, unpolished, and unemotional delivery that suggested a citizen new to politics rather than a seasoned politician, Goldwater quickly presented the themes of his campaign. He was disgusted with the Truman administration's "appalling record of waste, inefficiency, dishonesty, and failure both at home and abroad." He pledged to halt the "expanding governmental bureaucracy, government-created inflation, and . . . the highest taxes ever extracted from the American citizen." Although he had recently described the New Deal–Fair Deal as a "devilish plan to eventually socialize this country," Goldwater reassured listeners that his opposition did not mean elimination of federal programs.[6] "No responsible Republican has any intention or desire to abolish any one of them." He reiterated his support for the Federal Deposit Insurance Corporation, Social Security, unemployment insurance, the Federal Housing Authority, and the Securities Exchange Commission. Turning from domestic issues, Goldwater deviated from his prepared text to tie McFarland directly to the unpopular stalemate in Korea. He quoted McFarland, out of context, as suggesting that the Korean conflict was a "cheap war" because of the kill ratio of nine Chinese soldiers for each American combat death. In a telling blow, Goldwater challenged McFarland "to find anywhere within the borders of these United States a single mother or father who counts their casualties as cheap." Harry Truman's name was not on the ballot, but Goldwater assured Arizonans that they could still vent their anger by voting against his "personal spokesman," Ernest McFarland.[7]

Acting as the church amen corner, the *Arizona Republic* and *Phoenix*

Gazette gave the speech extended coverage and ran editorials that reiterated Goldwater's points. The *Republic* rejected McFarland as an "administration mouthpiece" and validated the "cheap war" charge, calling it a "dangerous rubber-stamping of the Truman Administration's timid and cynical forfeiture of lives in a war that could have been prevented and that is dragging on at terrific cost."[8] Five days after the Prescott speech the *Republic* endorsed Barry's candidacy and began merging the Eisenhower and Goldwater campaigns. The *Phoenix Gazette* similarly confirmed Goldwater's claim: "Mr. McFarland must stand or fall on the Truman record."[9] The Pulliam press would aid its champion in other ways. Ernest McFarland's picture rarely appeared in the newspapers, and news of his rallies and speeches was often consigned to the back pages. Along with a steady stream of enthusiastic editorials, Barry consistently received front-page, above-the-fold treatment.

Even with Ike's coattails and an attractive candidate, Steve Shadegg knew that he could not concede any votes to McFarland. He focused Goldwater's efforts on Maricopa (Phoenix) and Pima (Tucson) Counties, the state's major vote caches. Here were concentrated just over 70 percent of the state's electorate. Goldwater would win, Shadegg strategized, if he could come out of Maricopa County with a 10,000- to 15,000-vote lead and at least break even with McFarland in Pima County. With Republicans already corralled, he targeted independents, new residents, and conservative Democrats whose support for Governor Pyle over Ana Frohmiller suggested a less-than-firm commitment to their party. Still, Shadegg would not write off the heavily Democratic hinterlands. He scheduled Barry for campaign stops in Benson, Douglas, Nogales, Ajo, and other outlying Arizona communities. Shadegg also blanketed radio and television with campaign ads, in English and Spanish, ranging from one-minute jingles to thirty-minute formal presentations. Shadegg missed few opportunities to get his candidate's name and face before the voters. Those who escaped the electronic media blitz were reached with more traditional methods—postcards and billboards urging them to vote for Goldwater and Burma Shave–like signs reading:

> Mac is for Harry
> Harry's all through
> You be for Barry
> 'Cause Barry's for you
> GOLDWATER FOR SENATE[10]

Shadegg orchestrated an expensive campaign, and there was no shortage of funds. More than half of Goldwater's $45,000 war chest came from out-of-state contributors, including wealthy conservatives H. L. Hunt, E. L. Cord, Sid Richardson, and Joseph Pew. The Republican Senate Campaign Committee, sensing an upset, offered $7,000 to the cause. As in the Phoenix municipal elections, Harry Rosenzweig became an important conduit for campaign funds. Again he secretly gathered packets of money from Gus Greenbaum. "Hiding who gave it to me[,] I called up ten Democrats and put it under their names."[11] At one point he and Goldwater family friend Victor Armstrong stood on a downtown Phoenix corner and collected envelopes filled with money from area cotton and lettuce growers.[12]

The media barrage, ad campaign, and heavy speaking schedule had an effect. At the start of the fall campaign the *Arizona Republic* published a poll that showed the race had narrowed, with 49 percent of voters preferring McFarland; 45 percent Goldwater; and 6 percent undecided. Goldwater commanded strong support among Republicans, particularly professionals, managers, and businesspeople. To make up the difference between himself and McFarland, Barry needed to make inroads among men, blue-collar workers and farmers, and young voters. The poll results buoyed the Republicans and convinced them of their strategy's soundness. During the next month and a half they would accelerate a negative campaign while pressing their advantages.[13]

Barry Goldwater organized his offensive according to the Three C's, "Communism, Cronyism, and Chiseling," a slight modification of the national Republican election formula of K_1C_2.[14] Again and again he raked McFarland as the "leading light" of the Truman "gang," a "confused, greedy, conscienceless government composed of little men eager to feather their own nests."[15] The graft, deceit, and waste of the "rotten deal" must end, he told voters, and the "five percenters" and "influence peddlers" must be banished from Washington.[16] Deficit spending also drew the Republican candidate's ire, for it weakened America from within and left inflation in its wake. Asked Goldwater, "You know who's going to pay this bill we've allowed to accumulate don't you? Our children are going to pay it and live with it for a long time."[17]

He increasingly questioned the Democrats' commitment to America's foreign and domestic war against communism. Goldwater raised the specter of communist subversion and painted Franklin Roosevelt and Harry Truman with a red brush. He condemned "the appalling record of the New Deal and Fair Deal, of trusted elected government officials who were either duped into allowing communists to infiltrate into high places or sanctioned that infiltration." The moment of reckoning had come:

> Now is the time to discharge those who have coddled the communists. Now is the time to defeat those who have . . . failed to recognize the source and magnitude of this danger to our freedom.
>
> Now is the time to put men into political office who will give their first allegiance to the principles of American freedom. Now is the time to throw

out the intellectual radicals and the parlor pinks and the confused and the bumbling. Now is the time for change.[18]

He continued the attack in a radio address on October 5: "And I suggest to you the man in the striped pants with the English accent and the English relatives who rules our state department, Dean Acheson, is behaving a great deal like the man with the umbrella who went to Munich."[19] Following this line, Goldwater labeled as "appeasement" Truman's decisions not to seek a wider war by bombing Manchuria or allowing Nationalist Chinese forces to fight in Korea. There were, he concluded, but two options to the conflict: admit defeat and withdraw or win "by whatever means necessary."[20] Arizonans had little doubt where Barry stood.

Senators Joseph McCarthy and Robert Taft made campaign trips to Arizona and bolstered Goldwater's anticommunist credentials. McCarthy, notorious for his red-baiting activities, stumped the state twice for Barry, and at one press conference "in simulated absent mindedness, . . . mixed up the names of Adlai [Stevenson] and Alger Hiss."[21] Robert Taft, endorsing Goldwater as "a man of the highest character and ability," proceeded to substantiate the Arizona Republican's anticommunist charges. Said Taft, "The New Deal first recognized Russia and then permitted Communists to move into our government in powerful positions. They have affected the thinking of this New Deal crowd that runs the State Department. That's the crowd that has given the Communists what they wanted in Europe and elsewhere."[22]

By far the greatest boost to Goldwater's candidacy came in mid-October when the Eisenhower campaign train visited Phoenix and Tucson. Before an audience of twelve thousand Phoenicians, Ike endorsed Barry: "He was with me in a former crusade, and I am delighted to have him as an associate in this one."[23] The *Arizona Republic* captured the moment on film and decorated the event with large banner headlines. The handclasp before the crowd gave proof to Pulliam editorials that said the popular general and the local businessman were allies in a common cause. Goldwater ad copy, henceforth, played to the Eisenhower-Goldwater relationship and pleaded, "GIVE IKE A MAN HE CAN WORK WITH."[24]

Senator Ernest McFarland took the Goldwater candidacy seriously but was confident of reelection. He stood on his record in support of New Deal and Fair Deal legislation under the slogan "You never had it so good."[25] Perhaps statistically defensible, this theme seriously misgauged voters' perceptions. McFarland addressed the different Arizona constituencies, promising to work for the expansion of the livestock and tourism industries, for a copper excise tax to aid the mines, and for the Central Arizona Project. He challenged his opponent to stop speaking in "generalities" and to "name the laws, the measures, and the programs which . . . [he] would repeal or abolish." Confronting the charges of New Deal–Fair Deal socialism, McFarland berated Goldwater for resorting to "the fraudulent device of self-seeking politicians."[26] McFarland also condemned Barry for using "scare tactics," but he was not above his own hyperbole: "On the outcome of this election may depend war or peace, security or fear, freedom or slavery."[27] Arizona Senator Carl Hayden publicly endorsed McFarland, and stumping the state on his behalf were Speaker of the House Sam Rayburn and Senators Robert Kerr, Richard Russell, Estes Kefauver, and Lister Hill. Goldwater decried their visits, pointing out that it was a "sinister development when out-of-staters tell us how to vote."[28] Arizona unions backed McFarland and offered workers and funds to the campaign.[29]

Despite these efforts, McFarland's campaign never built momentum. Goldwater's attack was unlike any he had ever faced, and it left him bewildered. "I have been subjected to charges," he told a television audience, "which I have never dreamed would have been made by an opponent in any campaign."[30] Republican assertions that he was a Truman puppet stung him, and even in the last days of the campaign McFarland felt compelled to list administration measures that he had opposed. Nor could he shake off voter resentment aroused by Goldwater's "cheap war" accusation. Meanwhile, McFarland countered with charges of Republican corruption and distorted reporting in the Pulliam press, but he ignited little interest. A money shortfall also plagued the Democrat's campaign, and Goldwater outspent him more than two-to-one.[31]

Unable to stop Goldwater's drive or to catch voters' attention with his platform, McFarland changed the tone of his campaign. His supporters exposed as false Goldwater's claim that he was a University of Arizona graduate and attacked his war record, dismissing him as a "society soldier."[32] Pointing to his "palatial" La Jolla home, they asked voters to reassess the man "who seeks to be Arizona's winter senator—and California's third summer senator."[33] McFarland also trained his guns on Goldwater's out-of-state supporters and warned that the Republican was under the "remote control" of easterners.[34] A poll released at the end of October may explain this shift in tactics. In the last lap of the race, Goldwater had moved into the lead, with 49 percent of voters preferring him, 46 percent favoring McFarland, and 4 percent still undecided. Since September McFarland's support among men, young voters, and the elderly had slipped. During the same period Goldwater had padded his lead among women and white-collar workers and professionals. By a slim majority, new voters also backed Barry.[35]

Arizonans judged the two men on more than their platforms. Image was also important. The fifty-eight-year-old Ernest McFarland was, in Senator Carl Hayden's words, "a workhorse, not a show horse."[36] Progressive, intelligent, and hard-working, McFarland had effectively represented Arizona's interests in Washington. Though McFarland could operate behind the scenes, he was neither dynamic nor articulate. He was not a Washington power broker despite his position as Senate Democratic majority leader. McFarland had assumed the role in 1951 but remained in the background and allowed the whip, Texas Senator Lyndon Johnson, to plot legislative strategy. "I'm going to be more of a silent leader," he said. "I'm going to let them take the lead in certain things."[37] Consistent with this, he stressed to voters that his Senate seniority and Washington connections were his two greatest strengths. Such assets became liabilities in the anti-Truman atmosphere of 1952. Moreover, on the hustings, McFarland's roots in the Oklahoma countryside and in the Pinal County, Arizona, courthouse were clearly visible. He came across as a "good old boy from Oklahoma," said Democratic activist Charles Pine, "who used to brag that he was born in a log cabin. He was not the most colorful candidate."[38] Uncomfortable before television cameras, he appeared bumbling and inept. "His long suit," remembers Stewart Udall, "was shaking hands with everybody."[39] To newcomers to the state who lived in Phoenix and Tucson, he seemed a throwback to an earlier era; a man out of touch with postwar America.[40]

Barry Goldwater was a sharp contrast with McFarland. Barry's campaign literature described him as "tall, lean, hard muscled," and voters who pressed his flesh were not disappointed.[41] During the ten-month campaign, Goldwater had shown remarkable energy and endurance, delivering six hundred speeches and flying fifty thousand miles in his airplane. With each appearance Goldwater became more skilled and self-assured. At forty-three years of age, he was a comrade-in-arms of General Eisenhower, a pilot, an explorer, an Indian expert, and a photographer. His sharply angled face fit voters' image of the rough-hewn son of Arizona pioneers. So did his low-key speaking style, which jabbed listeners with exhortations to victory over grafters, liars, and communists. Goldwater was, in addition, a successful businessman who claimed experience in meeting payrolls and managing budgets. Here was the concerned patriot who sacrificed self to serve. Goldwater told voters it was time for a change, and they understood him with reference to both issues and personalities.[42]

The election confirmed Republican strategy nationally and in Arizona. Eisenhower handily defeated Stevenson, winning 55 percent of the popular vote and thirty-nine states with 442 electoral votes. The tide was so strong that it swept across the solid South, carrying Texas, Oklahoma, Florida, Tennessee, and Virginia into the Republican column. Although Ike outran Republicans everywhere, the GOP captured control of both houses of Congress. Eisenhower and Governor Howard Pyle, in winning Arizona by a two-to-one margin, gave Goldwater the edge that lifted him to a slim 6,725-vote victory over McFarland out of almost 260,000 ballots cast. Even with all of his assets, he had barely surmounted his state's traditional allegiance to the Democratic Party to become the first Arizona Republican since 1920 in the U.S. Senate. As Shadegg had planned, Barry's margins in urban Maricopa and Pima Counties were sufficient to offset McFarland's strength in the rural areas. Despite Goldwater's efforts and the combined popularity of Eisenhower and Pyle, national commentators judged the Arizona outcome as additional evidence of Joe McCarthy's prowess. Ernest McFarland was one of the four Democratic incumbents McCarthy had personally campaigned against and who were defeated for reelection. The election also marked the Republican Party's coming of age in Arizona. In addition to the Pyle and Goldwater triumphs, John Rhodes became the first Arizona Republican elected to the U.S. House of Representatives. In the state legislature, attorney Richard Kleindienst and twenty-nine Republicans won House races, up from eleven in 1951, and four Republicans began Senate terms, breaking the Democrats' monopoly in that body.[43]

Barry Goldwater arrived in Washington, D.C., or what he called the "land of oz," on his birthday, January 1, 1953.[44] Congressional leaders assigned the junior Senator from Arizona and his four-person staff to three small rooms in the Old (now Russell) Senate Office Building. Barry immediately established the routine that he would follow throughout his life in Washington: rising at 5 A.M., arriving at his desk between 7 and 8 A.M., and leaving for home after 6 P.M. In addition to the usual settling-in activities, Barry began his Alpha File, in which he collected important correspondence, his observations of events, and notes from meetings and telephone conversations with presidents and dignitaries. The family followed Barry east in stages. Daughter Joanne would enroll at Mount Vernon College, and little Peggy attended a private elementary school. Sons Barry Jr. and Mike entered nearby Staunton Military Academy, their father's alma mater.[45]

Keeping to a habit from his youth, Barry sought out mentors to assist in his transition to politics and to counsel him on his career. Robert Taft, who was known as "Mr. Republican" and was the party's leading conservative and the Senate's new majority leader, seemed a natural selection. "As soon as I got to the Senate, I had already picked out the man I admired and I made it a point to get very close to him. I pretty much let him guide me."[46] But owing to Taft's cold and reserved nature their relationship was never intimate, and Taft died in the summer of 1953. Barry did not appreciate Taft's assigning him to the Banking and Currency and the Labor and Public Welfare committees rather than the more prestigious committees—Armed Services and Interior and Insular Affairs—that he preferred. As Barry wrote home to brother Bob and

Bill Saufley: "I find myself in two committees one of which I may be of service to but the other . . . well, what the hell do I know about banking and currency. . . . [I] can't get four out of two and two more than once in three." He continued, "It's a slow process of learning, but by keeping my big mouth shut and my flap ears open maybe in a year or so I will venture forth with some sage observations."[47] Barry would find himself compelled to speak out long before the year was up. Meanwhile, conservative Senators Everett Dirksen and Styles Bridges proved more important than Taft in promoting Goldwater.[48]

Wisely, Barry deferred to Carl Hayden, Arizona's senior senator and an old family friend. Hayden had been accumulating seniority since 1927, and he had considerable influence within the Democratic Party and the Senate. Barry also realized that his inexperienced and small staff could not be as effective as Hayden's office in meeting constituent needs. "If you wanted something done," recalls friend Denison Kitchel, "you didn't go to Goldwater's office."[49] With Hayden charged with "delivering" on Arizona issues, Goldwater was able to move beyond state and even regional concerns to focus on national and international affairs. Thus, he left to Hayden, Stewart Udall, John Rhodes, and other members of the Arizona delegation the work of carrying the Central Arizona Project through Congress while he "never lifted very much."[50]

Goldwater aspired to the role that suited him temperamentally: a salesman-at-large for conservatism. He was out of place in Washington, a small-town businessman in a lawyer's world. He was unskilled in debate, unwilling to compromise his stands, and bored by legislative procedure. Few pieces of legislation would bear his name, and "he didn't fight hard for those bills he introduced."[51] As Goldwater had told Arizona voters, "My aim was not to pass laws, but to repeal them."[52] This disinterest in legislative matters led Utah Senator Wallace Bennett to conclude, "It became obvious he really didn't want to be a senator. Barry was ambitious early on. He was a little bit of a loner because of that."[53] For Goldwater the Senate became a means to a larger end. Not yet yearning for higher office, Goldwater found his calling peddling conservative ideas; he was a preacher who could rouse men and women to action and service to their principles and country. The Senate conferred stature and gave him a national pulpit from which to carry on the crusade. Colleagues soon recognized his strength and, at the prompting of Styles Bridges, appointed him to the Republican Senate Campaign Committee as a messenger to the party faithful.[54]

If he was a "luxury" for Arizona, voters did not resent him.[55] They delighted in the recognition Goldwater received and the attention he brought the state. Local opinion-makers encouraged this attitude. "Barry," noted Hayden staffer Roy Elson, "was the one that was always getting the ink. He was more quotable."⁵⁶ But overkill worried Stephen Shadegg, and he expressed concern about the "manufactured poop." Only a month after Goldwater left for Washington, Shadegg wrote to him: "The *Republic* and *Gazette* are giving you almost daily space and sometimes it appears they reach pretty far to make a story. It is my opinion that you would benefit from a little less publicity."⁵⁷

Even before arriving on Capitol Hill Goldwater had begun speaking to a national audience. Just three weeks after his coattail victory he told a *New York Times* reporter that he did not agree with the Point Four foreign aid program "in its entirety," favored an end to Korean War price and wage controls, and supported a national sales tax to raise revenues.⁵⁸ The *Times* found him again, after only ten days in Washington, insisting that there could be no tax cuts before the budget was balanced. "I intend to become," he wrote at the time, "rather unpopular by voting for economy all the way down the line come what mayish."⁵⁹ He also received media attention with his support of administration-backed legislation to grant states title to offshore oil lands and his own bill to expand government power in curbing communist influence in labor unions.⁶⁰

Goldwater was newsworthy in part because he had turned back the reelection bid of the Senate majority leader. He also was caught in the national spotlight that followed Joe McCarthy. More important, reporters quickly realized that Goldwater was no ordinary politician. Here was a maverick, a personable conservative with flash and color. Barry had broken the rule that said freshman senators were to be seen and not heard. Handsome and vigorous, candid and quotable, he personified for easterners the mystique of the West. What a contrast he made with the starchy Taft. Like the Phoenix newspapers, the eastern press would find that the Arizona senator made good copy. The attention did not make Barry arrogant. Behind the public man still huddled the private, insecure Goldwater. Feeling inadequate, he wrote to Steve Shadegg, who reassured him: "Don't let those bastards back there intimidate you with their snobbery and political connections or their anything else."⁶¹ Goldwater exposed the inner man rarely and only to such trusted Arizona friends as Shadegg, Denison Kitchel, and Harry Rosenzweig. Throughout his career he would look to them often to steel his resolve.

President Eisenhower's call for "dynamic conservatism" cheered Goldwater.⁶² The Arizona senator approved of the administration's efforts to restrain spending, pare bureaucracy, and reduce government competition with private industry, especially in the public power area. In scrutinizing the budget, Goldwater was not blind to military waste and inefficiency, and he demanded an accounting. "We'll see," he snapped, "whether the Pentagon or the civilians run this country."[63] He spoke on the Senate floor in February in support of a plan, proposed by Secretary of Agriculture Ezra Taft Benson, to reduce farm subsidies and price supports. Goldwater's work on the Banking and Currency committee led, in May, to his first major Senate speech, an attack on wage, rent, and price controls. He detailed the history of such restraints and decried them as effective only in breeding inflation, black marketeering, and crime. Ike was pleased. "Atta boy," he wrote Barry in a brief note after the speech.[64] Goldwater, meanwhile, voted for administration proposals extending Social Security coverage and increasing the minimum wage.[65]

As expected, Barry Goldwater was one of the senators who rode point on the administration's policy toward the nation's 400,000 Native Americans. Pressure had been building since the late 1930s to curtail the authority of the Bureau of Indian Affairs (BIA) and wean tribes from federal resources. A new relationship had begun to take shape during the Truman years, but the change in administrations accelerated the evolution of policy. In the early 1950s, demands to cut the budget and bureaucracy merged with pleas to "set the Indians free" and allow them to progress through free enterprise into the mainstream of American life. The new approach, called termination, was multifaceted. Short range, it sought the repeal of legislation that held Native Americans to second-class citizenship. The repeal would complement the larger goals of assigning BIA functions to federal agencies that performed similar services for other Americans and transferring to the states responsibility for their Native American populations. In the end, policymakers envisioned the elimination of federal services to the tribes and the abolition of the reservations. Regardless of motive, the program was an assault on tribalism. According to historian Donald Fixico, "In everything that it represented, termination threatened the core of American Indian existence—its culture. The federal government sought to de-Indianize Native Americans."[66] Termination would proceed in stages, with planners promising to take into account a tribe's level of acculturation, its resource base, and its motivation. Despite expectations, the policy was fully implemented only among the Klamath of Oregon, Wisconsin's Menominee, and small bands in Utah and Oklahoma.[67]

Since the mid-1940s Goldwater had wanted the federal government "out of the Indian business."[68] He was convinced that BIA control had stunted Native American social and economic growth and brought misery to the reservations. "If you want to see the end results of a welfare state look at our Indians."[69] Goldwater felt that Americans had a moral obligation to redress past wrongs, "for the lands that we've taken, for the promises that we've made, and we haven't done the job we should have done for them."[70]

His prescription for reform was "to make the Indian ready for white man's civilization."[71] Consistent with his personal philosophy, the Arizona senator contended that the state, and not the federal government, was the most effective and cost-efficient agency to bring amelioration and eventually assimilation. State authorities, over a lengthy transition period, would assume federal responsibilities and service the tribes with better hospitals, schools, and roads. As Native Americans "acquire the ability to learn,"[72] their special status would terminate, enabling them to "assume their rightful position in our society, alongside their white brothers."[73] In harmony with these beliefs, Goldwater introduced legislation, which President Eisenhower later signed, that gave Native Americans the right to buy weapons, liquor, and other goods denied them under discriminatory nineteenth-century laws. To end federal wardship, foster self-determination, and develop free enterprise skills, he sponsored bills broadening the allowable uses of leased Indian lands and enabling tribes to spend funds without federal approval. He also voted for proposals to extend state civil and criminal jurisdiction over reservations, transfer medical care for Native Americans to the Public Health Service, and initiate the termination process for the targeted tribes. If he mouthed the slogans, Barry was protective of those he knew. Washington slated no Arizona tribe for termination.[74]

By the mid-fifties, opposition had banked termination fervor. Democratic Party victories, Native American resistance, exposés of official deceit and pressure, and feedback about the destabilizing effect of termination brought pause. Goldwater and other termination advocates retreated. The Arizona senator maintained defensively, "I have never sensed that it was the opinion or the feeling that termination be pushed. . . . If the Indian tribes want to be terminated, they have a perfect right to ask it." And he changed his tack: "I do think we ought to find out why the Indian Bureau has not been able to do more good for the Indian with a billion dollars."[75]

President Eisenhower also counted on Goldwater to endorse the broad outlines of his foreign and military policies. Barry accepted the priority of resisting communist advances and approved of Secretary of State John Foster Dulles' intention to "roll back" the Reds and free captive nations. Goldwater, aware of budgetary constraints and consistent with his belief in technology, similarly backed the president's New Look defense strategy, which emphasized "more bang for the buck." This meant that the American response to the communist offensive would rely less on conventional forces and more on nuclear weapons and air power. In the face of communist aggression, the United States threatened to go to the brink of war, vowing massive retaliation in defense of its vital interests.[76]

At the same time, Goldwater did not hesitate to stand against the president and with Senate conservatives. He cast his first Senate vote against the nomination of Charles E. Bohlen as the U.S. ambassador to the Soviet Union. Eisenhower was strong in his support of Bohlen, a career foreign service officer whom he called "the best qualified man for the post."[77] But in the eyes of Goldwater and others on the Republican right, Bohlen was tainted, having served as adviser and interpreter to President Franklin Roosevelt at the much disparaged Yalta Conference of 1945. Bohlen was further damned for defending the Yalta agreements at his confirmation hearing. Senator Joseph McCarthy led the fight against Bohlen, suggesting darkly that declaring him a "security risk" was "putting it too weak."[78] Although the Senate confirmed Bohlen, Barry joined with McCarthy, Dirksen, John Bricker, William Jenner, and eight others against the president. Following the vote, Eisenhower wrote in his diary: "There were only two or three who surprised me by their actions; the others are the most stubborn and essentially small-minded examples of the extreme isolationist group in the party. I was surprised by the vote of Bricker and Goldwater. These two seemed to me a little more intelligent than the others."[79] Goldwater also bucked Eisenhower on the Bricker Amendment. This proposal sought to curb the president's constitutional treaty-making powers by requiring congressional approval of executive agreements and rejecting any accord that conflicted with the laws of the individual states. Although administration lobbying eventually defeated the measure in early 1954, Goldwater remained steadfast in his support of it. The budget-conscious Goldwater also consistently voted to reduce Eisenhower's requests for foreign aid.[80]

The drift of administration policy toward Southeast Asia was especially troubling to the Arizona senator. Rather than fall into lockstep behind the president, he refused to imagine Vietnam as vital to American interests. In 1953, during the debate on the foreign aid bill, Goldwater criticized France for "the perpetuation of a war in the face of the people's desire for freedom" and its failure to move Indochina toward independence. He offered an amendment to the bill denying aid to the French unless they gave "satisfactory assurances" of setting a "target date" for the end of colonial rule in Cambodia, Laos, and Vietnam. Senate rejection of his proposal, Goldwater warned, would bring deeper American involvement, for funding was "an open sesame to another war such as we have in Korea."[81] Massachusetts Senator John F. Kennedy's substitute motion offered a carrot to replace the Arizonan's stick: aid would be tendered to the French with the understanding that the decolonization process be accelerated. In the cold war atmosphere of the early 1950s, the motion was easily defeated. Almost a year later, in the aftermath of the French defeat at Dien Bien Phu, Goldwater remained focused on the danger of American involvement in Vietnam. Korea had convinced him of the risks of committing American troops to a ground war in Asia. Wars of liberation, he reasoned, were part of the "communist design to spread our strength out so thin in so many places that we will become more vulnerable in our more strategic areas."[82] As negotiators concluded their work on the Geneva Accords ending the war, Barry wrote, "We still don't know where we sit in regards to Indochina, and I am deeply concerned that there are people close to the President urging that we get into this thing. Believe me, that will be done over my loudest and strongest protests."[83]

Friction between Eisenhower and Goldwater was greater on domestic issues than it was on international ones. Goldwater hoped that Ike would not only roll back communism but also New Deal–Fair Deal programs. Instead, Eisenhower preserved the welfare state and, in accepting the expanded federal role in social and economic affairs, legitimized and consolidated liberal programs. He even took the lead in promoting federal aid to education and a national health insurance plan. Ike's failure to dismantle the welfare state or even halt the trend toward "centralism" was, for Goldwater, a betrayal of campaign promises and party principles.[84] In July 1953 he took the administration's request to raise the federal debt limit as an opportunity to question the president's commitment to a balanced budget and deficit reduction. "Our problem is not in Europe," declared the freshman senator. "It is not on the shores of Asia. It is wrapped up in the Treasury of the United States and the budget of the United States." While acknowledging that Ike had inherited the programs of liberal Democrats, he continued, "I am afraid we have embraced them and that in some instances we are fattening them."[85] He was more critical later in a letter to his brother and Bill Saufley: "It's obvious that the Administration has succumbed to the principle that we owe some sort of living, including all types of care to the citizens of this country, and I am beginning to wonder if we haven't gone a lot farther than many of us think on this road we happily call socialism."[86] It was more than the president's "metooism" that agitated Barry. Also nagging at him was Eisenhower's failure to act like a Republican. Having worked so hard to build the Arizona GOP, Goldwater was especially sensitive to the president's failure to use his patronage powers to reward loyalists and work through party channels. Eisenhower, he complained, "operated a nonpartisan administration."[87] I was "amazed what little grasp he had of real Republican problems. . . . He was not a political creature, he was a military man."[88]

Goldwater's association with Joseph McCarthy, of whom Eisenhower had said, "I just will not—I refuse—to get into the gutter with that guy," further distanced him from the president.[89] Barry had met McCarthy in the 1940s during one of the Wisconsin senator's visits to Arizona for health reasons. McCarthy had campaigned against McFarland, and Barry was indebted to him. As senators, their relationship tightened and they became friends. They corresponded frequently, saw each other socially, and exchanged Christmas gifts. "I was, what you might say, rather close to Joe and the people who were associated with him in Washington."[90] In part, the attraction was personal. Goldwater saw the private side of McCarthy and enjoyed sharing drinks with a man who could be gregarious and affable. He also admired the bravado and voiced the same concerns as "that fighting Irish Marine," the brawler who charged headlong into the anticommunist crusade.[91] Echoing McCarthy in April 1953, Goldwater demanded heightened vigilance of fellow travelers who "think that a little bit of socialism might not hurt. . . . In the federal government the woods are full of those who would like to see the government take over now privately owned means of production."[92] He defended his friend publicly: "Do I stick up for McCarthy? Yes, I always have and I shall continue to do so. . . . The people who want to get rid of McCarthy . . . are people who coddle communists."[93] In the same vein, he said in April 1954 that "I believe McCarthy will do a good job and has done a good job chasing down communists in our government."[94] Barry even assisted his friend's efforts, passing along to McCarthy's staff information about left-wing activity in Arizona.[95]

Friendship and their mutual cause did not conceal McCarthy's faults from Goldwater. Early on he confronted McCarthy about his accusations concerning communists in the U.S. State Department and found that "he couldn't name a single, solitary one. I told him that if he kept this up he was going to get into trouble—that you can't go around falsely accusing people when there's nothing to accuse them of."[96] Yet at the time, Goldwater did not go public with his misgivings. If McCarthy lied or was misinformed, rash, and abusive, he still had done service by focusing national attention on subversives. "I couldn't approve of some of the charges McCarthy was making, but there was a tremendous amount of evidence to support his allegations. . . . I supported McCarthy's efforts to bring this out in the open."[97] Goldwater justified the means and agreed with Senator John Bricker, who had once told McCarthy: "Joe, you're a dirty son of a bitch, but there are times when you've got to have a son of a bitch around, and this is one of them."[98] McCarthy was also a politically potent commodity. Reporting on his speaking trip to California and Arizona in September 1953, Barry wrote to Everett Dirksen, the chair of the Republican Senate Campaign Committee, that a brief defense of McCarthy had received "overwhelming applause. I feel, too, that we need not be afraid of the use of Joe's name, except, possibly, in the large industrial cities, which are pretty much under the control of the forces who hate McCarthy."[99] As late as January 1954 the Gallup Poll showed that 50 percent of Americans approved of McCarthy's work, with only 29 percent giving him an unfavorable rating. Equally important, Goldwater's sense of loyalty dictated his silence. He trusted his friends and stood by them regardless of their personal faults, the political fallout, and even the tactics they employed.[100]

Believing that McCarthy's recklessness was driven by a drinking problem, Barry tried to help his friend. He joined with Indiana Senator William Jenner to arrange a trip to the Bahamas where they could keep McCarthy from liquor and the press and "talk some sense into him."[101] McCarthy, however, frustrated their plan by flying south several days early and stashing bottles of liquor. He was "drunk as a skunk" by the time the Republican senators reached the islands.[102] On another occasion, Goldwater and other conservatives hid a "bad speech" that McCarthy was about to deliver on the Senate floor because they knew it would embarrass him.[103] Barry even called on Francis Cardinal Spellman of New York for help, asking him to intervene with McCarthy. McCarthy dutifully saw Spellman, but there was no change in the Wisconsin senator's behavior. Again, in March 1954, Barry and Senate conservatives William Knowland, Wallace Bennett, Everett Dirksen, and John Bricker attempted to rein in McCarthy. They hoped, in Bennett's words, to "avert the storm that was about to break over his head. . . . [N]eedless to say, . . . Joe refused to move to correct it. The storm has broken."[104]

The storm that Bennett had forecast was Joseph McCarthy's confrontation with the U.S. Army that played out before a large television audience from April 22 to June 17, 1954. Following up his investigations of subversion within the State Department's Voice of America and the libraries of the U.S. Information Agency, McCarthy targeted the army as "soft" on communism. His evidence was the army's promotion and then honorable discharge of a "pink" dentist who refused to sign a loyalty oath. The army defended itself by exposing McCarthy's efforts to wrangle special treatment for draftee G. David Schine, a member of his investigative staff. After months of accusations and countercharges, the hearings convened to resolve matters. For thirty-five days the television cameras exposed McCarthy to viewers, who were repelled by his hectoring and disregard for procedure. The hearings bloodied McCarthy, and his vulnerability encouraged opponents to attack. With President Eisenhower working behind the scenes, the Senate moved to censure McCarthy for conduct "contrary to senatorial tradition" and for bringing the body into "disrepute."[105]

Barry Goldwater again rose in his friend's defense. Goldwater condemned censure at length as "the culminating act in the merciless fight to destroy a United States Senator and the fight against communism which has been crackling on a score of left-wing fronts for over four years." Dismissing the charges as "technicalities and legal trivia," he looked for a hidden catalyst for McCarthy's pillorying.

It is buried beneath deceptive surface appearances of this case. Our search for that reason leads us to some extremely important men, some of them working in anonymity, who have vowed to drive McCarthy from a position of influence in this country.

Their motives are a criss-cross of spite, of fear of his political possibilities, and of the ever present and haunting dread that his ranging investigations might lead him into certain dark places in the Washington scene which they desperately want to keep covered up.

Goldwater warned that censure would only give aid and comfort to the "discredited and embittered figures of the Hiss-Yalta period of American dishonor [who] have crawled out from under their logs to join the efforts to get even." McCarthy was guilty merely of "excessive zeal," Goldwater concluded, and he cautioned the Senate to weigh censure's impact on the free world's struggle against international communism: "To remove such a man from honor and influence in America at this juncture would be a strong victory for Moscow."[106]

As events tilted against McCarthy, Goldwater became the key figure in a last-minute attempt to avert censure. Texas Senator Price Daniels approached him and suggested that if McCarthy would sign letters of apology to two senators he had insulted, southern Democrats would vote against the motion. With McCarthy's attorney Edward Bennett Williams, Goldwater drove to Bethesda Naval Hospital, where the Wisconsin senator was recuperating from an elbow injury. They entered the hospital through a side entrance to avoid reporters camped in the lobby and climbed the stairs to McCarthy's room. Goldwater knew immediately that McCarthy had been drinking; he had hidden a bottle of bourbon beneath his mattress. The men pleaded with him to sign the letters that Goldwater described as "short, mild in their language, and regret[ing] a discourtesy without really conceding any substantive error on McCarthy's part."[107] McCarthy picked up a pen to sign, and then, without warning or explanation, threw it across the room, cursed them, and ordered them out. As McCarthy later told Everett Dirksen, "I don't crawl. I learned to fight in an alley. That's all I know."[108]

On December 2, 1954, the Senate voted sixty-seven to twenty-two to condemn Joseph McCarthy, with Goldwater and most Republican conservatives remaining loyal to the end. As McCarthy fell into obscurity and deeper into alcoholism, he claimed fewer friends. Barry did not abandon him. McCarthy's death in 1957 at the age of forty-eight brought Goldwater to the Senate floor to remember his friend: "Because he lived, America is a brighter, safer, more vigilant land today."[109] Later, he filled seven pages of the *Congressional Record* with letters and clippings eulogizing Joseph McCarthy.[110]

Before McCarthyism departed the scene it claimed a last and most unlikely victim: the Republican Party. The November 1954 election returns gave control of the Senate and House to the Democrats. Barry was particularly distressed because the Democratic advance had overrun Arizona Republicans. While John Rhodes had barely managed to hold on to his congressional seat, former U.S. Senator Ernest McFarland had unseated Governor Howard Pyle, and Democrats had taken every state government office. The Democrats had also recaptured two seats in the state Senate and ten in the House, commanding lopsided majorities of twenty-six to two and sixty-two to twenty, respectively, in the legislative bodies. As every politically savvy Arizonan knew, McFarland's stay in the governor's mansion would be brief. He longed to reclaim his Senate seat from Barry Goldwater.[111]

In 1955 Senate Republicans handed Goldwater the opportunity to advance his political and ideological ambitions. Although he was in only his first term, they elected him chair of the Senate Republican Campaign Committee. Goldwater's selection reflected conservative clout in the party and came because the more senior Dirksen and California Senator William Knowland were, respectively, running for reelection and occupied as minority leader. The appointment was also a recognition of Goldwater's appeal to the rank-and-file, which was so clearly demonstrated in appearances around the nation during 1953 and 1954.[112]

The importance of this assignment to Goldwater's rise cannot be overemphasized. As campaign chair, he garnered prestige and influence and became a prime source for news reporters already attracted by his "lone-gun" image and off-the-cuff comments. The *New York Times* sharply increased its coverage of the Arizonan and moved news items about him from the back pages toward the front. He appeared on "Face the Nation," "American Forum," "Meet the Press," and other television news shows. Weekly newsmagazines carried stories about the Jet-Age Senator, usually accompanied by a photograph of Goldwater dressed in flight suit and helmet alighting from an Air Force fighter plane.[113] Here was a new kind of conservative, one who felt equally comfortable in the cockpit or the saddle. His heightened prominence created valuable contacts. General Douglas MacArthur wrote to Goldwater in 1955, "I admire so deeply what you are doing in the Senate."[114] Their association grew with time, and some years later, after lunching with the general, Barry gushed, "I felt then, as I do now, pretty much like a boy sitting at the feet of his father, as he outlined the ways a son should travel. With you, Sir, it was like an American sitting at the feet of the intelligence and courage of all Americans, listening to what I should do with the life that is left me."[115] The post also led to a working relationship, and then to a personal one, with Vice President Richard Nixon.

In a note to Barry, Dick Nixon declared his feelings: "In this political game, as you know, there are not too many people you can count on as real friends. I feel indeed most fortunate that I am able to include you in that category."[116] Barry agreed—"We were good friends, very close"—and the two men and their wives shared family news and formal and informal social occasions.[117]

Goldwater's impact beyond Washington, at the grassroots, was even more consequential. Eager to escape the Senate routine, he hit the chicken-and-peas circuit, pressing flesh, rallying the faithful, and raising money for candidates. Goldwater's personal magnetism and style made him a natural for the task. His small-town business background tightened the rapport with the audience. Talking extemporaneously or with notes scribbled on a napkin, he relaxed and gained confidence with every speech. His authority and command were even more palpable in the face-to-face bull sessions that followed the speeches and went on into the early morning hours. Barry would serve three two-year terms as campaign chair, 1955–56, 1959–60, and 1961–62. During his tenure he traveled more than two hundred thousand miles, gave two thousand speeches, and visited nearly every state in the union. This yeoman service laid the foundation for his political future, for he met, knew by name, and captured the loyalty of men and women down to the district and county levels of the Republican organization. Goldwater noted his accomplishment: "I don't think anyone in this Party knows more Republicans than I do."[118] Nor would they forget him. Few would disagree with Goldwater's observation that "the post opened the way to the GOP nomination."[119]

Goldwater did more than stroke Republican loyalists and regale them with campaign battle stories. Again and again he called his listeners to arms against their main enemy, organized labor. Goldwater had, since the 1946 right-to-work campaign in Arizona, resisted the economic and political power of labor unions. On the Senate floor and in Labor and Public Welfare Committee hearings, he championed legislation to expand federal authority to weed communists from unions, grant jurisdiction over labor relations to the states, clamp down on secondary boycotts and what he considered unfair labor practices, and create a national right-to-work law.[120] In the aftermath of the disastrous 1954 election and looking forward to 1956, Goldwater's pace quickened and he denounced unions for their political activities on behalf of Democratic Party candidates. He targeted, in particular, the Congress of Industrial Organizations (CIO), whose political action committee (PAC) had funded voter registration drives, radio broadcasts, polling, and leafleting campaigns for its candidates in 1954. In all, CIO-PAC spending climbed above $1 million in the campaign, an amount that other unions had matched. The money was well spent; candidates endorsed by CIO-PAC won in 126 House, fifteen Senate, and eight governors' races. Against this "conspiracy of national proportions," Goldwater demanded legislation to ban organized labor from political activity.[121] The unions, he charged, had become political machines, illegally using dues to build "slush funds" that were commanded by "power-hungry labor bosses" and beyond members' control.[122] Matters grew more serious for Republicans in 1955, when the American Federation of Labor and the Congress of Industrial Organizations merged, pooling the resources of their 15 million members. Organized labor, ready to flex its muscles, stood up to Goldwater's challenge. Walter Reuther, president of the United Automobile Workers, responded adamantly: "Our answer to you Senator is not less political action, but more political action on the part of the American labor movement."[123]

Yet those who listened to Goldwater's speeches detected a larger cause than the election of Republicans to the Senate or the defeat of organized labor. This cause was evident in the diverse speaking engagements that he shoehorned into his tight schedule. In addition to Republican groups, Goldwater appeared in 1955 before the American Legion, the Michigan Christian Endeavor Convention, the Marion County, Illinois, Soldiers and Sailors Reunion, the National Association of Manufacturers, and the Southern Nevada Knife and Fork Club, among others. To them he preached a gospel of modern conservatism-individualism, sanctity of private property, militant anticommunism, and the dangers of centralized power. Audience reaction encouraged Goldwater and he telephoned adviser Stephen Shadegg with the news: "Every place I have used it, which is damned near every speech I have made, it brings down the house."[124] Because Goldwater was less an original thinker than a merchant of ideas, he needed Shadegg's help to develop the message. Together they honed a Goldwater speech blueprint, the core of which Shadegg nutshelled as "collectivism versus personal faith and large federal bureaucracy versus our individualism."[125]

The Arizona conservative found other ways to win "this race for the minds of men."[126] Goldwater and Shadegg collaborated in 1956 on the script for the documentary film "For Freedom's Sake" to expose the danger the free world faced from "the insatiable brute forces of Russia." In the film, Goldwater narrates scenes of life behind the iron curtain, where "men and women and children disappeared in agony and terror to be regurgitated as listless, pathetic, human ciphers without meaning or dignity. Puppets in the Marxian program for world domination." The picture's climax comes when Goldwater, as prosecutor, cross-examines an actor playing Joseph Stalin and outwits him into revealing the "Marxian program for world domination." Fading to black in a montage of flag and church spire shots, the script conjures up George Washington, who solemnly intones: "Let us this day reject appeasement, refuse any compromise which requires denial of what is morally right. Let us dedicate our lives, our fortunes and our sacred honor to the cause of freedom in the service of mankind."[127] In addition to making speeches and movies, Goldwater encouraged his friend Denison Kitchel to write, and then supplied him with information for, a newspaper column called "Voice of Free Enterprise" that extolled the virtues of capitalism.[128]

These activities did not occur in isolation but drew significance as part of a "new" conservative impulse that moved beyond the "standpat" domestic agenda and foreign policy isolationism of the Old Guard. With raised expectations, conservatives of diverse stripes had welcomed the Eisenhower presidency as a remedy to the "creeping" socialism of the New and Fair Deals. Presidential performance, however, did not measure up to the promise. Deficit spending, the Bohlen nomination, the Bricker Amendment, and the censure of McCarthy had tainted Eisenhower in conservatives' eyes. So, too, did the president's preaching of "Modern Republicanism," which he described as "a type of political philosophy that recognizes clearly the responsibility of the Federal Government to take the lead in making certain that the productivity of our great economic machine is distributed so that no one will suffer disaster, privation, through no fault of his own."[129] Senator Bricker spoke for many when he alluded to such pronouncements: "Much that sails under the banner of Republicanism today is certainly not Republicanism as we know it in Ohio."[130] Nor did the administration's foreign policy initiatives draw conservatives' praise, for in the Korean truce they saw stalemate, and in the rhetoric of rollback they sensed the frothing of a paper tiger.[131]

In the age of "vital center" liberalism, conservatives of the 1950s could do little more than mount a rear-guard resistance. Even this was a difficult task. Outside the mainstream, stripped of authority in government, academia, and the media, conservatives had fractured into loosely structured ideological camps. Traditionalists condemned the twentieth century's rejection of moral absolutes and values and its worship before the new god of relativism. This, they believed, had spawned permissiveness and the decay of family, community, and American institutions. Libertarians summoned men and women to a defense of private property, the free market, and individualism as bulwarks against an aggrandizing central government bent on planning America into a regimented state. Anticommunists, tuned to the dangers within and without, rejected containment as appeasement and demanded to know, Why not victory? Although these currents of thought were not mutually exclusive, conservative proponents had yet to coalesce into a cause. No national leader or organization or forum had appeared to mark off the common ground that the three traditions shared nor to establish the bases for cooperation.[132]

Eisenhower's rejection of their cause added momentum to conservatives' efforts to rally and unite. Intellectuals like Russell Kirk, Frank Meyer, Milton Friedman, James Burnham, Wilmoore Kendall, William Rusher, E. Merrill Root, and William F. Buckley, Jr., opened a dialogue that convinced conservatives that their similarities were greater than their differences. Conservatives of all varieties would find unity in the fight against totalitarianism and its "Judas goat," liberalism.[133] In coalition, they championed private property as the foundation for liberty and progress, limited government against centralized power, belief in a higher moral order, and an end to coexistence with godless communism through victory in the cold war.[134]

Their work proved more than an intellectual exercise, for the "new" conservatives were proselytizers eager to spread the word. As Barry Goldwater labored at the grassroots, William Buckley reached for a similar mass audience. His *National Review* broadcast the message beyond the conservative core, and his jousting with liberals on television and radio talk shows attracted national attention and a following. Growing demand encouraged radio stations to join the net carrying the programs of conservatives Dan Smoot, Kent and Phoebe Courtney, and Notre Dame Law School Dean Clarence Manion. Robert Welch, soon to found the John Birch Society, became a much sought-after speaker. So, too, did Hollywood actor Ronald Reagan, who hosted the General Electric Theater. "The Speech," which Reagan delivered year after year to workers in GE plants and later to Chamber of Commerce and Kiwanis groups, was a searing indictment of big government and a call to arms in defense of personal freedom. Goldwater, Buckley, Reagan, and the other messengers of conservatism labored hard for their beliefs, and their efforts bore fruit. In their hands, conservatism began to lose its hard edge, its coldness, its reputation for being the property of the old, the elite, the rich, and the prejudiced. Conservatives had begun gathering resources and building a movement. Slowly shedding their defensiveness, they felt a heightened self-awareness and confidence, and they basked in a growing visibility. If the prairies were not yet on fire, they had begun to smolder.[135]

Despite the growing differences between them, Barry Goldwater worked hard to reelect President Eisenhower in 1956. "This administration," contended the Arizona senator, "has reversed the 20-year trend toward centralization of power in Washington. Free enterprise is again operating full steam ahead."[136] Opposing the president were the liberals, whom Goldwater blasted "as purposeful members of the world-wide conspiracy to destroy the genius of American freedom or unwitting dupes."[137] Goldwater, always the party loyalist, went on the stump for Ike, as a member of the Republican

National Committee's Speaker's Bureau, accusing Democratic presidential candidate Adlai Stevenson of "innocence and naivete in foreign affairs."[138] He also cautioned the United Automobile Workers against "meddling" in politics.[139]

Goldwater, considering himself a member of the president's team, was thus stunned when *Collier's* magazine published Paul Hoffman's article "How Eisenhower Saved the Republican Party." Hoffman, a former director of the Marshall Plan and an Ike confidante, disclosed the president's impatience with "Republican senators claiming the label Republican who embrace none or very little of the Eisenhower program and philosophy." While the article did not tag Goldwater as an "unappeasable," like Joe McCarthy or William Jenner, he did make the allied "faint-hope" group.[140] Goldwater was furious, convinced that the president had approved the piece. Republican National Committee member James Wood found Barry "so damn mad that he threaten[ed] to withdraw from the present campaign."[141] Goldwater wrote to Sherman Adams, the president's chief of staff, quoting the article and indignantly demanding "immediate answers": "I would like to know if the President feels that I am possessed of 'dangerous thinking and reckless conduct.' I want to know if the President feels I am one of those 'people you cannot afford to have as friends.'" Adams replied quickly and eased Goldwater's anger: "Does the President like Barry Goldwater? Answer: Yes."[142] The crisis passed and Goldwater continued to campaign, but the breach between him and the president had widened. Their personal correspondence remained thin and sporadic. Goldwater was surely not surprised that his name appeared only infrequently on the list of those invited to the White House for Ike's exclusive "stag" dinners.[143]

Eisenhower's reelection was never in doubt. A lackluster campaign by both sides and late October crises in Hungary and the Middle East produced a landslide for the president. In a staggering personal victory, Ike captured 457 of 530 electoral votes and became the first Republican since Reconstruction to carry a Deep South state. His coattails proved short, however, for the Democrats retained control of Congress. It was the first time since 1860 that a presidential candidate had won without his party gaining control of at least one house on the Hill. Meanwhile, in Arizona, Democrats bucked the Eisenhower tide and won all statewide races. Among the winners was Governor Ernest McFarland, who now looked to complete his comeback with a victory in the 1958 Senate race.[144]

Republican Party strategists, including Goldwater, gathered after the election to assess the results. Particularly eye-catching were the returns from the South. Eisenhower had repeated his 1952 victories in Texas, Florida, Tennessee, and Virginia while adding Louisiana to the Republican column. The Eisenhower surge went beyond the traditional pockets of southern Republican strength in eastern Tennessee, western Virginia, North Carolina, and the German counties of south-central Texas to envelop such southern cities as Montgomery, Birmingham, Savannah, Augusta, New Orleans, Baton Rouge, Shreveport, and their suburbs. There, the president had done well among white, upwardly mobile urban businesspeople and professionals. The gains galvanized Republicans, and they moved quickly to exploit the opportunity that Eisenhower had given them. As Barry Goldwater would later say, "We ought to go hunting where the ducks are."[145] In 1957 they created a southern division of the Republican National Committee that planned Operation Dixie as the lever to pry the Democratic grip from the South. This project pumped resources below the Mason-Dixon Line to recruit southern conservatives into the GOP, raise attractive candidates for state and local races, and subsidize their campaigns. The inauguration of Operation Dixie did not mean that the Republican Party had conceded African-American votes in the North or South to the Democrats. Eisenhower's percentage of the black vote had increased from 20 percent in 1952 to 40 percent in 1956. Republicans, like Democrats, were well aware of the political impact of the post–World War II migration of southern blacks into the electoral-vote-rich states of New York, California, Illinois, Michigan, Ohio, and Pennsylvania. These trends gave added impetus to Republican efforts to entice black voters back into the GOP fold, a tradition broken only in the 1930s. Taking a lesson from the Democrats, the Republicans dreamed of drawing African-Americans and southern whites into a coalition that would tilt the electoral balance on national, state, and local levels in their party's favor.[146]

Politics was Goldwater's prime focus during these early years in Washington, but family matters intermittently interrupted his routine. Meniere's syndrome, a condition that wife Peggy contracted immediately after coming east, created a physical barrier that handicapped the Goldwaters' relationship. She had awakened one morning to experience hearing loss, dizziness, and buzzing in her ears. Worsening over time, hearing impairment would cause Peggy great embarrassment. She bravely began wearing a button that read "Speak Up! I'm Deaf" and tried to continue her political chores. But feeling like the "village idiot," she shunned public gatherings more and more often.[147] Sons Barry Jr. and Mike, though at nearby Staunton Military Academy, still received their parenting "by letter."[148] Barry Jr., a member of the school diving team and ranked nationally in the sport at the high school level, resented the emotional distance, remembering that his father never saw him compete. Mike's "life-long habit" of not responding to the letters still did not dissuade his father from continuing to write them.[149]

More pressing for Barry was news of eldest daughter Joanne's pregnancy in late 1955. Nineteen-year-old Joanne had graduated from Mount Vernon College and returned to Phoenix to attend Arizona State College to complete her bachelor's degree. Meanwhile, Joanne's relationship with Tom Ross, a pre-med student at Arizona State, became serious, and they planned a June wedding. Both, however, were unprepared to add the burden of a baby to the difficulties of adjusting to marriage. Joanne approached her parents for help. In a letter written on December 31, 1955, just before her twentieth birthday, Barry counseled Joanne against abortion: "I want to ask you as a favor to me to remain calm and trust me in this instance. This can work out in a beautiful way to the eternal happiness of both of you and at the same time bring happiness to your mother and a same feeling to me. I have not felt other than compassion for both of you in this hour and that feeling will control my thinking but I do hope and Pray to God that you will allow us to explain to you where we sit and what we think is best for you."[150]

After weighing her parents' advice, Joanne decided to terminate the pregnancy. The decision was difficult for Barry and Peggy to accept, but their longtime work with Planned Parenthood had prepared them to support their daughter. Although abortion was illegal in the United States unless the mother's life was threatened, Barry made arrangements for the procedure. Joanne flew alone to Washington, D.C., and was taken to a designated street corner where she stood with a *Time* magazine folded under her arm for identification. A car soon stopped and took her and several other young women into the Virginia countryside, where the abortion was performed. The next day she was flown back to Phoenix. Although Barry Goldwater would never again confront abortion on so personal a level, the issue would resurface to test him.[151]

Barry Goldwater had come far and fast since his 1952 election to the U.S. Senate. Although only in his first term and representing a politically insignificant state, he had performed important party service and begun to shape a national profile. His defense of Joe McCarthy, prickly independence from the Eisenhower administration, and responsibilities as Senate Republican Campaign Chair had made him good copy and a familiar face in party circles. A growing conservative momentum further heightened his stature. Also facilitating his rise was a lack of competition. On the Republican right, Taft was dead, McCarthy disgraced, and MacArthur retired. Few other conservatives commanded the charisma to contest the mantle. Still, Goldwater's advance was hardly assured. He faced a tough campaign for reelection. His offensive against organized labor played well before the party faithful but was not yet salient to a national audience. While Goldwater was willing to lead conservatives, they had still not confirmed him as their political point man. Goldwater's relationship with Eisenhower remained unsettled. While Ike was now a lame-duck president, his authority was unequaled, and only the intrepid challenged him. Most followed Senator Bricker's counsel and fell in behind their president: "If we keep our places in the crew, we can probably have some influence in determining the final port reached by our good Ship of State."[152] Goldwater's conscience and ambition took him in a different direction. He soon would move to secure his constituencies and position himself to prepare the nation for a change in course.

6

"Let's Grow Up, Conservatives"

I am watching with growing hope and enthusiasm your political strategy. A great vacuum exists that you can fill. Never let up and never flinch. Dramatic and startling events lie just ahead.

—GENERAL DOUGLAS MACARTHUR

I have the unmitigated gall to think that I could lead men anywhere, business, politics or combat.

—BARRY GOLDWATER

In early 1957 political analyst Richard Rovere described Barry Goldwater as a "middling figure" in the GOP and a "paragon of party regularity."[1] Goldwater's hectic speaking schedule and work on behalf of President Eisenhower's reelection had certainly demonstrated allegiance. So had his voting record in the 84th Congress. During 1955 and 1956, Goldwater supported the administration with 66 percent of his votes, just under the average Republican senator's score of 72 percent. Although identified with the Senate's conservative bloc, Barry never ventured from the pack to oppose the president. He had, in fact, been the administration's voice on some issues. At the same time, Ike had not rejected Goldwater as he had William Jenner and Joseph McCarthy. Disagreements occurred, but they appeared insignificant to those outside the inner circles.[2]

Yet for some time Goldwater chafed under Eisenhower's leadership of the party and nation. He had grown impatient with the president over patronage issues and the administration's affirmation of New and Fair Deal programs. Eisenhower's short coattails in 1956 only confirmed for Goldwater that the White House had neglected political responsibilities. Moreover, Eisenhower's failure to intervene in the Hungarian Revolution of October 1956 had given lie to the policy of brinkmanship and the promise to roll back communism. With Ike in his last term as president, Goldwater became less hesitant. His support of the administration on the Senate floor dropped to 57 percent in 1957 and 1958 and then to 52 percent in the last two years of the Eisenhower presidency. Through confrontation, Goldwater defined himself and staked out a conservative alternative to Eisenhower's Modern Republicanism. His dissent, fused with a vision of change and new possibilities, quickly became the rallying cry for a generation of conservatives and made him a national figure.[3]

Barry Goldwater began his challenge in early 1957. The *New York Times* noted that he balked at President Eisenhower's call for congressional authorization to send U.S. forces to the Middle East if requested by a country being threatened by communist aggression. The proposal troubled Goldwater, for it portended an open-ended commitment that might escalate beyond congressional control. Moreover, ground wars in distant lands, he believed, accommodated the communists' long-range goals. A worried Goldwater telephoned Stephen Shadegg on January 4 and emphatically declared: "Now, Goddamn it Steve, . . . I just can't see how I can go for it. I hate like hell to start out voting against the Boss, but Christ, we criticized that action in Korea. We've criticized similar actions all along. . . . Who determines what the emergency is? Who says how many boys? What kind of equipment? What kind of forces?" Goldwater rejected the option of dispatching troops but would never advise backing down before the communist danger. As a committed brinksman and now a colonel in the Air Force Reserve, he recommended reliance on American technology to meet aggression. That meant the Strategic Air Command, "the strongest Goddamned club we'll ever have." He told Shadegg: "Now Goddamn it, we can't [beat] Russia on the ground now, or probably ever. We have this retaliatory force in the Air Force which we have promised to threaten Russia with, and to me, that's all we have to do, and I think it is the only reason we have peace today."[4] Despite his misgivings, Goldwater voted in March with the president and Senate majority to approve the Eisenhower Doctrine. "At that particular time," remembered Goldwater, "I had no outwardly expressed opinions in foreign policy."[5] His hesitancy in the face of administration decision-making would do much to change that.[6]

In April Goldwater mutinied and publicly flailed the president. The issue was Eisenhower's 1958 budget, the largest request yet made in peacetime, which included increases in spending for foreign aid, education, public housing, welfare, and the military. The size of the budget startled even George Humphrey, Eisenhower's secretary of the treasury, who told reporters that "there are a lot of places in this budget that can be cut"[7] and that unless Congress acted to reduce taxes and the deficit, "you will have a depression that will curl your hair."[8] The senator from Arizona needed little prompting, for the administration's spending requests violated his fundamental beliefs. Speaking from the Senate floor, Goldwater noted that until quite recently he had been convinced that Eisenhower "was providing the responsible leadership so vital to the maintenance of a strong domestic economy which, in turn, is a vital factor in maintaining world peace." The budget, however, represented a denial of campaign pledges and Republican Party principles, and "a betrayal of the people's trust." "A $71.8 billion budget not only shocks me, but it weakens my faith in the constant reassurances we have received from this administration that its aim was to cut spending, balance the budget, reduce the national debt, cut taxes—in short, to live within our means and allow our citizens the maximum personal benefits from their economic endeavors."[9]Unbalanced budgets and deficit spending, Goldwater argued, were merely symptoms of a deep-seated problem. He blamed the "faulty premises" of Modern Republicanism, "this splintered concept of Republican philosophy," for leading the president down a dangerous road. By "simply parrot[ing] the antics of its predecessor," the administration was "subvert[ing]" the American economy. Eisenhower's government, he continued, "was demonstrating tendencies to bow to the siren song of socialism."[10] No Senate Republican leader rose to rebuke Goldwater. He received positive reinforcement from the press. *Time* magazine breathlessly announced that with this speech, Barry Goldwater had "suddenly arrived."[11]

Making his declaration had not been easy. Barry sent the speech to the president the next day and in a cover letter wrote: "Believe me Sir, that was the most difficult task I ever assigned to myself and I debated this seriously for nearly a week, but I finally came to the conclusion that I could not in justice to my conscience and to the promises that I made to the people, leave what was in my heart and mind unsaid."[12] He attempted to soften the blow in other ways, telling a television audience that cabinet officers, not the president, were to blame. "None of us in the Republican Party," he contended, "seem to have any conception of what 'modern Republicanism' is. If it means continued deficit spending and continued higher taxes, I can't subscribe to it and I don't believe the President does."[13]

Eisenhower was not appeased. He had not received prior notice of the speech, which stunned him with its sharp, uncompromising tone. He contained his temper in public, asserting Goldwater's right to dissent but characterizing him as out of touch with twentieth-century realities: "In this day and time we cannot not use the government process or limit ourselves to the government processes that were applicable in 1890."[14] Ike was less restrained in private. According to aide Jack Anderson, "The President indicated in no uncertain terms his anger over the Senate speech on 'modern Republicanism' given by Senator Goldwater of Arizona."[15] In his response to Goldwater's letter, Ike described himself as "surprised and disappointed" by the speech. As adamant as Goldwater, he wrote icily: "The Party's 1956 Platform I consider a binding commitment on every responsible Republican.

Those Party pledges to the American people I will keep on doing my best to fulfill. I am sorry that our efforts to that end seem so distasteful to you."[16]

In July 1957 Barry Goldwater arranged a truce. He wrote again to the president, this time suggesting that "our differences are not as great as some people would like to have you believe. In fact, I have found it necessary to disagree with you on so few occasions that they are difficult to recall."[17] Ike reassured Barry the next day and acknowledged "that our areas of accord are larger, and certainly more significant, than any differences."[18] Open conflict had ceased, but the men had not bridged their growing disagreement. Goldwater's voting record on administration-backed measures did little to repair the breech. While Barry supported the 1957 and 1960 Civil Rights Acts and expansion of Social Security coverage and benefits, he voted against public housing, foreign aid, and increases in the minimum wage. Eisenhower, meanwhile, kept watch on the Arizona senator. Sensitive to criticism, the president assigned staff members to track Goldwater's comments about him and his administration. This practice would continue even after Eisenhower left the White House.[19]

Casting a national profile required more than a declaration of independence from the president. It demanded, as well, identification with and advocacy of a cause salient to the concerns of large numbers of Americans. In line with his Arizona experiences and businessman's antagonism to unions, Goldwater found his niche as a critic of organized labor. He had already won a reputation within the GOP for his fight against union power. He had jousted with the United Automobile Workers' president, Walter Reuther, and other union leaders in defense of free enterprise and against labor's interference in the political process. Before the election, the media and the public perceived such efforts as partisan tactics designed to curry voter favor. Beginning in 1957, however, Americans reinterpreted Goldwater's activities in light of a congressional investigation of labor union abuses. While following the contours of the administration's labor policies, Barry Goldwater rode the cause that enabled him to become his own man.

Goldwater's vehicle to heightened prominence was the Senate Select Committee on Improper Activities in the Labor or Management Field, known more popularly as the Senate Rackets Committee. The bipartisan committee, charged with investigating illegal activities in the labor movement, was headed by Arkansas Senator John McClellan with chief counsel Robert F. Kennedy and included Democratic Senators Sam Ervin, Frank Church, and John F. Kennedy and Republicans Karl Mundt, Carl Curtis, Irving Ives, and Barry Goldwater. The committee's work began in January 1957 and consumed 270 days in public hearings; the final report was not filed until early 1960. The investigation made startling discoveries that caused a national sensation. On television screens and in newspaper headlines, witnesses recited a litany of abuses: misuse of pension and welfare funds, bribery, extortion, kickbacks, rigged union elections, and collusion between organized crime and the labor movement. Malfeasance seemed to saturate the labor movement, with wrongdoing exposed in the unions representing meat cutters, carpenters, bakers, sheet metal workers, and textile workers, among others. In all, probers interrogated 1,526 witnesses, of whom 343 stood on their Fifth Amendment right against self-incrimination.[20]

For the Kennedy brothers and the committee's Democratic senators, these abuses paled before Dave Beck and Jimmy Hoffa's plundering of the Teamsters Union. Investigators had revealed the union leaders as driven by lust for personal wealth and power, unresponsive and irresponsible concerning the rank and file. To Goldwater and the Republicans, their crimes were reprehensible but less alarming than the threat other labor leaders posed to capitalism and American government. Goldwater, in questioning Jimmy Hoffa, alluded to his real target. Acknowledging a place for unions in modern America, he drew Hoffa into a discussion of labor's growing power and its ambitions beyond the bargaining table. "But to use it," argued Goldwater, "to advance a political theory or an economic theory is entirely another thing." Hoffa quickly grasped the Arizonan's thrust and concurred: "When you separate the political from the economic, you and I could have a different discussion, because I do not believe that it is the original intention of labor organizations to try and control any . . . political powers in this country for their own determination." Goldwater concluded later, "We both recognize that in the writing in the clouds today there is an individual who would like to see that happen in this country. I do not like to even suggest to let you and him fight, but for the good of the union movement I am very hopeful that your philosophy prevails."[21]

That individual was Walter Reuther, a socialist's son who joined the party in his own right in the 1930s. Intrigued by the Soviet experiment, he visited Russia during the depression, praising the system for creating jobs and expanding opportunities while deploring its authoritarianism. Returning from Russia, he helped organize the United Automobile Workers Union (UAW) despite fierce employer resistance and became its president in 1946. By then he had severed his Socialist Party ties and become a bread-and-butter unionist. Still, he enlisted the UAW in support of the Democratic Party and left-wing causes to pursue more sweeping political, economic, and social change.[22]

To Barry Goldwater, Reuther, not Hoffa, was the enemy within. "I would rather have Hoffa stealing my money than Reuther stealing my freedom."[23] Ideology and partisanship convinced Goldwater that Reuther's background and ability to marshal money and votes constituted a clear and present danger both to the nation and the Republican Party. Unsurprisingly, tension had been building between the men for years, but their antagonism became strident in 1957. "He has done," charged Goldwater, "more damage and violence to freedom than was accomplished by all the peculiar financial transactions of Mr. Dave Beck."[24] There was no concealing the UAW president's agenda from the Arizona senator: "What Mr. Reuther preaches is socialism."[25] In a Detroit speech in early 1958 Goldwater warned: "Underneath the Democratic label here in Michigan there is something new, and something dangerous—born of conspiracy and violence, sired by socialists and nurtured by the general treasury of the UAW-CIO. This is the pattern of political conquest."[26] Sometimes Goldwater tripped on his hyperbole. When his prepared remarks for a radio address fell short by thirty seconds, he ad libbed that Reuther was a "more dangerous menace than the sputnik or anything Soviet Russia might do to America."[27] He later regretted shooting from the hip: "It was one of those spur-of-the-moment things and if I had it to do over I never would have said it."[28] Reuther was not to be outdone. He returned the fire, dismissing the Republican as a "moral coward" and "political hypocrite."[29] Goldwater was "this country's . . . number one peddler of class hatred . . . a reactionary . . . a stooge for big business . . . mentally unbalanced and needs a psychiatrist."[30] The feud clarified few issues, but it did raise political capital for both men. Said Goldwater, "The battle made national headlines for a year."[31]

Goldwater and the Republicans were determined to expose Walter Reuther before the television cameras. Bobby Kennedy and committee Democrats resisted, insisting that investigators had found the UAW untainted by corruption. Suspicious of a "cover-up"[32] and convinced that the Kennedy brothers were "protecting"[33] Reuther for political reasons, the Republicans found a lever to open hearings: the UAW strike against the Kohler Company of Wisconsin. The strike against Kohler, a manufacturer of bathroom and plumbing fixtures, began in 1954 after the company rejected demands for a higher hourly wage, pension benefits, and union security.[34] When the company hired strikebreakers, beefed up its security force, and stockpiled guns and ammunition, the union answered with violence and with mass picketing that closed the plant.[35] To preserve bipartisanship and prevent a Republican bolt, the Democrats on the Senate Rackets Committee acquiesced, and Bobby Kennedy scheduled hearings. The Republicans eagerly awaited the opportunity to "embarrass" Reuther and the UAW, yet Kennedy was convinced that their strategy would fail. Events bore out his expectation.[36]

For five weeks, beginning in February 1958, the committee held hearings, calling seventy-nine witnesses to testify about the strike at Kohler. Tele-

vision viewers surely marveled at the spectacle, for the hearings were conducted in the same room as the Army-McCarthy showdown of 1954.
Despite the setting and the media hype, the public was sorely disappointed:
the UAW probe generated no bombshells. Even the much-publicized face-to-
face confrontation between the Republicans and Reuther proved anticli-
mactic. For three days they sparred with the UAW president but were unable
to land a telling blow. Reuther remained cool under the grilling, avoiding
traps and deftly turning aside Republican barbs. When Goldwater asked
him whether he felt responsibility for the rash actions of local unionists,
Reuther shot back, "Not any more than the President of the United States
feels obligated to repudiate every statement made by a Republican politician
when he says something the President doesn't agree with."[37] At the end of
Reuther's testimony, Nebraska Senator Karl Mundt regretfully admitted that
"there is no evidence before us of corruption insofar as your activities are
concerned."[38] Meanwhile, the Democrats hammered company representatives for their unenlightened labor policies and portrayed the response to
the strike as an overreaction. Goldwater later conceded to Bobby Kennedy,
"You were right. We never should have gotten into this matter. This investigation was not one in which we should have become involved."[39]

Nevertheless, Goldwater and the Republicans suffered no loss of face.
The issue of union corruption, made real by the expulsion of the Teamsters
from the AFL-CIO in December 1957 and follow-up indictments and trials of
labor leaders, had become a national priority. The proof of Reuther's wrongdoing may have eluded them, but in bringing him before the Rackets Committee they created in the public's mind an association with Jimmy Hoffa,
Dave Beck, and other discredited union leaders. Nor did the Republicans
leave the field in retreat; they attempted to fix their interpretation to events.
Although pleased with the investigation of the Teamsters, Goldwater complained to reporters that "Bobby Kennedy whitewashed Reuther."[40]
Kennedy later confronted Goldwater about the accusation and demanded to
know whether he wanted to continue the UAW probe. "No, no," Kennedy
remembered Goldwater saying. "I want to get back to Arizona now. I don't
want any hearings." Kennedy persisted, asking, "Then why did you say it?"
"That's politics," responded Goldwater. "You're in politics, Bob, whether you
like it or not."[41]

The effect of the hearings went beyond labor issues to touch the careers
of Goldwater and John F. Kennedy. The hearings had played well to the
media's tendency to simplify and personify complex problems. These two
attractive and engaging men, one just left of the political center and the
other on the right, offered observers mirror images who added color and
drama to the news commentaries. The comparison encompassed more than

political views. As one writer later noted, "Like Kennedy, he [Goldwater] has a devastating impact on the ladies; he also projects an aura of rugged masculine competence with which men like to identify."[42] The hearings certainly hastened Kennedy's ascent. Jumping from the springboard of his unsuccessful bid for the Democratic Party's 1956 vice presidential nomination to the Senate Rackets Committee, he had emerged as an uncompromising foe of labor corruption and a defender of honest unions. Barry Goldwater gained from the attention as well, strengthening his reputation with conservatives and GOP partisans and making his name and face known to a national audience. Still, their paths diverged. John Kennedy was priming for a run for the presidency while Barry Goldwater was drawn back to Arizona, where he faced a tough challenge to retain his Senate seat.[43]

The Democrats expected to make big gains in the 1958 elections. A sharp recession and rising unemployment, administration scandals, and federal intervention to enforce school desegregation in Little Rock had cut President Eisenhower's standing in public opinion polls and eroded Republican support nationwide. Crises in the Middle East and Asia and Russia's successful orbiting of Sputnik had heightened voter concerns about peace and further diminished GOP chances. To make matters worse, prominent Republican candidates antagonized organized labor by shaping their campaigns into referenda on the right-to-work issue.

All of this worked to the advantage of Arizona Governor Ernest McFarland. He was eager for a rematch with Barry Goldwater and confident of victory. This time he would not have to contend with the Truman albatross or Eisenhower's coattails. McFarland also took comfort in registration figures. Although state Republicans had begun to close the gap, Democrats still held a two-to-one voter edge. Thus, he wrapped himself in the party's banner and stumped Arizona hard as "Mr. Democrat," imploring voters to "Send Mac Back."[44] Goldwater, meanwhile, appeared vulnerable. McFarland noted his frequent absences from the Senate, missed roll-call votes, opposition to federal programs, and neglect of water issues. The Republican simply was a luxury that Arizona could not afford. Said McFarland, "Barry Goldwater is the sound effects man of the United States Senate. . . . [H]e is less a political figure than an entertainer. Like any other entertainer, he is more concerned about how he is received than about what he says."[45] With polls showing him in the lead, McFarland attempted to avoid controversy, telling voters that "Arizona Comes First" and presenting himself as a "builder" who could deliver on his promises.[46]

Stephen Shadegg, again Barry Goldwater's campaign manager, was worried. His candidate could not run on his legislative accomplishments nor prove an insider's relationship with the Eisenhower administration. If national party service had cheered state Republicans, Arizona was still a Democratic stronghold. Even Goldwater's stand against organized labor made Shadegg hesitate. Unions were weak in Arizona, and bossism and corruption were not local issues. Party activists, moreover, had informed Shadegg that Goldwater's activities had not played well at the grassroots. He wrote to Barry that "this is a good warning to us that we must concentrate our efforts on explaining and explaining and explaining your true position which is opposed to the corruption, graft, violence, and abuses and in support of individual working men."[47]

Shadegg did hold some high cards. The recession had not touched Arizona, and the local economy was booming. Goldwater's candidacy was uncontested in the Republican primary; the party was united behind him. Shadegg also knew that the influential Pulliam newspapers were eager to provide coverage and support. At the same time, infighting had splintered Democratic solidarity. McFarland, as governor, had antagonized key Democrats by ignoring their advice in patronage decisions and pressing a liberal agenda. As a result, he had faced a determined primary challenge from a conservative opponent who charged, in what would be a glimpse of the upcoming general election, that the governor had taken money from the Teamsters Union in exchange for "secret commitments."[48] Conservative Democrats surely could be enticed to bolt to the Goldwater camp as they had in 1952. Money did not concern Shadegg. He had more than $200,000 to spend, much of it contributed by Texas oilman H. L. Hunt and arch-conservative Robert Welch. Most important, Shadegg managed a candidate who symbolized to many Arizonans their imagined past. Blunt, unaffected, and tough-minded, Barry Goldwater could fire their hopes and enthusiasm.[49]

The Republican campaign packaged Goldwater as the "underdog, capitaliz[ing] on the drama of the lone knight on the white charger."[50] This was "a man of action, a man of decision, a man of courage, and a man who is dedicated to the service of the individual."[51] Opening his campaign in Prescott on September 10 with a speech carried to all Arizona through a twenty-station radio net, Goldwater evoked the pioneers as his role models: "These men and women, by individual initiative, by energy and hard labor and by sheer grit and courage, brought civilization to a wilderness, established a well-ordered society in a lawless land." Modern Arizonans, he believed, were cut of the same cloth and "want to recapture their own independence, reestablish personal responsibility, reduce and limit the concentration of power, and once more, work out their own destiny."[52] Throughout the campaign, Goldwater reminded voters that he had carried their message to Washington. But his battle for the people had not made him popular with the powerful. "I have kept my promise in office. I have fought the President, the party, and the administration to keep taxes down."[53] He had opposed, as well, the Democratic liberals and the Committee on Political Education (COPE), the campaign arm of the AFL-CIO. These collectivists, he warned, were close to their goal: "If you do not wake up, socialism will be a reality in the United States within another election."[54] "For Freedom's Sake," he asked them to join the cause.[55] In this vein, Republican rhetoric made Ernest McFarland a pawn, under the influence and control of sinister outside forces. Yet more than words were necessary to sway voters. To be successful Goldwater had to offer convincing proof that the national conspiracy had penetrated Arizona.[56]

Behind in the polls, Goldwater and Shadegg conceded no voter or precinct to the Democrat. They put their resources into a media blitz that filled the state's newspapers, billboards, and radio and television airwaves with Goldwater ads. Particularly effective in establishing Goldwater's credibility were his fifteen-minute television commercials. In "National Defense," viewers watched Goldwater, in flight jumpsuit, descend from the cockpit of a Air Force jet fighter to rattle off the names of the planes and missiles composing the American arsenal. His sober manner, technical knowledge, and military bearing conveyed authority and elicited confidence in the man and the system. "Compulsory Unionism," opened with Goldwater at his desk, framed by the Capitol dome. Here he attacked the "thugs" and "goons" of the labor movement who preyed on union members and denied them their rights and benefits.[57] The campaign, in addition, targeted minority groups, with Spanish and Native American speakers quoting and praising the Republican senator. For example, a radio commercial beamed at Arizona Apaches translated Goldwater's pledge, "I can tell you straight from the shoulder that it is not the intention of this administration to terminate any Indian tribe without the tribe wanting it, asking for it, participating in its plans."[58] Also, a direct-mail campaign was aimed at residents of small towns, tailoring the candidate's platform to local problems. "It was," said Shadegg, "a rifle approach that hit the target in the bull's eye."[59]

In the large cities, the campaign built a dense network of seven thousand "foot soldiers" who went door-to-door with "fact kits" to enlist their neighbors in the cause.[60] "Coffee break" gatherings held in Republican homes, of which Barry attended more than two hundred, complemented this canvassing and inspired workers to greater effort. In addition to party rank and file, such prominent Arizonans as William Rehnquist and John O'Connor and Sandra Day O'Connor volunteered as Goldwater campaign workers. Meanwhile, the candidate crisscrossed the state in his airplane, touching down to deliver his message wherever advance agents had prepared the way. Goldwater concentrated on heavily populated Phoenix and Tucson, but small towns like Window Rock, Elfrida, Show Low, Fredonia, Snowflake,

Seligman, and Gila Bend, among many others, were not neglected. Unusual for an incumbent, but in line with his underdog image, Goldwater challenged McFarland to a series of "face to face" television debates. The front runner rejected the proposal. While Barry flew, Governor McFarland traveled the state by bus. McFarland rented an airplane at one point; ironically, it ran out of gas and crash-landed in a field.[61]

Given Goldwater's stature, it was not surprising that the campaign attracted the national media. What was remarkable was the slanted coverage they gave to the Goldwater-McFarland race. More than a year before the election, *Newsweek* columnist Raymond Moley, a winter resident in Arizona, foreshadowed Goldwater's campaign plan, declaring the election a contest between "traditional conservatism and the collectivist aim of the political machine of the big unions."[62] He described Goldwater in a follow-up column in March 1958 as a "statesman" with "rare courage" and the Democrats as "mere figureheads . . . the real force will be COPE, operating by remote control from Detroit."[63] More flagrant was Paul Healy's *Saturday Evening Post* article titled "The Glittering Mr. Goldwater," published in June 1958. Healy was impressed with the senator from Arizona: "In his flying clothes he could pass for a character in the Steve Canyon comic strip; . . . As a man's man, he also appeals to women." McFarland, on the other hand, was "the red-faced, sixty-four-year-old governor who looks and acts like a farmer." Healy dismissed him as "bumbling," "slow speaking," and "burning with an ambition to regain his Senate seat."[64] *Time* magazine's correspondent drew a similar sketch, characterizing McFarland as "Homespun Ernie . . . [who] never missed a ribbon cutting" and Goldwater as the "tall, bronzed, lean-jawed, silver-haired man of 49." He completed Goldwater's portrait: "An experienced pilot, he flew over all 114,000 square miles of his state, landed long enough to fall in love with the landscape and the Indian tribes, snap thousands of color pictures, race down the perilous Colorado River in a flatboat—making friends everywhere."[65] Even the *New York Times* couldn't resist slamming McFarland as "portly, bucolic, benign" while mentioning Barry's youth, good looks, and sincerity.[66] Barry Goldwater would not always find the national media so complimentary.

The *Arizona Republic* and the *Phoenix Gazette* applauded Goldwater even more loudly than the national newspapers and magazines. To the *Republic* McFarland was "a last-century type of politico with a country fair type of oratory and a professed love for everybody at or near the voting age." Goldwater, was the "handsome jet pilot from a pioneer family with a long record of civic service . . . the energy and color as well as good name and stainless reputation."[67] The *Gazette* praised Goldwater as "the consistent champion of protecting the public and rank-and-file union membership from the abuses of labor monopoly power."[68] The Pulliam papers, however, went beyond mere cheerleading. Surveying the newspapers' activities, political scientists Frank Jonas and R. John Eyre described their performance as "political dynamiting," the use of "dynamite-laden, banner headlines, cartoon caricatures, yellow journalistic make-up, and a slanted presentation of meticulously researched quotations."[69] During the 1958 election, even more than in the 1952 race, the *Arizona Republic* and the *Phoenix Gazette* transformed themselves into the public-relations department of the Republican Party. They would soon go beyond reporting the news to making it.[70]

In spite of the advance billing and the determination of both sides, the Goldwater-McFarland rematch was, initially, a lackluster affair. Beginning in September and continuing into the third week of October, the men fenced with little effect. Goldwater's attempt to make McFarland a front man for Walter Reuther and Jimmy Hoffa would not catch fire. This did not, however, deter the *Republic* and *Gazette* from fanning the issue by insinuation in editorials, political cartoons, and news stories. When Goldwater failed to score with the labor issue he resurrected the ghosts of 1952, repeating charges of cronyism and McFarland's alleged statement that Korea was a "cheap" war. He also attacked McFarland as a "tax and spend" liberal whose "vague and obscure" program would erode living standards.[71] More positively, Goldwater vowed to continue his efforts for a strong national defense and against high taxes and union corruption. McFarland, meanwhile, rode his lead and was eager to remind voters of his fights for the GI Bill, tariff protection of Arizona industries, and reclamation projects. He took credit, as well, for bringing military and air bases to Arizona. McFarland cautioned voters that Barry Goldwater had canceled out the vote of Carl Hayden, the state's senior senator, on 320 occasions during the past six years; McFarland promised to work closely with Hayden.[72]

The *Arizona Republic* broke the campaign calm on October 19 with a stick of political dynamite. In banner headlines across page one of all editions, the paper blared: COPE AGENT 'MUSCLES' IN." The story—adorned with mug shots, photographs taken surreptitiously, and charts of evidence—detailed the Arizona activities of Charles "Al" Green, a COPE field director from California.[73] Arizona union leaders had recruited Green to create a telephone net and file card system that would get out the labor vote for the Democrats on election day. Although Green's work was open and lawful, the *Republic*'s presentation suggested criminality and conspiracy. "This is the man," claimed the paper, "sent to Arizona by Reuther and Hoffa to beat Goldwater . . . and get control of the Arizona State Legislature." The *Republic* alerted voters that the 1958 campaign was only the first stage of labor's offensive in Arizona. Following their pattern in Michigan and other labor-besieged states, Green and his "political muscle men" had begun the "takeover" that would deliver the Democratic Party and then Arizona government to the union bosses. Allegedly, COPE had earmarked $450,000 to ensure the success of the "purge effort."[74]

The *Arizona Republic* had received Green's mug shots, copies of his criminal record, and the surveillance photos from Stephen Shadegg. Shadegg had planted a spy in the Arizona labor leadership who daily informed him of union campaign activities. Through the summer and fall, Shadegg quietly compiled a dossier on Green and out-of-state union activists, waiting for the right moment and forum to bare his evidence. His candidate still trailing in the polls, he went to *Republic* and *Gazette* editor and publisher Eugene Pulliam with the material on Wednesday, October 16. Pulliam held the story for the Sunday edition to ensure the widest circulation of the charges and printed the Shadegg materials without reporter verification and before seeking rebuttal from Democrats or labor leaders. With the *Arizona Republic*'s help, the Republicans had forged the missing link between McFarland and the national union bosses whom Goldwater had fought for so long. The effort resulted in a "home run," Shadegg beamed.[75]

Thereafter, the labor question dominated the campaign and was contested on the Republican's terms. Goldwater charged forward, asking voters, "Does Arizona want to elect Jimmy Hoffa and Dave Beck in my place?"[76] He pressed the point home in two live television simulcasts seen on all Phoenix and Tucson channels on October 23 and 29. Interspersed with news clips of labor violence, mob scenes, and bullet-riddled automobiles, Goldwater's talk focused the issue of the campaign on "whether or not a United States Senator must be completely subservient to labor bosses and because of political fear, accede to their every demand." He wasted little time on McFarland, for his enemies were Reuther, Hoffa, and "the racketeers, and the gangsters, and the hoodlums." Speaking quietly and with a grim demeanor, Goldwater claimed to be the true friend of the rank and file, fighting in defense of their rights and promising to tear down "the union curtain of thought control." He assured voters, "I'll fight anyone who tries to destroy unions."[77] Validating Goldwater's contentions, the *Arizona Republic* reported threats made against Barry, his mother, and brother. Campaign aide Paul Sexson drew the connection after an abusive telephone call to JoJo Goldwater: "Has America come to this, where an Arizona Senator's mother is threatened because her son tells about the vicious racketeers who are exploiting the working man."[78] After security agents were assigned to guard Goldwater's plane, the *Republic* editorialized: "The fear among his supporters of physical violence to Goldwater adds a new twist in the senator's campaign."[79]

The assault stunned Ernest McFarland, and he never recovered. In retreat, he deplored the "smoke screen" of his "reactionary" opponent and the "fear and smear" newspaper campaign. "Guilt by innuendo, inference, and insinuation must not be permitted to prevail in this state."[80] McFarland also rejected the allegation that COPE had budgeted nearly half a million dollars for Arizona, and he denied receiving any of its money. The *Republic* quickly cracked that defense and, although uncovering a COPE allocation of only $14,000 to the state races, tracked $1,000 to the McFarland campaign. The paper also revealed a $4,500 Teamster contribution to McFarland's 1954 campaign for governor. The amounts were small, but they documented Goldwater's claims and gave the lie to McFarland's denials. In a clear sign of confusion, McFarland boasted of his own record of fighting labor racketeers and assured voters that he could do a better job than Goldwater against the union bosses. McFarland's lead in the polls quickly vanished.[81]

A bizarre incident in the last days of the campaign sealed McFarland's fate. On October 31, machinist union members Earl Anderson and Frank Goldberg (no relation to the author) inexplicably and without authorization distributed thousands of handbills depicting a winking Joseph Stalin smoking a pipe, with the caption, "Why not vote for Goldwater?"[82] This was a strained reference to the favorable reception Goldwater had received before the communist-tainted Mine, Mill and Smelter Workers Union and implied that Barry was pink. Rather than waste time deciphering the message, the *Arizona Republic* turned it to advantage: "Mac in Tears about Smears; What Does He Say Of This." The "slanderous cartoon" was "further evidence of the type of political campaign conducted by COPE."[83] Goldwater, too, saw his opening: "This operation has been planned for a long time, deliberately planned, diabolically planned by those outside forces who have been here since long before the beginning of this election. The union bosses have to get Goldwater, and this is their last desperate attempt."[84]

He immediately telephoned Senator John McClellan and demanded that the Senate Rackets Committee launch a "full-scale probe" of the incident.[85] Shadegg, meanwhile, sent out hundreds of copies of the handbill to supporters, newspapers, and radio and television stations around the state. The Pulliam press played the story repeatedly and the day before the election printed as a banner across the bottom of page one of all editions: "Don't Believe Any of COPE's Last Minute Smears; Keep Arizona Free—Vote For Senator Goldwater."[86] McFarland denied any involvement in the attempt to tar Goldwater, but no one was listening.[87]

Election night ended early for McFarland supporters. Steve Shadegg's intensive organizing, Goldwater's charisma, and Pulliam's war on the Democrats and labor had forged a 56 percent majority for the Republican, far from the close margin of 1952. Goldwater swamped McFarland, capturing 60 percent of the Phoenix-area vote, one-third of all Democrats, and ten of fourteen Arizona counties. He did particularly well among new residents, managerial and technical workers, the retired, and high-income voters. He even made inroads among unionists and carried the copper-mining precincts in Cochise County. Only black Arizonans resisted him. Other Republicans, jumping on the anti-COPE bandwagon, advanced with Goldwater. Paul Fannin won his race for governor, John Rhodes returned to the House of Representatives, and Republican candidates won twenty-five of the forty-two state legislative seats they contested.[88]

Goldwater's victory had more than local significance and was important for reasons other than its challenge to organized labor. His triumph came in the context of a Republican rout. Of the ten Republican senatorial candidates running for election west of the Mississippi River, Goldwater was the lone victor. In the worst Republican defeat since 1936, Democrats gained thirteen Senate seats and built a 64-to-34 advantage in the body. Conservatives, especially, were bloodied. William Knowland, who had retired from the Senate, lost his bid for the governorship of California. Defeat also claimed Senators John Bricker, William Jenner, and George Malone. The disaster was not confined to national office, for Republicans lost five governor's chairs and nearly seven hundred state legislative seats. The only other bright spots for the party were in Oregon, where Mark Hatfield was elected governor, and New York, where political newcomer Nelson Rockefeller easily beat his opponent by more than half a million votes.[89]

The election had a critical, defining effect for Goldwater and the Republican party. In surviving the Democratic wave, the Arizona senator had enhanced his standing with the rank and file and found open to him the leadership of the party's conservative wing. Vice President Richard Nixon, staking out his position in the center and preparing for 1960, was quick to recognize Goldwater's rise. In response to a letter from Barry calling on him to "rally the forces" in the wake of defeat and Eisenhower's lack of "interest," Nixon solicitously replied, "I am trying to arrange my schedule for the first two weeks in January so that I can spend a maximum amount of time with those who are vitally interested as you are in rebuilding the Republican Party."[90] As Goldwater represented the right and Nixon the center, the arrival of Nelson Rockefeller breathed life into progressive Republicanism. From his base in electoral-vote-rich New York and with seemingly unlimited resources, the popular Rockefeller laid claim to party leadership. His emergence would also galvanize the right. Rockefeller was liberal, ambitious, and bore the name that personified for western and southern conservatives—who were oriented to Main Street, not Wall Street—the hated Eastern

Establishment that had dominated their party for so long. Barry Goldwater shared their resentment. Though he was wealthy, he harbored a small-town businessman's suspicion of America's economic royalists. "Every movement needs a villain," wrote conservative William Rusher. "For the GOP Right, Nelson Rockefeller was it."[91] Barry Goldwater agreed: "They hate his guts."[92] The war for the party's future had begun. Each faction united behind its champion, with the moderates holding the center and encouraging consensus while the wings pressed their respective agendas.

Barry Goldwater's success as a politician was only a part of his growing appeal. Victory, after all, had come in remote Arizona, not the best lever to raise a national presence. More compelling, the Goldwater persona tripped a folk memory that was core to American culture. Like the characters in the westerns flooding television screens, here was a paladin who evoked a hallowed past and place. Goldwater was a westerner—a man of action, a rugged individualist, direct, virile, and tough. "For us," wrote conservative James Roberts, "the senator was the knight on the white horse, the Lochinvar riding out of the West to do battle with evil."[93] The image was in part real, in part promoted. On the stump or before television cameras, Goldwater evoked the western hero standing alone against all odds, imbued with frontier virtues, refusing to compromise his beliefs or country. The Arizonan's speaking style enhanced the impression. "His slightly twangy, dehydrated voice," wrote speech professor Ernest Wrage, "suggests that of cowboys of TV westerns."[94] Even Goldwater's tinkering with gadgets brought to mind the frontiersman, inventive, practical, and utilitarian. The senator's staff nourished the mystique, distributing publicity photographs of Goldwater clad in jeans and cowboy hat astride a horse. At other times he was pictured mounting the modern equivalent—an Air Force jet fighter. The national press picked up the theme and described Goldwater as the archetypical "cowboy" who, with "jaw squared," was "dynamic, lean, and bronzed."[95] If critics derided Barry as the Marlboro Man who shot from the hip, their words betrayed them.[96] They, too, were captives of the myth.

Also feeding his mystique was the American vision of the West's potential, and Goldwater's prestige soared as business boomed in Arizona. The warfare economy stimulated Arizona, and a modern job rush made it one of the nation's fastest-growing states. All economic indicators in Arizona moved upward: income, housing starts, bank deposits, Department of Defense contracts, and employment. With them, the state's population bulged 163 percent between 1945 and 1960 to more than 1.25 million people. Phoenix, in the same fifteen years, notched the highest rate of growth of the fifty largest U.S. cities. Quadrupling to become the home of nearly 440,000 men and women, Phoenix had grown into the urban center of the Southwest. The national press touted the "miracle in the desert" and fed the torrent.[97] Like the pioneers, modern Arizonans had found "a fresh start on a new frontier. . . . Even those without cash find it easier on the desert to try new jobs and to borrow money with no more collateral than a good idea."[98] Similarly, in an article about the new millionaires in Phoenix, *Saturday Evening Post* writer Harold Martin gushed: "They were young and strong and restless, and fired with the same westering spirit that had sent the covered wagons across the plains a hundred years ago. . . . They were moving across a continent . . . to make a new life for themselves under a bigger, brighter sky, in a vast empty land where it didn't matter who a man's family was, or how much money he had, or what school he'd gone to—or whether he'd gone to school at all. . . . None of them, when they arrived, had any resources except their wits."[99] For those on the make, the unbounded past had become the present again in the Grand Canyon state. Barry Goldwater, in style and message, locked into their aspirations and needs.[100]

If Arizona was in the lead, the rest of the West was not far behind. California, Texas, Washington, Colorado, and Utah were attached to the same military-industrial lifeline and experienced dramatic expansion in the fifteen years after World War II. While extractive industries remained important and the service sector created new opportunities, it was defense dollars that underwrote the advance and nurtured a new middle class. Seattle, Denver, Salt Lake City, and Albuquerque drew 25 percent of their income from defense spending, and one in ten Californians depended on defense contracts for a job. Economic growth sparked migration, and the western states gathered 13 million new residents between 1945 and 1960, most of them going to the Pacific coast states. The Southwest marked impressive gains as well. Consistent with trends in Phoenix, Albuquerque's population jumped from 50,000 in 1945 to 200,000 in 1960, and Dallas registered a sharp increase from 434,000 in 1950 to 680,000 ten years later.[101]

As the population moved west, so did influence in party and government. Astute observers quickly fixed on America's tomorrowland as the political pacesetter. They even had a gauge to measure its ascent: in 1940 westerners occupied forty-three seats in the House of Representatives; in 1960 it was sixty-nine and climbing. The emergence of the West as a key factor in the political equation enhanced Goldwater's credibility. Without a western brand, would Barry Goldwater have stirred as much enthusiasm? Would his rise have been so swift if the region was stagnant and unable to claim its reputation as the land of the boom and the second chance?[102]

In January 1959 Goldwater returned to Washington, D.C., and the labor wars. Following up the Senate Rackets investigation, committee members

John Kennedy and Sam Ervin introduced legislation that mandated union election by secret ballot and full disclosure of financial transactions. Goldwater dismissed this as a "panty-waist bill" that was "like a flea bite to a bull elephant."[103] He called, in addition, for tougher penalties for corrupt practices and a broadening of the Taft-Hartley Act's ban on secondary boycotts to cover union coercion of an employer that prevented business transactions with another employer. The unions had to be confronted, he argued, for "they stand now across the nation like a colossus and no power outside of Government can compare with them in magnitude."[104] Goldwater was correct that the Kennedy-Ervin bill was weak, but there was strong sentiment in the Senate for the passage of some labor legislation. On April 25, 1959, the Senate approved the measure by a vote of 90 to 1, with Goldwater standing alone in dissent. John Kennedy's assessment was too critical. It was "obvious that Senator Goldwater would be satisfied with no bill that did not destroy the organized trade union movement in America."[105] Retorted Goldwater, "It will remain one of the proudest votes I ever made."[106]

Goldwater remembered his vote as President Eisenhower's wake-up call on the labor issue. He has written that Eisenhower summoned him to the White House to explain his stand, and, taking this opportunity, he was able to convince the President to act. In fact, the administration had been involved in the issue for some time, and the president needed no prompting. Eisenhower had delivered a message to Congress in January 1958 that he repeated in 1959, recommending changes in the Taft-Hartley Act that would crack down on corruption, coercive picketing practices, and abuses of trust and power. Administration officials lobbied against the Kennedy-Ervin bill, deriding it as "a weak gesture . . . largely written by the unions. It contains none of the real reforms recommended by the President."[107] During debate in committee and on the Senate floor, Secretary of Labor James Mitchell fed Goldwater dozens of amendments to tighten the measure, none of which were accepted. With passage assured, the administration devised a counterstrategy that would orchestrate a future "grass roots" pressure campaign on the Senate while introducing stronger legislation in the more receptive House of Representatives.[108] The call went to Republican Congressman Robert Griffin and Democrat Philip Landrum to cosponsor a substitute measure capturing the president's directives. Eisenhower fought hard for the bill, and for the first time in his presidency used radio and television to encourage the passage of a specific piece of legislation. The president's public and private efforts were effective. The Landrum-Griffin Act passed the House and Senate, and Eisenhower signed it into law in September 1959. Administration records suggest only a minor role for Senator Goldwater in the law's enactment. President Eisenhower's papers offer no hint of his influence.[109]

Goldwater's reelection to the position of Republican Senate Campaign Chair in January 1959 provides some explanation. He was back on the road, encouraging partisans in anticipation of the 1960 presidential and congressional elections. In a slap at the president, he pledged during this second term as chair to return the party to the principles of Senator Robert Taft and oppose collectivism. Again he took the job seriously, traveling an average of ten thousand miles a month during the first half of 1959. His travel and his work in Congress allowed him only three weekends at home in Arizona with his wife. Although he made speeches, shook hands, and met Republicans all over the country, the emerging party in the South attracted his focused attention. Goldwater knew that weaning the region from the Democrats was critical to Republican chances and the success of modern conservatism.[110]

As Goldwater labored for conservatism on the stump, the movement advanced on other fronts. Conservatives shrugged off their losses in the 1958 elections and continued to develop a base. The *National Review*, after several lean years, built a circulation of thirty thousand readers while fifty thousand men and women subscribed to *Human Events* and ten thousand took *Modern Age*. Other conservative journals and magazines amassed a monthly readership of more than three hundred thousand. Presses like Henry Regnery and Victor Publishing Company solicited books by and for conservatives. The conservative impulse also took shape in such organizations as Americans for Constitutional Action, the Conservative Society of America, the Cardinal Mindszenty Foundation, and Defenders of the American Constitution. Particularly encouraging were inroads on campus. Conservative clubs appeared at Wisconsin, Yale, Harvard, and other academic bastions of liberalism. A spirit of defiance animated these campus conservatives. As one would later say: "You walk around with your Goldwater button and you feel the thrill of treason."[111] As the conservative net spread, interactions among movement leaders multiplied, creating personal and working relationships.[112]

Robert Welch was one of the conservative movement's insiders. Welch, a sixty-year-old candy manufacturer and a former board member of the National Association of Manufacturers, had founded the secret John Birch Society in December 1958. His organization honored a Baptist missionary killed by Chinese Communists just ten days after the victory over Japan in 1945. In the name of the "first" casualty of the cold war, he mobilized Americans against a communist conspiracy to dominate the world. The communists, said Welch, planned to encircle America, targeting Europe, then Asia, and finally Latin America and Africa. It was not invasion from without that would bring the United States down, but subversion from within. Increasing government control, high taxes, and unbalanced budgets meant the gradual death of capitalism and of the economic power to resist. Meanwhile, Welch detected a communist fifth column infiltrating the schools, media, and churches to brainwash Americans into accepting a hedonistic and immoral creed. Conspiracy-bred permissiveness and disrespect for law and order would mutilate the Constitution, religion, and the family. Once plunged into moral and social chaos, America would be the last domino to fall to the godless communist dictators. Thus, Welch concluded, patriots had to act quickly, for the traitors within already controlled 25 percent of the nation, and their timetable was ahead of schedule.[113]

Welch's message blended traditional fears of federal power with economic orthodoxy, militant anticommunism, and concerns about the weakening of America's moral fiber. In general tone and target, conservatives echoed Welch. According to FBI director J. Edgar Hoover, the communists "infiltrate every conceivable sphere of activity; youth groups, radio, television and motion picture industries; church, school and education groups; the press, nationality minority groups and political units."[114] Ezra Taft Benson, Eisenhower's secretary of agriculture and a Mormon church leader, called the anticommunist crusade "a fight against slavery, immorality, atheism, cruelty, barbarism, deceit, and the destruction of life."[115] Ronald Reagan clearly had Robert Welch in mind when he declared, "One of the foremost authorities in the world today has said we have ten years. Not ten years to make up our minds, but ten years to win or lose—by 1970 the world will be all slave or all free."[116] Barry Goldwater's works would resonate with Birchers, who sold his publications in the society's chain of American Opinion bookstores.[117]

Welch had approached Goldwater several years before founding the John Birch Society. Hinting of a matter of grave concern to the nation, Welch arrived at the Goldwater home in Phoenix with a nearly 300-page manuscript that he pressed the Arizona senator to read. In "The Politician," Welch traced the path of the communist conspirators to the White House. Both Franklin Roosevelt and Harry Truman, he argued, were under the control of communists. In Dwight Eisenhower "the Communists have one of their own actually in the presidency. . . . There is only one possible word to describe his purposes and his actions. That word is treason."[118] Goldwater skimmed the manuscript and immediately dismissed its allegations. The next morning he telephoned Welch: "I want no part of this. I won't even have it around. If you were smart, you'd burn every copy you have."[119] Welch was neither deterred nor alienated. He published the book in 1960 and contributed to the senator's 1958 reelection campaign, endorsing Goldwater in his *Blue Book*, the bible of the John Birch Society: "He is a superb political organizer, and inspires deep and lasting loyalty. He is absolutely sound in his Americanism, has the political and moral courage to stand by his Americanist principles, and in my opinion can be trusted to stand by them until hell freezes over. I'd like to see him President of the United States, and maybe some day we shall."[120]

What set Welch apart from Barry Goldwater and fellow conservatives was that he insisted on the existence of a plot. Where others attributed diplomatic setbacks, government action, and domestic controversy to the natural course of human events, Welch detected purpose and design. Nothing was a random occurrence or the product of error. All circumstances gained meaning when woven into a fabric of conspiracy. Conservatives recoiled as well from Robert Welch's key assumptions: the equation of liberalism with treason and his indictment of Eisenhower as a communist agent. Yet if Goldwater believed that Welch was "intemperate and unwise," the fledgling conservative movement could not repudiate Birch Society support.[121] "I disagreed with some of their statements," Goldwater later wrote, "but refused to engage in any wholesale condemnation of them. The last thing conservatives needed was to begin a factional war by reading small minorities or individuals out of our ranks."[122] In the rush to power, Birchers and their conservative allies became entwined in a "semialliance" that advanced the other's cause, and their own.[123]

By the end of 1959 the John Birch Society had planted chapters in sixteen states, including California, Massachusetts, New York, Illinois, Florida, and Texas. The society accelerated its efforts to expand in 1960, organizing active groups in thirty-four states and doubling membership every four months, reaching eighteen thousand men and women by year's end. Here was a sizable cache of resources available to promote conservative ends. Among the society's early recruits were Notre Dame Law School Dean Clarence Manion, former Internal Revenue Service Director T. Coleman Andrews, former Assistant Secretary of State Spruille Braden, and prominent Arizonans Frank Cullen Brophy and Denison Kitchel.[124] As Goldwater would later tell reporters, "[Birchers] are the finest people in my community."[125]

It was Birch Society national council member Manion who suggested to Barry Goldwater that he write a book outlining his conservative beliefs. Barry initially demurred, not because of Manion's tie to the Birch Society but from a sense of inadequacy: "I'm not a writer, I wouldn't know how to go about it."[126] Manion's solution was to find Barry a ghost. He hired L. Brent Bozell, an editor for *National Review* and the brother-in-law of William F. Buckley, Jr. Bozell crafted the book from Goldwater speeches, some of which Bozell himself had written, and his own research. Uncertain of demand, Manion ordered a run of ten thousand copies from his own Victor Publishing Company of Shepherdsville, Kentucky. *The Conscience of a Conservative* appeared in March 1960 and quickly became a best-seller, going through twenty printings in four years and eventually selling 3.5 million copies. Reading it, conservatives felt born again. Pat Buchanan bore witness and spoke for many men and women: *"The Conscience of a Conservative* was our new testament; it contained the core beliefs of our political faith, it told us why we had failed, what we must do. We read it, memorized it, quoted it. . . . For those of us wandering in the arid desert of Eisenhower Republicanism, it hit like a rifle shot."[127] Conservative theorist Russell Kirk concurred: "If one million people would read this book, it would change the world."[128]

The 123-page primer was bold and blunt. Goldwater demanded that Americans awaken to the dangers of liberalism and to the truth of conservative principles. Conservatism, he stressed, was not the servant of reaction or the privileged, but in applying the "wisdom and experience of the past" it offered solutions to modern problems. Unlike liberals, he continued, conservatives viewed each person as a complex and unique being who yearned for independence and responsibility. Conservatives championed this view and dedicated themselves to "achieving the maximum amount of freedom for individuals that is consistent with the maintenance of social order." The challenge exposed their foe; the federal government had become "a Leviathan, a vast national authority out of touch with the people, and out of their control." Hungry for power and corrupted by pursuit of it, federal managers had been slipping their restraints since the 1930s. In the Constitution, the founders had revealed the solution: limited government erected only to establish order, maintain the defense, and administer justice. The usurping of powers beyond those delegated, Goldwater maintained, was illegitimate and unconstitutional. A return to the constitutional path also entailed the restoration of states' rights, "our chief bulwark against the encroachments of individual freedom by Big Government." That government be constrained in its power and not interfere in the private lives of its citizens was a core belief for Goldwater. He had learned it in his youth, accepted it in the 1920s and 1930s, and enunciated it as a Phoenix city council member. Only rarely would he lose sight of it.[129]

Goldwater's agenda was clear: the federal government must "withdraw promptly and totally from every jurisdiction reserved to the states." This meant "freedom for farmers" through termination of subsidies and price-support programs. "Freedom for labor" would come by passing right-to-work laws and outlawing the closed shop. Because restrictions on property curtailed individual rights, Goldwater rejected the income tax as "confiscatory" and demanded cuts in federal bureaucracy and spending. He decried "Socialism-through-Welfarism" and suggested axing social, education, public housing, and urban renewal programs. Retreat from the welfare state, "the currently favored instrument of collectivization," would not be easy or immediate. "But I do suggest that we establish by law, a rigid timetable for a staged withdrawal."[130] It was a call to battle: "I have little interest in streamlining government or in making it more efficient, for I mean to reduce its size. I do not undertake to promote welfare, for I propose to extend freedom. My aim is not to pass laws, but to repeal them. . . . I will not attempt to discover whether legislation is 'needed' before I first determine whether it is constitutionally permissible."[131]

Southerners were particularly interested in Goldwater's chapter on civil rights. It offered them a defense of states' rights and a narrow interpretation of federal responsibilities. Differentiating civil from human or natural rights, the Arizona senator determined that the Constitution afforded blacks protection only in voting, contractual relations, and property holding. With Little Rock and other school desegregation actions in mind, he specifically denied the legitimacy of federal efforts to integrate educational facilities. "Despite the recent holding of the Supreme Court, I am firmly convinced—not only that integrated schools are not required—but that the Constitution does not permit any interference whatsoever by the federal government in the field of education. It may be just or wise or expedient for negro children to attend the same schools as white children, but they do not have a civil right to do so." Goldwater directly challenged the court and precedent: "I am . . . not impressed by the claim that the Supreme Court's decision on school integration is the law of the land." Ignoring power realities in the South and remaining consistent with his states' rights stand, Goldwater deemed segregation a problem best handled at the community level. Although Goldwater considered discrimination repugnant, he was unwilling "to impose that judgement . . . on the people of Mississippi or South Carolina." Racists would blink Goldwater's abhorrence of prejudice to embrace him as an ally. His constitutional opinions would sway few African-Americans; most dismissed the Arizona senator as an apologist for segregation.[132]

In the last chapter of *The Conscience of a Conservative*, which constituted a third of the book, Goldwater turned to foreign affairs. He condemned the "weak" response of American policy-makers to a "Soviet Menace" bent on world domination. "We have with great sincerity 'waged' peace, while the Communists wage war. We have sought 'settlements,' while the Communists seek victories. We have tried to pacify the world. The Communists mean to own it." The Soviets' military might and their direction of third-world revolutions were not the only causes of failure. Like Robert Welch, Goldwater targeted "an international fifth column that operates conspiratorially in the heart of our defenses" as a cause of American impotence.

The danger was immediate and, at least in this area, it tempered his fears about the swelling of federal authority.[133]

To turn the tide, Goldwater insisted that the United States repudiate all self-imposed restraints on the exercise of power and pursue total victory. The strategy of confrontation meant more than a flexing of military muscle, for Goldwater planned to exploit all economic, diplomatic, and political weapons in the American arsenal. He proposed cutting off foreign aid to communist and neutral countries and increasing technical and military assistance to American allies. He rebuffed negotiations and summit conferences that did not offer the United States the opportunity to make substantive gains. The cultural exchange program posed danger, as well, for it was a "Communist confidence game" run by "trained agents of Soviet policy." America's commitment to the United Nations required "reexamination" because the organization drained taxpayers and had become a communist-propaganda forum. He advocated the resumption of nuclear testing—calling it necessary for the development of weapons to offset Soviet superiority in conventional arms—and denounced the "Communist-induced hysteria on the subject of radio-active fallout" that led to suspension. Even diplomatic recognition of the Soviet Union could serve as a bargaining chip. The threat, or reality, of its withdrawal would stiffen American resolve in the cold war and boost the morale of men and women behind the iron curtain.[134]

For Goldwater, victory required more than stalemate. "In addition to guarding our frontiers, we must try to puncture his. In addition to keeping the free world free, we must try to make the Communist world free." Goldwater promised to make credible the policies of brinkmanship and communist rollback that the Eisenhower administration had decreed and deserted. Guerrilla operations by the Taiwanese against the Chinese mainland would have U.S. support. "Should the situation develop favorably, we should encourage the South Koreans and South Vietnamese to join the Free Chinese forces in a combined effort to liberate the enslaved peoples of Asia." Here was a domino theory in reverse, and it reflected the evolution of America's and Goldwater's thinking about Southeast Asia.[135]

He would invite the people of Eastern Europe to revolt and then would establish liaisons with underground leaders and supply them with radios, weapons, advisers, and "the paraphernalia of a full-fledged Resistance." With such encouragement came responsibility; the United States must be prepared to intervene militarily against "vulnerable" communist regimes. In the event of a revolt similar to that which occurred in Hungary in 1956, Goldwater would prohibit Russian intervention and be ready, "if the ultimatum is rejected, to move a highly mobile task force equipped with appropriate

nuclear weapons to the scene of the revolt. Our objective would be to confront the Soviet Union with superior force in the immediate vicinity of the
uprising and to compel a Soviet withdrawal." While going to the brink, Goldwater considered the possibility of war "unlikely," for "the mere threat of
American action" to save a people hostile to Soviet ambitions "would probably result in the communists' acceptance of the ultimatum." He concluded,
"Had we the will and the means for it in 1956, such a policy would have
saved the Hungarian Revolution." Perhaps words such as these would lead
Barry Goldwater in 1961 to say: "Because of some of the things I've said I
might never be President."[136]

In 1960 the *Los Angeles Times* presented the Arizona senator with
another opportunity to disseminate his views, inviting him to write three
columns per week under the title, "How Do You Stand, Sir?" The *Times*
began running the columns in January, and within six months more than fifty
newspapers carried them. By 1962 nearly one hundred fifty newspapers featured Goldwater's opinions on their editorial pages. Goldwater reviewed his
speeches and reread John Locke, but mostly he relied on Stephen Shadegg
to draft the columns. Interestingly, his aide and brother-in-law Paul Sexson
contacted Herbert Hoover staff member Bernice Miller for material: "In this
connection, do you suppose you could dig up a copy of the Chief's speeches
which were made between 1934 and 1936 which is the basic thinking of
Barry and has always been?"[137]

The center held the high ground in the Republican Party in 1960, and
Vice President Richard Nixon laid claim as Dwight Eisenhower's heir. Few
could challenge him. He had the look of a winner, was a dedicated party
man, and possessed strong anticommunist credentials. This, however, did
not deter some from pressing Barry Goldwater for president. On May 15,
1959, the Arizona senator met with Clarence Manion and a small group of
conservatives to discuss organizing a national campaign to mobilize sentiment and delegate votes. Manion told Goldwater that Nixon was not a "true
conservative" and that his nomination "would lead to defeat, which would
shatter the last chance of survival of the Republican Party." The Arizonan, he
maintained, was the "only hope for Republican victory. . . . Only a conservative can generate enough Republican enthusiasm to win." While reiterating his support for Nixon, Goldwater accepted Manion's assessment.
Catching the mood of the meeting, Goldwater disparaged the vice president
for joining the "one-worlders," a reflection of his "recent avowal for the
World Court." This concerned Goldwater, and he wondered aloud about
"just what Nixon might say or do next."[138]

Manion's proposal flattered Barry, who disclosed at the meeting that South
Carolina's Democratic senator, Strom Thurmond, and other southerners had

approached him as well. While pleased, he was sure that his "Jewish name" and lack of education would hamstring a run for national office. Manion continued to press, and Goldwater "assured us that he would not at any time repudiate the move." The minutes of the meeting show that a follow-up conference was scheduled for the next day with retired General Albert C. Wedemeyer, who would serve as national chair of the organization. A handwritten margin note reminded Manion to contact Arkansas Governor Orval Faubus to inform him of the operation. By the end of July 1959, Americans for Goldwater had mobilized in thirty-one states and the District of Columbia. Named to the group's organizing committee were Frank Brophy (Arizona), Eugene Pulliam (Indiana), Robert Welch (Massachusetts), Brent Bozell (Maryland), Spruille Braden (New York), Herbert Kohler (Wisconsin), J. F. Schlafly (Illinois), and actors Joel McCrea and Adolphe Menjou (California). Kent and Phoebe Courtney and Dan Smoot would soon enlist in the effort.[139]

Barry Goldwater was too realistic to take Manion seriously. Despite the success of *The Conscience of a Conservative* and the newspaper columns and his extensive party work, polls showed that he had the support of only 1 percent of Republican voters. Richard Nixon was clearly the overwhelming favorite of the rank and file. Nor did Barry yet hunger for the presidency. Though he could not be lured into a determined run, he refused to acquiesce to his party's embrace of Modern Republicanism. Nixon, the Eisenhower man, lacked the proper ideological moorings and was susceptible to liberal pressure, and he had to be convinced of the power of the party's right. Thus, while Americans for Goldwater built its mailing lists and distributed literature, Barry hit the banquet circuit in his role as Senate Republican Campaign Chair to rally the conservative troops. He spoke at twenty-three functions in thirteen states and the District of Columbia during January and February 1960. In May he visited eleven states and gave fourteen speeches. On the Senate floor he stepped up his criticism of the administration. Goldwater, in one particularly hard-hitting address, lashed the president's health care plan for the elderly as "socialized medicine" and just another feature of Eisenhower's "dime store new deal."[140]

A trip to Columbia, South Carolina, on March 26, 1960, sharpened the focus of the offensive. Goldwater's attempt to right Nixon's "complacent attitude" played to the needs of southern Republicans. At the request of Gregory Shorey, Jr.—the South Carolina Republican chair and Americans for Goldwater activist—the Arizona senator appeared before the state party convention. He roused the five hundred Republicans with an enthusiastic espousal of the states' rights position, and to Goldwater's surprise they pledged their thirteen national convention delegates to him for president. In the wake of South Carolina's vote, Arizona Republican leader

William Rehnquist wrote to Barry for instructions concerning the stance of the Arizona delegation. Goldwater replied on March 31 that Nixon was "our man" but noted that for six weeks "Dick has shown a decided tendency to drift far to the left, along the New Deal–Fair Deal lines . . . [and] we must employ means to get him back on the right track. . . . I do think . . . that opposition . . . will have a decided affect on him."[141] Goldwater felt, moreover, that if Arizona now deserted him for Nixon it would represent "a humbling political repudiation."[142] Arizona subsequently pledged its votes to Barry Goldwater for president. So, too, did Louisiana, and Texas Republicans proclaimed their preference for Goldwater for vice president. By July, Goldwater strategists counted one hundred delegates firm or leaning to their candidate on the first ballot, with two hundred more supporting him for vice president.[143] Said Goldwater, "We can't win, but we might make a respectable showing."[144] Nixon paid little attention to the Goldwater boomlet. He reasoned that the move was symbolic and that the conservatives, because they had little option, would have to unite behind him. The Nixon camp's only hint of concern came in the announced list of potential vice presidential nominees; it included Goldwater's name.[145]

In June, the month before the convention, the Goldwater campaign intensified. In addition to the four hundred Americans for Goldwater clubs, organizers had fielded the Goldwater Coordinating Committee, Youth for Goldwater, and dozens of ad hoc grassroots groups. Youth for Goldwater was especially active, forming chapters on sixty-four college campuses in thirty-two states. Stephen Shadegg opened a campaign clearinghouse in Yuma, Arizona, that maintained contact with the different wings, engineered telegram- and letter-writing efforts, and distributed literature, bumper stickers, books, and buttons. From the thousands of letters he received, Shadegg compiled a mailing list that served future Goldwater campaigns well. Barry, of course, was keenly aware of Shadegg's efforts. The John Birch Society, while not an official sponsor, also contributed to the cause. Birchers mailed to all Republican convention delegates postcards that read: "Nominate anybody you please. I'm voting for Goldwater."[146] At a Goldwater rally on the eve of the Chicago convention, Birch leader Robert Welch was a featured speaker. He circulated thousands of copies of the speech during the fall campaign and urged voters to write in Barry's name.[147]

The right was not alone in attempting to turn Richard Nixon. New York Governor Nelson Rockefeller balked at the proposed platform and threatened a floor fight unless the delegates made firmer commitments to supporting the civil rights movement and increasing defense spending. As Goldwater had feared, Nixon calculated that he could not win in November unless Rockefeller's organization delivered New York's electoral votes.

Believing the conservatives were under control, Nixon moved to quiet the revolt on his left flank. In line with terms dictated to him, the vice president left Washington, D.C., for New York City on July 22, just three days before the convention opened, and met with Rockefeller in the governor's Fifth Avenue apartment to hammer out an agreement. Nixon offered little resistance and even extended the vice presidency to Rockefeller; he declined. Early the next morning, aides telephoned the details of the deal to Chicago.[148]

News of Nixon's "compact" with their personification of the Eastern Establishment stunned conservatives. Texas Republicans went so far as to vote to release themselves from their commitment to Nixon. Goldwater was furious with the vice president. Nixon had not informed him of his mission to Fifth Avenue, and Barry opened fire, declaring this "surrender to Rockefeller" as "immoral politics" and the "Munich of the Republican Party."[149] Even worse, the incident came after Nixon had broken his promise to Goldwater to endorse a right-to-work plank for the platform. "The man," Goldwater wrote at the time, "is a two-fisted, four square liar."[150] Nixon supporters quickly calmed the convention but at great cost. "We collected," said a Nixon adviser, "every political IOU we held in the country that night."[151] As was his style, Barry would later forgive and forget his friend's dishonesty. It would not be the last time.[152]

Goldwater had planned to withdraw his name from consideration and release his delegates before the convention opened. Now, he said, "that could wait."[153] In defiance, boosters placed his name in nomination and paraded in support of their candidate. Their actions actually increased the conservatives' resentment, for they accused convention hall security of working on behalf of the Nixon forces to restrict the size and duration of their demonstration. Hardly reckless, and believing the point made, Goldwater strode to the speaker's platform to withdraw his challenge.[154] With his no-nonsense tone and black horn-rim glasses, he evoked a stern schoolmaster. He pleaded first for party unity. Goldwater insisted that conservatives unite behind Richard Nixon and support the platform "over the blueprint for socialism presented by the Democrats. . . . We must remember that Republicans have not been losing elections because of more Democrat votes—now get this—we have been losing elections because conservatives often fail to vote. . . . This country is too important for anyone's feelings; this country in its majesty is too great for any man . . . to stay home and not work just because he doesn't agree. Let's grow up, conservatives." Then he called them to action: "Let's if we want to take this party back—and I think we can some day—let's get to work."[155]

This moment became fixed in the conservative imagination. "I enlisted," recalls Pat Buchanan, marking the beginning of his life commitment to the movement.[156] He was not alone. "Now," said the *New York Times,* "their hearts belong to Barry."[157] The experience made Barry Goldwater heady as well. He left the speaker's stand and returned to his family's box, where youngest daughter Peggy rushed forward, hugged him, and asked: "Daddy, next time will it be for real?" Barry nodded vigorously and said yes.[158]

The convention enhanced Goldwater's standing beyond his conservative fold. Television cameras beamed his image and message from coast to coast. Ignoring Goldwater's double message, Republican moderates pegged him as a party stalwart. Rockefeller, on the other hand, left a poor impression. He was seen as a troublemaker, a spoiler who did not see beyond his own ambitions. As New York Congressman William Miller later observed: "Nelson shouldn't have tried to be captain till he was on the team awhile."[159] Goldwater bolstered his image with hard campaigning for the Richard Nixon–Henry Cabot Lodge ticket and against John Kennedy and the New Frontier. During the fall Goldwater traveled to twenty-six states, primarily in the West and South, and made 126 speeches. Again and again he targeted Kennedy for his "socialist and Left Wing" philosophy while accusing vice presidential candidate Lyndon Johnson of being a "counterfeit Confederate" who said one thing in the North and another down South.[160] Goldwater's southern exposure amused Kennedy, who joked about "that Confederate uniform that [Barry] has been using in the South."[161]

Goldwater did not confine his jabs to the Democrats. He criticized Nixon for "lackluster" campaigning and his "me-too" attitude. "He's been getting tougher, but he's still not tough enough."[162] Occasionally Goldwater ignored Nixon and Lodge while campaigning. When reporters questioned him about this, Goldwater replied, "I have voiced the cause of conservatism in my speeches, but I have never deliberately passed over Vice President Nixon as the man who should be elected President."[163] Reporters also noticed Goldwater's crowd appeal: "There was no lack of evidence that the Senator was attracting . . . a cult of personal enthusiasts even broader than that which revered the late Senator Robert A. Taft."[164] In early October, with the campaign just past the halfway point, Goldwater startled reporters with the off-the-cuff remark that if Nixon lost the election, he himself was available in 1964.[165]

John Kennedy bested Richard Nixon in November by fewer than 120,000 votes, or one-fifth of 1 percent, of the more than 68 million cast. The Democrat had done well in New England, carrying all but the traditionally Republican states of Maine, Vermont, and New Hampshire, and in the Middle Atlantic region. Similarly, Kennedy had picked up electoral votes in the South but snagged only Illinois, Michigan, Minnesota, and Missouri in the Midwest. The West, except for Nevada, New Mexico, and Hawaii, had gone to the Republicans.[166]

In spite of their party's defeat, Goldwater Republicans found solace in the returns from the South. Operation Dixie, combined with white southerners' dissatisfaction with liberal Democrats over racial issues, had enabled the Republicans to maintain and even expand their inroads below the Mason-Dixon line. Texas and Louisiana had returned to the Democratic column, but Nixon had held Florida, Virginia, and Tennessee. In capturing nearly half of the South's popular vote, Nixon had outrun Eisenhower in Alabama, Georgia, Mississippi, and South Carolina. Republicans also elected seven congressmen from the states of the old Confederacy. Just a glance at the 1960 electoral map was enough to convince conservative strategists that a western-midwestern-southern coalition was being born and that the White House was in reach. This did not distract Barry Goldwater from seeking out another cache of conservative votes. He reminded Republicans of the importance of augmenting their efforts in the South and West with a "serious, well thought-out campaign to show people in the large ethnic and religious groups in the cities who do not normally vote for us at national elections that we are the best party."[167]

Goldwater issued a quick election postmortem in which he wasted no time on the impact of the televised debates, the missile-gap issue, Nixon's knee injury and ill-advised pledge to visit all fifty states, or Kennedy's intercession on behalf of imprisoned civil rights leader Martin Luther King, Jr. Rather, Goldwater characterized Nixon's failure as a replay of the 1940, 1944, and 1948 elections, in which the Republican Party "offered voters insufficient choices with a 'me-too' candidate."[168] He repeated his message to *Time* magazine: "It's just what I've been saying. We cannot win as a dime-store copy of the opposition's platform. . . . We must be different."[169] In other words, Kennedy won because countless conservatives had folded their arms and refused to work or vote for Richard Nixon. When reporters asked about the 1964 race, Goldwater became cautious. "I want to figure in 1964, not necessarily as the top candidate. But I don't want Rockefeller in that spot."[170] Rockefeller had other ideas. Just a few weeks after Nixon's defeat he began to assemble a staff and plan for his political future.[171]

Barry Goldwater would not have the luxury of Rockefeller's studied and controlled approach. In 1960 he had activated a movement that he could not easily stop or channel. For example, Youth for Goldwater had refused to drop the banner. In September, less than two months after the convention, these campus conservatives evolved into the Young Americans for Freedom (YAF), a group launched from the lawn of the Buckley family estate in Sharon, Connecticut. The Goldwaterites of YAF claimed, after a year, twenty-seven hundred members in chapters on one hundred campuses. Barry was still the choice of Robert Welch and the John Birch Society. He complained ineffectually about the ad hoc groups that had mobilized in his support and then remained in place "without my permission[,] and they cause me deep embarrassment."[172] Yet his repeated cease-and-desist orders appeared hollow, for Steve Shadegg had never halted the bandwagon. Shadegg told Dan Smoot in a fall 1960 telephone conversation: "The thing that I want to show you is that we haven't given up. . . . Our problems are in practical politics . . . to get ahold of the machinery of the Republican Party in every state where we can. . . . It may take us four years, it may take us eight years, but to that objective we are committed. . . . Now there is only one man who [can] be the focal point of intelligent support for this and this is Barry."[173] Conservatives' expectations were on the rise, and Goldwater would find their fervor difficult to dam.[174]

In 1962 political commentator Jack Bell described Barry Goldwater's career during the 1950s: "The Arizona Senator was like a small cut of timber caught in a log run floating downstream. Now and then he could extract himself long enough to whirl rather fruitlessly in the current before the jam bore down on him again."[175] This assessment jibes with Goldwater's self-perception: "My life was certainly . . . without strategy or timetable."[176] These are surprising statements given that Goldwater soared in just eleven years from the Phoenix city council to nomination at the Republican Party convention in 1960. Four years later he emerged as the standard-bearer for the GOP. Compare his progress with the pace of two other men who certainly did not wait for their tides to rise. The pre-nomination careers of John Kennedy and Richard Nixon lasted fourteen years, and both began their political lives several rungs higher than Goldwater and on platforms far superior to Arizona.

Barry Goldwater harnessed ambition to a public persona that beckoned America to challenge, effort, and eventual victory. And, like nineteenth-century Tammany Hall boss George Washington Plunkitt, Goldwater could say, "I seen my opportunities and I took 'em."[177] With the backing of such powerful men as Eugene Pulliam, Everett Dirksen, Styles Bridges, Raymond Moley, and Clarence Manion, he was able to sell himself and his message. Even more neutral opinion-makers portrayed Goldwater as the embodiment of the western hero; a charismatic counterpoint to John Kennedy and Nelson Rockefeller. Goldwater was also bolstered by loyalists who learned well the arts of political organizing and the packaging of a public man. With vigor and skill, Barry Goldwater climbed to the upper circle of the Republican Party. Using the same abilities and resources he would initiate the rightward movement of the American mainstream.

7

Like a Desert Wash in Flood

I am sure you understand the political situation into which you have . . . no, not stumbled, but stepped; for it was by deliberate choice and by no accident that you flung your tribunate into the very crisis of things.

—CICERO TO CURIO
Cicero's Letters to His Friends

John Kennedy: So you really want this fucking job, huh?
Barry Goldwater: I do, but I don't know why.
—1961, *"I'd Have Ended the Vietnam War in a Week or Two"*

The sixties and President John Kennedy's opening of the New Frontier offered Barry Goldwater opportunities amid challenges. A few days into the decade, fellow Republicans reelected him to his third term as Senate Campaign Chair, with only scattered reservations from party liberals and admirers of Nelson Rockefeller. The post allowed him to continue what he had begun in 1955: gaining "exposure" and building "a line of credit" on which he could "draw when the need arises."[1] As before, he maximized his chance and scheduled 225 speaking engagements in 1961 and 200 more in the first nine months of 1962. Between January 1960 and November 1963 he made almost eight hundred speeches, two-thirds of them before party groups and many on college campuses. Senator Goldwater, since 1959 an Air Force brigadier general, also appeared frequently on radio and television talk shows. Newspapers and magazines gave him much space. He was, after all, "as handsome as a movie star," declared even solemn *Business Week*, and *Time* called him the "hottest political figure this side of Jack Kennedy."[2] Through his own efforts and those of the adoring press, he became the most visible critic of the New Frontier. His prominence as a leading Republican critic was particularly apparent in the context of Republican flux. President Eisenhower had retired; Richard Nixon, although beaten, still hoped to come back; and Nelson Rockefeller was strong but isolated.[3]

The intensity of his efforts led reporters to speculate about "Operation Goldwater" and its meaning for 1964.[4] "In spite of personal disavowals of candidacy," maintained *U.S. News and World Report,* "Goldwater is working hard and moving faster than many candidates do in a campaign."[5] The magazine estimated that the Arizonan would arrive at the Republican convention commanding between one-fourth and one-third of the delegates. If Goldwater was not, as he protested, a candidate for the nomination, he was eager to expand his factional base and increase conservative leverage over the party's platform and presidential choice. Soundings from around the nation encouraged him. In 1961 and 1962 Goldwater received eight hundred pieces of mail per day and averaged more than one hundred invitations to speak each week. *The Conscience of a Conservative* was in its twelfth printing, and he had been approached to write a second book. Conservative magazines *Human Events* and *National Review* soon successfully hawked Goldwater for President sweatshirts, bumper stickers, and lapel pins. Goldwater cautioned conservatives in March 1961: "Sometimes, the objectives we work toward can't be realized overnight and we must train ourselves to understand that there is such a thing as timing and patience in the conduct of political affairs. So, effort is needed and patience is needed."[6] The line between patience and effort was not obvious, however, and both Goldwater and his supporters would cross it instinctively.[7]

On January 11, 1961, nine days before John Kennedy's inauguration, Barry Goldwater marked the path of effort for his followers. Consistent with his belief that a conservative majority had only to be awakened, he advanced from the U.S. Senate floor "A Statement of Proposed Republican Principles, Programs and Objectives" as the lever to inaugurate a new era of GOP rule. Here were his standard themes, modified to fit the modern temper and harnessed to a plan for victory. In the declaration, written by the Senate Labor Committee's minority counsel Michael Bernstein, Goldwater described America as a nation of competing interest groups forged by Franklin Roosevelt's New Deal. These organizations, he contended, posed a danger to freedom. Americans, in the face of collective power, feel "virtually helpless to achieve what are, at bottom, individual goals"—economic betterment, educational advance, and "dignified human treatment in social and economic relationships." Becoming a member of these labor unions, farm associations, ethnic and religious societies, and consumer groups was no solution, for the individual is "often submerged, swamped and treated as a manipulated statistic" by leaders who sometimes act at "the expense of the membership." Goldwater reached out to what he called the "forgotten" and "silent" Americans "who quietly go about the business of paying and praying, working and saving. They mind their own business and meet their responsibilities on a day-to-day basis. They are the group who, for too long, have had their voices drowned out by the clamor of pressure groups which increases in volume as their numbers decline." They were, said Goldwater, the Republican Party's natural constituency and future majority. To turn the nation, the GOP had to become their vehicle; to retrieve their liberty and defend it, "to stem the seemingly inexorable march toward the automation of human beings."[8]

As the instigator of the "dehumanizing trend," the federal government had to be changed. Government downsizing, Goldwater was convinced, meant economic security, national progress, and a rebirth of individualism. Limits on federal growth and spending would stop the inflation-fed erosion of purchasing power and bring the tax relief necessary to fuel prosperity. The Arizona conservative did assign government an activist role in restricting the power of labor unions and other "pressure group organizations" to enhance individual economic and political decision-making. In sum, Goldwater's manifesto raised a new breed of conservative. His conservative was populist, unshackled from elite pretense and unafraid to rally the people. This sixties conservatism was especially convincing when voiced by a man of Goldwater's style and temperament.[9]

Human Events, the *Wall Street Journal,* and *U.S. News and World Report* gave Goldwater's "Platform for the Forgotten American" extensive coverage. They trumpeted its positive approach and appeal across economic, racial, and religious lines. Barry, however, had no illusion that large numbers of African-Americans might be drawn into the fold. So he continued to "hunt" his "ducks" among middle-class whites in the South, West, and Midwest and among blue-collar ethnics in the East.[10] Republicans like Richard Nixon, Ronald Reagan, and George Bush would heed the "Forgotten American" message, which came to frame Republican discourse for a generation. In 1961, as America entered the New Frontier, the message was still devoid of divisiveness and the politics of resentment. It would not remain so for long.[11]

Goldwater did not have high expectations of the new president. He met Jack Kennedy in Arizona in the 1940s while the future president was recovering from war wounds. Although political adversaries, they developed a friendship during their Senate service that Barry described as "warm."[12] Kennedy acquaintances attest to the president's personal regard for Barry. The Arizonan hung a photograph of Kennedy in his office foyer; the inscription read, "To Barry Goldwater, whom I urge to follow the career for which he has shown talent—photography."[13] Though Goldwater liked Kennedy, he did not want him in the Oval Office. He questioned Kennedy's commitment and focus: "He was not what one would call an educated man, although he had a brain that could absorb facts like a blotter. I've seen him come into a room many times not even knowing what was being discussed and within minutes arguing one side or the other with perfect clarity and within fifteen minutes he would have completely forgotten about it."[14] He believed Kennedy to be inexperienced and indecisive. Soon after Lyndon Johnson agreed to be Kennedy's running mate, Barry asked him why he had accepted the second spot on the ticket "to a weaker man."[15] Eisenhower's administration may have been a disappointment to Goldwater, but John Kennedy's presidency loomed as a disaster.[16]

President Kennedy's package of legislative requests confirmed Goldwater's expectations, and he reacted immediately. The New Frontier was simply New Deal–Fair Deal collectivism made fashionable for the sixties. The administration's proposals were, said the Arizona senator, "socialism of some order or another. [Soviet Premier Nikita] Khrushchev recently promised free housing, free medical care, and free transportation. And here we are with the New Frontier promising pretty much the same thing."[17] Goldwater rejected the administration's recommendations as inflationary and bureaucracy-building and joined the Senate's conservative coalition in blocking Kennedy's plans for health insurance for senior citizens, mass transit, and a department of urban affairs. He attacked aid to depressed areas as "a long step toward the point where [Washington] will be able to control, by executive order not only prices, wages, working conditions, and hours, but even the places of employment. . . . Nobody, least of all the administration—seems to know what the ultimate cost of these programs will be."[18] Still, Goldwater introduced legislation to authorize and construct the Central Arizona Project and its network of dams, pumping stations, and aqueducts. These reclamation activities, he maintained, were within the purview of the federal government because local communities did not command the resources to act. He reassured skeptics that 75 percent of such federal expenditures would be repaid.[19]

Although Goldwater missed 65 of 207 roll-call votes in 1961, he was out in front in opposing several Kennedy bills. He denounced the president's initiative for raising and expanding coverage of the minimum wage as "tampering with the natural laws of our free enterprise system by granting unearned wage increases through government edict."[20] A higher minimum wage, he prophesied, would bring unemployment because American jobs would be lost to cheaper labor markets overseas. He fought the allocation of funds for vocational training, insisting that proponents offer evidence that the program would actually lower unemployment. Goldwater was also active in the resistance against federal aid to education. He convincingly argued that the administration's proposal addressed a problem already past. Local communities had responded adequately to the crisis in the 1950s, and with baby boomers growing up, additional primary and secondary school classrooms and teachers were unnecessary. Goldwater's statistics even predicted a teacher surplus as early as 1970. These arguments, joined to states' rights convictions and concerns about federal control, mobilized a majority against the bill. Success strengthened Goldwater's resolve. He wrote to Stephen Shadegg, "I think that we have to hit, hit, hit at the radical philosophy pointing out the wrongness and stupidity of it and do it time and time again. . . . I am convinced we have them running. . . . Kick them real hard where it hurts."[21]

The new frontier of the sixties was also a matter of race. On February 1, 1960, four black college students sat down at a segregated lunch counter in Greensboro, North Carolina, and refused to leave when denied service. News of this simple act of defiance traveled quickly throughout the South and prodded black communities into a chain reaction of insurgency. By April 1, blacks had adopted the sit-in tactic in seventy cities from North Carolina and Virginia to Texas. Television cameras captured the protest for northern audiences. For many Americans, events became a twentieth-century morality play with the forces of good and evil, right and wrong personified before them. The sit-in campaign forced a dramatic shift in the civil rights movement. Confrontation replaced legalistic solutions and quiet negotiation. The large numbers of men and women engaged in direct action would have a ripple effect on local black populations, heightening the salience of discrimination and of a sense of personal efficacy.[22]

As a senator, John Kennedy had not been an active proponent of civil rights. During the 1950s, according to aide Theodore Sorensen, Kennedy "simply did not give much thought to this subject."[23] As president, Kennedy accelerated the federal government's hiring of blacks and directed the Justice Department under Attorney General Robert Kennedy to press litigation for school desegregation and voting rights. In the wake of the 1961 Freedom Rides, the Interstate Commerce Commission banned segregation in bus facilities. At the same time, Kennedy appeased white southerners by appointing avowed segregationists to the federal bench. Also disappointing to blacks was his reluctance to sponsor new civil rights legislation. If civil rights was an urgent issue to African-American activists, for John Kennedy it remained a political matter of low priority.[24]

Hoping to quiet confrontation and control the movement, Bobby Kennedy met with civil rights leaders in the summer of 1961 and suggested that they focus their efforts on a drive to register southern blacks to vote. Kennedy offered to arrange private funding for the operation, and to induce acceptance of the government's proposal he added tax exemptions for movement organizations and draft deferments for activists. Support of a voter registration drive provided the Kennedy administration with an escape from a difficult position and the means to build a reserve of voters. Jack and Bobby

Kennedy, looking back to the rise of the Irish to power in Boston and Massachusetts, saw the vote as the key to full citizenship for black Americans. With blacks voting as a bloc, they could elect their own while forcing southern white politicians to bow before a new electoral reality. Moreover, quiet voter registration drives would not spark white antagonism. At the same time, the growing black electorate in the North, South and West, aware of its benefactors, would reward Kennedy and the Democratic Party. While 68 percent of black voters supported Kennedy in 1960—8 percent more than Adlai Stevenson's 1956 total—their allegiance was not yet assured. Partly in response to Kennedy's proposition, civil rights workers targeted counties in the South to register voters, challenge local authority, and raise black power. Their efforts would provoke white resistance and bring about the crises that the Kennedys had tried to avoid.[25]

The black struggle posed a dilemma for Goldwater as well. Separating civil from human rights, the Arizonan vehemently supported black voting rights. "The right to vote," the conservative repeated, "is in the Constitution. There the federal government should act even if it means with troops."[26] He criticized Bobby Kennedy and the Justice Department for not prosecuting more vigorously "cases where they can prove that a man is denied the right to vote by reason of race, creed, or color."[27] Goldwater also supported a constitutional amendment to abolish the poll tax, which discriminated against blacks and the poor. In addition, he believed in the justice of the Freedom Rides and accepted as constitutional the desegregation of passenger terminals. But his states' rights stand barred him from following his personal feelings any further. He opposed federal action to bring desegregation and voted against the withdrawal of aid from segregated schools. When Mississippi Governor Ross Barnett defied a court order in 1962 and refused to allow James Meredith to enroll at the state university, Goldwater declared, "While I feel the governor was morally wrong in doing what he did, nevertheless, I felt that he was within his Constitutional rights." This startled even conservative and longtime friend Denison Kitchel, who advised that the Tenth Amendment's protection of states' rights did not permit defiance of a court order. Kitchel wrote to Barry: "I think you should admit that it was technically wrong and charge it off to human error in the face of great provocation. Then I think you should level your guns at the Court for its sociological jurisprudence and the Executive for its politically motivated haste and fire away for all you are worth. Make Barnett their victim, not your hero."[28] Goldwater stubbornly defended states' rights on philosophical grounds and refused to hedge. Still, politics figured into Goldwater's thinking, for Operation Dixie and the fragile gains that Republicans had made in the South were important to his plans. Goldwater thus reassured southern whites: "I would bend every muscle to see that the South has a voice in everything that affects the life of the South."[29]

A close reading of Goldwater's message suggests a slight but critical shift in the early 1960s. In *The Conscience of a Conservative* and before, his conservatism meant anticommunism, economic orthodoxy, and limited government. His comments about morality were vaguely stated and peripheral to his main themes. For Goldwater, moral issues were beyond the scope of government and more properly confined to the private sphere. Perhaps as a reflection of changing mores or the views of the conservative movement's growing number of traditionalists, he changed his focus and became more outspoken. At the American Hellenic Educational Progressive Association banquet in August 1962, he asked, "Have you looked at your TV sets lately? What wallowing in self-pity! What vast and contorted expression of emotion over trifling problems! What meaningless violence and meaningless sex! . . . Your ancestors would look upon us with pity. To them, we would be truly barbarians." He similarly dismissed modern art as the worship of "the cult of the ugly and common place."[30] The following year, after the Supreme Court had banned prayer in the public schools, he cosponsored a constitutional amendment to reverse the decision. It was only a beginning, but Goldwater had begun to validate the concerns of social conservatives, and in time they would grow bolder in shaping the movement's agenda.[31]

To Goldwater, the New Frontiersmen were as much a failure abroad as they were at home. "I suggest that men committed to collectivism and social engineering in domestic affairs are ill-equipped—indeed, almost incapable—of combatting the disease of worldwide collectivist slavery."[32] He dismissed Kennedy's foreign policy as "outmoded" and "weak-kneed," with Cuba his prime example.[33] In April 1961, fifteen hundred Cuban exiles who were trained by the CIA and had been promised American support invaded their homeland to spark an uprising against Communist leader Fidel Castro. Kennedy summoned Goldwater, who had just strapped himself into the cockpit of an F-86 Air Force fighter, to the White House for a briefing on the situation at the Bay of Pigs invasion site. When asked his advice, Goldwater bluntly told the president to order air strikes immediately or the mission would fail. Goldwater remembers that Kennedy agreed with his assessment, and he left the Oval Office sure that the operation would succeed. Kennedy's decision not to commit the Air Force, and the subsequent failure of the invasion, convinced Goldwater of the president's "rather gutless character as it applied to making decisions that amounted to something in the case of our country."[34] Kennedy, he concluded, "clearly had lost his nerve."[35] The crisis also had a liberating effect on the conservative: "For the first time, I saw clearly that I had the toughness of mind and will to lead the country."[36] In the wake of the Bay of Pigs fiasco, Goldwater would privately suggest to Kennedy that the United States invade Cuba "to rid the hemisphere of the threat of extended Communism," but the president rejected his counsel.[37] He later backed the administration's economic boycott of Castro's Cuba, yet in 1962 he condemned Kennedy's "do-nothing" policy.[38]

Goldwater offered other evidence for his stand. He gave Kennedy poor marks for appeasement before Khrushchev's rocket-rattling threats and the building of the Berlin Wall. Rather than placating the aggressors, said Goldwater, the president should order the wall torn down without delay. He labeled negotiations with the Soviets that eventually led to the formation of a neutralist-coalition government in Laos as an "acquiescence to their gruff freedom-killing demands."[39] The arrangement was "at the very best merely [a] way station on the road to Communist domination."[40] Kennedy's essential problem, said Goldwater, was a lack of an overall design to meet the Communist threat: "I suggest that we have been reacting frantically and separately to each Communist move as though it were a situation apart from Soviet grand strategy. We have been swatting one fly at a time and now the room is full of flies. We have been content with a patchwork, outmoded foreign policy which reeks of hesitation and uncertainty and ineptitude. . . . The need is for a policy grounded on strength which is willing to run some risk in the cause of freedom."[41]

Why Not Victory, published in early 1962, offered that policy. The book updated the foreign affairs chapter of *The Conscience of a Conservative* and showed Goldwater to be more concerned and insistent in light of what he saw as the continuing decline of American influence. The United States, he wrote, was fast losing the struggle for survival against a Moscow-directed "international conspiracy" to dominate the world. To awaken the nation, Goldwater evoked the 1930s and the Nazi menace: "We are dealing with an enemy whose appetite is insatiable, whose creed demands slavery for everyone, Americans included. The more we give in to that enemy, the more he wants; and the more we give in to him, the more he is encouraged to demand."[42]

Goldwater insisted that Americans shed their false faith in peaceful coexistence and mobilize all resources for the "dominant, proximate" goal of victory. Military superiority underwrote the offensive, with particular reliance on nuclear weapons to offset the communists' conventional advantage. He likened the current world situation to the Wild West, describing nuclear power as America's "pistol" against the Russian "giant," the "equalizer" that kept the enemy at bay. In the cold war climate, then, disarmament was an illusion and nuclear testing vital to American security. Goldwater looked to Cuba as the opening campaign in the struggle against international communism. In league with the member nations of the Organization of American States (OAS), the United States must "take whatever action is necessary to dislodge Communism from the front yard of the Western Hemisphere." If the OAS was not supportive of this aim, the United States "must take unilateral action." Goldwater rejected allegiance to the World Court and, in a not-so-veiled threat, announced that American support of the United Nations was assured "so long as the actions of the UN do not violate our national objectives and do not continue to serve the Communists as they have in the past." The admission of communist China to the organization, he said, should trigger the suspension of U.S. "political and financial support." Finally, to defeat Soviet-directed insurgencies in Africa, "where independence means Communist domination or a return to savagery," Goldwater proposed the establishment of western "protectorates" to "preside over a crash program preparing the African people economically, politically, and culturally for the responsibilities of self government." Against nations already under communist control, "we must proceed, overtly and covertly, to restore Western influence." As in *The Conscience of a Conservative,* Goldwater reassured Americans that his strategy would bring peace, not war. "Every time we have stood up to the Communists they have backed down. Our trouble is we have not stood up to them enough." *Why Not Victory* quickly became a best-seller.[43]

Goldwater and his conservative message gained credence because many Americans sensed that their nation was in retreat. The new administration seemed impotent while communism rooted at America's doorstep in Cuba, posed to penetrate the Western Hemisphere. The Kennedy administration appeared unable or unwilling to exert military power to counter communist thrusts in Vietnam, Laos, and Berlin. When combined with Russian space feats and boasts of hydrogen bomb megatonage, the communist threat became even more terrifying and immediate. At home, the New Frontier offered increased government spending, bureaucracy, and direction. In the civil rights movement, conservatives detected the danger of domestic turmoil and federal intervention to the detriment of community rights. Those schooled in anticommunist ideology were convinced of the relation between internal and external events.

The popularity of the Arizona senator was only a sign—though it was the most visible one—of the quickening conservative pulse. The readership of William F. Buckley, Jr.'s, *National Review* tripled between 1960 and 1964. In Texas, self-professed "Goldwater Republican" John Tower won a 1961 special election to fill Vice President Lyndon Johnson's vacant Senate seat. In the same year, the Wyoming state legislature passed a resolution calling for the repeal of the federal income tax amendment. Later it went on record opposing foreign aid and U.S. membership in the United Nations. In February 1962 the

Conservative Party was founded in Nelson Rockefeller's New York. Clarence Manion, Dan Smoot, Carl McIntyre, and other conservative commentators made five thousand radio and television broadcasts each week and were heard or seen in every state. Conservative organizations also registered impressive gains, with nearly fifteen hundred separate right-wing groups in existence. Keying this conservative organizational thrust was Robert Welch's John Birch Society.[44]

The conservative drive had stalled abruptly but briefly in early 1961 when the Birch Society's war on "subversives" attracted national attention. Many newspapers and magazines focused on *The Politician*—what *Time* called Robert Welch's *Mein Kampf*—and its labeling of President Eisenhower as a communist. The Birchers, *Time* concluded, were "a goose step away from the formation of goon squads."[45] The *Los Angeles Times* criticized the organization as authoritarian and irresponsible and warned that it posed "a peril to conservatives."[46] The *New York Times Magazine, Life, Newsweek, Look,* and the *Saturday Evening Post* ran similar articles about "extremism." The Justice Department also targeted the John Birch Society as "a matter of concern."[47] The media barrage soon lifted but was repeated in following years.[48]

In response to this negative publicity, conservative leaders moved to reassess their ties with the organization and gain distance. *National Review* attempted to steer a middle course through the media storm. Seeking no break in conservative ranks, William Buckley characterized the society as "an organization of men and women devoted to militant political activity." Few members, he was certain, fully subscribed to Robert Welch's sensational charges of communist influence in the White House. Although he disagreed with Welch on many issues, Buckley said of his friend, "I have always admired his personal courage and devotion to causes." "I hope it thrives," he concluded, "provided it resists such false assumptions as that a man's subjective motives can automatically be deduced from the objective consequences of his acts."[49] Barry Goldwater followed a similar tack. He told reporters that the Birch threat was exaggerated, for the society had "no more political effect than the American Legion, the Episcopal Church or any other organization."[50] "The Birch Society," he reiterated on NBC's "Meet the Press," "constitutes no danger. I am more concerned with the extremists to the left than I am with the extremists to the right."[51] Goldwater did concede that Welch hurt the conservative cause, having "said some very unfortunate things." The senator's solution was simple and took into account the philosophical ground he shared with members, personal relationships, and the political assets of the organization. He encouraged Birchers to "get rid" of Welch and continue the fight under new management.[52] Goldwater seriously misjudged members' allegiance to their leader, however.

Holding the middle ground did not appease the press, and the continuing exposé of the group embarrassed mainstream conservatives. Public opinion was influenced by the media, and polls showed that Americans were unfavorably disposed to the Birchers. Through a McCarthyism-in-reverse, Barry Goldwater was in danger of being tarred with an extremism brush. He was, in fact, vulnerable. Goldwater had defended the organization on several occasions. Most recently, in the January 20, 1962, issue of the widely read *Saturday Evening Post,* he had praised, in a clear reference to the Birchers, the "patriotic Americans who wish to remain vigilant to the threat of internal Communism and to socialist trends."[53] Also in January he unwittingly became a sponsor of the American Committee for Aid to Katanga Freedom Fighters, a Birch Society front organization that supported anticommunist secessionists in the Congo. Even before this he had agreed to serve on the executive council of the Committee Against Summit Entanglements, another Birch-affiliated group. Something had to be done to remove what Denison Kitchel called the "albatross around our neck."[54]

That same January conservatives John Hall, Russell Kirk, William Baroody, Stephen Shadegg, Barry Goldwater, and Bill Buckley met for two days at the Breakers Hotel in Palm Beach, Florida, "as an intellectual council of war" to review their strategy.[55] The problem was obvious: Welch was a liability, but the Birchers were critical to conservative success, and they could not be alienated. Buckley and Kirk pressed a hard line and proposed that responsible conservatives disassociate themselves from the society. Reminding the group of the absurdity of Welch's charges, Kirk joked, "Eisenhower isn't a communist, he's a golfer."[56] Goldwater and Baroody were more cautious and opposed open confrontation. There were, Goldwater noted, "nice guys" as well as "kooks" in the society, and he argued against a blanket condemnation.[57] Besides, Barry contended unconvincingly, while the society supported him, he didn't approve of it. The group finally agreed to subject Welch to high-profile censure and thus prod members to reject him. The tactic also shielded conservatives from media criticism. Goldwater would not be directly implicated in the anti-Welch effort. Buckley and Kirk would be his surrogates and deflect resentment.[58]

In follow-up, the editors of the *National Review* raised "The Question of Robert Welch" in the magazine's February 13 issue. They lashed Welch for "bearing false witness" and printed Russell Kirk's admonition: "Cry wolf often enough and everyone takes you for an imbecile or a knave, when after all there *are* wolves in the world."[59] Kirk, at the same time, contributed an article to the Catholic journal *America* in which he condemned the "fantastics" who "injure the cause of responsible conservatism."[60] In a letter to the *National Review* printed two weeks later, Barry Goldwater congratulated its editors and described Welch as being "far removed from reality and common sense." He called for Welch's resignation: "We cannot allow the emblem of irresponsibility to be attached to the conservative banner."[61] *Newsweek* quoted him similarly: "I wish he would step out so the fine, responsible people who are members could take charge."[62]

In spite of these efforts Goldwater and his friends gained only a partial victory. Goldwater remained the choice of the John Birch Society, but members refused to oust Welch. When the media siege lifted, Birch organizers took advantage of the surging enthusiasm for Goldwater to pump their membership to sixty thousand members in forty-eight states by the end of 1962. California alone housed three hundred Birch Society chapters. These recruiting efforts fortified the organization and allowed it to move up through conservative ranks. In the context of growing codependence, Goldwater supporters thereafter tempered their criticisms of Welch and his secret society. Barry Goldwater would, in turn, find himself increasingly exposed to extremist charges and in repeated denial.[63]

New York Governor Nelson Rockefeller watched these conservative maneuverings closely, for he had much at stake. Before any one else, he had determined to seek the Republican nomination for president in 1964. Born in 1908, the grandson of multimillionaire John D. Rockefeller, Nelson had been assistant secretary of state for Latin American affairs under Franklin Roosevelt, President Harry Truman's chair of the International Development Agency, and undersecretary of Defense and of Health, Education, and Welfare in the Eisenhower administration. Rockefeller, imbued with a sense of service, embraced politics, and in his first try for public office decisively won the New York governorship in 1958. He immediately aspired to higher office, his ambition facilitated and matched by the vast Rockefeller fortune. Supremely self-confident (the more cynical talked of hubris), Nelson was convinced that no obstacle or liability could keep him from his goal.[64]

In 1961 and 1962 the evidence confirmed his chances. Political professionals pegged him early on as the front runner for the Republican nomination. Though midwestern and western party leaders were to his right, Rockefeller's promise of victory quieted ideological concerns. Their hearts might belong to Barry, but they were certain that no candidate so right-of-center could win the White House. Richard Nixon, meanwhile, was handicapped: out of office, burdened with the reputation of having kicked victory away in 1960, and without a political base. Supporting the party kingmakers' assessment were public opinion polls that placed Rockefeller far in the lead among Republican voters with Goldwater a distant second. Square-jawed, handsome, and an energetic campaigner, Rockefeller offered the Republicans a viable alternative to Kennedy. The idea of a Rockefeller candidacy was still so bright in November 1961 that divorce from his wife of thirty-one years did not derail the bid.[65]

In spite of the positive press notices and polls, Rockefeller did not relax. He worried about his poor image within the party, a product of his actions during the 1960 convention and the "stigma" of the Rockefeller name. To repair the damage and quiet opposition to his advance, the New York governor attempted a rapprochement with conservatives. Kentucky senator and Republican National Chair Thruston Morton acted as his go-between and opened a channel to the party's leading conservative, Barry Goldwater. Their initial encounter in early 1961 went so well that the two men met monthly for breakfast for more than two years. Rockefeller hoped to win over Goldwater or at least neutralize him as an opponent. Thus, he appealed for Republican unity, always a high priority to party loyalist Goldwater. He gave a conservative spin to his positions, stressing individual initiative, private enterprise, fiscal responsibility, spending cuts, anticommunism, and a strong national defense. Disregarding Nelson's reputation for ruthlessness and guile, Barry took him at his word: "Rocky's really not such a bad fellow. He's more conservative than you would imagine."[66] "We were," remembers Goldwater, "in agreement on the majority of major issues."[67]

Nelson did more than charm Barry. He caused the Arizona conservative to pause and reassess his plans. Goldwater saw the governor as already in a commanding position for 1964, controlling New York's large bloc of convention delegates and possessing a well-funded and primed campaign machine. This especially impressed Goldwater, for in politics he was sure that "organization is the whole secret."[68] His backers, however, were unschooled in national campaigning and party politics—outsiders and mere amateurs compared to Rockefeller's staff. The right, Goldwater was convinced, was simply not ready to challenge the Eastern Establishment and had to set more realistic goals for 1964. As they did in 1960, conservatives should concentrate on shaping the party platform and educating the heir apparent. The 1968 election looked more promising and gave conservatives four more years to work the grassroots. In the face of Rockefeller's preparation, lead, and apparent ideological change of heart, Goldwater and his supporters would have to be patient. Little did Goldwater then realize that while the Rockefeller organization looked formidable, it was top-heavy and had spread shallow roots.[69]

Barry may have hesitated, but a small band of conservatives did not. Goldwater's withdrawal speech at the 1960 Republican convention had energized them, and they refused to take the long view. Their leader was forty-four-year-old F. Clifton White, a former Cornell University political science instructor who had become a Republican Party activist. He had been the chair of the Young Republicans (YR), an Eisenhower delegate at the 1952 convention, and the director for organization of Volunteers for Nixon-Lodge in 1960. He offered himself as an experienced political mechanic, a nuts-and-bolts specialist in movement-building and voter mobilization. In September 1961, White met with friends and former YRs William Rusher, an editor at *National Review,* and John Ashbrook, a newly elected Ohio Congressman, to discuss conservative possibilities. Rusher and Ashbrook, similarly under Goldwater's spell, encouraged White, and the three men combed their files to create a list of twenty-six members of the "old YR crowd" to invite "to talk politics."[70]

Twenty-two men responded, and on October 8 they secretly gathered in Chicago at a South Michigan Avenue motel. The group included two congressmen, three Republican state chairs, and several wealthy businessmen. White called the meeting to order and quickly focused the discussion. The goal, he told the group, was to transform the Republican Party into a force for conservatism. Rather than concentrate merely on platform shaping, conservatives had to capture the party machinery from the precinct organization to the national convention. With command of precinct caucuses and county conventions would come victories at state gatherings and the delegates necessary to nominate a conservative standard-bearer. The time was ripe, White continued, for losses in the 1960 elections had produced a leadership vacuum, with Republicans in control of only fourteen governorships and a handful of city halls. Moreover, 1964 held promise because one-fourth of the delegates to the Republican National Convention would be southerners.[71]

The capture of the Republican Party would not be a futile gesture, White assured them, for John Kennedy was vulnerable. Conceding the Northeast, middle Atlantic, and a scattering of midwestern and western states to Kennedy and even marking California as doubtful, White calculated a 301-electoral-vote majority from a coalition of Rocky Mountain, plains, border, central, and southern states. No one in the room doubted White. Nor could they conceive of success without Barry Goldwater. White, however, cautioned the men that it was too early to tie their efforts to a Goldwater candidacy. The group approved the strategy and charged White with developing a tactical plan and an operating budget. White announced at the meeting's close that he would inform Goldwater of the group's existence and intentions.[72]

In a visit arranged by Bill Rusher, Clif White and Nebraska state chair Charles Thone met Goldwater in his Senate office on November 11, 1961. White discussed the October meeting with the Arizona senator, detailing the group's plans and membership. He specifically dispelled any notion that this was a Goldwater for President operation, deferring any such decision until after the 1962 elections. That and the thrust of the effort pleased Goldwater:

"This is the best thing I've heard of since I became active in the Republican Party on the national scene."[73] His acquaintance with several members of the group also put him at ease. Barry offered White his support and agreed to spread the word to conservatives he encountered on his speaking trips. At the same time, Goldwater surprised White by baldly asserting that Rockefeller had the nomination all but "sewed up."[74] He suggested that White could better serve the cause by working to align the party platform with conservative principles. As White and Thone were leaving Barry wished them luck and asked them to keep in touch. Goldwater remained easily accessible to the group, says White. "I was usually put through to him immediately."[75]

The encounter buoyed White, who refused to be dismayed by Goldwater's comments about Rockefeller. Goldwater was more guarded, fearful of losing his freedom of action. Also, he had met Clif White before and was not enthusiastic about him. In 1958 White had offered his services to the senator's reelection campaign, prompting Goldwater to write to Steve Shadegg asking "whether or not he is effective."[76] White apparently did not pass muster and was not employed. Barry admired "the pros" and was always wary of those without established reputations and the proper credentials.[77] Four years had not changed Goldwater's opinion of White; he had no confidence in him. "Clif White," he told Shadegg, "doesn't know his ass from a hot rock about politics."[78] Yet even a good résumé would not have ensured White's inclusion in Goldwater's inner circle. Barry trusted his political career and sought advice chiefly from longtime Arizona friends like Shadegg, Harry Rosenzweig, and Denison Kitchel. Never was he eager to expand this nucleus. Though Goldwater supported White's greater purpose and maintained contact, he would never allow himself to become his puppet.[79]

White's group reconvened in Chicago on December 12. After reporting on his visit with Barry Goldwater, White set the conservatives' agenda. In preparation for 1964, he divided the United States into nine regions, each headed by a part-time director who would supervise state, county, and precinct organizations. These conservatives were instructed to learn the complex delegate selection process peculiar to each state, recruit leaders, and build a cadre. To cover the first year, White proposed a modest budget of $65,000, with allocations for his salary and office, secretarial, and travel expenses. The group approved the plan and budget unanimously. White initiated the operation soon after, renting a two-room office, known in the movement as Suite 3505, at Lexington Avenue and Forty-Second Street in New York City. Trips around the country followed to raise consciousness and prime conservatives for the task ahead. Group members, in turn, beat the bushes in their respective territories and sent information about volunteers and contributors to Suite 3505. The conservatives worked in secret, but news of their efforts leaked beyond the immediate group. William Rusher took fellow editors at the *National Review* into his confidence. Also, John Rousselot's attendance at the December 12 meeting ensured that Robert Welch and the John Birch Society were well informed of group activities.[80]

The conservatives' adrenaline was pumping, but funds were not. In election year 1962 other campaigns siphoned off contributions, and White's coffers were only half full by spring's end. June collections amounted to only $300. White, the true believer, refused to let his cause die. He borrowed $6,000 from his son's college education fund to shore up the effort. The situation did not improve significantly during the summer and fall, and White collected just two-thirds of the monies needed for the year.[81]

Adding to White's woes was Barry Goldwater's continued lack of enthusiasm. White pressed Goldwater with evidence of a "groundswell" of support, including an Associated Press poll of delegates to the 1960 convention that showed the Arizona senator in the lead for the 1964 nomination.[82] He might also have quoted Wisconsin's Democratic senator, William Proxmire, who noted in 1962: "Wisconsin visitors come to see me wearing Goldwater buttons. Letters praising Goldwater come to me almost as frequently as letters in praise of Kennedy."[83] Nor could Barry, as a devoted reader of *National Review*, miss the stream of ads selling Goldwater for President sweatshirts, bumper stickers, lapel pins, and key chains. Goldwater also knew, through his daughter Joanne, of the existence of the Californians for Goldwater clubs; organized in June 1961, they had mushroomed in six months to 600 members in eleven chapters. Still, he would not be turned from his fix on the GOP platform and the inevitability of Rockefeller's nomination. Besides, while White and the others had certainly raised conservative expectations, Goldwater perceived little substance in their efforts. He wrote Mississippian and White group member Wirt Yeager in September 1962: "I have never sought this nomination, as I have told you many times. I have many reasons, but I wouldn't put money and organization last and neither of these had reared its ugly head."[84]

Goldwater's activities in 1962 clearly showed that he had not deserted the conservative cause. Election year 1962 kept him on the road, where he repeatedly sniped at the Kennedy administration. In April he ripped Kennedy's jawboning of steel industry executives, which forced them to rescind a price increase, as "something you'd expect in a police state."[85] There was only one way to save the nation "from social regimentation," he said in May, and that was to vote Republican in November.[86] In June, Goldwater called for cuts in government spending and for rejection of Kennedy's public works bill as inflationary. Patrolling the New Frontier did not distract

Barry from happenings in his own party. Concerned that former President Dwight Eisenhower was organizing a draft for Richard Nixon if he won the California governorship, Goldwater rejected Modern Republicanism as "counter to the traditional principles" of the GOP.[87] Ike was again furious at Goldwater. He had already been roused by a September 1961 newspaper column in which Goldwater complained of "the inept handling of the Cuban situation by the Eisenhower administration."[88] In July 1962 Eisenhower blasted Goldwater: "I'm getting awfully sick of him. I'm beginning to feel that he is nursing this one ambition—to get the Republican nomination for the Presidency as the crowning achievement of his career. . . . He wants to set himself as the single authority and guiding voice for the Republican Party."[89]

The Cuban Missile Crisis of October 1962, coming on the eve of the midterm elections, would dash predictions of Republican gains. The fourteen-day crisis, set in motion by the discovery of missile sites in Cuba, brought the United States and the Soviet Union into direct confrontation and the world to the brink of nuclear war. Fortunately, Soviet Premier Nikita Khrushchev blinked first and agreed to American demands to dismantle the sites and remove the missiles from the island. Americans were pleased with the outcome, and public opinion polls registered a sharp rise in John Kennedy's popularity. But Goldwater saw the resolution of the crisis as another lost opportunity to roll back communism and as an American defeat. Tracing Russian boldness to Kennedy's failure of nerve at the Bay of Pigs, Goldwater had argued for decisive action. He went to the White House, this time holding the rank of Air Force Reserve major general, and advised the president "to move on Cuba militarily." The Russians were sure to back down before the Americans' nuclear superiority. Brinkmanship would not only force the Soviets to remove their missiles, it would also bring an end to the Castro regime. To Goldwater's chagrin, Kennedy "dwelt on the ultimate horror of thermonuclear warfare" and rejected his advice. "I came away from the meeting," he remembers, "with the impression that no amount of Soviet provocation would ever be sufficient in Kennedy's eyes to justify any action that might lead to the use of atomic weaponry."[90] To make matters worse, the easing of tensions had left Cuba fixed in Soviet orbit and Castro's government intact. "Once more the United States had retreated. Our action guaranteed the continued presence of a staging area for the Russian communistic ideological assaults on other countries in the Western Hemisphere and dealt a death blow to the Monroe Doctrine."[91]

In an October 30 letter to New Hampshire Senator Norris Cotton, Goldwater vented his frustration. "I think this whole Cuban episode has been one of the sorriest and saddest expeditions . . . I have ever witnessed." It was more than Kennedy's behavior during the crisis and in its aftermath that troubled him. "I wish the people were not so emotional so we could explore it."[92] If Kennedy had balked at the "horror" of nuclear war, the American people's attitude was "almost hysterical, unreasoned."[93] Brought to the brink during the Cuban Missile Crisis, many Americans now recoiled at the possibility of nuclear confrontation, at "thinking about the unthinkable."[94] Such perceptions, Goldwater believed, handcuffed America's defense against the vast conventional arms advantage that the communists possessed. For Goldwater the crisis fostered an urgency to air nuclear alternatives and convince the public that these were realistic options. His sense of mission often blinded him. It made him insensitive to a public rubbed raw by television and radio emergency tests, air raid warnings, school drills, programs to build fallout shelters, and media images of thermonuclear holocaust.

In November the Democrats scored the most impressive midterm election victory for a party in power since 1934, picking up four U.S. Senate seats while losing only two in the House of Representatives. Despite these outcomes, the elections boosted conservatives' hopes. Operation Dixie, while making no major breakthroughs, continued to show results. All six incumbent Republican congressmen won their races, and Texas, Florida, Kentucky, North Carolina, and Tennessee each elected a Republican to the House. There was a sharp increase in the number of Republican candidates for state and local offices, and in Georgia and North Carolina the party elected its first state senators since Reconstruction. In Alabama, Goldwaterite James Martin won 49 percent of the vote, coming within sixty-eight hundred ballots of upsetting veteran Democratic Senator Lister Hill. Meanwhile, the Republican candidate for governor in Texas claimed 46 percent of the vote. Regionwide, Republicans won more than 2 million votes in 1962, up 244 percent from just four years before.[95]

Conservatives also cheered returns in New York and California. Nelson Rockefeller had gained an unimpressive victory, running behind other Republican state candidates and beating a political unknown by a smaller margin than in 1958. The state Conservative Party had cut into his total, capturing more than 142,000 votes. California Governor Pat Brown, looking trim and enthusiastic on the campaign trail, thwarted Richard Nixon's comeback. Nixon had attacked the influence of extremist groups in the Republican Party, and the primary race with a Birch-backed opponent left him wounded. Nor could he convince Californians that the governorship was not just a stepping-stone back to the White House. A bitter Nixon blamed the press for his defeat and held his "last" press conference on November 7. Other races attracted national interest. Moderate Republicans George Romney and William Scranton claimed the governor's chairs in Michigan and Pennsylvania, respectively. While the progressive wing of the Republican Party had become crowded, the elections raised no new conservatives capable of challenging Barry Goldwater's leadership.[96]

Of particular importance to Goldwater were the results of the Arizona elections. Voters returned Governor Paul Fannin to office and awarded Republicans four more seats in the state House of Representatives. Although eighty-five-year-old Senator Carl Hayden was running for reelection, Republican leaders insisted on only a token resistance to his bid. Goldwater instructed Arizona Republican Chair Shadegg: "We don't want to beat Carl. He is the state's greatest asset in Washington." But "just in case" he died during the campaign, the party wanted a candidate available and in place.[97] Shadegg, eager to emerge from Barry's shadow and believing that he had the backing for at least a "token" campaign, declared and made the rounds implying a Goldwater endorsement. Feeling exposed and used, Barry "hit the ceiling" and personalized the dispute.[98] This opened a breech between Goldwater and his most astute political adviser that would take years to close.[99] In the Republican primary Goldwater assumed a neutral stance even though he opposed as too extreme Shadegg's opponent Evan Mecham, a Phoenix area car dealer with Birch Society backing. Mecham beat Shadegg only to lose to Hayden in the general election.[100]

Less than a month after the elections Clif White reconvened his group, now expanded to fifty-five members, to consider his state-by-state organizational chart, the 1963–64 budget, and the schedule of 1964 primary elections and state conventions. White updated the conservatives, reviewing his visits to twenty-eight states and contacts that he had established in fourteen more. He also informed them that Barry was well aware of their activities, for he not only provided the Arizona senator with copies of all memoranda but reported to him personally. Informally, group members had reached a consensus: the success of their efforts depended on Goldwater. White's last meeting with him, on November 12, was especially encouraging because he had sensed a cooling of the senator's relationship with Rockefeller. "I now felt we might well have cleared our highest hurdle."[101] Yet White was sure Goldwater would not act unless the group proved itself organizationally secure and financially viable. He proposed, then, hiring a public relations director, researchers, fund-raisers, and office support staffers to supplement his work as campaign manager. Crucial to staff effectiveness was the gathering of $3.2 million before the July 1964 convention. White predicted that Senator Goldwater could win on the first ballot, with more than the necessary 655 delegate votes coming from southern, western, and midwestern states. Success in the California primary was not necessary but would seal the conservative's victory. To facilitate these plans, White hoped to take the draft Goldwater operation public in March 1963. This did not require Barry's "overt approval," simply his "pledge not to disown the draft or repudiate his own possible candidacy."[102] As before, the group instructed White to see Goldwater and coax him with their progress.[103]

Unfortunately, what White might have outlined as a worst-case scenario occurred. The need to expand the group had increased exponentially the risk of a leak. Fourteen months of secrecy halted when Walter Cronkite's lead story on the CBS "Evening News" on December 3, 1962, exposed a conservative "plot" to stop the Rockefeller bandwagon. The report embarrassed Barry, and his reaction was predictable. He was in no mood to compromise when he met with White on January 14, 1963:

> *Goldwater:* Clif, I'm not a candidate. And I'm not going to be. I have no intention of running for the Presidency.
> *White:* Well, we thought we would have to draft you!
> *Goldwater:* Draft, nothin'. I told you I'm not going to run. And I'm telling you now, don't paint me into a corner. It's my political neck and I intend to have something to say about what happens to it.
> *White:* Senator, I'm not painting you into a corner. You painted yourself there by opening your mouth for the last eight years. You're the leader of the conservative cause in the United States of America, and thousands — millions — of people want you to be their nominee for President. I can't do anything about that and neither can you.
> *Goldwater:* Well, I'm not going to run. My wife loves me, but she'd leave me if I ran for this thing.[104]

White left Goldwater's office convinced that he had failed. He told Bill Rusher, "I'm going to give up politics and go back into business."[105] His discouragement quickly spread to the rest of the group. Said Texas member Peter O'Donnell: "We're like a wet noodle right now."[106]

But Goldwater had not been honest with White. He had no intention of quitting. Unbeknownst to White, Barry had already begun to hedge his bets on Nelson Rockefeller's nomination. His reevaluation came in the context of Nixon's defeat, Rockefeller's showing in New York, and the emergence of moderates Romney and Scranton. Perhaps White's cheerleading had also had an impact. Lacking confidence in White and seeking control, Barry prompted his advisers to draw a campaign blueprint for victory. The result was the brieflike "Program," written in longhand and dated December 23, 1962, just two weeks before Goldwater's meeting with White. The draft outlined as the first step to the nomination that Goldwater appoint an advisory group, "all of them to be personal friends in whom he has complete confidence as to their loyalty, ability and judgement." The group, which would be the organizational nucleus of the campaign, included fund-raising and public relations "experts," "an experienced political pro," and others to "carry out special missions." Operating from Washington, D.C., the group planned surveys in every state to assess voter sentiment, funding sources, and the potential for building "grassroots organizations." Barry's friends had obviously learned much from Clif White.[107]

Revealing the shift in thinking about 1964 were the thirteen "Premises" to guide the campaign that were laid down in the draft. Before all else, the draft argued, was a conviction that Barry's nomination was "within the realm of reasonable possibility." Failure to act now ensured the success of Nelson Rockefeller, who even if defeated by Kennedy would still be in a position to claim the party's nomination in 1968. If conservatives surrendered without a fight, "modern Republicanism" would vault to control of the party, and the right "might not recover for a generation." Goldwater had to run because he owed "an obligation to millions of Americans who believe firmly in the principles you have enunciated and who look to you for affirmative leadership." Although acknowledging Rockefeller's lead, the draft reminded the Goldwaterites of the vicissitudes of politics. Fortunes could change, and conservatives must not "be found wanting in the organization and groundwork essential to produce that action." There was even a script for Barry if the effort was discovered prematurely: "As for myself, it is my intention to seek re-election to the Senate in 1964. Whether or not that intention might have occasion to be changed is an eventuality which I do not foresee—it is one which would depend entirely on the wishes of the Republican Party."[108] In the wake of the 1962 elections, the Goldwater camp suddenly recognized its position of strength. Barry Goldwater was candid just three days before his meeting with White: "Assume I'm interested in the presidency. It still makes more sense for me to delay. I've done my backroom work already. Nobody's been around the country more in the last ten years than I have. I know the county chairmen. I know the potential convention delegates. Rockefeller and Romney still have to meet those people, but they're friends of mine. Another thing, I am the only conservative in the presidential picture. The others are . . . liberals. You might say, 'Let them fight it out for a while.'"[109]

In spite of rejection, a political fever burned intensely in Clif White. Prompted by group members he met with Goldwater on February 5, only to be rejected again. White summoned his executive committee to Chicago two weeks later to consider the future. He was surprised to find the mood of the members changed. Believing in the certain success of the cause, they had shaken off their discouragement and grown increasingly irritated at Goldwater's hesitancy. It was time to take the initiative from him. "There's only one thing we *can* do," snapped Indiana State Treasurer Bob Hughes. "Let's draft the s.o.b."[110] Members, without dissent, agreed to take the group public, reckoning they had time and room to maneuver if Goldwater did not disavow them. To lessen the likelihood of Goldwater's resistance, Peter O'Donnell, whom Barry respected, assumed the chair of the draft committee, and White accepted assignment as national director. For fear of provoking the press, the group decided that no John Birch Society member would hold a leadership position.[111]

The conservatives took their risk on April 8, when O'Donnell called a press conference in Washington, D.C., to declare his group's intention "to mobilize the tremendous spontaneous enthusiasm for Senator Goldwater that is sweeping the country."[112] Barry's response encouraged them: "I am not taking any position on this draft movement. It's their time and their money. But they are going to have to get along without any help from me."[113] The draft committee's announcement drew extensive media coverage, with several magazines detailing White's plans for the nomination and campaign against President Kennedy.[114]

Barry benefited from his position on the draft. He had distanced himself from the effort while enabling White to continue organizing and raising funds. His own camp was still in gear and proceeding with its plans. In evading "this President thing," he sheltered himself a little longer from attack. "The minute it becomes clear," observed Goldwater, "that a man is trying to get the nomination, he's a prime target for his enemies."[115] Also, the stand signaled reluctance but not intractability. This galvanized supporters, who, in turn, encouraged reporters to track signs of Goldwater activism. Barry surely found satisfying, yet hardly surprising, the news that Republican county chairs in Missouri and Illinois supported him by a two-to-one margin. Similarly, the *Atlanta Constitution* estimated that the Arizonan could count on a minimum of 250 of the South's 350 delegates to the 1964 convention. Backers in California, meanwhile, had collected 100,000 names on petitions imploring him to run. Insulated and with the campaign machinery humming, Barry could remain in a "fluid position," continuing his assault on the Kennedy administration's spending proposals and failure to cut the budget.[116] He also broadened his critique to suggest that the moon-landing program be deemphasized and more attention paid to developing a military-use policy for space. In just "pooping along," Goldwater was positioned to await the "breaks" of American politics.[117]

None of this really worried front-runner Nelson Rockefeller, who found his security in public opinion polls. Gallup's February survey of Republican voters gave him a lead over Barry of 49 percent to 17 percent. An end-of-April poll narrowed the distance but not alarmingly. Another report brought Rockefeller the glad tidings that two-thirds of the delegates to the 1960 Republican Convention checked his name as most likely to be nominated in

1964. Nelson still met monthly for breakfast with Barry, and his conservative fiscal proposals and support for Cuban "freedom fighters" played well to the party's right.[118]

On May 4, 1963, Rockefeller had called his friend Goldwater at home to tell him of his marriage that afternoon to Margaretta "Happy" Murphy. Goldwater sincerely wished the couple well, returned to his roof to fix a television antenna, and probably wasted little time speculating about how powerful a political bombshell had just exploded. He soon found out. Only one month before, thirty-six-year-old Happy Murphy had divorced her husband and surrendered custody to him of their four children, ages three to twelve. Many Americans quickly added up Rockefeller's sins, reinterpreting his 1961 divorce as the result of his relationship to this "other," younger woman. Their reaction was immediate, national, and intense. Phyllis Schlafly, a member of the Illinois Federation of Republican Women and a Goldwater supporter, was "disgusted with Rockefeller. A man who has broken up two homes is not the kind we want for high public office. The party is not so hard up that it can't find somebody who stuck by his own family."[119] Connecticut Senator Prescott Bush was similarly offended: "Have we come to the point in our life as a nation where the Governor of a great state—one who perhaps aspires to the nomination for President of the United States—can desert a good wife, mother of his grown children, divorce her, then persuade a young mother of four youngsters to abandon her husband and their four children and marry the Governor?"[120] The polls registered the reversal in popular sentiment: Gallup showed Goldwater in the lead for the first time, with 35 percent of the Republican vote to Rockefeller's 30 percent and Romney's 16 percent. Coincidentally, just two days before Rockefeller's marriage, Richard Nixon seemingly abandoned politics, giving up his California base for New York City and a private law practice. The two events dramatically altered the Republican equation for 1964.[121]

Rockefeller had seriously miscalculated. Perhaps the quiet after his divorce had lulled him. Maybe he was blindsided by an ambition too tightly wrapped in his overweening self-confidence. If initially stunned, Rockefeller quickly dismissed concerns about his character, sure that he could regain his stride. Others would not be so blind to the obvious. Political commentator Robert Novak was blunt when he wrote of Nelson and Happy Rockefeller's later appearance at a fairgrounds in Oregon, Illinois: "There was a smell of political death about the day in Ogle County. It was like observing a political corpse who did not realize that he was dead."[122] Nor did the fire cease after the initial volleys. In 1964 pollster Louis Harris reported on the candidate's gender gap: "Rockefeller's problem is his divorce and remarriage. . . . It is this one overriding problem that just crops out as soon as you mention

Nelson Rockefeller. Make no mistake about it, it is a crippling element particularly among women, and has just about destroyed his chances."[123] Republican politicians, never enamored with Rockefeller's politics, now had an excuse to write him off. Said one, "He might as well [have] take[n] the gaspipe."[124] Without at least the look of a winner, the governor's shallow base quickly eroded. Rockefeller looked for a scapegoat and blamed conservatives for the popular reaction. "You can't satisfy them. I've tried and it won't work. . . . They were the first to pounce on me when the marriage was announced. They hit me when I was down."[125]

The personal decisions of Rockefeller and Nixon had created a political vacuum that the Draft Goldwater Committee eagerly moved to fill. On June 10, Clif White transferred his headquarters from New York to the more choice Washington, D.C. Contributions increased and totaled almost half a million dollars, aiding the committee's activities in what was now a network of thirty-two state chapters. In some states, like South Carolina, the draft effort had completely absorbed the official Republican organization. To further press Barry, White planned a July Fourth rally at the Washington, D.C., National Guard Armory. Speakers were Barry's friends Arizona Governor Paul Fannin, Texas Senator John Tower, and Nebraska Senator Carl Curtis. Forty-two busloads of Goldwaterites from New York and thirteen from Connecticut, with contingents from as far away as Texas and Illinois, descended on the capital to produce a standing-room-only crowd of nine thousand that spilled from the building into the street. Barry had sensed a change in the political wind even before the rally. He told a UPI reporter, "I don't want this nomination, but it may be forced on me. If I'm put in the position where I have to take it, I won't be a reluctant tiger. I'll get out and fight."[126]

Nelson Rockefeller did not easily permit others to take the initiative. Nor could he remain idle while they trumped his ideals and ambitions. Polls in early July enhanced the urgency; Republican voters preferred Barry to him 38 percent to 28 percent. It was time to reassess campaign strategy. The Young Republicans' convention, held in Denver in June, gave him cause and pretext to return to the offensive. At the convention the Goldwaterites were out in force and assumed control. This alone concerned Rockefeller, but his aide George Hinman was troubled for other reasons. Hinman decried the infiltration of the organization by John Birchers and what he described as their harassment of Republican moderates. Also disquieting was the right's trumpeting of its southern strategy and intention of writing off the Northeast and the black vote in 1964. "There is," Hinman complained, "an insanity in the air around here."[127]

Rockefeller, after more than two years of courting Barry Goldwater, reversed course. Consistent with his liberal beliefs, angry over the response to his marriage, and eager to reignite the campaign, he moved to rally party moderates against conservatives. On July 14 the governor issued a press release reiterating his support for Republican doctrines of free speech, equal opportunity, fiscal integrity, and federalism. He then fingered the enemy: "Many of us have been taking too lightly the growing danger to these principles through subversion from the right."[128] The Young Republicans' convention, Rockefeller continued, gave proof of the danger, for "the proceedings there were dominated by extremist groups, carefully organized, well-financed and operating through the tactics of ruthless, rough-shod intimidation. These are the tactics of totalitarianism."[129] He concluded by condemning the southern strategy as an attempt "to erect political power on the outlawed and immoral basis of segregation."[130] In a follow-up press conference, Rockefeller left no doubt as to his real target. He challenged Barry Goldwater to disavow the John Birch Society before he became its pawn. Foreshadowing 1964, Rockefeller later declared that he could not support Goldwater "if he were a captive of the radical right."[131] In Rockefeller's absence—he was honeymooning in Venezuela—such liberals as California Senator Thomas Kuchel and New York Senators Jacob Javits and Kenneth Keating seconded his views. Former President Dwight Eisenhower, Richard Nixon, William Scranton, and George Romney withheld comment and left him isolated.[132]

Goldwater was furious at his friend's "doublecross"[133] and reacted immediately: "There'll be no more breakfasts. None at all." Senator Carl Curtis responded for Goldwater, decrying the "self-serving tactics by a man desperately trying to retrieve his declining political fortunes."[134] The attack by Rockefeller steeled Goldwater's political determination. It may also have accelerated his plans. In the summer Denison Kitchel opened an office in Washington ostensibly to campaign to reelect Barry Goldwater to the U.S. Senate. One of his first tasks was the purchase of a Recordak system for information storage to collect and sort the thousands of statements Goldwater had made since 1953. He also contacted Professors Milton Friedman and Robert Bork of the University of Chicago and Yale University, respectively, to entice them into joining a Goldwater brain trust. Political pro Ed McCabe enlisted in the effort, as did Dean Burch, Goldwater's legislative assistant, and William Baroody, the director of the American Enterprise Institute. Kitchel remained independent of the Draft Goldwater Committee, but as a political novice with few national connections, he approached Clif White for advice. Communication went one way, however, and White remained in the dark about Goldwater's plans. In fact, White's only interaction with Goldwater from May until October 1963 was by mail. Barry routed White's detailed reports of draft committee activities to Kitchel and blind copied his Arizona friend with the perfunctory replies.[135]

With politics in the hands of White and Kitchel, Goldwater turned fully to matters of state in the summer of 1963. Two issues fixed his and most of the country's attention. In the wake of demonstrations in Birmingham, Alabama, made powerful by television images of snarling police dogs and blacks violently thrown to the ground by the spray of fire hoses, the civil rights struggle had again become a national priority. This, plus Governor George Wallace's attempt to prevent black students from enrolling at the University of Alabama, prompted President John Kennedy to act. In June he submitted to Congress a civil rights bill with provisions strengthening voting rights laws, facilitating the attorney general's initiation of school desegregation suits, and, most important, outlawing discrimination in employment and in hotels, restaurants, theaters, and other public accommodations.[136]

Barry Goldwater could not follow the president's lead, objecting chiefly to the public accommodations section of the bill as an assault on property rights. Although believing that Kennedy's stand was morally correct, he was adamant: "I am completely opposed to this as being obtained through legislation." His solution was "voluntarism and not compulsion."[137] In regard to employment discrimination, he proposed a long-term emphasis on job training and vocational education. Also of concern to Goldwater was the spread of civil rights demonstrations from the South to the North and West. "I am somewhat fearful of what might happen in some of our large northern cities . . . if this type of fire-eating talk continues among the Negro leaders and those whites who would use them only as a means to gain power. . . . I am afraid we're in for trouble."[138] To those who saw the political future in a southern-western coalition, Kennedy's advocacy of the civil rights bill and the expansion of the movement beyond Dixie could only rebound to their advantage. To African-Americans, Barry Goldwater had failed another test of courage.[139]

Americans also focused that summer on John Kennedy's efforts to ease cold war tensions. With Berlin and Southeast Asian fronts seemingly quiet and the Cuban Missile Crisis still fresh in Americans' minds, the Kennedy administration successfully negotiated a nuclear test-ban treaty with the Soviet Union that outlawed explosions in the atmosphere and under water. Again, Goldwater could not support the president. The treaty was, he wrote, "the opening wedge to disastrous negotiations with the enemy, which could result in our losing the war or becoming a part of their system."[140] He took to the floor of the U.S. Senate repeatedly in August and September to debate the measure. Goldwater insisted that the treaty left America exposed, for it outlined no effective means to ensure Soviet compliance. Without testing, he argued, the United States would relinquish its nuclear lead and increase the risks of war. He rejected proponents' claims that technological means existed to monitor Soviet behavior and that the treaty would lessen conflict. In regard to the treaty's potential for reducing risks from nuclear fallout, Goldwater countered that the danger was less than that from "smog" and the "fumes of everyday life."[141] Contending that the Soviets were eager for the treaty's passage, the Arizona senator demanded evidence of their "good faith" and proposed linking ratification to on-site inspection or the withdrawal of communist troops from Berlin. All of Goldwater's amendments were overwhelmingly defeated, and the Senate passed the treaty by an 80-to-19 vote in late September. Explained Goldwater, "I do not vote against the hope of peace, but only against the illusion of it. I do not vote for war, but for the strength to prevent it. . . . If it means political suicide to vote for my country and against the treaty, then I commit it gladly."[142] His stand further endeared him to his supporters. But when added to his easy references to nuclear weapons or jokes about the military's ability to "lob" missiles "into the men's room at the Kremlin," the vote put him further out of step with the American majority.[143]

From the Goldwater camp during the autumn came the signs of a candidacy in motion. Political observers, keenly sensitive to changing nuances, discerned a softening of Goldwater's rhetoric; an increasing avoidance of "the phrase that stings." They reported that the senator relied less on raw verbs like "abolish, cancel, and terminate" and more on the soothing "study, rethink, and modernize."[144] In line with this, Goldwater shifted his position on some issues. He now favored sending troops into the South to enforce federal court orders on school desegregation. As recently as August he had reiterated his opposition to the progressive income tax. In September he called only for a review of the internal revenue system and "suggestions made in the whole [tax] field."[145] Commentator Walter Lippmann, considering this tilt toward the center as natural preparation for a presidential campaign, described Barry as "well on the road where he will sound less and less like Goldwater and more and more like Eisenhower. . . . [He] is now in the process of reshaping himself for the political realities of this country."[146] Goldwater was well aware of the transition: "There would be something wrong with any man in public life who didn't change some of his ideas to meet the developments of the time. Consistency is not necessarily a virtue."[147] Accompanying these shifts, Goldwater appealed for party unity while holding at arm's length former comrades Bill Buckley and Brent Bozell, whom the *New York Times* labeled as "far right" supporters.[148] Meanwhile, New Hampshire Senator Norris Cotton quietly agreed to head Goldwater's effort in the primary, and former Senator William Knowland assumed the leadership of a committee to advise Barry on his chances in the California contest. In September, Goldwater staffers reserved all fifty-one rooms on the fifteenth floor of the Mark Hopkins Hotel in San Francisco for the July Republican convention.[149]

A flood tide of poll results augured well for the Arizonan. Nationally, Goldwater captured the support of 45 percent of Republican voters to Rockefeller's 23 percent and Romney's 16 percent. New Hampshire Republicans preferred Barry over Rockefeller, 58 percent to 20 percent. In the South, Barry led Jack Kennedy by 20 percent, with only 12 percent undecided. A Texas straw poll in early November gave Barry a 52 percent to 48 percent edge over the president. According to John Tower, "There was a little bit too much Camelot going on. . . . And it was rubbing a lot of people the wrong way."[150] Pollster Samuel Lubell concurred. Citing a popular notion that Kennedy "gives in too much to the Negro," Lubell found in November 1963 a significant erosion in his popularity: "The president faces a close election with only a small edge in his favor."[151]

Public opinion polls greased the wheels of the Goldwater bandwagon, and Republicans scurried to climb aboard. Reporters counted thirty-five Republican state committees for Goldwater. He even picked up support in New England, where 134 of 179 party leaders backed Barry. In its October 7 issue, *Newsweek* estimated that Goldwater would reach the convention in July with 500 committed delegates and 82 leaning toward him. That share would put him within striking distance of a first-ballot victory. Barry was not passive before the tide. To assess his support first-hand, he scheduled a ten-state swing in September and October that took him through such electoral-vote-rich states as Ohio, Illinois, California, New York, Pennsylvania, and Texas.[152]

Goldwater's rise, meanwhile, blanketed enthusiasm for other candidates. The Arizonan had raised so much dust that Nelson Rockefeller's announcement of candidacy on November 6 went relatively unnoticed. Governors George Romney and Bill Scranton, who had just arrived on the political scene, had little support outside their home states. Goldwater's surging momentum worried Dwight Eisenhower. Although Ike vowed to back the party's nominee, he hoped it wouldn't be Goldwater. His staff was still under orders to gather "sundry documents which aggregate . . . the various criticisms leveled against you by Barry Goldwater."[153] He hinted at his concerns in October: "I am unclear on precisely what Senator Goldwater's views are."[154] While loath to head a stop-Goldwater movement, Eisenhower offered up, to Republicans soliciting advice, political unknowns like his Secretary of the Treasury Robert Anderson, Generals Alfred Gruenther and Lucius Clay, and brother Milton. He encouraged Henry Cabot Lodge, serving as the American ambassador to South Vietnam, to return home and force a dialogue within the party. Nixon, too, should have another look "because he is after all a very knowledgeable and very courageous type of person."[155] While prompting these men to throw their hats into the ring, Eisenhower shied away from endorsements. Not all of Ike's favorites would find obvious his distinction between encouragement and support.[156]

Goldwater's rise in the polls, his political activities, and his high-profile stands on current issues intensified the scrutiny of the media. Barry was not prepared for this. He had long been nurtured by the supportive Arizona press and national commentators receptive to his ideas and style. They had discarded his gaffes as not newsworthy or pressed him to amend and expand his off-the-cuff comments. Nor had he made the adjustment rhetorically from preaching to the converted on the Republican banquet circuit to addressing a national audience. In the late summer of 1963 his luxury of "free-wheeling" came to an abrupt end when political observers began to strain his every pronouncement and highlight spontaneous slips.[157] Goldwater, whom *Newsweek* had tagged the "fastest gun," was now fair game.[158] One of the first pieces to make Goldwater's handlers blanch was an August interview with Stewart Alsop of the *Saturday Evening Post*. Here Goldwater admitted, "You know, I haven't got a really first-class brain." Without prompting, he volunteered, "You know, I think we ought to sell TVA (Tennessee Valley Authority)." Alsop couldn't believe his ears: "You really do?" "Yes, yes, I do," confirmed the Arizonan.[159] A Tennessee Goldwaterite was stunned: "TVA ranks behind God, mother and country down here, and Barry knows that damned well; yet he still goes around shooting from the hip."[160] Wrote Tom Wicker about the senator's "habit of oversimplification": "It is as though a child were speaking on the problems of the times, with a child's directness and lack of complexity."[161] Walter Lippmann weighed in with similar hyperbole, dismissing Goldwater's philosophy as "radically opposed to the central traditions of the Republican Party and . . . wholly alien to the moderate and conservative character of the American party system."[162] In the November 1 issue, the editor of *Life* magazine was direct, "'Guts without depth' and 'a man of one-sentence solutions' are the epithets of his critics. The time has come for him to rebut them if he can."[163] Probing for errors, reporters dogged Goldwater to state and restate his positions on the John Birch Society, TVA, civil rights, and nuclear war, dissecting even the slightest of shifts to make news. John Kennedy voiced the conventional wisdom: "Barry won't last a month."[164]

Peter O'Donnell of the Goldwater Draft Committee responded immediately, meeting with Barry to caution him about his quips and extemporaneous remarks. Damage control, O'Donnell stressed, forced the conservatives on the defensive, pitted Goldwater's image, and inhibited the mobilization of supporters and funds. Part of Goldwater's problem was habit: "I don't devote an overabundance of time to my thoughts. I've been through the situation so often, so long, the answers just sort of pop out."[165] Also important were grammatical and syntactical lapses that left Goldwater exposed. First at a press conference in late October and then in an interview reprinted in the *Congressional Record*, Goldwater suggested: "I think we could probably return a third—maybe—half of our [European] forces if we gave the NATO command the right to use nuclear weapons—tactical weapons—when *they* [emphasis added] were attacked."[166] John Kennedy was quick to pounce, joking, "He has had a busy week, selling TVA and giving permission or suggesting that military commanders overseas be permitted to use nuclear weapons. . . . So, I thought it really would not be fair for me this week to reply to him."[167] If Kennedy's motivation was political, his interpretation was understandable. Barry was not receptive to the criticism of friends or foes. "If they want Goldwater they're going to have to take him the way I am. I'm not going to change my spots."[168]

John Kennedy and Barry Goldwater had already discussed the 1964 presidential race. Their mutual admiration outlined an issues-oriented, high-road strategy, with neither resorting to negative campaigning. They even talked of barnstorming the country together, appearing repeatedly in a debate format before the voters. This would be, Kennedy told Secretary of the Interior Stewart Udall, a "great campaign"[169] that offered Americans a "clear choice" between liberalism and conservatism.[170] Philosophical issues aside, Kennedy was eager to face Goldwater because he was sure of victory. "The trouble is," confided Kennedy to friend Ben Bradlee as early as May 1963, "if he's the nominee, people will start asking him questions, and he's so damn quick on the trigger that he will answer them. And when he does, it will be all over."[171] Kennedy was convinced that a decisive win in 1964 would provide the mandate that had eluded him in 1960 and halt the spread of the American right. While confident, the president was cautious. The White House staff had begun to file Barry's legislative votes and public statements. In the fall John Kennedy scheduled political trips to the Pacific coast, Rocky Mountain states, and Texas to mend fences in preparation for the coming campaign.[172]

The shots in Dallas that snuffed out John Kennedy's life also destroyed any chance Barry Goldwater had of being president of the United States. Goldwater heard the news in Chicago while accompanying the coffin of his wife's mother to Muncie, Indiana, for burial.[173] He told reporters, "The President's death is a profound loss to the nation and free world. He and I were personal friends. It is also a great loss to me."[174] Goldwater was among the mourners at Kennedy's funeral. In his grief, Goldwater canceled forthcoming television appearances and halted the work of Kitchel and White.

The Phoenix City Council, from left, Hohen Foster, Frank Murphy, Margaret Kober, Nicholas Udall, Barry Goldwater, Harry Rosenzweig, Charles Walters, 1949. (Arizona Historical Foundation)

Campaigning for the U.S. Senate in 1952 with General Dwight Eisenhower and
Governor Howard Pyle. (Arizona Historical Foundation)

In the cockpit of an Air Force fighter. Photographs like this one frequently appeared in newspaper and magazine articles about Goldwater. (Arizona Historical Foundation)

Goldwater on the Senate Rackets Committee in 1957. Seated at the table are John Kennedy at bottom right, Robert Kennedy at center right, and Goldwater at top right. (Arizona Historical Foundation)

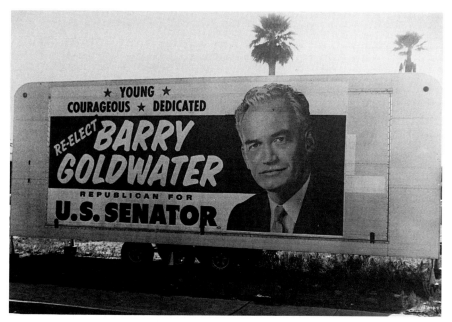

Scene from the 1958 Senate reelection campaign.
(Arizona Historical Foundation)

Stalin handbill smear from the 1958 campaign.
(Courtesy of William Saufley)

Goldwater with Rogers C. B. Morton at the podium of the 1960 Republican convention. (Arizona Historical Foundation)

Arizona Representative John Rhodes, Vice President Richard Nixon, and
Goldwater in the late 1950s. The same three men would meet again in August
1974, just before Nixon resigned the presidency.

With Nixon on the campaign trail in 1960. From left: Peggy Goldwater, Barry
Goldwater, unidentified, Pat Nixon, unidentified, Richard Nixon.
(Arizona Historical Foundation)

The mix of signs was Goldwater's usual view during the 1964 campaign.
(Arizona Historical Foundation)

Goldwater postcard urging Arizonans to vote on election day. Billboards and TV ads with Goldwater pictured against the Grand Canyon and Monument Valley evoked the western hero but prompted opponents to call him the Marlboro Man. (Author's collection)

At the podium of the 1972 Republican convention with conservative heir-
apparent Ronald Reagan standing by. (Arizona Historical Foundation)

Goldwater at the close of his fifth Senate term, in the mid-1980s.
(Courtesy of Joanne Goldwater)

In his seventies, Goldwater was still at the controls of an airplane.
(Courtesy of Joanne Goldwater)

Goldwater in the 1980s. (Courtesy of Joanne Goldwater)

Goldwater's skill as a photographer is evident in this self-portrait, probably from the 1930s. (Courtesy of William Saufley)

Particularly onerous for Goldwater at the time was the hate mail he received, accusing him of playing a role in the president's death. Seemingly, Goldwater's repeated criticism of the New Frontier had provoked a right-wing extremist to act. This sentiment was not confined to Barry's enemies, and even aide Dean Burch feared that Kennedy's assassin might have been "some nut with a Goldwater sticker on his forehead."[175] In early December Goldwater decided to reevaluate the campaign. He called Burch: "You know, I think this blows the whole deal. It's just not the same."[176] Soon after, "I told Kitchel to pass the word. I would not run."[177]

His supporters could not let that decision stand. On December 12, Norris Cotton, Carl Curtis, Denison Kitchel, Dean Burch, William Knowland, John Rhodes, William Baroody, speech writer Karl Hess, and political analyst Jay Hall met with Barry in his Washington apartment to discuss the race.[178] Initially, Goldwater resisted their urging to stay in the race and ticked off his reasons for bowing out. With Kennedy dead, the strategy that had animated the campaign meant nothing politically or personally. Voters, numb and craving respite and the familiar, would never reject Kennedy's successor after so brief a time in office. Besides, Goldwater held Lyndon Baines Johnson in contempt. Johnson was "treacherous," a "hypocrite," a man "who never cleaned that crap off his boots."[179] Goldwater had no desire to enter into a campaign against such an opponent.[180]

The Goldwaterites, however, were insistent. With Norris Cotton in the lead, they argued that the assassination had not changed the conservative indictment of the New Frontier as collectivism at home and retreat abroad. The conservative movement could not be halted in mid-stride, and Goldwater owed a debt to his supporters. Most important, Cotton appealed to Goldwater's sense of patriotism. "America," contended the New Hampshire senator, "was getting soft. It needed a new commander."[181] He likened Barry to France's General Charles De Gaulle—two men who heard their nation's call and sacrificed in its service. Having made their case, the men left without knowing if they had prevailed. As Barry sat with Kitchel nursing a bourbon and water in the darkening apartment, his decision began to firm. He asked his friend for advice. "Barry, I don't think you can back down."[182] Thinking only briefly of Peggy's opposition, Barry replied, "Alright, God damn it, I'll go."[183]

Ambition, hard work, and luck had made Barry Goldwater the front runner for the Republican nomination for president of the United States. But now that he claimed the lead, he did not want it. The heat from the media had drained him of his easygoing manner and the assassination of President Kennedy of his will to win. Defensive, humorless, and deprived of his freedom of action, Barry Goldwater was more a hostage than a political hopeful. Said Clif White: "He went through the motions of campaigning for the nomination and election, but his heart was never in it."[184] John Tower agreed: "He ran like a man who didn't expect to win and that had an awful psychological drag on the campaign."[185] Barry sensed, clearly and early on, a martyrdom in an impossible cause. With martyrdom came zealotry in defense of his beliefs and moderation in pursuit of compromise and consensus. If Goldwater could not right the country, he was grimly determined to right his party.

8

The Woodstock of American Conservatism

This is not a stopgap election in 1964. This is not just one for the record books. This is one for the history books. We stand at the latter end of the second century of the American experience, the American Revolution.

—BARRY GOLDWATER

No historical montage of the 1960s is complete without images of the August 1969 Woodstock music festival. During its three days, nearly half-a-million "flower children"—enveloped in music, love, and marijuana—descended in peace on Max Yasgur's six-hundred-acre farm in New York. For those who participated, actively or vicariously, Woodstock was the crucible for birthing a better world. Those who go nostalgia tripping into the sixties, however, rarely make tracks for the Woodstock of the right—the primary campaign of Barry Goldwater that culminated in the four-day Republican convention in San Francisco. Unlike Woodstock's new world, the world birthed by the Goldwater convention was not stillborn. In 1964 conservatives emerged from their wilderness of isolation to see a political promised land. They developed a sense of personal efficacy and collective solidarity. They learned new skills and saw their expectations rise. This was only a beginning, for the taste of power did not slake their thirst. The karma of the convention may have differed from that of Woodstock, but it would prove more powerful.

On January 3, 1964, just two days after his fifty-fifth birthday, Barry Goldwater declared his intention to seek the Republican nomination for president. He summoned reporters to his Scottsdale, Arizona, home and read a prepared statement pledging "an engagement of principles," not personalities. He would campaign for limited government and "individual responsibility against regimentation" that threatened to make "us, our lives, our property, our hopes and even our prayers . . . just cogs in a vast government machine." He was not, as he had said so many times before, "a 'me-too' Republican," and he promised, "I will not change my beliefs to win votes. I will offer a choice, not an echo."[1] The press conference also served to introduce the Goldwater campaign team, quickly dubbed the Arizona mafia by reporters. Goldwater appointed Denison Kitchel as general director, Dean Burch as Kitchel's assistant, and Richard Kleindienst as director of field operations. No one from the draft committee was assigned a place in the organization, and Kitchel and Goldwater privately suggested to Clif White that his group be dissolved.[2]

In the follow-up question session Goldwater told reporters that he planned to enter primaries in New Hampshire, Illinois, Oregon, and California. Victories in these contests would prove Goldwater's popularity with the rank and file, build momentum, and drive the work of his supporters in nonprimary states. Still, he had agreed only reluctantly to take the primary path. Goldwater was more comfortable with an "insider" strategy that harvested delegates in state and district conventions and party committees. The primaries posed high risks while offering only a minority of the convention's delegates. As pollster Louis Harris noted, "Many people . . . don't quite understand that the bloodiest wars in politics are the primaries. These are played for keeps. People chop each other up and blood flows and the scars are made forever."[3] Goldwater, however, had no choice. Nelson Rockefeller's financial resources, strength as a campaigner, and weakness outside his home base called for an appeal to the "people" over the "politicians." Primary wins might make his candidacy viable, and Goldwater had to join the fray to deflect him.[4]

Barry Goldwater had stumbled badly off the blocks. Personal insecurities prescribed loyalty as the chief criterion for appointment to his campaign team. Even the goal of conservative hegemony did not overcome his inadequacies and fear of betrayal. Estranged from Steve Shadegg, Goldwater turned to Denison Kitchel, who had neither the skill nor the temperament to direct a national campaign. John Tower dismissed him as a "neophyte" with "no real sensitivity for politics."[5] Goldwater's congressional aide Dean Burch had participated only in the senator's reelection campaign and in Paul Fannin's successful run for the governorship in 1958. An observer described Richard Kleindienst as a "Western cowboy roughneck: tactless, boisterous and professionally profane in two languages (English and Navajo)."[6] Like Kitchel and Burch, Richard Kleindienst's knowledge of politics was restricted to Arizona. Goldwater had made his decisions without respect to expertise and in haste. When Barry contacted him about the director of operations position only two hours before the announcement, Dick Kleindienst asked, "What the hell's that?"[7] Goldwater explained bluntly to Kleindienst: "Listen, and get this straight. I'm not going to turn my life over to people I don't know and trust if I'm going to go through with this."[8] In defense, Goldwater later reflected, "We would have lost even if Abraham Lincoln had come back and campaigned with us."[9]

Two days later, on January 5, Kitchel, Burch, and Kleindienst met with Clif White and members of the draft group in Washington, D.C. Kitchel, coldly, gave White a choice—either serve as Kleindienst's assistant or quit the campaign. Aware that he was clearly out of his league, Kleindienst interrupted and offered to work with White like "partners in a law firm."[10] White would be the "coordinator of field operations," subordinate on the organizational chart but equal in responsibility. Hiding his hurt, White accepted the demotion immediately. Kleindienst's instinctive gesture did much to secure the nomination for Barry Goldwater. Clif White's political acumen was unmatched in the Goldwater camp. He alone had an intimate knowledge of the politics of delegate-selection and the personalities of grassroots activists. Although the primaries grabbed the most attention and more would be added to Goldwater's calendar, it was Clif White's steady pick-up of delegates that created the conservative power base. Despite all his work, White never entered Goldwater's inner circle.[11]

In addition to the Arizona mafia and Clif White, three other men were important to the Goldwater campaign. Ed McCabe, a former Eisenhower aide and a seasoned politician, served as director of research. Goldwater selected Karl Hess, a *Newsweek* editor with libertarian sentiments, to be his chief speech writer. William Baroody of the American Enterprise Institute, as resident ideologue and minister without portfolio, positioned himself as head of Goldwater's brain trust. Baroody's personality, however, hamstrung his efforts and hurt the campaign. Kitchel characterized him as "a real Machiavellian type, a schemer, [who] loved power plays." Driven by a feeling of "possessiveness," Baroody isolated Goldwater and alienated such conservatives as Bill Buckley, Bill Rusher, and Brent Bozell.[12] Baroody drew the curtains so tightly that Buckley was relegated to advising Barry Goldwater through the pages of *National Review*. Like the Arizonans, McCabe, Hess, and Baroody had the credentials to enter the inner circle. Said Goldwater, "They were part of the team for one reason: I trusted them."[13]

Goldwater began his campaign in New Hampshire on January 7, already on the defensive. Two days before he had made a poor showing on NBC's "Meet the Press," his appearance marred by his factual errors and seemingly impulsive answers. He threatened, if elected, to make diplomatic recognition of the Soviet Union a bargaining chip to secure concessions, initiate a blockade of Cuba to force Soviet withdrawal, and scrap the Nuclear Test Ban Treaty "if it appeared to our advantage to test in the atmosphere." He added unnecessarily, "There are risks in all of these things."[14] Supporters found his answers candid and refreshing. Others shared the concerns of the *Washington Evening Star* about Goldwater's "information gap" and an "inattention to detail and an impreciseness of utterance that could be troublesome."[15]

The flak was still flying when Goldwater touched off another controversy. At his first New Hampshire press conference he suggested "one change" in Social Security—that it be made "voluntary . . . if a person can provide better for himself, let him do it."[16] Social Security, like nuclear weapons, was an emotional issue, and Goldwater appeared to raise it indifferently and without laying a foundation for discussion. Retired people were particularly sensitive to any hint of tampering with their entitlements, and New Hampshire had the fourth highest proportion of men and women over sixty-five years of age of any state in the union. The *Concord Monitor*'s distorted headline—"GOLDWATER SETS GOALS: END SOCIAL SECURITY, HIT CASTRO"—only intensified their fears.[17] That same day, news wires reported that the senator favored, as he had stated before, authorizing the NATO supreme commander's use of tactical nuclear weapons "without referral to the White House."[18] In this shorthand, off-the-cuff restatement of his position, Goldwater again mistakenly assumed a level of knowledge clearly beyond the average voter. In Portsmouth, New Hampshire, two days later, Goldwater said: "I don't feel safe at all about our missiles. I wish the Defense Department would tell the American people how undependable the missiles in our silos actually are. I can't tell you—it's classified." Concluded Barry in understatement, "I'll probably catch hell for this."[19] Voters could not but question Barry's judgment in broaching an important topic carelessly and with little effort to suggest solution through serious dialogue. The initial trip to New Hampshire had certainly been memorable, and Goldwater left a lasting first impression in voters' minds. Barry seemed oblivious to his impact. "If we can just keep this up, I think we have it made."[20]

But Goldwater continued to stumble. On January 16 he made his first major speech of the campaign before the Economic Club of New York. Much of the address was a spirited defense of conservative economic principles and an attack on federal spending, "the Santa Claus of the free lunch, the government hand-out, the Santa Claus of something-for-nothing and something-for-everyone." These comments, however, were lost in the uproar that greeted Goldwater's assertion about the causes of poverty: "We are told that many people lack skills and cannot find jobs because they do not have an education. That's like saying that people have big feet because they wear big shoes. The fact is that most people who have no skill, have no education for the same reason—low intelligence or low ambition."[21]

The confidence that marked the Goldwater campaign in the fall had disappeared by winter. Despite the firm support of New Hampshire Senator Norris Cotton and William Loeb, the editor and publisher of the powerful Manchester *Union-Leader*, Goldwater had squandered his lead in the polls. This decline was caused in part by the eclipse of the draft committee by the

Arizona mafia. Kitchel and Kleindienst were unprepared for New Hampshire, printing too little campaign literature and scheduling inadequate radio and television time. They attempted to compensate by overbooking their candidate, who made as many as nineteen appearances in eight or nine towns during sixteen- and eighteen-hour days. Their minimal advance work was readily apparent. "We flew up and down the state in random leaps that made no sense," wrote Goldwater. "I often spoke to as few as a dozen people. Just about everything we did was extemporaneous."[22] That included speechmaking. Rather than deliver a "formula" talk, Goldwater's handlers allowed him to speak at will. Kitchel recalled: "It was a hand-to-mouth operation; Barry ad libbed his way through that campaign."[23] Adding to these problems, Goldwater was on crutches, recovering from surgery that removed a bone spur from his right heel. "I remember every footstep of that campaign."[24] In pain, unaccustomed to the cold New Hampshire winter, overexposed, and exhausted, Barry was unsmiling and disinterested, without emotion or energy. "I'm no baby-kissing, handshaking, blintz-eating candidate," Goldwater maintained, and no one disagreed.[25]

He became easy prey. Many reporters followed the lead of Walter Mears of the Associated Press: "All we had to do was keep hitting him with questions and then wait until he slipped and we had our headlines."[26] Yet the press did not feast gleefully. One voiced the dilemma: "How could we be fair to Goldwater—by quoting what he said or by explaining what he thought? To quote him directly was manifestly unfair, but if he insisted on speaking thus in public, how could one resist quoting him?"[27] Even the protective *National Review* was dismayed by Goldwater, citing "weaknesses in the presentation of ideas and policy."[28] Perhaps this is what led Bill Buckley to counter with "Answers for Conservatives," a primer of Goldwaterisms to reassure conservative troops about their leader's positions. Goldwater, never thick-skinned, became surly with reporters, and they noted every incident. The press-friendly environment of Arizona had become a distant memory.[29]

It was more than poor organization, physical pain, and media harpies that made trouble for Goldwater. Barry could be his own worst enemy. After John Kennedy's assassination and in confrontation with a desperate Nelson Rockefeller in New Hampshire, Goldwater became less cautious, less willing to yield to his advisers. His temperament and style, which had played so well when he was a senator, betrayed him. Voters reassessed his bluntness and tough talk and condemned it as shoot-from-the-hip recklessness. "Why, he would have us in a war in a minute," feared a Manchester housewife.[30] Nor were Americans prepared for the blunt, direct discussion that Goldwater believed his mission demanded. Beyond style and message, however, was another problem. Clouding his judgment and escalating the commitment to confrontation was Barry's tendency to personalize issues and controversies. The matter of the NATO commander's control over tactical nuclear weapons is the critical case in point. As Barry Goldwater knew, the NATO commander, since the Eisenhower administration, was authorized, in time of communication breakdown, to deploy and use tactical nuclear weapons to meet a Soviet attack against Western Europe. Although the matter was an operating policy and a nonissue, Goldwater felt compelled to raise it repeatedly and open himself to the charge of being "trigger-happy." What spurred Goldwater beyond discretion was the Johnson administration's political decision not to join the debate and even to deny standard procedure. The lie infuriated Goldwater, who focused his anger against Secretary of Defense Robert McNamara, a man he had on several occasions praised.[31] When asked about his nuclear refrain, Goldwater explained: "Oh, shit! I brought it up because of McNamara. . . . McNamara made some crack about some speech that I had made that had reference to nuclear weapons. His remarks indicated that . . . the only person in the world that could use nuclear weapons, or order them, was the President. And that's when I made the statement [about] . . . the commander of NATO. . . . That was McNamara's [fault], he started it."[32] The secretary compounded his sins when he described Goldwater's allegation that American missiles were undependable as "completely misleading, politically irresponsible, and damaging to the national security."[33] McNamara took the offensive, making Goldwater the liar and even questioning his patriotism. Much less was necessary to ignite a vendetta with Barry Goldwater.[34]

Political opponents were quick to exploit every Goldwater gaffe, real and imagined. Surveying polls results that showed New Hampshire voters opposed to Goldwater's stands on Social Security, nuclear issues, and the United Nations, Nelson Rockefeller portrayed himself as the mainstream candidate and the Arizonan as dangerous and radical. Rockefeller asked in Concord: "How can there be security when he wants to take the United States out of the United Nations? How can there be sanity when he wants to give area *commanders* [emphasis added] the authority to make decisions on the use of nuclear weapons?"[35] Rockefeller, needing a win to revive his candidacy, wheeled his campaign machine into line and barnstormed New Hampshire for weeks in a whirlwind of speech-making, back-slapping, and flesh-pressing. He charmed voters with his folksy approach and good humor, even conversing in French to woo French Canadian voters, who constituted 18 percent of the state's population. Yet he could not counter suspicions concerning New York liberals and Rockefeller money. Especially damaging was the divorce and remarriage issue, which the *Union-Leader* framed as a question, asking whether voters wanted a "wife-swapper in the White House."[36]

Rockefeller, however, was never in contention. In the lead was Henry Cabot Lodge, Richard Nixon's running mate in 1960 and then the American ambassador to South Vietnam—a man whose name was not even on the ballot. His supporters, attuned to voters' dissatisfaction with the alternatives, organized a write-in campaign that played to Lodge's New England roots and presence on the front line against the communist menace. Rockefeller, convinced that Lodge cut into his base, telephoned Saigon and asked the ambassador to come home or renounce the effort. Lodge refused to do either, and on election day in March he won 33,000 votes and a first-place finish. Barry trailed with 20,700 votes (23 percent) and Rockefeller with 19,500. Rockefeller had edged noncandidate Richard Nixon by fewer than 4,000 ballots.[37]

The political ground shifted in the wake of the election. New Hampshire spawned a Lodge boomlet, and the April Gallup poll showed the ambassador winning the approval of 42 percent of the Republican rank and file. His supporters looked to the Oregon primary in May to prove their candidate's viability as they foraged outside of New England to build an instant Lodge for President movement. Nelson Rockefeller also believed that Oregon would be decisive, and he departed for the West Coast the day after the New Hampshire primary. His adamant refusal to reconsider the race forestalled other moderate or liberal Republicans from mounting a challenge. Behind Lodge, Richard Nixon was the biggest winner in New Hampshire. If the convention deadlocked, he was available as the compromise candidate.[38]

The Goldwater camp's reassessment was especially thorough, as its candidate had lost the most ground. Blaming the media and a grueling campaign schedule, Goldwater's advisers pared back the number of press conferences and personal appearances. The new campaign format mandated tighter control to reduce Barry's tendency, especially when tired, to blurt comments without elaboration. He would relax his pace, speak from prepared texts, and make better use of radio and television. Barry was amenable to these suggestions, realizing that he had no lock on the nomination. Because he had never been beaten before, New Hampshire embarrassed him. The defeat "got his dander up," said Clif White. "Now he decided that he wanted to win."[39] Dick Kleindienst also noticed a change in his candidate. "What happened was, I think, unique. New Hampshire was like a catalytic agent; it heightened determination . . . brought things down to a realistic basis . . . to where it should have been all along."[40] Even more important, the defeat actually enhanced Goldwater's chances, for it brought about the redemption of Clif White. Appointed codirector of field operations, White was now Kleindienst's equal. While Kleindienst took responsibility for primary contests in fourteen states, they shared tasks in the Illinois and California contests, and White directed the effort in nonprimary states.[41]

Goldwater's tactical shift was temporarily effective. He did not fumble into the headlines, and descriptions of him as reckless and radical disappeared from news copy. He preached unity to fellow Republicans and couched his proposals more moderately. Thus, at a Madison Square Garden rally in New York City, he advocated "Immediate and serious study . . . to determine every area in which the administration of Federal programs, to any degree, can be turned over to the states or local government, without injury to the program."[42] He reiterated his support for a "sound" Social Security system: "I want to see it strengthened."[43] Broaching issues for the fall campaign against the Democrats, Goldwater advocated tougher policies against the communists in South Vietnam. Specifically, he proposed interdicting the supply lines that funneled guns and other materiel into the south. Still, he was careful not to arouse concern. Shutting down these routes did not require the bombing of the Vietnamese or their cities. "It could mean messing up some roads, hitting some depots, and stopping some shipping."[44] Morality in government was another Goldwater agenda item, and he targeted for attack the influence peddling of Bobby Baker, a protégé of Lyndon Johnson's. Under the Democrats, Goldwater charged, "call girls, Bobby Baker, and motels" had become the watchwords of Washington power brokers.[45] In the same vein, he wondered aloud how Lyndon Johnson had been able to amass a personal fortune during his tenure as a public servant. The changed context of the campaign also facilitated Goldwater's mid-course corrections. The Lodge effort distracted reporters, and their anticipation of the next head-to-head primary in May gave Barry breathing room during the "dead time" of March and April. Still uncertain was Goldwater's ability to internalize these modifications and thus alter voters' perceptions.[46]

The wisdom of Clif White's strategy to pursue the nomination through the precinct, county, district, and state delegate-selection process became evident even before the returns were in from New Hampshire. In late February, Oklahoma named twenty-two Goldwater delegates, and North Carolina pledged twenty-five of its twenty-six delegates to the Arizonan. The Goldwater campaign also picked up support in Tennessee and Kansas. Goldwater's delegate count continued to grow in March, April, and May. Republicans in South Carolina, Louisiana, Georgia, and Mississippi went on record for Goldwater. At the convention, Barry would hold the votes of 271 of the 278 southern delegates, almost a third of his first-ballot strength. Additional support came from the Midwest and Rocky Mountain states. Clif White even found Goldwater delegates in Maine, Massachusetts, Vermont, and Pennsylvania. Primary wins in Illinois on April 14, Indiana on May 5, and

Nebraska on May 12 padded the lead.[47] By mid-May, 555 delegates were firm or leaning toward the Arizona senator. He needed only one hundred more delegates to secure the nomination. Future selections in Alabama, Colorado, Montana, New Mexico, Utah, and Washington promised ninety additional first-ballot votes for Barry. In contrast, Pennsylvania's favorite son, Governor William Scranton, figured his support at sixty-three delegates; and Ambassador Lodge claimed forty-three. The Goldwater bandwagon, quietly and with only token opposition, had regained its momentum. National newsmagazines, having counted the conservative out after New Hampshire, now wondered, "Can Barry Goldwater be stopped?"[48]

In light of this advance and the obvious risks, Goldwater's advisers decided to sidestep the May 15 Oregon primary. Rockefeller, with nothing to lose, poured his energy and nearly half a million dollars into the contest. His efforts paid off, and Oregon Republicans rewarded the only candidate "who cared enough to come" with a fourteen thousand–vote victory over second-place finisher Henry Cabot Lodge (33 percent to 27 percent). Goldwater ignored the results and the size of the moderate-liberal majority but certainly was disappointed with his 17 percent share. Oregon derailed Lodge, once more making Rockefeller the moderates' only hope. It also convinced Rockefeller that he had finally downed his "character" problem. The New York governor believed that his campaign had hit its stride, and he predicted victory in California on June 2. The Oregon results cheered Richard Nixon. If Rockefeller could beat Goldwater in California, convention stalemate was a real possibility. Barry Goldwater, although building a commanding delegate lead, also looked to California for a showdown. This was an opportunity to convince the skeptics of his appeal, knock Rockefeller out of the race, and clinch the nomination.[49]

The Rockefeller strategy in California was simple. Said his public relations expert Stuart Spencer, "We had to destroy Barry Goldwater as a member of the human race."[50] That meant turning up the volume on the accusations that Nelson Rockefeller had tested in New Hampshire. Goldwater, he charged, was trigger-happy and likely to embroil the United States in nuclear war. "WHO DO YOU WANT IN THE ROOM WITH THE H-BOMB BUTTON?" asked a Rockefeller campaign flier.[51] Goldwater was the enemy of the elderly and was bent on taking Social Security checks away from the needy. Goldwater will "turn back the clock of social progress," Rockefeller declared.[52] Goldwater was a dangerous extremist who had the backing of the John Birch Society and Ku Klux Klan. By word, deed, and the company he kept, argued Rockefeller, Goldwater had turned his back on the Republican mainstream. Reaching for every voter, he attacked Goldwater for "hijacking" California's Colorado River water for the benefit of Arizona.[53] At the same time, Rockefeller claimed to be as hawkish on Vietnam as Goldwater. He advocated a policy of "hot pursuit" by the South Vietnamese against Viet Cong sanctuaries in Laos and North Vietnam.[54] Still, Rockefeller's offensive did not disguise his flaws. He remained vulnerable because of his divorce and remarriage. His negative campaign lacked substance, offering moderates and liberals little more than anti-Goldwater planks. On the hustings he shunned specifics and loaded his speeches with banal generalities, a style reporters derisively labeled as BOMFOG after Rockefeller's favorite phrase: "Brotherhood of Man, Fatherhood of God."[55]

Although he was given to "foggy bombast" and headed an operation that was paper-thin and top-heavy, the New York governor had a real chance to win in California.[56] Goldwater's negative image was a partial explanation. Money was more important. Rockefeller hired the premier public relations firm Spencer-Roberts and put more than $2 million at its disposal. "These boys," wrote commentators Rowland Evans and Robert Novak, "are running a dream campaign with all the money they need."[57] Rockefeller's funds bought an organization of hired "volunteers" who engineered a direct-mail campaign and staffed "telephone mills" to reach every registered Republican. Billboards were plastered and radio and television saturated with Rockefeller commercials. This effort and the win in Oregon had effect. Five days after the Oregon primary, the Field Poll showed Rockefeller with a 46 percent to 33 percent lead over Goldwater. Just weeks before, Goldwater had held the advantage, 43 percent to 27 percent.[58]

Barry countered Rockefeller with a grassroots army of activists recruited through Young Republicans, Young Americans for Freedom, and John Birch Society channels. Particularly strong in Los Angeles and Orange Counties, these conservatives worked the precincts, seeking out every potential Goldwater voter in their neighborhoods. In one massive drive on May 23, eight thousand men and women canvassed six hundred thousand homes door-to-door, taking stock of the Arizonan's support and the needs of loyalists. Organizers would be ready on election day, tending children, making telephone calls, and carpooling every Goldwaterite to the polls. California conservatives, however, did more than master the election process and deliver Goldwater votes. The campaign offered them the opportunity and inspiration to take control of the Republican machinery and become the party's new cadre. The difficult and tedious labor of right-wing organizers, dating back to the 1950s, had begun to bear political fruit.[59]

While the grassroots stirred, Goldwater toured the state, speaking in support of the United Nations, Social Security, and "strong, affirmative action" in Vietnam.[60] Repeatedly, he refused to disavow Birchers' backing and "welcome[d] their votes."[61] Goldwater, following his aides' advice, confined his appearances to large rallies and limited his access to the press. Hollywood lent Barry a hand, and Ronald Reagan, John Wayne, Robert Stack, Rock Hudson, and Raymond Massey charged the campaign with star power. With the tide of financial contributions running high, Goldwater matched Rockefeller's spending and relied heavily on television and radio to present his message and fire the faithful. Sensing the closeness of the race, Goldwater organizers even asked out-of-state supporters to check "mailing lists for relatives, school chums, business associates, old army buddies and Christmas card lists for persons you know that are living in California. Sit down and write each a personal note requesting that they . . . vote for the Senator."[62] The growing intensity of the campaign heightened interest and inflamed passions. Both Goldwater and Rockefeller campaign headquarters received bomb threats, and security was tightened around the candidates. Hecklers became more aggressive and taunted the candidates with placards reading, "Goldwater: The Fascist Gun in the West" and "Do you want a leader, or a lover in the White House?"[63]

Abruptly, the Goldwater campaign was forced from mobilization to damage control. On May 24 Barry appeared on ABC's "Issues and Answers" and, in response to Howard K. Smith's question about interdiction of communist supply lines in Vietnam, offered: "There have been several suggestions made. I don't think we would use any of them. But defoliation of the forests by low-yield atomic weapons could well be done. When you remove the foliage, you remove the cover." Smith followed up: "Would you have to take action within Red China, on the Red Chinese side of the border?" Goldwater did not hesitate: "You might have to, but we are confronted with that decision. Either that, or we have a war dragged out and dragged out. A defensive war is never won. . . . If we decide to go into this war in a full-scale way, certainly we would have to make the decision on strategic supplies for the enemy at the same time."[64]

Reporters rushed the story into print. Both United Press International and Associated Press distorted Goldwater's remarks as a call to use atomic weapons in Southeast Asia. The *San Francisco Examiner* headlined: "Goldwater's plan to use Viet A-Bomb."[65] The article in the *Los Angeles Times* was more sedate: "A-arms could aid Viet fight, Goldwater says."[66] Rightfully, Goldwater cried foul and contended that he had been "misinterpreted."[67] "I outlined the low-yield defoliation idea which has been talked of and talked of and talked of by the highest levels in the Pentagon. This is nothing new and I made it perfectly clear, I thought, that this was not a suggestion of mine."[68] Yet even in explaining his stand he could stumble. At a press conference in the offices of the *San Diego Union,* he announced without prompting: "If I had my choice, I would go into South China. It would be fairly easy. You have one railroad. You have a number of bridges. You would knock out the railroad; if that did not convince them, you would knock out the roads." Despite the obvious news value of these remarks, reporters smothered them, aware of Goldwater's tendency to speak off the cuff. Rather than exploit Barry, they brought him "back to zero," repeatedly questioning him to "clarify his statements" until "we understand what he means. This is sometimes hard to figure out."[69]

Was Goldwater seeking to awaken Americans to the danger before them in Vietnam? Was he attempting to demonstrate his military expertise and thus a fitness for the presidency? Had old habits simply resurfaced? Whatever the reasons, he had again misfired and fueled concern about his recklessness and irresponsibility. But it was more than what he said or his seemingly uncontrollable compulsion to prick the boil of America's nuclear anxieties that led to controversy. Also causing apprehension in voters' minds was Goldwater's "barracks bull-session" manner about confrontation with China and about atomic weapons, as if he were game-playing war scenarios with fellow military men.[70] "You can't pin it down," said Jack Stewart over the telephone to his friend, former President Herbert Hoover, "but the feeling is that he might get us into war."[71] Goldwater legitimately decried his treatment by the press, yet his deepest wounds were self-inflicted.

As Goldwater attempted to douse the controversy over the "Issues and Answers" interview, another blaze engulfed his campaign. On May 25 the New York *Herald-Tribune* published and the *Los Angeles Times* reprinted an eleven-hundred-word statement written by Dwight Eisenhower that outlined the positions he expected the eventual Republican nominee to champion. Ike, doggedly refusing to endorse anyone, backed the candidate pledged to "responsible, forward-looking Republicanism," the United Nations, and the foreign aid program. He dismissed as unworthy of consideration those who were prone to "impulsiveness" in the conduct of foreign policy and in the use of nuclear weapons. In addition, Eisenhower specified that a "particular obligation to be vigorous in the furtherance of civil rights" was vital to a candidate's chances.[72] Ike's sentiments were no secret to his friends and aides, who had urged him to make public his private concerns. In Eisenhower's mind, Goldwater did not measure up, for he had opposed Modern Republicanism since its inception. Rockefeller, at the same time, was too self-serving and critical of the actions of the Eisenhower administration. What Ike wanted was a Rockefeller win in California that would stop Goldwater. With the two main contenders deadlocked, the convention might open to men Eisenhower preferred—like Dick Nixon or Bill Scranton. Eisenhower had for months prepared the ground for this scenario, making telephone calls and meeting with Nixon, Scranton, and supporters of Henry Cabot Lodge.[73]

Goldwater, clearly Ike's target, had received a strong rebuke. Lamely, he professed to fit Eisenhower's description of the perfect candidate and welcomed the reaffirmation "of those basic Republican principles upon which my candidacy is based."[74] He tried to laugh the incident away, appearing at a rally with a trick arrow sticking out of his back. More darkly, he absolved Eisenhower of responsibility and blamed instead "this mysterious clique in the East that nobody seems to know anything about . . . the nebulous mysterious wing of the party that I've never been able to figure out who they are."[75]

Rockefeller eagerly exploited the opening. He claimed Eisenhower's blessing and promised to continue his fight to uphold the tenets of Modern Republicanism. The effect of the statement was minimal, however, because the day before the primary Ike repudiated its implications. "You people," he snapped at reporters, "read Goldwater out of the party, I didn't."[76] Eisenhower retreated when confronted, unwilling to incur conservative rage as the "hatchetman" of an anti-Goldwater movement. He was reluctant, as well, to risk embarrassment and his prestige in a losing cause. He figured the odds realistically: "You can't canter without a horse."[77] Unless a contender incited a groundswell of support, Eisenhower would not commit. But in light of Goldwater's lead, how could a candidate reach viability without Ike's nod?

In a parallel ploy, Rockefeller presented himself as the candidate of the Republican mainstream and in campaign literature implied the backing of moderates Nixon, Scranton, and Romney. The scheme backfired when all three immediately denied Rockefeller and mollified Barry by disavowing any role in a stop-Goldwater effort. "It's understandable," remarked a bitter Rockefeller. "They're all available and hoping for lightning to strike."[78] This was unfair to Scranton and Romney; the former did not yearn for the presidency, and the latter's personal dislike of Rockefeller kept him at arm's length. The New York governor did peg Nixon correctly. Nixon's ambitions were barely concealed, and he even scheduled a meeting with advisers on May 30 to review his political options. Despite these outcomes, the Louis Harris Poll released on May 29, the last Friday of the campaign, encouraged Rockefeller. It showed Goldwater closing in, but the New York governor remained the front runner, 49 percent to 40 percent.[79]

There were early warnings that this lead was not firm. Rockefeller's divorce and remarriage became an issue again on May 27, when the board of trustees of the Jesuit-run Loyola University in Los Angeles withdrew an invitation to Rockefeller to speak on campus. The following day, sixteen Protestant ministers from Southern California congregations issued a joint statement, calling on Rockefeller to quit the race because he had "struck a serious blow against the Christian concept of marriage."[80] The worst was yet to come. On May 30, just seventy-two hours before the polls opened, Happy Rockefeller gave birth to Nelson Jr. The proud father interrupted his campaign and flew back to New York to be with his family. The Goldwater campaign reacted quickly and bumped standard themes to fill the air waves and newspapers with copy asking: "Why are women for Goldwater? Because he is a responsible family man . . . a fine example of . . . loyalty for the White House."[81] In another ad, a child asked: "Mother, . . . *why* are *we* for Barry Goldwater?" She replied, "Because: Children need the inspiration of example. If all children are to grow up respecting truth, morality, courage, and justice, we must show them that we too respect these principles."[82] Decorating the prose were large pictures of Barry surrounded by Peggy and the extended Goldwater clan of children and grandchildren. Moral concerns weighed heavily on Republicans, and undecided voters and those leaning to Rockefeller switched to Goldwater. The Harris Poll, conducted over the weekend and released on June 1, showed a surge for the conservative; he trailed the New York governor only slightly, 40 percent to 42 percent.[83]

On election day Goldwater volunteers made sure that every one of their charges went to the polls. It was critical that they did. The Arizona senator maintained a narrow lead of 58,231 votes to capture 51.4 percent of the more than 2 million ballots cast. Nelson Rockefeller carried northern California by over 100,000 votes, but he stumbled in the south, where a heavy conservative turnout in Orange and Los Angeles Counties brought victory to Goldwater. Under the rules of California's winner-take-all primary, the state's eighty-six-member delegation would be pure Goldwater. He now had more than enough support to claim the Rep·blican nomination for president on the first ballot. Nelson Rockefeller was stoic: "Sometimes with a defeat there's a gain—there are things you don't have to worry about any more, like do you have to take the country into war over Vietnam."[84] Dejectedly, Dwight Eisenhower confided to a friend, "We have lost a major battle and [it] may be a decisive one. I don't see how with this man we can carry more than ¼ the states."[85]

In triumph and looking ahead to the fall campaign, Barry Goldwater was magnanimous. He preached unity in his victory statement and invited "all Republicans to join our crusade so that this year the Republican party will offer a choice, not an echo, to the American people."[86] A few days after the California primary he sent Rockefeller supporter and New York Senator Jacob Javits a booklet explaining his positions on the issues. In the cover letter Goldwater assured Javits that his stand on world affairs "is the Eisenhower-Dulles foreign policy which I feel is the only one that will work." On states' rights, "I find myself in absolute agreement with General Eisenhower and I am certain the majority of the Republican Party as well." Goldwater concluded: "If you have any questions or need any clarification, I'd be very happy to provide it."[87] Goldwater aides also leaked to the press that moderate Bill Scranton was the leading choice for the vice presidential nod. Conservatives prepared, as well, to compromise on the party platform. Their "kill-em-with-kindness strategy"[88] led Pennsylvania's Senator Hugh Scott to joke that Goldwater's people were willing "to accept anything short of the *Communist Manifesto*."[89] Continued conservative flexibility, however, would depend on the behavior of the moderates and liberals.[90]

The Republican center and left refused to accept the California results or the growing Goldwater delegate count. Eisenhower's hidden hand orchestrated the discontent once more. On June 6, four days after the California primary, he invited Bill Scranton to his Gettysburg farm to discuss the political situation. Ike liked the Pennsylvania governor, who had served in the State Department during his administration and whose Republican family lineage could be traced to the party's founding in the 1850s. The men had met socially several times before, and Eisenhower was particularly fond of Scranton's wife, Mary. In behavior now ritualized, the former president pressed Scranton to declare his candidacy for the nomination. His "theory" was that the convention should have a variety of candidates "across the spectrum" from which to choose. He was impressed with Scranton's record as governor.[91] Besides, Goldwater's nomination would have a disastrous effect on the party's chances in November. As Scranton recalls: "He never said that he would support me and come out and declare himself, but he made it very clear that he wanted me to run."[92] The implied endorsement persuaded the governor to act. On June 7 he traveled to Cleveland for the Republican governors' conference while his aides hurriedly prepared a statement of candidacy to be delivered on television's "Face the Nation" that same day.[93]

Scranton found the Cleveland meeting rife with dissension over Goldwater's looming nomination.[94] Surely he was encouraged by the efforts of Rockefeller and Michigan Governor George Romney to mount a last-ditch resistance. As Scranton was about to leave for the television station, he returned a telephone call that Eisenhower had placed to him earlier that morning. Scranton was dumbfounded as Ike backed away from an endorsement, declaring his intention not to join any "cabal" to stop Goldwater. "My God," Scranton remembers thinking, "how am I going to run for president if it's 'yes, no, yes, no'?"[95] Goldwater's campaign manager, Denison Kitchel, was the prime mover behind the call. Having caught wind of the Eisenhower-Scranton rendezvous, Kitchel informed Goldwater supporter George Humphrey, Ike's secretary of the treasury. Humphrey had immediate access to Eisenhower, for the former president, also in Cleveland for the conference, was his houseguest. Eisenhower, convinced by Humphrey of his responsibility to remain neutral and above the fray, backed away from the Pennsylvania governor. Wondered *The New Republic* columnist TRB, "How in the world Ike ever put over D-Day really is a question."[96] Scranton pocketed his statement; there would be no surprises that Sunday on "Face the Nation." Demoralized, he fidgeted and responded indecisively to questions about the race. "I reverted to type because I'm a party man. It was the worst thing on television that I've ever done."[97]

The intensity of the anti-Goldwater sentiment at the governors' conference grew in Scranton's absence. Breaking his strict no-politics-on-Sunday rule for the only time in his career,[98] George Romney demanded in a press statement that Goldwater meet privately with him and explain his positions. If Barry was not in tune with Republican principles, Romney vowed to "do everything within my power to keep him from becoming the party's presidential candidate."[99] Rockefeller took Romney at his word and offered to donate staff and work for the anti-Goldwater cause. Ohio Governor James Rhodes and later Bill Scranton also promised their support. Romney, however, hesitated at the brink, citing a pledge to the people of Michigan to complete his term as their governor. Perhaps as important was Oregon Governor Mark Hatfield's sobering assessment: "George, you're six months too late. If you can't add, I'll add it for you. Goldwater's got it."[100] This did not discourage Richard Nixon, also in Cleveland, from taking a shot: "It would be a tragedy if Senator Goldwater's views as previously stated were not challenged and repudiated."[101] In the end, the moderates' frantic maneuvering produced much sound and fury that signified nothing; it was "an exercise in ineptness, vacillation and rear-view heroism," wrote a *Time* magazine reporter.[102] Dubbed the "The Hamlet of Harrisburg," a humiliated Scranton returned to Pennsylvania resigned to the inevitability of Goldwater's nomination.[103]

The pending civil rights bill of 1964, then delayed by filibuster in the U.S. Senate, caused Scranton to reconsider. Barry Goldwater and a handful of Republicans had joined southern Democrats to oppose the bill when it was introduced by John Kennedy in 1963, and it had bogged down, as had so many New Frontier requests. Now, with President Lyndon Johnson floor-managing the measure from the White House, passage was imminent. Goldwater, following Kitchel's advice and armed with the seventy-five-page critique written by Yale Law School Professor Robert Bork, voted against cloture of debate and offered amendments to delete from the legislation those sections prohibiting discrimination in public accommodations and mandating fair employment practices. Although a foe of segregation, he opposed the public accommodations clauses because they "would force you to admit drunks, a known murderer or an insane person into your place of business," while the fair employment provisions would lead to the hiring of "incompetent" employees.[104] The federal government, he argued, had no constitutional authority in such areas, which were better left within the jurisdiction of state and local officials. Enforcement of these provisions, moreover, meant "the creation of a Federal police force of mammoth proportions. It also bids fair to result in the development of an 'informer' psychology in great areas of our national life—neighbors spying on neighbors, workers spying on workers, business spying on businessmen."[105]

In spite of great pressure to reconsider, Goldwater held his ground on the measure's unconstitutionality. On June 18 he was one of twenty-seven senators to vote no, reiterating his belief that the racial issue was "fundamentally a matter of the heart. The problems of discrimination can not be cured by laws alone." Goldwater realized the potential fallout from his vote. "If my vote is misconstrued, let it be, and let me suffer its consequences. . . . This is where I stand."[106] Later in June his advisers attempted to repair some of the damage with the promise that, if elected, Goldwater would do a "better" job enforcing the act than Lyndon Johnson.[107]

Goldwater's vote was a matter of principle, a reflection of his sense of the Constitution and belief in limited government. It was also a gamble that could yield a big political payoff. Convinced that he needed to hold the South if he was to have any chance in November, Goldwater had already begun to back away from offering full support to voting rights for blacks. He thus declared before a Republican meeting in North Carolina that federal law pertained only to national elections and defended the states' "right to judge the qualifications" of voters as long as it was done in a nondiscriminatory manner.[108] This he contended, despite the record of southern registrars' systematically denying black voters the franchise. Nor could he ignore the evidence of the much-discussed "white backlash" among northern voters. In May, the Field Poll in California found that 79 percent of white voters believed that blacks were "pushing too hard for integration."[109] A Harris Poll released in July revealed that white Americans feared that blacks wanted to "take over" their jobs (58 percent), move into their neighborhoods (43 percent), and "take over" schools (35 percent).[110] Even more convincing was the showing of Alabama's segregationist Governor George Wallace in the northern Democratic primaries. Running against Lyndon Johnson or his surrogates, Wallace had gathered 34 percent of the Democratic vote in Wisconsin, 30 percent in Indiana, and 43 percent in Maryland. He ran particularly well in white ethnic neighborhoods, areas that Goldwater had long targeted as containing the "ducks" that Republicans should be hunting. Stoking prejudice was foreign to the Arizona senator. Still, with the civil rights movement mobilizing in Mississippi and racial tensions building in northern ghettos, race was the wild card of the 1964 election.[111]

General Eisenhower telephoned Bill Scranton on June 10 just after Barry Goldwater voted against cloture of debate on the civil rights bill. He asked Scranton, "Now, how do you feel?" Said Scranton, "I'm sick." "So am I," replied Eisenhower. Goldwater's vote infuriated the Pennsylvania governor, and he did not wait for Ike's prompting or endorsement: "I no longer cared." To Scranton, Goldwater's stand on civil rights was central to his own decision to enter the race. "I was determined that the country realize that there were people within the Republican Party who did not agree with him on this subject. The party would not go down in history as the white-supremacy party."[112] With the support of his wife and without an Eisenhower commitment, Scranton went before the Maryland delegation to the Republican convention and, on June 11, announced his candidacy: "I have come here to offer our party a real choice. I reject the echo we have thus far been handed—the echo of fear and reaction—the echo from the never-never land that puts our nation on the road backward to a lesser place in the world of free men. . . . Can we in good conscience turn our backs on the century-old progressive history of our party? You and I know we cannot."[113] His cause assumed a greater urgency eleven days later with news that civil rights workers James Chaney, Andrew Goodman, and Michael Schwerner were missing in Mississippi.[114]

Bill Scranton made an attractive candidate. Handsome, wealthy, and committed to serve, he had been christened by reporters the Republican John Kennedy. He possessed Eastern Establishment breeding and connections and a good relationship with the Republican right. Scranton and Barry Goldwater were friends. The Arizona senator had been Bill's senior officer in their Air Force Reserve unit on Capitol Hill. In deciding to seek the Pennsylvania governorship in 1962, Scranton had solicited Barry's advice. As a newcomer to politics, Scranton had few enemies. He appealed to all the party's wings: "I am a liberal on civil rights, a conservative on fiscal policies, and an internationalist on foreign affairs."[115] Now the last moderate in the race, he could count on the aid of Rockefeller and Lodge, who had just resigned his post in Saigon and returned to campaign for him. Perhaps, too, Eisenhower would finally line up against Goldwater.[116]

With only five weeks left before the convention, Scranton plotted a desperate strategy. Using the issues that Rockefeller pioneered, he hoped to generate media flak and rank-and-file indignation. Goldwater might even be goaded into overreaction or blunder. If convinced that Goldwater could not win in November and impressed with popular dissatisfaction, delegates might pause and favorite sons stand firm in their decision to hold supporters. Once past the first ballot, moderates convinced themselves that they had a chance to regroup and even to recapture the party.[117]

Scranton hit Goldwater hard. He went on the road, traveling more than twenty thousand miles and visiting delegates in twenty-five states. In Topeka, Kansas, Scranton predicted Republican ruin if the Democrats "can accuse us—and be believed—of an irresponsible defense policy that would turn over the decision to use nuclear weapons to field commanders. Suppose they can accuse us of trying to destroy the Social Security system? . . . Suppose they show that when the chips are down, Republicans won't stand for equal rights for all Americans?"[118] Before the Florida delegation, he denounced Goldwater for believing "that 'total victory' can be won simply by standing up to the Russians, both guns drawn. [He] reduces the complexities of foreign policy to simple emotional terms that have wide appeal . . . the rugged individualism of the pioneer, the gun slinging marshal of the frontier town."[119] Barry even gave Scranton an opening. The June issue of *Science and Mechanics* carried Barry Goldwater's article "A Realistic Space Program for America." In a vision of things to come, Goldwater broached a "four-point program" that shifted America's energies away from exploration to the seeding of space with military satellites that can "detect and destroy enemy ICBMs . . . minutes after they are launched." Using the laser as a "death ray," the United States could secure itself from communist attack.[120] The article also reiterated Goldwater's objections to the 1963 Nuclear Test Ban Treaty.[121]

None of this, however, made any difference. Goldwater did not respond publicly to Scranton and privately asked supporters to show the Pennsylvania governor every courtesy. Opinion polls indicated that Scranton was the overwhelming choice of the Republican rank-and-file (62 percent to 38 percent) but confirmed that he did little better than Goldwater when matched with Lyndon Johnson. Both Republicans could look forward to a rout at the hands of the Democrat in November. Scranton's staff was inexperienced; Congressman Silvio Conte dismissed them as "white-sneakered amateurs."[122] There was insufficient time to raise necessary funds, and the campaign relied on the demoralized organization donated by Rockefeller. The Pennsylvania governor found little support among party cadres. "We called all the old names," said one moderate, "but they weren't there any longer, or they weren't in politics any longer. It was as if the Goldwater people had rewired the switchboard of the Party and the numbers we had were all dead."[123] Thus, Texas gave Goldwater fifty-six delegates on June 16, and selection contests in Montana, Utah, Colorado, and Arkansas were fattening his lead. In Illinois, said Everett Dirksen, delegates were "as tight as wallpaper" for Goldwater, and the Pennsylvania governor salvaged only eight uncommitted votes.[124] What Scranton did succeed in doing was offending Barry Goldwater. The conservative perceived his friend's actions as a betrayal. In late June, in an interview for the German newsmagazine *Der Spiegel*, Goldwater was asked about Scranton as a running mate. "I would say he has completely ruled that out. At one time there was a strong possibility for it. But when he has turned to attacking personally a man that I always thought he considered a friend—well, the old Et Tu, Brutus."[125]

In succession, Hugh Scott, brother Milton Eisenhower, and Rockefeller beseeched Eisenhower to commit. Scranton called him on July 6, warning that unless an endorsement was forthcoming, Goldwater was sure to be nominated. Eisenhower was unmoved. Although still bridling over Goldwater's attack on his administration in 1957 as a "dime-store New Deal" and over the "insults" he has "gratuitously heaped upon me" over the years, Ike had convinced himself "that my function is to bring harmony to the Party . . . and that I am going to try to do."[126] There would be no last-minute reprieve from the general. On July 9 the Scranton campaign collapsed for all practical purposes when Ohio's favorite son, Governor James Rhodes, released his delegates and they stampeded to Goldwater. Denison Kitchel counted Scranton out on the eve of the San Francisco convention: "The Scranton mine caved in. Flooding at one end of the shaft, it was now burning at the other."[127]

The Pennsylvania governor did not yet see the handwriting on the wall. Prodded by his staff, he consented just fifteen hours before the convention's start on July 13 to a "very dramatic" gesture.[128] Supporters distributed to all delegates an open letter addressed to Barry Goldwater that Scranton had neither read nor signed. The letter was intentionally provocative and blistered the conservative. It chided him: "You have too often casually prescribed nuclear war as a solution to a troubled world. You have too often allowed the radical extremists to use you. You have too often stood for irresponsibility in the serious question of racial holocaust." It dismissed "Goldwaterism" as a "whole crazy quilt collection of absurd and dangerous positions that would be soundly repudiated." And it demanded that the Arizonan appear with Scranton before the convention and the nation so that "the Goldwater philosophy [could] . . . stand public examination." The letter concluded, "The issue is extremely clear. . . . Will the convention choose the candidate overwhelmingly favored by the Republican voters, or will it choose you?"[129] The tone and content of the letter stunned even Scranton. Still, he refused to disavow the deed before NBC's television cameras and declared it "entirely my responsibility, and I stand on it."[130]

The scheme, contrived to pry delegates loose from Goldwater, failed miserably, in fact quickening the movement of the uncommitted to the conservative. Barry, of course, was "boiling mad."[131] Conciliation no longer concerned him; there would be no concessions to the moderate wing. Supporters shared his anger. Said a Goldwaterite: "If Scranton gets the [nomination] there'll be blood three feet deep on the convention floor, and the nomination won't be worth the powder to blow it to hell."[132]

Goldwater's interview in *Der Spiegel* also produced a squall. It was not so much what Goldwater said, though he made his handlers cringe with renewed mention of giving the NATO commander "great leeway in the decision to use [nuclear weapons]" and of defoliating the jungle cover in Vietnam—"one possible way of doing it even though I made clear this would never be done, would be the use of low-yield nuclear devices."[133] Rather, it was CBS News correspondent Daniel Schorr's framing of the circumstances of the interview that was so damaging. Schorr reported from Germany on July 11: "It is now clear that Senator Goldwater's interview with *Der Spiegel* with its hard line appealing to right-wing elements in Germany was only the start of a move to link up with his opposite numbers in Germany."[134] Schorr went further, announcing that Goldwater planned to visit Germany, speak in Bavaria, and stay at Berchtesgaden, Adolf Hitler's former retreat.[135] The implications were obvious: the grandson of the Jewish peddler was in league with neo-Nazis and an admirer of Der Führer. Scranton lieutenants reproduced the text of the Schorr broadcast and circulated it among convention delegates.[136]

The smear that Schorr later dismissed as "one sloppy and unfortunate sentence" did not die, for others took up his theme.[137] *Life* magazine reported that "the G.O.P. was seized by its unyielding right wing," engulfed in a "tide of zealotry" and "raw power."[138] An editorial in *The Reporter* condemned the "conquest of the Republican Party" by "fanatics."[139] Goldwater, said Protestant theologian John Swomley, Jr., "is hardly a candidate who would share the Christian concern for peace and world order."[140] According to syndicated columnist Drew Pearson: "The smell of fascism has been in the air at this convention."[141] Some made their allusions more obvious. Norman Mailer, in an *Esquire* piece, described the Republican convention as "murderous in mood. The mood of this convention spoke of a new kind of society. Chimeras of fascism hung like fogbank. . . . There was an éclat, a bull roar, a mystical communion in the sound even as Sieg Heil used to offer its mystical communion."[142] Roy Wilkins of the National Association for the Advancement of Colored People warned: "Those who say that the doctrine of ultra-conservatism offers no menace should remember that a man came out of the beer halls of Munich, and rallied the forces of Rightism in Germany. All the same elements are there in San Francisco now."[143] Through repetition, the big lie took on its own truth.

While these happenings disturbed the press and the nation, they raised no dust on the five-acre floor of the New Deal–built Cow Palace. "It was my convention," boasted Barry, "from the day the doors opened."[144] If Goldwaterites were a minority of the larger Republican Party, at the convention they constituted a two-thirds majority. Goldwater delegates were firmly committed to their candidate, with 80 percent having read *The Conscience of a Conservative*, 75 percent having attended a rally, and 70 percent already in his camp before he entered the race. The most densely packed Goldwater delegations carried the banners of southern and western states, while northeastern contingents seated few conservatives in their ranks. Mostly, the Goldwater delegates were under fifty years of age, male, middle- and upper-middle class, and white. African-Americans were visible by their absence; NBC News counted only twenty-five among the 1,308 delegates and 1,008 alternates. The Georgia delegation was entirely white for the first time in fifty years. About one hundred members of the John Birch Society took seats on the convention floor.[145]

While confident of their allegiance, Clif White diligently shepherded the party's new activists. He bought time on a San Francisco station and directed his charges to carry transistor radios and tune in for instructions. His thick black loose-leaf notebooks bulged with information on each delegate's occupation, education, club memberships, and wife's and children's names. To deter raiding, White's staff paired the delegates in a buddy system. "The Kennedy organization at Los Angeles in 1960 was impressive," reported *The Nation's* Carey McWilliams, "but this one was awesome."[146] Taking no chances, the Goldwaterites monitored the walkie-talkies of Bill Scranton's floor managers. They also identified every television and radio cable that snaked through the loft of the Cow Palace. Barry explained: "If anybody got a little too obnoxious to us, they could always have cable trouble."[147]

With the preliminaries over, the convention moved to consider the party platform. The Goldwater forces, because of their delegate share, dominated the platform committee and hammered together planks that mirrored their candidate's views. Long gone was the spirit of compromise that animated the committee during its early deliberations. The platform focused on the federal government as the source of the country's domestic problems. It traced America's "moral decline and drift" to a "leadership grown demagogic and materialistic through indifference to national ideals." Adding layers of overlapping bureaucracy to government and restricting freedom with expanding regulatory controls, the "federal extremists" had accelerated the decline toward centralization of power in the hands of the few. The Republicans vowed to fight the faceless, bureaucratic managers to cut spending, balance the budget, lower taxes, and begin retiring the debt. To enhance America's moral fiber they proposed curbing the flow of pornography through the mails and passing a constitutional amendment to restore prayer to the schools and other public places. Platform writers needed only sixty-six words to draft the civil rights plank, the core of which was a promise of "full implementation and faithful execution of the Civil Rights Act of 1964." Tempering this was the party's ardent opposition to "Federally-sponsored 'inverse discrimination,' whether by the shifting of jobs, or the abandonment of neighborhood schools, for reasons of race." At the same time, the platform reassured Americans of its support of a "strong, sound system of Social Security." The committee members' reading of *Why Not Victory?* was apparent in the sections devoted to foreign affairs. The platform called generally for "victory over Communism" and specifically for the "eventual liberation" of Eastern Europe, aid to Cuban "freedom fighters," and the removal of the Berlin Wall before entering into future negotiations with the Russians. In regard to Vietnam, the Goldwaterites censured the administration for encouraging "an increase of aggression in South Vietnam by appearing to set limits on America's willingness to act." They continued: "We will move decisively to assure victory in South Vietnam while confining the conflict as closely as possible."[148]

The proposed platform dismayed the moderates. They dismissed it as a retreat from the platform adopted at the 1960 convention and its commitment to social welfare programs, federal aid to education, and negotiations with the Russians. Particularly disturbing was the contrast between the 1964 plank on civil rights and the strong 1960 statement, advocating "vigorous enforcement" of civil rights statutes and "the full use of the power, resources and leadership of the federal government to eliminate discrimination."[149] For reasons of principle and politics, the moderates moved to confront the conservatives in a floor fight over the platform. Scranton and Rockefeller supporters set the terms of the debate, proposing planks that repudiated the John Birch Society and similar extremist groups, advocated the president's sole control of nuclear weapons, and strengthened the party's stand in defense of civil rights. George Romney, independently, offered additional motions on civil rights and political extremism that he cleared with Arizonans John Rhodes, Paul Fannin, and Dick Kleindienst. Believing the nomination already cinched, the Michigan governor described his effort as issues-oriented and designed "to wake up the delegates."[150] Press reports on July 13 that Goldwater had suggested to Governor George Wallace that he drop out of the presidential race surely firmed the moderates in their plans.[151]

The platform fight on the evening of July 14 was the moderates' last stand, and the conservatives gave them no quarter. Conceiving the challenge as a cynical and arrogant refusal to accept the new Republican reality, Goldwaterites beat down every Scranton-Rockefeller motion. Parliamentary victory, however, was insufficient to ease the anger and animosity of some conservatives. Nelson Rockefeller, long the enemy of the right, gave them opportunity to vent their hostility. Speaking in support of the motion on extremism, his words about "goon squads, bomb threats, . . . and Nazi methods" were drowned out in a chorus of boos and chants of "We want Barry, we want Barry."[152] The men and women in the gallery, not the delegates, shouted him down, their roar rising in volume to meet his every effort to continue talking. Rockefeller did not miss the opening, stood his ground, and wore a wry smirk that meshed self-satisfaction with disgust. He knew how the scene would play on televisions in Peoria. "This is still a free country ladies and gentlemen,"[153] he scolded them, and ABC's Sam Donaldson reported, "The 'bund' booed louder."[154] Jacob Javits's appearance provoked the same reaction: "It chilled me with the thought that I might be seeing the beginnings of an American totalitarianism."[155] The demonstration was neither officially orchestrated nor sanctioned. It did, however, mirror the Goldwater campaign's bitterness and determination to resist compromise. Thus, George Romney's less objectionable amendments were similarly defeated. This occurred despite Clif White's contention that the proposals were acceptable and that it made political sense to be flexible. When he approached his superiors, however, they rejected any such truce as a "sign of weakness."[156]

In the same spirit, Barry Goldwater refused to balance the ticket ideologically, bypassing Scranton and other well-known moderates to chose upstate New York Representative William Miller as his running mate. Miller, a six-term congressman, former chair of the Republican National Committee, and a Catholic, had a "slashing style" that Goldwater liked.[157] According to a National Committee staffer, "He's a guy who can look into the TV and snarl, and his mind works fast, and he's willing. Also, he's a gut cutter."[158] Goldwater was more diplomatic: "One reason I chose Miller is that he drives Johnson nuts."[159]

The convention turned to its main business, the nomination of a presidential candidate, on July 15. Scheduled for prime time, managers staged the nominating speeches and demonstrations to spike viewer interest for the coming drama of the roll of the states. While there were no surprises that night, conservatives on the convention floor and across the nation waited with quickening anticipation for their moment in the sun. Alabama, Arizona, Florida—the tide was rising. By Mississippi's turn, the count was Goldwater 430 delegates, everyone else 87. With Ohio, the vote was 618 to 123. South Carolina, which had nominated Goldwater for president at the 1960 convention, put him over the top by casting its sixteen votes for the Arizonan and bringing his total to 663, eight more than needed to win. Barry telephoned Clif White in the Goldwater convention trailer: "Clif, you did a wonderful job, all of you fellows. I can't thank you enough."[160] (Soon afterward the nominee named Dean Burch as chair of the Republican National Committee and demoted White to the "meaningless letterhead" group called Citizens for Goldwater-Miller.)[161] In the end, Goldwater won 883 of the 1,308 delegate votes, and Scranton finished a distant second with 214 votes. The roll taken, Scranton made his way to the convention, mounted the podium, and graciously asked that the vote be made unanimous. Scattered diehards in the New York, New Jersey, and Oregon delegations, among others, refused to go along. Only one thing dampened the conservative mood that day: a public opinion poll put Johnson out in front of Goldwater in the race for president, 80 percent to 20 percent.[162]

A nominee's acceptance speech is traditionally a healing act, a rallying cry on shared ground against a common foe. But Barry Goldwater was unable to reach out to his opponents. He felt personally vilified, his cause slandered by men he had considered friends. He had no patience for those who snubbed him as an illegitimate heir to the Republican throne. This, after conservatives had lost in other conventions yet remained loyal and worked for the ticket. There would be no bribe, no balm to ease the hurt of the moderates and liberals. Instead, his acceptance speech signaled a "historic break," an uncompromising, ideological appeal that set forth division as the strategy of conquest.[163] "Any who join us in all sincerity, we welcome. Those who do not care for our cause we do not expect to enter our ranks in any case."[164] In light of the opinion polls that predicted disaster in November, he realistically targeted his own party for salvation. The country's turn would come later.

The themes of Goldwater's speech to the convention on July 16 were familiar. America, he warned, had been misled by "false prophets" who would have us "stagnate in the swampland of collectivism" and "cringe before the bullying of communism." At home, "we are plodding at a pace set by centralized planning, red tape, rules without responsibility, and regimentation without recourse." We endure scandals and corruption in the highest offices of government, "aimlessness" among our young people, and "violence in the streets." Abroad, we suffer repeated failure. "We have weakly stumbled into conflict—*timidly* refusing to draw our lines against aggression . . . and *tragically* letting our finest men die on battlefields unmarked by purpose, pride or prospect of victory. Yesterday it was Korea. Today it is Vietnam." The time has come for Americans to renew the national purpose and reclaim their role as "freedom's missionaries in a doubting world." Restoration at home demanded that men and women take back from government control over their own lives. Government must be curbed so that it performed "only those needed and Constitutionally-sanctioned tasks."

America, as the defender of world peace, must steel itself against communism: "We must make clear that until its goals of conquest are absolutely renounced, and its relations with all nations tempered, Communism and the governments it now controls are enemies of every man on earth who is or wants to be free." He closed: "Our Republican cause is to free our people and light the way for liberty throughout the world."[165]

While the delegates cheered, commentators analyzed the speaker and the speech. They noted that Goldwater had shown no joy or excitement as he stood before the convention and cameras. He appeared grim-faced, his words tough and body tense. Black-rimmed eyeglasses made him look sterner. A flat affect only enhanced the picture. They criticized the speech as rambling and too abstract. Goldwater had offered no specifics regarding the government programs that he would continue or abandon. Several noted that while Goldwater had used the words "free," "freedom," and "liberty" forty times, he made no mention of blacks or civil rights. More spontaneous was a reporter's assessment: "My God, he's going to run as Barry Goldwater."[166]

The speech troubled leading Republicans. Congressman Walter Judd questioned not only the content of the speech but its style. "Barry, who is always warm and charming in person, seemed more defiant than conciliatory, militant than magnanimous. It is hard to see how he can win on that basis."[167] Richard Nixon, preparing to campaign for Goldwater in the fall, judged it "strident, divisive . . . if he ever had a chance to win the presidency, he lost it that night with that speech. . . . I felt almost physically sick as I sat there."[168] Dean Burch defended his mentor: "If Goldwater had recited the Lord's Prayer, there were certain people at the convention who were going to object to it."[169] Clif White, however, was more objective. Goldwater "stunned" him with the "abrasive quality of his words."[170] Stephen Shadegg was similarly affected, believing that the "harsh, almost belligerent delivery overshadowed the good points." Shadegg was amazed that Goldwater had failed to use the speech to reunite the party and instead had "ripped open old wounds and erected barriers which were never broken."[171] Barry disagreed: "I didn't write it, but it's the best speech I ever made."[172]

Most comment and concern focused on a phrase that came at the end of the speech and that Goldwater had underlined in pencil for emphasis: *"Extremism in the defense of liberty is no vice. Moderation in the pursuit of justice is no virtue."* The statement, which lacked either explanation or example, was inspired by Aristotle and created by Claremont College history professor Harry Jaffa, a member of the Goldwater brain trust. When chief speech writer Karl Hess reviewed Jaffa's suggestion, he immediately realized the impact it would have. "It was as if I stepped on a land mine. But everyone on staff, including Goldwater[,] loved it."[173] Goldwater interpreted the lines, without reference to context, as an expression of unvarnished patriotism and love of liberty. A desire for revenge also drove the candidate, and he and campaign manager Kitchel planned it as a "deliberate" jab at their opponents.[174] It had its intended effect. As Richard Nixon observed, it bit like salt in "new wounds."[175] Clearly the conservatives' political instincts had deserted them, and they were unprepared for the reaction. Goldwater "didn't see anything coming when he said that," maintains Benjamin Bradlee, "and neither did the dumb bastards around him."[176] Nelson Rockefeller described the statement as "dangerous, irresponsible and frightening."[177] California Governor Pat Brown, applying a now standard theme, told reporters that "Goldwater's acceptance speech had the stench of fascism. . . . All we needed to hear was 'Heil Hitler.'"[178] The Goldwater camp lamely attempted to cover itself. Kitchel claimed that "we were talking about the good extremists, not the idiots. There is a difference."[179] Contended Goldwater, "I wanted to smoke this 'extremism' thing out and find what the devil they were talking about. Well, it didn't work."[180] It did work in another way. It gave moderates and liberals another reason to bolt.[181]

Particularly unnerving to Goldwater and Kitchel was Dwight Eisenhower's response. Ike called Goldwater after the speech and requested that he appear the next morning in his hotel with an explanation. Goldwater and Kitchel arrived at the general's suite at 10:30, only to be kept waiting for another quarter of an hour. When Eisenhower appeared, still in pajamas and dressing gown, he confronted Goldwater as he would a junior officer: "Barry, what the hell did you mean last night about extremism . . . ? I couldn't make any sense out of it and I thought it was a damn silly thing to say." Goldwater tried several approaches but could not wean Eisenhower from the conclusion that the statement attempted to use the end to justify the means. Finally, Barry reached the general. "I reminded him that if my remark was not true then he was probably the most extreme extremist of all time, because he led millions of men into what is the most extreme action men can take—war."[182] That was all Ike needed. He put his arm around Barry: "By golly, I do understand. Barry, that's marvelous."[183]

Most Americans were not so easily convinced, for they could not divorce the phrase from its historical context. Coming after years of controversy about extremist groups, the remarks seemed to sanction those who resorted to witch hunting, intimidation, and even violence. Experiences in the California primary and, most recently, the disorder that accompanied Rockefeller's appearance before the convention gave the issue a raw salience. Again, Goldwater could blame only himself for breathing life into the caricature of recklessness that his opponents had drawn. Liberals, moderates, and conservatives could only wonder at his bent for self-destruction. Despite the uproar, Barry Goldwater never doubted the wisdom of his pronouncement. Nearly thirty years later he was still bound to a literal reading and insensitive to the implications of his words. He declared defiantly: "I think it's the best statement I ever made. The opponents were a bunch of jackasses from New York. . . . The word extreme would mean anything to them."[184] Patrick Buchanan's father had better insight. On hearing Goldwater make his remark on extremism, he said simply, "He's finished."[185]

The consensus across the political spectrum in July 1964 was that the events of the previous seven months and especially during the week in San Francisco would have longterm significance. A power shift had occurred that signaled the rise of a western-southern coalition and the decline of the East in Republican Party politics. The new conservative elite rejected Modern Republicanism's acceptance of New Deal social programs, the activist role of the federal government, and the importance of the black vote. Although conservative control of the party machinery was still firming, liberal and moderate factions were in disarray and on the defensive. Their comeback could be accomplished only precinct by precinct. Ideology determined the spin given to these happenings. According to NBC anchor Chet Huntley, the Republican Party had rejected the twentieth century and "will reflect the nostalgic yearning for a return to the simplicity of a frontier society, where there were no Social Security numbers, no labor contracts, no welfare bureaus, and where government—like the discouraging word—was seldom heard. . . . It has no patina of quiet reserve and great dignity. It is new and shiny money and it rings with brashness on the political counter."[186] Tom Wicker of the *New York Times* labeled the convention a coup d'état,[187] while *Newsweek* editorialized, "It was a revolt against frustration, against the pressures and the complexities of the modern world."[188] Phyllis Schlafly, on the right, saw a new dawn because Goldwater had broken the "New York kingmakers" conspiracy and chased them from the political temple.[189] Goldwater was less dramatic, but agreed: "We knew that the only thing we could accomplish would be moving the Republican headquarters from New York to the West Coast, and we did that. We got it away from the money."[190] Bill Rusher of *National Review* cheered the new reality: "The upsurge of the conservative movement in this country is a development of the first rank. Win or lose in November, we are here to stay."[191]

Even in triumph Barry Goldwater had no illusions about the coming campaign against the Democrats. "Frankly, I think I was beaten July 15."[192] He predicted defeat because of the "stiletto job Rockefeller and Scranton and others had done on me" in the fratricidal campaign.[193] At their hands, and his own, Goldwater had been seriously wounded. Still, it would be of little matter in light of what was to come. Barry Goldwater was about to encounter a political infighter with an instinct for the jugular, a top graduate of the tough Texas school of politics, Lyndon Baines Johnson. The defamation of Barry Goldwater by the Democrats and their accomplices would be unprecedented in American political history.

9   Martyr to the Cause

The point is . . . to win recruits whose attention we might never have attracted but for Barry Goldwater; to win them not only for November the third, but for future Novembers.
                                                                —WILLIAM F. BUCKLEY, JR.

I've often said that if I hadn't known Barry Goldwater in 1964 and I had to depend on the press and the cartoons, I'd have voted against the son of a bitch.
                                                                —BARRY GOLDWATER

The mood was certainly upbeat at the White House in mid-July 1964. Few candidates for the presidency had ever held higher cards than Lyndon Baines Johnson. With the theme "Let Us Continue" he had moved rapidly after the tragedy in Dallas in November 1963 to enact into legislation the promises of John Kennedy. He had pushed through Congress the Civil Rights Act, the Wilderness Preservation Act, and the War on Poverty's Economic Opportunities Act, with its Head Start, VISTA, Job Corps, and Community Action programs. Nor was this the end of the Great Society agenda. With a mandate from the voters, the Democrats pledged at their Atlantic City convention in August to go forward with Medicare, Medicaid, aid to education, regional redevelopment, and urban renewal legislation. President Johnson, at the same time, wooed the business community with a tax cut and budget- and deficit-reduction initiatives. Organized labor had enlisted in the Johnson campaign without coaxing. Long antagonistic to Barry Goldwater, it would provide $2 million to elect the president. Lyndon Johnson summarized the Democratic package: "I just want to tell you this— we're in favor of a lot of things and we're against mighty few."[1]

Meanwhile, Americans had enjoyed forty-one consecutive months of economic growth under the Democrats. The gross national product was up, as were industrial production, consumer spending, and business profits. The Democrats boasted that nearly 4 million jobs had been created since 1961 and that the unemployment rate had dipped below 5 percent in July 1964. All economic indicators pointed to continued prosperity. There was good news from abroad as well. Tension with the Soviet Union had eased since the Cuban Missile Crisis and the enactment of the Nuclear Test Ban Treaty. In Southeast Asia, America's commitment appeared measured and manageable.[2]

Added to this were the benefits of incumbency. Presidents make news and order events, their every statement and action devoured by the copy-hungry reporters stationed in the White House. Johnson's flair for the dramatic played well to press needs, and his announcements were often highlighted in news bulletins that preempted regular television programming. At the president's disposal was Air Force One, and every entrance and exit was orchestrated to the strains of "Hail to the Chief." Government was also a presidential and political resource, providing information and advocates for the campaign trail. Opinion polls reflected Johnson's advantages and America's contentment. The Kennedy mantle, prosperity, peace, the presidency, and now the Republican civil war gave him an enormous lead over his conservative challenger.

The Democrats fashioned an appeal that raised hope while inspiring fear. Taking the high road, LBJ claimed the mainstream and waged a nonpartisan campaign that focused on past accomplishments and his and John Kennedy's dream of the Great Society. Johnson spoke of a national calling to relieve suffering and end injustice, with the federal government his catalyst for change. The promise of prosperity and federal spending, he hoped, might overshadow racism and deliver the South to the Democrats. As a southern businessman asked, "Who can shoot Santa Claus?"[3] Looking beyond the nation's borders, Johnson pledged, "I will go to any remote corner of the world to meet anyone, any time, to promote freedom and to promote peace."[4] Johnson nevertheless advocated a strong defense because America could not let down its guard in a dangerous world. Commander-in-Chief Johnson, aware of his awesome responsibilities, vowed never to yield control of the nuclear button. In 1964, this was the essence of responsible leadership.

Appearing "presidential" enhanced the rhetoric. "The-best-politics-is-no-politics," Johnson believed, and in the initial stage of the campaign reporters and photographers found him in the Oval Office or Rose Garden tending to the nation's business.[5] Only after the image had been fixed would he venture out in the trappings of presidential power to battle for voters' allegiance. Even then he did not engage in political rough-and-tumble, never deigning to recognize his opponent by name. Here was a builder, leader, and statesman—the president of all the people—and he welcomed Democrats, independents, and disaffected Republicans under his banner.[6]

Complementing Johnson's effort was the underside of the campaign. Its purpose was to make Barry Goldwater a central issue, to give Americans something to vote against. Vice presidential candidate Hubert Humphrey and Johnson loyalists Bill Moyers, Abe Fortas, and Clark Clifford, among others, planned a negative campaign that caricatured Goldwater as a dangerous radical bent on war and in league with extremists. A vote for Goldwater was a vote against the elderly and Social Security. Elect Goldwater and scuttle aid programs for the deserving poor. Goldwater as president would unleash nuclear war. As Democrats wrote on campaign placards, "In your heart, you know he might." Humphrey set the stakes: "What we are talking about in this election is life itself, the future of the planet, the salvation of the species."[7] Compare this with President Johnson's somewhat less dramatic sketch of the alternatives in his acceptance speech before the Democratic Convention on August 27, 1964: "It is between courage and timidity. It is between . . . those who see what can be and those who want only to maintain the status quo. It is between those who welcome the future and those who turn from its promise."[8] The stakes were clearly too high for voters to stay home or to vote for Goldwater on November 3.

This negative campaign escalated because Lyndon Johnson wanted to do more than merely win. To surpass Franklin D. Roosevelt and exorcise John Kennedy's ghost from the White House, LBJ demanded the greatest mandate in American history. He conceded no state to Goldwater, not even Arizona. Few things would deter him from his prize. According to aide Bill Moyers, "He felt that anything that could help . . . was worth the price."[9] Thus the Johnson White House established the Five O'Clock Club, which planted spies like E. Howard Hunt (on leave from the Central Intelligence Agency) in the Goldwater camp. Reporters were encouraged to feed Goldwater's off-the-record remarks to White House staffers and to provide advance copies of the Republican's speeches for simultaneous rebuttal. The "Anti-Goldwater Program" also led to collusion between the press and the government to manipulate the news.[10] The Department of Defense supplied facts and figures to seemingly neutral journalists to bolster Democratic claims and refute the Republicans. White House aide Walter Heller furnished "ammunition" to syndicated columnists Walter Lippmann and Sylvia Porter. The selection of financial adviser Porter resulted from Heller's suggestion to the president that "it might be healthy to get some respected columnist to give broader circulation to the adverse Goldwater impact on the stock market and the economy. It might heighten market fears temporarily, but it would help put the blame where it belonged." Porter complied, and her column, appearing in 350 newspapers, warned that a Goldwater victory "injects an uncertainty into the calculations of business analysts, business executives, and investment managers."[11] Another such broadside followed a few weeks later.[12]

Advertising was LBJ's most prized weapon. The Democrats planned their television and radio ad campaign in tune with polls indicating that

Goldwater's stands on Social Security and nuclear weapons raised serious concern. Among Bill Moyers' suggestions to the advertising firm Doyle Dane Bernbach was a television spot in which "he [Goldwater] could have his finger—or that of some field commander—on the nuclear trigger."[13] Agency executives accepted the theme and developed it further. The images of Goldwater they eventually pitched to the American people remain case studies in the art of negative campaigning.[14]

President Johnson had well-laid plans, yet he was vulnerable on two fronts. As the Republicans adjourned their convention in San Francisco, the Harlem ghetto in New York City convulsed in racial rioting. The tinder of unemployment and slum life soon spread the violence beyond Manhattan to the Bedford-Stuyvesant section of Brooklyn. The city quieted after five days, but two weeks later violence in Rochester, New York, led Governor Nelson Rockefeller to order one thousand National Guardsmen to the community. In August, rioting jolted Jersey City, Paterson, and Elizabeth, New Jersey. Similar disturbances rocked Toledo, Ohio; Medford, Massachusetts; Kansas City and St. Louis, Missouri; and Dixmoor, Illinois, with the violence finally ending in Philadelphia, Pennsylvania, at the end of August. The rioting left nine dead and 580 wounded, with more than 2,000 arrested. Thus began the sixties' cycle of long, hot summers. The intensity of violence and the toll of casualties would mount significantly in later years.[15]

Racial tensions spiraled, worrying Democratic precinct captains and union local presidents who remembered well the inroads that Alabaman George Wallace had made just months before in their white working-class, ethnic neighborhoods. A union leader spoke of the members' concerns: "They fear Negroes will take their jobs, overrun their schools, move into their neighborhoods and downgrade their property, and I admit there is some rationality to this."[16] Yet it was more than contested turf that fueled anger and apprehension. The rioting seemed to whites another symptom of the widespread breakdown in law and authority that mounting police statistics on murder, robbery, and rape had already detailed. For many, an economic explanation of violence and crime proved less convincing than a racial one. In this context, Wallace's decision on July 19 to quit the race made northern Democratic politicians uncomfortable. The white backlashers among their constituents were vocal and might be less hesitant to desert to the relatively more respectable Goldwater.[17]

But LBJ dismissed the importance of the backlash vote, certain that a "frontlash" of moderate Republicans and independents would turn the issue to the Democrats' advantage by a margin of three to one.[18] He surely welcomed the efforts of the Reverend Dr. Martin Luther King, Jr., of the Southern Christian Leadership Conference, Roy Wilkins of the National

Association for the Advancement of Colored People, and Whitney Young of the Urban League to dampen white resentment with a moratorium on civil rights demonstrations until after election day. The August 4 discovery in Mississippi of the bullet-riddled and mutilated bodies of missing civil rights workers James Chaney, Andrew Goodman, and Michael Schwerner stunned Americans and added to frontlash sentiment.[19]

Similarly, Lyndon Johnson refused to surrender the South to the Republicans and attempted to appease all but the most die-hard racists. At the Democratic convention he brokered a deal that recognized the legitimacy of the all-white Mississippi delegation and offered the challenging Mississippi Freedom Democratic Party only two token at-large seats. Most blacks swallowed Johnson's terms, for Goldwater's candidacy gave them no bargaining power. Alabama and Mississippi delegates walked, but the rest of the South pledged allegiance to the Democratic Party and its standard-bearers. Yet the racial truce was fragile, and the backlash remained a risk factor in the Democratic profile.[20]

The president's other problem was Vietnam. Johnson had inherited it from Kennedy and, like his predecessor, could neither retreat nor yet justify a full-scale commitment. Soon after taking office he had authorized covert military action against North Vietnamese targets. Begun in February 1964, the American-conceived Operation Plan 34A deployed South Vietnamese forces in sabotage activities, commando raids, and the shelling of northern coastal facilities to escalate gradually the pressure on Hanoi to halt its support and supply of the Viet Cong insurgency in the south. U.S. Navy destroyers, while not officially part of these actions, patrolled in close proximity, monitored North Vietnamese responses, and gathered military information. By spring, staffers had designated targets in North Vietnam for a future air war if the battlefield situation deteriorated to the point of imminent communist victory. To effect this, they drew plans for the deployment of U.S. air strike forces to Southeast Asia. Policy-makers, meanwhile, circulated a draft resolution that gave congressional approval for the prosecution of a wider war. Publicly, Johnson reiterated America's intention to support the defense of South Vietnam, a domino whose fall would send shock waves throughout Southeast Asia. Hoping that the escalations that he had ordered would have the desired effect, the president gave no hint of Operation Plan 34A and did not reveal administration scenarios to increase America's military commitment. Barry Goldwater knew that his calls for decisive action to cut off Viet Cong supplies were not sounded in a void. His Pentagon contacts had apprised him of the covert war being waged in the north and of military plans for the escalation of the conflict.[21]

Vietnam emerged briefly from the back pages of American newspapers during the first week of August 1964. President Johnson announced that Navy destroyers *Maddox* and *C. Turner Joy* had been subjected to "unprovoked" attack in the Tonkin Gulf off the North Vietnamese coast. On August 7, Congress took Johnson at his word and approved the Tonkin Gulf Resolution, giving the president authority to "take all necessary measures to repel any armed attack against the forces of the United States and to prevent further aggression."[22] American warplanes proceeded, in a response that *Time* described as "carefully measured and fitted to match the challenge," to bomb naval and storage facilities along the northern coast.[23] Goldwater voted for the resolution and supported the president. "I believe that it is the only thing he can do under the circumstances. We cannot allow the American flag to be shot at anywhere on earth if we are to retain our respect and prestige."[24]

The public and press response to his initiative pleased Johnson. He had flexed American military muscle yet was still perceived as the peace candidate. Under Congress' broad mandate, planning to increase military involvement proceeded on schedule. It would rise in intensity as analysts concluded that South Vietnamese forces were unable to contain the Viet Cong without American ground and air support. Johnson knew that he would have to deal with Vietnam eventually, but he did not welcome a public debate during the campaign. Better, he thought, to delay decision-making until after the election, when politically unpopular options became more feasible. Through the end of the year, the almost twenty-five thousand American troops stationed in Vietnam would avoid a direct combat role and maintain their status as advisers to anticommunist forces.[25]

To Lyndon Johnson's surprise, Barry Goldwater volunteered to relieve him of his campaign liabilities. In the wake of the Harlem riot, Barry asked to see Johnson privately, and a meeting was set for July 24 in the Oval Office. Goldwater's request propelled Johnson staffers into a flurry of conferences and memo writing. They arrived at a consensus that Goldwater would broach the civil rights issue, and they advised LBJ to avoid agreement on "specific matters" and to "take the initiative."[26] The president responded with a press conference two hours before Goldwater's arrival, in which he reiterated to prearranged questions his stand for equal rights for all Americans. In contrast to White House cynicism, Goldwater acted from a sense of patriotism and fear of exacerbating racial tensions. He said later, "I am scared to death of [the backlash]. I know your big cities in the Northeast and in the Middle West—not only on the West Coast—are just tinder boxes, and I'll be darned if I will have my grandchildren accuse their grandfather of setting fire to it [*sic*]."[27] During the sixteen-minute meeting, Goldwater suggested to the president, who quickly concurred, that they mute the civil rights issue. "I told him I would not attack his position. I hope he would refrain from challenging mine."[28] The two candidates released a joint statement: "The President met with Senator Goldwater and reviewed the steps he has taken to avoid the incitement of racial statements. Senator Goldwater expressed his position, which was that racial tensions should be avoided. Both agreed on this position."[29]

Unmentioned was Goldwater's other suggestion. To maintain a united front before the communist enemy, he promised to hold his fire on Vietnam. He offered, surely to Johnson's relief, to desist from raising the issue to attack the president. No pictures were taken of the meeting because of another staff recommendation that Goldwater be denied the "use [of] the White House as a backdrop for a television presentation."[30]

The press gave extensive coverage to the meeting and praised the candidates for their wisdom. But the reporters failed to grasp the critical importance of the event. Even later, when the racial rhetoric of presidential politics changed and the candidates' agreement to veil their discussion of Vietnam became known, no deeper analyses ensued. Despite the candidates' efforts, civil rights proved too immediate to be ignored. Their decision, while made to ease tensions, would cause the issue to mutate into new political images and code words of racial antipathy. Democrats, reluctant to threaten their own bases of support, rarely confronted the Republicans. Instead, they chose to undermine the backlash by fanning fears of a Goldwater presidency and waving the wand of federal largess.

Goldwater did act from the best intentions in regard to Vietnam, but had he done the nation a disservice? By refusing to challenge LBJ with a hawkish alternative and force a public examination of the emerging policy, Goldwater robbed Americans of their last opportunity to debate the war before the beginning of a large-scale military buildup. Johnson faced no serious test, no need to justify his course, and his aides continued to develop their scenarios without hesitation. Even when the candidates allowed Vietnam to surface, their treatment belied its importance and deferred scrutiny. They made Vietnam a secondary issue, one mentioned intermittently, vaguely, and on stumps far off the main campaign trail. Gentle reassurances from one candidate and, from the other, nonspecific declarations to pursue victory, could not awaken Americans to the involvement both men privately predicted. Meanwhile, reporters gave priority to other stories and accepted without question the candidates' constructions of reality. Americans were not so much deceived about Vietnam during the 1964 election as they were lulled into sleepwalking toward their future.

The Goldwater camp followed the opinion polls as avidly as the White House. The results, repeated in survey after survey, were disheartening. Voters preferred Johnson in every region of the nation, except the Deep

South. Sixty-eight percent of women, 70 percent of those between the ages of twenty-one and thirty-four, 73 percent of Catholics, and 86 percent of African-Americans wanted to go all the way with LBJ. To 45 percent of the American electorate, Barry Goldwater was a "radical."[31] Goldwaterites, however, discounted these findings, for they were convinced that the poll takers had failed to gauge accurately the depth of conservative sentiment in America. As their leader had assured them so many times, there existed a forgotten majority of Americans who either did not vote or unwillingly followed the dictates of Democratic and union bosses. Goldwater had championed the cause of these Americans against big government and big labor in the 1950s. From the podium of the 1960 Republican convention he had appealed to these men and women, imploring them to "grow up" and work for the cause. Surely, they would finally respond, awakening to a conservative candidate who voiced a choice rather than echoed the refrain of "metooism." In the West and South, in the ethnic communities of the East and Midwest, this silent majority, once roused, could bring victory to conservatives in November.[32]

Barry Goldwater was less sanguine than his backers, but pessimism did not paralyze him. Competitive and proud, Goldwater refused to concede the election, especially to a man he disliked and distrusted. He also felt obligated to fellow conservatives. A vigorous campaign would draw people and resources to the conservative movement and tighten its grip on the Republican Party. Yielding to defeatism, moreover, would ensure a rout in November that would certainly stall, if not reverse, conservative momentum. Besides, a post-convention bounce in the opinion polls had boosted Goldwater's ratings ten points in August. Was this the beginning of a trend or the ceiling of his support? The election was still months away, and anything was possible in politics.[33]

If, as the Arizonan believed, the majority was conservative in heart and mind, there was no need to moderate positions or blur ideology. Americans already approved of his standard themes of peace through strength, individual responsibility, limited government, and free enterprise. Yet Goldwater realized that these doctrines alone were insufficient to pry voters loose from the bosses and to end apathy. To galvanize men and women he had to expose their feelings of vulnerability and confront the problems that other politicians evaded. As Goldwater had foreshadowed in the primary campaign, he now pioneered in presidential politics an agenda that commentators labeled the "social issue."[34]

Lyndon Johnson, Goldwater declared, had infected the White House with "corruption, immorality, and cynicism."[35] What kind of a role model, he asked, was a Texas "wheeler-dealer" who had parlayed three decades of government service into a personal fortune and spawned a cronyism that brought the U.S. Senate into disrepute? He contended that, despite evidence of wrongdoing, the president's backroom influence had forced Congress to halt inquiries of misconduct in high places. Goldwater also indicted the president for compromising the Constitution by steamrolling legislation that voided community authority, states' rights, and the "freedom of association." In supporting racial quotas LBJ had launched a frontal assault on basic American values of self-reliance and individual initiative. "All men are created equal at the instant of birth, Americans, Mexicans, Cubans and Africans," Goldwater reminded his listeners. "But from then on, that's the end of equality."[36] The conservative repudiated, as well, Supreme Court decisions that coddled criminals, prohibited prayer in the schools, and permitted pornographers to continue to prey. Barry Goldwater, like his opponent, offered Americans a clear choice: "Either we continue the suicidal drift of the last generation away from constitutional government, away from moral order, away from freedom, and away from peace and order in the world community. Or we chart a new course of peace, freedom, morality, and constitutional order based on the wisdom of our history."[37]

Even more dangerous to Goldwater, the moral decay that shrouded Washington now infected America beyond the Beltway. Republican National Chair Dean Burch explained: "We're trying to sell the idea that there's something wrong in this country." We've got riots in our cities. Our kids aren't turning out worth a darn—every other one is a delinquent."[38] A corrupt president thus incited challenges to parental authority, jeopardized the family, and brought all institutions under suspicion. Wielding the related "switchblade issue," Goldwater attributed rising crime rates to declining moral standards. He condemned the "bullies and marauders" who acted without fear of retribution and made Americans anxious even in their own homes. "I don't have to quote the statistics to you," he said grimly. "You know. Every wife and mother—yes every woman and girl knows what I mean."[39]

While Goldwater never explicitly linked blacks to urban violence and street crime, his words and images were charged with innuendo. His campaign literature was more direct and quoted him as pigeonholing with criminals and thugs the black activists "who take to the streets in violation of the law dishonor their cause, default their leadership and defame this nation."[40] It framed civil rights demonstrations within the context of the "growing menace to personal safety . . . in homes, churches, playgrounds and places of business." African-Americans read Goldwater and rallied en masse against him. For many whites, the conservative's rhetoric on race was one more reason to back Johnson. Yet to those whites most threatened by racial change a vote for Goldwater offered a means, at last, of resistance. Did Goldwater not realize that he was inciting the very tensions that he sought to curb with his initiative to the White House? Was he blind to a racism that scarred black and white Americans as deeply as segregation?[41]

Goldwater's handlers set a campaign schedule that took him to forty-five states, with most time booked in the electorally rich battlegrounds of the Midwest and Pacific coast. They also allocated one-third of their budget to television. This was still insufficient, the conservatives knew, to energize what they conceived as the forgotten majority. Reviewing their come-from-behind win in the California primary, they were convinced that the election would be won across the back fences and on the front porches of America. Pinning its hopes on the neighborhood activist, the Goldwater campaign subordinated party regulars. This, in turn, raised conservative power both inside and outside the party. The campaign beckoned to young conservatives and facilitated their advance through party ranks; a climb that would certainly have been slower in a more traditional effort. It enhanced the prestige of such right-wing groups as the John Birch Society, whose scaffolding around the Republican Party was already in place. Collaterally, the society fed off enthusiasm for Goldwater, and membership applications flooded its Belmont, Massachusetts, headquarters. Fervor for Goldwater did not always instill party discipline. Wayne Hood, a Montana Republican, complained, "We were penalized by the over-zealous Goldwater people who had been carrying on a constant war with the Party organization."[42] "I was plagued," wrote Republican Jeb Stuart Magruder, "by zealots who flocked to the cause. They were uncontrollable. They cared nothing about the Republican Party, only about their hero."[43] Regardless, the Goldwater campaign served well a generation of conservative activists. It was basic training that prepared them for future combat.[44]

Mounting evidence of a groundswell assured the Goldwater leadership that confidence in the grassroots activists was not misplaced. At campaign rallies, audience enthusiasm for the Arizonan awed his team. Fund-raising efforts brought additional proof. With the political fat cats making safe wagers on Johnson, Republicans initiated a direct-mail campaign that targeted Goldwaterites, veterans, magazine subscribers, small-business owners, middle-income families, and professionals. The results were unprecedented. Fifteen million letters brought in $5.8 million, one-third of the campaign's income. Six hundred and fifty thousand men and women responded to direct mail and television appeals with checks of one hundred dollars or less. Only 28 percent of the Republicans' income, as compared to the Democrats' 69 percent, came in donations of five hundred dollars or more.[45]

Flush with the possibilities, Goldwater acted to quell the rebellion in Republican ranks. Campaign manager Denison Kitchel prompted Richard Nixon to send Goldwater a letter asking him to explain, again, his statement on extremism. Nixon complied, calling on Barry "to clear the air once and for all" about a "manufactured, false issue." After citing examples of what Abraham Lincoln described as "firmness in the right," Goldwater rendered the phrase harmless: "If I were to paraphrase the two sentences in question . . . I would do it by saying that wholehearted devotion to liberty is unassailable and that half-hearted devotion to justice is undefensible." For many Americans, Goldwater's offer was too late and a rationalization that did little to modify their perceptions.[46]

General Eisenhower's continuing complaints about Goldwater's lukewarm support of the Civil Rights Act and his failure to condemn the Ku Klux Klan and other "vigilantes" were the stimuli for the conservative's most important effort to heal wounds.[47] He offered to meet with the leaders of the moderate and liberal wings of the Republican Party in Hershey, Pennsylvania, on August 12, 1964, to discuss differences and concerns. Hershey was a true party summit, with Eisenhower, Nixon, Goldwater, William Miller, Bill Scranton, George Romney, and Nelson Rockefeller attending the closed meeting. During the nearly three-hour gathering, Goldwater made a strong appeal for party unity. He scored with Ike by pledging "an immediate return to the proven Eisenhower-Dulles policy of peace through strength," support for the United Nations and Social Security, and "faithful execution of the Civil Rights Act." The general was also pleased with Barry's promise to "seek the support of no extremist of the left or the right" and repudiation of "character assassins, vigilantes, Communists, and any group such as the Ku Klux Klan which seek[s] to impose its views through terror, threat or violence."[48] After the meeting, Eisenhower told reporters, "I am right on Senator Goldwater's team as much as he wants me."[49]

Romney and Rockefeller, however, found Goldwater's efforts inadequate. Governor Romney wanted a stronger commitment to civil rights, believing that Goldwater planned to "finesse the issue" to "take advantage of the backlash."[50] Goldwater's assertions that he had worked for integration in Phoenix, had attempted to conciliate civil rights leaders, would appeal to black voters, and wished to dampen racial tensions did not sway Romney. Goldwater bristled and allowed his pledge on civil rights to stand without further elaboration. Rockefeller focused on Goldwater's revised stance on extremism. The New York governor called for a "forthright" declaration that not only promised not to "seek" but "completely reject[ed]" the support of extremists. With the John Birch Society in mind, he also suggested that acts of "conspiracy" be specifically cited as another reason to spurn such groups.

Barry, with Eisenhower's support, rejected this advice and claimed that his new statement satisfied Rockefeller's concerns. The Democrats easily secured a transcript of the secret meeting and it circulated among the White House staff.[51]

Reporters described the meeting as the beginning of the Republicans' healing process. There was still, however, a long way to go before recovery. Privately, Eisenhower backed away from his support of Goldwater. Nixon remembers the general saying, "You know, before we had this meeting, I thought that Goldwater was just stubborn. Now I am convinced that he is just plain dumb."[52] He told Nelson Rockefeller in a telephone conversation, "We have to recognize what we got—a man who is not bad—he is honest. . . . I will not do much because of age."[53] After the election Eisenhower informed Bill Scranton, "I voted for Goldwater but I did not vote for him, I voted for the Party."[54] For his part, Rockefeller pocketed the Goldwater for President buttons that Barry pressed into his hand at the meeting and disclosed to reporters that he had no plans to campaign outside New York state. He would neither bolt to the Democrats nor endorse Goldwater. Romney, while "accepting" his party's decision, also refused to back its standard-bearer.[55] Such liberal Republicans as California Senator Thomas Kuchel, New Jersey Senator Clifford Case, and New York Senators Kenneth Keating and Jacob Javits followed a similar path. Scranton bucked the trend, endorsed Goldwater, and campaigned for him in Pennsylvania and the Midwest. Goldwater's strongest backer was Richard Nixon, who traveled fifty thousand miles and made more than 150 appearances in thirty-six states on the Arizonan's behalf. In light of these efforts, Goldwater forgave Nixon's past indiscretions and would never forget his support. Nor would Barry forget the men who had deserted him "when the chips were down and the going was hard."[56]

With the style and substance of campaign '64 already set, Barry Goldwater returned to the steps of the county courthouse in Prescott, Arizona, on September 3, to launch formally the drive for the presidency. He delivered one of his most powerful speeches. Confronting the warmonger caricature head on, he spoke of peace repeatedly and vowed, "I do not intend to be a wartime president." He offered proof, a pledge to abolish the "outmoded and unfair" military draft. Goldwater also continued his assault on "Big Brother" and the "cancerous growth" of the federal bureaucracy, but declared that "we . . . shall never abandon the needy and the aged—we shall never forsake the helpless." He made sure to stress the "social issue," citing "the sick joke, the slick slogan, the off-color drama, and the pornographic book" as evidence of America's moral decline. He reminded his listeners of the related crime problem: "Our wives, all women, feel unsafe in our streets."

And he tied the civil rights movement to lawlessness: "mobs in the street restrained only by the plea that they wait until after election time to ignite violence again." Goldwater ended with great expectations. Americans, he believed, welcomed the task of renewal. America's rebirth, in turn, would transcend the nation's shores and "illuminate the world."[57]

Goldwater continued the offensive in Los Angeles, where he called for a 25 percent tax cut spread over five years. "This reduction would represent part of the increase in revenues that our growing economy is producing. The balance of that increase would be used to eliminate our present deficit."[58] Following stops in Seattle, Minneapolis, and upstate New York, he visited Chicago on September 11. There he championed the principles of limited government and "judicial restraint," especially in regard to the Supreme Court's school prayer decision and its "obsessive concern for the rights of the criminal defendant."[59] Law, he argued, must adapt to changing times, but reform was accomplished most effectively through the legislative process. On September 15 Goldwater was in St. Petersburg, Florida, to began a four-day, eight-city swing through the South. The St. Petersburg speech surprised reporters because the community's large senior citizen population offered him a high-profile opportunity to ease concerns about his stand on Social Security. Instead, he maintained the focus on crime and lawlessness. Large numbers of men and women turned out for Goldwater rallies everywhere. In Memphis, police estimated the crowd at 30,000; in Montgomery, 24,000; and in New Orleans, 27,000. Goldwater went on to St. Louis on September 20 and raised Vietnam. He deplored LBJ's pursuit of "a policy of weakness, a policy of indecision, a policy of indirection." He also challenged the pollsters: "Against the polls, against the newspapers and against the Federal pocketbook, we are getting the support of the people."[60] Three days later he was in Dallas, advocating peace through preparedness.[61]

National newsmagazines and the "prestige" press gave Goldwater extensive coverage and, occasionally, high marks on the campaign's first twenty days.[62] At the same time, they criticized his apparently deliberate intention to prick local sensitivities. In Knoxville, Tennessee, he proposed the sale of the TVA's steam-generating plants. In Charleston, West Virginia, he attacked the War on Poverty as a "hodgepodge of handouts" and a "phony, vote-getting scheme."[63] He was savvy, at the same time, in avoiding certain critical concerns. Most obvious, he made no mention of segregation or civil rights issues during his southern swing.[64]

The crowds that greeted Goldwater in September were large and enthusiastic. Yet in the face of roaring ovations at rallies of the faithful, Barry Goldwater stood impatient, remote, even withdrawn, pulling no energy from the mass. Reporters noted that his sharpest jabs lacked fire and revealed no deep feeling. He became increasingly defensive. In part, his flat delivery was habit, a career-long wooden style that endeared him to loyalists and resisted coaching. Goldwater also came off poorly in comparison to Lyndon Johnson, whose flesh-pressing exuberance played to favorable reviews. More important, appearances reflected increasing realism about the nature of the campaign and the chances for an upset. A month after the Hershey conference it was evident that Goldwater had mended few fences. Moderate and liberal Republicans refused to campaign or appear with him on the same platform. This was mirrored at the precinct and county levels, where party regulars were "lying down on the job."[65] Infighting between Goldwater enthusiasts and Republican stalwarts further choked momentum.[66]

Even worse was the general media reaction to his campaign. Photo magazines like *Life* and *Saturday Evening Post* raked Goldwater and continued their pre-election assaults. The *Atlantic Monthly* condemned Goldwater's "simplistic views" and "rebellion against the problems of modern life."[67] An editorial in *The Christian Century* compared the Goldwater campaign with the Nazi rise to power in 1933. "We hear again the appeal to national pride and self-justification; we hear the brandishing of weapons—any kind of weapons—to fulfill our purposes; we hear the gods invoked in alliance with our claims; we even notice subtle and implicit appeals to those among us who are racist. We have cause to be uneasy."[68] The most scurrilous piece was *Fact Magazine*'s "The Unconscious of a Conservative: A Special Issue on the Mind of Barry Goldwater." Editor Ralph Ginzburg peddled the sheet as a psychological exposé, printing the assessments of hundreds of psychiatrists, who called Goldwater mentally unfit to be president. Fabricating and doctoring quotations, Ginzburg indicted Goldwater as "a dangerous lunatic" and "paranoid schizophrenic" given to "unconscious sadism" and "suicidal tendencies." The *Fact Magazine* portrait was not complete without the now-standard historical parallel: "I believe Goldwater," wrote an Atlanta, Georgia, psychiatrist, "has a mask of sanity covering an inner political madness. . . . I find myself increasingly thinking of the early 1930s and the rise of another intemperate, impulsive, counterfeit figure of a masculine man, namely, Adolf Hitler."[69]

Goldwater received little succor from the local press. In an unprecedented reversal of the pattern, most daily newspapers tilted against the Republican candidate. Lyndon Johnson won endorsements from 445 newspapers (42 percent of all U.S. papers), with a combined daily circulation of 27.6 million readers (61.5 percent of all U.S. readers), to Goldwater's 368 dailies, with 9.7 million readers. Even Republican presidential candidate Alf Landon in 1936 had won the backing of a majority of the nation's newspapers against Franklin Roosevelt. While Barry gained the support of the *Los*

Angeles Times and *Chicago Tribune,* he counted only one-half as many endorsements as Richard Nixon had in 1960, and they were from newspapers with a total circulation but one-fourth of those championing the former vice president. Some newspapers pulled no punches. The *Sacramento Bee* editorialized: "Practically all of Goldwater's votes and views tend toward the enslavement of Americans."[70] Others made a blanket condemnation. The *Denver Post* reminded voters that "the Republican Party had its eyes open when it nominated Senator Barry Goldwater. It took the step deliberately; it knew what it was doing, and it must be held accountable for the results."[71] Even erstwhile mentor Eugene Pulliam and his *Arizona Republic* were only halfhearted in their support of Goldwater. Pulliam privately dismissed the conservative as "flighty" and a "lightweight," and he confided to William Mahoney, an Arizona Democrat and the U.S. ambassador to Ghana, that "you and I both know that Barry Goldwater is not qualified to be President of the United States."[72]

The conservative attacked the double standard of journalism, and press fairness quickly emerged as a campaign issue. Many reporters and editors did in fact favor the election of Lyndon Johnson. He had impressed them as a strong and effective leader who had under the most difficult of circumstances moved the country forward. But it was not love of Johnson so much as fear of Goldwater that fueled press animosity. Barry Goldwater threatened to disrupt the status quo of domestic progress. Journalists were certain that his policies would end the thaw in the cold war. He kept company with and attracted the wrong kind of friends. Reporters and editors thus deemed it a public service to "unmask" Goldwater, even to the point of overkill. They projected onto the conservative any guilt that arose. Goldwater's press was poor because of his impulsive answers during spontaneous exchanges. His statements and addresses were not carefully prepared or presented. Even his supporters realized this, the press observed. Correspondent Sam Donaldson, an admirer of Goldwater, remembered one speech in which the candidate was "saying things that seemed to be poorly thought out, at least poorly explained." A Goldwaterite approached Donaldson and pleaded: "Listen here. Write what he means, not what he says."[73] Donaldson was not the first nor would he be the last to face this quandary. They did their "duty," but as Ben Bradlee, who was a *Newsweek* editor in 1964, maintains, "I don't know a reporter who isn't a little bit ashamed of picking on Barry the way they did."[74] The press censure embittered Goldwater: "I've never seen or heard in my life such vitriolic . . . attack on one man as has been directed at me. I think these people should frankly hang their heads in shame because . . . they made the fourth estate a rather sad, sorry mess."[75] In later years, he would be strongly supportive of men he considered victims of media witch hunts.[76]

The Democratic campaign strategy frustrated Goldwater. President Johnson remained on the front porch of the White House during most of September, sallying forth only on "nonpolitical" trips to Florida to survey hurricane damage and to the Pacific Northwest to meet with Canadian Prime Minister Lester Pearson. Johnson's refusal to enter the fray threw the Republicans off balance. "We couldn't find an opponent," complained Denison Kitchel. "We were punching at a pillow."[77] While Johnson waited to strike, vice presidential candidate Hubert Humphrey carried the campaign to Goldwater. Humphrey, possessed of a seemingly endless supply of energy, crisscrossed the nation, alternating humor with dire warnings of impending doom to skewer the conservative. Cabinet members, except Secretary of State Dean Rusk and Secretary of Defense Robert McNamara, joined Humphrey on the hustings. Their presence in Washington was not missed, noted *Time,* for they had "long since been campaigning from within their offices, issuing instant replies to every criticism Goldwater has made of their departments."[78] Conservatives even accused the Post Office Department of having enlisted in the effort. In September, it issued a postcard with a stamp declaring, "For the People — By the People — Social Security."[79]

Democratic tactics infuriated Barry Goldwater. On September 7, during a commercial break in NBC's popular "Monday Night at the Movies," the Democrats struck a blow that left Goldwater reeling. Their ad opened on a little girl picking a daisy in a sunny field and counting as she plucked its pedals. A male voice, military and authoritative, growing stronger and stronger, began counting down after the little girl had reached ten. At zero, the screen filled with the sight of a nuclear blast. "These are the stakes," declared the voice of Lyndon Johnson. "To make a world in which all of God's children can live, or go into the dark. We must either love each other, or we must die." A male voice directed: "Vote for President Johnson on November 3rd. The stakes are too high for you to stay home."[80] Johnson telephoned Bill Moyers soon after: "I guess it did what we Goddamned set out to do, didn't it."[81] The ad aired only once. Although the commercial made no mention of Barry Goldwater, surveys found that listeners made the connection and were convinced that he was named. Five days later, another spot drove the connection home. This one featured a little girl licking an ice-cream cone as a female voice recounted that before passage of the Nuclear Test Ban Treaty atomic bombs were exploded in the atmosphere. The resulting radioactive fallout caused children to die. Now, the voice continued, a man who voted against that treaty wants to be president. "His name is Barry Goldwater, so if he's elected, they might start testing all over again."[82] It, too, was shown only once. What Goldwater had inspired, Rockefeller had fashioned, and Scranton had validated, the Doyle Dane Bernbach agency now imprinted on the American consciousness. Meanwhile, Republicans at the National Committee headquarters in Washington, D.C., were convinced that their telephones were bugged.[83]

The ads prompted the media, as the Democrats hoped, into another series of stories on what *Newsweek* called "the nuclear issue."[84] *Time,* putting the daisy girl on its cover, reviewed Goldwater's "itchy-finger image."[85] Johnson emerged from the press flurry as the "responsible, restrained keeper of nuclear peace."[86] Journalists rarely challenged his depiction of Goldwater, describing him with "Dr. Strangelove–type images of the 'madman' who unleashes nuclear war."[87] Goldwater's nuclear problem perplexed the Republicans. They tried to counter with commercials that showed Goldwater as calm, caring, and concerned, a family man who was neither warlike nor impulsive. They filmed Goldwater with Eisenhower at his Gettysburg farm, where the general reassured the American people of his friend's peaceful intentions. None of this worked. "When I went to bed," said campaign manager Kitchel, "I would lie awake asking myself at night, how do you get at the bomb issue? My candidate had been branded a bomb-dropper—and I couldn't figure out how to lick it."[88] The press offered Kitchel little help. In accepting Democratic rhetoric as truth and repeating it, few commentators attempted to engage either candidate in a serious discussion about strategic policy or the arms race. Then again, most Americans no longer cared; they had already made up their minds on the nuclear issue. Barry Goldwater scared them. They had no patience with his intention "to educate the American people to lose some of their fear of the word 'nuclear.'"[89]

Goldwater's Republican opponents similarly cued the Democratic strike on domestic issues. Social Security became the measure of the conservative's interest in the elderly, poor, and challenged. Democrats repeatedly broadcast a television commercial that showed disembodied hands ripping a Social Security card. Again the Arizonan was found wanting and unreliable: "On at least seven occasions Senator Barry Goldwater said that he would change the present Social Security system. But even his running mate, William Miller, admits that Senator Goldwater's voluntary plan would destroy the Social Security system. President Johnson is working to strengthen Social Security."[90] Skillfully, the image-makers had fed on past accusations and hardening predispositions. The damage was apparent to Karl Hess, Goldwater's chief speech writer, when people confronted him several times during the campaign and swore that they had seen his boss tearing apart Social Security cards on television. "They could not be shaken in their conviction."[91]

A semi-official literature, malevolent and distorted, supplemented these efforts. Presses printed millions of copies of *Barry Goldwater: Extremist of the Right, The Case Against Barry Goldwater, Barry Goldwater: A Political Indictment,* and *Goldwater from A to Z.* There was even a *Goldwater Coloring Book* that offered children the opportunity to color Goldwater in the guise of Napoleon and as a member of the Ku Klux Klan. Nor were Goldwaterites above this level of campaigning. They produced 16 million copies of such vicious tracts as *A Texan Looks at Lyndon, None Dare Call It Treason,* and *A Choice Not an Echo.*[92]

The opinion polls that bulged from LBJ's pockets testified to the Democrats' success in September. Goldwater's ratings were stagnant at 30 percent, showing no change from the readings taken at August's end. But the Johnson campaign team did not relax. It feared voter complacency and indications that the president's support was "broad but shallow." Moreover, while Goldwater had not picked up any ground, he had tagged Johnson as a "wheeler-dealer" and raised suspicions of presidential chicanery. Summing up the growing consensus in the White House, aide John Martin wrote that the president "has given the people something to vote against—Goldwater. Perhaps now he should give them something to vote for." It was time to "fire the second stage of the rocket" and begin active campaigning.[93] Johnson welcomed the advice. He thrilled at the prospect of a political fight, especially when the odds were so favorable. Besides, his pride and sense of history demanded that he not only maintain the advantage but devastate his opponent.[94]

On September 22 he lunged into the campaign, addressing the receptive delegates at the United Steelworkers convention in Atlantic City. The president was upbeat and even inspirational. "We will extend the helping hand of a just nation to the poor and the helpless and the oppressed. We will do all these things because we love people instead of hate them, because we have faith in America, not fear of the future." He also was on the attack. "It takes a man who loves his country to build a house instead of a raving, ranting demagogue who wants to tear down one."[95] While Goldwater was not named, no one missed the reference. Aides half-heartedly attempted to convince reporters that the president meant to say demagogues and had no particular individual in mind. The following day LBJ spoke to the International Union of Electrical Workers in Washington, D.C., and lifted lines from Nelson Rockefeller's speeches. "Americans are faced with a concerted bid for power by factions which oppose all that both parties have supported. It is a choice between the center and the fringe, between the responsible mainstream of American experience and the reckless and rejected extremism of American life."[96] Two days later Johnson was in Eufaula, Oklahoma, where he offered reassurances about Vietnam. "We don't want American boys to do the fighting for Asian boys," he said. "We don't want to get involved in a nation with 700 million people and get tied down in a land war in Asia." Nor would he give Goldwater an opening. "There are some that say we ought to go south and get out and come home, but we don't like to break our treaties and we don't like to walk off and leave people who are searching for freedom."97 On September 28 the president charged into the Northeast, making thirty speeches in twenty hours in six states. He returned briefly to the subject of Vietnam in Manchester, New Hampshire: "What I have been trying to do, with the situation that I found, was to get the boys in Vietnam to do their own fighting with our advice and with our equipment. . . . We are not going north and drop bombs at this stage of the game, and we are not going south and run out and leave it for the Communists to take over."98 By the end of September Johnson had traveled seventy-eight hundred miles in pursuit of votes. In forty-two days of active campaigning he would cover more than sixty thousand miles and give as many as two hundred speeches.99

Only a part of the Johnson message was delivered in formal speeches. The campaign medium was equally important. Despite security-sensitive aides, he demanded access to voters and worked them, as often as he could, person to person. At campaign stops he waded into crowds and used both hands to grab those outstretched to him, sometimes two and three at a time. He winked and nodded at those he could not reach, the personal connection made. Frequently he stopped his motorcade to shake more hands and distribute Johnson for President buttons. The Johnson touch also worked well from the stump. He evoked drama, leaning into audience members' faces, gesturing with both hands, and pointing upward to remind listeners that John Kennedy's spirit was "there in heaven watching us."100 Few would forget Johnson's imagery when he conjured up international crisis and asked: "Which man's thumb do you want to be close to that button now, which man do you want to reach over and pick up that hot line when they say, 'Moscow calling'?"101 No wonder that the Johnson campaign became, in sixties terms, a "happening," and that crowds of 30,000, 75,000, and as many as 175,000 mobbed him.102

Goldwater put on a brave face before the poll results and the Johnson onslaught. On September 28 he embarked on a five-day whistle-stop train tour that took him to thirty-three towns and cities in Ohio, Indiana, and Illinois. He repeated set speeches, holding to the themes of peace, limited government, and individual freedom. In Columbus, Ohio, on October 1, he made one of his few references to Vietnam. "I promise you that we would bend every effort to see that decisions were made in South Vietnam, and you people would be part of them to the end, that some day we could hope and pray that we could end that terrible conflict."103 He later released a statement to the press, pledging, if elected, to send former President Eisenhower to South Vietnam. "I intend to come to grips with this vital question and, at that time, I want the very best and soundest advice available."[104] But when restricted to a defensive crouch, even advocacy of moderation and peace could pose problems. Thus, just halfway through his speech in Hammond, Indiana, commentators had already counted almost thirty references, even if negative, to "push the button," "holocaust," and "atomic weapons."[105] The crowds of five thousand to ten thousand that greeted the presidential candidate pleased Republicans. Disconcerting, however, were those who jeered Goldwater or mocked him with placards reading: "Vote for Goldwater and go to war," "Welcome Doctor Strangewater," and "In your gut you know he's nuts."[106] Their numbers and intensity would grow with the campaign.[107]

Goldwater had scored no breakthroughs, and his offensive had stalled. Worse, he counterpunched with no effect on the nuclear issue and was exposed on Social Security. The Goldwater team feared a disaster in November. "Without something," recalled Texas Senator John Tower, the results were certain to be "cataclysmic" and Republicans would be "like lemmings marching to the sea."[108] Clearly the campaign demanded a mid-course correction. With few other options, Goldwater agreed with his advisers to press Johnson even harder on morality, corruption, crime in the streets, and the other social issues. Polls confirmed that these were real concerns and that Johnson was vulnerable. Maybe there was still time to push Johnson onto the defensive and persuade conservatives to surface. He would continue to raise defense and foreign policy matters but with less intensity, hoping that events might validate his positions. Goldwater's team did note one bright spot. Its grassroots army of almost 4 million activists had mobilized. Campaign workers personally contacted more than 12 million households by mid-October, 4 million more than the Democrats. Yet even that was insufficient to offset growing pessimism. "We were like the officers of the *Titanic*," joked Tower. "We knew what was happening, but those folks down below who were drinking and dancing didn't."[109]

Goldwater's speeches in Salt Lake City on October 10 and in Chicago on October 16 intensified the thrust on social concerns. Choosing as his forum the Mormon Tabernacle on Temple Square in downtown Salt Lake, Goldwater asked: "Why do we see wave after wave of crime in our streets and in our homes? Why do we see riot and disorder in our cities? A breakdown of morals of our young people? . . . A flood of obscene literature?" He answered: "The moral fiber of the American people is beset by rot and decay. And the most tragic thing of all is that this decay has made its most virulent attack on our young people." Goldwater's solutions to America's social ills were the removal of Lyndon Johnson—"immorality always starts at the top"—and the return of prayer to the public schools. Republicans replayed the speech to a national television audience later in the month.[110]

In Chicago, Goldwater focused on race. He prefaced his remarks by asserting that equality before the law did not mean "all men's accomplishments must be equal, that their skills must be equal. . . . On those levels, there is no equality, there is only opportunity." The goal of American society, he contended, "is neither to establish a segregated society nor to establish an integrated society as such. It is to preserve a *free* society." Under these assumptions, Goldwater scorned quotas in hiring and education. "One thing that will surely poison and embitter our relations with each other is the idea that some predetermined bureaucratic schedule of equality—and worst of all, a schedule based on the concept of race—must be imposed. . . . That way lies destruction." Similarly, he rejected busing to achieve racial balance in schools as "morally wrong," a "hypothetical goal of perfect equality imagined by the theorists of the so-called Great Society." Government's proper role in racial matters was to "offer moral leadership and persuasion" and guarantee the "freedom of association." As he had said so often, "No law can make one person like another if he doesn't want to." The speech was broadcast nationally on October 22.[111]

On October 14 a story broke that reified Goldwater's charges and was, potentially, a serious setback for the Johnson campaign. The week before, Walter Jenkins—the father of six, a trusted Johnson family aide for twenty-five years, and a special assistant to the president—was arrested for committing homosexual acts in a men's room at the YMCA in Washington, D.C. Johnson immediately dispatched Abe Fortas to obtain Jenkins' resignation. Fortas and Clark Clifford then made the rounds of newspaper offices, asking editors to hold the story temporarily to protect the Jenkins family. To distance himself further, Johnson even contrived to implicate Goldwater, for the Arizona senator had been Jenkins' commanding officer in their Air Force Reserve unit. Sources at the FBI had tipped the Republicans to the incident within forty-eight hours, and staffers informed Goldwater on October 12. When the news became public, the president commissioned the FBI to investigate any breaches in security. Meanwhile, LBJ ordered a crash poll and other damage control procedures to assess the impact. In her husband's silence, Lady Bird Johnson publicly expressed sympathy for Jenkins and his family.[112]

The "social issue" was powerful, but Goldwater's integrity set limits on its use. His initial reaction was to lash the president for "using every power of his great office, right now, yesterday and tomorrow, to cover-up one of the sorriest rumors we have ever had in the nation's capital. . . . The White House remains silent in the face of scandal, grave suspicion and a sense of national doubt unequalled in our time."[113] Barry Goldwater, however, would not stoop to conquer. Thereafter, he confined his remarks to suggestions that more "thorough security checks and investigations" be prescribed for those occupying "highly sensitive position[s] in the White House."[114] He reacted similarly when Clif White, now director of Citizens for Goldwater-Miller, sought permission to show on national television a twenty-eight-minute documentary titled "Choice." Designed to display graphically America's "moral rot" and make the race issue obvious, it was a montage of teenage gangs, women in topless bathing suits, pornography, black rioters, and strip-tease shows. Goldwater previewed the film, deemed it "racist," and canceled it.[115]

To Lyndon Johnson's great relief, international events smothered the "social issue" for the remainder of campaign '64. Within forty-eight hours of the appearance of the Jenkins story, newspapers headlined the ouster of Soviet Premier Nikita Khrushchev, the victory of Great Britain's Labour Party over the Conservatives, and the explosion of communist China's first atomic bomb. The president made a special broadcast from the Oval Office on October 18 to quiet concerns. He calmly reassured Americans that their nation was prepared militarily for any eventuality and that, at the same time, the "quest for peace . . . has never been more determined than it is now."[116] In contrast, recent events alarmed Barry Goldwater. The administration had been caught "flat-footed," he charged, and "the Communist threat to our security had become grave." He derided "peaceful coexistence" as "simply the Communist strategy for world conquest" and pointed to the Chinese bomb as convincing proof that his vote against the Nuclear Test Ban Treaty was justified. Now more than ever it was time for America to "confront Communism with a firm policy of resistance."[117] There was little doubt in most Americans' minds that events had made Lyndon Johnson's election even more imperative.

In the last weeks of the campaign Johnson hammered Goldwater where he was most vulnerable—on the issue of war and peace. He was so adept that he could flay Goldwater on nuclear policy and guerrilla war in the same breath. In Akron, Ohio, Johnson observed: "Sometimes our folks get a little impatient. . . . They rattle their rockets some, and they bluff about their bombs, but we are not about to send American boys nine or ten thousand miles away from home to do what Asian boys ought to be doing for themselves."[118] Nor would he let audiences lose sight of his Great Society: "It's the time—and it's going to be soon—when nobody in this country is poor. It's the time—and there's no point in waiting—when every boy or girl can have all the education . . . [they] can put to use. It's the time when there is a job for everybody who wants to work. . . . It's the time of peace on earth and good will among men."[119]

Barry Goldwater was fatigued, demoralized, and defeated, yet went through the final motions, appearing in Maryland, New York, Tennessee, Kentucky, Iowa, Wisconsin, Illinois, Ohio, Pennsylvania, Wyoming, Nevada, South Carolina, Texas, and California. He talked of Vietnam in Pikesville, Maryland: "American sons and grandsons are being killed by Communist bullets and Communist bombs. And we have yet to hear a word of truth about why they are dying."[120] In the wake of the Viet Cong attack on Bienhoa air base on November 1 that killed five Americans, Goldwater said, "We are down there at war, and I think it is high time that the President tells the people we are . . . and what he plans to do."[121] He reiterated, in Cleveland, his opposition to the Civil Rights Act, busing, and racial quotas. In Columbia, South Carolina, he appeared with recent GOP convert Senator Strom Thurmond, and in a speech carried on television throughout the South he reminded listeners: "We are being asked to destroy the rights of some under the false banner of promoting the civil rights of others."[122] During a national television broadcast the night before the election, Goldwater still tried to convince voters that he wasn't "trigger-happy."[123] As was his custom, he ended the campaign in Fredonia, a small Arizona town north of the Grand Canyon. He finished speaking to the sparse crowd, then, squinting into the setting sun, said, "If Jack were here, we would have had a good campaign."[124]

At 6:29 P.M. on November 3, before the polls had closed, NBC News predicted a Johnson landslide. By 7 P.M. the other networks had concurred. The president had slaughtered Barry Goldwater by a 16 million–vote margin (43 million to 27 million; 61 percent to 39 percent) that translated into a 486 to 52 electoral-vote blowout. In the size of his popular vote and plurality, LBJ had even bested Franklin Roosevelt's crushing of Alf Landon in 1936. His was a national triumph. In New England, Johnson handily captured the traditional Republican bastions of Maine (69 percent), New Hampshire (64 percent), and Vermont (66 percent). Goldwater could muster only 39 percent of the region's tally. Johnson scored impressively in the Middle Atlantic states (66 percent), with New York giving him a 2 million–vote edge. In the Midwest (61 percent), he won Illinois by more than 1 million votes and took Michigan and Ohio by nearly that many. Republican Kansas, Iowa, Nebraska, South Dakota, and North Dakota all went to LBJ. Goldwater's totals in the farm belt did not even match Herbert Hoover's 1932 figures. The vote was somewhat closer out West, but Goldwater posed no threat to the Democratic sweep. Johnson carried the Rocky Mountain states with 56 percent of the vote and the Pacific Coast with 59 percent. California voters preferred Johnson over Goldwater by almost 1 million ballots, with about one-third of the difference amassed in Los Angeles County. Johnson faltered only in the

Deep South, losing Mississippi, Alabama, South Carolina, Georgia, and Louisiana, and in Goldwater's native Arizona.[125]

The victory was broad-based. Reviving the New Deal coalition, the president united farmers, blue-collar workers, the poor, professionals, minorities, and the middle class. He captured 62 percent of women voters and 90 percent of the Jewish vote. Johnson even expanded the coalition, raiding the Republican Party of 20 percent of its supporters, or 7 million "frontlashers." The competition between Republicans and Democrats for the African-American vote ended in 1964 with lopsided results. In four black precincts of Knoxville, Tennessee, the tally was Johnson's 5,468 to Goldwater's 62. In Richmond, Virginia, two black precincts went to Johnson, 3,395 to 18. Overall, the 94 percent of black men and women who voted against Goldwater are credited with delivering Virginia, Florida, Tennessee, Arkansas, and North Carolina to LBJ. Johnson won a majority of white votes nationally and is the last Democratic presidential candidate to do so.[126]

Barry Goldwater followed the returns briefly, turned off his television, and worked alone in his room until going to bed at 11 P.M. In anger, he refused to concede that night, and his belated congratulatory telegram defiantly focused less on the election than on the problems of Vietnam, Cuba, and law and order. At a press conference held in the Camelback Inn in Scottsdale the next morning he lambasted the press and moderate and liberal Republicans who refused to work for the ticket. He gave no indication of his plans. Observers reeled off other reasons for his defeat, including the brilliance of the Johnson campaign, peace and prosperity, and Goldwater's missteps. But they agreed with Goldwater that no Republican could have upset Johnson in 1964.[127]

A chagrined Barry Goldwater later apologized to fellow Republicans: "I accept the full responsibility for it. I'm sorry I couldn't produce better results. I'm sorry that so many good men . . . went down with me."[128] The election was a decisive defeat for the GOP but not as staggering as the 1958 debacle. The Republicans lost two seats in the U.S. Senate, thirty-seven in the House of Representatives, and 541 in state legislatures. They gained one governor's chair. While there was much ticket splitting, and although many Republicans contesting state office ran ahead of the national ticket, the casualty list was long. Of the fifty-seven Republican members of the House of Representatives who endorsed Goldwater before the July convention and then ran for reelection, twenty were defeated. Such promising and strong candidates for the Senate as Howard Baker in Tennessee, Claude Kirk in Florida, Paul Laxalt in Nevada, Charles Percy in Illinois, Robert Taft, Jr., in Ohio, and Bud Wilkinson in Oklahoma waged losing efforts. In Texas, George Bush, the son of Connecticut Senator Prescott Bush and an ardent Goldwaterite, carried on a vigorous campaign against incumbent Senator Ralph Yarborough. Like Goldwater, Bush opposed the Civil Rights Act as unconstitutional and refused to repudiate the John Birch Society. The burden of Goldwater and the popularity of Johnson in his native Texas proved too much to overcome. Bush ran seven points ahead of Goldwater but could muster only 44 percent of the vote. The Arizona returns offered some consolation. Republican Paul Fannin won election to Goldwater's Senate seat, but Dick Kleindienst's bid for the governorship was defeated. As important as the sum of the actual damages was the lost opportunity that 1964 represented to the Republicans. Vulnerable first-term Democratic liberals elected in 1958—such as Vance Hartke (Indiana), Philip Hart (Michigan), and Gale McGee (Wyoming)—rode the president's coattails and survived.[129]

There were a few Republican winners besides Paul Fannin. California voters elected conservative George Murphy over Kennedyite Pierre Salinger. Conservative Roman Hruska won reelection in Nebraska. Republican liberals did better, with New Yorker John Lindsay elected to the House of Representatives and Michigan Governor George Romney and Pennsylvania Senator Hugh Scott returned to office. Indeed, liberal Republicans counted only one important loss as Bobby Kennedy captured the New York Senate seat of Kenneth Keating. The Republican who made the most gains in 1964, Richard Nixon, did not run for office. Nixon had campaigned hard for Goldwater and defended him after the election: Goldwater, declared Nixon, "had the problem of constant sniping from the rear from defectors within his own ranks. . . . I think there has been enough bloodletting."[130] He called Rockefeller a "divider" and snapped: "I would suggest that anyone who sits on the sidelines can't step in and be captain of the team."[131] Barry was indebted to his friend and announced in a meeting of Republicans after the election, "Dick, I will never forget it. I know that you did it in the interests of the Republican Party and not for any selfish reasons. But if there ever came a time I can turn those into selfish reasons, I am going to do all I can to see that it comes about."[132]

Commentators quickly weighed the evidence and pronounced the Goldwater movement an aberration now dead. According to *New York Times* columnist James Reston, "Barry Goldwater not only lost the presidential election yesterday but the conservative cause as well. He has wrecked his party for a long time to come and is not even likely to control the wreckage."[133] *Time* magazine prophesied: "The conservative cause whose championship Goldwater assumed suffered a crippling setback. . . . The humiliation of their defeat was so complete that they will not have another shot at party domination for some time to come."[134] Chet Huntley of NBC dismissed Goldwater voters as "classic Republicans, segregationists, Johnsonphobes, desperate conservatives, and radical nuts . . . the coalition of discontent."[135] There was soon more proof that the conservative thrust was spent. Moderate and liberal Republicans purged Goldwater protégé Dean Burch as national party chair and put forward Ray Bliss, a pragmatic politician without ties to any faction. *Newsweek* described this coup as the "end of an era."[136] Having escaped the Goldwater nightmare, General Dwight Eisenhower also vowed to do his part. "If the Lord spares me for 1968, I am going to come out for somebody at least 18 months ahead of time. This year I tried to do what was decent."[137]

The reports of conservatism's demise were greatly exaggerated because they neglected crucial changes at the grassroots. Commentators portrayed Goldwater's victories in the five Deep South states as exceptions that proved the breadth of Johnson's accomplishment. They derided the Republican vote in Mississippi (87 percent), Alabama (69 percent), and the other states as racist. And they belittled the significance of these inroads, reviewing the success of Eisenhower and Nixon in capturing upper southern states and a higher percentage of the vote in the region at large. Subsequent analysis, however, revealed what Goldwater had achieved. Of the 507 southern counties he carried, 233 had never voted Republican. One hundred and thirty-eight rural black-belt counties with nonwhite majorities went strongly for Goldwater. Race, in fact, proved a key variable throughout the South, and Johnson received a clear majority of the white vote only in Texas. Thus, the 1964 campaign accelerated the regional reversal and polarization of the parties on race, with blacks rallying to the Democratic standard and whites quelling their hostility to the GOP. Goldwater, in other words, carried a different South than did Eisenhower and Nixon. As his predecessors had begun to turn the allegiance of whites in the upper South to the Republican Party, Goldwater began the transformation of loyalties in the heart of Dixie. This was apparent not only in the presidential figures but also in the returns for congressional races. Of the ten House seats won from Democrats nationally, Republicans captured seven in Alabama, Mississippi, and Georgia. The results might have been even more dramatic, but Republicans contested only two-thirds of these elections.[138]

There was also movement in the North, particularly in urban, ethnic-Catholic strongholds. The 1964 campaign brought no Republican erosion in heavily Irish, German, and Italian Catholic precincts. In the New York City boroughs of Queens, the Bronx, and Staten Island, Goldwater even exceeded the small but noticeable support among the Irish and Italians that Nixon garnered in 1960. Designating these areas an "early and accurate litmus of Northeastern Catholic politics," Republican strategist Kevin Phillips suggested that 1964 foreshadowed a realignment similar to that which portended in 1928.[139] As Al Smith's failed campaign drew the new immigrants into the

Democratic fold and presaged the party's ascendancy, Goldwater's ruin fore-shadowed a similar fate for the Republicans. Peace, prosperity, and racial quiet smothered the "backlash" in 1964. When the "social issue" became more charged, a growing number of Goldwater Democrats would cause the political balance of power to shift.[140]

Conservatives meshed the returns from New York and the South with data gathered in the West. The Rocky Mountain states were the most closely contested. Southern California's fast-growing San Diego and Orange Counties went to Goldwater. Surely, even for the most disappointed, it was too early to abandon the possibilities that a southern-western-urban ethnic coalition offered.[141]

Signs from the grassroots that conservatives were refusing to give up the fight braced these hopes. Bumper stickers defiantly attested to a continuing loyalty: "One of 27,000,000 and Proud of It" and "27 million Americans Can't be Wrong."[142] George Bush spoke for many: "I am convinced that conservatism was not beaten on November 3. Goldwater was beaten, Bush was beaten, . . . but I don't think we can say conservatism was beaten."[143] The 1964 campaign was an incubator that accelerated the maturation of a generation of conservatives. Michael Deaver, James Edwards, Jake Garn, Jesse Helms, Phyllis Schafly, David Stockman, and George Will, to mention only a few, either began their political lives in the Goldwater campaign or honed critical skills there. Shortly after the election, campaign worker Richard Viguerie gathered lists of Goldwater contributors. From them he developed a national direct-mail network to provide information and raise funds for conservative causes. None of these vibrations surprised Richard Nixon, who was well informed about the strength and tenacity of Republican conservatism. Looking ahead to 1968, he was keenly aware that white southerners would constitute one-fourth of the delegates to the Republican convention, with many other veterans of the Goldwater campaign in attendance.[144]

In their hearts, conservatives knew that Barry Goldwater was right, but their heads denied another leap of faith with the Arizonan. They were eager to raise a new political hero, and the 1964 campaign offered them that opportunity in Ronald Reagan. Well known to conservatives, Reagan had served Goldwater as the co-chair of the California campaign. To do more, he offered to deliver a nationally televised speech titled "A Time for Choosing," a variation of a talk that he had given for years on the Rotary Club–Chamber of Commerce banquet circuit. Goldwater's advisers previewed the speech and were reluctant to let Reagan go on the air, fearing that he would reignite the Social Security issue after, they naively believed, it had been neutralized. Goldwater overruled them, and the program appeared on October 27. Skilled in the medium, reassuring, and friendly, Reagan offered Goldwaterisms about high taxes, "intellectual elites," bureaucracy, and "compulsory government programs." Using the soft sell, he neither alienated nor frightened listeners, a sharp contrast with Goldwater's stridency. A flood of telephone calls and contributions followed the telecast, testifying to Reagan's appeal.[145]

On election night Reagan consoled and cheered his fellow conservatives in their adversity: "But, we're just starting out. God bless all of you and I'm sure that in the days ahead we won't lack for ammunition."[146] The next day conservatives in Owosso, Michigan, formed a Republicans for Reagan organization. On January 31, 1965, Clif White and members of his Draft Goldwater committee met at the O'Hare Airport Inn outside Chicago. They soon made overtures to Ronald Reagan. In light of Barry Goldwater's sense of martyrdom, the rush to the new champion must have been hard to bear.[147]

When Ronald Reagan won the presidency in 1980 and the mainstream shifted to the right, American conservatives became conscious of their history. They explored the past and discovered the bench marks from which they measured their movement's progress: the publication of Friedrich von Hayek's *Road to Serfdom*, Robert Taft's defeat at the 1952 Republican convention, the appearance of *National Review*, and the aborted presidential bids of Ronald Reagan in 1968 and 1976. None of these events, however, compares in the conservative imagination to Barry Goldwater's campaign for the presidency in 1964. Those who fought the odds that year, first in the primaries and state conventions and then against the Democrats, wear special badges of identity and honor. They stand apart as the founding generation that in defeat marked future victory. Patrick Buchanan wrote later: "Like a first love, the Goldwater campaign was, for thousands of men and women now well into middle age, an experience that will never recede from memory, one on which we look back with pride and fond remembrance. We were there on St. Crispin's Day."[148] Paul Weyrich spoke similarly for a younger generation: "Even if we did nothing but wear a Goldwater button, or attend a rally—and some of the New Right are so young [that] is all they did—it made a mark, and had an impact."[149] Even today conservatives assess allegiance according to a personal carbon dating that makes 1964 the touchstone of commitment. Perhaps it was, as Buchanan suggests, a first love, an initial call to service at a time when many Americans looked beyond themselves for meaning. Sacrifice in a lost cause is also empowering, especially when the future is read as a validation of the past. As John Tower noted: "The '64 campaign was the Alamo before San Jacinto, to put it in Texas terms."[150] Both politically and personally, 1964 would prove a pivotal election, a beginning rather than an end.

Part III   From Martyrdom to
            Canonization

10 Rising from the Ashes

Was he beaten as his beater has been? Did he suffer such slaughter as his slayers?
—ISAIAH 27:7

Friends and family agreed that defeat left no deep scars on Barry Goldwater. The size of Lyndon Johnson's mandate denied second-guessing, and his understanding of its creation headed off self-doubt. Forced retirement briefly gave Barry time to get reacquainted with his wife, Peggy, and grown children, with Arizona, and with long-neglected hobbies. He relaxed and his sense of humor returned. "Peggy and I just [sit] on the hill," he told journalist David Broder, "watching the sunsets, and occasionally humming to ourselves, 'Hail to the Chief.'"[1]

If Goldwater's intellectual and emotional moorings were intact, he found his public role in flux. Defeat made the Arizonan a private citizen for the first time in fifteen years and stripped him of a formal pulpit. He retained the respect of conservatives, which was even enhanced, yet he no longer held their confidence as leader. Barry Goldwater was able to forgo riding point— it clearly had drawbacks—but he had no intention of leaving the public scene. The impact of the 1964 campaign was evident in this refusal to retreat. Goldwater's pride and principle demanded vindication. His sense of responsibility to the conservative movement also necessitated a continued public presence. Besides, he joked, "I am too old to go back to work and too young to get out of politics."[2]

First as a critic and then again as a U.S. senator, he pressed his positions. Feedback was immediate and encouraging. National and international events convinced the Arizonan of his course and reassured him that the effort of 1964 was not in vain, just premature. The fall of Lyndon Johnson and the rise of a Republican Party shaped to Goldwater's strategy and appeal shifted popular perceptions of the conservative. So did a style that was usually less shrill and more deliberate than before. Americans began to imagine him a prophet in his own time. Defeat touched Barry Goldwater in another way. It intensified his already fierce loyalty to friends and party, even to the point of overriding ideology. In the coming years, Goldwater's partisanship deepened, and he would cleave to those who had stood by him in his time of need.

In early 1965, with funds from the party, Barry settled into an office in the basement of the Goldwater's store in Scottsdale. Only his longtime secretary, Judy Rooney (later married to Dwight Eisenhower's nephew and Goldwater aide Earl Eisenhower), made the transition with him. Despite their hopes, or fears, it was not a tranquil time. Up to one thousand letters per week showered the office from all over the United States. Each day Goldwater received thirty invitations to speak. He resumed his frenetic pace, scheduling more than a speech a day during 1966 and 1967. He appeared often at Arizona Republican functions, a renewal of his hands-on approach to party-building. "I travel all over the state, almost constantly, just working for the party."[3] He also worked for himself. In June 1965 he announced to Yuma Republicans that he would seek reelection to the U.S. Senate in 1968. Early on, his polls showed him ahead of possible opponents Senator Carl Hayden, Secretary of Interior Stewart Udall, Congressman Morris Udall, and Roy Elson, Hayden's administrative assistant. "I am conducting," he confided to a friend in early 1966, "what I might call a low-key campaign speaking daily with groups of all ages."[4] Goldwater brushed up his Spanish to enhance his appeal to Hispanic voters. He even worked the high schools in search of future conservatives. Conveniently, he had renewed the lease on his Washington, D.C., apartment.[5]

Goldwater, meanwhile, drew handsome speaking fees from national groups, with earnings mounting to as much as $150,000 per year. "I was making money," he wrote, "more than ever in my life."[6] Increasing his exposure, he returned to the editorial pages of the *Los Angeles Times* with three columns per week on national and international affairs. Seventy-five dailies across the United States, including the *Arizona Republic,* showcased his views. Repeated appearances on such network news programs as "Issues and Answers," "Meet the Press," and "Face the Nation" similarly testified to Goldwater's continuing national stature and appeal. Despite these heavy commitments, the Arizonan did much traveling during the time away from Washington. In addition to speaking tours in the United States, he visited Vietnam, Australia, and Europe. The pace was such that Judy Rooney noticed little break in the customary routine. "Those four years we were here, it was like we were still sitting in the Senate."[7]

A busy speaking schedule and the election of another right-minded member of Congress, Goldwater knew, was not enough to secure the future of the conservative movement. During his post-election vacation to Jamaica in early 1965 he and Denison Kitchel explored options to marshal the resources of the 27 million men and women who had voted for him. They announced, in June 1965, the formation of the Free Society Association (FSA) as a "haven" for conservatives who might "either lose interest entirely or, in search of action, be siphoned off by . . . the so-called 'extreme right.'"[8] In a nod to the recent past, they specifically excluded from membership Ku Klux Klansmen and active John Birchers.[9] With Goldwater as honorary board chair and Kitchel as president, the group laid plans to launch a television and radio campaign to awaken Americans to conservative principles, organize "think-ins" on college campuses, create a speakers' bureau, publish scholarly monographs, and recruit a membership of 150,000. The FSA offered, as well, to coordinate the efforts of conservative groups while "strengthen[ing] and complement[ing] the activities and the functions of the Republican Party."[10] To facilitate mobilization, the FSA drew funds from the coffers of the now-defunct Citizens for Goldwater-Miller organization and began soliciting members from 1964 campaign mailing lists. Such prominent conservatives as Raymond Moley, Clare Booth Luce, George Humphrey, William Rehnquist, and Robert Bork were early members.[11]

The performance of the FSA never matched Goldwater's expectations or temperament. Only 38,500 men and women paid the five-dollar membership fee. Budgets soon grew tight, and officers shelved television and publication plans. At the same time, other conservative groups—like the American Conservative Union, Americans for Constitutional Action, and Young Americans for Freedom—were experiencing surging memberships and resisting subordination to what Stephen Hess and David Broder dismissed as a "tract-writing outfit."[12] Goldwater quickly lost interest, for he was more comfortable rallying conservatives with speeches, in newspaper columns, and on television. Although FSA leaders recognized their failure early on, they did not announce their organization's demise until 1969.[13]

Barry Goldwater's rapid resurgence had come in the wake of foreign and domestic events that gave his words new meaning and urgency. The message had not changed but Americans had. In early 1965, President Lyndon Johnson responded to attacks on American advisers with Operation Rolling Thunder, the bombing of North Vietnam to interdict supplies and soldiers bound for southern battlegrounds. In March the first American combat troops landed in South Vietnam and, a few months later, pursued the Viet Cong in "search and destroy missions." Johnson had committed 184,000 American soldiers to Vietnam by the end of 1965; a year later the number had more than doubled.[14]

The war in Vietnam "became one of the driving forces of my life," wrote Goldwater.[15] Subordinating political and economic issues and merging Viet

Cong with North Vietnamese, he consistently offered a military solution to the conflict. The quick destruction of North Vietnam through massive air power was his prescription for victory, because he was certain that the guerrilla war could not continue in the south without logistical support. Reflecting his Air Force training, he rejected, like General Douglas MacArthur, a ground war on the Asian mainland as too costly. He thus praised the president for initiating the bombing of supply routes and smugly declared in April 1965: "Today, the United States is moving firmly and decisively on a foreign policy course charted straight out of the Republican campaign of 1964."[16]

He urged the president on, suggesting he leave the war to the "pros" in the Pentagon. "The Vietnamese targeting smacked heavily of armchair political thinking. It is not tough, win-the-war military thinking, thus the imagined need for ground troops."[17] Goldwater recommended following the military's advice that bombers hit "industrial complexes" near Hanoi, agricultural dikes, and the port facilities and supply depots of Haiphong.[18] He became exasperated when the president restricted these targets: "Why the hell we don't hit Haiphong, I don't know. So long as your enemy continues to get supplies, he will fight. . . . Hanoi gets the bulk of its supplies from Russia through the port of Haiphong. Therefore we ought to put it out of business."[19] To the same end, he advocated blockading or mining Haiphong harbor. To complement the air war in the north, Goldwater insisted that sorties be launched against Viet Cong sanctuaries in Cambodia and Laos. There were, however, limits to total war. The conservative rejected the targeting of residential areas: "We are not people killers."[20]

Goldwater downplayed the fear that intensifying the war would provoke Soviet or Chinese intervention. Overwhelming American air and naval power, he was convinced, held these communists at bay. He even told a European audience that "I pray that Communist China gives us provocation to attack their nuclear possibility."[21] Intelligence reports maintaining that bombing was more effective in conventional wars against industrialized foes did not sway the Arizonan. He also rejected evidence that the guerrilla war in the south would continue even without northern supplies. Similarly, the sustained high morale of the Vietnamese in the face of air attack was of little import before American technology and resolve.[22]

Goldwater formed his opinions about the war from experience, meetings with military leaders, and on-site inspections in Vietnam. While in country, Goldwater flew over North Vietnam and the Ho Chi Minh Trail network. He visited U.S. soldiers manning front-line positions. Although neither of Barry's sons served in Vietnam, he did establish a personal bond to the battlefield. In 1967, ham operator Goldwater tied his K7UGA station into the Military Affiliate Radio System (MARS). With the assistance of thirty-five volunteers working in shifts that ensured twenty-four-hour-a-day coverage, Goldwater patched almost 200,000 telephone calls from American soldiers in Vietnam to their families in the states. The link brought the war home to Goldwater: "You'd hear the soldiers just moaning and groaning."[23]

These activities and his interpretation of patriotism firmed support for the war and opposition to dissent. He demanded that Arkansas Senator J. William Fulbright, a critic of the war, resign as chair of the Committee on Foreign Relations. "I am ashamed to watch a television set and see Democratic members . . . telling the American people that our power has made America arrogant and self-righteous and expansionist and immoral. No American has the right to or the justification to level such charges against his country. And that goes double for doing it in a time of war and in a fashion that lends aid and comfort to our enemies." Goldwater characterized "doves" as "lunatic crowds of appeasers, pacifists, and pro-Communists and just plain Communists." He was adamant that draft evaders be punished severely, "imprisoned for ten to twenty years." The morality of American involvement, he bristled more candidly than he realized, "can be debated after the war is over." In an incident during his first tour of Vietnam in 1965, he was abusive. "I wish," CBS reporter Morley Safer remembers him saying, "they would let me have my way out here. There wouldn't be a gook or fucking reporter left in six months."[24]

As the president raised the stakes in Vietnam, racial fires engulfed American cities. On August 11, 1965, five days after the passage of the Voting Rights Act, the black ghetto of Watts in south Los Angeles erupted in violence. Thirty-four died in the rioting and almost nine hundred were wounded, with property damage mounting to $30 million. The violence spread throughout black America, for joblessness, crowded and substandard housing, inadequate services, and police brutality were common. In 1965 the casualty list ran to twenty-two cities, and in 1966 it was at forty-four, including Chicago and Cleveland. It was more than a concern for law and order and property damage that spurred white anger. The violence seemed irrational or the work of black radicals because it coincided with a flood of legislation designed to redress grievances. In addition to the Voting Rights Act, Congress rapidly passed the Great Society's War on Poverty. Coming in a context of resentment against African-Americans, who were seen as having already pushed too far and too fast, such government programs suggested preferential treatment and exacerbated white rancor. The emergence of the civil rights movement in the North also challenged whites who believed that their schools, jobs, and communities were under siege. The meaning of black rights had changed for white Americans. And the sixties had yet to see its most violent summer.[25]

For many Americans, the black uprising was only one symptom of a profound breakdown in authority, traditional values, and personal security. They
fingered federal bureaucrats as the enemy for raising already-high tax bur-
dens and elevating welfare over work and minority over majority. Paternalistic and out of touch, the "social engineers" had compounded their sins with
forced busing and affirmative action programs without regard to the will or
rights of those affected. Americans accused the liberal Supreme Court of
sanctioning these abuses while coddling criminals and easing restrictions on
pornography. They bemoaned the blunted influence of church and family,
condemning as causes the changing sexual lifestyles and the youth rebellion.
A countercultural plague of crime and violence, divorce, sexual promiscuity,
teenage pregnancy, and drug abuse was the result. Voters had ignored Goldwater in 1964, when he targeted liberalism as the culprit and declared it
bankrupt. Now, more and more men and women accepted his verdict. The
president and the Democrats had betrayed them. Their promises of peace
and prosperity had shattered in domestic war, foreign conflict, permissiveness, and governmental incompetence.[26]

Although he had the opportunity, Goldwater did not pummel the
Democrats with the "social issue." His priority was Vietnam, and he left the
domestic arena to other conservatives. Still, he lashed the president on
spending, predicting growing deficits and rising inflation. Racial violence
was of even greater concern. After the riots in Watts he called for job training
and economic investment in the ghettos. "The thing that happened in Los
Angeles . . . was caused by people . . . just being fed up with not being able
to get jobs, with not being able to live as well as other people live." At the
same time, he blamed civil rights activists for fomenting violence, and he
linked their tactic of civil disobedience to the rioting. "I think it's time that
the leaders, both Negro and white, quit saying that if the law doesn't suit
you, go ahead and violate it."[27] Later, his accusations became more specific:
"As long as people are told they are allowed to break the law, as Dr. Martin
Luther King is doing, urban riots will continue."[28] In 1966 he again blamed
King and the civil rights movement: "I think they're going ninety miles an
hour toward anarchy. King has stated he doesn't feel people are required to
obey a bad law. This is open advocacy of disrespect."[29] Goldwater wasn't
above red-baiting. "Although I don't accuse anybody," he said as he role-
played a communist leader, "I would be involved in black organizations right
up to my ears."[30]

Conservatives looked to the 1966 midterm elections for validation. The
returns were mixed. Collectively, Republicans staged a major comeback,
winning twenty-five of thirty-five governors' races, eighteen of thirty-two
Senate contests, and forty-seven House seats. In state legislatures, they

recovered nearly all of the seats lost in 1964. Liberal Republican Governors Nelson Rockefeller, George Rommey, and John Volpe claimed victory in New York, Michigan, and Massachusetts, respectively. Mark Hatfield, Edward Brooke, and Charles Percy won U.S. Senate seats. These successes, however, disguised further erosion of moderate and liberal influence within the GOP. Of the forty-seven House seats gained, only two were in northeastern districts. Conservatives had, moreover, made additional advances, with primary election victories in New York, Pennsylvania, and Maine.[31]

More satisfying to conservatives was the reelection of Senators John Tower, Strom Thurmond, Karl Mundt, and Carl Curtis. Victories in Senate races in Wyoming and Oklahoma added to the Senate's conservative bloc. In the South, where Goldwater had campaigned for local candidates, conservatives more than balanced their loss of congressional seats in Alabama and Mississippi with gains in Arkansas, Florida, Georgia, North Carolina, South Carolina, Tennessee, Texas, and Virginia. In all, southern Republicans netted nine House seats to increase their total to twenty-six. The Republican right's greatest gains were in governors' mansions. Conservatives captured ten governorships, of which eight were in southern and western states. Their biggest coup was California. Hiring Rockefeller choice Stuart Spencer as campaign manager and asking Barry Goldwater to stay out of California during the campaign, Ronald Reagan rolled over Democratic Governor Pat Brown by almost one million votes. Reagan telephoned the Arizonan the next day and acknowledged his debt: "If it hadn't been for what you did [in 1964], I could not have won yesterday."[32] Barry Goldwater was particularly pleased with results in conservative bellwether Arizona. Supreme Court–ordered reapportionment combined with the rising population of Phoenix to deliver the state Senate to the Republicans for the first time. They similarly took a majority of seats in the state House of Representatives. Meanwhile, Arizonans elected Republicans as governor, attorney general, and state treasurer. Two of the state's three congressional seats went Republican. The 1964 disaster was now behind Goldwater and his fellow conservatives. The future again offered promise. Surveying the results at home and nationally, Goldwater judged the election a repudiation of Lyndon Johnson and the Great Society, "a backlash against dishonesty in government, runaway inflation, welfare-state socialism and a no-win policy in Vietnam."[33]

Political affairs and a national focus during these years did not distract Goldwater from his other interests. Peggy rejoiced in his heightened attention and their togetherness. He returned to the Colorado River, this time with his grown daughters and sons, to retrace part of the 1940 rafting trip. He enjoyed boosting Arizona, encouraging tourism with articles and talks on history and sites of interest. Goldwater published *People and Places,* a fine collection of

portraits and Arizona landscapes. In 1967, in a reflection of changing national
perceptions, he served as tour guide on the CBS television special *Barry Goldwater's Arizona*. Boosterism yielded to environmental awareness when he
joined Margaret Kober, who had served with him on the Phoenix city council,
to co-chair the campaign to shield from developers the summit of Valley of the
Sun landmark Camelback Mountain. A matching grant from the federal government guaranteed the success of the effort. Wielding his national influence,
he worked in support of Arizona's congressional delegation, lobbying for passage of the Central Arizona Project (CAP). In speeches, letters, and telephone
calls, he assured conservationists that the project would not damage the
Grand Canyon ecosystem, and he appealed to Senate friends for support as a
"personal favor."[34] These activities bolstered Senator Carl Hayden's main campaign, which achieved victory when President Johnson signed legislation
authorizing the CAP in September 1968. "WATER! WATER! WATER!" headlined
the *Arizona Republic*, heralding the last major federal water project in the
West.[35] Designed to rescue Arizona's desert agriculture by the mid-1980s, the
CAP's pumping plants, storage dams, aqueducts, and coal-fired power plant
were pricetagged at an estimated $1.3 billion. These were also years of tran-
sition for Barry Goldwater. His mother, JoJo, died in December 1966. After
thirty-seven years in uniform, he reached mandatory retirement age in 1967
and left the U.S. Air Force Reserve as a major general.[36]

The pace stayed hectic in 1967 and 1968. Barry and Peggy traveled to
Asia, with stops in Taiwan, Vietnam, Japan, and Thailand. In Taiwan, Goldwater renewed friendships with Chinese pilots he had trained during World
War II who were now high-ranking officers in the Republic of China air
force. He met with Generalissimo Chiang Kai-shek. "I have long been an
admirer of his," he wrote to his children, "and have long agreed completely
with his policies."[37] The Goldwaters also toured Southern Rhodesia and
South Africa. Perhaps it was his conviction that South Africa was a key ally in
the war against international communism that led him to racial appeasement: "I feel very strongly about this apartheid thing, not that I am 100 percent in favor of it or that I think it should be extended into eternity, but I do
think the United States is making a dreadful mistake in not allowing the
thing to be tested [in South Africa]."[38] On tours of American cities and college campuses, the conservative continued to support the president's
Vietnam policies, objecting only to bombing halts and restrictions on air
strikes. Referring to Lyndon Johnson, Goldwater beamed, "In his heart, he
knows I was right."[39] Massive antiwar demonstrations and the Tet Offensive
in early 1968, which witnessed devastating Viet Cong attacks throughout
South Vietnam and even into the U.S. embassy compound in Saigon, did not
cause him to doubt a military solution.[40]

The growing intensity of racial violence in America may have led Barry Goldwater to review his domestic policies. The summer of 1967 was the most bloody of the sixties, with seventy-one cities, including Phoenix, suffering disturbances. The worst rioting occurred in Detroit, where tanks and troopers from the 101st Airborne Division quieted violence that left the city burning and forty-three dead and seven thousand arrested. Keying on economic reform, Goldwater wrote friends to praise University of Chicago Professor Milton Friedman's negative income tax plan, which proposed federal cash payments to supplement the income of the poor. Rather than a "handout," conservatives conceived the funds as compensation to poor Americans for exemptions they would have declared if they had filed income tax returns. Government payments would serve as a base allowance and, consistent with conservative philosophy, bring cuts in costs and bureaucracy. Goldwater, in turn, suggested to Friedman a "hypothetical idea" based in the post–New Deal reality that "there have been many changes made through legislation and court decisions . . . [that] are not going to be reversed or thrown out overnight and probably most of them never."[41] Goldwater proposed to recognize federal initiatives and national guidelines but to delegate to the states the funds and responsibility for program administration. His plan, which resembled that for block grants, promised not only to reduce the size of the federal government but to strengthen states' rights. Goldwater did not pursue these ideas methodically or vigorously. Rather, he tinkered with them in private for a time, then let others take the lead.[42]

The Goldwater Senate campaign was already primed in early January 1968, many months before election day in November. Campaign manager Dean Burch had begun to tap the list of contributors to the 1964 presidential race and dust off the old speeches. Although Goldwater faced no challenger in the Republican primary, Burch soon held sufficient funds to allocate $150,000 to the campaign. He bankrolled $400,000 more for the fall race against the Democrats. In May, Goldwater formally announced his bid. Comparing 1968 to 1952, the year of his first Senate run, he proclaimed: "Leadership needed then is lacking now. Chaos which merely threatened then, engulfs us now. The crisis then has become the disaster of today." Goldwater pledged to protect the freedom of America's "forgotten men and women" from bureaucrats: "We are all being rapidly reduced to the status of numbers in a government computer." He condemned deficit spending that "mortgaged" the nation and ranked an anti-crime effort high on his list of priorities. He reproached the Democratic administration for its "quicksand policies abroad," which produced jungle war on the Asian mainland. Victory in Vietnam was, he later promised, as close as two weeks away with the "proper targeting."[43] To no one's surprise, he concluded, "I have not changed or compromised."[44]

Taking advantage of his high name recognition and strong identification with the state, the Republicans presented Goldwater "more as a national monument than as a political candidate."[45] Campaign workers erected billboards and sent repeated mailings of Goldwater portrayed against the painted backdrop of majestic Monument Valley, the site of numerous John Ford–John Wayne westerns. Dressed in Levis, boots, and cowboy hat and shirt, he was the western legend come to life. Despite his advantages, Goldwater planned a rigorous campaign—making three appearances per day, including Sundays—and neglected no section of the state. To preserve their candidate and protect him from fatigue-generated irritability and missteps, aides set a schedule that had Goldwater sleeping in his bed at home every night. In the hands of efficient and enthusiastic party workers, the Goldwater charisma easily translated into votes.[46]

A changing Arizona also benefited the Republican. Between 1953 and 1970 the state's population doubled to 1.7 million, with the heaviest migration flooding metropolitan Phoenix, which housed half of Arizona's people. Almost one in five of the new citizens of Phoenix came from California, and almost half of them were from Goldwater country—Los Angeles and Orange Counties. The lure of Phoenix was its continuing economic boom, fueled by defense spending, in manufacturing and service industries. As urban Arizona grew, Democratic-dominated rural areas dependent on cattle, mining, and agriculture languished economically and demographically. Forced retirement in 1964 had been to Goldwater's benefit, for it kept him in touch with the new Arizona. He had personally courted residents, longtime and new, and stayed attuned to their concerns. State Democrats still held a fourteen-point voter registration lead, but Republicans hardly considered themselves underdogs.[47]

Such leading Arizona Democrats as Secretary of the Interior Stewart Udall and his brother Congressman Morris Udall recognized Goldwater's advantages and were reluctant to challenge him for the seat of retiring Senator Carl Hayden. The candidacy fell by default to thirty-eight-year-old Hayden aide Roy Elson, who had been defeated in a bid for Goldwater's Senate seat in 1964. Born in Pennsylvania, Elson had come to Arizona as a child and grew up in Tucson. Upon graduating from the University of Arizona he went to work for Senator Hayden in Washington. Elson remained with Hayden, except for a two-year military commitment, and eventually became the senator's administrative assistant. As age slowed octogenarian Carl Hayden, his right-hand-man assumed more responsibilities. Elson, recalled a congressional associate, "was the U.S. Senate's 101st senator. He had indeed more power than many of the junior senators."[48] He was particularly influential in steering the Central Arizona Project through Congress and to the president's desk. But his influence did not enhance name recognition nor erase the impression that his ties to Arizona were Hayden-mediated. Moreover, as Elson suggested, CAP was "too complicated for the average person. . . . It was not a good issue. . . . they still had their pools, their communities were growing and they didn't see any water shortage. . . . I don't think the people really cared."[49]

Hayden held Elson in high esteem, but he did not initially endorse him. In accordance with the Democratic pecking order, the senator sent Elson to the Udall brothers with his pledge of support if either decided to make the race against Goldwater. Only after they deferred did Hayden back Elson. This exacerbated the animosity that already existed between Elson and the Udalls and further handicapped his Senate race. The lack of funding and cooperation would seriously undercut Elson's effort. Stewart Udall withheld his support until a few days before the election. In the absence of money and organization, Elson placed his faith in fate. "Of course, in any election, you always think that you might get a break. For instance, Barry might have dropped dead."[50]

Barry Goldwater, running unopposed in the primary race, focused on national Republican politics in the spring and summer of 1968. His candidate for president was Richard Nixon. He had praised the former vice president consistently since 1964, and in March 1968 he reaffirmed his commitment. In a slap at the party's moderates and liberals, he also served notice that 1964 had not faded: "I am not a sometime Republican. I have always been a Republican and have always supported the nominee of my party, and this I will do in 1968."[51]

Goldwater was not the only prominent conservative to jump on the Nixon bandwagon. In 1966 and 1967 Nixon had courted and won endorsements from John Tower, Strom Thurmond, William F. Buckley, Jr., John Ashbrook, and Peter O'Donnell. Richard Kleindienst, Goldwater's director of field operations in 1964, filled the same role in the Nixon campaign. Nixon's overtures to the right reflected his recognition of new GOP realities. He had told Bill Buckley, "If Barry showed that the Republicans can't win with just the right wing, I showed in 1962 that we can't win without them."[52] With the southern states and Arizona holding 388 of the 677 votes needed for nomination, Nixon had figured the political equation astutely. He would get the rest of his support by claiming Barry Goldwater's bases in the Rocky Mountain, Plains, and Midwestern states. Nixon, however, had no illusions about his conservative supporters: "They don't like me, but they tolerate me."[53] Conservatives, in turn, tempered their enthusiasm, aware that Nixon was not ideologically dependable. Yet he was acceptable, especially in the face of a challenge from old nemesis Governor Nelson Rockefeller, and they were determined to win in November.[54]

Rockefeller, who opened a late challenge to Nixon, saw his only chance of nomination in a splitting of the conservative vote. He found an unlikely bedfellow in California Governor Ronald Reagan. Many conservatives saw Reagan as Goldwater's heir. They agreed with an observer: "He is Goldwater mutton, dressed up as lamb."[55] While publicly disavowing presidential aspirations, Reagan had connected soon after his 1966 gubernatorial victory with Clif White and the former draft-Goldwater group, still headquartered in Suite 3505 in New York City. In 1968 he kept his options open, the favorite son of the large California delegation.[56]

Barry Goldwater was quite comfortable approaching the California governor about his intentions. They were longtime friends, having met in the late 1940s through Reagan's father-in-law, Dr. Loyal Davis, a Phoenix winter resident and neighbor of Goldwater's. Reagan was still a liberal at the time, and Barry remembers: "He was so far to the left, he wouldn't talk to me. In fact, he called me a black fascist bastard one day."[57] Under the tutelage of the Davis family, Reagan eventually embraced conservatism and became Goldwater's ideological soul mate. Reagan was strong for Goldwater in 1964, but mutual friend Bill Buckley believes that the campaign left "some bad blood between the two."[58] In particular, Reagan was upset because Goldwater had not fully appreciated his effort, especially the highly successful October speech. Reagan, perhaps responding to Goldwater's prompting, showed disinterest in the nomination on several occasions. After a meeting in August 1967, Goldwater confided his thoughts to friend Hubert Humphrey, which the vice president set down in a memo to the files: "He said he told Reagan that this was not his time and that Reagan shouldn't kid himself into believing that he could beat Johnson. . . . He also told me that he didn't think Reagan was ready for the Presidency."[59] In January 1968, at Reagan's Pacific Palisades home in California, Goldwater broached the subject of the nomination. Reagan again denied any desire to be the Republican standard-bearer.[60]

President Lyndon Johnson's decision not to seek reelection and the assassination of New York Senator Robert F. Kennedy caused Ronald Reagan to rethink his future. Coached by Clif White, Reagan avoided the primaries only to become an official candidate on August 5, just hours before the Republican convention opened in Miami. Paralleling Rockefeller's strategy, Reagan and White hoped to ignite a bolt of Nixon conservatives and stop a first-ballot nomination. Nixon personally called on Barry Goldwater, John Tower, and Strom Thurmond to intercede and calm the conservative troops. They were effective and held Reagan to scattered gains among southern delegations.[61] Nixon was grateful: "Barry, if there is ever anything you want, just ask it."[62] Initially, he gave Goldwater and the other conservatives no reason to doubt their efforts. Nixon framed his campaign in terms of law and order, a strong national defense, free enterprise, suspicion of the federal bureau-cracy, and resistance to busing. He adopted Barry Goldwater's southern-western strategy while conceding the Northeast to the Democrats. His acceptance speech must have been especially gratifying to Goldwater. Nixon praised Barry's "forgotten Americans—the non shouters, the non demon-strators. They're not racists or sick; they're not guilty of the crime that plagues the land. . . . They work in American factories, they run American businesses. They serve in government; they provide most of the soldiers who die to keep it free. They give drive to the spirit of America. They give lift to the American dream."[63]

With the easing of the summer heat in mid-September, the Arizona Senate race began in earnest. The omens boded ill for Roy Elson. While Elson had easily brushed aside his opponents in the Democratic primary, Goldwater had gathered nearly as many votes running unopposed on the Republican ballot. Polls a week later showed Goldwater far ahead, with a 61 percent to 31 percent margin. Playing catch-up, Elson stressed his legisla-tive expertise and youth and Goldwater's record. Senator Goldwater, he told voters, had opposed Medicare, aid to college students, the Civil Rights Act of 1964, and the Nuclear Test Ban Treaty. He was "an expensive luxury" that the state could not afford.[64] "I challenge him to just tell us one thing he did to help the State of Arizona—name one project, name one program. And when he does I'll tell him how the work was done. It was done by Hayden's office."[65] Echoing Elson, Senator Carl Hayden alluded to Goldwater's prior service: the U.S. Senate is "not just a place to make speeches and expound political theory. It is a place to work and it seems to me Arizona would do well to send a working senator to Washington."[66] None of this was new. Ernest McFarland had tried the same approach in 1958. Now Elson would find few Arizonans willing to enlist in a losing cause. Elson likened his money-starved campaign to a "floating crap game, preparing speeches as we go, flying tourist class, and taking out my own laundry."[67] He had no illusions. "I got to say about everything I wanted . . . , but no one was particularly lis-tening. After a while, I was just hoping that I could make it respectable and be able to at least walk away with my head high."[68]

According to custom, Barry Goldwater opened the campaign in Prescott, and in a single sentence set his themes: "The basic political question is whether individual men and women are to live free of force or the fear of force from aggressors in the world, from oppressors at home, or from trans-gressors in our streets." Ignoring Elson, Goldwater blamed the Johnson administration for a breakdown in law and order, the "no-win" war in Vietnam, and an acceleration toward "centralism."[69] Lowering the voting age to eighteen years, establishing a volunteer army, and supporting the Central

Arizona Project completed his agenda but attracted less interest. Determined to return to the Senate, he refused to rest on his lead and pushed himself and his staff hard.[70]

The campaign played according to Goldwater's plan. He appeared all over the state, fresh and vigorous, delivering set speeches. Political ads identified him as "Mr. Arizona" and the state's respected and tested envoy to the nation and the world. A highly effective television commercial displayed him in the Arizona outback, appropriately attired, as an announcer declared: "Barry Goldwater is above all else a product of the land he loves. He had roamed Arizona's canyons and valleys . . . camped on her wind-chilled mesas . . . found a great message in this rawboned land . . . self reliance . . . hard work . . . rugged, determined stick-togetherness. . . . Arizona's lesson is America's lesson . . . but much of America has forgotten. . . . That's why Barry Goldwater must be returned to the United States Senate . . . Senator Barry Goldwater. Doesn't that sound great?"[71]

Reporters and voters responded to the cues. Speaking appearances and press conferences became deferential question-and-answer forums that provoked no serious screening or challenge. Goldwater adopted a disappointed "I told you so"[72] tone and proclaimed the voice of authority: "Four years ago we asked the people to face the perils threatening to destroy this land. We failed. Oftentimes, the truth is harsh and unappealing, but the perils persist . . . uncertainty continues . . . terror stalks our cities . . . brave men die in a distant war . . . there is economic and social injustice at home. Our leaders, trapped by indecision, offer no positive course."[73] He now gave voters another chance. To resolve the "ugly war" in Vietnam, he placed a "fish or cut bait" time limit of "ten days or maybe two weeks" on the Paris peace talks. If negotiators did not end the conflict, "then we will assume a new military posture and use our full power to force the enemy into submission."[74] The solution to rising crime was to "get rid of poor judges who allow permissiveness to influence their judgements. We must stand behind our law enforcement community; when that is done, the rate of crime will diminish."[75] Headlines in the Arizona papers announcing Viet Cong offensives, crime waves, the high cost of living, campus unrest, the Soviet invasion of Czechoslovakia, and the capture of the U.S.S. *Pueblo* crew by Korean communists seemed to bear testimony to his foresight. In this context, Goldwater's refusal to debate Roy Elson sparked no criticism. His standing was such that *Arizona Republic* reporter Bernie Wynn noted, only half in jest, that Goldwater "could recite 'Little Bo Peep' from the political platform this year and Arizona audiences would cheer."[76]

The *Arizona Republic* balanced its reporting throughout the campaign and endorsed both Elson and Goldwater for the U.S. Senate seat. Arizona citizens would have none of that. Goldwater beat Elson by fifty thousand votes and took 57 percent of the tally. For the first time in Arizona's history, both U.S. senators were Republicans. Richard Nixon won the state's electoral votes but ran behind Goldwater. Arizona Republicans continued to surge, sweeping all but one of the state offices, picking up a seat in both houses of the legislature and electing two of three U.S. congressmen.[77]

The Arizona race absorbed most of Barry's time and energy, but commitment to a Nixon victory required that he do his part. Richard Nixon and Barry Goldwater were in close contact throughout the campaign, sharing advice and information. Mostly, the Nixon staff counted on Goldwater to turn conservative supporters away from American Independent Party candidate George Wallace. Goldwater did his best, arguing that a vote for Wallace was a blow at the conservative movement. Such a vote, he argued, went nowhere "but right down a rathole" and profited "only one person—our friend Hubert Horatio Humphrey. Is that what you really want?" Support Dick Nixon, for he, like Wallace, was tough on crime, expected Supreme Court justices to heed the Constitution, and opposed federal "handouts."[78] In what was a very tight race, Goldwater surely had an impact, though Wallace was not a significant factor outside the South. Although Goldwater failed to persuade erstwhile supporters in Alabama and Mississippi, and Wallace did win the electoral votes of Georgia and Louisiana, Nixon collected 30 percent and 23 percent of the popular vote, respectively, in the latter states. Nixon's 38 percent share of the South Carolina tally was sufficient in the three-way race to keep it in the Republican column. As in 1964, the South was clearly contested ground.[79]

The 1968 election resulted in a narrow popular-vote victory for Richard Nixon. He won 43.4 percent of the vote, edging Hubert Humphrey's 42.7 percent; George Wallace gained 13.5 percent. At the same time, Nixon had fashioned an indisputable 301 to 197 electoral-college triumph that united the trans-Mississippi West with the industrial Midwest and the southern fringe, except for Texas. In the West, and specifically the Southwest, the Republicans had found their base of operations. The choice demonstrated remarkable acuity. Republicans flexed political muscle in a region that was rising in population and on the make economically. Humphrey's electoral vote, harvested primarily in the Northeast, revealed the increasingly peripheral electoral nature of the region and confirmed Republican wisdom. Nor did victories here offer Democrats much solace, for blue-collar Irish and Italian-Catholic constituents were in revolt. Nixon dramatically expanded Goldwater's 1964 gains, capturing 33 percent of their vote, with Wallace taking 8 percent. Crime and racial violence had fueled anger and fear. Welfare programs, busing, and affirmative action in hiring and promotion had threatened core interests. Closer to their values were the Republican populists with the slogans of equality of opportunity and law and order. The 1964 pattern of racial polarization had stabilized. Eighty-five percent of blacks, but only 38 percent of whites voted Democratic in 1968. Nixon had taken a third of the African-American vote in 1960; in 1968 he won only 12 percent. Finally, simple arithmetic revealed a transformed political landscape. Combining the Nixon and Wallace totals, 57 percent of the American people had repudiated Democratic liberalism. In politics, the velocity of change is accelerated, its trajectory unknown. Conceived by Barry Goldwater and given birth by Richard Nixon, what Kevin Phillips called the Emerging Republican Majority had become the new reality.[80]

Arizona's sixty-year-old junior senator made a smooth transition back to Washington, D.C. With the help of Dean Burch and Judy Rooney, he assembled a young staff and quickly returned to his routine. Goldwater, as he did in his previous terms, arrived early to work each morning and insisted on the punctuality of staff and fellow senators. Other old habits persisted. His impatience with the legislative process resurfaced, and he was absent for more than half of the floor votes, the worst record of any senator in the 91st Congress. He did little to improve this record in subsequent sessions. Although representing a small state and having no reputation for legislative expertise, Goldwater did exert considerable clout. He was the vindicated elder statesman. Cast in his image were twenty-seven of the forty-three Senate Republicans who were conservative and represented mostly western and southern states. There were four times that many on the House side with similar credentials. Even among liberals his prestige had risen with Lyndon Johnson's disgrace and the rightward shift in the national mainstream. Goldwater's appointment to the Armed Services and Aeronautical and Space Science Committees reflected his standing and pleased him.[81]

Easing the return and heightening his influence was the crowd of Arizonans that the Nixon administration enticed into federal service. President Nixon named Dean Burch to chair the Federal Communications Commission and Richard Kleindienst, William Rehnquist, and Richard Burke to the Department of Justice. Bob Mardian, John Pritzlaff, and Isabel Burgess also took positions in the administration, as did many veterans of 1964. In May 1969 the ranks of the Goldwaterites grew by another member. Barry Jr. won a special election in Southern California to fill the U.S. House seat of a Nixon-administration appointee. "It was the biggest thrill in my life," wrote Barry Sr. "I had no real interest in politics," said the son, running only to please his father.[82]

Senator Goldwater did not hesitate to inform Richard Nixon of his expectations. Long suspicious of the power of the federal bureaucracy, he urged the president to reorganize the government "in depth" and remove all Kennedy-Johnson appointees.[83] Writing ten days before the inauguration, Goldwater insisted that Nixon replace those "in a position to do you damage and through you, the Republican Party."[84] He advised Nixon eight days later to sweep from the State Department those Democrats who seek "the disarmament of our country."[85] Nixon's delay spurred Goldwater into a thoroughgoing review and determined refrain. His scrutiny of the Voice of America program revealed that "we really haven't been cleaning the rascals out."[86] The Office of Economic Opportunity suffered from "Democratic drags" who "undermine . . . the President day after day and whose allegiance is pledged to the Kennedy wing of the Democratic Party."[87] Goldwater found little change after a year. "With the exception of the White House staff, the Department of Defense, and the Attorney General's office, the bureaus of our government are shot through with Johnson and Kennedy holdovers who have no intention of helping you or our government." It was impossible to place the Nixon stamp on policy, he pressed, "when these people are cutting your throat every time you turn around."[88] His drumbeat of complaints was still strong late in the summer of 1970.

The White House was more deeply concerned about the need to tame the bureaucracy than he knew. Richard Nixon, in particular, was distressed when government officials leaked information to journalists about Vietnam and foreign policy initiatives. The FBI's reluctance to intervene led the president and his men to take matters into their own hands. In midsummer 1969, Nixon instructed aide John Ehrlichman to create "a little group right here in the White House. Have them get off their tails and find out what's going on and figure out how to stop it."[89] Ehrlichman recruited Egil Krogh, David Young, E. Howard Hunt (who had spied on Barry Goldwater in 1964), and G. Gordon Liddy as "plumbers" to plug the leaks. Observing few restraints on their mission, they initiated illegal burglaries and telephone wiretaps of the president's "enemies." Later they expanded their charge to the domestic arena and performed "dirty tricks" and stockpiled information against political opponents. The first steps had been taken on the road to Watergate.[90]

A failure to secure patronage appointments added to Goldwater's frustration with the president. It also fanned his insecurities. Uncomfortable asking for favors, yet holding political IOUs, Goldwater was shocked by the administration's indifference, especially its rejection of a longtime friend, retired General William Quinn, as ambassador to Greece. Depressed, he yielded to self-doubt: "I am beginning to think that because my name is Goldwater and because I lost in 1964, . . . that the White House is going out of its way to see that nothing that I desire is to be granted."[91] There were other signs of an apparent fall from grace. In February his name had been inadvertently left off a White House guest list. Although promised easy access to the president and "meetings at regular intervals," Goldwater had trouble scheduling an appointment.[92] After repeated attempts, he finally visited with the president in early March 1969. He would not confer again with the president in private for six months, and after that not until December 1970. Clearly there was substance to his grievance: he was "never consulted about political matters."[93]

Although White House staffers jealously guarded the appointment calendar, at Nixon's insistence they did not want to alienate the senator. He carried weight with conservatives, and they needed his support. To keep the "crotchety" Arizonan loyal and to salve his "feeling . . . that he is not appreciated," they suggested that the president "pay homage" and "schmooze him."[94] Charles Colson suggested that the president handle Goldwater in brief, regularly scheduled White House visits. "Every time he meets with the President he is good for several weeks thereafter, but then he begins to feel neglected, used and out of the mainstream. Goldwater is terribly important to us."[95] The president apparently gave more weight to Dick Kleindienst's advice that the Arizona senator be cultivated by telephone, "giving him individual and personal attention every three or four weeks."[96] Invitations from Nixon to play golf at Burning Tree Country Club, calls to serve as the president's representative at foreign air shows, and attendance at White House ceremonies were also features of this "stroking" campaign. So, too, were promises to consult on matters of special interest to the senator.[97]

The Arizonan devoured the attention, and it made him receptive to administration direction. When joined to party and personal loyalties, it could even override strong convictions. Still, flattery did not blind Goldwater to the dangers inherent in the White House screening strategy. In a March 24, 1970, note to the Alpha File, he wrote that Nixon "has drifted more and more . . . from availability and whether he realizes it or not, a very effective shell has been constructed around him."[98] He criticized the president ten months later for allowing himself to be "surrounded by people who really aren't too smart in the field and he is not allowed to know what is going on."[99] As these statements suggest, Goldwater saw Nixon as naive, an unknowing prisoner of his staff. He had yet to conceive the White House as afflicted with the mentality of the besieged and his friend as an accomplice in his own isolation.[100]

The senator might be cantankerous and bruise easily, but the administration's congressional liaisons were secure in his support. He backed President Nixon's anticrime initiatives on the Senate floor, and in his new book *The Conscience of a Majority* he dismissed the "overweening concern for the rights of the accused criminal."[101] He approved the administration's sounding of delay, if not retreat, on busing and other liberal initiatives. The president's proposals to share federal revenues with the states and create a Family Assistance Plan with negative-income-tax features accommodated his own ideas. The conservative appreciated Nixon's efforts to bridle the activist Supreme Court and create "a court oriented more toward law and the Constitution than sociological influence."[102] He defended Richard Nixon's choices for the bench, including segregationist G. Harold Carswell. "The President of the United States," he argued, "should be given broad leeway in choosing judicial nominees who might reflect the same broad philosophy as his own."[103] Goldwater was particularly interested in the administration's review of federal policy toward Native Americans. In a reversal of his 1950s position, he sustained its renunciation of termination and endorsement of self-determination, the strengthening of tribal communities, and the return of tribal lands. With memories of the 1964 campaign still vivid, the Arizonan championed Vice President Spiro Agnew's offensive against the news media. He even endorsed a phonograph record titled "Spiro T. Agnew Speaks Out," urging Republicans to buy this "collector's item" and listen to its "hard-hitting, headline-making attacks on the Liberal Left."[104]

Sometimes allegiance demanded the dousing of cherished beliefs. He blanched when Nixon declared himself a "Keynesian" and watched uneasily as federal spending increased, the deficit soared, and the administration affixed new layers to the Washington bureaucracy. Despite his long opposition to wage and price controls, Goldwater swallowed hard and stood by the president in his call for a ninety-day freeze in August 1971 and mandatory guidelines that lasted until 1974. Publicly, he blamed "liberal extravagance" for inflation and unemployment and the necessarily bitter medicine needed to ease "stagflation."[105] Said Goldwater, "I know of nothing any President could have done to protect the American consumer short of imposing temporary government controls."[106] Privately, he was stunned. He confided to Milton Friedman: "President Nixon's economics has me hanging on the ropes, and frankly, his casual observance of deficit spending leaves me very close to not being able to support him, but when I think of the alternatives it scares the living hell out of me."[107]

In light of Goldwater's interest in aviation and his fear of America becoming a second-rate power, it was less surprising that he enthusiastically endorsed the administration-promoted Supersonic Transport (SST). "I do not see anything new," contended the pragmatic conservative, "about the Federal Government being in the transportation business."[108] It still must have been embarrassing when fellow Republican Senator Charles Percy gingerly reproached him by reading Goldwaterisms against federal aggrandizement from the pages of *The Conscience of a Conservative*. South Dakota Senator

George McGovern was less charitable and accused the Arizonan of "sheer demagoguery" on the issue.[109] Goldwater's support of these Nixon policies disturbed many conservatives. Karl Hess, chief speech writer during the 1964 campaign, was disgusted and voiced their anger: "Goldwater used to be against kings, now he seems for them."[110]

The Arizona senator, with administration backing, also pursued a personal agenda. Consistent with campaign pledges, he successfully advocated the lowering of the voting age to eighteen years and the creation of a volunteer army. He offered legislation to ban pornography from the mails, basing his case on "the constitutional guarantee of freedom of privacy . . . among the fundamental rights reserved to the people by the Constitution."[111] He cosponsored, as well, a constitutional amendment to permit school prayer. Assuming Carl Hayden's role, Goldwater lobbied for subsidies for Arizona cotton farmers and funding for the CAP and solar energy research. He worked to expand the boundaries of Grand Canyon National Park and railed against the smog that obstructed his view of the Valley of the Sun. "I don't care how tough we have to get, even if it means an economic loss to the state."[112] In *The Conscience of a Majority*, he declared: "While I am a great believer in the free competitive enterprise system and all that it entails, I am an even stronger believer in the right of our people to live in a clean and pollution-free environment."[113] The Sierra Club still criticized him as "oriented toward economic rather than environmental issues" and cited his votes to weaken antipollution legislation and permit prospecting and mining in wilderness areas.[114] Conservationists also chafed at Goldwater's exhortation to exploit space in a manner that evoked the "pioneer" tradition: "The vast reaches of space in a dynamic universe offer mankind its greatest opportunity to again achieve, through exploration and change involving new frontiers, new lands to conquer and new civilizations to build."[115] Meanwhile, he continued his long campaign against "union arrogance" and invited a "thorough reexamination" of all relevant laws to the end of reducing organized labor's "overconcentration of power."[116]

During the early 1970s the conservative felt the pressure of social change as women mobilized in a rebirth of feminism and young people challenged traditional values and lifestyles. He responded, like most politicians, by skimming his personal experiences and constituent mail. In 1969, with little correspondence on the subject, he introduced a joint resolution endorsing the Equal Rights Amendment (ERA). This was a symbolic act, for the ERA had drawn bipartisan support since the 1940s. Seemingly a simple guarantee of individual rights, it had also appeared as a plank in the 1964 Republican platform. Goldwater's office prepared a form letter on the issue, announcing the senator's cosponsorship of the resolution and backing of "the philosophy behind the effort to gain an equal status with men in matters of competing for salary promotions, rising to executive positions, and being free to enter upon a career of their own choosing."[117] By 1971, when passage became a real possibility, growing anti-ERA agitation nationally and in Arizona persuaded him to reverse course. He now rejected the amendment, believing that it would compel the drafting of women, destroy women's colleges, and cause the "forced mixing of male and female students in the same dormitories."[118] Later he developed his rationale more fully: "The basic reason behind my vote is the fact of nature that when God created mankind, He created them male and female, and no law can change His works by making men and women identical."[119] At other times, Goldwater cited the Fourteenth Amendment, Equal Pay Act of 1963, and 1964 Civil Rights Act as making the legislation unnecessary. While he voted no, Congress approved, and President Richard Nixon signed the amendment, sending it to the states for ratification.[120]

In a libertarian vein, and consistent with his defense of "a man's right to be let alone," Goldwater reassessed his views on the legalization of marijuana.[121] His family's experience during Prohibition colored his perception. So did widespread use of marijuana in the Southwest during his youth. Goldwater flirted with changes in the drug laws only briefly. After soliciting an array of legal and medical opinions during 1969 and 1970, and in the face of heavy constituent mail demanding strict enforcement, he concluded "that nothing can be gained by legalizing marijuana, and I will vigorously oppose any movement in that direction."[122] Years later, following his retirement from public life, Goldwater was again open to change: "I'd support it [legalization of marijuana and cocaine] just to see what would happen."[123]

In foreign policy, President Nixon's pursuit of détente with the communists worried Goldwater, but he eagerly embraced the administration's commitment to a strong national defense. Critical to the Arizonan's support was a conviction that American influence and power had seriously eroded during the sixties. Goldwater warned that Russian aggressiveness in Eastern Europe and the Middle East marked the beginning of a "determined drive" for "undisputed world leadership."[124] He claimed other evidence of communist intentions—a military build-up that had drastically diminished U.S. superiority and allowed the enemy to gain parity and even claim an advantage in critical defense areas. Aggravating the threat, he argued, was Secretary of Defense Robert McNamara and his "civilian cadre" of "whiz kids," who had fostered waste and mismanagement while ravaging military morale.[125] Now, America was in danger of succumbing to a "new isolationism."[126] This retreat, "scripted and orchestrated" by "left-wing political elements," was an unrealistic and irresponsible yearning to flee the world in the wake of the Vietnam nightmare. With America in harm's way, Goldwater decried any attempt to reduce defense spending as "part of an overall strategy to bring about unilateral disarmament of this nation."[127]

Determined to repair the damage and blunt the communist offensive, Goldwater as a member of Senate Armed Services Committee championed Pentagon requests for weapons procurement and research. He concentrated his efforts, in accordance with his Air Force experience, on the development or upgrading of the B-1 bomber, C-5A cargo plane, F-111 tactical fighter, P-3C anti-submarine airplane, C-9 medium transport, F-4E fighter, and the Chaparral, Hawk, Pershing, Lance, Poseidon, Sidewinder, Shrike, and Minuteman missile systems, among others. In addition, he fought for the Anti-Ballistic Missile (ABM) program even though he confessed, "Frankly, I think I could debate both sides of this ABM issue and convince no one, including myself."[128] Goldwater was known as Mr. Air Power[129] in Washington, and, according to White House congressional liaison Tom Korologos, "If there was a problem with the Air Force, you went to Goldwater. He was for anything that flew."[130] Goldwater did not hide his passion; on his desk sat a plaque reading, "Air Force Spoken Here."[131]

While Goldwater opposed efforts to trim the defense budget, he occasionally complained about military duplication and waste. Goldwater wrote to Secretary of Defense Melvin Laird in late 1971, noting that although he had voted to authorize funding for the Harrier, Cheyenne, and F-14 aircraft, he found the four separate tactical air forces of the armed services "extremely expensive."[132] A few months later he told an *Arizona Republic* reporter that Pentagon procurement practices were a "godawful waste of money."[133] Goldwater, however, cautioned Americans that "the mere existence of waste and cost overruns and similar problems must not be allowed to blind this country to the need for keeping its defenses strong. Nor should the inflated cost of military hardware become the overriding consideration in determining our level of defense expenditure."[134] The conservative was more open with his Senate colleagues. He confided to South Dakota Senator George McGovern that the military budget could probably be cut by "10 to 20 percent without any harm," but his Arizona and conservative constituencies prevented him from publicly taking such a stand. And defense spending was of no small import to the Grand Canyon State. In 1972 about one in five Arizona jobs was tied to prime defense contracts and the presence of military bases. Observed McGovern: "It is a curious contradiction of the deserved reputation he has as a man of candor, who says what he thinks and lets the chips fall where they may."[135]

Barry Goldwater's resistance to the "new isolationism" demanded a solution to Vietnam that caused no loss of American face, will, or influence. The stakes were as high in the early seventies as they had been ten years before: "I am convinced that the Chinese communists and the communists' aim, generally, is to dominate the Far East. This entire area has great strategic value, and whoever controls Southeast Asia will have a stranglehold on the rest of Asia. . . . I firmly believe that if we don't stop them in Vietnam, we will be trying to stop them in the rest of Southeast Asia."[136] The Arizona senator accepted Nixon's call for an "honorable peace" through the "Vietnamization" of the war. This entailed the gradual withdrawal of U.S. troops, the strengthening of the South Vietnamese armed forces, and the expansion of the air war in the north and south. Impatiently, he repeated his advice to remove all restrictions on targeting: "I would suggest a complete bombing of Haiphong and the opening of the Red River dikes, even though the Navy seems to think this is not a profitable venture."[137] It was worth the risk of a wider war: "I say, if a Russian ship is bombed at Haiphong, that's too damn bad. I hope we hit them all. They have no business being in Haiphong. They are our enemy."[138] He supported the invasion of Cambodia in 1970, convinced that widening the war would shorten it by forcing the North Vietnamese to "sue for peace."[139] According to Barry Goldwater: "Nixon will get his greatness from this decision."[140]

For a time, the conservative softened his stand on antiwar dissenters. He went into the streets and talked to protesters during demonstrations in Washington, D.C., and was particularly impressed with the Vietnam veterans who had "good, solid stories to tell and good, solid arguments to use."[141] The disruptive tactics of some, however, incensed him. In May 1971 antiwar activists forced their way into his Senate office suite, screamed obscenities, and spray painted the walls. Furious at these "professional agitators" and "anarchists,"[142] Goldwater confronted the president about the breakdown in law and order: "Unless some leadership was shown from the White House and . . . the police were allowed to act in a free manner unhampered by the Democratic leadership, . . . I would find it very difficult to support [you] for renomination."[143] A year later he was more inflammatory, alleging Democratic Party collusion with the enemy. "I begin to wonder," he declared during a Senate debate on the war, "if our friends on the other side of the aisle have received another letter of direction from Mrs. Nguyen Binh, the chief Viet Cong negotiator at the Paris peace talks."[144]

The key to American survival in a dangerous world, Goldwater believed, was a strong commander-in-chief able to react quickly to crisis, unhindered by Congressional "micromanagement," partisanship, or indecision.[145] He thus took the lead in opposing the War Powers resolution, an attempt by "new-isolationist" critics of the administration's Vietnam policy to reassert congressional control over presidential war-making. The resolution required formal authorization of military action taken without a declaration of war and fixed presidential adherence to a strict timetable. Goldwater's resistance required philosophical realignment. He disputed the wisdom of generations of conservatives who denounced the menace of executive power. He was also compelled to reinterpret his own positions. In his first year in the U.S. Senate, Goldwater had supported the Bricker Amendment with its restrictions on presidential treaty-making.[146] He had tensed in 1957, when President Eisenhower responded to events in Lebanon with a request for a broad congressional mandate to order military action against the general threat of communist aggression.[147] On the CBS television show *The Great Challenge* in 1961 he declared, in regard to foreign policy, that "the President now has more power in this field than the Constitution ever intended."[148] In defense of the presidential power, Goldwater had become a loose constructionist of the Constitution. "It is my strong belief that the Framers intentionally painted with a broad brush."[149]

Working closely with aide Terry Emerson, Goldwater became the administration's chief advocate against the bill. He cited American history and the Constitution to prove that the president as "primary author of foreign policy has both a duty and a right to take military action at any time he feels danger for the country or its freedoms."[150] The president alone was entrusted with the right to deploy troops "whenever and wherever he chooses."[151] The same sources convinced him that "Congress can aid the President in the exercise of his functions, but it cannot interfere with or limit his discretion in carrying out his separate powers."[152] According to Goldwater, Congress had the power only to "declare" war (he interpreted this to mean "announce") and could not effect policy except through appropriation decisions.[153] Under these assumptions, he dared opponents to act on their convictions and end the war in Vietnam by refusing to fund it. The majority found Goldwater's arguments unpersuasive, and the War Powers Act passed in November 1973 after years of debate. Two decades later, Goldwater remained adamant: It was "the most stupid piece of legislation ever passed by Congress."[154]

Also forcing the Arizonan to reposition himself was President Nixon's decision to make an opening to the communist People's Republic of China. "Ping-pong" diplomacy quickly gave way to a presidential visit and meetings with Mao Tse-tung and Chou En-lai in February 1972. Normalization of relations between the countries seemed only a matter of time. The new policy jolted Barry Goldwater and fellow conservatives. For decades Goldwater, Richard Nixon, and the supporters of Chiang Kai-shek had vigorously upheld his Republic of China regime on Taiwan as the legitimate authority over the mainland. In March 1971, Goldwater caught wind of a possible change in administration thinking and wrote to the president for information: "Anything you can tell me about your long-range plans for Red China, either in recognition or admission to the United Nations would certainly be appreciated."[155] Following administration reassurances, he had responded to the expulsion of Taiwan from the United Nations with a call to "cut off all financial help, withdraw as a member, and ask [it] to find a headquarters location outside of the United States."[156] Nixon, realizing that the China initiative had ignited a rebellion on his right flank, attempted immediately to defuse it through Goldwater. He asked the Arizonan to accompany him to China. Goldwater promptly declined. To Nixon's relief, however, the conservative agreed to withhold comment until a White House briefing was held after the president's return.[157]

On February 29, 1972, congressional leaders and Barry Goldwater met with the president in the Oval Office. Goldwater was apprehensive, for he had read in the newspapers about the Shanghai Communiqué and its apparent revision of American-Taiwanese relations. Nixon attempted to relax the conservative, joking, "I can see Chou En-lai with his Chinese Goldwaters having the same trouble that Barry is having now." He then stressed, to Goldwater's relief, that the U.S. remained committed to Taiwan. In regard to Goldwater's "biggest worry," the president declared "forcefully" that diplomatic recognition of the People's Republic of China was not a possibility.[158] Goldwater remained silent but was still uneasy. As Goldwater knew, the Shanghai Communiqué had reiterated the claim of the People's Republic as the ruling government and Taiwan as a part of China. The communists also called for the removal of U.S. forces from Taiwan. The accompanying American statement said nothing of rollback, contained no references to treaty obligations with Taiwan, and did not challenge Peking's assertion of hegemony. Instead, it emphasized the U.S. desire for peaceful settlement of all disputes and, for the first time, affirmed the ultimate objective of American military withdrawal. Clearly the United States had made concessions and retreated from its many steadfast declarations of support for the Republic of China.[159]

Barry Goldwater returned to his Senate office and dictated a note to the Alpha File. How did he stand? Should he back the president or criticize the policy shift? The conservative searched his conscience, allegiances, and experiences. He felt real conflict between his loyalty to Richard Nixon and his sense of personal obligation to friends on Taiwan, between sustaining a Republican administration in foreign affairs and a commitment to allies in the war against communism. "If I am pressed," he resolved finally, "I will have to say I support the President and the language of the Communique."

He reassured himself, perhaps less than half-convinced: "To sum it up, if I cannot believe my President, then I have lost all my faith in men, in friends and in leadership. I think he has told us the truth."[160]

Other conservatives were not at all convinced. William F. Buckley, Jr., took Goldwater to task publicly for his support of Nixon's China policy. Goldwater "is living in his own world," wrote the editor of the *National Review*, if he believes that the U.S. made no major concessions to the Chinese communists. "It is bad enough to lose Taiwan. The prospect of losing Barry Goldwater is insupportable, and terribly, shatteringly sad."[161] Such leading conservatives as William Rusher, John Ashbrook, and James Burnham were also concerned about Goldwater's turn to regular Republicanism and his loss of ideological fire. In addition to the president's initiative toward China, they cited Goldwater's acceptance of détente with the Soviet Union, the no-win policy of Vietnamization, wage and price controls, and continued deficit spending. Nixon had long been suspect in their eyes. Now they judged Goldwater guilty by commission and omission.[162]

The Arizonan rejected their reproach. He defended the conservatism of the administration, certifying its proper selection of Supreme Court justices and nominees to the federal district and appeals courts. President Nixon, after some prompting, had launched a crippling attack on liberalism by appointing conservatives to the federal bureaucracy. To these accomplishments Goldwater added Nixon's veto of the Child Care bill, refusal to replace J. Edgar Hoover as head of the Federal Bureau of Investigation, opposition to busing, pursuit of a strong defense, continuation of nuclear testing, and efforts to destabilize the Allende government in Chile. He pleaded with conservatives to be realistic, for all their desires could not be satisfied. In a curious endorsement, he praised Nixon to William Loeb, the editor and publisher of the Manchester, New Hampshire, *Union Leader:* "There are many things that the President has done that I don't like any part of, but I have to say that on the whole, he's given us a much better government than we've had since Truman."[163] Besides, as Goldwater bluntly reminded conservatives, there were few alternatives. Election year 1972 was upon them, and the "left-wing agitators" in the Democratic Party had nominated Senator George McGovern. In the face of this danger, conservative antagonists threatened "the entire party, the entire country, the entire free world, and freedom itself." Conservatives, in crisis, had to "choke back" their criticism and stand "shoulder to shoulder with Richard Nixon." The stakes were too high to stay at home.[164]

In spite of his concerns, Goldwater almost sat out the 1972 campaign. He expected Nixon to ask him to address the convention, but the invitation was still not forthcoming a week before the convention was to open. Prickly after years of feeling ignored, the Arizona senator took this as a personal rejection. Apparently the Nixon camp would not even perform the rituals of respect due a party war-horse. Demoralized, he wrote a note to the Alpha File: "I don't want to become just another hasbeen as I see so many pathetically wandering around convention halls where they are no longer needed and no longer wanted or no longer thought of. . . . It is kind of hard to realize that the end of the road is in sight and that the Party you have worked so long for and so hard for is no longer in need of your kind of leadership or help."[165] Even after the White House switchboard put the call through, he was still hurting. He petulantly refused a request to switch the day and time of his speech—it was opening day at 8:30 P.M. or "not at all." He rejected all suggestions for changes in his text as well.[166]

Stroking from the president and his staff helped to heal Goldwater, who backed up his admonitions to conservatives by logging almost fifty thousand miles, making more than one hundred speeches, and visiting twenty-two states on behalf of the ticket. Democratic allegations of Republican "dirty tricks" did not bother Barry Goldwater. The bugging of the Democratic Party headquarters at the Watergate complex in Washington, D.C., on June 17, 1972, was "unimportant" and, he alleged, the listening devices "were deliberately planted by Democrats to create an issue." As he reminded reporters, "They did the same things to me [in 1964]—taping speeches, bugging, spying. . . . I even did some myself."[167] On the Senate floor, Goldwater attacked the media's calumny in deceiving "the public to believe that in some sinister way one of the greatest Presidents this country ever had was personally pulling the strings to have his campaign workers engage in illegal pursuits."[168] Later, Goldwater blamed himself for not having been more suspicious of the campaign practices of the Committee to Re-elect the President (CREEP). In particular, he had received $750,000 from Maurice Stans to buy a jet aircraft for his campaign trips. "Right there is where I should have smelled a rat because the Republican Party never had that much money laying around at anytime in my memory."[169]

Richard Nixon campaigned for reelection on his accomplishments in foreign affairs, including the withdrawal of all U.S. combat troops from Vietnam by the late summer. As the Republicans told voters on election eve, peace was at hand. Domestically, the president followed the emerging Republican pattern with calls for law and order and individual responsibility and against busing and affirmative action. The Democratic Party's opposition to the Vietnam War and approval of Great Society welfare programs thinned its ranks. New party rules that ensured convention representation to women and people of color also fueled desertion by confirming white voters' notions of Democratic gender and racial favoritism.[170]

The 1972 election was 1964 in hard reverse. The Nixon landslide smothered George McGovern. The president won over 60 percent of the popular vote, just below Lyndon Johnson's winning margin. Nixon's 520 electoral votes rivaled Franklin Roosevelt's greatest victory, with only Massachusetts and the District of Columbia remaining in the Democratic column. The South was now solidly Republican, as were the West and Midwest. The Republican tide was strongest in the Sunbelt, where such counties as Orange (Florida), Dallas (Texas), Maricopa (Arizona), and Orange (California) counted more than two-thirds of their vote for the president. Meanwhile, a majority of blue-collar urban ethnics abandoned the Democratic coalition, with only Jewish and African-American voters holding fast. Political realignment was in full swing at the presidential level and promised to accelerate in the wake of migration to the South and West. In 1948, Arizona, Florida, California, and Texas combined for sixty votes in the electoral college; in 1972, they cast ninety-four votes. Massachusetts, Pennsylvania, and New York, in comparison, had seen their collective ninety-six electoral votes in 1948 diminish to eighty-one in 1972.[171]

Nixon's personal victory masked the continuing transformation of the GOP. Seventy-five percent of Republican senators in 1972 represented areas outside New England and the Middle Atlantic states. In the 1930s these two regions had accounted for half of the Republican bloc. During the same period, the Republican House delegation from the East had been cut in half. Conservatives made their greatest gains in the South. Republicans now held one-third of the South's U.S. Senate seats, up from 10 percent just eight years before. Southern Republican members of the House of Representatives had doubled in number since 1964, and they formed one-third of the region's delegation. The seeds of Goldwaterism had not only sprouted but also produced a bountiful harvest.[172]

Two weeks after the election Barry Goldwater visited with Richard Nixon at Camp David for one of their rare private meetings. Goldwater's eyes were on the second term, and he urged the president to proceed boldly. The great mandate, contended the conservative, gave Nixon the leverage to confront the Pentagon and force a restructuring of the military's procurement and supply systems. The armed services wasted too much money, fostered duplication, and acquiesced to unreasonable delays in developing new weapons. Also, as he had done so many times before, the Arizonan advised his friend to take control of the bureaucracy and remove all Democrats from executive office.[173]

Another of his suggestions was already moving toward implementation. After the South Vietnamese stalled the Paris peace talks during the final phase of negotiations, President Nixon ordered Operation Linebacker II, the saturation bombing of North Vietnam. The "Christmas Bombing," which began on December 17 and lasted for eleven days, engaged B-52 aircraft in the dropping of more than 15,000 tons of explosives. The purpose of the operation was to convince the South Vietnamese of America's stake in their future and the North Vietnamese of its willingness to use all means to effect and maintain a settlement. The talks resumed soon after the bombing ended, and all parties signed an agreement in January 1973 that provided for the release of American prisoners of war, set a date for U.S. withdrawal, allowed northern and southern armies to remain in place, and outlined the eventual formation of a coalition government for South Vietnam. To quell last-minute hesitation on the part of reluctant South Vietnamese President Nguyen Van Thieu, the Nixon administration enlisted Goldwater's help. Nixon had the Arizonan and conservative Mississippi Senator John Stennis publicly caution Thieu that hesitation imperiled congressional funding. The president also ordered aide General Alexander Haig to forward to the South Vietnamese a warning from Barry Goldwater: If Thieu "bucks much more," the United States should withdraw and "to hell with him."[174]

To Goldwater, Operation Linebacker II proved the case he had been making since the mid-1960s: "When the U.S. policy makers decided to take advantage of our superior military capabilities, they brought the war to an end in approximately twelve days. It might have been twelve weeks had we waged an all-out air and naval offensive earlier."[175] This was the conventional Air Force wisdom then, and it remains so today. It ignores, however, the changes that transpired over time in the nature of the war and American objectives. The administration designed Linebacker II to revive a negotiation process that was already in its endgame. It followed the 1968 Tet offensive, which began the transformation of Vietnam from a guerrilla to a conventional war, requiring the north to create an extensive and vulnerable logistical support base. Détente, too, had caused the Soviet Union and the People's Republic of China to diminish their support for the Vietnamese communists. After these changes, dreams of giving the Air Force "free rein" were, by 1972, no longer politically feasible. Finally, the administration did not plan the operation to achieve military victory. The president ordered the Christmas Bombing to complete the safe evacuation of American troops, bring the POWs home, and create a "decent interval" that would permit America to save face.[176]

At their Camp David meeting in November, Barry Goldwater had made a personal request of the president. He was thinking of retirement from the Senate in 1974. Approaching his sixty-fifth birthday, he realized that it was time to allow "young men to rise." This was good for the Republican Party and would "avoid dissention and disruption."[177] Besides, as he told Arizona governor and longtime friend Jack Williams, "I have watched too many men slip between the age of sixty-five and later in the Senate."[178] Also beckoning him home was his wife, Peggy, who continued to suffer from hearing loss and had become an infrequent visitor to Washington, D.C. His children's marital problems—only son Mike would escape divorce—had dealt a blow to his sense of family. Guilt born of a history of neglect had been rekindled. Finally, he now felt a vindication that justified the martyrdom of 1964. He had won back his Senate seat, and "the whole of the Nixon organization was the guts of the Goldwater organization."[179] Thus, the Arizonan asked the president, barring a change of mind about the 1974 Senate race, for appointment as ambassador to Mexico. He did not report Richard Nixon's response. But Barry Goldwater's needs and loyalties would keep him on the Washington stage for a while longer, as the president soon had more pressing problems to consider.[180]

11

Staying the Course

What in hell has happened to my America?

—BARRY GOLDWATER
The Coming Breakpoint

Republicans were in a dream state as 1973 began. They bubbled with talk of the now-emerged Republican majority that would ensure their hold on the country for a generation or more. Euphoria, however, became despair within twenty months as the Nixon presidency unraveled in scandal, and America was in retreat at home and abroad. The worst was yet to come. In the aftermath of Republican disgrace, the Democrats reclaimed the White House. National decline and drift led Barry Goldwater to pessimism and historical analogy. In *The Coming Breakpoint,* he warned, "We are in about the same position as was Rome before she collapsed."[1] Despite Goldwater's jeremiad, there was accumulating evidence of Republican revival. It would be born of a rising on the right. Filling the vacuum in a Republican Party gutted of moderates and liberals, an evolving conservative movement maneuvered to turn domestic change and foreign setbacks to advantage. A new conservatism would not only make the Carter years a brief interregnum in Republican rule but stake claim to the American future as well.

No one was more attuned to the meaning of his election mandate or more determined to seal a place in history than Nixon. With America's formal withdrawal from Vietnam at hand, the president envisioned bold foreign policy initiatives that would build on first-term accomplishments. Domestically, he aimed to roll back federal power with program and spending cuts while bolstering state and local governments. Barry Goldwater cheered Nixon's shift to the right, and in line with proposed bureaucracy-pruning, again strongly encouraged the administration to "clean out" the State Department of its Democratic holdovers. Presidential speech writer Patrick Buchanan echoed the Arizonan: "Our fault in the first four years was that we never came to grips with government. . . . We've been a thin film of dust on a hardwood table; if we left now, we'd blow away. . . . We have to get control before we reorganize them. We can't even trust our own phones, you never know when one of our phone calls is going to pop up in the *Washington Post*."²

Barry Goldwater also urged Nixon to take a "tough" stance against Republicans who refused to follow the administration's lead. "I mean tough like not building projects in their states, not having Republicans attend their functions, etc." Toughness fit the Nixon game plan, and in the margin of the Goldwater letter the president jotted, "E[hrlichman]—Note[,] He is right."³ Richard Nixon had already planned to carry the matter a step further. In September 1972 he confided to presidential counsel John Dean, "I want the most comprehensive notes on all of those that have tried to do us in. . . . We have not used the power in the first four years, as you know. We have never used it. We haven't used the Bureau and we haven't used the Justice Department, but things are going to change now."⁴

Amid the ruffles and flourishes that inaugurated the second term and pressured by the ambitions of younger men, Barry Goldwater assessed his political future. He set down on paper the pros and cons of a 1974 Senate race. Among those opposed to his seeking reelection were Peggy and family members who wanted him to return to private life. He saw his wife only on trips to Arizona and California every other weekend. He visited with his children and grandchildren even less. Another negative for Goldwater was his "loss of drive" and "no real burning desire to run again." He asked himself, "Is there more I can do?" noting his minimal influence as a minority party junior senator. Filling Carl Hayden's role had become burdensome, and he likened the routine to operating a "sort of a pimp's office." He said, "I am besieged by requests for jobs here, jobs there, money, money, money." Financial security was also a consideration.⁵ Although he earned about $100,000 per year, and the family's net worth was more than $1 million, what Barry described as an "extravagant life" forced him to raid the family stock portfolio and erode principal.⁶ Finally, the lure of retirement and hobbies became more tantalizing as he grew older.⁷

A powerful array of responsibilities and needs, however, overcame any temptation to leave Washington. He could not wean himself from the call to service that his mother had sounded so loudly and so often. Events had convinced him that one person could make a difference. Arizona's future demanded funding for the Central Arizona Project and solar energy development. The Grand Canyon had to be protected and the park area expanded. His work regarding Native Americans was unfinished. The nation needed his strong voice for national defense. He was the conservative movement's patriarch. Nor could he relinquish the senatorial perks and privileges to which he had grown accustomed; the prestige and power that he had long pursued and that gave meaning to his life. And as always there was loyalty to party and friends. Now was no time to desert, for the critics of Richard Nixon and the Republican Party had threatened to halt the victory march even before it had begun.[8]

In the context of the 1972 campaign Goldwater had been suspicious and disdainful of Democratic allegations of Republican "dirty tricks." He dismissed the Watergate break-in as an isolated incident—politics as usual—and the Democrats' whining did not shield them from blame for similar ploys in past battles. Watergate, he believed, was perpetrated by "some crazy crew of political neophytes who had been swept up in the excitement of the campaign"[9] and was "not anything of a massive moral issue."[10] He became more disturbed, however, as the continuing probe yielded startling revelations of a money trail from the burglars to the Committee to Re-elect the President (CREEP). The possibility of White House complicity led the Senate to authorize a select committee, chaired by North Carolina's Samuel Ervin, to investigate and hold hearings. Also of concern was growing evidence that Watergate was not an anomaly but a small piece of a larger pattern of administration espionage and sabotage. Early on, some Republicans privately entertained doubts about the president's integrity. While convinced that Nixon did not have prior knowledge of the Watergate break-in, they felt he was implicated in its cover-up. "This," said a cagey Senator John Tower, "was not necessarily untypical of Nixon. He just thought he could get away with it."[11] Barry Goldwater, too, had stories to tell. At the "Munich of the Republican Party," the 1960 convention, he called Nixon "a two-fisted, four-square liar."[12] Nixon's overweening ambition during the 1964 campaign had also exposed serious character flaws.[13]

In spite of such memories, Barry Goldwater did not raise his guard. Denial was more comfortable, because suspicion was inconsistent with a mental map that put loyalty to friends and party in bold relief. Instinctively, the Arizonan rushed to their support. He projected onto Nixon his own protectiveness of staff as the cause of the president's intransigence to investigators. He read his 1964 experiences into Nixon's ordeal. "I am convinced that there was a determined effort on the part of the majority of the major press . . . to misrepresent me because just as [with] Nixon, the eastern and some western liberal press members want no part of a conservative President."[14] His faith in the presidency and desire to bolster the power of the commander-in-chief made him receptive to defenses of executive privilege and national security. Thus, in 1973 he wrote, "I am persuaded that the exercise of executive privilege in matters of national security and foreign policy, confidential conversations, and papers by persons who are in direct relationship with the President, personal files and court litigation preparation are firmly rooted on sound constitutional ground."[15] Besides, the encircled GOP needed him. Goldwater's behavior during the controversy, observed *Washington Post* editor Benjamin Bradlee, smacked of "knee-jerk partisanship. He hated to see the Republicans take a black eye. . . . He did not do any homework on this issue as on all other issues. And, if you don't do your homework, you are at the mercy of what other people tell you."[16] Even after many Americans had answered the two key questions—"What did the President know?" and "When did he know it?"—Barry Goldwater remained captive to his loyalties. He became emotionally invested in support of the president. This prevented him from assimilating new evidence and discerning the pattern of duplicity and wrongdoing. Only years after the events did he shed his blinders to "see the real Nixon."[17] Only then could he confess to Denison Kitchel, "I suppose if I have one weakness that is greater than any other of many that I have, it has been loyalty to friends."[18]

Yet as his mother had instructed him so well, Goldwater demanded honesty. Trusting in his friend's innocence, blaming the president's subordinates, and pressing to get on with the nation's more important business, he consistently advised Richard Nixon "to come clean, lay the whole thing on the table, tell everything about it that [you] had not told the people and everything would be all right."[19] In April 1973, when private urging failed to persuade the president to stop stonewalling, Goldwater made a public plea. He told the *Christian Science Monitor* that the crisis demanded that Richard Nixon come forward and give "assurances" to the American people. "The Watergate. The Watergate. It's beginning to be like Teapot Dome. I mean, there's a smell to it. Let's get rid of the smell." Goldwater restated his faith in the president but noted, "I might not support him if it turns out he knew all about this and kept his mouth shut. But I don't think he knows about it." Substantiating this, the conservative reported a conversation with John Dean, who had been Barry Jr.'s roommate at Staunton Military Academy. He asked Dean, "Is there any truth in this?" to which the president's counsel replied, "Not at all." Said Goldwater, "I believe this kid." Goldwater also noted that the scandal was hurting party fund-raising. "I've been getting letters and calls from Republican friends of mine all around the country. They are saying, 'No more money to the Republican National Committee until this is cleared up.'" Curiously, most reports of the Goldwater interview did little more than inform readers that Teapot Dome referred to the scandals of the Warren Harding administration (1921–24), the most notorious of which was the bribery of Secretary of Interior Albert Fall in exchange for oil leases on federal lands. Reporters missed a critical nuance, as perhaps did Goldwater, and did not follow the historical logic to its conclusion. The Arizonan's analogy recalled a president who presumably did not know of his cronies' wrongdoing.[20]

Richard Nixon could not comply with Goldwater's advice. He was fully implicated in the cover-up, having already attempted to use the Central Intelligence Agency to derail the FBI probe of Watergate. In March he authorized the payment of hush money to the burglars. The president, after the failure of a "limited hangout" strategy and the ploy of an in-house investigation, moved to distance himself from the spreading net. On April 30, 1973, he accepted the resignations of H. R. Haldeman and John Ehrlichman and fired John Dean. Nixon told the American people in a televised address that he assumed "responsibility" for his aides' actions but not the "blame."

Barry Goldwater praised the president's handling of the situation, doubting that he "has withheld anything."[21] He defended Nixon on the Senate floor: "I believe implicitly that the President knew nothing at all about any matter in relation to the so-called Watergate affair. I believe that he is completely honest."[22] To resolve the matter and prove Nixon's innocence, Goldwater joined other senators in cosponsoring a resolution authorizing the president to appoint a special prosecutor. Soon after, Goldwater and Senator Alan Cranston of California asked that the special prosecutor's charge be broadened to cover allegations of corruption beyond the Watergate break-in. Goldwater, meanwhile, rejected demands for Nixon's impeachment that followed the Ehrlichman and Haldeman resignations. Impeachment "is not something that's done willy-nilly," he argued. However, if the president had "been dishonest about this, then I think impeachment would certainly come."[23]

On May 16, the day before the televised hearings of the Ervin Committee were to begin, Senator Goldwater reiterated his position in a press release. He pleaded with Americans to end their obsession with Watergate and for the president to redress concerns candidly. Although Goldwater realized that the scandal was a "blot" on the nation's history and still wanted answers to who, what, and why, more pressing affairs of state demanded attention. "We are witnessing," he warned, "the loss of confidence in America's ability to govern." As proof, he cited the president's failure to fill a growing number of vacant positions in the Department of Defense. Discouraging economic news also put the nation at risk. "We have a far greater responsibility to our children and I might say to ourselves than to allow the sordid Watergate to wash out all other concepts of responsibility. . . . I urge my President to start making moves in the direction of leadership, which has suffered from lack of attention because of an understandable concern about Watergate."[24] Not surprisingly, presidential aide Alexander Haig telephoned the next day to express Nixon's interest in Goldwater's comments. Although disappointed that the president had not called, the Arizonan was pleased to have sparked a White House reaction. Yet in his enthusiasm Goldwater undercut the impact of the message with reassurances: "I told [Haig] I felt that the majority of Americans did not associate Mr. Nixon in a guilty way with this sordid mess and that he should be out in front leading the people."[25]

Impatient for direct word from the president, Goldwater pounded out a follow-up letter on his portable typewriter. It reflected his belief in Nixon's innocence and the marginal meaning of Watergate. He wrote as an ally: "I want you to understand that what I am saying to you comes right from the heart, comes from years of friendship and comes from deep devotion to everything you and I believe in." Goldwater then offered the president the means to reassert influence. It was important "to get acquainted with the Congress . . . getting down to the little fellow who has to go out and in his district or his state to keep the Republican Party going, to keep the radicals out of office and to support you." He suggested that the president "stop living alone. You have to tear down that wall that you have built around you. . . . No one who I know feels close to you. I will make one possible exception. I feel close to you." On a happier but not necessarily candid note, Goldwater maintained that Republicans were beginning to "shrug off" Watergate, and he urged the president to grasp the reins of party leadership. "I will continue to support you," he concluded, "back you, and as I have often told you, do anything you want me to." Again, Richard Nixon made no response, but he surely felt that his right flank was, for the present, secure.[26]

Goldwater went public on Watergate again in June. In an interview with CBS news correspondent Dan Rather, he dismissed talk of resignation and impeachment as premature, certain that Nixon's full airing of the facts would cause Watergate to fade as an issue. Still, he was frank about the scandal's political fallout and his priorities: "The thing that bothers me is here I have spent a third of my life trying to build the Republican Party, adding my little bit to it, having been successful in the South and in the Southwest, and then all of a sudden, as I near the end of my time in politics, I wonder—what the hell's it all been for?"[27]

John Dean was scheduled to testify before the Ervin Committee on June 25, 1973, and commentators expected him to give evidence damaging to the president's case. In anticipation of his appearance, Dean solicited the advice of the Arizona senator, conferring with him at the home of Barry Jr. "He told my dad what was going on," remembers the younger Goldwater. "He wanted to know whether he should be guarded or wide open in his testimony."[28] The senator listened to Dean's story, believed him, and responded automatically, "John, march your ass up there to the Senate, in front of those cameras, and tell 'em what you know as best you can." The strain of dual loyalties caused Goldwater distress. Dissonance brought a flash of acceptance, and he instinctively recoiled, unable to suppress his memories: "That goddamn Nixon has been lying all of his life."[29] Goldwater's insight, however, was fleeting. He did not absorb fully the impact of John Dean's words, and there was no significant alteration in his mind-set. Even after Dean's appearance before the committee and the resulting public uproar, he reverted to type. "I haven't decided on what his testimony means yet," the *Arizona Republic* quoted him. "I have to study it first."[30] It is uncertain whether he ever took that opportunity.[31]

A few months later the politics of Watergate once more became personal for Goldwater. In September, White House aides informed him that Spiro Agnew was under investigation for accepting bribes from contractors while governor of Maryland and vice president of the United States. Goldwater's high regard for Agnew brought him to the defense. Agnew was "not guilty of anything," and Goldwater supported his nomination for president in 1976.[32] Inner conflict, at the same time, provoked more doubt concerning the president's integrity. He wrote his suspicions into the Alpha File: "If someone were to ask me if I could suggest someone to write a scenario for a Watergate type of operation [to disgrace Agnew], I would turn to one man and he happens to be the President of the United States, Richard Nixon. It has his hand, a hand that I have known for a long time. . . . I now sit . . . with the dreadful feeling that maybe Mr. Nixon has more power than is good for him and is using it in a way that is not good for any of us."[33]

Goldwater's anxiety over Spiro Agnew's difficulties quickly subsided, however, as it had with John Dean's. His public posture showed no change. Just days after the Alpha File entry he published a series of articles in the *New York Times* repeating his seemingly unconflicted call for Nixon to clear the air of Watergate so that he could get on with the business of government. "I happen to feel he is completely innocent of charges that he knew about the Watergate break-in ahead of time or was cognizant of the massive attempt to cover up this episode and its related incidents." To end the crisis, Goldwater proposed that Nixon release "selected portions" of the tape recordings he had made in the Oval Office, debate Senator Ervin on national television, and hold more press conferences. He expected Senate critics to show their good faith by suspending the televised hearings. In a reflection of his sense of Watergate, Goldwater further proposed that Senate investigators end their "double standard" and expand the probe of dirty tricks to include past Democratic campaigns against Republicans.[34]

Goldwater stayed the course through the trials of October. He supported the president when he induced the "Saturday Night Massacre," ordering special prosecutor Archibald Cox fired and accepting the resignations of Attorney General Elliott Richardson and Deputy Attorney General William

Ruckelshaus, who refused to comply. Said Goldwater, Cox was "getting a little far afield" in his attempt to take the president to court to obtain tapes of presidential conversations. "The whole operation was beginning to have a political undertone."[35] More troublesome were revelations that the White House could not locate some tapes and that suspicious gaps existed in the taped evidence. "As one schooled in electronics," countered the conservative, "I can understand it."[36] By the end of the month, Goldwater regretfully concluded that Nixon's credibility was at "an all-time low from which he may not be able to recover."[37]

The situation had reached a critical stage, and Barry Goldwater believed that Richard Nixon had to seize the initiative to save his presidency. To jar Nixon, to break down the "wall" that isolated him from political realities, the conservative prodded more critically and insistently. Nixon's handling of the tapes had been "clumsy." He was a "loner," never one of the boys, and when he ignored his friends' advice, trouble pursued him.[38] The fundamental issue was personal integrity, and the president had to confront it. "I don't think it's Watergate, frankly, as much as it's just a question in people's minds of just how honest is this man? I hate to think of the old adage, 'Would you buy a used car from Dick Nixon?'—but that's what people are asking around the country."[39] Crisis times demanded desperate actions. Nixon could save himself and the nation by discarding the defense of executive privilege, answering questions, and providing investigators with all relevant evidence. "There is no sensible reason for him to resign," Goldwater persisted. "He's not guilty of anything."[40] To facilitate Nixon's coming out, Goldwater called for calm, for Americans "to check their wild stampede, to pause a moment in their tumult and trumpeting" and to, "in God's name, cool it."[41]

The senator felt he had scored a breakthrough when Nixon rewarded his stubborn allegiance with an invitation to dine at the White House on December 13. The small gathering included loyalists Pat Buchanan, Bryce Harlow, Ray Price, Pat Nixon, and Julie and David Eisenhower. Having not visited with the president in more than a year, Goldwater was shocked at the impact of Watergate on his friend. "His mind seemed to halt abruptly and wander aimlessly away. Each time, after several such lapses, he would snap back to a new subject. I became concerned. . . . Is the President coming apart?" At one point, Goldwater interrupted the "gibberish," impatiently snapping at Nixon: "Act like a President." The uncomfortable silence that followed ended when Nixon renewed his "ceaseless, chippy chatter." Later, abruptly and without context, he turned to the Arizonan: "How do I stand, Barry?" "People are divided," Goldwater responded, initiating another break in the conversation until the president returned to his rambling. "The evening was a watershed for me," wrote the Arizonan later.

"Nixon appeared to be cracking. The presidency was crumbling. I would not stand idly by if the situation worsened." What action did Goldwater have in mind? He would, as he had for months, press Nixon to "come clean, one way or another."[42]

Although 1973 had been a bad year for the president, it accelerated the rehabilitation of Barry Goldwater. Remaking him in their own image and scoffing at suggestions that his criticisms had been "tactical,"[43] liberals praised the conservative for his "blunt talk."[44] They raised him as a GOP icon. "He is now," wrote Roy Reed of the *Los Angeles Times,* "the Dwight D. Eisenhower of the Republican Party."[45] Such a judgment required some manipulation of history and a willingness to ignore Goldwater's recent resistance to détente, busing, the halting of trade with Southern Rhodesia, the school lunch program, and mass transit. It also acknowledged the impact of Lyndon Johnson's fall, for his "deception somehow legitimized the Goldwater war policy."[46] Goldwater's stand on Watergate had also impressed the American people. They placed him tenth in the Gallup "Most Admired Men" poll in 1973, and a year later raised him to the sixth spot. Heeding the voice of the people, 6 percent of Republican county chairs checked his name as their nominee for president in 1976.[47]

The new year brought Richard Nixon no respite. In January, Egil Krogh was sentenced to prison for his activities with the White House plumbers. In February, Nixon's lawyer Herbert Kalmbach pleaded guilty to campaign irregularities. The following month, H. R. Haldeman, John Ehrlichman, Charles Colson, John Mitchell, and Robert Mardian, among others, were indicted as conspirators in the obstruction of justice. The grand jury also secretly named Nixon as an unindicted participant in the coverup. In all, thirty of the president's men, including four cabinet officers, would be convicted and imprisoned.[48]

With the beginning of election year '74 and in the face of preliminary polls predicting heavy losses, Republican leaders became restless under their Nixon albatross. As early as January they began to hint that the president should resign for the good of the party. This disturbed Nixon, especially when he was informed that an "Arizona mafia" was orchestrating the putsch. Alexander Haig calmed him, finding that Barry Goldwater "appeared to be standing firm."[49] Other Republicans proved less reliable. On March 19, conservative Senator James Buckley of New York, the brother of William F. Buckley, Jr., called on the president to resign. Nixon's ploy on April 29, in which he released edited transcripts of White House conversations rather than the actual tapes, caused further erosion. Pennsylvania Senator Hugh Scott withdrew his support when Nixon's profanity-laced transcripts revealed a "deplorable, disgusting, shabby, immoral performance."[50] Arizona

Congressman and House Minority Leader John Rhodes seconded Scott, describing the transcripts' contents as "devastating."[51]

In spite of the rising tide of indictments, convictions, and revelations, Barry Goldwater continued to resist the flow. He would not ask the president to step down because "I don't think it's the prerogative of one man to put himself above 46 or 47 million Americans who voted for Mr. Nixon or the 23 or 24 percent of the American people who still believe he should be President."[52] In January he blamed the Democrats for "dragging" the matter out for "no better reason than to gain political advantage."[53] When experts discovered as many as nine deliberate tape erasures of a crucial White House conversation, Goldwater resolved: "It's nothing more than technicians explaining how eighteen minutes of silence occurred on tape. My confidence in the President is still strong."[54] In March, he rallied California Republicans around the president, urging them to resist the divide-and-conquer tactics of the "liberal press."[55] As late as April 1974 he wrote to constituents that it was "time to put Watergate behind us and get on to some of the most pressing problems facing our nation. . . . However, the Congress and all of its committees are controlled by the Democrats, and frankly, I think they are going to drag Watergate out for some time to come."[56]

Goldwater even took the release of the tape transcripts in stride. He applauded Nixon: "In this, I believe, the President has gone as far as he possibly could on the question of materials sought by the House Judiciary Committee." If Nixon had not appeased the House Committee, then surely it was playing a "partisan role aimed at vote-getting rather than truth-getting."[57] Goldwater's defense went beyond Senate speeches. He circulated a sixty-page defense of the president's decision to withhold the tapes; it was written by "the smartest lawyer I ever met." *Washington Post* editor Ben Bradlee found it "the shoddiest piece of scholarship I ever saw. He omitted everything that hurt his case and exaggerated everything that helped. It was unforgivable."[58] When Bradlee confronted him, Goldwater denied having even read the document. Goldwater's legal counsel, Terry Emerson, also aided the president's case, preparing a brief supporting his decision to withhold materials from the courts. Emerson concluded: "President Nixon's reading of executive privilege as being based in the actions and rulings of the Founding Fathers is verified by both the Washington and Jefferson precedents."[59] White House aide Tom Korologos was appreciative: "It seems that all we do down here is thank you and the Senator for the good fight . . . and what a fight you're putting together."[60] Ignoring these efforts, the House Judiciary Committee voted to pursue the issue in the courts.

May 1974 brought a more visible show of support. Guaranteed a warm welcome, the president flew to Phoenix for his first outing since the release of the edited transcripts. The state Republican organization obliged, turning out sixteen thousand enthusiastic men and women for "a straight-out party pep rally . . . in the heart of Barry Goldwater country."[61] Even more pleasing to the president was the conservative senator's pledge of confidence tendered later at a reception in Goldwater's Scottsdale home.[62]

Behind the resolute public mask was Barry Goldwater the practical politician. In the spring he began to doubt the president's chances of survival. The unraveling of Nixon's defense and the potential political fallout for Republicans led him and John Rhodes to discuss, on several occasions, the possibility of suggesting resignation to Nixon: "Frankly, it gets down to one question: Does the President want to see the destruction of the two-party system which will most certainly occur if he remains in office, or would he, in the interest of maintaining that system, step down? . . . If we continue to lose elections, and there is no indication that we will not, then the politics of America will come under the domination of the labor movement, all of the radical groups who have crept in bed with government."[63]

Other Republicans on Capitol Hill, braced by editorials in the conservative *Chicago Tribune* and *Omaha World Herald* advocating resignation, urged the leadership to act. At the end of May, Goldwater publicly broached the resignation option in a *Newsweek* interview. A heavy outpouring of mail, ten-to-one in the president's favor, downed this trial balloon, and Republicans resolved to stave off impeachment until after the November elections, unless new disclosures made that impossible.[64]

The Supreme Court's unanimous ruling on July 24 that the president surrender his tapes began the countdown of Nixon's final days in the White House. On July 27 the House Judiciary Committee passed the first article of impeachment, outlining an obstruction of justice charge. Within a few days it voted two more articles: abuse of power and defiance of committee subpoenas. The president vowed to fight, and Senate leaders met to begin arrangements for a trial. Head counters gave Nixon twenty to twenty-six hard-core votes with another ten to fifteen senators leaning in his favor. Barry Goldwater was not among them. He had concluded reluctantly that Nixon was exposed on the abuse of power article and that he might have to vote to convict. The release on August 5 of the "smoking gun" transcript removed any lingering doubt from Goldwater's mind. It revealed that on June 23, 1972, within a week of the Watergate break-in, Richard Nixon was the prime mover in the cover-up, having directed the CIA to smother the FBI investigation. Goldwater was furious: "He had lied to the people, had lied to his friends in the Congress, including me. . . . That was the last straw. . . . I was wrong in protecting him as long as I did. . . . I was through with him."[65] Later he fumed to Senate colleagues, "There are only so many lies you can take and now there has been one too many. Nixon should get his ass out of the White House — today!"[66]

The question was no longer whether but how. Nixon was defiant, and a trial would embroil the nation for months more in Watergate. To spare the country that turmoil, Alexander Haig engineered the effort to convince the president that his deteriorating Senate base would not support continued resistance. Goldwater — as the leader of the Republican right wing, party patriarch, and Nixon friend and loyalist — was the obvious choice to present the case. Republicans delegated the task to him, but at Nixon's insistence on a "broader picture," they asked Hugh Scott and John Rhodes to join the mission to the White House.[67] Haig instructed the men that a consensus on the bleakness of the situation but not an insistence on resignation would nudge the skittish Nixon toward the right decision.[68]

At 5 P.M. on August 7 the three Republicans were ushered into the Oval Office. Nixon joined them within minutes. The atmosphere was tense and emotional. "I was literally on the verge of tears," remembers Goldwater, "and I could see glistening in the others' eyes." Dick Nixon, to the last, concealed himself. "He acted as though he had just shot a hole in one. I had never seen him so relaxed."[69] After reminiscing about past political battles, the president cut the small talk and came to the point:

> *Nixon:* Okay, Barry, go ahead.
> *Goldwater:* Things are bad.
> *Nixon:* Less than a half dozen votes?
> *Goldwater:* Ten at most. Maybe less. Some aren't firm. I took a nose count in the Senate today. You have four firm votes. The others are really undecided. I'm one of them . . .
> *Nixon:* Do I have any options?
> *Rhodes:* I want to tell the people outside that we didn't discuss any options.[70]

The meeting lasted less than thirty minutes. Nixon then joined his family in the White House solarium and announced his decision: "We're going back to California."[71]

The next day, the president invited Barry Goldwater and forty-five other congressional loyalists — "those he felt close to" — to the White House.[72] He talked of his mother and family. He told them he was not a quitter, but to fight was not in the national interest. "I just hope . . . ," Nixon sobbed, "I haven't let you down."[73] As the men filed out of the room, Barry stopped and hugged his friend. Twenty minutes later, Richard Nixon went before the television cameras and became the first president to resign his office.

The swearing-in of Gerald Ford as president temporarily eased Goldwater's concerns about the future of the nation and Republican Party. He felt close to Ford; both had been football centers, served in Congress, and were conservatives. After Nixon, the country needed a "Mr. Clean. He's an All-American boy. Everybody likes him."[74] Disconcerting, however, was Ford's selection of longtime adversary Nelson Rockefeller as vice president. When asked, Goldwater had put forward the name of party stalwart George Bush, the Republican National Committee Chair. Goldwater himself had won the nod of nearly 25 percent of Americans in a poll on vice presidential candidates, and the Ford administration was inundated with letters endorsing him. Believing Ford to be weak and "not the smartest man who ever came down the pike," Goldwater was worried that the ambitious New York governor had positioned himself well for 1976.[75] "I prophesy that within six months to a year the country will hear more of Rockefeller than of Ford and Ford will gradually fade into the background as Rockefeller moves in with all of his power accumulated over the years."[76] In December he was one of seven senators to vote against Rockefeller's confirmation. Many conservatives were as disturbed with the nomination as Goldwater. The right, wrote William Rusher, felt "deliberately slapped in the face by the new president."[77] Argued William Buckley, Jr., conservatives now had to regroup and formulate their own approach to the economic, social, and foreign challenges of the 1970s. Also troubling to Goldwater was President Ford's pardoning of Richard Nixon in September. If Goldwater publicly supported the decision as "the only decent and prudent course," in private he was perplexed. It was premature, he groused, for Nixon was innocent until proven guilty; he had not even been charged with a crime.[78]

Curiously, the events of the Watergate years did not seal Nixon's guilt for Barry Goldwater. In denial, and following a visit with Nixon in his San Clemente exile, the Arizonan advised on January 30, 1975: "Even though you have a Presidential Pardon I would, when your health is sufficiently good, waive your pardon and offer to appear before any court in the Capital City to, in effect, stand trial for whatever charges might be brought against you, keeping in mind that none have. . . . This would accomplish several things; it would show you as a man of courage, as a man of decency, as a man of respect for the law and as a man who is determined to allow justice to clear his name."[79]

On the eve of his Senate reelection campaign, Barry Goldwater feared that in prodding Nixon's resignation he had "killed" himself politically in conservative Arizona.[80] He could not have been further from the mark. Goldwater returned home as a conquering hero who, announced the *Arizona Republic,* was "one of Arizona's most popular figures and one of the nation's leading Republicans."[81] The primary results in early September offered strong evidence of his stature. Although Goldwater ran unopposed, his vote total was nearly as great as the sum of support received by the three candidates contesting the Democratic primary. Barry, rarely able to hold a grudge and most secure with men he had known for decades, offered Stephen Shadegg the job of campaign manager. Shadegg eagerly accepted and chose as Goldwater's theme a slogan tuned to the popular sentiment: "Arizona needs him . . . The nation needs him!"[82]

The senator was absent from Arizona for most of September, but the outlines of his campaign were fixed early in voters' minds. As expected, he blamed inflation on federal spending and called for a balanced budget amendment and a reduction in the size of the Washington bureaucracy. The growing deficit, he warned, was not simply a problem of the present: "We must stop borrowing the earnings of future generations."[83] Familiar to voters, as well, were his stands for a strong military and against busing and crime-generating "permissiveness."[84] While approving the Nixon pardon, he adamantly resisted the Ford administration's amnesty plan for draft evaders and deserters. He likened it to "throwing mud in the faces of millions of men who served this country."[85] Goldwater promised to continue his work to protect the Grand Canyon and develop solar and geothermal energy sources. And he reminded voters of his efforts in creating the volunteer army and reducing the voting age to eighteen years.[86]

There were new planks in his platform. As he had during his review of drug policy, Goldwater championed the privacy rights of Americans. Fearing the growing threat of federal "social manipulation or conditioning" posed by fast-developing computer technology, he had written a bill to restrict the government's use of personal information and give citizens ready access to their files. "It is time," he declared, "to halt this drift towards reducing each person to a number. . . . We would all become marked individuals. . . . Privacy as liberty is all too easily lost." In raising "the right 'to be let alone' from intrusions by Big Brother in all his guises," Goldwater footnoted the Supreme Court's *Roe v. Wade* decision making abortion a matter between a woman and her physician. As the court found, the right to privacy is "so rooted in the traditions and conscience of our people as to be ranked as fundamental."[87]

The controversy over abortion, while just beginning, also demanded attention. In his 1973 constituent form letters about *Roe v. Wade*, Goldwater had disagreed with the "length to which it went" but believed that "abortion should be legalized because whether it is legal or not women are going to have it done."[88] He was consistent in the 1974 campaign: "I don't want to see promiscuous abortion. If a life is in danger, it's OK, but otherwise, the pill ought to be enough. If it isn't, they ought to say 'no.'"[89] Informing this position were family experiences, the influence of his wife, and his belief in individual rights. When the abortion debate in Arizona grew more polarized, however, candor would yield to calculation. As son Mike explains, "He jumped that fence a couple of times."[90]

Jonathan Marshall accepted the challenge of running against what he called a "national monument."[91] Born in New York, the fifty-year-old Marshall came to Arizona in 1963 after buying the *Scottsdale Progress,* a small suburban Phoenix newspaper. As editor and publisher, he offered Maricopa County a liberal alternative to the conservative Pulliam press. Marshall, a political unknown, took to the campaign trail because "we need a national house cleaning. We need new leaders who will restore faith in the minds of the American people. . . . It is time for Arizona to have a working senator, a senator who is in tune with the times."[92] Promising an issues-oriented campaign, the Democratic contender produced position papers outlining his ideas on mass transit, energy self-sufficiency, environmental protection, and education reform. He pledged if elected to work for the expansion of Medicare benefits, more stringent pollution controls, and the creation of a Consumer Protection Agency. In foreign affairs he favored détente and the withdrawal of all aid to repressive regimes. With Watergate the backdrop, Marshall attacked the Nixon pardon and charged that Goldwater had naively backed the president "right down the line" and now "suddenly became this great moralist."[93] Marshall, like Democratic candidates before him, reviewed Goldwater's attendance record. He charged that Arizona's "absentee" senator neglected his duties, having missed 50 percent of the roll-call votes, the worst record in the chamber.[94] Unlike Democrats campaigning in other states, Marshall would not have the economy as an ally. Arizona was booming, stimulated by defense spending. In the first half of the 1970s, Arizona was the nation's fastest growing state, registering a population leap of 25 percent.[95]

The fall campaign was devoid of revelation, incident, and energy. A shortage of funds hamstrung Marshall's effort. Without a history of party service and the proper pioneer bloodlines, Marshall could count on little assistance from Democratic regulars. "We are going to run an austerity campaign, which means doing a lot of walking and riding of buses."[96] Besides having no funds to rent an airplane, mailings were ruled out as too expensive, and television and radio advertising was kept to a minimum. Marshall's "reserved" nature and minimal campaign flair deepened the hole.[97] So, too, did building tensions within his organization that led him to fire two campaign managers and conduct the effort alone in the last weeks. Barry Goldwater, meanwhile, marshaled his usual full store of resources to reach every receptive voter. Although relying heavily on television and radio to carry the message, his October schedule was full and he was a presence throughout the state. Goldwater often spoke off the cuff before large groups on "whatever world trouble spot is brewing at the moment."[98] Also particularly effective was his turning of Watergate to advantage. Goldwater wooed his audience and highlighted his influence by retelling the "inside story of Richard Nixon's resignation."[99] Still, observers noted that there was "no particular zest to his campaign appearances."[100]

Election day brought no surprises to either camp. Barry Goldwater won an impressive victory, capturing 58 percent of the vote. Republicans were also successful in holding on to their two House seats. The Watergate fallout did reach Arizona, however. Democrats regained control of the state Senate and the governor's mansion. The post-Watergate Democratic resurgence in Arizona was mirrored nationally, for the party picked up forty-six seats in the House of Representatives and four in the U.S. Senate. Democratic majorities in both houses were the largest since 1936.[101]

Although he was victorious, his dismal showing among the Navajo in northeastern Arizona infuriated Goldwater. He prided himself on his relationships with Arizona's Native Americans, particularly the Navajo. Throughout his life he had been a frequent visitor to the reservation, running supplies, exploring, and taking photographs of the land and people. He relished their names for him—"Chiidee Naa Taah" (man with automobile that flies) and "Hosteen Bitsiisheh' illii" (man with curly hair). He christened his Scottsdale home "Be-Nun-I-Kin" (house on top of the hill) and filled it with Navajo rugs and Hopi Kachinas. In previous campaigns, the Arizona conservative had claimed a majority on the reservation. In 1974, Marshall won the backing of nine of every ten Navajos.[102]

The Navajos had turned against Goldwater because of his decisive support of the neighboring Hopi in a land dispute that had embroiled the tribes since 1882. For almost a century the seminomadic Navajo had followed their sheep herds west, encroaching more and more on the land and water supplies of the vastly outnumbered Hopi settled in farming villages atop narrow mesas. Rights to oil, gas, and coal deposits further complicated the matter. In 1962 a federal court ruled that the tribes jointly owned the contested 1.8 million acres even though the Navajo occupied most of the land. The court left to Congress the task of partitioning this "Joint Use Area." Barry Goldwater, who had ties to both tribes, remained neutral, attempting to prod compromise "that will not cause a hardship on the Navajos and will be of justice to the Hopi."[103] When that failed, Goldwater sided with the Hopi and introduced legislation to divide the area equally between the tribes. This would force relocation of 160 Hopi and more than 10,000 Navajo. He believed the solution just, for the Navajo "have 16 million acres . . . , literally tens of thousands of acres that are not being used."[104] In 1974 Congress followed Goldwater's lead and passed the partition bill, with relocation scheduled to be completed in 1986. What Goldwater underestimated, however, was the impact of relocation on the Navajo people. Forced off land to which they had deep religious and ancestral ties, the Navajo felt an intense spiritual loss. Relocation destroyed traditional lifestyles and aggravated stress, seen in a rising incidence of alcoholism, divorce, and physical illness. Navajo resistance slowed the timetable and brought stalemate. Twenty years after the passage of the law, hundreds of Navajo families remain on Hopi land.[105]

Barry Goldwater lost his focus on these problems when he became entangled in a personal feud with Navajo tribal chair Peter MacDonald. MacDonald was a Goldwater protégé who carried the proper credentials from the 1964 campaign and was being groomed for Republican Party leadership. The Arizona senator was so impressed that he had pushed forward MacDonald's name to second Richard Nixon's nomination for president at the 1972 convention. But when Goldwater tilted toward the Hopi in the land dispute, MacDonald bolted. He enlisted Democratic aid to defeat the Goldwater partition effort and supported George McGovern for president. Equally provocative, MacDonald requested that the AFL-CIO organize the Central Arizona Project's power plant located on the reservation and conduct a voter-registration drive among the Navajo. His endorsement of Jonathan Marshall was, in Goldwater's mind, the final act of betrayal. The senator charged soon after the election that a "conspiracy" between organized labor and MacDonald had led to a "transfer of union funds" that produced the "high Navajo turnout" against him. Later, he prodded the General Accounting Office to audit Navajo tribal funds.[106] Furious at MacDonald and bound by promises to the Hopi, Goldwater refused to compromise as the consequences of relocation came to light. He was adamant: "The law is the law and the Navajos should get off the land."[107] Yet Goldwater was torn, for he felt a sense of obligation to the Navajo people. He coped by blocking the reality of relocation. Thus, when the Arizona senator appeared on the reservation at Big Mountain a few years later, Goldwater astounded the Navajo by asserting: "There has been no decision that says you have to move or what you have to do. And until that happens, and I don't think it's very close to happening or the way it looks now will happen, I won't say don't worry, but nobody can push you around."[108]

Barry Goldwater anticipated his fourth Senate term to be his last. He would be seventy-two years old at its end, and a host of health problems—including pain in his hips, knees, shoulder, and back—nagged at him. Peggy Goldwater also hoped that this was his last hurrah. An infrequent visitor to Washington, she felt a growing distance from her husband. Their time together in Arizona and California was often tense. Peggy had little interest in politics, and Barry was bored with his wife's friends and activities. He

showed no patience with her hearing problem. Rumors of Barry's "woman-
izing" exacerbated Peggy's fears, and he was compelled to reassure her.[109]
"Just you remember that I am in love with you—*ONLY*. . . . You have no one
or nothing to be jealous of—I love you."[110] The Goldwaters also continued
to drain their estate. Capital gains taxes and the annual expenses of maintaining California and Washington apartments, the Phoenix home, and a
boat, paying domestic help and country club fees, and meeting the needs of
the children took twice as much as Goldwater earned from his Senate salary.
Retirement in 1981 offered an opportunity to make up lost economic
ground. Finally, in contemplating a last term, Barry Goldwater probably felt
emancipated, ready to bask in a maverick's role.[111]

As a member of the Armed Services Committee and the Senate Select
Committee to Study Governmental Operations with Respect to Intelligence
Activities, the Arizonan in 1975 and 1976 was primarily focused on military
and foreign affairs. In a series of speeches he attacked the Ford administration's pursuit of détente with the Soviet Union as a "policy of mortal
danger."[112] Goldwater was certain that the Russian communists exploited
détente as a "tactic of warfare" to neutralize American nuclear power, obtain
Western technology, and distract world opinion from human rights concerns.[113] Meanwhile, the fall of South Vietnam and Cambodia to communist
troops in spring 1975 validated for him, once again, the domino theory. It
was useless to "cozy up to the Chinese Communists," he argued, for they
sought world power, not peace.[114] "They can march their armies all the way
down to the Straits of Malacca and they can take all of that rich country in
there, country that frankly we're very dependent on."[115] To abandon Taiwan
to false hopes compounded the Vietnam disaster and gave proof of America's
failure of commitment and nerve. Goldwater, unwilling to countenance further retreats, also backed a Strom Thurmond–initiated resolution warning
the Ford administration against surrender of rights or sovereignty over the
Panama Canal. Because the "basic aim of Communist hegemony is alive and
well," the conservative renewed his call for a build-up of the U.S. arsenal.[116]
Americans, he complained, "are buying too little security while wasting
more and more tax dollars on ineffective domestic programs."[117]

These views informed his position on the Senate investigation of the
intelligence community that came in the wake of Watergate-like domestic
operations and allegations of assassination plots against foreign leaders and
of attempts to destabilize foreign governments. He called for a halt to the
probe, fearing that it "blackened the reputation" and eroded the effectiveness of agencies vital to the security of the United States.[118] Goldwater dismissed the committee's final report as "free-wheeling, self righteous, and
frequently moralizing" and refused to sign it.[119] Rejecting enhanced con-

gressional oversight as an invitation to leaks, the conservative reiterated his conviction that a broad mandate for covert action was an indispensable part of American foreign policy. It provided "the President . . . with a range of actions short of war to preserve the free world and to thwart the global ambitions of Communist imperialism. Covert operations can and should be used in circumstances which might not be described as 'vital' but are nevertheless necessary to prevent a crisis from occurring."[120]

The Arizonan was more in tune with the Ford administration on domestic issues. In unison, they resisted Democratic spending initiatives and emergency job programs designed to combat stagflation and rising unemployment. The cure for American economic ills, Goldwater believed, could be found in a balanced budget, retirement of the national debt, and an end to federal "red tape, waste, and boondoggles."[121] He thus opposed emergency aid bailouts to New York City and the Penn Central Railroad and the creation of the Consumer Protection Agency. Condemning the "quasi-judicial rulings" of regulatory agencies for shackling American business, the conservative urged delays in the imposition of stricter water and air pollution standards.[122] Insulated in his final term, Goldwater also suggested to Milton Friedman and Denison Kitchel that he make public his prescription for stronger medicine. "One of the things I can do for my country," he wrote them, is advocate the repeal of Social Security and its "drastic tax."[123] They dissuaded him from bringing up the issue because it would, Kitchel cautioned, "lower your leadership rating."[124] Meanwhile, the Arizona senator could still be counted on to vote against busing as a means to school integration and for law and order, finding solutions in tougher judges and mandatory jail sentences.[125]

Under the circumstances of Watergate and Gerald Ford's rise to the presidency, Republicans began to maneuver early in preparation for the 1976 campaign. Because of his standing, Barry Goldwater found himself in a powerful but delicate position. Ford, with few presidential credentials and unproven in a national campaign, began courting the conservative in May 1975. Goldwater was well aware of Ford's predicament but was initially noncommittal. Ford had disappointed him: "The country in its history has never been so badly in need of a leader, and Ford is not giving us that leadership, at least not in consistent quantity and quality." He was still suspicious of Rockefeller's ambitions and even conjured up a scenario in which the president is "reelected, Rockefeller being the Vice President and then the President bowing out."[126] Jockeying for advantage, Goldwater relayed the message to Ford through Dean Burch, that "I'm not sewed up, I'm not on the team and maybe will not be on the team unless a change is made on . . . the Vice Presidency." At the same time, Goldwater was aware of a building momentum for undeclared candidate and conservative heir-apparent

Ronald Reagan. The former California governor was in close contact with him, and while he had not made his presidential intentions explicit, Goldwater sensed that "it's almost impossible to fail to detect . . . in all probability he will run. . . . I suspect he is expecting my assistance."[127]

Although it was "the most painful political decision of my public life," Goldwater chose his candidate before the year was out.[128] The Arizonan, as was his custom, worked through his thoughts in writing. He denied disagreements with the administration over détente, amnesty for antiwar dissidents, and deficit spending to conclude that Reagan and Ford were both ideologically sound. It was "an actual toss-up" as to which man was more conservative. The more important consideration was winning in November, for Democratic victory would be "a disaster to the United States."[129] On pragmatic grounds Goldwater counted out Ronald Reagan. "The men in charge of the Reagan campaign had never impressed me as possessing any degree of political skill."[130] Even if Reagan beat the odds and won, he lacked Ford's experience in handling Congress. Any break in Republican continuity "would be dangerous," for "the Democratic Congress could continue to cut this country into ribbons."[131] Moreover, Ford was the incumbent president and party leader and deserved continued support. "Traditionally, you don't turn on a sitting President," explained Ford-backer John Tower. "Barry Goldwater is a party loyalist."[132] Goldwater did not note it, but a lingering resentment of his conservative successor may have colored the decision as well. Ford's dropping of Rockefeller from the ticket clinched the matter. The Arizona senator confided to the president in October 1975 that "if I could help [you] in any way that would be more or less behind the scenes[,] to count me in."[133] Later, Ford sweetened the deal by promising a solar-energy research project for Arizona. Sensitive to all the players and looking to victory, Goldwater offered a compromise for the sake of party unity. He proposed that Reagan accept the vice presidential nomination and Rockefeller replace Henry Kissinger as secretary of state. There is no indication that any of the men gave the matter serious consideration.[134]

Ronald Reagan took his friend's decision with grace and in stride. Acknowledging Ford's incumbency, he said, "I can understand that very easily."[135] His wife, Nancy, was not so forgiving, and a coldness stilled the Reagans' relationship with the Goldwaters. The senator's decision stunned conservatives. During the campaign, William Buckley, Jr., repeatedly lectured Goldwater for his retreat from stands that Reagan now advanced. William Rusher was more confrontational, accusing Goldwater of "brutally undercutting Ronald Reagan's authentically conservative bid." Reviewing the past, he contended: "Goldwater's grip on conservative principles just isn't (and perhaps never was) the absolutely dependable thing we believed it to be."[136] The young Goldwaterites of 1964, now come of age, were especially critical. Alan Crawford, in the Young Americans for Freedom magazine *New Guard,* editorialized after a Goldwater attack on Reagan that the Arizonan "had either abandoned the conservative philosophy for which he is known or the sportsmanship and sense of fair play that have endeared him to millions. . . . [Goldwater] has let conservatives down."[137] In a *Conservative Digest* article, direct-mail activist Richard Viguerie and political science professor Lee Edwards raked Goldwater for his poor Senate attendance record and subsequent lack of leadership. They questioned his commitment to the conservative movement, citing missteps on wage and price controls, Nixon's China policy, and abortion. This should come as no surprise "because he is a Republican first, last and always."[138] Had he also, they wondered, become comfortable as the liberals' conservative, a pet the left stroked to gain political advantage?[139] To the younger generation, the founding father of conservatism had betrayed the revolution.[140]

The campaign for the Republican nomination must have evoked painful memories and caused Goldwater much anguish. As Goldwater had so many times before, Ronald Reagan preached the conservative catechism of balanced budgeting, retirement of the national debt, law and order, and a transfer of power from Washington to local communities. In an echo from the past, he suggested the sale of the Tennessee Valley Authority (TVA) as "something to look at."[141] Détente with the Russians, the Californian argued, was "a one-way street which the enemy is using to further his aims toward the eventual domination of the world."[142] Reagan observed, in a nod to his mentor, that "Goldwater tried to tell us some things that maybe eleven years ago we weren't ready to hear. He was possibly a little ahead of his time."[143] The Ford campaign also cribbed from the past, denouncing Reagan as out of the Republican mainstream and an extremist.

After stumbling in the early primaries, the Reagan campaign recharged with broadsides against the administration's efforts to renegotiate the status of the Panama Canal. Secretary of State Henry Kissinger, carrying forward negotiations pursued under President Nixon, had reached an understanding with the Panamanians that the United States would eventually cede jurisdiction and responsibility for the canal. The talks deadlocked, however, on the length of American control and the extent of a continued U.S. military presence. In a decade of economic and foreign-policy setbacks, the threatened "loss" of the canal became emotionally symbolic of America's relative decline. Reagan, with his finger on the pulse of conservative Republicanism, refused to compromise the Canal Zone. It is "sovereign United States territory," he declared, "and we intend to keep it."[144]

The Ford camp countered the right-wing offensive with Barry Goldwater. The Arizonan took issue with Reagan over the means of policy, not its ends. He, too, wanted to preserve U.S. control, but he believed that concessions were necessary before the demands of Panamanian nationalism and regional geopolitics. If the United States didn't "bend a little bit," Goldwater warned, "we are going to be faced with the problem of guerilla warfare, whether we like it or not. Are you willing to go to war over Panama?"[145] In addition, there was no guarantee that "shooting trouble" would not spread to the "whole section of Central America."[146] Muffling points of agreement, Goldwater exaggerated Reagan's jingoism while reminding conservatives of the pecking order in their movement. In a one-minute radio spot that flooded the air waves before the Nebraska primary, he scolded Reagan for "public statements concerning the Panama Canal [that] contained gross factual errors. I know his statements . . . could needlessly lead this country into open military conflict. He has clearly represented himself in an irresponsible manner on an issue which could affect the nation's security."[147] Goldwater also tendered "a little fatherly advice,"[148] encouraging the California challenger to study the issue, for "if he knew more about it," his position would change.[149]

At the same time, Gerald Ford's rank did not insulate him from a Goldwater reprimand. The Arizonan barked out his political counsel: "You are the President. Do not stupe [sic] to arguing with another candidate. Your speeches are a little bit too long. Get a good speech that is short and use it and use it. Reagan's trick, as you know, is to have a whole handful of cards and he shuffles out whatever comes out to be ten minutes of speaking, and I don't think the deck has changed much over the years. . . . You are not going to get the Reagan vote. These are the same people who got me the nomination and they will never swerve, but ninety per cent of them will vote for you for President, so get after middle America. . . . For God's sake, get off Panama, but don't let Reagan off that hook."[150]

As a byproduct of the primary season, Goldwater came to a final reckoning with Richard Nixon. The Chinese announced that the ex-president had accepted their invitation to visit the mainland on February 21, 1976, the fourth anniversary of his initial trip. The timing could not have been worse for Gerald Ford, because it revived Watergate memories and the controversy over China policy just three days before the New Hampshire primary. Goldwater was furious at Nixon for putting his interests before the needs of the president and party. What months of Watergate had failed to kindle came in an instant with the trip to China. A flash of insight hit Goldwater during his appearance on "Good Morning America." "Within a millisecond, our entire experience together came apart, just like that."[151] He scowled before the television cameras: "As far as I'm concerned Mr. Nixon can go to China and

stay there."[152] Their friendship was over. "I don't think he should ever be for-
given. He came as close to destroying this country as any one man in that
office has ever come. . . . This guy's dishonest."[153] Time has not cooled his
anger. "I wouldn't speak to that sonofabitch if he was dying of thirst out in
this desert."[154] Nor did Richard Nixon's death in 1994. Goldwater was visible
by his absence from the former president's funeral.[155]

Hip surgery in June 1976 sidelined Barry Goldwater until the Republican convention in August. Speaking to the gathering, he implored the delegates to unite behind the party's nominee and fight the Democrats. "I have
seen Mr. [Jimmy] Carter's future and it doesn't work. I have seen Mr.
Carter's future and it is Lyndon Johnson's past."[156] The Republicans treated
him with the respect due the "elder statesman of the party," interrupting his
speech twenty-one times with applause.[157] In close balloting, Ford nosed out
Ronald Reagan for the nomination. Conservatives, however, could hardly be
disappointed; the party was theirs. Accompanying the rise of Republicanism
in the South and West, the increasing number of presidential primaries had
given greater voice to the conservative rank and file and whittled away at liberals' efforts to secure blocs of delegate votes. The liberal eastern wing was
so decisively routed that it could not even mount a challenge to the rightward shift of the party. Few could be found to come forward to replace the
aging Rockefellers or Romneys on the party's shrinking left. Conservatives
nominated Senator Robert Dole of Kansas as Ford's running mate, discarding any need to balance the ticket with a progressive. They also gained
revenge. At their hands, Nelson Rockefeller had became a vice presidential
footnote.[158]

The choice between Jimmy Carter and Gerald Ford was obvious to the
Arizona conservative. "At stake for the nation in the election is our economy,
security and freedom."[159] Goldwater praised President Ford for his efforts to
restore America's prestige in the world while reining in inflation with
budget and bureaucracy cuts. Carter's election would bring back Great
Society "social engineering" and lead to "nationalization" of the "oil
industry, railroads, airlines, and trucking firms." Also making him suspect,
Carter had fallen under the spell of "extremists in the fields of consumerism
and environmental control." Declared Goldwater: "Either we stick with the
steady, responsible and proved leadership of President Ford, or we gamble
on an untried, unsure challenger committed to a program of state-con-
trolled socialism."[160] Despite the stakes, economic hard times and Watergate backlash gave the Georgia governor a narrow popular and electoral
vote victory. Conservatives could take heart not only in the closeness of the
margin. Carter's election, while interrupting Republican rule, reflected a
new political equation in presidential politics. The Democrat was a born-

again Christian who rode to victory on the back of the now Republican South. Although conservatives were wary, he promised to balance the budget by 1980, make the federal bureaucracy more responsive, and ease controls on American business. Republicans, meanwhile, cheered victories of conservative candidates in Senate races in Delaware, Indiana, Utah, Wyoming, and California.[161]

Barry Goldwater had not served as a member of the Senate's loyal opposition since the early 1960s. Illness and age now required him to choose his battles, with Carter's foreign and defense policies becoming primary targets. As he had throughout his career, Goldwater keyed on the threat of international communism, and Soviet adventurism in Africa and the invasion of Afghanistan in 1979 gave credence to his concerns. He quickly grew impatient with the president's efforts at strategic arms limitation and what he believed was a misreading of communist intentions. "I think we are wasting our time and the time of the world by even trying to put up with the Russians when they want everything and we have given them everything but the flagpole."[162] Better to build the B-1 bomber, perfect the neutron bomb, and refine the cruise missile. He criticized as shortsighted and unfair the administration's human rights initiatives that made outcasts of American allies. Thus, on his return from a trip to South Africa and Southern Rhodesia, he presented the case of these "two very potentially valuable friends" to Carter's national security adviser, Zbigniew Brzezinski.[163] It was time to make amends, and Goldwater called for an end to "meddling" in South Africa and a lifting of the U.S. arms embargo.[164] He demanded, as well, that the president be consistent and condemn abuses in China and Cuba. "I'll be darned if I can see any sense in preaching human rights in one part of the world and not in another where the exhortation is badly needed."[165] The Arizonan also renewed his drive against the War Powers Act for creating "535 Secretaries of State,"[166] and tying "the hands of the Commander-in-Chief."[167] He pressed on Jimmy Carter a broad interpretation of executive power. "Frankly, I don't think it is any business of the Congress what the President is planning in the way of covert or clandestine movements that are in the interests of the freedom of our people."[168]

High on President Carter's agenda was Senate ratification of the Panama Canal treaties, and he designated a pivotal role for Goldwater. The treaties provided for a phased U.S. military and administrative withdrawal to be completed by the end of 1999, yet they recognized America's right to defend the canal indefinitely. With Goldwater's 1976 stand in mind, both Jimmy and Rosalynn Carter vigorously pursued his vote. Not only was every vote critical, but Goldwater's support, in turn, offered cover to Senate conservatives fearful of constituent flak. Initially, the Arizonan promised the president "to maintain an open mind."[169] Although he accepted the importance of improving relations with Latin America, concerns about American security nagged him. "I do think," he wrote to Carter, "some adjustments are needed. I don't think we have to give away the moon to keep the Panamanians happy."[170] To help Goldwater resolve his doubts the administration arranged a trip to the Canal Zone and meetings with Panamanian leaders in January 1978. General Omar Torrijos impressed Goldwater, who called him "a most interesting man, certainly not the Castro-type dictator."[171] Yet to Carter's disappointment, the inspection confirmed the senator's preconceptions that the Panamanians could neither defend, operate, nor maintain the canal. Denison Kitchel's book opposing the treaties—Goldwater contributed the book's introduction—and Arizona's hostility to any change in the canal's status bolstered his decision. Goldwater took an active role in the Senate debate, emphasizing U.S. defense needs and the financial cost of implementing the treaties. In spite of conservative opposition, however, the president achieved a narrow victory, winning just two votes over the necessary two-thirds majority.[172]

The administration's China policy provoked an even more vigorous reaction. Developing Nixon and Ford initiatives, Jimmy Carter restored diplomatic ties with the People's Republic of China in December 1978. Normalization, however, required a simultaneous severing of relations with Taipei and termination of the 1954 U.S.–Chinese Mutual Defense Treaty. Goldwater was irate about the "Taiwan sellout," a "double-crossing" that was characteristic of the administration's "appeasement" policies.[173] "Any president who would violate the Constitution on such a major matter in breaking faith with the nation's treaty obligations would run the risk of impeachment."[174] He had believed, perhaps too naively, the repeated assurances of Nixon and Ford that the United States would never abandon the Republic of China. "The treatment of Taiwan," he said bitterly, "calls into question the honor, the very soul, of America's word."[175] Realizing that Senate action could not revoke Carter's diplomacy, Goldwater took a different tack. He counseled with legal advisers and decided to take the president to court for terminating a treaty without Senate consent. On December 22, 1978, he filed, with twenty-five other senators, *Goldwater v. Carter,* asking the federal court to declare the president's action unconstitutional and illegal. It was a dangerous precedent, argued his brief, that usurped the principle of checks and balances and was tantamount to unilateral repeal of a law of the land. Although long an advocate of expanding presidential authority, Barry Goldwater now resisted the "untrammeled power of the President to annul any treaty he wishes."[176] The senator followed the judicial proceedings closely and felt vindicated when the district court found in his favor. To Goldwater's chagrin, however, the Supreme Court vacated the case. Refusing to rule on the merits, the justices deemed the matter a "political" issue and therefore "nonjusticiable."[177] The court's timidity in the face of the president's "obvious usurpation of legislative power," said a disgusted Goldwater, left "the road . . . open to a dictator."[178] The United States would continue to furnish arms and maintain trade and cultural ties with Taipei, but the future now lay in Beijing.[179]

Frustrated by foreign policy setbacks, Barry Goldwater looked for a hidden hand behind events. He, like Robert Welch of the John Birch Society, fingered the Trilateral Commission as the concealed agent of change. This "international cabal" had orchestrated a campaign for one-world government, Goldwater insisted: "a skillful coordinated effort to seize control and consolidate the four centers of power—political, monetary, intellectual, and ecclesiastical." The "nonelected rulers" of the commission, with banker David Rockefeller a key player, had begun to break down American resistance by infiltrating government and boring from within. As part of their scheme, they invited Jimmy Carter to join the commission in 1973 and "immediately commenced grooming him for the presidency." Echoing Welch, Goldwater concluded, "The outsider had been co-opted by the insiders." It was no surprise to the Arizona senator that Vice President Walter Mondale, Secretary of State Cyrus Vance, Brzezinski, and nearly half of the president's cabinet were members of the Trilateral Commission. Clearly, the commission was well on its way to "multinational consolidation of the commercial and banking interests by [having seized] control of the political government of the United States."[180] The Panama Canal treaties offered more evidence of "unknown influence," a commission attempt to secure its Panamanian investments.[181] Goldwater went public with the evidence in the *Congressional Record* in 1977 and 1978, and then in his memoirs, *With No Apologies*, in 1979.[182]

He also discovered commission intrigue in Arizona. Its agent was the Arizona Project, a journalistic probe of organized crime in the wake of the 1976 murder of *Arizona Republic* reporter Don Bolles. In a series of reports, investigators reviewed allegations that linked Goldwater's brother Bob and friend Harry Rosenzweig to the underworld. By implication, they tarred Goldwater, concluding that he had "condoned" the presence of organized crime in the state.[183] The Arizona senator was convinced that this was a Trilateral ploy, and he confided to Stephen Shadegg the real purpose of the investigation, "the need for silencing one guy named Goldwater." He continued, "So what happens? They start out, as I told you in prior papers on dictators, to destroy first the reputation of people, then the reputation of the press that destroyed those people. . . . [I]s it impossible to believe that the

Arizona Republic and the Indianapolis Star and the other papers have been sucked into the idea that some how they have to discredit Goldwater regardless of whoever else they discredit?"[184] But Goldwater's flirtation with conspiracy theory did not outlast the Carter administration. Looking back, he frowns on his "too hasty opinion about the Trilateral Commission. Maybe these are some of the words I wish I could take back."[185]

During the Carter presidency, Goldwater allowed other conservatives to take the lead on domestic issues. Remaining consistent, he voted against a higher federal debt ceiling, amnesty to antiwar dissidents, the creation of the Departments of Energy and Education, the windfall-profits tax, additional funding for food stamps and public housing programs, busing, public assistance to the Chrysler Corporation, and an extension of the deadline for ratification of the Equal Rights Amendment. He supported, at the same time, tax cuts, balanced budgets, and school prayer. To address the energy crisis and relieve business of what he considered unfair constraints, Goldwater favored exempting states from federal strip mining regulations and provisions of the Clear Air Act, sought delays in implementation of Federal Water Pollution Control Act programs, and rejected the Alaska Land Bill, which removed more than one-fourth of the state from energy development. These positions raised the wrath of conservationists, who relegated Goldwater to the bottom rank of senators on environmental issues. Also troubling them was Goldwater's contention that "if we stop construction of nuclear power plants, this country is through industrially. If we're going to use coal, we'll have to knock down the Environmental Protection Agency. The sooner we do that the better off this country's going to be. Coal produces some crappy air, but we control it a lot better than we used to."[186]

Goldwater was more zealous when he perceived that Arizona's future was in danger. President Carter posed a threat in 1977 when he sought to trim the federal budget by cutting the funding for nineteen western reclamation projects. Although only half built, the expensive Central Arizona Project was a high-profile target. Goldwater came quickly to the defense and vouched for the CAP's indispensability: "Having spent my entire life on this desert, I can tell you that if supplementary water is not clearly available by 1980 that part of our country is going to start growing backward and . . . will rapidly become the dregs of the rest of the states."[187] Goldwater and the other western senators were stubborn; Carter would have to find savings elsewhere in the budget. Their determined resistance and presidential ineptness combined to protect the water projects and force the administration to retreat.[188]

In the spring of 1979, Barry Goldwater admitted the approach of retirement and began to settle his affairs in Washington. He had prepared a last, uncompromising shot at his opponents in a Stephen Shadegg–ghosted memoir, *With No Apologies*. Also, he had renewed his pledge to Peggy not to seek another term and promised an announcement on New Year's Day 1980, his seventy-first birthday. The decision brought him relief. The seventies were a disappointing time, riddled with setbacks at home and abroad. Not only had the nation and Republican Party faltered, but Goldwater also felt a sense of personal failure. He was pessimistic about the future and wrote to Peggy, "The entire world is changing and I honestly think that you and I and others in our age group have lived through the best of America."[189] Knee injuries, spurs on both heels, a troublesome hip, and assorted illnesses frustrated and depressed him as well. Also having an effect were the blows he had absorbed from the critics of the new conservative generation and from the crime probe in Arizona. There were other signs of withdrawal as well. He made fewer appearances both on and off the Senate floor. Goldwater had neglected political business in Arizona and was out of touch with constituent needs and community change. Administrative assistant Judy Eisenhower responded to the cues, efficiently screening him from telephone calls and appointments. Yet the Arizonan hesitated. He sensed a change in the political wind. How could Barry Goldwater desert the ranks when the conservative movement was readying to enter the promised land?[190]

In spite of initial setbacks, the 1970s had proved a boom time for conservatism. Already reeling from the turbulence of the sixties, Americans found no relief in the new decade. They had believed the Nixon administration's tough talk and promises to rein in the counterculture and vigorously defend traditional values. In fact, in the early 1970s feminists had sought congressional passage and presidential approval of the Equal Rights Amendment, which conservatives feared would undermine the family, obscure sex roles, and encourage homosexuality. The Supreme Court's *Roe v. Wade* decision opened another wound, seemingly making life a matter of choice. America's moral reserves were further depleted during the Watergate scandals. Deceit and improper conduct at the political pinnacle numbed those anxious about the nation's moral future. An energy crisis, shortages, recession, and double-digit inflation signaled a decline that was economic as well as spiritual.

Conservatives gained little solace from international events. They denounced détente with the Soviet Union and rapprochement with the People's Republic of China as appeasement and policies of retreat. Relaxation of cold-war tensions, arms limitation agreements, and budgetary restraints surely meant the loss of American military superiority. Meanwhile, few could claim victory in the withdrawal of American troops and the Vietnamization of the war in Southeast Asia. News footage of the hurried helicopter evacuation from the roof of the embassy in Saigon stunned a nation already sobered by the heavy losses in blood and materiel after a decade of war. The dominoes did not stop falling with the "loss" of Vietnam, Cambodia, and Laos. Communist gains were also recorded in Africa and the Middle East. Despite a grassroots campaign, conservatives could not prevent the passage of the Panama Canal treaties. As the 1970s ended, the failure of U.S. policy in Iran placed in bold relief a decade of malaise and drift. The seizure of the American embassy revealed the limits of power and provoked a public soul-searching unseen for three decades.

Discontent was widespread but unfocused, making effective protest difficult. As conservatives perceived it, the government, the media, and other institutions were in liberal hands and unresponsive to conservative grievance. To effect mobilization and change, activists developed a phalanx of single-issue movements, multipurpose political organizations, think tanks, and religious federations united in support of conservative candidates and issues. This generation of conservatives, called the New Right by commentators, practiced fund-raising via direct mail, a communication tool that enabled them to reach targeted, single-issue constituencies. When direct mail was fused to the political action committee (PAC), a response to legal restrictions on personal campaign contributions, conservatives could gather scattered grassroots interests into a focused and national force.[191]

The diverse camps of American conservatism united under this broad tent. Dramatic growth in such conservative and fundamentalist churches as the Southern Baptist, Assemblies of God, and Church of Christ made resources available to activist ministers preaching a right-wing social agenda. Entering the public sphere, these ministers galvanized support for the Moral Majority, America for Jesus, and the National Christian Action Coalition. At the same time, Americans donated heavily to the nearly sixteen hundred televangelists who were broadcasting a conservative socioreligious message. And many Catholics accepted the conservative social program and joined with Protestants in Right to Life, the Eagle Forum, Pro-Decency, and Stop-ERA. To restore prosperity conservatives advocated a "supply-side" agenda. Tax cuts would revive the American economy and pay for themselves by generating increased production and government revenue. Deregulation of business, government budget cuts, and reduction of the federal bureaucracy were also prescribed for recovery. These proposals, when added to concern over declining productivity and profits, made business receptive. In 1976, executives had organized 433 PACs, and by 1982 there were 1,467 to focus corporate clout. Militant anticommunists enlisted with social and economic conservatives in such groups as the American Freedom Coalition, the Conservative Caucus, and the Committee for the Survival of a Free Congress. Allied but separate, neoconservative academics and journalists condemned the assault on traditional authorities and values by government and left-wingers. The leaders of the New Right had built an alliance reaching across the religious, class, ethnic, and regional divisions of American life.[192]

These New Right activists moved against diverse targets in the 1970s. They boycotted television programs and their sponsors to protest the exploitation of violence and sex. Anti-abortionists marched, picketed, gathered petitions, and wrote to legislators to show support for a constitutional amendment reversing *Roe v. Wade*. Some invaded clinics, destroying property and intimidating patients and staff members. Conservatives mobilized to defeat gay-rights referenda in Florida, Minnesota, Kansas, and Oregon. Women and men in Stop-ERA and the Eagle Forum confronted feminists and stymied ratification of the Equal Rights Amendment. Tax opponents achieved their greatest victory in California with the Proposition 13 rollback of property levies.

Although there was some discussion about creating an inclusive political vehicle, and a Libertarian party did appear, most conservatives felt comfortable retaining their Republican credentials. Working with ideologically compatible party regulars, they ably combined single-issue constituencies into winning coalitions on election day. This did not occur in a vacuum. White Democrats in the South and in northern ethnic communities reexamined their partisan loyalties in light of foreign policy failure, economic stagnation, inflation, the loss of jobs overseas, "tax bracket creep," and a declining standard of living. They felt betrayed by party leaders who pressed busing, affirmative action, and welfare programs. To them, this was rank favoritism toward minorities that they understood only in zero-sum terms. A hemorrhaging of members and funds from organized labor, meanwhile, had removed key resources from Democratic war chests. Defections helped topple liberal Democrats running for state and national office and bolster the conservative bloc in Congress. In 1980 conservatives reached higher and prepared to rally their troops behind Ronald Reagan for president. With enhanced respectability, strong organizational and communication skills, and an army of volunteers, New Rightists had firmly established their position in the Republican Party.[193]

The New Right was an evolutionary stage of the conservative movement rather than a break with the past. As such, it owed much to Barry Goldwater. Not only had the 1964 campaign been the coming of age for many New Rightists, but Goldwater had long championed the multifaceted platform of social, economic, and foreign policy issues they now claimed as their own. The Arizona conservative had long confronted big government, welfare spending, unbalanced budgets, and high taxes. Since the 1960s he had been on the front line against busing, pornography, affirmative action, and crime in the streets. He did this while advocating private virtue, public morality, and school prayer. Goldwater prided himself, as well, for making anticommunism and military preparedness the linchpins of his career. Nor did the New Right invent the means to influence. The Goldwater team in 1964 had worked direct mail vigorously and demonstrated its reach and potential power. Similarly, Goldwater had beckoned to the "forgotten Americans," and his populism helped scuttle Republicanism's elitist image. As *Newsweek* noted, "He is to conservatism what Elvis is to rock and roll: he repackaged the raw goods for a mass audience."[194]

Yet there were important differences. Goldwater veered from New Rightists in his assignment of priorities. Anticommunism, peace through military strength, and limited government topped the Arizona senator's agenda. The New Right coalition, and especially its fundamentalist wing, emphasized "family" values—morality, antifeminism, and the right to life. Goldwater regarded the right to privacy as fundamental and rejected government encroachment against personal freedoms. "The conservative movement," he repeated, "is founded on the simple tenet that people have the right to live life as they please, as long as they don't hurt anyone else in the process."[195] The new generation, on the other hand, was prepared to enlist the government to police even the most private behavior of Americans. Moreover, rather than assess the entire record, New Rightists expected a candidate to pass a battery of single-issue litmus tests to garner approval. Also troubling to Goldwater was the involvement of organized religious groups in the political process. The Arizonan was convinced that their absolutism, their "organ-tone" rhetoric, endangered constitutional protections.[196] Goldwater remembered his family's resistance in the 1920s to Prohibition, a law he condemned as spawned by the unholy union of religion and politics. While serving on the Phoenix city council he had opposed the interference of religious groups in policy-making.[197]

Yet Barry Goldwater was a well-seasoned politician, savvy at figuring the political score. As the senator became more and more reluctant to leave the public stage, expediency demanded that he bend before the power of the New Rightists. In his last campaign, he would muffle conflict and even compromise his views to win their support.

12 Conservatism Triumphant

I campaigned for a man who we can see now was a prophet in his own time. I hope the ideals he spoke about then, that those ideals will remain our ideals. . . . I think he walked his lonely road; it was necessary that as a John the Baptist someone do that, or maybe what we're enjoying tonight wouldn't be happening here.

—RONALD REAGAN
November 19, 1980

Ronald Reagan was never a conservative. . . . I don't think he ever thought anything through.

—BARRY GOLDWATER
September 24, 1992

There was no press conference on January 1, 1980, to announce Barry Goldwater's retirement from public life. In spite of past signals, poor health, and the emergence of attractive Republican candidates, he had decided on a final run for the Senate. Goldwater, though at career's end, remained ambitious and was receptive to those who argued that he was indispensable to country, party, and conservative movement. He had to make the race, for Democratic victory would seal the nation's fate: "I'll give this country five years."[1] Especially tantalizing was that the 1980 elections offered Republicans their best chance for control of the Senate in three decades. A Richard Wirthlin poll in July 1979 predicted an easy victory for Goldwater and assured him that he would do his part to secure GOP rule. Moreover, how could he abdicate the service responsibilities that, above all else, gave him meaning? "Arizona was my home, but the Senate had become my life. I couldn't give it up. . . . I was more than a husband, more than a father. I was a man—a political animal."[2] Besides, the golden years had lost their allure. "I would be a complete basket case within six months if I were forced into retirement before my time."[3]

Peggy Goldwater seemed to be the only obstacle to reelection. Barry had promised her repeatedly that he would not again seek office, and she eagerly anticipated his return to private life. For long periods they had lived apart, and weekend visits and daily telephone calls did not adequately renew past intimacy or allow their marriage to grow. Also, Peggy was ill, suffering from emphysema and the effects of a lifelong smoking habit. Barry realized that Peggy was lonely and insecure, and his conflict made him feel guilty. Still he attempted to obtain release from his pledge. He coaxed her with his Senate seniority and the importance of protecting the U.S. military and intelligence communities from their critics. He pointed out his responsibilities to twenty-five staffers and noted that, even in retirement, the family's financial situation would require him to spend much time away. While Barry was apprehensive, Peggy would not disappoint him, for she would never allow her needs to trump his. "I'm not going to tell him he can't do it. I've never been able to do that and I'm not going to start now."[4]

To ease their father's guilt, the Goldwater children offered a face-saving solution. As daughter Peggy Goldwater Clay remembers, they "recognized in Dad the absolute, dire need to run for the Senate. It was important to his self-esteem. What the hell was he going to do sitting around in Phoenix?"[5] At the same time, their mother deserved tenderness and respect, and they scolded their father for his inattention and impatience. "You can be cruel and inconsiderate," wrote son Mike, "because of her hearing problem." He advised his father to "make your peace with Mom however you can. She's a lot stronger physically and mentally than you think she is."[6] In a trade-off for a final Senate term, they suggested that their parents share "quality time" during which Barry and Peggy Goldwater could revitalize their relationship and look toward Arizona retirement in 1986. This pleased Barry, and he convinced himself that Peggy "ordered me to run again."[7]

Caught up in the national rush of conservative momentum and cheered by the Wirthlin poll, Barry Goldwater did not realize how vulnerable he was to challenge. Believing that he would retire in 1980, Goldwater had neglected both constituent and political "local work" during his last term.[8] He had lost touch with Arizonans and had, in six years, not even visited Holbrook, Winslow, Douglas, Nogales, and other sizable communities outside metropolitan Phoenix and Tucson. This created the impression, when added to his habitually weak Senate attendance and voting record, that he was bored, or too old, or even lazy. Making the issue particularly potent was the changing face of the Arizona electorate. The Arizona boom had attracted half a million new residents, raising the state's population 53 percent during the 1970s to more than 2.7 million in 1980. Forty percent of those registered to vote in 1980 had not lived in the state six years before. Many were young voters casting their first ballots. To large numbers of recent residents and new voters, Goldwater "was lore; they never knew him, they never met him."[9] He had become a stranger in his native land. An April 1979 poll revealed evidence of trouble ahead. Half of the Arizonans questioned gave

Goldwater a "fair to poor" rating as senator, with another 14 percent undecided. Goldwater's own surveys found him lagging among young voters and
new residents. Concluded political analyst Earl de Berge, the "softening" of
Goldwater's support portended a "tough uphill battle" for reelection.[10]

Nor could Goldwater count as heavily as he had in the past on the
Republican organization to mobilize the vote. The Goldwater loyalists who
built the Arizona Republican party in the 1940s and 1950s were retiring
from politics, and New Right activists had moved to take their places. Many
of the new generation remembered Goldwater's apostasy in 1976, when he
supported Gerald Ford over Ronald Reagan. In defiance, several Arizona
delegates had refused to applaud his convention speech. Goldwater was also
suspect because of his position on abortion. Awakening to political realities,
the senator acknowledged the growing power of the faction to his right and
the ascent of new party leaders. In particular, he reversed his longstanding
opposition to Phoenix-area car dealer and archconservative Evan Mecham,
endorsing him as "an honest man, a religious man" in the 1978 gubernatorial
race.[11]

To confront what he characterized as his "problem of reidentification"
with Arizona and to manage the campaign, Goldwater succumbed to habit
and called once more on Stephen Shadegg.[12] This handicapped the effort
from the start, because Shadegg was out of touch with recent campaign
trends, styles, and techniques. According to Judy Eisenhower, "Shadegg was
still living in 1958."[13] Arizona's Republican National chairwoman, Kit
Mehrtens, agreed: "We're a little bit too old. It's not a modern campaign.
We're still back twenty years ago."[14] Rather than deflect Goldwater's liabilities or restore his image as a candidate of Arizona's present and future, the
dated campaign approach suggested a man past his prime.[15]

Although Goldwater dismissed opponent Bill Schulz as the "bald-
headed guy," the Democrats could not have fielded a stronger candidate.[16]
Schulz was a graduate of the U.S. Military Academy, where Goldwater had
dreamed of going, and had a degree from the Harvard Business School. An
owner of apartment complexes and a land developer, the forty-nine-year-old
Republican-turned-Democrat had parlayed the Arizona boom into a multimillion-dollar fortune. As a political "nobody," he began to campaign early
and saturated television with his name and face.[17] Schulz astutely rejected
a frontal assault on Barry Goldwater. He disarmed voters by telling them of
his admiration for the conservative senator and admitting to voting for
him in the past. In recognition of Goldwater's service and Arizona's climate
of opinion, the challenger even promised, only half in jest, "to introduce
a bill to have his face carved on Mount Rushmore. . . . I'm not contesting
Barry's greatness, just his next term."[18] Unfortunately, Schulz observed,

the senator had become exhausted in defense of state and national interests. He confided to voters that former classmates at West Point, now serving in the Pentagon, had urged him to run because Goldwater was no longer effective. "They want new blood on the Military Affairs Committee. When they testify on the Hill, they say he's not into what's going on—even when he's there."[19] To bolster his claims, Schulz repeated rumors that Goldwater longed to retire but had been "hot boxed" into running by self-interested politicians.[20] "The job of being a United States senator," he repeated throughout the campaign, "takes a lot of energy and I'm going to put all of my energy into being a good senator. When I run out of energy, I'll get out."[21] Until then, Arizonans could be assured that the Democrat would pick up Goldwater's cudgels and battle for a strong military and against inflation, high taxes, and big government.[22]

Bill Schulz, unlike Roy Elson and Jonathan Marshall, had the resources to mount an effective challenge. He was confident—some say arrogant—bright, and combative. Aggressive on the stump, he impressed *Phoenix Gazette* columnist John Kolbe with "enough persuasive power to sell Chryslers to Henry Ford."[23] Still, Schulz's greatest asset was his personal wealth. To overcome Goldwater's advantages of incumbency and name recognition, Schulz allocated more than $2 million dollars to his campaign. Much of it was budgeted for television advertising tuned by a professional staff to eighties' styles and tastes. For the first time, Barry Goldwater was at a disadvantage financially. His team would cry foul about the money Schulz pumped into the race, and spending did become a campaign issue. Yet that did little to dampen the effectiveness of the Democrat's media blitz and election strategy.[24]

Events in the summer of 1980 confirmed Schulz's choice of "Energy for the '80s" as his campaign slogan. In June, Barry Goldwater cut short a plan to visit "every little town between now and Labor Day" and entered a Washington, D.C., hospital to repair the artificial right hip inserted in a 1976 operation.[25] Shortly after his release he began to hemorrhage; he lost consciousness and was rushed back to the hospital. His incision became infected and further complicated recovery. Through July and most of August, Goldwater was bedridden in the capital, rising only to appear at the Republican convention. Television captured that moment of determination, but the haggard image on the screen stunned viewers. His perspiring face, grimaces, and hobbled walk gave evidence of great pain. It also played to Schulz's advantage by sanctioning the senator's age and health as critical issues in the Arizona race. The Democrat's staff immediately went to work preparing television ads for the fall campaign that showcased a weakened Goldwater and implied his inability to serve. Even Goldwater's own commercials could not disguise his exhaustion and pain.[26]

Everything appeared routine as Barry Goldwater kicked off his last campaign from the steps of the Prescott courthouse on September 10, 1980. The speech was vintage Goldwater—tough, conservative, and partisan. The enthusiastic crowd cheered his efforts to cast Jimmy Carter's foreign policy and economic sins upon Bill Schulz. A vote for Goldwater was a vote for Ronald Reagan and fiscal responsibility, individual freedom, and limited government. The voice was still strong, but no one could miss his exhaustion and pronounced limp. Reporters noted that the Goldwater campaign planned to wade into the Arizona backcountry during the first weeks of September and then focus on Phoenix and Tucson, home to 85 percent of the state's registered voters. Optimistic before the challenge, the senator vowed: "I won't do anything different than I've done in the past. I'm just going to try and smoke him out and see where he stands."[27]

This, however, would not be a typical Goldwater Senate campaign. Fresh from his decisive victory in the Democratic primary, Bill Schulz relentlessly hammered the Republican in person and with a series of continually fresh television ads. Questions about Goldwater's health created the context as Schulz worked to link absenteeism to ineffectiveness. He demanded to know why Arizona's senior senator was "not showing up for his job."[28] The challenger similarly confronted a key Goldwater asset: "What is seniority worth when you can't get the job done? A hard-working junior or senior senator can get more done than a senator who isn't working."[29] The issue was simple: whether because of age or lack of commitment, "Goldwater just didn't hustle enough."[30] Schulz supplemented this negative campaign with Arizona-sensitive stands for a balanced budget, redistribution of federal tax dollars to the states, military superiority, cuts in the Washington bureaucracy, and deregulation of American business. He also distanced himself from Jimmy Carter, labeling such identification a "red-herring."[31] While chasing conservative votes, Schulz counted on support from middle-class moderates and liberals, African-Americans, Hispanics, Navajos, conservationists, and union members.[32]

Schulz had drawn blood and forced the Goldwater campaign to retreat. Defensively, Goldwater maintained that experience had taught him to answer the Senate bell only on important votes and to avoid roll calls that merely decided procedural issues. His staffers hurriedly reviewed the legislative record to counter Democratic charges that the senator could claim few accomplishments during twenty-four years in office. When this did not halt the slippage, he reached for Reagan's coattails. "I believe my experience—my seniority—my understanding of how the system works will enable me to do more for the people of Arizona. I believe we are going to have a Republican president. I want to finish the job I started."[33]

Beyond issues, images turned voter opinion. Schulz ran like the Goldwater of campaigns past. Embodying dynamism and accentuating the contrast, he held a flurry of press conferences and made multiple campaign appearances daily in communities across the state. Shadegg, meanwhile, insulated his candidate. "We were fooling ourselves," Goldwater later wrote, "by in effect talking to nothing but the choir such as Sun City, Fountain Hills."[34] On occasion, Barry Goldwater seemed confused about matters for which he claimed expertise. His criticism of Titan 2 missiles as having "outlived their usefulness" drew a strong rebuke from the secretary of the Air Force and forced a retraction.[35] He rambled to reporters and was quoted about his tax problems: "I'm in the process of finding someone who can loan me some money so I can pay my next quarter's taxes. I made more money last year than ever and still can't pay my taxes."[36] Goldwater's refusal to debate Bill Schulz only enhanced voters' impression that the conservative Republican could not meet the challenge of the younger man. Fixated by his opponent, Goldwater lamely countered, "I am running with all the energy at my command."[37]

The private polls of both candidates registered significant erosion in Goldwater's support. Schulz released a survey that put him ahead of Goldwater everywhere but Maricopa County (where more than half of Arizona voters resided) and behind by only four percentage points overall. Goldwater's poll taker Richard Wirthlin concurred, describing the race as a dead heat. Schulz's attacks had an effect, and Wirthlin found defections among college graduates, senior citizens, white-collar workers, and other Goldwater constituencies. Schulz also scored well with voters under thirty-five years of age, new residents, and traditionally Democratic groups. More than 20 percent of Arizona voters who had switched to Schulz gave their negative perception of Goldwater's job performance as the chief reason.[38]

In an urgent memo to Goldwater, Wirthlin suggested a mid-course correction framed by the insight that "image, not issue position, will be the prime determinant of who wins or loses." He proposed to erase voters' doubts about age and health with an aggressive, high-profile campaign that raised Goldwater's visibility and stressed his Arizona roots. Playing to the conservative's experience and clout, it would focus on "uniquely" state concerns about the Central Arizona Project's future, growth and development, and the environment. While Goldwater sought "maximum media impact," his ailing hip limited exposure to two appearances a day, with weekends reserved for rest and recovery. Thus, television spending needed to be increased appreciably, the old commercials discarded and new production begun immediately. Finally, Wirthlin called for a redoubling of direct mail campaigning, door-to-door canvassing, and absentee-ballot gathering to ensure that every Goldwater supporter voted. "Television alone created William Schulz," Wirthlin reassured his candidate. "He doesn't have a strong organization." Wirthlin's suggestions encountered no resistance, and Goldwater asked Ronald Crawford, a Washington, D.C., political consultant and longtime supporter, to manage the new thrust. Stephen Shadegg, recuperating at home after a series of accidents, was "fenced-off," and the transition to modern campaigning went smoothly.[39]

Running scared, Goldwater cast for every vote. This led him to deal with the powerful pro-life lobby in Arizona. Although he opposed abortion on demand and federal funding of abortion, the conservative had consistently supported a woman's right to choice, in consultation with her physician. Goldwater had stubbornly objected to what he believed was a minority's refusal to compromise and an attempt to legislate "morality in absolute terms."[40] Thus, he voted against the Human Rights Amendment because it made no exceptions for abortion to safeguard the life or health of the mother or in cases of rape and incest. He would, as late as September 23, 1980, deny that "the federal government has any business deciding the wrongness or rightness of a woman having an abortion."[41] Yet a week later Goldwater won the endorsement of Arizonans for Life, having signed a statement approving a strict "human-life amendment that would prohibit abortion except to prevent the death of the mother."[42] To avoid the wrath of his pro-choice wife, Barry had waited for Peggy to leave the house before allowing abortion opponents to appear with the statement. An anti-abortionist remembered Goldwater's words on the occasion: "I may have many faults, but my word is my honor."[43] Conflict between principle and political expediency would plague him for the remainder of the campaign, and he attempted to obscure his position. At a campaign stop in Bagdad, Arizona, he affirmed his pro-life stand but remarked, "I've always felt that it was up to a woman and her doctor to decide if a baby is to be aborted."[44]

During October, Schulz held to his successful game plan. Goldwater was "a folk hero" and "the legend," but age and health problems had robbed him of effectiveness.[45] Citing Arizona's loss of the federal Solar Energy Research Institute to Colorado, Schulz scoffed, "He ain't got what he claims and he ain't using what he's got."[46] The Democrat was prepared for the Senate's challenge and eager to do the "nitty-gritty" work that the office demanded.[47] Responding to charges that he waged only a negative campaign, Schulz proposed a seven-point economic plan to reduce inflation and unemployment while increasing industrial productivity. Also in his platform were planks supporting the Equal Rights Amendment and choice. Endorsements from Governor Bruce Babbitt and Senator Dennis DeConcini conferred the regular Democratic organization's blessing and bolstered his network of support.[48]

The Goldwater campaign, meanwhile, seemed recharged. Ron Crawford, in line with Richard Wirthlin's suggestions, doubled the television advertising budget and even outspent Schulz in the closing weeks of the race. New and improved commercials filled the screen. They reminded Arizonans: "Senators come two to a state. Leaders come once in a lifetime . . . Now, more than ever."[49] As they aired, the senator made news in appearances throughout the state, recounting legislative victories and preaching the conservative gospel. He also restructured, in typical Goldwater fashion, the issue of his Senate record: he was just too busy with the needs of Arizona constituents to wait on the Senate floor to vote on "some rubbish."[50] Goldwater also promised Arizonans that he would fight, if reelected, for a national health plan and a voluntary Social Security system. To ease the concerns of Jewish voters he reiterated his support for the state of Israel even though he had repeatedly opposed foreign aid requests. The strenuous schedule worsened the extreme pain Barry Goldwater felt from his hip wound, which a nurse packed daily with gauze. On some days his shirt was soaked with blood. Yet despite the growing intensity of the campaign, neither Goldwater nor Schulz made a breakthrough, and they remained deadlocked on the eve of the election.[51]

If there was no movement in the polls, the *Arizona Republic* wavered under the impact of the Schulz campaign. At the beginning of the race, the newspaper's columnists and editorial writers assailed the Democrat's spending as extravagant and criticized his "blank record"[52] and attempt to "buy a seat in the U.S. Senate."[53] Schulz, in addition, had no popular support, and his "staged candidacy" was "the creation of media advisors, well-prepared scripts, [and] careful editing of recordings."[54] By mid-October, *Republic* columnists and reporters had become more even-handed and began to ignore the editorials favoring Goldwater's reelection. Tom Fitzpatrick reproached the Republican for "duck[ing] hard questions" and taking a "free ride," by not giving voters "a full-faced view of [his] total performance as a senator." Fitzpatrick asked: "Could it be that he has been around so long that we may mistake longevity for excellence?"[55] The newspaper's Marilyn Taylor, apparently not schooled in Pulliam-style journalism, was bemused by Goldwater's attitude "that reporters should have enough sense to use discretion when quoting him."[56] At the campaign's close, the *Republic* printed syndicated columnist Charles Bartlett's piece "Goldwater—Schulz: The Two Candidates Typify the Past and Present of Arizona." Bartlett pointedly suggested that Arizona create a "third legislative house" so that those "of long service and special distinction can be elevated so that their wisdom can be heard after their energies diminish."[57] Like the *Arizona Republic,* the *Phoenix Gazette* backed Barry because of his experience and seniority, but its endorsement reflected how Schulz had shaped the debate: "For energy in the '80s, Arizona is fortunate to have an outstanding freshman in Dennis DeConcini."[58] In the few years since Eugene Pulliam's death, his newspapers had gone a long way toward journalistic objectivity.[59]

The race spurred a heavy turnout, and 79 percent of Arizonans went to the polls on election day. They gave Ronald Reagan more than half a million of their votes and a crushing two-to-one margin of victory over Jimmy Carter. Ticket-splitting, however, locked Barry Goldwater and Bill Schulz in a tight race. After 434 of Arizona's 1,224 precincts had been counted, Schulz was ahead by 3,141 votes; after 766 precincts he had built his lead to 7,774 votes. The Democrat was winning in fourteen of the state's sixteen counties, but a heavy Republican vote in Maricopa (Phoenix) and Yavapai (Prescott) counties kept Goldwater in contention. Exit polling showed that the senator had captured the white-collar and senior citizen vote but by smaller margins than in the past. Voters under twenty-four years of age and men and women residing in Arizona for fewer than five years went strongly for Schulz.[60]

At 1:00 A.M., with 85 percent of the vote tabulated, the race was too close too call. Barry Goldwater, with each indecisive hour, became depressed and embittered as he watched the national triumph of the conservative movement. He felt rejected and humiliated; his neighbors had turned against him, ignoring decades of public service. Barry began to drink. Soon he ordered Harry Rosenzweig, brother Bob, his children and grandchildren from the house. Only Peggy and Judy Eisenhower were allowed to remain, and they comforted him as he wept. Goldwater's reprieve did not come until just before the sun rose. Unlike the Schulz campaign, the Goldwater team had aggressively shepherded absentee voters, traditionally affluent, well educated, and Republican. The effort paid off, for Goldwater won 16,000 of Maricopa County's 22,000 absentee ballots, enough to eke out a 9,399-vote victory from the more than 850,000 votes cast. A shift of only eight votes per precinct would have given the race to Schulz. Ron Crawford realized how close his candidate had come to defeat: "If the campaign had lasted another week, Goldwater would probably have lost."[61]

Goldwater had not regained his composure by the start of his postelection press conference the next morning. In the tense atmosphere, he was abrupt and irritable:

> *Question:* "Will you try to improve your voting record?"
> *Answer:* "I won't break my back at it. If I have something to vote for, I'll be there, but I'm not gonna just go put my tail on the floor of that Senate."
> *Question:* "Why did you do so poorly? What was the message of the voters?"
> *Answer:* "I don't know and I don't particularly care."[62]

Missing his hurt, a reporter accused Goldwater of being "boastful, insensitive, and more than a little arrogant."[63] Confirming Schulz, he observed that Goldwater "had nearly blown his job by not taking it seriously enough." A *Republic* editorial agreed, warning in "A Message to Barry" not to take the people for granted.[64] Because Barry Goldwater had been confident of an easy victory, and because he took political matters personally, the closeness of the race was devastating. He confided to former Governor Howard Pyle, "I came out of this campaign feeling worse than any experience I have ever gone through."[65] Goldwater soon shrugged off the pain, however. He apologized for his "abrasive"[66] behavior and in a full-page newspaper ad pledged to work "with the kind of dedication and enthusiasm you have a right to expect."[67] But the memory haunted him. Although the fact was unspoken, he and every other Arizonan knew that the coming Senate term would be his last.

None had predicted that from the ruins of the 1964 Goldwater for President campaign would emerge a national conservative victory just sixteen years later. Yet Ronald Reagan had reason to acknowledge Goldwater's role, for the scenario of his 1980 triumph was scripted in that defeat. Reagan reiterated 1964 appeals for curbs on federal authority, for tax cuts, for military superiority, and for confrontation with communism. Similarly, he emphasized the social issue with opposition to affirmative action, busing, and pornography. What Reagan learned so well from Goldwater's experience was the power of image. Relaxed before the cameras and without stridency, Ronald Reagan comforted Americans with his aphorisms about hard work and individual responsibility. If Carter lambasted Ronald Reagan's prescriptions as simplistic and out of date, for many Americans they enhanced the Republican's reputation as populist and patriot. Like LBJ, Jimmy Carter hurled the epithets of warmonger and racist, but scare tactics had little effect against the affable Republican. The pattern of the Democratic attack amused Barry Goldwater. Remembering 1964, he joked: "I guess the guy who did the television spots for Johnson died."[68] Nor would the press, now antagonistic to the president, do its part and corroborate the charges. Voters' choices in 1980 reflected not only dissatisfaction with the occupant in the White House but also how much the mood and mind of America had shifted to the right.[69]

The Reagan team also perfected the campaign strategy of 1964. Time had shown the wisdom of fusing the West and South, popularly but too narrowly known as the Sunbelt, into a fulcrum to the presidency. The Census Bureau had recorded dramatic growth in the two regions since World War II. In 1980, one in five Americans lived in the western states, up from one in nine in 1947. The population of America below the thirty-seventh parallel had more than doubled in the forty years since 1940. It was in these regions that Republicans mobilized most aggressively and effectively. Here, too, the New Right made significant inroads. On this common ground, the GOP and the new conservative generation became entwined, sharing candidates and agendas. To the western-southern coalition Republicans welcomed northern blue-collar Catholic defectors from the Democratic Party. African-Americans, finding no home in the Republican Party since 1964, continued their tradition and voted nearly unanimously for the Democratic contender.[70]

History wrote a better role for Reagan than for Barry Goldwater. Incumbency did not benefit the president in 1980. Economic stagnation, inflation, the hostage crisis in Iran, and other measures of the "misery index" convinced Americans that they were better off without Jimmy Carter. Campaigning as an outsider, Reagan took advantage of accumulating anger about welfare, taxes, and government bureaucracy. Reagan, however, was more than the candidate of resentment. He promised Americans prosperity through supply-side economics, and he renewed international prestige with an activist foreign policy. In a reversal of 1964, the business community poured its resources into the Republican campaign while organized labor continued to decline. Reagan won 51 percent of the popular vote in the three-way race with Jimmy Carter and independent John Anderson and a 489-to-44 electoral college landslide. The Democratic ticket captured only the District of Columbia and six states, almost a mirror image of 1964.[71]

Conservatives cheered more than the capture of the White House. Shifting with the population to the West and South was congressional power. Led by the California delegation, about half of the seats in the body were in southern and western hands. Together, Florida, Texas, Arizona, and California gained thirty-nine seats in the House of Representatives between 1940 and 1980. From these regions the congressional elections raised a bumper crop of conservatives. Republicans picked up eleven seats to take control of the U.S. Senate. In coalition with "boll weevil" southern Democrats, House Republicans had enough votes to pass the new president's legislative requests.[72]

In spite of ideological resonance and stature, Barry Goldwater was an outsider in Reagan's Washington. Illness helped keep the Arizona senator from the foreground. In November 1981 doctors replaced his troublesome left hip with a prosthetic device. He underwent triple bypass heart surgery the following year. These setbacks, plus age and habit, gave Goldwater the worst attendance record of any senator in the 97th Congress. Nor did the administration make it a point to solicit his advice and consent. Reaganites dutifully performed their ritual recognition of the conservative patriarch, but Barry Goldwater had ceased being someone they needed to coax or accommodate. The close Arizona election alone was sufficient to convince them that his prime was past. Thus, Barry Jr. complained: "They didn't treat my Dad real well. . . . He wasn't getting service out of the White House that even a normal Senator would expect."[73] This handling extended to the Republican organization as well. Said the Arizona senator, "The Party doesn't seem to give a darn whether I live or not."[74]

Ronald Reagan did not call his aides to task. The two conservatives had grown apart in accelerating trajectories since the 1976 campaign. On inauguration day Goldwater deepened the divide when he upbraided the populist-turned-President and Nancy Reagan for the extravagant festivities: "I've seen seven of them. When you gotta pay two thousand dollars for a limousine for four days, seven dollars to park, and two dollars and fifty cents to check your coat at a time when most people in this country can't hack it, that's ostentatious."[75] The Reagans would invite him to few White House social functions, and he rarely accepted their hospitality.[76]

The senator played the backbencher as the Reagan team put forward its domestic agenda. Promising a "new beginning," the president proposed to restrict the federal government's role in the social and economic life of America. He called for deep spending cuts and a tightening of eligibility requirements in Medicare, Medicaid, food stamps, school meals, child nutrition, job training, and public housing programs. Still, Reagan insisted, a "safety net" of support remained for the "truly needy." To stimulate the economy, the president looked to supply-side economics, now known as Reaganomics. Tax cuts that primarily benefited affluent Americans and business corporations would bring prosperity by stimulating saving and investment that, in turn, promised new plants, more jobs, and higher productivity. This quickening tempo of economic growth, Reagan was sure, would provide government, even at the lower tax rates, with the revenue to balance the budget and eventually retire the national debt. Attempting to enhance incentive while shoring up the competitive advantage of American business, Ronald Reagan also declared war on federal regulations that restrained the free market. He backed legislation to deregulate the savings and loan industry. He authorized budget cuts for the Environmental Protection Agency and Occupational Safety and Health Administration that reduced staff and crippled enforcement. Appointing opponents of regulation to such agencies impeded their mission further. Collaterally, Reagan appointees to the National Labor Relations Board reflected the administration's hostility to organized labor, as did the presidential busting of the Professional Air Traffic Controllers Organization in 1981. New marching orders to the Justice Department's Civil Rights Division and Equal Employment Opportunities Commission similarly stalled affirmative action and antidiscrimination efforts.[77]

Critics decried Reagan's proposals as "trickle down" economics, no different from the policies pursued under Secretary of the Treasury Andrew Mellon during the 1920s. They said the budget ax was cutting beyond fat and striking bone. Repeating George Bush's derision of supply-side theories as "voodoo" economics, the president's opponents compiled data showing a further skewing of the distribution of wealth in favor of upper-bracket taxpayers, a continuing decline in investments for new plants and machinery, and a growing number of business and farm failures. They also assailed business deregulation plans that culled targeted industries, bringing unemployment and job insecurity. Losses here, when added to those already amassed in auto, steel, rubber, and other smokestack industries, sent the national unemployment rate to 8 percent in 1981 and 10 percent a year later. Deregulation posed another danger. With government watchdogs on a tight leash and spoils worth the risk, opportunities lured corporate raiders with few qualms about business ethics. Finally, tax cuts and a military build-up that projected a 56 percent increase in defense spending over five years meant massive deficit spending. America was in danger not only of abandoning its poor, argued liberals, but also of mortgaging itself to foreign bondholders.[78]

Barry Goldwater stayed the course against the president's critics. Reaganomics made sense to Goldwater as a means of "reversing the welfare state," enhancing individual incentive, and securing market freedom.[79] "Supply side economics was nothing but free enterprise," he contended. "I've been a free enterprise man all my life. . . . It was nothing but the encouragement of the system that made us economically great. Yes, I was for it."[80] He did his part, sponsoring a bill to amend the Communications Act of 1934 that would deregulate radio stations. The soaring national debt did not deter him. "The first year it's going to cause a very large deficit. But in the succeeding years, we probably should grow rapidly enough to provide a minimum of 10 million new jobs."[81] He advised President Reagan to "stand by his guns, not back up one inch from his plan to let the capitalist system function, and to give the business community hell for not showing enough confidence in his program."[82] Goldwater also favored deregulating the savings and loan industry and, despite warnings from opponents, "didn't worry about it."[83] He similarly encouraged the president against an old adversary, organized labor.[84]

Recovery from the 1981–82 recession cheered him, but his euphoria soon vanished as the deficit continued to mount. Like many conservatives, Goldwater initially faulted congressional Democrats for allocating funds beyond the president's spending requests. Later, he spread the blame, grousing about Ronald Reagan's disregard for the principles of fiscal conservatism. As he would tell William Buckley, Jr., "We used to say about the

Democrats: 'They spend and spend and elect and elect.' Now, the Republicans—'They borrow and borrow and elect and elect.' So, there's basically no difference."[85] He observed subsequently: "Had I been in Reagan's place, this country never would have gone $3 trillion in debt."[86] Growing concern about the deficit forced an uncharacteristic Goldwater retreat on defense spending. A strong military was necessary, he insisted, but the Reagan administration was "overbuilding."[87] Competition between the services led to expensive duplication, and military contractors felt no obligation to contain their production costs or meet contract deadlines. "I think the defense industry has such a hold on buying and selling of military equipment that they can damned near do what they want."[88] Now insulated from voter retribution and "scared to death" by the exploding costs of weaponry, Goldwater took a stand. He objected, for example, to the Apache helicopter that was scheduled for Arizona manufacture. "They think that will influence me? Hell, they could build it in my living room, and I won't go along till they get the price down."[89] Goldwater even called on the president to freeze military spending to bring deficit reduction.[90]

When friends were under attack and political matters became personal, the fiery Goldwater of old returned to the headlines—as he did in the summer 1981, when Ronald Reagan nominated Goldwater protégé and Arizona Court of Appeals Judge Sandra Day O'Connor as the first woman to serve on the Supreme Court. The nomination disturbed elements of the New Right, particularly anti-abortion groups that questioned O'Connor's commitment to the right to life. Goldwater immediately went to her defense. After Moral Majority leader Jerry Falwell was misquoted as saying that good Christians should be concerned about O'Connor, Goldwater barked: "Every good Christian ought to kick Falwell right in the ass. I get damn tired of these political preachers telling me what to believe in and do."[91] As before, the Arizona senator rejected abortion, school prayer, or any single issue as the test of conservatism. He broadened the context, alerting Americans to the danger inherent in "the uncompromising idealism of religious groups": "The religious factions that are growing throughout the land are not using their religious clout with wisdom. They are trying to force government leaders into following their positions 100%. If you disagree with these religious groups on any particular moral issue, they cajole, they complain, they threaten you with loss of money or votes or both. . . . I am warning them today, I will fight them every step of the way if they try and dictate their moral convictions to all Americans in the name of conservatism."[92] For good measure and in protest, he resigned his membership in Right to Life.[93]

Goldwater was true to his pledge and continued the fight against the "muscle of religion toward political ends."[94] In early 1982 he joined liberals in attacking New Right efforts to legislate limits on the jurisdiction of the Supreme Court. Goldwater concurred with critics that Supreme Court decisions on school prayer, abortion, and busing were in error but believed that the Congress should not "meet judicial excesses with legislative excesses."[95] Basing his position on the principle of "judicial independence," he opposed "a frontal assault" on the judiciary as "a dangerous blow to the foundations of a free society." Goldwater responded to the chorus of dissent that greeted his stand in characteristic fashion: "If they don't like it, to hell with them." Besides, as he candidly noted, serving his final term gave him the luxury to follow his conscience. "When you don't have to worry how people at home will vote, you feel much more free to tell what you really think."[96]

Barry Goldwater's most important assignment during Reagan's first term was to the chairmanship of the Senate Select Committee on Intelligence. This troubled those who demanded that the intelligence community be tightly leashed. In light of Goldwater's often-stated views on covert operations and congressional oversight, they had good reason to question his commitment to scrutiny. Covert operations, the Arizona senator had long maintained, were critical to American security, and he advocated wide presidential discretion in their authorization. During the 1970s Goldwater had rejected the findings of a Senate probe that detailed intelligence agencies' abuses and had dissented from its recommendations for restraint. Goldwater had even voted against the creation of the committee he now chaired. During the Carter administration he had charted further erosion of the morale and resources of the intelligence community and blamed Central Intelligence Agency Director Stansfield Turner for "damn near ruin[ing] the C.I.A."[97] Now, with the White House and Senate intelligence committee in sympathetic hands, the rebuilding process could begin, and Goldwater was determined to do his part. To secure the intelligence community's confidence, he supported increased funding for the CIA and promoted a less-than-rigorous exercise of his committee's oversight function. In July 1981, Chairman Goldwater observed: "I don't even like to have an intelligence committee. I don't think it's any of our business."[98] He planned to minimize "meddling" with legislation. "My only hope was to change the law to allow less congressional intrusion."[99] In a similar vein, he told the *New York Times*, "I'm a bit old-fashioned. When it comes to covert operations, it would be best if they didn't have to tell us anything."[100] Such attitudes firmed the passive role his committee already played, for it was dependent for information on those it policed. He would have to trust Reagan administration officials to obey the law and be sufficiently intelligent to avoid embarrassing the nation, the Senate, and him.[101]

For these reasons Goldwater made what was for him an unusual request.

Believing that the position of CIA director was "owed" to him, he asked
Ronald Reagan to appoint Admiral Bobby Inman, a career naval intelligence
officer and former head of the National Security Agency in the Carter White
House.[102] The CIA needed Inman, Goldwater insisted, because he was a professional, a man of integrity, and highly regarded on Capitol Hill. To Goldwater's dismay, Reagan had already promised the job to Bill Casey, his 1980
campaign manager. The president assured Goldwater that Casey, a former
member of the Office of Strategic Services (OSS), which preceded the CIA
during World War II, had the qualifications. A New York attorney with a
sharp intellect and excellent administrative skills, Casey shared with the two
men a fervent anticommunism. Goldwater persisted: "I did not think that
experience in a war fought forty years ago qualified anybody to run a modern
intelligence service." The president, however, was adamant and direct. "He
reminded me that we wouldn't be having this conversation if it weren't for
Bill Casey. He was sending Casey to the CIA and I might as well forget it."[103]

Inman's appointment as deputy director of the CIA did not appease Goldwater, who looked for an opening against Casey. In this he found allies, for
Casey inspired little confidence and much concern. The CIA director gave
the appearance of someone who could not be trusted. He disdained congressional oversight and held the watchdog committees in contempt. Casey
was "smart like a fox," according to Utah senator and intelligence committee
member Jake Garn, and would divulge nothing unless tightly cornered.[104]
"He was almost an impossible man to do business with," said Goldwater.
"He'd sit in front of you and testify and you knew goddamn well he wasn't
telling the whole story."[105] Further undermining credibility was his speaking
style. Goldwater called Casey "Flappy" or "Flapper Lips" because he was
often unintelligible—mumbling, garbling, and disguising his words.[106] John
Tower was equally critical: "Casey would dissemble, temporize, engage in
double speak. I don't know whether he did it for enjoyment or it was just his
nature. . . . He did not serve the president well."[107] More damaging to Casey
were persistent allegations of questionable business dealings and his
appointment of men with reputations like his own. In summer 1981, Goldwater made his move and called for Casey's resignation. He backed down,
however, before determined opposition from the White House and the clear
signal that Inman would not be appointed to the directorship, regardless of
Casey's fate. Casey survived the probe into his business dealings despite its
fainthearted conclusion, which judged him not "unfit" to serve.[108]

Thereafter, Goldwater embraced what he could not change. He was
patient with his "problem child" and tolerated Casey's behavior.[109]
According to Goldwater: "Casey just said to hell with Congress. He would
find a way around us. I phoned him on various occasions and raised the

roof with him. Bill would mumble and stumble around, but I knew he was going to march his own way."[110] Realizing this, and aware that Casey's zealotry might need a tight rein, Goldwater still did not raise his guard. He distrusted Casey, but partisanship and ideological resonance fed Goldwater's forbearance. The Arizona senator relaxed also because he sympathized with Casey's complaints about congressional "meddling" in intelligence work. In common cause, he blinked Casey's deceit. Nor was Goldwater temperamentally suited to perform the rigorous work of scrutiny. "He was not one to look deeply into issues," said Vermont senator and intelligence committee member Patrick Leahy. "He wouldn't bestir himself to look for things, even things that looked very obvious."[111] Most members of the intelligence committee, Democrats as well as Republicans, followed Goldwater's lead. They either approved the administration's policy or found ignorance and cynicism more comfortable than confrontation. During the calm of the early 1980s an image of routine surrounded the relationship between Casey and the committee, giving the appearance that the CIA was under control and that congressional oversight was operating smoothly and effectively. Countering critics, Goldwater gave assurances that fostered an impression of vigilance. He told a reporter in May 1982, "I would agree that none of the intelligence family breaks down the door trying to see the committee, but I think that Casey has pretty well kept us abreast of what's going on."[112]

If Reagan's choice at CIA was not to Barry Goldwater's liking, the president's anticommunist crusade was. The Reagan administration, in a return to rhetoric of the Eisenhower-Dulles years, promised to "roll back the Reds" in Africa, Asia, and Central America. The president and Bill Casey reserved a major part in the offensive for the CIA. To carry forward the rebuilding, the administration increased the CIA's budget by 50 percent between 1981 and 1983, and the agency expanded its work force by more than a third. Bill Casey was eager to take advantage of the new resources, and he planned a significant escalation in covert operations. Congress, however, had placed some obstacles in his path. Before initiating any operation, the president was required to sign a "finding" about the nature of the proposed action and its importance to national security. In addition, oversight legislation made the CIA director accountable and obligated him to keep the Senate and House intelligence committees "fully and currently informed" of such activity and explain its scope "in a timely fashion." There was even provision for prior notification of the committees "of any significant anticipated intelligence activity." These requirements slowed Casey's initiative only temporarily. Reagan was receptive to his requests, and between 1980 and 1986 he authorized a fivefold increase in the number of covert operations. Said an insider at the CIA's Langley headquarters: "Reagan is the Will Rogers of intelligence—he never met a covert operation he didn't like."[113]

Central America was the critical theater of operations for Reagan and the Casey. Here, in an area long considered vital to national security, the administration chose to flex its muscles and demonstrate America's new resolve. Recent events gave urgency to the mission. In 1979 the Sandinista National Liberation Front overthrew the Somoza dictatorship and established a leftist government in Nicaragua. This concerned Barry Goldwater, for it "could well have a domino effect running through the entire area of Central America. Communism is on the march."[114] The Reagan administration agreed and claimed that the Sandinistas and their Cuban sponsors were exporting revolution by funneling munitions to left-wing guerrillas in neighboring El Salvador. In December 1981, President Reagan signed a finding that authorized the CIA to train and equip the anti-Sandinista Contras for the purpose of blocking arms shipments to Salvadoran leftists. Casey dutifully reported this to the congressional intelligence committees. He neglected, however, to disclose that the covert operation went beyond arms interdiction. Aid to the Contras—or freedom fighters, as Reagan called them—was the administration's means to destabilize and eventually overthrow the government of Nicaragua.[115]

Press reports in March 1982 revealed more than Casey did and exposed the already intense U.S. efforts to undermine the Sandinista government. The CIA director again appeared on Capitol Hill, insisting that the war in El Salvador was the administration's focus. He stressed Nicaraguan interference in the Salvadoran civil war but provided little evidence of Sandinista traffic in arms. Most intelligence committee members accepted his reassurances, agreeing on the necessity of stopping any arms flow. They primarily pressed him about the size and tactics of the Contra force. Some, like Representative Norman Mineta, still were suspicious: "He treats us like mushrooms—he keeps us in the dark and feeds us manure."[116] Barry Goldwater, believing in the administration's thrust, did not press Casey at all. He was even pleased that the *Washington Post* had revealed CIA covert activity in Nicaragua and told reporter Bob Woodward that "a lot of this stuff should be made public. The American people should know what is being done." While Goldwater acknowledged to Woodward his concern about Casey's "forthrightness" and lack of professionalism, he praised the CIA director as "a fine man. Honest. A real spy when he was with the OSS, a real guy with a dagger."[117] Bobby Inman's resignation from the CIA, coming the same month, did not arouse Goldwater's concern, and he remained at ease and consistent with Casey.[118]

Continuing reports of significant Contra military action against the Sandinistas but of little arms interception alerted congressional opponents of the administration's policy. In December 1982 they overwhelmingly passed the Boland Amendment, written by the chair of the House Intelligence Committee, which prohibited covert operations to overthrow the government of Nicaragua. The president signed it into law, but his policy did not change. Nor did Barry Goldwater's support and faith. He denounced the Boland Amendment as "unconstitutional," an infringement upon "the power of the President to be the Commander in Chief and formulate foreign policy."[119] Later, he wrote the editor of the *Washington Post:* "I do not believe the CIA is violating the law. . . . Time and again, we have been reassured that the Agency is within the law."[120]

In May 1983, when dissatisfaction again intensified and Congress threatened to cut off Contra aid, Goldwater huddled on the telephone with Ronald Reagan to review options. "We have got to continue this program without interruption," Reagan told Goldwater. "We cannot go on this way. Lordy, that is how we lost Vietnam. The Congress did it with shutting off of the funds. We lost Angola in the same way. And here we are now, right in our own backyard." With his mind on the despised War Powers Act, Goldwater agreed: "These damn fool members of Congress are . . . going to change the whole way we do things if they are not careful." In line with "alternative number 3," the Arizona senator promised to corral enough votes on the intelligence committee in support of a compromise to maintain funding until September 30, 1983, contingent on a new presidential finding.[121] In it the president would delineate U.S. policy toward Nicaragua. Intelligence committee members supported their chair, and Congress voted to continue support. As agreed, Reagan issued a finding in September that announced the goals of the covert program as diverting the Sandinistas from revolutionary agitation and pressuring them into negotiations. Neither the president nor his CIA director interpreted this as mandating a change in course in Nicaragua. Activity organized by the CIA continued as before, but it gained momentum.[122]

The cease-fire between congressional critics and the Reagan administration was temporary. Authorized by a new presidential finding in December, "unilaterally controlled Latino assets" departed a CIA mother ship to plant magnetic mines in the harbors of three Nicaraguan ports in January 1984.[123] The CIA placed the mines to halt trade and provoke economic emergency. By the end of February mines had disabled nine ships, with seven more damaged in March. Despite the history of CIA involvement in Nicaragua, there was little questioning in Washington of Contra claims of sole responsibility. Bill Casey had given neither Senate nor House intelligence committee members prior notification of the covert operation.[124]

Nor would the members be informed "fully" or in a "timely fashion." Casey postponed his scheduled February 20 appearance before the Senate intelligence committee until March 8. His testimony at that briefing, the first since September 1983, filled fifty-four pages of the record. He briefed the committee again the following week for more than two hours; this time the presentation consumed eighty-four pages. Yet on both occasions, his reference to the mining was buried in the text and conveyed in a single, twenty-seven-word sentence. "Magnetic mines have been placed in the Pacific harbor of Corinto and the Atlantic harbor of El Bluff as well as the oil terminal of Puerto Sandino."[125] Set in a context of Contra achievements and delivered in the passive voice and in the Casey style, the significance of the action eluded the senators and committee staff. Only Senators Jake Garn and Patrick Leahy, who had missed Casey's appearance and later received private briefings, perceived the extent of the CIA's role.[126]

On April 5, while participating in Senate debate over an administration request for additional Contra funding, Barry Goldwater became fully aware of CIA involvement. Tired and feeling the weight of his seventy-five years, Goldwater casually began to read from a classified memo prepared by his committee's staff. He spoke "in a tone of would-you-believe-this," and then, grasping the import of the words, became red-faced and angry.[127] Casey had "lied" to him.[128] The CIA was the prime mover in the mining incident. On hearing Goldwater, Maine Senator William Cohen rushed to his side and whispered that he was revealing raw intelligence data about a secret operation. Humiliated, Goldwater stopped immediately and for the only time in his thirty-year career asked that his remarks be stricken from the *Congressional Record*. Intelligence committee vice chair Daniel Moynihan would be similarly surprised. He learned about the CIA's involvement in the next day's edition of the *Wall Street Journal*.[129]

"I was devastated," said Barry Goldwater.[130] He told friends, "I've pulled Casey's nuts out of the fire on so many occasions. I feel like such a fool."[131] In a letter leaked to the press, he berated Bill Casey: "I am pissed off. . . . The President has asked us to back his foreign policy. Bill, how can we back his foreign policy when we don't know what the hell he is doing? Lebanon, yes, we all knew that he sent troops over there. But mine the harbors in Nicaragua? This is an act violating international law. It is an act of war. For the life of me, I don't see how we are going to explain it."[132] Because of his conservative credentials and reputation for intense partisanship, Goldwater's rebellion "sent shock waves up and down the line" and touched off an uproar in Congress over administration policy.[133]

Yet it was not the act of mining itself that incensed the Arizonan. In a letter to the editor of the *Washington Times* he professed, "Had I been President, I would have ordered the mining of these harbors myself, only I would have done it a little differently. I would have told the American people about it and this would have removed many of the objections that I would have."[134] In fact, he opposed a resolution condemning the mining that later passed the Senate and House by large majorities. Rather, what Goldwater objected to was "that the CIA had completely failed in its responsibilities to inform our Committee of this covert action."[135] A single sentence hidden in reams of text hardly met the requirement to keep his committee informed. Having worked so hard to restore CIA influence, relax supervision, and cover Casey's missteps, Goldwater felt personally "betrayed."[136] Of no small matter was Barry Goldwater's honor. Bill Casey had embarrassed him before his colleagues. On the Senate floor he declared: "I am forced to apologize to the members of my committee because I did not know the facts on this case, and I apologize to all Members of the Senate for the same reason."[137] Casey's insistence that he had fulfilled his legal responsibilities only escalated Goldwater's fury.[138]

Goldwater's embarrassment deepened when his leadership drew fire. While vice chair Moynihan backed him and nearly resigned in protest from the committee, Minnesota's Republican Senator David Durenberg was critical: "I had begged Barry for months to get Casey in to find out just what the hell the administration was doing under the finding [in September] on Nicaragua. As I recall we hadn't had him before us since the previous fall when we should have had him in monthly."[139] Joseph Biden of Maryland spread the blame: "There was not enough due diligence. We have lost the resolve to make the system work. . . . It would be nice to have an infusion of backbone, myself included."[140] From the right flank, meanwhile, Utah Senator Jake Garn came to Casey's defense and pilloried Goldwater. He was blunt: "Goldwater blew it. Neither he nor Moynihan did their homework. Some senators can't cope with doing their own work and rely on staff." At a closed meeting of the intelligence committee, Garn exploded: "You're all a bunch of assholes. It's your fault, not Casey's."[141] The *Washington Post* echoed Senate critics. The incident, wrote the editor, showed a "failing of oversight" in that the Senate panel had attempted "to forgo the cross-examination style in favor of cultivating a relationship of trust with the CIA."[142] Ben Bradlee was more harsh in private: "Casey probably played Goldwater like a violin."[143] The *New York Times* concurred with the *Post* and condemned congressional "timidity." In taking Casey's reassurances at "face value," the committee was not so much "misled" as "asleep or dreaming."[144] Wrote *Times* columnist William Safire, Goldwater had become "the grand old toothless tiger."[145]

A seemingly contrite Bill Casey petitioned Goldwater for peace at the end of April. In a handwritten note and then before a closed session of the Senate intelligence committee, he apologized for "misunderstandings and failures in communication."[146] Goldwater and Moynihan, however, demanded a more complete surrender. They required him to sign the Casey Accords, which left no doubt of their expectations and tightened oversight guidelines. Henceforth, Casey promised to provide the committee with the written texts of presidential findings initiating operations and of briefing papers detailing the scope and purpose of covert activity even when it did not require Reagan's approval. He also agreed again to inform the committee "as soon as practicable and prior to implementation of the actual activities."[147] Despite this, the administration had no intention of being bound by the new rules. President Reagan, running for reelection in 1984 and unwilling to furnish the Democrats with any ammunition, had ordered a "holding action" in Nicaragua until after November.[148] Casey, as always, justified the means with the end. He confided to CIA deputy director John McMahon: "I only apologized to save the Contras."[149]

Goldwater and Moynihan should have been more wary. Although thrilled by Casey's written promises, had they any cause to place their faith in them? As the Arizonan observed when Casey put his name to the accords, "He dropped the pen, as if it had been poisoned."[150] Casey, the true believer, would neither cease nor desist from his covert efforts against communism, and he began immediately to circumvent congressional authority and the revised guidelines. In April, with congressional funding in jeopardy, he made his first contacts with overseas contributors to arrange financing for the Contras. Future funding arrangements would be more creative. Casey rarely fretted over congressional reaction to his efforts. For four years he had played to senators' ideological and partisan needs and lulled them into a false sense of vigilance. He had tested their scrutiny and found it wanting. They, in turn, had tolerated Casey's neglect of his responsibilities and never impressed on him their oversight prerogatives. If an opportunity had existed to rein in Casey, it was long since past. On stepping down from the committee after the maximum eight years of service, Barry Goldwater may even have heightened Casey's contempt. The Arizona senator, despite his suspicions and Casey's record of deceit, wrote on October 1, 1984: "I just wanted to take these few minutes to tell you how much I have enjoyed working with you and at times, for you. . . . I think you've done a heck of a job and you've certainly brought the intelligence group a long way up the road that the Church committee darned near destroyed you on. . . . I appreciate it as an American citizen, not just as a United States Senator."[151] He went public with his praise, as well, telling *U.S. News and World Report* that "Bill Casey is doing a great job."[152]

On Mother's Day 1984, as the controversy over the Nicaraguan mining waned, family matters briefly distracted Goldwater. He weighed Peggy's plea that he retire before the end of his Senate term, and he acknowledged her lament that "all you have done for most of our forty years together has been to say goodbye." But repeating his mother's lesson "never to quit," he denied her request.[153] There was unfinished business, and Goldwater was determined to complete his mission of service.

Of first importance was the reelection of Ronald Reagan. Goldwater's most memorable moment in the campaign came at the Republican convention when he linked the past and present of conservatism and framed his own place in its history. With no apologies, he raked the Democrats and reminded Americans that "extremism in the defense of liberty is no vice. . . . Members of the convention, we have a leader, a real leader, a great commander in chief: President Ronald Reagan. And in your hearts, you know he's right."[154] Reagan's reelection was never in doubt. His slogans "America is back" and "It's morning again in America" reflected the national confidence that came from an assertive foreign policy, low inflation, and high productivity. Similarly, the rollback of social and affirmative action programs symbolically lifted working-class and lower-middle-class white voters, as did a tax cut that actually redistributed resources to those in upper-income brackets. Walter Mondale could neither arouse enthusiasm nor shake the onus of the Carter years. His promise to attack the deficit by raising taxes was fatal. In even greater numbers than before, northern ethnics voted with white southerners and westerners for the Republican candidate. On the other side of the color line, African-American allegiance to the Democratic Party held firm. Minnesota, in supporting its native son, was the only state to buck the Reagan tidal wave. According to conservative pundits, the results went beyond the effects of prosperity and incumbency. The Reagan coalition of social, economic, and political conservatives had consigned the class-based, interest-group alignment of New Deal creation to the historical ash heap. Surely it was a sign that Ronald Reagan's tally of 59.2 percent of the vote matched exactly Franklin Delano Roosevelt's victory margin in 1932.[155]

In the midst of conservative celebration, Barry Goldwater held a series of interviews with reporters. The discussions were wide-ranging, but as the incoming chair of the Senate Armed Services Committee, his views on defense policy were particularly newsworthy. The deficit demanded immediate action, said Goldwater, and he called for a freeze on military spending. This meant scrapping the MX missile system, but "I think we have enough missiles anyway." Besides, "the Russians don't want to get into war with us."[156] While provocative as usual, Goldwater refrained from announcing the main agenda for his last two years. Now in position and banking on his stature as a strong proponent of the Pentagon, he had begun to review plans for an extensive reorganization of the defense establishment. If enacted, his reforms would combine two cherished goals—fortifying the national defense while making government more efficient and economical. The effort yielded the most important legislative achievement of his career.[157]

Since the 1960s the Arizona senator had sounded warnings about American military decline. He had decried civilian management of the war in Vietnam and laid the blame for defeat on Secretary of Defense Robert McNamara and President Lyndon Johnson. New failures highlighted his charges and exposed to him the multifaceted character of defensive decay. If the takeover of the U.S. embassy in Teheran frustrated Goldwater, the planning and implementation that doomed the mission to rescue American hostages in 1979 appalled him. So, too, did the deaths of 241 Marines left vulnerable to a terrorist bombing in Beirut in 1983. Even the "successful" invasion of Grenada, which overthrew the nation's leftist government, revealed to Goldwater a "minefield of errors" in military thinking, coordination, and execution.[158] Nor did he believe that the large Reagan defense budgets provided the answer. Instead, they exacerbated service rivalries, fostered duplication, bared procurement snafus, and produced scandalous examples of waste and extravagance.[159]

Continuing the work begun by Senators John Tower and Henry Jackson, Goldwater analyzed the strengths and weaknesses of a military establishment last reorganized in 1947. He found that the crisis in defense went to the core of the system—a "cultural" frame of reference that sanctioned "a single service rather than a joint perspective."[160] Specifically, Goldwater targeted for reform a weak chain of command, inadequate overall strategic and budget planning, and the absence of a unified command in combat operations and theaters. The Arizonan went high profile in the cause in early 1985. With Senator Sam Nunn and Representatives William Nichols and Les Aspin, he lobbied friends in the Pentagon and on Capitol Hill while hammering out legislative detail. Reform advocates fought an uphill battle, for the issue had little popular urgency, and they faced a resistant organization with muscle in Congress. They made gradual headway with the logic of reorganization but were also willing to play "hardball," at one point putting the defense budget and all military promotions on hold.[161] With the final hearings scheduled for November and December, reformers looked toward passage of their bill during the next session of Congress.[162]

A family emergency made these matters secondary to Goldwater. Emphysema, severe arthritis, and heart disease had taken Peggy Goldwater's strength. "She stayed home," remembers her husband, "and became a hermit."[163] In late November, her condition deteriorated, and Barry rushed home to Phoenix. Soon she fell into a coma. Complications led doctors to amputate her leg and place her on life support, but she continued to fail. On December 11 the family accepted her physician's advice and allowed Peggy to die.[164]

A grief-stricken Goldwater returned to Washington in January and became single-minded in his advocacy of the military reform bill. The legislation passed by lopsided majorities in the Senate (95 to 0) and House (406 to 4) in the spring of 1986, attesting to his efforts.[165] Said Sam Nunn: "Without Senator Goldwater's leadership, without his determination and his sense of humor, this bill would not be here . . . for consideration."[166] The Goldwater-Nichols Department of Defense Reorganization Act created a strong chair of the Joint Chiefs of Staff (JCS), making the holder of the post the "principal" military adviser to the president, with a more prominent role in a coordinated strategic-planning and budget-making process. It also fixed accountability by establishing a direct chain of command from the president to the secretary of defense through the JCS chair to the commanders in chief of the ten world area commands. These commanders gained effective control over all air, ground, and naval forces in their theaters of operation. Finally, to diminish "servicism" and reorient military focus, the act linked promotion to general or flag rank with prior service in joint-duty assignments.[167]

Barry Goldwater was particularly proud that the most extensive military reorganization in forty years had not added a single layer of bureaucracy to government. He was also pleased when the legislation showed a quick return. The reforms eased the defense establishment's transition from cold war and flush funding to a new world order and fiscal austerity. Similarly, battlefield results would soon prove the value of the law. Goldwater was candid in his triumph: "It's the only goddamn thing I've done in the Senate that's worth a damn. I can go home happy."[168]

As the year and a career that spanned six Senate terms ebbed, Goldwater found other reasons to rejoice. He had seen the triumph of Republican conservatism in the 1980s. Not only had his principles gained legitimacy, but they now framed debate about public policy. The senator's conservative successor, Ronald Reagan, had slowed the expansion of government, cut taxes, and contained Soviet advances. Two of Goldwater's Arizona protégés sat on the Supreme Court, and Reagan's appointment of one-half of the federal judiciary had decidedly shifted legal opinion in a conservative direction. Liberals joined in the tribute, remembering Goldwater's lifelong defense of personal freedoms. Even defense establishment adversaries gave Goldwater his due. At Pentagon ceremonies Secretary Caspar Weinberger presented him with the Department of Defense Distinguished Service Medal, and the secretaries of the four armed services followed with their individual civilian service awards. The Arizonan wept. In final recognition, Ronald Reagan awarded "Mr. Conservative" the Presidential Medal of Freedom, the highest civilian honor for dedication to the national interest.[169]

The closing of his public life revealed frustrations as well. The Navajo-Hopi land dispute remained unresolved more than a decade after congressional action and the expenditure of $300 million. Nine years later the Navajo would continue to resist resettlement. Goldwater had targeted the Department of Education for termination, but it survived. The War Powers Act still defied repeal. Few responded to his fears about the influence of the Israel lobby on Congress and the danger of its tampering with foreign policy. The mixed record of the Reagan administration disappointed him. He complained that Reagan had slowed the rates of federal growth and spending but did not reverse them. Nor did the rollback in social programs cut dependence on government. Most disconcerting, the deficit clouded the American future. Election day 1986 added to his discontent. While Goldwater's hand-picked successor, Representative John McCain, was victorious, the Republicans lost control of the Senate. With it went hope of a renewed conservative advance. On the same day came startling revelations that members of the Reagan administration had ignored a standing pledge not to negotiate with terrorists and had sold arms to secure the release of American hostages in Lebanon. Ignoring congressional prohibitions against military assistance to the Contras, CIA Director Casey orchestrated a scheme to use the profits from the arms sales to support the overthrow of the Sandinista government. Goldwater did not doubt the gravity of the affair or Reagan's complicity in it—"a dreadful mistake, probably one of the major mistakes the United States has ever made in foreign policy."[170] Looking back on the Reagan years, he could agree with Patrick Buchanan's assessment: "In many ways, conservatives served America well, but we accepted truces in too many battles, we surrendered, outright, on too many fronts. Ours is thus, an unfinished revolution."[171] More darkly, Goldwater confided: "There's a lot of things that happened under Reagan that future years are going to turn up that will not hold him in the great position that he now occupies. I think we all know that."[172]

With the final round of award presentations, tributes, and press interviews completed, Barry Goldwater said a tearful goodbye to his staff and closed his Senate office. His papers were boxed and labeled for Arizona delivery to serve as material for a new memoir. After thirty-seven years of public service, it would be a hard transition to retirement. And he would have to make it alone.

13 Mr. Conservative

History has to judge every man who served. . . . I don't know how they're going to treat me. I may be the worst S.O.B. that ever came down the pike. But I won't lose any sleep over it. I just like to be remembered as an honest person who tried.
—BARRY GOLDWATER

A quiet retirement would not cap so vibrant a life as Barry Goldwater's. Alone and relieved of influence, he was drained by depression. He mourned, "You are nobody when you are gone."[1] Service to the nation and conservative movement had driven him throughout his career, and without its press he was a man waiting to die. Resurrection came in causes tied to personal experiences and interpreted according to his conservative perspective. Goldwater chose to contest the social issue that he had introduced into presidential politics but which had evolved by the 1980s into patterns now offensive to him. With principles intact, he reemerged as a national figure, a statesman above politics. Also renewing him was a recognition of his part in the shaping of modern America. Goldwater had pioneered a conservative movement, helped carry the West to political prominence, and championed vigorous anticommunism. Victory would bring new challenges. As Barry Goldwater contemplated his accomplishments he confronted coming breakpoints.

It wasn't easy to go home again. Boomtown Phoenix was no longer a familiar or comfortable place; many friends were gone. Recalled Barry Goldwater: "I'd say, 'Where's Sam?' and they'd say, 'Oh, Sam died.' I quit asking questions."[2] The Goldwater name even disappeared from storefronts as a California retailer absorbed the Arizona chain. Approaching his seventy-eighth birthday, he felt the drag of fifteen medical operations. "The pain seems to reach everywhere—my heels, shoulders, back, neck, both artificial hips, elbows, chest."[3] He tinkered with his hobbies, but they provided only brief escape. Family offered little solace. He lost Peggy and felt estranged from his children. In a revealing letter on the occasion of Barry Jr.'s defeat in the California Republican Senate primary in 1982, Goldwater had been introspective about his parental role modeling: "As I think back on my youth,

my father was a distant person from me. His father was a distant person from
him, as were all the men on my side of the family. Although I never knew
your grandmother's family too well, the little bit I learned of her father
would put him in the same class. Namely, that they were men who believed
that life always presents its challenges and the challenges should be
answered, as far as possible, by the one receiving the challenge. That has
been my guiding light, but now that I approach the status of an old man, I
can look back and see where maybe I was wrong."[4] Though feeling guilty, he
was still "fed up" with his children's "money talk" and the financial responsibilities that they expected him to assume. Goldwater was proud that "it
cost me a million dollars to be a Senator," yet he was forced to sell off half the
land from around his home to satisfy family needs. Arizona would attempt to
succor its most famous son, naming a college building, high school, bombing
and gunnery range, lake, street, the state Republican headquarters, and an
airport terminal for him. This did little to lift him. Lonely, depressed, and
insecure, he sought professional help.[5]

Dealing with the turmoil that embroiled Arizona under Governor Evan
Mecham brought him no relief. Although hesitant initially, Goldwater had
again backed Mecham, a man to his political right, this time in the 1986
gubernatorial campaign. Arizona politicos judged the nod decisive in
enabling him to win a plurality in the three-candidate race. The former senator soon regretted his decision, for the new governor was an instant embarrassment. Ill-advised appointments to state offices, mismanagement, and
insensitive comments about blacks, Hispanics, gays, and Jews convinced
many voters that Mecham was both incompetent and a fool. Within a year
of the election Goldwater added his voice to the opposition and called on the
governor to resign to save the state and Republican Party from further dis-
cord. But there was no reasoning with Mecham. "He's a very, very religious
man," remarked Goldwater, "and I think he honestly feels that he has an 800
line straight up to God."[6] In February 1988, Goldwater became the honorary
chair of the campaign to recall the governor from office. "He screwed up too
much. You look back over all the governors we've had in this state. We've had
some darn good ones and we've had some mediocre ones, but it took us a
long time to get a really bad one."[7] Mecham's impeachment, conviction, and
removal a few months later did not cheer Goldwater, yet it enhanced his reputation locally and nationally, particularly among moderates and liberals.[8]

By the time Mecham was removed Barry Goldwater's attention had
shifted to other matters. Vice President George Bush, in a race with Kansas
Senator Bob Dole for the Republican presidential nomination, solicited the
Arizonan's help in the New Hampshire primary. Goldwater flew to New
England and endorsed Bush as "the most qualified candidate of my lifetime,

except me."[9] The Bush campaign also scheduled appearances for Goldwater in the South and, in triumph, honored him at the 1988 Republican convention. While remaining loyal to Bush in the fall, Goldwater bristled over the vice president's tactics against Democrat Michael Dukakis. He felt that Bush's flag-waving and exploitation of the social issue with thrusts against Willie Horton and "Harvard boutique liberals" ignored the critical matters of war and peace and the deficit.[10] When Bush's running mate, Senator Dan Quayle, made a campaign stop in Phoenix, Goldwater barked a rebuke: "I hope you take this kindly, but I want you to go back and tell George Bush to start talking about the issues, OK?"[11] Some might have replied that Bush was only elaborating on the anticrime message first enunciated in 1964. Goldwater reflected pessimistically a few years later, "I happen to believe that the time of the Liberal is over. They don't have anything to offer, but on the other hand, the Conservatives aren't offering too much either."[12]

These forays into politics did not renew him. While searching for his role, Goldwater made endorsements. He appeared in an advertisement for the National Rifle Association, and in the spirit of the Old West he praised guns as America's equalizers. "We have the right [to bear arms] regardless of station, title, or wealth. In America, a man who toils with his hands has the same rights as a czar or a king."[13] Goldwater also made a service announcement on national television, calling on Americans to preserve ancient Native American sites from plunder. More commercially oriented, he endorsed the Pritikin Longevity Center, "where you learn to live better . . . and longer," for helping to lower cholesterol levels and blood pressure.[14]

What was missing from his life was a sense of purpose, a calling beyond himself. Barry Goldwater found it again in his mother's words, which he repeated during an interview on his birthday in 1989: "Barry, all of us have to pay rent for the space we occupy on earth."[15] The catalysts for the Arizonan's revitalization emerged from within his community and family. In making the abstract immediate and personal, they would carry a powerful charge.

The challenge began in January 1989, when Mecham supporters joined with the followers of the Reverend Pat Robertson to signal their control of the Arizona Republican Party. At the state convention they passed a resolution that declared the United States "a Christian nation . . . a republic based upon the absolute laws of the Bible, not a democracy."[16] The uproar that greeted this action disturbed the resolution's sponsor. He later said, "We wanted things to settle down without alienating the Jews. They're the ones who carry the purse strings of the party."[17]

The incident ignited Goldwater. The party he had built into a contender had been seized by a "bunch of kooks." In a letter to the editor of the *Arizona*

Republic, he described himself as "upset, mad, and disgusted," and then denied the New Rightists' legitimacy: "They are not Republicans of the same cast that I and many, many others are."[18] Goldwater would make no retreat, and he resumed his attack on the religious right. Accordingly, he made what was for him an extreme gesture to the goal of reconstructing his party. In 1992 he endorsed Karan English, the Democratic candidate for the U.S. House of Representatives, against Republican Douglas Wead. Wead, an Assemblies of God minister and former Bush administration liaison to evangelical conservatives, had arrived in the state in 1990, proclaiming himself a "Goldwater Republican." Taking Goldwater's name in vain was not Wead's only sin. Goldwater rejected him for mixing religion and politics and for carpetbagging in Arizona. The former senator ignored the torrent of conservative criticism and relished English's victory. Republican moderates took heart from Goldwater's example. Those who felt as he did about "the crackpots and nuts" rallied and eventually forced the radicals from power.[19]

Prodded by his conservative instincts, he opened other fronts. No longer constrained by political considerations, Goldwater "returned to his maverick ways" and championed abortion rights.[20] "Well, personally, I think it's a woman's decision, I don't think we should legislate for it or against it. If a woman feels she'd be better off not having a baby, that's her own damn business."[21] He joined the National Republican Coalition for Choice and agreed to serve on its national advisory board. In the summer of 1992 he publicly objected to the national Republican Party platform plank on abortion and prophesied that if it were adopted "the convention will go down in a shambles as well as the election." Declared the senator: "I say as a lifelong Republican, as one who has followed the party through thick and thin . . . : I don't want to see it destroyed now. . . . Abortion is not something the Republican Party should call for the abolition of, by legal means or by any other means. There is no way in the world that abortion is going to be abolished. It has been going on ever since man and woman lived together on this earth."[22] In Arizona, he opposed Proposition 110, a pro-life ballot measure that would ban abortion except to save a mother's life. Pro-choice advocates attributed its overwhelming defeat to Goldwater's opposition.[23]

In the same election Goldwater endorsed a referendum making the birthday of the Reverend Martin Luther King, Jr., a state holiday. Boosterism provides a better explanation for his stance than does a heightened appreciation of King's role in the fight against racism. Arizona's resistance to the holiday had caused it to lose a Super Bowl date and revenues from convention business.[24]

Gay and lesbian rights became another Goldwater cause. Arguing in favor of privacy and individual freedom, he urged the Phoenix City Council in June 1992 to adopt a civil rights ordinance that would protect homosexuals from discrimination in employment, housing, and public accommodations. "Under our Constitution, we literally have the right to do anything we may want to do as long as the performance of those acts do[es] not cause damage or hurt to anybody else. I can't see any way in the world that being gay can cause damage to somebody else."[25] Although weakened to prohibit discrimination only by businesses with city contracts, gay rights activists recognized Goldwater's role in the passage of the law. Said Charlie Harrison: "We didn't get everything we wanted, but what we did get was 100 percent because of Barry."[26] Later, Goldwater endorsed federal legislation to protect gays and lesbians against job bias. He scolded opponents: "Anybody who cares about real moral values understands that this isn't about granting special rights; it's about protecting basic rights."[27]

In 1993, Goldwater joined the attack on the U.S. military's policy of discrimination against gays and lesbians. He appeared on television on "Larry King Live" and snapped, "Government should stay out of people's private lives."[28] In a letter to the *Washington Post* that was reprinted in twenty-one newspapers, he rejected the Clinton administration's "don't ask, don't tell" compromise on gay rights: "Lifting the ban on gays in the military isn't exactly nothing, but it's pretty damn close." He drew comparisons to past discrimination against women and African-Americans and announced that it was "high time to pull the curtains on this charade of policy." The issue was clearly drawn in his mind: "You don't have to be 'straight' to fight and die for your country. You just need to shoot straight."[29] When President Bill Clinton called him for advice Goldwater was blunt: "The President of the United States is the commander in chief of the armed forces, and if he says to drop the ban, by God, everybody should do an about-face or get out of the service. . . . Give the order and then shut up about it."[30]

Many conservatives decried the former senator's positions as betrayals of the movement. They searched for the cause of their patriarch's disloyalty, with some attributing it to senility. Others found it in his new wife, Susan Wechsler, whom he married in February 1992. Wechsler, a single parent and health care administrator, had met Barry several years before; she was called to his Scottsdale home when he complained of chest pains. Goldwater acknowledges his wife's strong influence, particularly on gay rights, and her encouragement to speak out. Other family ties reinforced her efforts and enhanced the salience of the issue. Goldwater's grandson Ty Ross as well as a grandniece are openly gay.[31] "When you have gays in your family," he said candidly, "you don't go around knocking [homosexuality]."[32] Loyalty to friends bolstered him as well: "I was really amazed at the people I had known all my life who were gay."[33] Also encouraging Goldwater's candor was his retirement from office. With electoral campaigning behind him he no longer had to muffle unpopular opinions. Looking back, he feels guilty about remaining silent and failing to take a public stand when his voice might have made a difference. "Perhaps," he confided to his daughter Joanne, "I'm one of the reasons this place is so redneck."[34]

Most important in understanding these views is Barry Goldwater's commitment to conservative principles. A grandfather's legacy, parents' example, and his experiences in depression America blessed the rugged individualist and fixed him in defense of personal freedom. Men and women whose exercise of rights did not impinge upon their neighbors' rights demanded protection from authorities intent on meddling with their lives, homes, and pocketbooks. "The least government," he repeated in 1993, "is the best government, and I believe in that."[35] This belief was at the crux of his dispute with the religious right, and he fought its attempts to expand government's reach into the private sphere. Rooted in this unyielding stand was Goldwater's determination to expand the scope of privacy rights and defend choice in abortion, between consenting adults, against forced busing, and in drug use. Only in the face of irresponsible behavior harmful to others and to protect children would he accept the exercise of governmental power in private life. The social issue, which he had broached in 1964, had clearly changed through the efforts of the new generation of conservatives. As Goldwater held fast to his beliefs, the movement had passed him on the right and entrenched itself in positions he could not support.

While conservatives still claim him, liberals have welcomed Barry Goldwater into their fold. They interpret his gay rights and pro-choice positions and resistance to the religious right as a shift to the left that, in turn, validates their own beliefs. Yet the liberal embrace is possible only by ignoring the Arizonan's enduring conservatism. He disparages government's role in society and the economy and calls for federal withdrawal from social programs. He opposes gun control and believes that getting tough with criminals will restore law and order.[36] To repair the family and society, Goldwater believes, women should leave the work force and return home to raise their children. In muting his persistent antipathy to their assumptions, Goldwater has facilitated liberals' acceptance. Now, after decades of confrontation, he is content to bask in the public acclaim. Yet Goldwater never surrendered. He simply heeded the wisdom gathered in growing old.[37]

National recognition years after his retirement nourishes Goldwater's self-esteem, but there are other reasons he feels a heightened sense of fulfillment. The movement he fathered helped shift America to the right, and liberals have been forced to adapt to conservative initiatives. Organized labor, his old foe, has fallen on hard times, stripped of its power and influence. President George Bush, pursuing the course charted by Goldwater in the 1950s, vowed to enforce a 1988 Supreme Court decision and "take steps to prevent unions from using money collected from non union workers for political activities that those workers oppose."[38] After years of vigorous anti-communist crusading, he lived to see the dismantling of the Berlin Wall and the fall of Marxism in Eastern Europe and the Soviet Union. He was gratified when military commanders credited the Goldwater-Nichols Reorganization Act for underwriting the successful invasion of Panama in 1989 and Operation Desert Storm against Iraq in 1991. In his 1992 State of the Union address, President Bush acknowledged Goldwater: "This is a fact: Strength in the pursuit of peace is no vice; isolation in the pursuit of security is no virtue."[39] The Republican contest for the presidential nomination that year also testified to Goldwater's impact on party politics. George Bush and Patrick Buchanan constituted the party's presidential candidate pool, as no liberal Republican commanded a sufficient following to make the race. Bill Clinton's victory in November provided new evidence that Republican chances hinge on a southern-western coalition.[40]

In spite of the return of the Democrats to power in 1992, Barry Goldwater had no reason to mourn. In his speech accepting the Democratic nomination, Bill Clinton had tied into conservative appeals and stirred memories of Goldwater's forgotten Americans by running "in the name of all the people who do the work, pay the taxes, raise the kids and play by the rules—in the name of the hard-working Americans who make up our forgotten middle class."[41] The Clinton administration's task force on welfare reform outlined plans to make government assistance transitional and compel recipients to find private sector or community service jobs. While lobbying for a new crime bill, the president again echoed Goldwater: "The American people increasingly feel that they're not secure in their homes, on their streets, or even in their schools."[42] So, too, did candidates for state and local election across America in 1993 who replayed Goldwater's 1964 domestic themes on crime and taxes. Members of Congress validated another Goldwater position when they decried the dangers to privacy posed by advanced computer technology and when they proposed legislation to safeguard individual rights. In foreign policy matters, Bill Clinton's promise to "strongly oppose" congressional efforts to restrict the president's military authority in Somalia and Haiti surely cheer the former senator. Resonance with Clinton on these issues explains, in part, the Arizonan's defense of the president in the Whitewater affair. "I haven't heard anything yet," declared Goldwater, "that says this is all that big of a deal. It's making it awful hard for him to be president. I just wish they'd get off his back."[43] These words also reflect Goldwater's lifelong awe of the presidency and echo his defense of Richard Nixon during Watergate.[44]

Perhaps Barry Goldwater was even prouder of the growth and development of Arizona. When Goldwater was born the Arizona territory counted a population of just over 200,000 men and women. Now, 3.9 million people live within its borders, and the Valley of the Sun swells below his hilltop home. He boasts that by the year 2000, Phoenix will be the nation's fifth largest city and that twenty years after that it will have merged with the Tucson metropolitan area to create a vast desert megapolis. A longtime booster of his community and state, Goldwater sees no limit to growth, for technology will secure the future. Thus, if Colorado River water proves insufficient to meet demand, there is another option. "This may sound crazy, but we're going to be able to drop a big hose in the Pacific Ocean. We'll all be drinking ocean water."[45]

Barry Goldwater's prestige grew in recognition of his achievements and through his identification with Arizona's success. Yet more is necessary to account for his growing national stature. He stands well in comparison with politicians like Lyndon Johnson, Richard Nixon, and even Ronald Reagan. Goldwater was victimized in 1964, and many Americans felt similarly abused at Lyndon Johnson's hands. They warm to a man temperamentally incapable of brutalizing an opponent in the Johnson style. Perhaps they have convinced themselves as well that the Vietnam War might have been won quickly and decisively if America's leaders had only accepted his military advice. Nor do scandals like Watergate or Iran-Contra tarnish Goldwater. He never appeared devious or conspiratorial; deception was not his method or purpose. While he was no more candid than many politicians, his bluntness suggests a golden time, before photo-ops and spin doctors. It is hardly surprising that this inherently decent man earns the respect of even those who disagree with his views.

Beyond this he commands a charisma energized by myth. Fostered by the politician himself and nurtured by the media for a receptive public is a casting of Goldwater in the role of the western hero. He is the forthright, tough-minded, man of action who speaks plain truths regardless of consequence. No one doubts his sincerity or patriotism or the appropriateness of the slogan "In your heart, you know he's right." He still evokes the magic, appearing in 1993 on the cover of *Parade Magazine* wearing a worn cowboy hat. Interviewer Dotson Rader followed the well-marked trail: "He seems to represent an era fast retreating into memory. He stands as a kind of icon of the American West; a man of fortitude and honesty from a time and place forever lost to us."[46] When Americans look at Barry Goldwater, they see their mythic past.

In the national celebration of Barry Goldwater a measure of forgetfulness is necessary, for he offers up a record layered in contradiction. He has

continuously resisted the dispatching of American troops to distant land
wars and believes in military superiority to avert conflict. Yet during cold
war crises and war in Vietnam he urged the military option with little attention to consequences. It was Goldwater who led the opposition to the
Nuclear Test Ban Treaty and belittled the effects of nuclear fallout. His personal abhorrence of prejudice pressed him to a private activism on behalf of
minorities. Publicly, however, he kept a low profile and did not challenge
community mores. Goldwater continues to oppose the Civil Rights Act of
1964 as a violation of the constitutional rights of property owners. He served
thirty years in the U.S. Senate, but his chief legislative accomplishment did
not occur until the end of his career. He was impatient with the legislative
routine, frequently absent during committee work, and indifferent to constituent service. Political ambition meant the neglect of wife and family.
While honesty is his core value, expediency has shadowed his personal
views about abortion, military spending, and federal aid to Arizona. Partisanship and a sense of loyalty blinded him from the truth about Joseph
McCarthy, Richard Nixon, and William Casey. As a marketer of ideas, rather
than as their creator, Goldwater played his greatest role.

A long life is a double-edged sword. Not only have the years made Barry
Goldwater a respected elder of the American society, they also have enabled
him to sense the possibility of coming breakpoints. The conservative movement did secure legitimacy and liberals are still regrouping, but its future is
uncertain. The decline of communism and the closing of the cold war
robbed the right of a central focus. For half a century anticommunism had
cemented the heterogeneous elements of the conservative coalition, providing target, unity, and identity. A new world order with diverse centers of
political and economic power denies the catalytic symbolism culled from a
confrontation between freedom and slavery. A failure of leadership has frustrated the response to changing circumstances. First Barry Goldwater then
Ronald Reagan personified the conservative movement and gave it a continuity of contention. At the end of the twentieth century, no heir has emerged
to unite the right, and dissension erodes its base. The sins of the televangelists, fallout from the Iran-Contra and savings and loan scandals, and the
press of factional agendas have bled the movement of resources and fostered
a tribalism that denies the inclusiveness vital to victory.[47]

The struggle for the soul of the movement and its Republican Party
vehicle is only beginning. "Moderate" Republicans have called for a return
to their party's roots—a modern Goldwaterism that stresses the three "pillars": fiscal responsibility, limited government, and peace through strength.[48]
Eager for battle are the supporters of Patrick Buchanan, Pat Robertson, and
Phyllis Schlafly. In their name, Buchanan has sounded the attack on abor-

tion, gay rights, racial quotas, and multiculturalism: "We cannot raise a white flag in the culture war because that is who we are. If our leaders have lost the stomach and will to fight, you don't abandon the field, you go out and find new leaders."[49] Conservative Christian activists have responded, and Republican party organizations in Minnesota, Texas, Virginia, Oregon, Iowa, Washington, and South Carolina, among others, are in their grasp. Ironically, as the Republican mainstream flows to his right, Barry Goldwater finds himself in the position that Nelson Rockefeller, William Scranton, and George Romney had occupied in 1964.[50]

Perhaps more profoundly troubling to the conservative future, as R. Emmett Tyrrell, Jr., argues, was the failure during the 1980s to force "revision in the Liberal legends." Even after Reagan, the American people approve an activist role for the federal government and imagine: "Liberalism is for progress, freedom, defense of the little guy; conservatism is the opposite. . . . The conservatives are Robber Barons, racists, squirrelly military officers, Senator Joseph McCarthy, drunk drivers, cigarette smokers, all the stoopnagels of the West and all the criminals not of the Robin Hood variety."[51] During the conservative moment, the liberal grip on the universities, media, and opinion- and image-making institutions of American society never loosened. Was conservatism's victory, then, merely a tactical one that flared from specific and time-bound circumstances? Had the right's strategic goal of inaugurating a pervasive philosophical transformation been checked?[52]

Another potential breakpoint is emerging in the desert. Heralded as part of the southwestern "New California"[53] and the "end of the funnel of white flight,"[54] Arizona has grown dramatically. Development, however, has occurred in ignorance and often in defiance of the environment. Fueled by U.S. defense spending and risky savings and loan investments, the desert has disappeared under housing and condominium tracts, malls, and asphalt. Arizonans, meanwhile, submerge themselves in a visual "illusion of water abundance," creating artificial lakes, building waterfalls, and digging swimming pools.[55] Consumers have begun flocking to stores to buy misters that expand their living space by emitting a fine, evaporative spray of cooling water into the desert air. While they tout themselves as the descendants of the rugged individualists of the Old West, and even dress that way, Arizonans have always been pragmatic about their needs. Their lifestyle is subsidized by the $3.6 billion Central Arizona Project that was designed to water desert agriculture but now underwrites urban growth.[56]

Will the future return the promise of the past? Defense spending, always critical to Arizona's health, may no longer power growth. In the early 1990s social-service poor Arizona saw statistics on homelessness rise, and it counted one in seven of its inhabitants, mostly children, as living below the poverty line. Pollution obscures Grand Canyon vistas, and Phoenix residents face repeated warnings that area air has been fouled by automobile exhaust and wood burning. Congestion, downtown decay, and sprawl reveal other signs of urban blight. Judgment day on the over-allocation of Colorado River water is fast approaching as the mushrooming populations of California, New Mexico, Utah, and particularly Nevada compete with Arizonans to slake their thirst. Perhaps the half of the West that lives in California has already seen the future. There, as the cold war ended, population pressure on a fragile land made the dream unsustainable.[57]

The environmentalist and booster instincts of Barry Goldwater, as with most westerners, coexist in tension. Goldwater acknowledges the problems inherent in development but says with resignation, "That's progress."[58] In a statement that belies his entire life, he reflects: "One man is not going to have an influence on that."[59] In his sense of service, however, may be found the means to confront coming hard times and hard choices.

"I've got one hell of a good life," Barry Goldwater has said.[60] In his ninth decade he devotes his days to projects, tinkering with gadgets, model building, photography, and the ham radio. He is in good health—as wife Susan observes, "His organs are perfect."[61] He remains active, occupying the Goldwater Chair for American Institutions at Arizona State University and teaching a political science class. Invitations still flood his office, and he is unable to keep up with the volume. Unsurprisingly, Barry Goldwater continues to heed his mother's words and to speak out on issues. Disproving those who see a new mellowness, Goldwater remains as intense in his beliefs as ever. The spit and spirit were evident in a May 1993 letter to old friend Bill Saufley: "I don't know what's going to happen to all of us in this country, and while I shouldn't say it, in a way, I'm glad I'm getting so damned old. I probably won't be here to see the disaster that's heading our way. Can it be stopped? Yes, but I don't know where they are going to find the guts to do it."[62]

Notes

Chapter 1: Legacy

Epigraph: Interview with Barry Goldwater, September 24, 1992.

1. Browne, *Adventures*, 288–89.

2. Ibid., 75, 131, 134, 278; Fireman, *Arizona*, 6–8; Yates quoted in Powell, *Arizona*, 43.

3. Rigby, *Desert Happy*, 24, 108; Abbey, *Cactus Country*, 19; Van Dyke, *Desert*, 24–26; Worster, *Rivers of Empire*, 67; Krutch, *Desert Year*, 243, 270; Krutch, *Voice*, 221.

4. Wyllys, "Historical Geography," 123.

5. Krutch, *Voice*, 17; Sellers and Hill, *Arizona Climate*, 5–6; Abbey, *Cactus Country*, 112; Powell, *Arizona*, 10; Fireman, *Arizona*, 21; Browne, *Adventures*, 56.

6. Krutch, *Desert Years*, 56, 60, 70; Krutch, *Voice*, 43–45, 133; Abbey, *Cactus Country*, 21–23; Van Dyke, *Desert*, 133–36; Woodin, *Home*, 8, 10; Rigby, *Desert Happy*, 108, 118–19.

7. Lamar, *Far Southwest*, 2–3; Fireman, *Arizona*, 134; *New York Times*, August 22, 1886, 1.

8. Nadeau, *Water Seekers*, 139.

9. Lamar, *Far Southwest*, 433, 437.

10. Fireman, *Arizona*, 150; McDowell, *Barry Goldwater*, 33; Smith, *Goldwaters*, 19–25. I am greatly indebted to Dean Smith for his careful research into the history of the Goldwater family.

11. Goldwater, *With No Apologies*, 17; Goldwater, *Goldwater*, 44; Smith, *Goldwaters*, 5.

12. Dubnow, *History of the Jews*, I: 343, 405–7; II: 13–26, 30–41, 61, 110, 144; Baron, *Russian Jew*, 22, 39–42; Greenberg, *Jews in Russia*, I: 29–30.

13. Smith, *Goldwaters*, 5–9; Goldwater, *With No Apologies*, 17.

14. Smith, *Goldwaters*, 8–9.

15. More formally, Michel Goldwater served as the vice president of Sonora's Hebrew Benevolent Society, a mutual benefit association. See Kramer and Stern, "Early Associations," 176.

16. Smith, *Goldwaters*, 4; Goldwater, *Goldwater*, 43.

17. Goldwater, *Goldwater*, 43; Smith, *Goldwaters*, 11–13.

18. Smith, *Goldwaters*, 15–17.

19. Ibid., 18.

20. Browne, *Adventures*, 76.

21. Smith, *Goldwaters*, 23–25; Stern and Kramer, "Early Associations," 181.

22 McDowell, *Barry Goldwater*, 34; Smith, *Goldwaters*, 26; Pitt, *Decline of the Californios*, 244–46.

23. *Los Angeles Star*, May 24, 1862.

24. Goldberg, "Reminiscences," 175.

25. Lamb, "Jewish Pioneers," 31–34; Lingenfelter, *Steamboats*, 31, 36; Smith, *Goldwaters*, 25–27; Romer, "From Boulder," 69; Fireman, *Arizona*, 151.

26. Goldwater, "Arrival of the Anglos," 81; Lamb, "Jewish Pioneers," 135; Smith, *Goldwaters*, 28–31.

27. Lamb, "Jewish Pioneers," 35; Smith, *Goldwaters*, 31.

28. Lamb, "Jewish Pioneers," 95, 137, 148, 151, 153, 180; Stocker, *Jewish Roots*, 18–25; Stern and Kramer, "Major Role," 335; Glanz, "Notes," 244–46; Fierman, "Drachmans," 148; Fierman, "Goldberg Brothers," 4–8; Karsh, "Heyman Mannasse," 39–40; Stern and Kramer, "Who Was Isaacson," 121. For more on the Jewish presence in the West see Rochlin and Rochlin, *Pioneer Jews*, and Rischin and Livingston, *Jews*.

29. Meinig, *Southwest*, 57.

30. Fierman, "Jewish Pioneering," 57–66; Lamb, "Jewish Pioneers," 4–6, 60–61, 258–59, 266–68, 279–92; Stern, "Mayor Strauss," 347, 353, 356.

31. Lamb, "Pioneer Jews," 247–58; Stocker, *Jewish Roots*, 1.

32. Stern and Kramer, "Some Further Notes," 37.

33. Kramer and Stern, "Early Associations," 186–87; McDowell, *Barry Goldwater*, 43–44; Lamb, "Jewish Pioneers," 37; Stocker, *Jewish Roots*, 13–14; Smith, *Goldwaters*, 36–37, 73–75, 116, 120.

34. Fireman, *Arizona*, 141.

35. Fireman, *Arizona*, 141; Lamb, "Jewish Pioneers," 44–47; Eggenhofer, *Wagons*, 90–92; Smith, *Goldwaters*, 32–34.

36. Census Data Files, 1860–1880, Arizona Historical Foundation; Lingenfelter, *Steamboats*, 36–37; Goldwater, *With No Apologies*, 19; Smith, *Goldwaters*, 34–40.

37. Bureau of the Census, *Ninth Census of the United States, 1870: Population and Social Statistics*, I: 568, 720; Bancroft, *History of Arizona and New Mexico*, 481–82, 536, 581, 603; Lamar, *Far Southwest*, 6, 13, 430, 441, Wyllys, *Arizona*, 115–17, 139, 273–74; Lyon, "Corporate Frontier," 6; Thompson, "Arizona's Economic Development," 33; Wilson, "Pioneer Jews," 232–33.

38. Quoted in Lamar, *Far Southwest*, 448.

39. Ibid., 451.

40. Ibid., 432.

41. Lamar, *Far Southwest*, 446; Wyllys, *Arizona*, 113, 124, 187–89, 191, 194, 196, 209.

42. Miller, "Civilian and Military Supply," 116–17, 122, 133; Lamar, *Far Southwest*, 47, 194, 202; Goldwater, "Arrival of the Anglos," 79; Smith, *Goldwaters*, 44, 47; Wood and Smith, *Barry Goldwater*, 23; Watkins, *High Crimes*, 38.

43. Luckingham, *Phoenix*, 12–16; Fireman, *Arizona*, 42, 117, 218; Johnson, *Central Arizona Project*, 1; Glanz, "Notes," 250.

44. Lamb, "Pioneer Jews," 301; Smith, *Goldwaters*, 48–53.

45. Lamb, "Pioneer Jews," 302; Smith, *Goldwaters*, 49; Pry, "Uncertain Enterprises," 1–4.

46. Meinig, *Southwest*, 41–42; Goldwater, "Three Generations," 145; Fireman, *Arizona*, 139; *New York Times*, July 1, 1877, 5; Lamb, "Fifty-four Years," 130–31; Smith, *Goldwaters*, 56.

47. Yenne, *History of the Southern Pacific*, 31; Wyllys, *Arizona*, 213; Fireman, *Arizona*, 141, 152; Lamb, "Jewish Pioneers," 48, 59; Smith, *Goldwaters*, 55–57.

48. Census Data File, Arizona Historical Foundation.

49. Goldwater, *Goldwater*, 50.

50. Smith, *Goldwaters*, 160; Goldwater, "Three Generations," 155.

51. Goldwater, "Three Generations," 154; Smith, *Goldwaters*, 94–96, 157–58; Lamb, "Pioneer Jews," 223–34, 290.

52. Smith, *Goldwaters*, 92–93; Barry Goldwater, *With No Apologies*, 20; Stern and Kramer, "Some Further Notes," 36–39.

53. Kramer and Stern, "Early Associations," 187; Fireman, "Bar Mitzvah," 341; Smith, *Goldwaters*, 67, 128; McDowell, *Barry Goldwater*, 44.

54. Goldwater interview, September 24, 1992.

55. Interview with Barry Goldwater, August 30, 1990.

56. Smith, *Goldwaters*, 131; Bell, *Mr. Conservative*, 30; Goldwater interview, August 30, 1990.

57. Smith, *Goldwaters*, 122, 128; Schlereth, *Victorian America*, 143.

58. Fireman, "Bar Mitzvah," 342.

59. Goldwater interview, September 24, 1992; Stocker, "Jewish Roots," 12; Lamb, "Jews in Early Phoenix," 310–12; *Arizona Republican*, September 30, 1905; Interview with Harry Rosenzweig, November 16, 1989; Interview with Esther Fireman, September 24, 1992; Interview with Josephine Goldwater by Bert Fireman, February 5, 1959, Arizona Historical Foundation.

60. Meinig, Southwest, 41–43; Nash, "Reshaping Arizona's Economy," in Luey and Stowe, *Arizona*, 75, 131, 135–36; Fireman, *Arizona*, 143–45, 147, 157, 164; Lamar, *Far Southwest*, 465–66; Thompson, "Arizona Economy," 29–31; Bureau of the Census, *Eleventh Census of the United States, 1890: Population*, I: Part 1, 8; *Twelfth Census of the United States, 1900: Population*, I: Part 1, 10; *Thirteenth Census of the United States, 1910: Population*, II: 66.

61. *New York Times*, June 17, 1885, 2.

62. Quoted in Luckingham, *Phoenix*, 27.

63. Meinig, *Southwest*, 43, 50–51; Luckingham, *Phoenix*, 2, 21, 27–31, 42; Fireman, *Arizona*, 145; Kotlanger, "Phoenix," 22; Ehrlich, "Arizona's Territorial Capital," 231, 239; Bureau of the Census, *Eleventh Census of the United States, 1890: Population*, I: part 1, 58; *Twelfth Census of the United States, 1900: Population*, I: part 1, 609.

64. Smith, *Goldwaters*, 123, 128; Schlereth, *Victorian America*, 146–49; Ewen, *Channels of Desire*, 68–69, 193–94; Leach, "Transformations," 319–42.

65. Quoted in Smith, *Goldwaters*, 125.

66. Ibid., 127.

67. Ibid., 125.

68. Ibid., 130; Pry, "Uncertain Enterprises," 4.

69. Luckingham, *Phoenix*, 43; Johnson, *Central Arizona Project*, 2; Cross, Shaw, and Schifele, *Arizona*, 116; Watkins, *High Crimes*, 39; Erna Fergusson, *Our Southwest*, 161; Worster, *Rivers of Empire*, 172.

70. Worster, *Rivers of Empire*, 135, 147, 180; Luckingham, *Phoenix*, 43–46; Johnson, *Central Arizona Project*, 3–4; Reisner, *Cadillac Desert*, 118–19; Wiley and Gottlieb, *Empires*, 12–13, 176; Fireman, *Arizona*, 219.

71. Conners, *Who's Who*, 21.

72. Powell, *Arizona*, 77–79; Thompson, "Arizona's Economic Development," 22–23; Cross et al., *Arizona*, 117; Fergusson, *Our Southwest*, 162, 165.; Luey and Stowe, *Arizona*, 157.

73. Conners, *Who's Who*, 21.

74. Bureau of the Census, *Thirteenth Census of the United States, 1910: Population*, II: 82; Thirteenth Census of the United States, Population by Counties and Minor Civil Divisions: 1910, 1900, 1890, 19; Smith, *Goldwaters*, 142; Fergusson, *Our Southwest*, 165; Thompson, "Arizona's Economic Development," 23–24.

75. Quoted in Luckingham, *Phoenix*, 53–54.

76. Josephine Goldwater interview.

77. Interview with Barry Goldwater, Jr., July 29, 1991.

78. Fireman, "Most Unforgettable Character," 3, typescript in File 44, Goldwater Family Papers; Smith, *Goldwaters*, 137–38; Stolley, "Senator's Pioneer Mother," 25; Josephine Goldwater interview; Wood and Smith, *Barry Goldwater*, 32–33.

79. Stolley, "Senator's Pioneer Mother," 25.

80. Goldwater, *With No Apologies*, 21; Smith, *Goldwaters*, 138; *Phoenix Gazette*, April 21, 1961; Wood and Smith, *Barry Goldwater*, 34.

81. Shadegg, *Barry Goldwater*, 47.

82. Goldwater, *With No Apologies*, 21–22; Smith, *Goldwaters*, 133, 135, 139; *Arizona Gazette* (Phoenix), January 2, 1909.

83. Goldwater, "West That Was," 13, 16.

84. Interview with Barry Goldwater, September 24, 1992.

Chapter 2: Coming of Age

Epigraph: Interview with John Tower, September 14, 1990.

1. Bureau of the Census, *Thirteenth Census of the United States, 1910: Population*, II: 77; *Agriculture*, VI: 74; *Manufactures*, IX: 48.

2. Pry, "Uncertain Enterprises," 3; "Goldwater History," Alpha File, Barry Goldwater Papers, Arizona Historical Foundation; Bureau of the Census, *Thirteenth Census of the United States, 1910: Manufactures*, IX: 37, 48.

3. Quoted in Powell, *Arizona*, 67.

4. Arizona State Constitution; Lamar, *Far Southwest*, 503–4; Wyllys, *Arizona*, 304–9, 312.

5. Quoted in McDowell, *Barry Goldwater*, 49.

6. Smith, *Goldwaters*, 142.

7. Interview with Josephine Goldwater by Bert Fireman, February 5, 1959; Smith, *Goldwaters*, 143–44; Shadegg, *Barry Goldwater*, 49–50.

8. Interview with Barry Goldwater, August 30, 1990.

9. Ibid.

10. Goldwater, *With No Apologies*, 22.

11. Goldwater interview, August 30, 1990.

12. Interview with Jack Williams, December 16, 1991.

13. Interview with Paul Fannin, September 1, 1990.

14. Interview with Harry Rosenzweig, November 16, 1989; Goldwater interview, August 30, 1990; Interview with Bette Quinn, September 13, 1990; Interview with Paul Sexson, September 1, 1990; Fireman, "Goldwater Family Notes," Goldwater Family Papers, Arizona Historical Foundation; Goldwater, *With No Apologies*, 20.

15. Josephine Goldwater interview.

16. Barry Goldwater has said that he was not raised as a Jew because of the absence of Jewish religious institutions in Phoenix. In 1910, the year after Barry was born, Phoenix's forty Jewish families organized Congregation Emanuel holding services in a rented hall. They also established a school to teach their children Hebrew and Jewish customs. Phoenix's first permanent synagogue and religious school were built in 1920. See Lamb, "Jews in Early Phoenix," 312–14; Stocker, *Jewish Roots*, 31–32; *Arizona Republican*, December 9, 16, 1910; Herzberg, "Cornerstone Laying"; Bureau of the Census, *Census of Religious Bodies: 1916*, Part I: 152.

17. Interview with Robert Goldwater, November 17, 1989.

18. "Goldwater's Faith," *Time*, August 28, 1964, 56.

19. "Goldwater History," Alpha File; Josephine Goldwater interview; Kleindienst, *Justice*, 16.

20. Barry Goldwater to Stephen Shadegg, March 11, 1957, Box 480, Barry Goldwater Collection, Barker Texas History Center.

21. Goldwater, *Goldwater*, 36.

22. Josephine Goldwater Papers, Arizona Historical Foundation.

23. Shahin, "Desert Patriarch," 66; "Goldwater's Faith," 56.

24. Interview with Robert Goldwater by Dean Smith, January 7, 1985.

25. Quoted in Bernstein, "AuH$_2$O," 49.

26. Quoting Robert Creighton in Perry, *Barry Goldwater*, 21.

27. "Goldwater History," Alpha File; Smith, *Goldwaters*, 148–49; McDowell, *Barry Goldwater*, 51–52; Interview with William Saufley, August 31, 1990; Goldwater, *Goldwater*, 40; Shadegg, *Barry Goldwater*, 55; Chanin and Chanin, *This Land*, 188.

28. Rosenzweig interview; Saufley interview; Goldwater, *Goldwater*, 50.

29. Smith, *Goldwaters*, 146.

30. Interview with Paul Sexson, September 1, 1990.

31. Interview with Peggy Goldwater Clay, July 30, 1991.

32. Interview with Carolyn Goldwater Erskine, October 26, 1990.

33. Goldwater interview, August 30, 1990; Interview with Harry Rosenzweig by Dean Smith, April 30, 1984, Arizona Historical Foundation; Josephine Goldwater interview; Paul Sexson interview; Goldwater, "Arrival of the Anglos," in Chanin and Chanin, *This Land*, 82; Robert Goldwater interview; Goldwater, *With No Apologies*, 23; Goldwater and Harvey, *Goldwater Kachina Doll Collection*, 2–3; Smith, *Goldwaters*, 167; Ensenberger, "Barry Goldwater," 13; Erskine interview.

34. "Salesman for a Cause," *Time*, June 23, 1961, 13.

35. Bell, *Mr. Conservative*, 37.

36. The IQ score was measured by the Terman Psychological Test in 1925 when Barry Goldwater was sixteen years old. Barry Goldwater transcript, Registrar, University of Arizona. See Terman, *Measurement of Intelligence*, 79, 94.

37. Josephine Goldwater interview.

38. Goldwater interview, August 30, 1990.

39. Interview with Denison Kitchel by Dean Smith, April 9, 1985; Interview with Barry Goldwater, Jr., July 29, 1991; Interview with Tom Korologos, September 11, 1990; "Goldwater . . . The Man," KOOL-Channel 10 broadcast, Phoenix, Arizona, 1984, Arizona Historical Foundation.

40. Goldwater, *Goldwater*, 34.

41. Goldwater, *With No Apologies*, 101.

42. "Goldwater History," Alpha File; Robert Goldwater interview; Thomas Martin, "The Country I Love," *Saturday Evening Post*, October 24, 1964, 30.

43. Goldwater, *With No Apologies*, 22.

44. Erskine interview.

45. "Goldwater History," Alpha File; Goldwater interview, August 30, 1990; Robert Goldwater interview; McDowell, *Barry Goldwater*, 56; Goldwater, *Goldwater*, 36.

46. Goldwater, *Goldwater*, 33.

47. Recorded during an interview with General William Quinn, September 11, 1990.

48. U.S. Senate, 83rd Cong., 1st sess., July 11, 1953, Reprint of Senator Barry Goldwater Fourth of July Speech, *Congressional Record* 99: A4281.

49. Robert Goldwater interview.

50. Goldwater, *Goldwater*, 36.

51. Interview with Benjamin Bradlee, September 10, 1990; Bell, *Mr. Conservative,* 13; Barry Goldwater to William Saufley, October 30, 1991, in the author's possession; Rosenzweig interview; Kleindienst, *Justice,* 38; G. A. Harrison, "Way Out West," *New Republic,* November 23, 1963, 19.

52. Stolley, "Senator's Pioneer Mother," 26.

53. Barry Goldwater to Dean Smith, May 30, 1985, Barry Goldwater Papers, Arizona Historical Foundation.

54. Interview with Michael Goldwater, August 29, 1990.

55. Gilbert, "Love, Dad," 23.

56. Goldwater interview, August 30, 1990.

57. Tower interview; Telephone interview with William F. Buckley, Jr., August 10, 1990; Quoted in Bell, *Mr. Conservative,* 45.

58. William Quinn interview.

59. Paul Sexson interview; Interview with Joanne Goldwater, September 1, 1990; Barry Goldwater, Jr., interview; Miller, *Drama,* 7–8, 14, 19, 95; Miller, *Your Own Good,* 97–98; Osherson, *Finding Our Fathers,* 4, 24.

60. *Arizona Republic,* January 18, 1987.

61. Barry Goldwater, Jr., interview.

62. Interview with Bill Schulz, August 29, 1990.

63. Barry Goldwater, Jr., interview.

64. *Phoenix Gazette,* December 3, 1986.

65. Quoted in Kramer and Roberts, *"I Never,"* 267.

66. Interview with Phyllis Thompson, September 12, 1990.

67. Clay interview; Bette Quinn interview; Paul Sexson interview; Barry Goldwater, Jr., interview.

68. U.S. Senate, 87th Cong., 1st sess., April 18, 1961, *Congressional Record* 107: 6113.

69. Stolley, "Senator's Pioneer Mother," 26.

70. Radin, "The Role of the Father in Cognitive, Academic, and Intellectual Development," in Michael Lamb, *Role of the Father,* 241, 268; Henry B. Biller, "The Father and Personality Development: Parental Deprivation and Sex-Role Development," in Lamb, *Role of the Father,* 93, 99; "Goldwater Family," Alpha File; Wood and Smith, *Barry Goldwater,* 42; *Arizona Republic,* June 16, 1977; Kotlanger, "Phoenix," 356.

71. Erskine interview.

72. Ibid.

73. Stolley, "Senator's Pioneer Mother," 26.

74. Rosenzweig interview.

75. "Goldwater History," Alpha File; Wood and Smith, *Barry Goldwater,* 39; Bernstein, "AuH$_2$O," 49; Fireman, "Goldwater Family Notes"; Goldwater, *Goldwater,* 51.

76. Goldwater interview, August 30, 1990.

77. "Goldwater History," Alpha File; Interview with William W. Dick, October

25, 1990; Barry Goldwater transcript, Phoenix School District; Goldwater interview, September 24, 1992; Smith, *Goldwaters*, 151; Peplow, "Goldwater Mystique," 106.

78. Goldwater, *Goldwater*, 52.

79. "Goldwater History," Alpha File.

80. Ibid.; Interview with Barry Goldwater by Dean Smith, July 5, 1984, Arizona Historical Foundation.

81. Goldwater interview, August 30, 1990; Barry Goldwater transcript, Staunton Military Academy; Telephone interview with Paul J. Kivlighan, January 25, 1991; Saufley interview; Harrison, "Way Out West," 18.

82. Staunton, *Kablegram*, 1928; Telephone interview with David McCampbell, January 7, 1991; and Telephone interview with J. Howard Fry, Jr., January 4, 1991.

83. Ibid.

84. Quoted in Shadegg, *What Happened*, 77.

85. Goldwater, *Goldwater*, 53.

86. Ibid., 58.

87. *Who's Who in America, 1946–1947*, 1822; William Quinn interview; Goldwater, *Goldwater*, 52–54; Rosenzweig interview; "Goldwater History," Alpha File. Alexander Patch later served in World War II, commanding American forces on Guadalcanal during the final phase of fighting and the Seventh Army in Europe after the relief of General George Patton. See Weigley, *Eisenhower's Lieutenants*, 221, 637.

88. Goldwater transcript, Staunton Military Academy.

89. Goldwater, *Goldwater*, 54–55; Goldwater transcript, Staunton Military Academy; Fry interview; McCampbell interview; Kivlighan interview; *Kablegram*, 1928.

90. Bureau of the Census, *Fourteenth Census of the United States, Population: 1920*, III: 74; *Agriculture: 1920*, VI, Part 3: 229–39; *Manufacturing: 1919*, IX: 47; *Fifteenth Census of the United States: 1930*, III, Part 1: 150; *Agriculture: 1930*, II, Part 3: 342; Wyllys, *Arizona*, 331; Thompson, "Arizona Economy," 23–24.

91. Kotlanger, "Phoenix," 223–24, 230–32; Malone and Etulain, *American West*, 44.

92. Nash, *American West*, 106; Meyer, "Federal Grants," 92, 104, 115, 121, 125, 167.

93. Quoted in Luckingham, *Phoenix*, 81.

94. Charles A. Selden, "Prosperity and Progress in the Opulent Southwest," *New York Times*, February 1, 1920, sect. 8, p. 1.

95. Bureau of the Census, *Fourteenth Census of the United States, Population: 1920*, II: 60, 1329, *Manufacturing: 1920*, IX: 48–49; *Fifteenth Census of the United States, Population: 1930*, III, Part 1: 153–54, *Manufacturing: 1930*, III: 51; Johnson, *Central Arizona Project*, 3; Luckingham, *Phoenix*, 79, 106.

96. Weisberg, "Panorama," 103.

97. Kotlanger, "Phoenix," 337.

98. Bemis, "Agriculture," 40.

99. Kotlanger, "Phoenix," 334, 342–43, 366–67.

100. *Phoenix City Directory*, 1920.

101. Quoted in Kotlanger, "Phoenix," 430.

102. In 1909, the territorial legislature passed over the governor's veto a law giving each Arizona school district the authority to segregate its schools. The Phoenix district created separate elementary, secondary, and high schools for blacks. See, Kotlanger, "Phoenix," 296–97, 430, 444–45, 456; *Fifteenth Census of the United States, Population: 1930*, III, Part 1: 153, 157; *Arizona Republic*, April 6, 1991; Luckingham, *Phoenix*, 58–65; Gill and Goff, "Joseph H. Kibbey," 411–22.

103. Quoted in Shadegg, *Barry Goldwater*, 59.

104. "Who Barry Goldwater Is," *U.S. News and World Report* July 27, 1964, 38.

105. Barry Goldwater says of this restriction, "I never heard of that." Goldwater interview, September 24, 1992.

106. Goldwater interview, September 24, 1992; Chanin and Chanin, *This Land*, 188; Wood and Smith, *Barry Goldwater*, 46; and Goldwater transcripts, University of Arizona.

107. An Episcopal church service was performed for Baron Goldwater and he was later cremated. Barry's account of his father's passing is matter-of-fact and without emotion: "When Mun reached home, my father was still in bed—a most unusual thing for him. He appeared to be in great pain. Mun called the doctor and did what she could to make my father more comfortable. He was dead when the doctor arrived." Goldwater, *With No Apologies*, 23–24.

108. Quoted in Bell, *Mr. Conservative*, 36.

109. "B. M. Goldwater," 9–10; "Goldwater's Faith," 56; Fireman, "Goldwater Family Notes;" Goldwater, *With No Apologies*, 24–25; Interview with Robert Goldwater by Dean Smith, February 10, 1984; Smith, *Goldwaters*, 166.

110. William Saufley Papers, Arizona Historical Foundation.

111. Goldwater, *With No Apologies*, 24–25, 29, 31; Smith, *Goldwaters*, 166–67; Robert Goldwater interview; Saufley interview; Bernstein, "AuH$_2$O," 50; Weinstock, "Senator," 12.

112. Niebur, "Social and Economic Effect," 13, 17–18, 24, 38, 45; Shirer, "Business in Arizona," 1; Luckingham, *Phoenix*, 202; Kotlanger, "Phoenix," 249; Wyllys, *Arizona*, 352; Robert Goldwater interview; Goldwater, *Goldwater*, 85–86.

113. Wood and Smith, *Barry Goldwater*, 118; *Arizona Republic*, January 20, 1991; "Goldwater History," Alpha File; Interview with Denison Kitchel, November 18, 1989; Interview with Denison Kitchel by Dean Smith, April 9, 1985.

114. Military Records of Barry Goldwater, Department of Defense; *Phoenix Gazette*, October 19, 1979; Saufley Papers; "Goldwater History," Alpha File.

115. Goldwater, *With No Apologies*, 28.

116. Ibid., 27–28.

117. Smith, *Goldwaters*, 176–77; Kleindienst, *Justice*, 13; Thomas Martin, "The Country I Love," *Saturday Evening Post*, October 24, 1964, 30.

118. *Arizona Republic*, June 10, 1934.

119. Interview with Peggy Goldwater by Dean Smith, May 2, 1984; Lynds, *Middletown*, 7–8; Miscellaneous Diaries, Peggy Goldwater Papers, in the possession of Peggy Goldwater Clay; Interview with Ray Johnson, December 16, 1991; Toffler,

"Woman," 62; Interview with Alice Johnson McGreavy, December 15, 1991; Telephone interview with Isabel Wise, January 2, 1992.

120. Peggy Goldwater interview, May 2, 1984; *Arizona Republic*, December 12, 1985; Wood and Smith, *Barry Goldwater*, 64; Polly Surrey, Mount Vernon College, to the author, March 30, 1992; Mount Vernon College, *The Cupola*, 1929.

121. Quoted in Toffler, "Woman," 60.

122. Clay interview.

123. Goldwater, *With No Apologies*, 29–30; Peggy Goldwater interview, May 2, 1984; Shadegg, *Barry Goldwater*, 71, 77; Wood and Smith, *Barry Goldwater*, 66; Johnson interview; Goldwater to Casserly, April 24, 1986, Alpha File; Goldwater, *Goldwater*, 30, 364; McGreavy interview; Clay interview.

Chapter 3: The Consciousness of a Conservative

Epigraph: Barry Goldwater to William Saufley, February 23, 1953, Saufley Papers, Arizona Historical Foundation.

1. *New York Times*, September 20, 1931, sect. 3, p. 8.

2. Niebur, "Social and Economic Effect," 13–18, 23; *New York Times*, December 29, 1929, sect. 3, p. 2, September 30, 1931, sect. 4, p. 8, June 11, 1933, p. 7; Arrington, "Arizona," 11; Wyllys, *Arizona*, 352;

3. Niebur, "Social and Economic Effect," 21–22, 31–32, 38–39, 43–46, 50–55; Quoted in Luckingham, *Phoenix*, 102–3.

4. The Grand Coulee Dam alone, note historians Michael P. Malone and Richard W. Etulain, "irrigated more land and generated more power than all the dams of the Tennessee Valley Authority combined" (*American West*, 98).

5. Nash, *American West*, 162–65, 172, 180; Malone and Etulain, *American West*, 97–98, 106; Wiley and Gottlieb, *Empires*, 2, 5–6, 19.

6. Arrington, "Arizona," 11–12, 14–16, 18; Niebur, "Social and Economic Effect," 63–64; Luckingham, *Phoenix*, 103–5, 109–13, 126–27; Kotlanger, "Phoenix," 27–28, 110, 159, 166, 170, 208.

7. Quoted in Wiley and Gottlieb, *Empires*, 166.

8. Niebur, "Social and Economic Effect," 16, 18, 30, 76, 84; Luckingham, *Phoenix*, 103; Arrington, "Arizona," 12, 14, 19.

9. Goldwater, *With No Apologies*, 44.

10. Interview with Barry Goldwater, August 30, 1990; Interview with Robert Goldwater, November 17, 1989; Rice, "Arizona: Politics in Transition," in Jonas, *Politics*, 47.

11. *Arizona Republic*, December 1, 1933; Goldwater, "Retailing in Phoenix, 1930–1940," in Horton, *Economic, Political, and Social Survey*, 145.

12. Goldwater, *With No Apologies*, 44.

13. Goldwater, "Retailing," 145.

14. Quoted in Shadegg, *Barry Goldwater*, 113.

15. *Arizona Republic*, April 2, 1934; Robert Goldwater interview.

16. Interview with Denison Kitchel, November 18, 1989.

17. Horton, *Economic, Political, and Social Survey,* 168.

18. Ibid., 42.

19. Goldwater, *With No Apologies,* 44.

20. Barry Goldwater to H. B. Watkins, April 10, 1952, Box 70, Herbert Hoover Post-Presidential Papers, Herbert Hoover Library.

21. Interview with Barry Goldwater by Stephen Feeley, November 30, 1971, Hoover Library.

22. *Phoenix Gazette,* June 23, 1938.

23. Barry Goldwater to Herbert Hoover, June 27, 1938, Box 70, Hoover Post-Presidential Papers.

24. "Store-Employee Relations," Box 3Y332, Barry Goldwater Collection, Barker Texas History Center.

25. Bell, *Mr. Conservative,* 59; Interview with Barry Goldwater by Ed Edwin, June 15, 1967, Dwight David Eisenhower Presidential Library; Interview with William Saufley, August 31, 1990.

26. Saufley interview; McDowell, *Barry Goldwater,* 59–60; Yambert, "Flying Clerks," 56–58, 128; Bill Saufley to Mel and Kay, "Notes on History of Goldwater's," in William Saufley Papers, Arizona Historical Foundation.

27. Quoted in de Toledano, *Winning Side,* 120.

28. Saufley interview; Interview with Robert Goldwater by Dean Smith, November 5, 1984, Arizona Historical Foundation; "Store-Employee Relations"; Bell, *Mr. Conservative,* 58–59; Jackie Hedges to Barry Goldwater, April 12, 1940, in Fireman, "Goldwater Family Notes," Goldwater Family Papers, Arizona Historical Foundation. Morris Goldwater's death on April 11, 1939, marked the end of his generation's influence on the store.

29. Goldwater, "Arrival of the 'Anglos,'" in Chanin and Chanin, *This Land,* 82.

30. Goldwater, *With No Apologies,* 26–27.

31. Kotlanger, "Phoenix," 382.

32. Bill Saufley to the author, February 6, 1991, December 1, 1992; Michael Goldwater Papers, copies in the author's possession; Parker, *When the Smoki Dance,* 1–8. On the heel of Barry Goldwater's left hand are tattooed four blue dots that signify his participation in Smoki ceremonies.

33. Kennedy, *Birth Control,* 105.

34. Ibid., 121.

35. Kennedy, *Birth Control,* 73–74, 91, 100, 108–19, 140–41, 165–69; Hull, "Margaret Sanger," 8–9, 17; *Arizona Republic,* December 7, 1936, February 19, 1937, October 1, 1937; Interview with Alice McGreavy, December 15, 1991; "Clippings," Box 1, Planned Parenthood of Central and Northern Arizona Papers, Arizona Historical Foundation; Barry Goldwater to Wilbur Asbury, February 1, 1949, Saufley Papers.

36. Goldwater, *Arizona Portraits*; Goldwater, *Goldwater,* 78; Ensenberger, "Barry Goldwater," 13–14.

37. Norman Nevills to Barry Goldwater, January 22, 1940, Box 10, Norman D. Nevills Papers, University of Utah.

38. Mrs. R. P. Johnson to Nevills, no date, Box 10, Nevills Papers.

39. Goldwater to Nevills, April 13, 1940, Box 10, Nevills Papers.

40. Goldwater to Nevills, January 22, 1940, Box 10, Nevills Papers.

41. Goldwater, *Odyssey*, 62. It was reprinted in 1970 under the title *Delightful Journey* by the Arizona Historical Foundation.

42. Ibid., 14.

43. Interview with Esther Fireman, September 24, 1992.

44. Quoted in Bernstein, "AuH$_2$O," 52.

45. Elizabeth Simon, "From Desert, Store Oasis Sells Smart Fashions to Women of U.S.," *Women's Wear Daily*, March 2, 1939.

46. Robert Goldwater interview; Saufley interview; "Goldwater's: A Century of Service," Saufley Papers; Bernstein, "AuH$_2$O," 52; Faber, *Road*, 84.

47. Quoted in Keith Wheeler and William Lambert, "The Easygoing Man Behind the Image," *Life*, October 23, 1964, 95.

48. Saufley interview.

49. Ibid.; "Campaign Materials," Box 143, Ernest McFarland Papers, McFarland State Historical Park.

50. Goldwater, *Goldwater*, 85.

51. Quoted in Wheeler and Lambert, "Easygoing Man," 96.

52. Quoted in Toffler, "Woman," 62.

53. Wood and Smith, *Barry Goldwater*, 51.

54. *Arizona Republic Magazine*, August 23, 1964.

55. Robert Goldwater interview; Interview with Margaret Kober, December 16, 1991; *Arizona Republic*, January 18, 1987.

56. Saufley interview.

57. Goldwater, *Odyssey*, 51.

58. Saufley to author, September 8, 1991; *Newsweek*, March 6, 1989, 15.

59. Fergusson, *Our Southwest*, 170.

60. Horton, *Economic, Political, and Social Survey*, 121.

61. Bureau of the Census, *Sixteenth Census of the United States, 1940: Population*, I: 89, 92; Shirer, "Business," 1; Horton, *Economic, Political, and Social Survey*, 41; Cunningham, "Box," 163–172; Luckingham, *Phoenix*, 111; Goldwater, "Retailing," 145.

62. Nash, *American West*, 174; Malone and Etulain, *American West*, 105; Athearn, *Mythic West*, 100.

63. Perry, *Barry Goldwater*, 24; Saufley to author, November 18, 1992.

64. Goldwater interview, August 30, 1990.

65. Interview with Jim Byrkit, November 15, 1990.

66. Saufley interview; Robert Goldwater interview; Goldwater to Nevills, January 30, 1941, April 2, 1941, Box 10, Nevills Papers; Goldwater, *Goldwater*, 78; Quoted in Bernstein, "AuH$_2$O," 52.

67. Interview with Joanne Goldwater, September 1, 1990.

68. Interview with Paul Sexson, September 1, 1990.

69. Interview with Barry Goldwater, Jr., July 29, 1991.

70. Barry Goldwater, Jr., interview.

71. Goldwater, *With No Apologies,* 32.

72. Ibid., 31–32; "3–15–1977," Alpha File, Barry Goldwater Papers, Arizona Historical Foundation; Goldwater interview, August 30, 1990.

73. Jamestown *Post Journal,* October 25, 1941, Saufley Papers.

74. Goldwater, *With No Apologies,* 33.

75. Goldwater's "Newsletter," September 5, 1941, Saufley Papers.

76. Military Records of Barry Goldwater, Department of Defense; "April 21, 1986," Alpha File; Barry Goldwater to Ernest McFarland, July 11, 1941, Box 142, McFarland to Goldwater, no date, Box 143, McFarland Papers; Carl Hayden to Barry Goldwater, July 28, 1941, Personal Files of Barry Goldwater, Arizona Historical Foundation; *Arizona Republic,* March 31, 1991; Interview with Barry Goldwater, September 24, 1992.

77. Stolley, "Senator's Pioneer Mother," 26.

78. Goldwater Military Records; Goldwater, *With No Apologies,* 34.

79. Interview with Samuel Goddard, October 24, 1990.

80. Goldwater Military Records; "Goldwater History," Alpha File; Goldwater, *With No Apologies,* 35; Goldwater, *Goldwater,* 59–60; *Arizona Republic,* September 13, 1942, January 18, 1987.

81. Moser, *China,* 84.

82. Goldwater Military Records.

83. Ibid.; "Goldwater History," Alpha File; Goldwater, *With No Apologies,* 36–37; La Farge, *Eagle,* 65, 247; Spencer, *Flying,* 94; Tunner, *Over,* 39.

84. Goldwater Military Records; Moser, *China,* 80; Tunner, *Over,* 58.

85. Tunner, *Over,* 73.

86. Ibid., 74.

87. Thorne, *Hump,* 29, 35, 114; La Farge, *Eagle,* 87, 90, 109–11, 118; Tunner, *Over,* 75, 129.

88. Moser, *China,* 58, 80, 84; Tunner, *Over,* 46–47, 62, 70; La Farge, *Eagle,* 118, 125, 204; Thorne, *Hump,* 37; Spencer, *Flying,* 9, 47, 100; Goldwater Military Records.

89. Goldwater, *With No Apologies,* 38; Goldwater Military Records.

90. Barry Goldwater, Jr., interview.

91. Barry Goldwater to Joanne Goldwater, no date, Joanne Goldwater Papers, copies in the author's possession.

92. Goldwater to Joanne, June 30, 1944, Joanne Goldwater Papers.

93. Goldwater to Joanne and Barry Jr., August 1943, Joanne Goldwater Papers.

94. Goldwater to Michael Goldwater, May 10, 1944, Michael Goldwater Papers, copies in the author's possession.

95. Goldwater to Joanne, August 1943, December 1943, February 1944, March 14, 1944, July 10, 1944; Goldwater to Joanne, Barry Jr., and Michael, April 1944, June 30, 1944, Joanne Goldwater Papers.

96. Goldwater to Joanne, November 1943, Joanne Goldwater Papers.

97. Goldwater to Michael, March 13, 1945, Michael Goldwater Papers.

98. Goldwater to Joanne, December 1943, Joanne Goldwater Papers.

99. "April 21, 1986," Alpha File.

100. Joanne Goldwater interview.

101. Quoted in Gilbert, "Love, Dad," 23.

102. Barry Goldwater, Jr., interview.

103. Thomas B. Morgan, "Life Without Father," *Good Housekeeping*, November 1962, 236.

104. Barry Goldwater, Jr., interview.

105. Quoted in Gilbert, "Love, Dad," 173.

106. Interview with Peggy Goldwater Clay, July 30, 1991.

Chapter 4: Take-Off

1. Wiley and Gottlieb, *Empires*, 31.

2. Ibid., 29, 33, 110, 122–23, 145; Nash, *American West*, 195–96, 202, 204, 214; Nash, *American West Transformed*, 17–30; Malone and Etulain, *American West*, 109, 115–19.

3. Nash, *Impact*, 218, 222; Luckingham, *Phoenix*, 136–41; Fireman, *Arizona*, 231–33; Gerald Nash, "Reshaping Arizona's Economy: A Century of Change," in Luey and Stowe, eds., *Arizona*, 130, 132–33, 138, 140.

4. Fireman, *Arizona*, 233.

5. Goldwater, *Goldwater*, 87.

6. Weinstock, "Senator," 12–13.

7. Interview with Robert Goldwater by Dean Smith, January 7, 1985, Arizona Historical Foundation.

8. Wade, *Bitter Issue*, 1–5, 10, 18, 31–34, 99.

9. Quoted in Wade, *Bitter Issue*, 35.

10. *Arizona Republic*, July 3, 1946, November 4, 1946; Konig, "Toward Metropolis Status," 218; Reinhard, *Republican Right*, 13–14; Wade, *Bitter Issue*, 35–37, 72.

11. Wood and Smith, *Barry Goldwater*, 76–77; Phillippi, "Arizona," 29–31; Interview with Malcolm Straus, September 27, 1991.

12. Chafe, *Unfinished Journey*, 91–97; Wade, *Bitter Issue*, 43, 75, 82; Konig, "Toward Metropolis Status," 224.

13. Quoted in Wade, *Bitter Issue*, 78.

14. Ibid., 43–46, 82; Wiley and Gottlieb, *Empires*, 276–77; Gall, *Politics*, 13.

15. Wade, *Bitter Issue*, 125; Interview with Denison Kitchel, November 18, 1989.

16. *Arizona Labor Journal* (Phoenix), May 29, 1947.

17. *New York Times*, April 18, 1948, sect. 4, p. 6.

18. Barry Goldwater to Norman Hull, December 26, 1946, William Saufley Papers, Arizona Historical Foundation.

19. Goldwater, *Goldwater*, 87; Harold H. Martin, "The New Millionaires of Phoenix," *Saturday Evening Post*, September 30, 1961, p. 25; Barry Goldwater to

Frank Hill, March 7, 1947, Saufley Papers; *Arizona Times* (Phoenix), April 6, 1948; *Arizona Republic,* April 6, 1948; Fireman, *Arizona,* 233.

20. Johnson, *Central Arizona Project, 1918–1968,* 38–41; Goldwater, *With No Apologies,* 39–40.

21. An acre-foot is the amount of water that will cover an acre of ground to a depth of one foot. It is also the amount of water the average family will consume in a year.

22. The compact also allocated 7.5 million acre-feet to the upper basin states of Wyoming, Colorado, Utah, and New Mexico. Mexico was to receive the remaining 1.5 million acre-feet. Karen L. Smith, "Water, Water Everywhere, Nor . . . ," in Luey and Stowe, *Arizona,* 159; Nadeau, *Water Seekers,* 186, 188; Nash, *American West,* 95; Fireman, *Arizona,* 220–21; Reisner, *Cadillac Desert,* 129–30.

23. Quoted in Nadeau, *Water Seekers,* 190.

24. Reisner, *Cadillac Desert,* 266.

25. California agreed on an annual diversion of 4.4 million acre-feet, which left 300,000 acre-feet for Nevada and 2.8 million acre-feet for Arizona. Ibid., 129–31, 266; Johnson, *Central Arizona Project,* 7, 55; Nadeau, *Water Seekers,* 208.

26. Fireman, *Arizona,* 223; Nadeau, *Water Seekers,* 245–46; Wiley and Gottlieb, *Empires,* 177.

27. See, e.g., Barry Goldwater to Cavanaugh Luggage Company, April 9, 1947, Saufley Papers.

28. Barry Goldwater to California customers, n.d., Saufley Papers.

29. *Arizona Republic,* September 28, 1949.

30. Barry Goldwater to Raymond Moley, September 17, 1949, Box 19, Raymond Moley Collection, Hoover Institution Archives. Emphasis added.

31. U.S. House, 81st Cong., 1st sess., *The Central Arizona Project, Hearings Before the Subcommittee on Irrigation and Reclamation,* 1949, 210–11.

32. Johnson, *Central Arizona Project,* 58, 85.

33. Reisner, *Cadillac Desert,* 126.

34. Ibid., 271, 305. See also Worster, *Rivers of Empire.*

35. Quoted in Worster, *Rivers of Empire,* 279.

36. Clive S. Thomas, "The West and Its Brand of Politics," in Thomas, *Politics,* 8–9; John G. Francis and Clive S. Thomas, "Influences on Western Political Culture," in Thomas, *Politics,* 38; Malone and Etulain, *American West,* 226–27.

37. Barry Goldwater, letter to the editor, *The Reporter,* November 22, 1962, p. 6.

38. Don O. Berdorfer, "CAP and TVA: Barry's Fine Distinction," *The Reporter,* September 10, 1964, p. 36.

39. Johnson, *Central Arizona Project,* 98; Interview with Barry Goldwater, September 24, 1992.

40. Goldwater interview, September 24, 1992.

41. Military Records of Barry Goldwater, Department of Defense; Goldwater, *With No Apologies,* 38; *Phoenix Gazette,* July 13, 1963; Interview with William Saufley, August 31, 1990; Interview with Orren Beaty, Jr., September 14, 1990; Wood and Smith, *Barry Goldwater,* 62; "Goldwater History," Alpha File, Arizona

Historical Foundation; Interview with Ronald Reagan, August 7, 1991; William Saufley to the author, July 20, 1991.

42. William Saufley to the author, November 18, 1992.

43. Beaty interview; William Saufley to the author, November 18, 1992; *Mohave County Miner* (Kingman), April 1, 1948; KRUX radio broadcast, May 23, 1947, Saufley Papers; Bert Fireman, "Under the Sun" column, *Phoenix Gazette*, July 3, 1948, October 9, 1948.

44. Interview with Ben Avery, October 26, 1990.

45. Quoted in Wiley and Gottlieb, *Empires*, 187.

46. Saufley interview.

47. Avery interview.

48. Goldwater, *Goldwater*, 73.

49. Beaty interview; Avery interview.

50. Luckingham, *Phoenix*, 66–67, 73, 147; Leonard E. Goodall, "Phoenix: Reformers at Work," in Goodall, *Urban Politics*, 113–14; Goldwater, *Goldwater*, 87–88.

51. Quoted in Luckingham, *Phoenix*, 148.

52. Interview with Barry Goldwater, August 30, 1991.

53. Interview with Margaret Kober, August 30, 1991.

54. Quoted in Luckingham, *Phoenix*, 144.

55. Konig, "Toward Metropolis Status," 24–29; Beaty interview; Goldwater, *Goldwater*, 87; Goldwater, *With No Apologies*, 41–42; Murphy, "Visit," 128; Luckingham, *Phoenix*, 144–47. In the immediate postwar period, Phoenix was not alone in the quest for political change. Coalitions of business and civic groups in Albuquerque, Portland, San Antonio, Oklahoma City, and Denver launched similar campaigns. See Bernard and Rice, *Sunbelt Cities*; Abbott, *New Urban America*; and Luckingham, *The Urban Southwest*.

56. Luckingham, *Phoenix*, 148; Goldwater, *With No Apologies*, 42–43; Konig, "Toward Metropolis Status," 31–41; Kelso, *Decade*, 8; Kober interview.

57. Interview with Harry Rosenzweig, November 16, 1989; Goldwater interview, August 30, 1990.

58. Goldwater, *Goldwater*, 89.

59. Kober interview; Konig, "Toward Metropolis Status," 58–59; Bell, *Mr. Conservative*, 46; Kleindienst, *Justice*, 18; Beaty interview; Orren Beaty, Jr., to the author, August 4, 1992; Goldwater interview, August 30, 1991.

60. *Arizona Republic*, September 9, 1949, October 13, 1949; Luckingham, *Phoenix*, 153.

61. Eugene Pulliam was the grandfather of Dan Quayle, the former senator from Indiana and vice-president of the United States.

62. Kober interview.

63. Interview with Jack Williams, December 16, 1991.

64. *Arizona Republic*, September 9, 10, and 11, 1949, October, 28, 1949, November 2 and 5, 1949; Konig, "Toward Metropolis Status," 53, 64; Luckingham, *Phoenix*, 150–51; Interview with Charles Pine, October 26, 1990; Murphy, "Visit," 130.

65. *Arizona Republic,* November 3, 1946.

66. Rosenzweig interview.

67. Goldwater interview, September 24, 1992.

68. Interview with Charles Walters, August 31, 1990; *Arizona Republic,* November 18, 1949; Goldwater interview, September 24, 1992; Wendland, *Arizona Project,* 21.

69. *Arizona Republic,* October 25, 1949.

70. Ibid., October 21, 1949.

71. Ibid., October 14, 1949.

72. Ibid., October 21–23, and 27, 1949, November 1–5, and 7, 1949.

73. Ibid., October 30, 1949.

74. Ibid.

75. Walters interview; Goldwater, *With No Apologies,* 41; *Arizona Republic,* September 17 and 29, 1949, October 25–27, 1949; Rosenzweig interview.

76. *Arizona Republic,* November 3, 1949.

77. Ibid., November 1, 1949.

78. Ibid., November 9–11, 1949; Phoenix City Council "Minutes," November 15, 1949, p. 169.

79. Walters interview.

80. Williams interview; Interview with Paul Fannin, September 1, 1990.

81. Phoenix City Council "Minutes," January 3, 1950, p. 297.

82. Weinstock, "Senator," 15.

83. Konig, "Toward Metropolis Status," 289–301, 313–14; Kelso, *Decade,* 35–37, 42, 44, 58–59; Kober interview; Straus interview.

84. Phoenix City Council "Minutes," January 3, 1950, pp. 303, 307, January 31, 1950, p. 356, February 15, 1950, pp. 393, 405, April 25, 1950, pp. 527–28, October 10, 1950, p. 217; Williams interview; Straus interview.

85. Phoenix City Council "Minutes," June 20, 1950, p. 36.

86. Ibid., May 16, 1950, p. 561.

87. Ibid., February 13, 1951, p. 397.

88. "Reelection of the Charter Committee" pamphlet, in the author's possession.

89. McDowell, *Barry Goldwater,* 91; Phoenix City Council "Minutes," July 11, 1950, p. 79; Konig, "Toward Metropolis Status," 101, 305; Bureau of the Census, *Seventeenth Census of the United States, 1950: Population,* II: Part 3, 3–5, 9, 15.

90. Barry Goldwater to Richard Kleindienst, June 9, 1972, Alpha File.

91. Interview with Samuel Goddard, October 24, 1990.

92. Kelso, "1948 Elections," 96; Fannin interview; Berman, *Parties,* 20, 31.

93. Quoted in Chafe, *Unfinished Journey,* 98.

94. Griffith, *Politics of Fear,* 52.

95. Ibid., 49.

96. Interview with Howard Pyle by Ed Edwin, May 11, 1967, Dwight David Eisenhower Presidential Library.

97. Shadegg, *Arizona Politics,* 32–33; Pyle interview by Edwin; Goldwater, *With*

No Apologies, 45; "Nonpolitical Politician," *Time,* March 26, 1951, p. 26; *Arizona Republic,* May 28, 1950; Rosenzweig interview.

98. Jones, "Ana Frohmiller," 349–50, 360–61; Houghton, "1950 Election," 91.

99. Interview with Gene Karp, September 1990. Karp is an aide of Arizona Senator Dennis Deconcini.

100. Interview with Roy Elson by Donald A. Ritchie, June 20, 1990, Senate Historical Office, U.S. Senate Library. Elson was Arizona Senator Carl Hayden's administrative assistant and ran for the U.S. Senate against Barry Goldwater in 1968.

101. Shadegg, *Arizona Politics,* 42; Beaty interview.

102. Interview with Stewart Udall, July 14, 1992; Kleindienst, *Justice,* 23.

103. Jones, "Ana," 363.

104. Ibid., 361.

105. Bernstein, "AuH$_2$O," 54; "Republican Party Platform, 1950," Box 108, Howard Pyle Papers, Arizona State University; Fireman, *Arizona,* 207; Jones, "Ana," 361, 363–64;

106. Avery interview.

107. Shadegg, *Barry Goldwater,* 88.

108. Phoenix City Council "Minutes," August 31, 1951, p. 147.

109. "Reelection" pamphlet.

110. Kelso, *Decade,* 11–12; Fireman, *Arizona,* 233–34; *Arizona Republic,* February 16, 1952; Konig, "Toward Metropolis Status," 205–14, 227; Phoenix City Council "Minutes," February 27, 1951, p. 411, November 20, 1951, p. 282A.

111. Saufley Papers.

112. Nogales *Daily Herald,* October 19, 1951.

113. Hayek, *Road to Serfdom;* Goldwater, *Goldwater,* 110; *Arizona Daily Star* (Tucson), October 19, 1951.

114. Quoted in Tindall, *America,* 1267.

115. Phoenix City Council "Minutes," April 24, 1951, p. 515. Barry Goldwater had first encountered Douglas MacArthur in 1927 during army reserve training exercises. "I have always been proud to brag," Goldwater later wrote MacArthur, "that I served under you." Barry Goldwater to Douglas MacArthur, February 5, 1955, General Correspondence, U.S. Senate, Barry Goldwater Papers, Arizona Historical Foundation.

116. Goldwater, *With No Apologies,* 48.

117. Goldwater Military Records. The Korean Conflict would eventually cost America more than 33,000 combat deaths; 103,000 were wounded and missing. South Korean, North Korean, and Chinese casualties mounted to more than 2.5 million.

118. Goldwater, *Goldwater,* 94.

119. Goldwater, *With No Apologies,* 225; Barry Goldwater, "Scrapbooks," Arizona Historical Foundation.

120. Telephone interview with Lincoln Ragsdale, December 12, 1990.

121. Interview with Otis T. Burns, April 5, 1991.

122. Melcher, "Blacks and Whites," 209.

123. Interview with William Mahoney, October 24, 1990.

124. *New York Times*, September 11, 1964, p. 20; Melcher, "Blacks and Whites," 195, 198, 201; Gill and Goff, "Joseph H. Kibbey," 420–22; Williams interview; "Goldwater's Good Deeds in Arizona," *New Republic*, August 22, 1964, p. 9; Mahoney interview; Joseph Stocker, "Remembering a Challenge to Segregation," *Arizona Republic*, December 11, 1988; "Campaign Materials," Box 142, Ernest McFarland Papers, McFarland State Historical Park; Goldwater interview, September 24, 1992. The court case was successful. In 1953, Maricopa Superior Court judge Fred Stuckmeyer, Jr., declared school segregation in Arizona unconstitutional.

125. Goldwater interview, September 24, 1992.

126. Telephone interview with Ruth Finn, February 5, 1991.

127. Quoted in "Goldwater's Good Deeds," 10.

128. Stocker, "Real," 7.

129. Telephone interview with Sonoma Smith, December 20, 1990; Interview with Joseph and Ida Stocker, October 26, 1990; Finn interview; Telephone interview with Fran Waldman, December 20, 1990; Straus interview; Rosenzweig interview; Telephone interview with Rabbi Albert Plotkin, December 20, 1990; Telephone interview with Fran Frazin, December 20, 1990; *New York Times*, October 17, 1964, p. 16.

130. Telephone interview with Junius A. Bowman, January 30, 1991.

131. Telephone interview with James R. Green, January 4, 1991.

132. Goldwater interview, September 24, 1992; Bowman interview.

133. *New York Times*, October 28, 1964, p. 26.

134. *New York Times*, September 11, 1964, p. 20.

135. Ragsdale interview.

136. Telephone interview with Clovis Campbell, November 26, 1990; Telephone interview with Thomasena and Eugene Grigsby, December 20, 1990.

137. Ragsdale interview.

138. Goldwater interview, September 24, 1992.

139. Rosenzweig interview; Straus interview.

140. *Arizona Republic*, September 17–19, 1952; Finn interview; Williams interview; "Campaign Materials," Box 143, McFarland Papers; Phoenix City Council "Minutes," September 23, 1952, pp. 294–95. Blacks protested discrimination in Phoenix hotels, restaurants, and other public accommodations into the 1960s. The city council passed a public accommodations ordinance in 1964. *Arizona Republic*, February 28, 1993.

Chapter 5: In the "Land of Oz"

1. McMillan, "McFarland," 412; Goldman, *Crucial Decade*, 224; Alexander, *Holding the Line*, 9.

2. *Arizona Republic*, April 25, 1952.

3. Interview with Barry Goldwater by Ed Edwin, June 15, 1967, Dwight David Eisenhower Presidential Library.

4. *Arizona Republic,* March 16, 1952, April 25 and 27, 1952, July 3, 1952, September 10, 1952; *Arizona Daily Star,* July 31, 1952; Shadegg, *Arizona Politics,* 56; Shadegg, *How to Win,* 34; Interview with Stephen Shadegg by Ed Edwin, Oral History Collection, Columbia University; Goldwater, *With No Apologies,* 50–53; Barry Goldwater to Howard Pyle, June 24, 1960, Box 76, Howard Pyle Papers, Arizona State University.

5. Shadegg, *Arizona Politics,* 58.

6. *Arizona Republic,* April 25, 1952.

7. Ibid., September 19, 1952; McMillan, "McFarland," 421; Goldwater, *With No Apologies,* 53.

8. *Arizona Republic,* September 23, 1952.

9. *Phoenix Gazette,* September 20, 1952.

10. Stephen Shadegg to Barry Goldwater, July 15, 1952, Box 475, "1952 Schedule," Box 477, "Radio Schedule," Box 476, Barry Goldwater Collection, Barker History Center; *Arizona Republic,* October 9, 1952; Shadegg, *How to Win,* 20–22; McDowell, *Barry Goldwater,* 99.

11. Quoted in Bernstein, "AuH$_2$O," 55.

12. Willie Bioff, a convicted extortionist and racketeer and later an adviser to Goldwater on organized labor, also contributed to the campaign. The amount of his donation is unknown; Goldwater put the figure at $1,300, and Harry Rosenzweig claimed that it was $10,000. Bioff was assassinated in a car bombing in 1955. Goldwater, *Goldwater,* 11, 103–4; Bell, *Mr. Conservative,* 53; *Arizona Republic,* October 26, 1952, November 2, 1952, January 18, 1987; C. E. Tuttle to Stephen Shadegg, October 10, 1952, Melva Harris to Shadegg, October 13, 1952, Shadegg to Vernon Barrett, October 14, 1952, Robert Muckler to Shadegg, October 28, 1952, Box 475, "Financial Donations," Box 477, Goldwater Collection, Barker History Center; Interview with Victor Armstrong, September 1, 1990; Interview with Harry Rosenzweig, November 16, 1989. See also Reid and Demaris, *Green Felt Jungle,* 42–43, 202, 206.

13. *Arizona Republic,* September 23, 1952.

14. Ibid., October 1, 1952.

15. Ibid., October 22, 1952.

16. *Arizona Daily Star*, October 1, 1952; "Goldwater for Senate" Election Pamphlet, Arizona Historical Foundation.

17. *Arizona Republic,* September 7, 1952.

18. Radio address, September 3, 1952, Box 475, Goldwater Collection, Barker History Center.

19. Radio address, October 5, 1952, Box 475, Goldwater Collection, Barker History Center.

20. *Arizona Republic,* October 7, 15, and 22, 1952.

21. Ibid., October 19, 1952.

22. *Arizona Daily Star,* October 30, 1952; *Tucson Daily Citizen,* October 20, 1952; *Arizona Republic,* September 14, 1952, October 19 and 30, 1952.

23. *Arizona Republic*, October 11, 1952.

24. Ibid., September 26, 1952, October 11 and 25, 1952, November 1, 1952.

25. Ibid., August 23, 1952.

26. Ibid., October 1 and 18, 1952.

27. Ibid., October 1, 1952.

28. Ibid., October 22, 1952.

29. McMillan, "McFarland," 5; *Arizona Republic*, September 30, 1952, October 3, 4, 7, 9, 23, and 26, 1952.

30. *Arizona Republic*, November 2, 1952.

31. McMillan, "McFarland," 424.

32. *Arizona Republic*, October 30, 1952.

33. Ibid., October 29 and 31, 1952.

34. Ibid., October 18, 1952.

35. Ibid., October 16, 17, 21, 22, and 28, 1952.

36. Interview with Roy Elson, December 14, 1991.

37. McFarland, *MAC*, 9.

38. Interview with Charles Pine, October 26, 1990.

39. Interview with Stewart Udall, July 14, 1992.

40. Carlson, "McFarland," 5; Interview with Orme Lewis by Thomas Soapes, July 19, 1976, Eisenhower Presidential Library; Stocker, "Pleasant Primitive," 11; Wood and Smith, *Barry Goldwater*, 87.

41. "Goldwater for Senate" pamphlet.

42. "Jet-Age Senator with a Warning," *Time*, March 7, 1955, 23.

43. Kelso, "1952 Election," 100–102; *Arizona Republic*, November 4 and 5, 1952; Mason, *Arizona*, 18; Berman, *Parties*, 22; Richard G. Kleindienst, *Justice*, 19. Republican Evan Mecham lost his bid for a seat in the Arizona House of Representatives in the 1952 elections.

44. Barry Goldwater to Joanne Goldwater, January 1956, Joanne Goldwater Papers, copies in the author's possession.

45. Goldwater, *Goldwater*, 6, 28; Goldwater, *With No Apologies*, 13; Interview with Judy Rooney Eisenhower, October 26, 1990; Interview with Michael Goldwater, August 29, 1990; Interview with Joanne Goldwater, September 1, 1990.

46. *New York Times*, October 4, 1988, p. 28.

47. Barry Goldwater to Bob Goldwater and Bill Saufley, January 1953, Saufley Papers, Arizona Historical Foundation.

48. Wood and Smith, *Barry Goldwater*, 16. On Robert Taft see Patterson, *Mr. Republican*; and Kirk and McClellan, *Political Principles*.

49. Interview with Denison Kitchel, November 18, 1989.

50. Elson interview; Pine interview; Fradkin, *River No More*, 249; Udall interview.

51. Interview with Frank Moss, September 24, 1990.

52. Goldwater, *Conscience*, 23.

53. Interview with Wallace Bennett, September 8, 1990.

54. Interview with Judy Rooney Eisenhower by Dean Smith, November 13, 1984, Arizona Historical Foundation; Judy Rooney Eisenhower interview; *Arizona Republic*, September 27, 1953.

55. Elson interview.

56. Interview with Roy Elson by Donald A. Ritchie, June 14, 1990, U.S. Senate Historical Office.

57. Shadegg to Goldwater, February 2, 1953, Box 479, Goldwater Collection, Barker History Center.

58. *New York Times*, November 26, 1952, p. 12.

59. Goldwater to Bob Goldwater and Bill Saufley, January 1953, Saufley Papers.

60. *New York Times*, January 10, 1953, p. 11, January 13, 1953, p. 33, March 16, 1953, p. 9.

61. Stephen Shadegg to Barry Goldwater, February 23, 1953, Box 479, Goldwater Collection, Barker History Center.

62. Goldman, *Crucial Decade*, 282.

63. *Arizona Republic*, May 25, 1953.

64. Goldwater, *With No Apologies*, 68.

65. U.S. Senate, 83rd Cong., 1st sess., May 12, 1953, *Congressional Record* 99: 4766–93; U.S. Senate, 83rd Congress, *Standby Economic Controls*, Hearings before the Committee on Banking and Currency, 1953, Part 1, 275, 277, 293–5, Part 2, 480, 739; Goldman, *Crucial Decade*, 241–43.

66. Fixico, *Termination*, 183.

67. Tyler, *Indian Affairs*, 22–32, 44–46; Tyler, *History of Indian Policy*, 151–53, 162, 164–72; Interview with S. Lyman Tyler, August 15, 1990. For more on termination see Fixico, *Termination;* and Burt, *Tribalism in Crisis*.

68. Barry Goldwater to Carlos Emery, December 24, 1952, Box 65M143, Carlos Emery Papers, University of Kentucky Libraries.

69. *Arizona Republic*, September 25, 1952.

70. Goldwater interview by Edwin.

71. Barry Goldwater to Ernest McFarland, February 15, 1949, Box 143, Ernest McFarland Papers, McFarland State Historical Park.

72. U.S. Senate, 83rd Cong., 1st sess., January 16, 1953, *Congressional Record* 99: 394.

73. Barry Goldwater to Carlos Emery, January 21, 1953, Box 65M143, Emery Papers.

74. When asked in 1990 about the policy of termination, Barry Goldwater responded: "It was never big; a minor problem." Goldwater interview, August 30, 1990. Barry Goldwater to Ernest McFarland, December 27, 1947, June 21, 1949, Box 143, McFarland Papers; *Arizona Republic*, October 15, 1952, January 17, 1953, May 29, 1953, January 28, 1954, July 11, 1954; *Arizona Daily Star*, May 27, 1953; U.S. Senate, 83rd Cong., 1st sess., January 16, 1953, 99: 394; U.S. Senate, 83rd Cong., 2nd sess., June 25, 1954, 100: 8960, 8970, 8973, 9136, 9138, *Congressional Record*; U.S. Senate, 83rd Cong., 2nd sess., *Transfer of Indian Hospitals and Health*

Facilities to Public Health Service, Hearings Before a Subcommittee on Interior and Insular Affairs, 1954, 86–90; *Phoenix Gazette,* August 15, 1953.

75. U.S. Senate, 85th Congress, 1st sess., *Federal Indian Policy, Hearings Before the Subcommittee on Indian Affairs,* 1957, 194, 202.

76. Interview with Barry Goldwater by William Cooper, Jr., May 14, 1979, University of Kentucky Libraries. See also Goldwater, "Airpower as Our National Strategy," *Vital Speeches of the Day* 21 (May 15, 1955): 1233–36.

77. Quoted in Greenstein, *Hidden-Hand Presidency,* 166.

78. Ibid.

79. Dwight David Eisenhower, "Diary," April 1, 1953, Eisenhower Diary Series, Eisenhower Presidential Library. In 1959 Barry Goldwater supported Charles Bohlen's selection as special adviser to the Secretary of State on Soviet affairs. Said Goldwater: "I wrote him a couple of years ago that I had made a mistake in opposing him in 1953." *New York Times,* July 13, 1959, p. 1.

80. Alexander, *Holding the Line,* 53, 71; Rosenau, *Nomination,* 2–15; U.S. Senate, 83rd Cong., 1st sess., March 23, 1953, *Congressional Record* 99: 2187–2208, 2277–2300, 2392.

81. U.S. Senate, 83rd Cong., 1st sess., June 30, 1953, *Congressional Record* 99: 7597.

82. Barry Goldwater to Edith Cott, May 27, 1954, General Correspondence, 1954, U.S. Senate, Goldwater Papers, Arizona Historical Foundation.

83. *New York Times,* July 2, 1953, p. 6, July 15, 1953, p. 33; *Arizona Republic,* May 22, 1954; Barry Goldwater to William Saufley, June 7, 1954, Saufley Papers.

84. Goldwater interview by Edwin.

85. U.S. Senate, 83rd Cong., 1st sess., July 31, 1953, *Congressional Record,* 99: 10632–33.

86. Barry Goldwater to Bob Goldwater and William Saufley, January 30, 1954, Saufley Papers.

87. Goldwater, *With No Apologies,* 101.

88. U.S. Senate, 83rd Cong., 2nd sess., August 4, 1954, *Congressional Record,* 100: 13270; Goldwater interview by Edwin.

89. Quoted in Griffith, *Politics of Fear,* 199.

90. Goldwater interview, August 30, 1990.

91. The quote is attributed to Idaho Senator Herman Welker and is found in Rovere, *McCarthy,* 57.

92. *Arizona Republic,* April 22, 1953.

93. Ibid., November 30, 1953.

94. Ibid., April 10, 1954.

95. Goldwater interview, August 30, 1990; Barry Goldwater to Joseph McCarthy, November 30, 1953, January 11 and 30, 1954, and General Correspondence, 1953 and 1954, passim, U.S. Senate, Goldwater Papers; Bernstein, "AuH$_2$O," 56; Oshinsky, *Conspiracy,* 307–8; Buckley and Bozell, *McCarthy,* 53, 55, 57, 60, 74, 161, 189.

96. Quoted in Bernstein, "AuH$_2$O," 56.

97. Goldwater, *With No Apologies*, 59.

98. Quoted in Rovere, *McCarthy*, 65.

99. Barry Goldwater to Everett Dirksen, September 9, 1953, Box 171, Republican National Committee, Office of the Chairman (Leonard W. Hall) Records, 1953–1957, Eisenhower Presidential Library.

100. Goldwater, *With No Apologies*, 60; Goldwater interview, August 30, 1990; Griffith, *Politics of Fear*, 263.

101. Goldwater, *Goldwater*, 130.

102. Goldwater interview, August 30, 1990.

103. Quoted in Bernstein, "AuH$_2$O," 56.

104. Goldwater, *Goldwater*, 129–30; Goldwater interview, August 30, 1990; Wallace Bennett to the Bennett Family, March 25, 1954, Box 2, Wallace Bennett Papers, University of Utah.

105. Rovere, *McCarthy*, 5, 207, 222, 226, 229; Griffith, *Politics of Fear*, 207, 213, 217, 219, 243–69; Oshinsky, *Conspiracy*, 356, 474–81; Greenstein, *Hidden-Hand Presidency*, 198, 200, 206.

106. U.S. Senate, 83rd Cong., 2nd sess., November 12, 1954, *Congressional Record*, 100: 16001–16005; Griffith, *Politics of Fear*, 271–311; *New York Times*, November 13, 1954, p. 8.

107. Goldwater, *With No Apologies*, 61.

108. Goldwater interview, August 30, 1990; Rovere, *McCarthy*, 56. Quoted in Thomas, *Man to See*, 80.

109. U.S. Senate, 85th Cong., 1st sess., May 8, 1957, *Congressional Record*, 103: 6572.

110. Griffith, *Politics of Fear*, 312–13; *New York Times*, June 9, 1957, p. 60; U.S. Senate, 85th Cong., 1st sess., August 14, 1957, *Congressional Record* 103: 14687–94.

111. Houghton, "1954 Elections," 595; Shadegg, *Arizona Politics*, 70.

112. Goldwater interview by Edwin.

113. "Jet Age Senator," 23.

114. General Douglas MacArthur to Barry Goldwater, January 20, 1955, Douglas MacArthur Papers, City of Norfork, Virginia.

115. Barry Goldwater to Douglas MacArthur, April 28, 1959, MacArthur Papers.

116. Richard Nixon to Barry Goldwater, January 12, 1956, Richard M. Nixon Vice Presidential Papers, National Archives, Pacific Southwest Region.

117. *New York Times*, January 12, 1955, p. 12, February 21, 1955, p. 8, February 28, 1955, p. 6, September 8, 1955, p. 22, April 30, 1956, p. 12; Barry Goldwater to Stephen Shadegg, July 18, 1977, Alpha File; "Goldwater" file, Nixon Vice Presidential Papers; Goldwater interview, September 24, 1992.

118. Quoted in Rovere, *Goldwater Caper*, 35.

119. Interview with Carl Hayden by Joe B. Frantz, October 28, 1968; Goldwater interview by Edwin; Goldwater, *Goldwater*, 113; Goldwater, *With No Apologies*, 96, 309.

120. Although critics pointed out how backing a national right-to-work law was inconsistent with his states' rights principles, Goldwater remained steadfast in support.

121. *New York Times,* October 25, 1955, p. 24.

122. Ibid., December 5, 1955, p. 20.

123. Goldwater, *Goldwater,* 110, 118; Richberg, *Labor Union Monopoly,* 40–45; Gall, *Politics,* 65, 68, 76, 98; U.S. Senate, 83rd Cong., 1st sess., March 9, 1953, *Congressional Record* 100: 1724, 2nd sess., May 4, 1954, 100: 5949–5954, May 5, 1954, 100: 5994–6005; Barry Goldwater to Karl Mundt, April 30, 1954, Box 628, Record Group III, Legislation, Karl Mundt Papers, Karl Mundt Foundation, Dakota State College; Foster, "1954," 393–398, 400–404; *Arizona Republic,* March 16, 1953; *New York Times,* March 16, 1953, p. 9, May 4, 1954, p. 1, May 7, 1954, p. 16, October 25, 1955, p. 24, October 30, 1955, p. 76, November 20, 1955, p. 42, December 5, 1955, p. 18 (quote).

124. Transcript of telephone conversation between Barry Goldwater and Stephen Shadegg, June 13, 1955, Box 479, Goldwater Collection, Barker History Center.

125. Ibid. Goldwater Scrapbooks, nos. 25–29, Goldwater Papers, Arizona Historical Foundation. See also Goldwater speech delivered to Sigma Chi Fraternity, June 28, 1955, Box 479, Goldwater Collection, Barker History Center.

126. Goldwater, Sigma Chi Fraternity speech, June 28, 1955.

127. "For Freedom's Sake," Box 480, Goldwater Collection, Barker History Center.

128. Denison Kitchel to Barry Goldwater, January 16, 1956, Box 2, Denison Kitchel Collection, Hoover Institution Archives, Stanford, California.

129. Eisenhower statement to reporters, November 14, 1956, Box 717, Official File, White House Central Files, Eisenhower Presidential Library.

130. Quoted in Reinhard, *Republican Right,* 137.

131. Rusher, *Rise of the Right,* 22, 26, 64–65; Nash, *Conservative Intellectual Movement,* 253–54; Himmelstein, *To the Right,* 23–25.

132. Nash, *Conservative Intellectual Movement,* xiii–xiv, 3–4, 40–53, 85–91; Himmelstein, *To the Right,* 8, 14, 38–42, 45–46, 49–51, 62; Rusher, *Rise of the Right,* 36; Blumenthal, *Rise of the Counterestablishment,* 4.

133. Nisbet, *Conservatism,* 50.

134. Nash, *Conservative Intellectual Movement,* 82, 128, 131, 172–75, 178–81; Rusher, *Rise of the Right,* 29–30; Himmelstein, *To the Right,* 77; Frank S. Meyer, "The Recrudescent American Conservatism," in Buckley, *American Conservative Thought,* 76–83; Kirk, *Program,* 41–42, 162, 169–71, 251, 256; Kirk, *Conservative Mind,* 8–9.

135. Nash, *Conservative Intellectual Movement,* 148–52, 163; Rusher, *Rise of the Right,* 55, 85; Reagan, "Where's," 303–11; Reagan, *American Life,* 126–32, 137; Wills, *Reagan's America,* 278, 283, 285–86; Noonan, *What I Saw at the Revolution,* 279.

136. U.S. Senate, 84th Congress, 2nd sess., January 12, 1956, *Congressional Record,* 102: 489.

137. *Arizona Republic,* March 12, 1956.

138. *New York Times,* October 23, 1956, p. 28.

139. Ibid., November 4, 1956, p. 52.

140. Paul G. Hoffman, "How Eisenhower Saved the Republican Party," *Collier's,* October 26, 1956, 44–47. The Marshall Plan was proposed in 1947 by the Truman administration. It was designed to finance European economic recovery.

141. James C. Wood to Leonard Hall, October 13, 1956, Box 187, Republican National Committee, Office of the Chairman Records, Eisenhower Presidential Library.

142. Barry Goldwater to Sherman Adams, October 12, 1956; Adams to Goldwater, October 16, 1956, Box 712, Official File, White House Central Files, Eisenhower Presidential Library.

143. Official File, White House Central Files, Eisenhower Presidential Library, *passim.*

144. Houghton, "1956 Election," 96.

145. Quoted in Tindall, *Disruption,* 60.

146. Wolfe, "Southern Strategy," 20, 24, 29–30, 36, 109; Tindall, *Disruption,* 52–53; White, *Making of the President 1964,* 142; McAdam, *Political Process,* 157; Piven and Cloward, *Poor People's Movements,* 215, 217. See also Lawson, *Black Ballots.*

147. Interview with Alice McGreavy, December 15, 1991.

148. Interview with Michael Goldwater.

149. Goldwater, *Goldwater,* 369; Interview with Barry Goldwater, Jr., July 29, 1991; Barry Goldwater to Michael Goldwater, January 13, 1958, Michael Goldwater Papers, copies in the author's possession.

150. Barry Goldwater to Joanne Goldwater, December 31, 1955, Joanne Goldwater Papers.

151. Interview with Joanne Goldwater; Joanne Goldwater to the author, April 4, 1993.

152. Quoted in Reinhard, *Republican Right,* 137.

Chapter 6: "Let's Grow Up, Conservatives"

Epigraphs: Douglas MacArthur to Barry Goldwater, February 3, 1961; "June 23, 1978," Alpha File, Barry Goldwater Papers, Arizona Historical Foundation.

1. Richard H. Rovere, "Letter from Washington," *The New Yorker,* April 27, 1957, 70.

2. "Public Record of Barry Goldwater," *Congressional Quarterly 21* (September 20, 1963): 1622.

3. Ibid.; Reinhard, *Republican Right,* 150; Annunziata, "Revolt," 256.

4. Transcript of a telephone conversation between Barry Goldwater and Stephen Shadegg, January 4, 1957, Barry Goldwater Collection, Box 480, Barker History Center.

5. Interview with Barry Goldwater by Ed Edwin, June 15, 1967, Eisenhower Presidential Library.

6. *New York Times*, January 5, 1957, p. 1, January 6, 1957, pp. 1, 34, 35.

7. Quoted in Hughes, *Ordeal*, 236.

8. Quoted in Reinhard, *Republican Right*, 138.

9. U.S. Senate, 86th Cong., 1st sess., April 8, 1957, *Congressional Record* 105: 5258–65 (quotations found on 5259).

10. Ibid., 5260–61.

11. Reinhard, *Republican Right*, 139–42; Alexander, *Holding the Line*, 191–93; *Chicago Tribune*, April 9, 1957; *New York Times*, April 9, 1957, p. 27, April 28, 1957, sect. 4, p. 3; "People of the Week," *U.S. News and World Report*, April 19, 1957, 20; "The Backward Look," *Time*, April 22, 1957, 25–26; "The Republican Split," *Time*, May 20, 1957, 26. In the end, Congress cut about $4 billion from the Eisenhower budget.

12. Barry Goldwater to Dwight Eisenhower, April 9, 1957, Box 514, Official File, White House Central Files, Eisenhower Presidential Library.

13. *Chicago Tribune*, April 23, 1957.

14. *New York Times*, April 11, 1957, p. 11.

15. Jack Z. Anderson to Ann C. Whitman, April 13, 1957, Box 23, DDE Diary Series, Ann C. Whitman File, Eisenhower Presidential Library.

16. Dwight Eisenhower to Barry Goldwater, April 23, 1957, Box 514, Official File, White House Central Files, Eisenhower Presidential Library.

17. Goldwater to Eisenhower, July 1, 1957, Box 370, Official File, White House Central Files, Eisenhower Presidential Library.

18. Eisenhower to Goldwater, July 2, 1957, Box 370, Official File, White House Central Files, Eisenhower Presidential Library.

19. "Public Record," 1585, 1594, 1601.

20. Goldwater, *Goldwater*, 100; McClellan, *Crime*, 18, 208; Kennedy, *Enemy*, 23–24, 166; Barnard, *Walter Reuther*, 163.

21. McClellan, *Crime*, 21, 53, 71–72, 93, 104, 114, 143, 147, 161, 176, 180, 209–10; Kennedy, *Enemy*, 42, 88, 92, 136, 154, 161–62, 190, 196, 200, 207, 212; Lee, *Eisenhower*, 60–63; U.S. Senate, Select Committee on Improper Activities in the Labor or Management Field, 85th Cong., 1st sess., 1957, Part 13, 4964–65.

22. Barnard, *Walter Reuther*, 4, 8, 12, 15–16, 37, 56–57, 155, 213.

23. Quoted in Smith, *Goldwaters*, 207.

24. Quoted in Lee, *Eisenhower*, 66.

25. Goldwater speech to the Chamber of Commerce, in *Congressional Digest* 36 (October 21, 1957): 238.

26. "Salt and Pepper," *Time*, February 3, 1958, 13.

27. Detroit *Times*, January 21, 1958. See also, Detroit *News*, February 1, 1958, March 9, 1958.

28. Quoted in McDowell, *Barry Goldwater*, 123.

29. *Arizona Republic*, March 30, 1958.

30. "Salt and Pepper," 13.

31. "Goldwater's Racket," *New Republic*, September 23, 1957, 4–5; Lee, *Eisenhower*, 70; Goldwater, *Goldwater*, 101.

32. Quoted in Lee, *Eisenhower*, 71.

33. *New York Times*, March 2, 1958, sect. 4, p. 4.

34. Herbert Kohler was a supporter of conservative causes with strong ties to Clarence Manion and Robert Welch. Kohler advertised his company in the John Birch Society magazine, *American Opinion*, and he sat on the national advisory board of the Young Americans for Freedom.

35. In 1960 the National Labor Relations Board found the Kohler Company guilty of unfair practices that prolonged the strike and aimed to destroy the union. The U.S. Court of Appeals sustained this judgment, and in 1965 the company and union agreed to a $4.5 million settlement providing for back pay and pension credits. See Uphoff, *Kohler*, 389, 420–21.

36. Uphoff, *Kohler*, 2, 121–29, 132, 146–47, 182–84, 195, 383–84; Kennedy, *Enemy*, 266–85, 290–95.

37. Select Committee Hearings, 85th Cong., 2nd sess., 1958, Part 25, 10053.

38. Ibid., 10252.

39. Ibid., Parts 21 and 25, passim; Uphoff, *Kohler*, 271–88; Kennedy, *Enemy*, 297.

40. Quoted in McDowell, *Barry Goldwater*, 127. See also *New York Times*, February, 16, 1960, p. 30, for the Republican minority report that accused Robert Kennedy of a cover-up in refusing to investigate a "clear pattern of crime and violence" in UAW activity.

41. Uphoff, *Kohler*, 291; Lee, *Eisenhower*, 81–90; U.S. Senate, 85th Cong., 1st sess., June 13, 1958, *Congressional Record* 103: 11080; Kennedy, *Enemy*, 298–99. The hearings produced the Kennedy-Ives Bill, which proposed stricter regulation of union pension and welfare funds, a secret ballot in union elections, and curbs on unfair picketing. Although Goldwater initially condemned the legislation as a "weak, mousy bill" and a "sweetheart bill," amendments strengthened its terms and he backed passage. The bill passed the Senate in the summer of 1958, but it was defeated in the House of Representatives.

42. *New York Post*, May 8, 1961.

43. "Goldwater vs. Kennedy," *Commonwealth*, June 20, 1958, 293.

44. *New York Times*, October 13, 1958, p. 32.

45. Speech by Ernest McFarland, "Campaign Materials," 1958, Box 142, Ernest McFarland Papers, McFarland State Historical Park.

46. Berman, *Parties*, 20; Rice, "1958 Election," 267; *New York Times*, October 13, 1958, p. 32; *Arizona Republic*, October 5, 1958; "Campaign Materials," Box 142, McFarland Papers.

47. Ross R. Rice, "Arizona: Politics in Transition," in Jonas, *Politics*, 66; Stephen Shadegg to Barry Goldwater, June 27, 1958, Box 480, Goldwater Collection, Barker History Center.

48. *Arizona Republic*, September 6, 1958.

49. Frank H. Jonas and R. John Eyre, "The Newspaper as a Giant Public Relations Firm in Politics," in Jonas, *Political Dynamiting*, 144; Rice, "Arizona," 52–53, 67; Wood and Smith, *Barry Goldwater*, 119.

50. Shadegg, *How to Win*, 19.

51. "Proposed Campaign Strategy," Box 489, Goldwater Collection, Barker History Center.

52. *Arizona Republic*, September 11, 1958.

53. Ibid., October 16, 1958.

54. Ibid., September 5, 1958.

55. Ibid., September 8, 1958.

56. *Phoenix Gazette*, May 24, 1958; *Arizona Republic*, May 4, 1958.

57. "Compulsory Unionism," Box 3y330, Goldwater Collection, Barker History Center.

58. Barry Goldwater to Nelson Lupe, October 1, 1958, Box 487, Goldwater Collection, Barker History Center.

59. "Compulsory Unionism," Box 3y330, "National Defense," Box 3y332, "Radio Spots," Box 487, Goldwater Collection, Barker History Center; Rice, "Arizona," 51; Shadegg, *How to Win*, 163.

60. Shadegg, *How to Win*, 126.

61. Ibid., 26, 129–30; Stephen Shadegg to Frank Jonas, December 18, 1958, Frank Jonas Papers, University of Utah; Goldwater, *With No Apologies*, 90; *Arizona Republic*, September, 14, 1958, October 20, 1958, November 1, 1958; *Phoenix Gazette*, December 3, 1986; "Itinerary," Box 489, Goldwater Collection, Barker History Center; "Campaign Materials," Box 142, McFarland Papers.

62. Raymond Moley, "The Issue in Arizona," *Newsweek*, September 23, 1957, 120.

63. Raymond Moley, "Test in Arizona," *Newsweek*, March 24, 1958, 112.

64. Paul Healy, "The Glittering Mr. Goldwater," *Saturday Evening Post*, June 7, 1958, 39, 116.

65. "Personality Contest," *Time*, September 29, 1958, 15.

66. *New York Times*, October 13, 1958, p. 32.

67. *Arizona Republic*, March 24, 1958, October 19, 1958.

68. *Phoenix Gazette*, April 18, 1958.

69. Jonas, *Political Dynamiting*, 2.

70. Jonas and Eyre, "Newspaper," 169, 175–76; *Arizona Republic*, November 1, 1958. More restrained was the support Goldwater received from the *Arizona Daily Sun* (Flagstaff), the *Arizona Daily Star* (Tucson), the *Yuma Sun*, the *Prescott Courier*, and the *Douglas Dispatch*.

71. *Arizona Republic*, October 1, 1958.

72. Ibid., September, 11, 20, 21, 29, and 30, 1958, October 1, 2, 5, 8, 10, 12, 14, 16, 17, and 18, 1958.

73. Green had been involved in strike violence and arrested twice during the 1940s.

74. *Arizona Republic*, October 19, 1958; Jonas and Eyre, "Newspaper," 157–58.

75. Stephen Shadegg to Frank Jonas, May 27, 1959, Jonas Papers; Jonas and Eyre, "Newspaper," 143–44, 147, 152–54, 175; Frank H. Jonas and R. John Eyre,

"The Unintentional Smear," in Jonas, *Political Dynamiting,* 188; Shadegg, *Arizona Politics,* 85–87, 91, 93 (quote); *Arizona Republic,* October 20, 1958.

76. *Arizona Republic,* October 21, 1958.

77. Copies of speeches found in Box 487, Goldwater Collection, Barker History Center; *Arizona Republic* October 24 and 30, 1958.

78. *Arizona Republic,* October 24, 1958.

79. Ibid., October 21, 25 (quote), 29, and 30, 1958.

80. Ibid., October 21 and 26, 1958.

81. Ibid., October 25, 1958; McFarland, *MAC,* 296; Jonas and Eyre, "Newspaper," 164.

82. *Arizona Republic,* November 1, 1958.

83. Ibid.

84. Ibid., November 4, 1958.

85. Ibid., November 2, 1958.

86. Ibid., November 4, 1958.

87. Jonas and Eyre, "Unintentional Smear," 183–98, 204–7; Shadegg, *Barry Goldwater,* 138; *Arizona Republic,* October 20, 1958, November 2 and 3, 1958; *Phoenix Gazette,* February 10, 1959; *New York Times,* February 14, 1959, p. 10; Transcript of a telephone conversation between Barry Goldwater and James Duffy, October 1958, Box 2.325/SI, Goldwater Collection, Barker History Center.

88. *New York Times,* November 5, 1958, pp. 1, 20; *Arizona Republic,* November 5, 1958; Stephen Shadegg to Barry Goldwater, January 10, 1958, Box 506, Goldwater Collection, Barker History Center; Rice, "1958 Election," 271–73.

89. Hess, *In a Cause,* 9; Evans, *Future,* 222; *New York Times,* November 5, 1958, p. 1.

90. Barry Goldwater to Richard Nixon, December 16, 1958, Richard Nixon to Barry Goldwater, December 30, 1958, Richard M. Nixon Vice Presidential Papers, National Archives, Pacific Southwest Region.

91. Quoted in Kramer and Roberts, *"I Never,"* 5.

92. Ibid.

93. Roberts, *Conservative Decade,* 26.

94. Wrage, "Little World," 115.

95. "This Lively Man—Goldwater," *Newsweek,* July 4, 1960, 26.; "The Conservative King," *Time,* August 8, 1960, 16; "A New Force for '64: Goldwater Builds a Following," *U.S. News and World Report,* April 10, 1961, 65.

96. Interview with Jonathan Marshall, October 25, 1990.

97. "Miracle in Arizona: Phoenix Rises and Soars," *Newsweek,* January 4, 1960, 45.

98. "The American Desert, 1955: A New Way of Life in the U.S.," *Time,* July 25, 1955, 44, 53.

99. Harold H. Martin, "The New Millionaires of Phoenix," *Saturday Evening Post,* September 30, 1961, 26–27.

100. Leggett, "Arizona," 51–52; Leonard E. Goodall, "Phoenix: Reformers at Work," in Goodall, *Urban Politics,* 110; Tansik and Billings, "Current Impact," 11–12.

101. Sale, *Power Shift,* 148.

102. Nash, *American West,* 217, 233–36, 248; Clayton, "Impact," 449–50, 453–54, 462, 464, 467, 471, 473.

103. *New York Times,* April 20, 1959, p. 2; Goldwater, *With No Apologies,* 74.

104. Address to the Traffic Club of Pittsburgh, Pennsylvania, *Congressional Digest,* August 1959, 218.

105. Quoted in Sorensen, *Kennedy,* 54.

106. *New York Times,* January 31, 1959, p. 22; U.S. Senate, 86th Cong., 1st sess., April 21, 1959, *Congressional Record* 105: 6389–90; Lee, *Eisenhower,* 115; Barry Goldwater to Stephen Shadegg, July 29, 1977, Alpha File.

107. Edwin McCabe to Bob Gray, April 6, 1959, Box 631, Official File, White House Central Files, Eisenhower Presidential Library.

108. Ibid.

109. "Staff Notes," July 21, 1959, Box 43, DDE Diary Series, Whitman File, Eisenhower Presidential Library; Lee, *Eisenhower,* 100–101, 105–8, 117, 123–24, 127, 130–31, 135, 156–57.

110. *New York Times,* January 22, 1959, p. 17, March 12, 1959, p. 28, April 18, 1959, p. 18; Barry Goldwater to Elizabeth Brown, July 22, 1959, Box 2, Elizabeth Churchill Brown Papers, Hoover Institution Archives.

111. "Campus Conservatives," *Time,* February 10, 1961, 38.

112. Nash, *Conservative Intellectual Movement,* 152; McEvoy, *Radicals or Conservatives,* 18–20; Evans, *Revolt,* 32, 59–60; Milton Friedman to Barry Goldwater, December 12, 1960, Box 73, Milton Friedman Collection, Hoover Institution Archives. Stephen Shadegg was in contact with such conservatives as Dan Smoot, J. Howard Pew, and W. Cleon Skousen. See Shadegg to Barry Goldwater, March 8, 1961, Box 506, Goldwater Collection, Barker History Center.

113. Welch, *Blue Book,* 9, 18–28, 33, 59–64, 104, 141; Broyles, *John Birch Society,* 12, 17, 102–12, 118.

114. Kolkey, *New Right, 1960–1968,* 82.

115. Ibid., 79.

116. Ibid., 77.

117. Pasted on the front of American Opinion bookstore copies of Goldwater's *The Conscience of a Conservative* was a sticker reading: "This book belongs to, and has been approved by, the JOHN BIRCH SOCIETY." In the author's possession.

118. Forster and Epstein, *Danger,* 42. Compare quotations in *Danger on the Right* with those toned down in subsequent editions of *The Politician.* For example, see Welch, *The Politician,* 5–6, 277–79.

119. Goldwater interview by Edwin.

120. Welch, *Blue Book,* 119–20.

121. Goldwater interview by Edwin.

122. Goldwater, *Goldwater,* 127.

123. Rusher, *Rise of the Right,* 63. In 1961, the Justice Department leaked information that Barry Goldwater had, in May 1959, joined the Committee Against

Summit Entanglements, a Birch Society front organization. *Newsweek*, April 17, 1961, 32.

124. Denison Kitchel resigned from the John Birch Society after reading *The Politician*. His resignation letter was blind copied to Barry Goldwater. Denison Kitchel to Robert Welch, June 8, 1960, Box 3, Denison Kitchel Collection, Hoover Institution Archives.

125. Goldberg, *Grassroots Resistance*, 116–40; Quoted in Kolkey, *New Right*, 209.

126. Interview with Barry Goldwater, September 24, 1992.

127. Buchanan, "Voice," ix.

128. Goldwater interview, September 24, 1992; *Phoenix Gazette*, December 3, 1986; Goldwater, *Goldwater*, 120; Goldwater, *With No Apologies*, 99–100. Kirk is quoted on the flyleaf of *The Conscience of a Conservative*.

129. Barry Goldwater, *Conscience*, 5, 9, 10, 13, 20, 22.

130. Ibid., 30, 32, 42, 69, 51, 54, 66, 70.

131. Ibid., 23.

132. Ibid., 31, 33, 34, 37.

133. Ibid., 87, 89–90, 95–99.

134. Ibid., 100–101, 105–11, 114, 118–20.

135. Ibid., 121–22.

136. Ibid.; Robert Sheehan, "Arizona Fundamentalist," *Fortune*, May 1961, 254.

137. Shadegg, *Barry Goldwater*, 154; Goldwater to Shadegg, January 20, 1960, Shadegg to Goldwater, January 12, 1960, Box 506, Goldwater Collection, Barker History Center; Stephen Shadegg, *What Happened*, 7, 25–26; "The Senator-Columnist," *Newsweek*, February 2, 1960, 49–50; Paul Sexson to Bernice Miller, January 19, 1960, Box 70, Herbert Hoover Post-Presidential Papers, Herbert Hoover Presidential Library. Goldwater donated to charity the $1,600 he received each month for his columns.

138. "Strictly Confidential" meeting minutes, May, 15, 1959, Box 147, J. Bracken Lee Papers, University of Utah.

139. Ibid.; "Goldwater Committee," July 31, 1959, Box 147, Lee Papers; Box 505, Goldwater Collection, Barker History Center.

140. Hammerback, "Barry Goldwater's Rhetoric," 175; Bell, *Mr. Conservative*, 10; Raymond Moley to Barry Goldwater, May 26, 1960, Box 19, Raymond Moley Collection, Hoover Institution and Archives; "Itinerary for 1960," Box 506, Goldwater Collection, Barker History Center; *New York Times*, May 8, 1960, p. 32.

141. William Rehnquist to Barry Goldwater, March 28, 1960, Goldwater to Rehnquist, March 31, 1960, Box 506, Goldwater Collection, Barker History Center.

142. Goldwater, *With No Apologies*, 103.

143. Stephen Shadegg estimated that Goldwater could win as many as 275 first-ballot votes for president but listed only sixty-seven as firm. In addition to votes from Arizona, Louisiana, and South Carolina, Shadegg marked scattered support in the California, Tennessee, Nebraska, Mississippi, Washington, Georgia,

Virginia, Pennsylvania, North Carolina, Idaho, Wisconsin, Wyoming, and Nevada delegations. Nixon adviser Leonard Hall put the Arizonan's strength at three hundred delegates. Barry Goldwater "counted 59 at the top." Reinhard, *Republican Right*, 154; Transcript of a telephone conversation between Stephen Shadegg and Dan Smoot, September 16, 1960, Box 506, Barry Goldwater to Shadegg (letter), September 1, 1961, Box 3J7, Goldwater Collection, Barker History Center.

144. Quoted in Shadegg, *What Happened*, 32.

145. White, *Suite 3505*, 19; Goldwater, *With No Apologies*, 101–2; *New York Times*, March 27, 1960, p. 31, May 15, 1960, p. 1, June 15, 1960, p. 24.

146. "Campaigns," Box 9, Series 5, Jacob K. Javits Collection, State University of New York at Stony Brook.

147. Evans, *Revolt*, 91; Gregory Shorey, Jr., to Barry Goldwater, July 11, 1960, and Shorey to L. Brent Bozell, July 6, 1960, Box 506, and Boxes 505 and 506, passim, Goldwater Collection, Barker History Center; Elizabeth Brown to Barry Goldwater, August 9, 1960, Box 2, Brown Collection.

148. White, *Making of the President 1960*, 210–18, 424–26; Rae, *Decline*, 41–43; Kramer and Roberts, *"I Never,"* 230–34.

149. *New York Times*, July 24, 1960, p. 38.

150. Goldwater, *Goldwater*, 256.

151. Quoted in White, *Making of the President 1960*, 223.

152. *New York Times*, July 24, 1960, p. 38; White, *Making of the President 1960*, 219; Reinhard, *Republican Right*, 152.

153. Goldwater, *With No Apologies*, 112.

154. Louisiana's ten delegates refused to switch to Richard Nixon and cast their votes for Barry Goldwater.

155. Goldwater, *With No Apologies*, 111–12; Shadegg, *Arizona Politics*, 106; Evans, *Revolt*, 102–3; *New York Times*, July 28, 1960, p. 14. Barry Goldwater underestimated the power of his words and the will of conservatives. A little more than a month after the convention, he wrote: "Conservatives are not interested . . . in the dirty, hard work of obtaining control of the political party. They would much rather sit around their tea tables, their gin rummy games, or their meetings agreeing with each other instead of taking on the opposition." Barry Goldwater to Elizabeth Brown, September 1, 1960, Box 2, Brown Collection.

156. Buchanan, "Voice," ix.

157. *New York Times*, August 7, 1960, p. 9.

158. Harry Jeffrey to the author, September 28, 1991.

159. Quoted in Kramer and Roberts, *"I Never,"* 235.

160. *New York Times*, October 23, 1960, p. 26.

161. Quoted in White, *Making of the President 1960*, 356.

162. *New York Times*, October 12, 1961, p. 31.

163. Ibid., October 9, 1960, p. 48.

164. Ibid., October 12, 1960, p. 31.

165. Ibid., October 9, 1960, p. 48; "Conservative Crusader," *Time*, October 17, 1960, 23.

166. White, *Making of the President 1960*, 382–83. An Oklahoma presidential elector cast his vote to elect South Carolina Senator Strom Thurmond as president and Barry Goldwater as vice president.

167. Ibid., 391; Quoted in Bell, *Mr. Conservative*, 130.

168. "Press Release," November 9, 1960, Box 68, Lewis L. Strauss Papers, Hoover Presidential Library.

169. "The Mourning After," *Time*, November 21, 1960, 21.

170. *New York Times*, November 10, 1960, p. 38.

171. Connery and Benjamin, *Rockefeller*, 74.

172. Barry Goldwater to Elizabeth Brown, December 13, 1960, Box 2, Brown Collection.

173. Transcript of a telephone conversation between Shadegg and Smoot, Box 506, Goldwater Collection, Barker History Center.

174. Telephone interview with William F. Buckley, Jr., August 10, 1990; Evans, *Revolt*, 108–10.

175. Bell, *Mr. Conservative*, 64.

176. Goldwater, *Goldwater*, xii.

177. Riordan, *Plunkitt*, 3.

Chapter 7: Like a Desert Wash in Flood

Epigraph: Goldwater and Kennedy cited in Michael Leahy, "I'd Have Ended the Vietnam War in a Week or Two," *New Choices*, December 1992–January 1992.

1. *New York Times*, July 3, 1961, p. 1.

2. "Apostle of Conservatism," *Business Week*, March 25, 1961, 34; "Salesman for a Cause," *Time*, June 23, 1961, 12.

3. Novak, *Agony*, 36–38; *New York Times*, July 24, 1959, p. 15, January 6, 1961, p. 14; "Making the Rounds," *Time*, June 16, 1961, 16; Faber, *Road*, 75; Evans, *Revolt*, 106; Murray Gait, "Green and Fertile Field for the Goldwater Rush," *Life*, November 1, 1963, 32; Rusher, *Rise of the Right*, 98.

4. *New York Times*, July 3, 1961, p. 1.

5. "The Goldwater Story—How It Is Growing," *U.S. News and World Report*, August 7, 1961, 58.

6. Text of Barry Goldwater's speech to the Young Americans for Freedom Rally, March 3, 1961, New York City, Box 38, Jacob K. Javits Collection, University of New York at Stony Brook.

7. Shadegg, *Barry Goldwater*, 172; *New York Times*, July 3, 1961, p. 1; White, *Suite 3505*, 31; Gilbert A. Harrison, "Carry Me Back: Some Notes on Barry Goldwater," *New Republic*, March 27, 1961, 13.

8. U.S. Senate, 87th Cong., 1st sess., January 11, 1961, *Congressional Record* 107: 576–85; Bell, *Mr. Conservative*, 175. New Left groups like the Students for a

Democratic Society (SDS) shared such sentiments. See SDS's *The Port Huron Statement*.

9. U.S. Senate, 87th Cong., 1st sess., January 11, 1961, *Congressional Record* 107: 576–85.

10. Quoted in Bass and DeVries, *Transformation*, 27.

11. "Goldwater's Platform for 'The Forgotten American,'" *U.S. News and World Report*, January 23, 1961, 52–54; "The Forgotten American," parts 1 and 2, *Human Events*, January 27, 1961, 57–60, 61–64; Novak, *Agony*, 25–31.

12. Goldwater, *With No Apologies*, 137.

13. Barry Goldwater Papers, Arizona Historical Foundation.

14. Barry Goldwater to Stephen Shadegg, March 18, 1977, Alpha File, Goldwater Papers.

15. Goldwater, *With No Apologies*, 122. Lyndon Johnson's reply deflected Goldwater's characterization of Kennedy to focus on his comments about the Democratic Party's "socialist platform." The Texas senator wrote that "all of us have to decide for ourselves what represents a 'socialist platform.'" Johnson, *Vantage Point*, 102.

16. *Arizona Republic*, January 1, 1989; Interview with Benjamin Bradlee, September 10, 1990; Interview with George McGovern, September 12, 1990; O'Donnell and Powers, *"Johnny,"* 213; Sorensen, *Kennedy*, 754.

17. Quoted in Bell, *Mr. Conservative*, 148.

18. U.S. Senate, 87th Cong., 1st sess., June 12, 1961, *Congressional Record* 107: 9955.

19. *New York Times*, January 21, 1961, p. 36, January 31, 1961, p. 1; McDowell, *Barry Goldwater*, 168–71; Barry Goldwater, letter to the editor, *The Reporter*, November 22, 1962, 6, 8.

20. Quoted in Wood and Smith, *Barry Goldwater*, 170.

21. Bell, *Mr. Conservative*, 65; U.S. Senate, 87th Cong., 1st sess., April 18, 1961, *Congressional Record* 107: 6111, May 23, 1961, 8664–72, May 24, 1961, 8720–33; Matusow, *Unraveling*, 97–107; Barry Goldwater to Stephen Shadegg, July 24, 1961, Box 3J5, Barry Goldwater Collection, Barker History Center.

22. Goldberg, *Grassroots Resistance*, 141–66.

23. Quoted in Sorensen, *Kennedy*, 471.

24. Lawson, *Black Ballots*, 255, 259–60; Piven and Cloward, *Poor People's Movements*, 227–29; Miroff, *Pragmatic Illusions*, 223–70.

25. Lawson, *Black Ballots*, 261–66; Piven and Cloward, *Poor People's Movements*, 225–32; Sorensen, *Kennedy*, 478–79; McAdam, *Political Process*, 157–58.

26. *New York Post*, May 11, 1961.

27. *New York Times*, April 8, 1963, p. 2.

28. Denison Kitchel to Barry Goldwater, November 12, 1962, Box 2, Denison Kitchel Collection, Hoover Institution Archives.

29. Bell, *Mr. Conservative*, 67, 137; McDowell, *Barry Goldwater*, 177; *New York Times*, November 19, 1961, p. 70 (quote), July 17, 1964, p. 12.

30. *New York Times*, August 23, 1962, p. 59.

31. U.S. Senate, 88th Cong., 1st sess., June 19, 1963, *Congressional Record* 109: 11084.

32. Address to the Young Americans for Freedom, March 7, 1962, Barry Goldwater Speeches, January–May 1962, vol. 1, Goldwater Papers.

33. *New York Times,* July 15, 1961, p. 12.

34. Barry Goldwater to Stephen Shadegg, March 18, 1977, Alpha File, Goldwater Papers.

35. Goldwater, *Goldwater,* 137.

36. Ibid., 136.

37. *New York Times,* August 2, 1971, p. 1.

38. Goldwater, *With No Apologies,* 138–40; Goldwater, *Goldwater,* 134–37; Lawrence O'Brien to Barry Goldwater, May 9, 1961, White House Staff Files, John F. Kennedy Papers, John F. Kennedy Presidential Library; Quote in *New York Times,* September 15, 1962, p. 1.

39. U.S. Senate, 87th Cong., 1st sess., April 20, 1961 *Congressional Record* 107: 6349.

40. *New York Times,* January 20, 1962, p. 9.

41. Goldwater, *Why?* 32; *New York Times,* July 14, 1962, p. 11; Address to the Annual United Press International Conference of Editors and Publishers, in U.S. Senate, 87th Cong., 1st sess., June 12, 1961, *Congressional Record* 107: 9953.

42. Goldwater, *Why?* 24, 155.

43. Ibid., 39, 87–88, 97, 115, 133, 138–39, 142, 154.

44. Himmelstein, *To the Right,* 67; Rusher, *Rise of the Right,* 97; White, *Making of the President 1964,* 94; Epstein and Forster, *Radical Right,* 6–7; *New York Times,* March 10, 1961, p. 60.

45. "The Americanists," *Time,* March 10, 1961, 22.

46. *Los Angeles Times,* March 12, 1961.

47. "Storm Over Birchers," *Time,* April 7, 1961, 18.

48. *New York Times,* April 8, 1961, p. 13; George Barrett, "Close-up of the Birchers' Founder," *New York Times Magazine,* May 14, 1961, sect. 6, pp. 13, 89, 91, 92; "The John Birch Society: Patriotic or Irresponsible, it is subject of controversy," *Life,* May 12, 1961, 124–30; "Wide-Swinging Bitter-Enders of the Right," *Newsweek,* April 10, 1961, 43–44; Chester Morrison, "The Man Behind the John Birch Society," *Look,* September 26, 1961, 23–27; Stephen M. Young, "Danger on the Right," *Saturday Evening Post,* January 13, 1962, 6–7.

49. William F. Buckley, Jr., "The Uproar," *National Review,* April 22, 1961, 242–43.

50. *New York Times,* September 29, 1961, p. 15.

51. Quoted in Bell, *Mr. Conservative,* 89.

52. *New York Times,* April 6, 1961, p. 16.

53. Barry Goldwater, "Danger on the Left," *Saturday Evening Post,* January 20, 1962, 8.

54. Bell, *Mr. Conservative,* 89; *New York Times,* April 6, 1961, p. 16, November

19, 1961, p. 70, November 20, 1961, p. 34, January 12, 1962, p. 2, October 10, 1964, p. 16; Broyles, *John Birch Society*, 107; Interview with Denison Kitchel, November 18, 1989.

55. Kirk, "Sword," 471.

56. Quoted in Judis, *Buckley*, 198.

57. Ibid.

58. Kirk, "Sword," 471–74; Judis, *Buckley*, 198–99.

59. *National Review*, February 13, 1962, 83–88.

60. Russell Kirk and Benjamin L. Masse, "The Birchers," *America*, February 17, 1962, 643.

61. *National Review*, February 27, 1962, 140.

62. "Newsmakers," *Newsweek*, February 19, 1962, 57.

63. Goldberg, *Grassroots Resistance*, 125–30.

64. Telephone interview with George Romney, April 6, 1992; Desmond, *Rockefeller*, 22, 114, 138, 144.

65. Connery and Benjamin, *Rockefeller*, 73; White, *Making of the President 1964*, 80; "Left and Right," *Newsweek*, March 19, 1962, 37.

66. Quoted in Novak, *Agony*, 74.

67. Goldwater, *Goldwater*, 139; Novak, *Agony*, 39, 69–76; Interview with Barry Goldwater by William Cooper, Jr., May 14, 1979; Goldwater, *With No Apologies*, 158.

68. "Goldwater's Look Ahead," *U.S. News and World Report*, October 22, 1962, 62.

69. Novak, *Agony*, 77–78.

70. Ibid., 122–24; White, *Making of the President 1964*, 94–95; White, *Suite 3505*, 24, 26–28, 31–35, 38; Rusher, *Rise of the Right*, 101.

71. White, *Suite 3505*, 37–40, 56; Rae, *Decline*, 55–56.

72. Rusher, *Rise of the Right*, 103–4.

73. Quoted in White, *Suite 3505*, 46.

74. Ibid., 45.

75. Rusher, *Rise of the Right*, 104–6; White, *Suite 3505*, 44, 45 (quote), 46.

76. Barry Goldwater to Stephen Shadegg, April 23, 1958, Box 480, Goldwater Collection, Barker History Center.

77. Rusher, *Rise of the Right*, 88.

78. Quoted in Shadegg, *Arizona Politics*, 122.

79. White, *Suite 3505*, 43; Rusher, *Rise of the Right*, 88, 144.

80. White, *Suite 3505*, 47–48, 52–55; Rusher, *Rise of the Right*, 107–11, 135.

81. White, *Suite 3505*, 61–62, 75–76; Rusher, *Rise of the Right*, 137.

82. White, *Suite 3505*, 56.

83. Quoted in Dudman, *Men of the Far Right*, 23.

84. Lorene and Phil Le Feurne to James J. Barry, January 6, 1962, Box 507, Goldwater Collection, Barker History Center; White, *Suite 3505*, 55–56, 79 (quote), 85–86.

85. *New York Times*, April 15, 1962, p. 49.

86. Ibid., May 8, 1962, p. 50.

87. Ibid., July 3, 1962, p. 10.

88. Barry Goldwater to Dwight Eisenhower, November 14, 1961, Box 8, Principle File, Post-Presidential Papers, Dwight David Eisenhower Presidential Library.

89. Dwight Eisenhower to Charles Jones, July 3, 1962, Special Names Series, Post-Presidential Papers, Eisenhower Library.

90. Goldwater, *With No Apologies,* 146.

91. Ibid., 148.

92. Barry Goldwater to Norris Cotton, October 30, 1962, Box 17, Norris Cotton Collection, University of New Hampshire.

93. Goldwater, *With No Apologies,* 149.

94. From the title of Herman Kahn's 1962 book on nuclear war.

95. Barry Goldwater, "The G.O.P. Invades the South," *Saturday Evening Post,* April 13, 1962, 10, 12; Reinhard, *Republican Right,* 164; White, *Making of the President 1964,* 97; Mayer, *Republican Party,* 518; Tindall, *Disruption,* 60.

96. Novak, *Agony,* 84, 86–88; Desmond, *Rockefeller,* 308; Reinhard, *Republican Right,* 166–67.

97. Quoted in Shadegg, *Arizona Politics,* 113.

98. Kitchel interview.

99. Shadegg exacerbated the dispute in 1965 when he sold to the Barker History Center files from Goldwater's Senate races in 1952 and 1958 and from his bid for the Republican nomination for president in 1960.

100. Shadegg, *What Happened,* 52–53; Shadegg, *Arizona Politics,* xix, 113; Kitchel interview; Watkins, *High Crimes,* 30–31.

101. White, *Suite 3505,* 91.

102. Ibid., 101.

103. Ibid., 88–101; Rusher, *Rise of the Right,* 138–39.

104. White, *Suite 3505,* 117.

105. Ibid., 118.

106. Ibid., 102–18; Telephone conversation between Stephen Shadegg and Peter O'Donnell, February 1963, Box 3J9, Goldwater Collection, Barker History Center.

107. "Program," December 23, 1962, Box 4, Kitchel Collection.

108. Ibid.

109. *Arizona Republic,* January 12, 1963.

110. Quoted in White, *Suite 3505,* 123.

111. Rusher, *Rise of the Right,* 144–45; White, *Suite 3505,* 119–28, 158.

112. Ibid., 132.

113. Rusher, *Rise of the Right,* 146.

114. "Goldwater for President? A Drive is Launched," *U.S. News and World Report,* April 22, 1963, 25; "'Draft Goldwater' Move Starts—Its Meaning," *U.S. News and World Report,* April 29, 1963, 42–44; *New York Times,* April 9, 1963, p. 25.

115. "This Presidential Thing," *Time,* June 14, 1963, 30.

116. Novak, *Agony,* 128.

117. *New York Times,* April 24, 1963, p. 32, April 26, 1963, p. 12, July 16, 1963, p. 1; Barry Goldwater to Leeland R. Corbett, May 24, 1963, Orren Beaty Jr., Papers, in the author's possession; Shadegg, *What Happened,* 64.

118. White, *Suite 3505,* 145–46; Novak, *Agony,* 174.

119. Quoted in Toledano, *Winning Side,* 144.

120. "This Presidential Thing," 26–27.

121. Novak, *Agony,* 140; White, *Making of the President 1964,* 86.

122. Novak, *Agony,* 224.

123. Quoted in Wolfe, "Southern Strategy," 145.

124. "G.O.P. Opens with a Pair," *Business Week,* May 5, 1963, 36.

125. Novak, *Agony,* 149–50; "The Block-Goldwater Movement in the GOP," *Newsweek,* July 22, 1963, 19.

126. White, *Making of the President 1964,* 97, 99; White, *Suite 3505,* 162 (quote), 181–86; Rusher, *Rise of the Right,* 146.

127. "He's Rolling Along Like a Tumbleweed," *Life,* July 12, 1963, 23; White, *Suite 3505,* 168–71; Novak, *Agony,* 176 (quote), 177–80, 195–202.

128. Quoted in Kramer and Roberts, *"I Never,"* 274.

129. White, *Suite 3505,* 173.

130. Novak, *Agony,* 210.

131. Ibid., 216.

132. "Time to Hear From Goldwater," *Life,* July 26, 1963, 4; Novak, *Agony,* 203–11, 215–16; Goldwater, *Goldwater,* 142–44; Kramer and Roberts, *"I Never,"* 276–77.

133. "The Wraps are Off," *Newsweek,* July 22, 1963, 41.

134. Novak, *Agony,* 212, 213.

135. Rusher, *Rise of the Right,* 157; White, *Suite 3505,* 199–207, 214, 217; Kitchel interview; White, *Making of the President 1964,* 99; Clif White to Barry Goldwater, June 7, 1963, Goldwater to White, June 12, 1963, Box 4, Kitchel Collection.

136. Matusow, *Unraveling,* 85–93.

137. Barry Goldwater to Denison Kitchel, June 19, 1963, Box 2, Kitchel Collection.

138. Barry Goldwater to Elizabeth Churchill Brown, July 19, 1963, and July 27, 1963, Box 2, Elizabeth Churchill Brown Collection, Hoover Institution Archives.

139. "Where Barry Stands," *Time,* August 13, 1963, 13; *New York Times,* June 21, 1963, p. 1, June 23, 1963, p. 8.

140. Barry Goldwater to William Saufley, September 27, 1963, William Saufley Papers, Arizona Historical Foundation.

141. U.S. Senate, 88th Cong., 1st sess., September 19, 1963, *Congressional Record* 109: 17557.

142. Ibid., September 19, 1963, 109: 17558.

143. Ibid., August 8, 1963, 109: 14545, August 13, 1963, 109: 14849–50, August 19, 1963, 109: 15287–91, August 23, 1963, 109: 15743–44, August 27, 1963, 109: 15927–28, September 5, 1963, 109: 16408–12, September 19, 1963, 109: 17557–58,

September 23, 1963, 109: 17723; *New York Times*, July 25, 1963, p. 2, August 20, 1963, p. 1, September 6, 1963, p. 1, September 20, 1963, pp. 1, 9, September 24, 1963, p. 1; *Arizona Republic*, September 20, 1963; Quoted in Hess, *In a Cause*, 85. In 1992 Congress imposed a moratorium on all nuclear testing until July 1, 1993. President Bill Clinton announced on its expiration that the United States would follow a "no-first-test option" and not resume testing unless other nations did.

144. "For Goldwater There's No More Free-Wheeling," *Business Week*, October 5, 1963, 30.

145. *New York Times*, September 20, 1963, p. 22.

146. "In Front and Getting Farther," *Time*, September 27, 1963, 23.

147. Gilbert A. Harrison, "Way Out West," *The New Republic*, November 23, 1963, 17.

148. *New York Times*, September 16, 1963, p. 30.

149. *New York Times*, September 20, 1963, p. 22, September 21, 1963, p. 12, November 23, 1963, p. 30; White, *Suite 3505*, 205; Stanley Meister, "The Two Goldwaters," *The Nation*, October 26, 1963, 256–59; Faber, *Road*, 32; Goldwater, *Goldwater*, 147; *Congressional Quarterly, Public Records*, 1580.

150. Interview with John Tower by Joe B. Frantz, August 8, 1971.

151. White, *Suite 3505*, 213, 224, 244; Novak, *Agony*, 219, 249–50; *New York Times*, October 23, 1963, p. 18; Parmet, *JFK*, 272; "The Polls," *Time*, November 8, 1963, 25.

152. "Will it be Goldwater, Rockefeller, or ___?" *U.S. News and World Report*, October 7, 1963, 46–48; "The Jet Bandwagon," *Newsweek*, October 7, 1963, 33–34; *New York Times*, August 26, 1963, p. 1, September 2, 1963, p. 1, November 1, 1963, p. 22.

153. Bryce Harlow to Dwight Eisenhower, July 15, 1963, Box 7, Special Names Series, Post-Presidential Papers, Eisenhower Papers.

154. "For Goldwater," 30.

155. Quoted in Ambrose, *Nixon: Triumph of a Politician*, 31.

156. Novak, *Agony*, 256, 259; White, *Making of the President 1964*, 74–75, 88; Jerry Landauer, "Goldwater's Warm-Up," *Wall Street Journal*, October 15, 1963; Dwight Eisenhower to Clarence Hill, September 3, 1963, Convenience File, Post-Presidential Papers, Eisenhower Papers.

157. "For Goldwater," 30.

158. "Fastest Gun," *Newsweek*, January 20, 1964, 20.

159. Stewart Alsop, "Can Goldwater Win in 1964?" *Saturday Evening Post*, August 24, 1963, 21.

160. "The Finger of Fate?" *Time*, November 8, 1963, 25.

161. "Anatomy of the Goldwater Boom," *New York Times Magazine*, August 11, 1963, pp. 7, 9.

162. "Somewhat Nonconformist," *Time*, September 6, 1963, 18.

163. "Goldwater's Foreign Policy: Let's Hear More," *Life*, November 1, 1963, 4.

164. "Fastest Gun," 20.

165. Interview with Barry Goldwater, September 24, 1992.

166. U.S. Senate, 88th Cong., 1st sess., November 27, 1963, *Congressional Record* 109: 22875.

167. Quoted in O'Donnell and Power, *"Johnny,"* 385, and Novak, *Agony,* 243.

168. "Something's on the Move?" *Time,* November 22, 1963, 17.

169. Interview with Stewart Udall, July 14, 1992.

170. Quoted in Bradlee, *Conversations,* 230.

171. Ibid., 179.

172. Goldwater, *With No Apologies,* 156; Bradlee interview; O'Donnell and Powers, *"Johnny,"* 13, 384–85; Sorensen, *Kennedy,* 754; Pierre Salinger to Thomas Schreth, October 9, 1963, White House Staff Files, Kennedy Papers, Kennedy Presidential Library.

173. Walter Cronkite had erroneously reported on the CBS News that Goldwater was on his way to Muncie for a political rally.

174. *New York Times,* November 23, 1963, p. 8.

175. Quoted in Perry, *Barry Goldwater,* 81.

176. *Arizona Republic,* January 18, 1987.

177. *New York Times,* November 23, 1963, p. 8, November 26, 1963, p. 11; White, *Suite 3505,* 244–51; White, *Making of the President 1964,* 6–7, 19, 100; *Phoenix Gazette,* December 7, 1963; Goldwater, *Goldwater,* 149.

178. For a version of these events that describes a two-meeting sequence see White, *Suite 3505,* 254–55.

179. Goldwater, *Goldwater,* 151–52.

180. Kitchel interview; White, *Making of the President 1964,* 100–101; Goldwater, *With No Apologies,* 163; Goldwater, *Goldwater,* 151–52.

181. Goldwater, *Goldwater,* 152.

182. Ibid., 153.

183. Hess, *In a Cause,* 134; Shadegg, *What Happened,* 81; Goldwater, *Goldwater,* 152–54; *Arizona Republic,* January 18, 1987; Kitchel interview.

184. Quoted in White, *Suite 3505,* 410.

185. Interview with John Tower, September 14, 1990.

Chapter 8: The Woodstock of American Conservatism

Epigraph: "Westward Ho!" *Time,* October 18, 1963, 30.

1. *New York Times,* January 4, 1964, p. 1.

2. Ibid.

3. Louis Harris, "Decisive Elements in the 1964 Presidential Election," in Van den Bosch, *Political Issues,* 36.

4. *New York Times,* January 4, 1964, p. 1; Shadegg, *What Happened,* 92; Novak, *Agony,* 264; Kessel, *Goldwater Coalition,* 59.

5. Interview with John Tower, September 14, 1990.

6. Novak, *Agony,* 285.

7. Goldwater, *Goldwater*, 159.

8. Kleindienst, *Justice*, 30.

9. "His Kind of Campaign," *Business Week*, July 25, 1964, 122–24; Novak, *Agony*, 285; Goldwater, *With No Apologies*, 165–66, 170; White, *Suite 3505*, 263–64; Interview with Denison Kitchel, November 18, 1989; Goldwater, *Goldwater*, 189.

10. White, *Suite 3505*, 266.

11. Kleindienst, *Justice*, 33; White, *Suite 3505*, 265–66.

12. Kitchel interview.

13. Shadegg, *What Happened*, 67–70; Kitchel interview; Telephone interview with William F. Buckley, Jr., August 10, 1990; Goldwater, *Goldwater*, 158.

14. "Goldwater Begins Work on Platform," *The Christian Century*, January 15, 1964, 69.

15. *New York Times*, January 6, 1964, p. 17; *Washington Evening Star*, January 7, 1964.

16. White, *Suite 3505*, 289.

17. Ibid.

18. *New York Times*, January 8, 1964, p. 1.

19. "Giving It and Catching It," *Time*, January 17, 1964, 13.

20. Kleindienst, *Justice*, 35; "Fastest Gun," *Newsweek*, January 20, 1964, 20–21; *New York Times*, January 10, 1964, p. 1; "Giving It," 13.

21. *New York Times*, January 16, 1964, p. 1; "The Poverty Issue," *Time*, January 24, 1964, 12–13.

22. Goldwater, *Goldwater*, 160.

23. Quoted in Perry, *Barry Goldwater*, 87.

24. Quoted in White, *Making of the President 1964*, 110.

25. Perry, *Barry Goldwater*, 87–89; Shadegg, *What Happened*, 97–98; Faber, *Road*, 24–25; "Goldwater Itinerary," Box 17, Norris Cotton Collection, University of New Hampshire; Interview with Richard Kleindienst by Stephen Shadegg, November 18, 1964, Box 3J9, Barry Goldwater Collection, Barker History Center; White, *Suite 3505*, 292; Novak, *Agony*, 307–11; Robert Ajemian, "The Senator Finds the Trail Icy," *Life*, March 6, 1964, 31.

26. Quoted in Hess, *In a Cause*, 26.

27. Quoted in White, *Making of the President 1964*, 112.

28. "Bell for Round One," *National Review*, February 11, 1964, 94.

29. William F. Buckley, Jr., "Answers for Conservatives," *National Review*, February 25, 1964, 145–46, 148–49.

30. "Two Down, Three to Go," *New Republic*, March 21, 1964, 4.

31. "May I tell you," wrote Barry Goldwater, "that I think you are doing a good job in a very difficult position, and I find this feeling to be reflected generally throughout your command." Goldwater to Robert McNamara, December 15, 1961, Box 68, Lewis L. Strauss Papers, Herbert Hoover Presidential Library. Goldwater also described McNamara as "one of the best Secretaries of Defense ever—an IBM machine with legs." *New York Times*, February 20, 1962, p. 22.

32. Interview with Barry Goldwater, September 24, 1992.

33. "Giving It," 13.

34. "How Good Are U.S. Missiles—Is Goldwater Right?" *U.S. News and World Report,* January 27, 1964, 44–45; Interview with William Scranton, March 7, 1992.

35. "Toward the Day of Reckoning," *Time,* January 10, 1964, 22.

36. "Ambassador Lodge—Running Strong," *Newsweek,* March 23, 1964, 22; McDowell, *Campaign Fever,* 21–24, 33; "Hi-Ho New Hampshire! Barry Goes Galloping In," *Life,* November 1, 1963, 33.

37. "New Hampshire Poll: Write-In Fever Gains," *Newsweek,* March 9, 1964, 18–21; Faber, *Road,* 28; White, *Making of the President 1964,* 114–16; *New York Times,* March 11, 1964, p. 1, March 12, 1964, p. 1.

38. Kessel, *Goldwater Coalition,* 64, 72–75; White, *Making of the President 1964,* 117.

39. Interview with F. Clifton White by James Cannon, 1964, Columbia University Oral History Collection.

40. Quoted in Perry, *Barry Goldwater,* 92.

41. Kessel, *Goldwater Coalition,* 68–69; White, *Making of the President 1964,* 131; White, *Suite 3505,* 304–5; Denison Kitchel, Richard Kleindienst, and Clif White to Norris Cotton, March 14, 1964, Box 17, Cotton Collection.

42. *New York Times,* May 13, 1964, p. 22.

43. *Straight Forward! That's Goldwater,* campaign pamphlet, author's collection.

44. Speech to the American Society of Newspaper Editors, Washington, D.C., April 18, 1964.

45. *New York Times,* March 22, 1964, p. 52.

46. Faber, *Road,* 30, 53–54; *New York Times,* March 17, 1964, p. 20, April 21, 1964, p. 23 (quote), May 14, 1964, p. 26.

47. The results were: Illinois—Goldwater 63 percent to Margaret Chase Smith 20 percent (with write-in votes, Goldwater's share drops to 49 percent); Indiana—Goldwater 67 percent to Harold Stassen 27 percent; Nebraska—Goldwater 50 percent to Richard Nixon 31 percent.

48. White, *Suite 3505,* 301–7, 313–18, 324–25, 329, 332; Faber, *Road,* 33–34; Novak, *Agony,* 368; Cosman, *Five States,* 40; *Newsweek,* May 18, 1964, 27–31.

49. White, *Suite 3505,* 325–28; White, *Making of the President 1964,* 118–21; Herbert E. Alexander, "Financing the Parties and Campaigns," in Cummings, *National Election,* 163; *New York Times,* May 17, 1964, p. 72.

50. "Campaigning for the Presidency," PBS, August 19, 1992.

51. Kessel, *Goldwater Coalition,* 85.

52. *Los Angeles Times,* May 21, 1964.

53. Ibid.

54. Ibid., May 20, 1964.

55. Ibid., May 25, 1964; Rowland Evans and Robert Novak, "Showdown in California: Big Crisis for Goldwater" *Saturday Evening Post,* May 30, 1964, 17.

56. Evans and Novak, "Showdown," 17.

57. Ibid., 19.

58. White, *Making of the President 1964*, 125–28; Alexander, "Financing," 163; *Los Angeles Times*, May 17 and 27, 1964.

59. Andersen and Lee, "1964 Election," 456–57, 472; Rae, *The Decline*, 57; White, *Making of the President 1964*, 124–25.

60. *Los Angeles Times*, May 14, 1964.

61. Ibid., May 23, 1964.

62. Clif White and Richard Kleindienst to Norris Cotton [form letter], May 19, 1964, Box 17, Cotton Collection.

63. *Los Angeles Times*, May 12, 19, 24, 28, and 31, 1964; Kessel, *Goldwater Coalition*, 87–88; White, *Suite 3505*, 337, 339.

64. "Issues and Answers," ABC, May 24, 1964.

65. *San Francisco Examiner*, May 25, 1964.

66. *Los Angeles Times*, May 25, 1964.

67. Ibid., May 27, 1964.

68. Quoted in Faber, *Road*, 169.

69. "Covering the Candidates," *Newsweek*, July 20, 1964, 72.

70. Novak, *Agony*, 402.

71. Telephone conversation between Jack Stewart and Herbert Hoover, May 28, 1964, Box 70, Post-Presidential Papers, Herbert Hoover Presidential Library.

72. *Los Angeles Times*, May 25, 1964.

73. Ambrose, *Eisenhower*, II, 651; Conversation between Dwight Eisenhower and Bryce Harlow, May 15, 1964, telephone conversation between Eisenhower and Colonel Saloman, May 19, 1964, telephone conversation between Eisenhower and Richard Nixon, May 19, 1964, Box 2, Appointment Book Series, Post-Presidential Papers, Dwight Eisenhower Presidential Library.

74. *New York Times*, May 26, 1964, 18.

75. "Ike Takes a Stand," *Newsweek*, June 8, 1964, 40.

76. *Los Angeles Times*, June 2, 1964.

77. Conversation between Eisenhower and Harlow, May 15, 1964, Box 2, Appointment Book Series, Eisenhower Post-Presidential Papers, Eisenhower Presidential Library.

78. *Los Angeles Times*, May 29, 1964.

79. Scranton interview; Telephone interview with George Romney, April 6, 1992; Kessel, *Goldwater Coalition*, 82–83; *Los Angeles Times*, May 28, 30, and 31, 1964, June 1, 1964.

80. *Los Angeles Times*, May 29, 1964.

81. Ibid., May 31, 1964.

82. Ibid., June 1, 1964.

83. Ibid., May 28, 29, and 31, 1964, June 1 and 2, 1964.

84. Quoted in White, *Making of the President 1964*, 145.

85. *Los Angeles Times*, June 4, 1964; White, *Suite 3505*, 351; Telephone conversation between Dwight Eisenhower and Walter Thayer, June 4, 1964, Appoint-

ment Book Series, Box 2, Post-Presidential Papers, Eisenhower Presidential Library.

86. *New York Times,* June 4, 1964, p. 22.

87. Barry Goldwater to Jacob Javits, June 9, 1964, Box 9, Series 5, Jacob K. Javits Collection, State University of New York at Stony Brook.

88. "The Clinched Nomination," *Time,* July 17, 1964, 22.

89. Quoted in McDowell, *Campaign Fever,* 79.

90. Novak, *Agony,* 435.

91. Scranton interview.

92. Ibid.

93. White, *Making of the President 1964,* 150; Scranton interview.

94. For detailed discussions of the Cleveland meeting see White, *Making of the President 1964,* 151–60, White, *Suite 3505,* 362–68, and Novak, *Agony,* 416–38.

95. Scranton interview.

96. "Heads-Off," *The New Republic,* June 20, 1964, 2.

97. Kitchel interview; Scranton interview.

98. George Romney is a devout member of the Church of Jesus Christ of Latter-Day Saints.

99. Quoted in Schlesinger, *History,* vol. 4, 3662.

100. Quoted in White, *Suite 3505,* 364.

101. Ibid., 367–68.

102. "I am a Candidate," *Time,* June 19, 1964, 14.

103. Ibid.; Romney interview; Scranton interview.

104. *New York Times,* February 15, 1964, p. 11.

105. Kitchel interview; Perry, *Barry Goldwater,* 125; "The Covenant," *Time,* June 19, 1964, 15; *New York Times,* June 7, 1964, p. 72, June 9, 1964, p. 1, June 10, 1964, p. 32, June 13, 1964, p. 1, June 16, 1964, pp. 1, 24; June 19, 1964, p. 1, 27; U.S. Senate, 88th Congress, 2nd sess., June 18, 1964, *Congressional Record* 110: 14319.

106. June 18, 1964, *Congressional Record* 110: 14319.

107. Whalens, *Longest Debate,* 215; *New York Times,* June 27, 1964, p. 10.

108. *New York Times,* March 1, 1964, p. 61.

109. *Los Angeles Times,* May 21, 1964.

110. Louis Harris, "The 'Backlash' Issue," *Newsweek,* July 13, 1964, 24–26.

111. *New York Times,* May 2, 1964, p. 22, May 2, 1964, p. 72, June 17, 1964, p. 23; White, *Making of the President 1964,* 245.

112. Scranton interview.

113. "I Am a Candidate," 13.

114. Telephone conversations between Eisenhower and Scranton, June 10 and 11, 1964, Appointment Book Series, Box 2, Eisenhower Post-Presidential Papers, Eisenhower Presidential Library; White, *Making of the President 1964,* 162–63.

115. "I Am a Candidate," 15.

116. White, *Suite 3505,* 220; Novak, *Agony,* 94, 442; White, *Making of the President 1964,* 164, 203.

117. "Barry's Blitz," *Newsweek*, July 13, 1964, 28, 30; White, *Making of the President*, 165; Novak, *Agony*, 445–46.

118. "Mission: A Winner's Image," *Time*, June 26, 1964, 18.

119. "Let's Not Kid Ourselves," *Time*, July 3, 1964, 18.

120. *Science and Mechanics*, June 1964, 109. Goldwater's plan was among several precursors of the Strategic Defense Initiative (SDI) put forward by the Reagan Administration during the 1980s. See Baucom, *Origins of SDI*.

121. Ibid., 46–47.

122. "Clinched Nomination," 22.

123. Quoted in White, *Making of the President 1964*, 166.

124. Quoted in McDowell, *Campaign Fever*, 73.

125. Barry Goldwater to Norris Cotton, June 17, 1964, Box 17, Cotton Papers; "Clinched Nomination," 21; "Back to the Wars," *Newsweek*, July 6, 1964, 20, 23; White, *Making of the President 1964*, 167; White, *Suite 3505*, 369; *New York Times*, July 11, 1964, p. 10.

126. "Memo to the Files," July 8, 1964, Box 68, Strauss Papers.

127. Telephone conversations between Eisenhower and Hugh Scott, June 12, 1964, and Milton Eisenhower, June 12, 1964, and Nelson Rockefeller, June 16, 1964, and William Scranton, July 6, 1964, Box 2, Appointment Book Series, Eisenhower Post-Presidential Papers, Eisenhower Presidential Library; White, *Making of the President 1964*, 205; Quoted in Norman Mailer, "In the Red Light: A History of the Republican Convention in 1964," *Esquire*, November 1964, 88.

128. Scranton interview.

129. Scranton letter is reprinted in McDowell, *Campaign Fever*, 108–10.

130. Quoted in Shalit and Grossman, *Somehow*, 66.

131. *New York Times*, July 14, 1964, p. 22.

132. Stewart Alsop, "Crisis at the Cow Palace," *Saturday Evening Post*, July 11, 1964, 20.

133. *New York Times*, July 9, 1964, p. 20.

134. Quoted in Goldwater, *Conscience of a Majority*, 180.

135. Goldwater planned to visit his friend General William Quinn, commander of the U.S. Seventh Army stationed in Germany, after the convention. In the wake of Schorr's broadcast, Goldwater canceled the trip. Now public and controversial, Quinn's friendship with Goldwater became a professional liability, and he retired prematurely in 1966. Interview with William Quinn, September 11, 1990.

136. Schorr, *Clearing*, 7–8.

137. Ibid., 8.

138. "The Big New Face of the G.O.P.," *Life*, July 24, 1964, 23.

139. Max Ascoli, "The Runaway Republicans," *The Reporter*, August 13, 1964, 26.

140. "Goldwater: Yes or No?" *The Christian Century*, July 8, 1964, 882.

141. Quoted in William F. Buckley, Jr., "Tribute to Goldwater," *National Review*, November 9, 1973, 1265.

142. "In the Red Light," 170.

143. *New York Times,* July 14, 1964, p. 30.

144. Quoted in Bernstein, "AuH$_2$O," 63.

145. Cosman, *Case,* 22–24, 55; McDowell, *Campaign Fever,* 100; Stephen Shadegg, *What Happened,* 265; Shalit and Grossman, *Somehow,* 59; Telephone interview with John Roussellot by Stephen Shadegg, February 1, 1965, Box 3J9, Barry Goldwater Collection, Barker History Center.

146. Carey McWilliams, "High Noon at the Cow Palace," *The Nation,* July 27, 1964, 94.

147. White, *Suite 3505,* 382–83; Rusher, *Rise of the Right,* 165; *Washington Post,* September 19, 1967.

148. "The 1964 Republican Party Platform," reprinted in Schlesinger, *History,* 3634–55.

149. "The 1960 Republican Party Platform," in Schlesinger, *History,* 3532–33.

150. Romney interview.

151. "1960 Republican Party Platform," 3510–35; White, *Making of the President 1964,* 202, 206–7; Bates, "Race," 2–3; Kessel, *Goldwater Coalition,* 111–13; Romney interview; George Romney to Barry Goldwater, December 21, 1964, Michael Goldwater Papers, in the author's possession; *New York Times,* July 13, 1964, p. 18.

152. *New York Journal-American,* July 15, 1964.

153. Ibid.

154. Donaldson, *"Hold On,"* 232.

155. Javits, *Autobiography,* 351.

156. Rosenthal, "Republican," 398–99; White, *Making of the President 1964,* 211–12; Tower interview; White, *Suite 3505,* 399.

157. McDowell, *Campaign Fever,* 132.

158. Ibid., 115.

159. *New York Journal-American,* July 15, 1964; *New York Times,* July 17, 1964, pp. 1, 11; Goldwater, *Goldwater,* 185; Perry, *Barry Goldwater,* 129 (quote), 130–31.

160. Quoted in White, *Making of the President 1964,* 216.

161. Rusher, *Rise of the Right,* 170.

162. White, *Suite 3505,* 399–405; White, *Making of the President 1964,* 213–16; *Arizona Republic,* February 16, 1992.

163. Goldwater, *Goldwater,* 186.

164. Acceptance Speech reprinted in Goldwater, *Where I Stand,* 16.

165. Ibid., 9–17.

166. James O'Gara, "The Man Who," *Commonweal,* August 7, 1964, 530; Rosenthal, "Republican," 397–98; Dell, "Republican Nominee," 403–4; Quoted in White, *Making of the President 1964,* 228.

167. Walter Judd to Stanley Hornbeck, July 20, 1964, Box 210, Walter H. Judd Collection, Hoover Institution Archives.

168. Nixon, *RN,* 260.

169. Telephone interview with Dean Burch by Stephen Shadegg, December 1964, Goldwater Collection, Barker History Center.

170. White, *Suite 3505*, 407.

171. Shadegg, *What Happened*, 166–67.

172. Quoted in Leahy, "I'd Have Ended," 45.

173. *Salt Lake Tribune*, November 17, 1990.

174. Kitchel interview.

175. Nixon, *RN*, 260.

176. Interview with Benjamin Bradlee, September 10, 1990.

177. "The New Thrust," *Time*, July 24, 1964, 17.

178. "Tribute," 1265.

179. Kitchel interview.

180. "Goldwater Speaks His Mind," *U.S. News and World Report*, December 21, 1964, 48.

181. Harry Jaffa to Denison Kitchel, March 11, 1969, Box 5, Denison Kitchel Collection, Hoover Institution Archives; Goldwater, *Goldwater*, 186.

182. Barry Goldwater to Lewis Strauss, July 22, 1964, Box 68, Strauss Collection.

183. Kitchel interview. For a slightly different account see Denison Kitchel, "Explaining Things to Ike," *National Review*, April 30, 1976, 447–48.

184. Interview with Barry Goldwater by Hugh Downs, ABC, "20/20," July 23, 1993.

185. Quoted in Buchanan, *Right*, 307.

186. Quoted in Shalit and Grossman, *Somehow*, 73–74.

187. Quoted in Faber, *Road*, xiii.

188. "A Choice—Not an Echo," *Newsweek*, July 27, 1964, 18.

189. Schlafly, *Choice*.

190. *Arizona Republic*, February 16, 1992.

191. Rae, *Decline*, 198; Reinhard, *Republican Right*, 197; William A. Rusher, "Lessons of the Nomination Drive," *National Review*, July 28, 1964, 643.

192. "Goldwater Speaks his Mind," 47.

193. Barry Goldwater to Stephen Shadegg, June 23, 1965, Box 3J13, Goldwater Collection, Barker History Center.

Chapter 9: Martyr to the Cause

Epigraphs: Buckley quoted in Judis, *Buckley*, 231; Goldwater quoted in "Goldwater? Goldwater!" *National Review*, May 24, 1974, 571.

1. Herbert E. Alexander, "Financing the Parties and Campaigns," in Cummings, *National Election*, 185–86; "Nowhere to Go But Johnson," *Business Week*, July 25, 1964, 47–48; Quoted in White, *Making of the President 1964*, 365.

2. Matusow, *Unraveling*, 56; "Going into Next Year at a Gallup," *Business Week*, September 19, 1964, 27–29.

3. "Businessmen's Vote: It's Going To Be a Tough Decision," *Business Week,* September 5, 1964, 25.

4. Quoted in Goldman, *Tragedy,* 224.

5. Quoted in Faber, *Road,* 45.

6. Johnson, *Vantage Point,* 104; White, *Making of the President 1964,* 373; Goldman, *Tragedy,* 221–22.

7. *New York Times,* September 12, 1964, p. 10.

8. Reprinted in Schlesinger, *History,* vol. 4, 3674–78.

9. Quoted in Jamieson, *Packaging,* 177.

10. "Anti-Goldwater Program," memo to Bill Moyers, September 10, 1964, Box 117, "Republican Party," Subject File, White House Central Files, Lyndon Johnson Presidential Library.

11. Walter Heller to Lyndon Johnson, August 4, 1964, September 10 and 16, 1964, White House Central Files, Lyndon Johnson Presidential Library.

12. *Los Angeles Times,* December 20, 1973; *New York Times,* December 31, 1974, p. 4; White, *Breach,* 132; Goldman, *Tragedy,* 170–71; White, *Making of the President 1964,* 367; Glenn Pool to Lyndon Johnson, August 31, 1964, Shannon H. Ratliff to Glenn Pool, September 5, 1964, Cliff Carter to Jack Valenti, September 16, 1964, Box 117, "Republican Party," Subject Files, White House Central Files; Kermit Gordon to Paul Southwick, September 3, 1964, Southwick to Bill Moyers, September 14, 1964, Box 481, Frederick Panzer Papers, Johnson Presidential Library.

13. Bill Moyers to Lloyd Wright, September 14, 1964, Box 481, Frederick Panzer Papers, Johnson Presidential Library.

14. Jamieson, *Packaging,* 177.

15. White, *Making of the President 1964,* 232–45; Fletcher Knebel, "Race Riots: Goldwater Boon," *Look,* September 22, 1964, 36; Flemmer, "New York," 1–2, 17, 18; Stanley Kelley, Jr., "The Presidential Campaign," in Cummings, *National Election,* 66.

The first race riots have been lost in the wake of Mississippi's Freedom Summer and the Watts violence of 1965. They offer historians important entry points to study northern race relations, racial perceptions, and ghetto conditions before events transformed patterns.

16. "Union's War on Goldwater—AFL-CIO Plans its Strategy," *U.S. News and World Report,* August 17, 1964, 13.

17. "Worse Than Mississippi," *Time,* July 24, 1964, 29.

18. Quoted in Faber, *Road,* 146.

19. Ibid., 158.

20. Goldberg, *Grassroots Resistance,* 159; White, *Making of the President 1964,* 292–95.

21. Sheehan, Smith, Kenworthy, and Butterfield, *Pentagon Papers,* 234–63; 274–77, 283–88; Baritz, *Backfire,* 120–28; *New York Times,* June 14, 1971, p. 18; Barry Goldwater to Stephen Shadegg, May 15, 1978, Alpha File, Barry Goldwater Papers, Arizona Historical Foundation.

22. Quoted in Baritz, *Backfire*, 129–30.

23. "A Measured and Fitting Response," *Time*, August 14, 1964, 11.

24. Baritz, *Backfire*, 128–30; *New York Times*, August 5, 1964, p. 4.

25. Sheehan et. al., *Pentagon Papers*, 264–69, 294–98, 300–302, 307–8; Matusow, *Unraveling*, 149–50; Goldman, *Tragedy*, 175–76, 183; Baritz, *Backfire*, 133.

26. "Meeting with Goldwater," Bill Moyers to Lyndon Johnson n.d., Box 32, Bill Moyers Papers, Johnson Presidential Library; "Meeting with Senator Goldwater," n.d., Box 7, Appointment File (Diary Backup), White House Central Files, Johnson Presidential Library.

27. Quoted in Hess, *In a Cause*, 206.

28. Goldwater, *With No Apologies*, 193.

29. "Civil Rights: The White House Meeting," *Newsweek*, August 3, 1964, 15.

30. Goldwater, *With No Apologies*, 192–93; "The Proper Stance," *Time*, July 31, 1964, 9; "Meeting with Senator Goldwater." Lyndon Johnson's memoir, *Vantage Point*, makes no mention of the meeting.

31. Charles Jones, "The 1964 Presidential Election," in Crotty, *Public Opinion*, 393.

32. "Lyndon Johnson—Will He Win?" *U.S. News and World Report*, September 7, 1964, 44–47; Goldman, *Tragedy*, 24; Jones, "The 1964 Presidential Election," 390; White, *Making of the President 1964*, 332, 361.

33. Jones, "Presidential Election of 1964," 390.

34. Scammon and Wattenberg, *Real Majority*, 35.

35. "The Candidates Spell Out the Issues," *New York Times Magazine*, November 1, 1964, sect. 6, p. 23.

36. *New York Times*, July 21, 1964, pp. 1, 21.

37. "Bobby Baker Again," *Newsweek*, September 14, 1964, 22; Emmet Hughes, "Crime and Politics," *Newsweek*, October 19, 1964, 25; "LBJ's Wealth Grows as an Issue," *Business Week*, August 22, 1964, 32; Faber, *Road*, 126, 232–35; Scammon and Wattenberg, *Real Majority*, 35–40, 42–43; *New York Times*, October 11, 1964, p. 76, October 14, 1964, p. 28, October 29, 1964, p. 1; "The Candidates Spell," 23.

38. "The 'Something's Wrong' Theme," *Time*, August 28, 1964, 24.

39. "'Something's Wrong' Theme," 24.

40. *Straight Talk*, campaign pamphlet (New York: New Yorkers for Goldwater-Miller, 1964), author's collection.

41. Faber, *Road*, 235; McDowell, *Campaign Fever*, 206.

42. Wayne Hood to Stephen Shadegg, November 2, 1964, Box 3J8, Barry Goldwater Collection, Barker History Center.

43. Magruder, *American Life*, 42.

44. Shadegg, *What Happened*, 191, 195; Jay Klopfenstein to Denison Kitchel, September 26, 1965, Kathryn Shyrock to Barry Goldwater, September 30, 1965, Box 7, Denison Kitchel Papers, Hoover Institution Archives.

45. Stans, *Terrors*, 122; Walter Pincus, "The Fat Cats Are Hard to Find," *The*

Reporter, August 13, 1964, 34–36; Alexander, "Financing," 161, 172, 178–79, 182; Kessel, *Goldwater Coalition,* 146; Kelley, "The Presidential Campaign," 47, 56–58; Crawford, *Thunder,* 46–47.

46. Denison Kitchel to Richard Nixon (draft), no date, Barry Goldwater to Richard Nixon, August 7, 1964, Box 3, Kitchel Papers.

47. Telephone conversation between Dwight Eisenhower and George Romney, August 4, 1964, Box 2, Appointment Book Series, Post-Presidential Papers, Dwight Eisenhower Presidential Library.

48. Transcript of Hershey meeting in Hess, *In a Cause,* 180–83.

49. "Toward Nov. 3," *Time,* August 21, 1964, 15.

50. Telephone interview with George Romney, April 6, 1992.

51. Hess, *In a Cause,* 200, 204, 206, 208, 210–13, 222–23; "Republican Party," July 20, 1964 to September 19, 1964, Subject File, Box 117, White House Central Files, Johnson Presidential Library.

52. Quoted in Nixon, *RN,* 262.

53. Telephone conversation between Dwight Eisenhower and Nelson Rockefeller, August 14, 1964, Box 2, Appointment Book Series, Post-Presidential Papers, Eisenhower Presidential Library.

54. Telephone conversation between Dwight Eisenhower and William Scranton, December 1, 1964.

55. Romney interview.

56. "There was Plenty of Give and Take," *Newsweek,* August 24, 1964, 19–20; "As Republicans Close Ranks," *U.S. News and World Report,* August 24, 1964, 34–35; "Toward Nov. 3," 13–15; Kelley, "Presidential Campaign," 69; Interview with William Scranton, March 7, 1992; Ambrose, *Nixon: Triumph of a Politician,* 56; "Nixon Schedule," Box 515, Goldwater Collection, Barker History Center; Reinhard, *Republican Right,* 198, 202; Barry Goldwater to George Romney, December 8, 1964, Romney to Goldwater, December 21, 1964, Michael Goldwater Papers, in the author's possession.

57. *New York Times,* September 4, 1964, p. 12.

58. "Goldwater: 'Republicans Will Cut Taxes, Reduce Debt,'" *U.S. News and World Report,* September 21, 1964, 117.

59. Quoted in Erickson, "Reporting," 61.

60. *New York Times,* September 20, 1964, pp. 1, 70.

61. "In the Thick," *Time,* September 18, 1964, 32; Erickson, "Reporting," 47, 60, 76; *New York Times,* September 11, 1964, pp. 1, 21, September 16, 1964, pp. 1, 12, September 17, 1964, pp. 1, 28; "Marching Through Dixie," *Time,* September 25, 1964, 20–21.

62. Prestige press refers to such influential newspapers as the *Wall Street Journal, New York Times, Los Angeles Times, Washington Post, Chicago Tribune, Atlanta Constitution, Baltimore Sun,* and *Christian Science Monitor.*

63. *New York Times,* September 19, 1964, 1.; "Marching Through Dixie," 20.

64. Stempel, "Prestige Press," 15–17; "The Kickoff," *Time,* September 11, 1964,

20. "They're Off: The Long, Hot Campaign," *Newsweek*, September 14, 1964, 19; "Getting Across to the Voters," *Business Week*, September 19, 1964, 32–33.

65. "Getting Across," 32.

66. Faber, *Road*, 260; White, *Making of the President 1964*, 351.

67. "Goldwater's Views," *Atlantic Monthly*, September 1964, 6.

68. "The 1964 Religious Issue," *The Christian Century*, October 7, 1964, 1228.

69. Ralph Ginzburg, ed., "The Unconscious of a Conservative: A Special Issue on the Mind of Barry Goldwater," *Fact Magazine*, September–October 1964, 28, 40, 56, 57, 58; *New York Times*, September 15, 1964, p. 23. Barry Goldwater sued *Fact* magazine for libel in September 1965. He told William Buckley, Jr., who had advised him not to bring suit: "If you can say that kind of thing about a man who is running for public office, then decent men are going to stop running . . . ." Goldwater won the case in 1968 and the court awarded him $150,000 in damages. William F. Buckley, Jr., "Goldwater v. Ginzburg," *National Review*, June 18, 1968, 624; *New York Times*, May 5, 1968, p. 62, May 8, 1968, p. 28, May 9, 1968, p. 35, May 15, 1968, p. 27, May 25, 1968, p. 1, July 19, 1969, p. 12, January 27, 1970, p. 32.

70. Quoted in "Covering the Campaign," *Time*, October 2, 1964, 74.

71. Ibid.

72. Interview with Ben Avery, October 26, 1990; Edward, "Press Support," 485–88; Faber, *Road*, 174, 256; Hess, *In a Cause*, 113; Erikson, "Influence," 207, 209, 215; Interview with William Mahoney, October 26, 1990.

73. Donaldson, *"Hold On,"* 47.

74. Interview with Benjamin Bradlee, September 10, 1990.

75. *New York Times*, November 5, 1964, p. 20.

76. Hedley Donovan, "The Difficulty of Being Fair to Goldwater," *Life*, September 18, 1964, 93–96.

77. Quoted in White, *Making of the President 1964*, 347.

78. "In the Thick of It," *Time*, September 18, 1964, 30.

79. Faber, *Road*, 179, 182; "49–44 for Medicare," *Newsweek*, September 14, 1964, 23.

80. Quoted in Lokos, *Hysteria*, 147.

81. Quoted in Jamieson, *Packaging*, 200.

82. Quoted in Faber, *Road*, 168.

83. Jamieson, *Packaging*, 186–87, 198, 200–201; Charles A. H. Thomson, "Mass Media Performance," in Cummings, *National Election*, 127; Shadegg, *What Happened*, 238.

84. "The Nuclear Issue," *Newsweek*, September 21, 1964, 33–34.

85. "The Itchy-Finger Image," *Time*, September 25, 1964, 15.

86. Ibid., 15.

87. Ibid., 17.

88. Quoted in White, *Making of the President 1964*, 347.

89. Jamieson, *Packaging*, 205–6; Thomson, "Mass Media," 123–24; "Itchy Finger Image," 16.

90. Quoted in Matusow, *Unraveling*, 148.

91. Jamieson, *Packaging*, 190; Hess, *In a Cause*, 100.

92. McDowell, *Campaign Fever*, 176; Hess, *Cause*, 126–29; Shadegg, *What Happened*, 262.

93. "General Strategy," John Martin to Bill Moyers, October 1, 1964, Box 25, Moyers Papers, Johnson Presidential Library.

94. Jones, "1964 Presidential Election," 390.

95. "Promises and Punches," *Time*, October 2, 1964, 42.

96. Quoted in Faber, *Road*, 208.

97. Quoted in Goldman, *Tragedy*, 235.

98. Ibid., 236.

99. "Goldwater in the Old Confederacy," *Newsweek*, September 28, 1964, 28; McDowell, *Campaign Fever*, 198; Goldman, *Tragedy*, 230.

100. Quoted in White, *Making of the President 1964*, 379.

101. Quoted in Goldman, *Tragedy*, 234.

102. McDowell, *Campaign Fever*, 211–12; Goldman, *Tragedy*, 232; Rovere, *Goldwater Caper*, 161.

103. *New York Times*, October 1, 1964, p. 24.

104. Ibid., October 6, 1964, pp. 1, 29. Goldwater was more specific about Vietnam in writing. In his campaign book *Where I Stand*, Barry Goldwater argued that "there was no substitute for victory. We are at war in Vietnam, and we must have the will to win that war." He called for the interdiction of supply lines in neutral areas and the end to "privileged sanctuaries." He concluded: "The security of all Asia hinges on this crucial battle." *Where I Stand*, 28, 29. A pamphlet from the Citizens for Goldwater-Miller Committee titled *Barry Goldwater Speaks Out on the Issues*, quoted him: "The nation must back up its resolve with whatever manpower, equipment, and weaponry it may take."

105. Quoted in White, *Making of the President 1964*, 342; *New York Times*, October 2, 1964, p. 21.

106. Quoted in White, *Making of the President 1964*, 345.

107. McDowell, *Campaign Fever*, 180, 194; White, *Making of the President 1964*, 340–43.

108. Interview with John Tower by Joe B. Frantz, August 8, 1971.

109. Goldman, *Tragedy*, 228; Kelley, "Presidential Campaign," 47; Interview with John Tower, September 14, 1990.

110. *Salt Lake Tribune*, October 11, 1964; *Deseret News*, October 12, 1964.

111. *New York Times*, October 17, 1964, p. 16; "The Free Society," Alpha File, Goldwater Papers.

112. Faber, *Road*, 236–37; White, *Making of the President 1964*, 386–88; Kalman, *Abe Fortas*, 226–27; Matusow, *Unraveling*, 145–46; Goldman, *Tragedy*, 249–50.

113. *New York Times*, October 15, 1964, pp. 1, 24.

114. Ibid., October 20, 1964, pp. 1, 28.

115. Matusow, *Unraveling*, 146; "The Morality Issue," *Newsweek*, November 2, 1964, 25–26; White, *Suite 3505*, 414; Interview with Denison Kitchel, November 18, 1989; *New York Times*, October 24, 1964, pp. 1, 14.

116. Reprinted in Schlesinger, *History*, vol. 4, 3692.

117. *New York Times*, October 22, 1964, p. 46.

118. Quoted in Goldman, *Tragedy*, 237. See also Connelly, "Some Questions," 11–20.

119. White, *Making of the President 1964*, 392–93; *New York Times*, October 27, 1964, p. 21; Faber, *Road*, 242–43, 246; Quoted in Rovere, *Goldwater Caper*, 166.

120. *New York Times*, October 21, 1964, pp. 1, 33.

121. Ibid., November 2, 1964, p. 19.

122. Quoted in Shalit and Grossman, *Somehow*, 203.

123. *New York Times*, November 3, 1964, p. 21.

124. *New York Times*, October 28, 1964, pp. 1, 26; White, *Making of the President 1964*, 350, 357; McDowell, *Campaign Fever*, 230; Goldwater, *Goldwater*, 220.

125. McDowell, *Campaign Fever*, 235; *New York Times*, November 4, 1964, p. 1; Faber, *Road*, 270, 275; White, *Making of the President 1964*, 400–404.

126. Faber, *Road*, 277; Goldman, *Tragedy*, 255; "The Elections," *Time*, November 4, 1964, 3–5, 12; Bass and DeVries, *Transformation*, 350.

127. *Los Angeles Times*, November 14, 1972; Kitchel interview; *New York Times*, November 4, 1964, p. 23, November 5, 1964, p. 20.

128. U.S. House of Representatives, 89th Cong., 1st sess., January 27, 1965, *Congressional Record* 111: 1422.

129. "The Elections," 12; "The Liberal House," *Time*, November 13, 1964, 38; Hess, *In a Cause*, 8–9; Milton C. Cummings, Jr., "Nominations and Elections for the House of Representatives," in Cummings, *National Election*, 230; Morley, "Bush," 20–21; Wills, "Hostage," 21–22; Jones, "1964 Presidential Election," 401.

130. "The Republican Future," *U.S. News and World Report*, November 16, 1964, 69.

131. "The G.O.P.: A Trunkful of Troubles," *Newsweek*, November 16, 1964, 26.

132. *Congressional Record*, January 27, 1965, 1421.

133. *New York Times*, November 4, 1964, p. 23.

134. "The Elections," 5.

135. Quoted in Shalit and Grossman, *Somehow*, 215.

136. "End of an Era," *Newsweek*, January 25, 1965, 23.

137. "Clearing the Underbush," *Time*, December 18, 1964, 24; "Pen Pal for Dean," *Time*, January 8, 1965, 17; *New York Times*, December 29, 1964, pp. 1, 12; Hess and Broder, *Republican Establishment*, 32, 39–42; Telephone conversation between Dwight Eisenhower and William Scranton, December 1, 1964, Box 2, Appointment Book Series, Post-Presidential Papers, Eisenhower Presidential Library.

138. Wolfe, "Southern Strategy," 193–98, 215; Cosman, *Five States*, 43–44,

51–55, 64–66, 72, 93–99, 112, 131; Bass and DeVries, *Transformation*, 28–29, 79, 164, 202, 256.

139. Phillips, *Emerging*, 168.

140. Ibid., 74–78, 166–69; Tindall, *Disruption*, 65.

141. White, *Making of the President 1964*, 354; Phillips, *Emerging*, 403, 440, 445.

142. Author's collection.

143. "The Republican Party and the Conservative Movement," *National Review*, December 1, 1964, 1053.

144. John Dos Passos, "What Hope for Maintaining a Conservative Opposition," *National Review*, October 20, 1964, 907; Bass and DeVries, *Transformation*, 256; Barrett, *Gambling*, 193, 259; *Los Angeles Times*, July 18, 1974; Interview with Jake Garn, November 26, 1990; Viguerie, *New Right*, 26–27; Rusher, *Rise of the Right*, 161.

145. Goldwater, *Goldwater*, 209; Kitchel interview; Reagan, *American Life*, 139–43; Reagan, *Speaking*, 22–36; Interview with Ronald Reagan, August 7, 1990.

146. Quoted in Loudon Wainwright, "It's Too Early To Bind Wounds," *Life*, November 13, 1964, 31.

147. Hess and Broder, *Republican Establishment*, 254; Rusher, *Rise of the Right*, 204; White, *Why Reagan Won*, 66.

148. The English victory over the French at Agincourt in 1415 occurred on the feast day of St. Crispin. Buchanan, *The Conscience of a Conservative*, x.

149. Paul Weyrich, "Blue Collar or Blue Blood? The New Right Compared with the Old Right," in Whitaker, *New Right Papers*, 51.

150. Tower interview. The Mexican army annihilated the 187 Texican defenders of the Alamo on March 6, 1836. Regrouping, General Sam Houston surprised and defeated Santa Anna's forces at San Jacinto on April 21, 1836.

Chapter 10: Rising from the Ashes

1. David S. Broder, "There's No Radical Change in Goldwater," *New York Times Magazine*, June 19, 1966, p. 9.

2. Quoted in Hess, *In a Cause*, 216.

3. Broder, "There's No Radical," 10.

4. Barry Goldwater to Robert Wood, February 25, 1966, Box 6, Robert E. Wood Papers, Herbert Hoover Presidential Library.

5. Goldwater, *Goldwater*, 221; Interview with Judy Rooney Eisenhower, October 26, 1990; Interview with Barry Goldwater by Ed Edwin June 15, 1967; *New York Times*, June 16, 1965, p. 31; *Arizona Republic*, April 30, 1966, October 4, 1968, November 7, 1968, January 18, 1987.

6. Goldwater, *Goldwater*, 221.

7. "Column Right," *Newsweek*, January 18, 1965, 55–56; "Trip Itinerary," Peggy Goldwater Papers, private collection of Peggy Goldwater Clay; Barry Goldwater to

the Goldwater children, February 6, 1965, January 21, 1967, Michael Goldwater Papers, in the author's possession; *New York Times*, December 6, 1967, p. 16, December 16, 1967, p. 3; Judy Rooney Eisenhower interview.

8. Denison Kitchel to John J. Kennedy, June 25, 1965, Box 2, Free Society Association Collection, Hoover Institution Archives.

9. In October 1965 Goldwater called on Birchers to resign from the society and pledge allegiance to the Republican Party because their leader, Robert Welch, has "generally been wrong, ill-advised, and at times, ill-tempered" in his remarks. Goldwater now regretted the exclusion of an anti-extremism plank from the Republican Party's 1964 platform. *New York Times*, October 12, 1965, p. 33.

10. Barry Goldwater to Russell Kirk, July 21, 1965, Russell Kirk Papers, Central Michigan University.

11. Denison Kitchel to Barry Goldwater, April 11, 1965, Box 5, Goldwater to Stetson Coleman, April 15, 1965, Box 5, "Press Release," June 17, 1965, Box 13, Kitchel to Kennedy, June 25, 1965, Box 2, Goldwater to Kitchel, August 2, 1966, Box 5, "Bylaws" and "Articles of Incorporation," Box 1, Free Society Association Collection, Hoover Institution Archives; *New York Times*, June 18, 1965, pp. 1, 20.

12. Hess and Broder, *Republican Establishment*, 53.

13. *Arizona Republic*, April 10, 1966; Ronald Crawford to Denison Kitchel, December 6, 1965, Box 3, Barry Goldwater to John Saloma III, February 8, 1966, Box 5, Kitchel to Saloma, February 23, 1966, Box 5, Goldwater to Lynn Mote, April 6, 1966, Box 2, Free Society Association Collection; Goldwater to Elizabeth Brown, May 27, 1966, Box 2, Elizabeth Churchill Brown Collection, Hoover Institution Archives.

14. Baritz, *Backfire*, 137, 165.

15. Goldwater, *Goldwater*, 221.

16. *New York Times*, April 2, 1965, p. 24.

17. Barry Goldwater, "President Johnson Overrides the Military on Vietnam Fighting," *Human Events*, July 10, 1965, 13.

18. *New York Times*, November 15, 1965, p. 1.

19. *Arizona Republic*, January 1, 1967.

20. Goldwater, *Goldwater*, 222; Barry Goldwater, *With No Apologies*, 202; Barry Goldwater to Chet Huntley, January 10, 1973, Alpha File, Barry Goldwater Papers, Arizona Historical Foundation; *Washington Post*, January 21, 1967, February 18, 1967, August 24, 1967, October 29, 1967; *Arizona Republic*, December 14, 1966, March 30, 1967, April 4, 1967; "Issues and Answers," ABC, November 13, 1966; *New York Times*, January 22, 1965, p. 14, February 22, 1965, p. 2, June 17, 1965, p. 4, September 6, 1965, p. 6, November 3, 1965, p. 3 (quote), January 15, 1966, pp. 1, 8, April 19, 1966, p. 25.

21. *New York Times*, April 28, 1965, p. 14.

22. Goldwater, *Goldwater*, 224; *New York Times*, June 14, 1965, p. 28; Clodfelter, *Limits*, ix, 35–36, 117–19, 125, 134–35, 141, 145, 205, 208, 210; Summers, *On Strategy II*, 113; Baritz, *Backfire*, 40, 183.

23. Goldwater, *Goldwater*, 76, 223–24; Stilp, "Operation MARS," 20–21; Barry Goldwater to Stephen Shadegg, May 15, 1978, Alpha File, Goldwater Papers; Quoted in Bernstein, "AuH₂O," 64.

24. *New York Times*, May 6, 1966, p. 6.; *Arizona Republic,* April 3, 1966, March 19, 1967; Goldwater, *Goldwater*, 249; Quoted in Safer, *Flashbacks*, 140.

25. Matusow, *Unraveling*, 360–62; Wolfe, "Southern Strategy," 259–62.

26. Matusow, *Unraveling*, 160, 395; Edsall and Edsall, *Chain Reaction*, 7–8, 10, 45, 57, 69, 122.

27. *New York Times*, August 24, 1965, p. 15.

28. Ibid., November 3, 1965, p. 3.

29. Quoted in Newhall, "Barry Goldwater," 19.

30. *New York Times*, January 15, 1966, p. 25, July 28, 1966, p. 18.

31. Rae, *Decline*, 86–87; Hess, *In a Cause*, 172; Phillips, *Emerging*, 101; U.S. House, 89th Cong., 2nd sess., October 11, 1966, *Congressional Record* 112: 26118–19.

32. Interview with Denison Kitchel, November 18, 1989.

33. White, *Suite 3505*, 418–20; Wolfe, "Southern Strategy," 363–64; Shadegg, *Arizona Politics*, 146; Ross H. Rice, "Arizona: Politics in Transition," in Jonas, *Politics*, 57–63; *New York Times*, November 10, 1966, p. 31.

34. Barry Goldwater to Thruston Morton, August 2, 1967, Box 24, Thruston Morton Papers, University of Kentucky.

35. *Arizona Republic*, September 13, 1968.

36. Barry Goldwater with Richard Joseph, "Traveler, Consider My Arizona . . . ," *Esquire*, October 1966, 124–26; Goldwater, *People and Places;* Interview with Margaret Kober, December 16, 1991, Margaret Kober Papers, private collection; Goldwater to Robert Wood, August 12, 1966, Box 6, Robert Wood Papers, Hoover Presidential Library; Interview with Roy Elson by Donald A. Ritchie, July 6, 1990; Reisner, *Cadillac Desert*, 282–83, 300–301, 304–5; Worster, *Rivers of Empire*, 275–76; *New York Times*, May 19, 1965, p. 37, July 28, 1966, p. 21, December 28, 1966, p. 37, October 7, 1967, p. 17; *Arizona Republic*, March 1, 1967.

37. Barry Goldwater to the Goldwater children, January 13, 1967, Michael Goldwater Papers.

38. Barry Goldwater to Michael Goldwater, December 18, 1967, Michael Goldwater Papers.

39. *Scottsdale Progress*, December 4, 1967.

40. "Trip Itinerary," Peggy Goldwater Papers; *New York Times*, April 10, 1967, p. 1; *Arizona Republic*, March 18 and 30, 1967, April 4 and 7, 1967, September 12, 1967, December 2, 1967.

41. Barry Goldwater to Milton Friedman, July 5, 1967, Milton Friedman Papers, private collection.

42. Matusow, *Unraveling*, 362–63; Wolfe, "Southern Strategy," 468–69; Barry Goldwater to Lewis L. Strauss, April 30, 1968, Box 68, Lewis L. Strauss Papers,

Hoover Presidential Library; Milton Friedman to Barry Goldwater, August 3, 1967, Friedman Papers.

43. ABC "Evening News," October 19, 1968, Arizona Historical Foundation.

44. *New York Times*, January 9, 1968, p. 27, May 28, 1968, p. 35; *Arizona Republic*, May 28, 1968, October 4, 1968; "Statement," May 27, 1968, Box 2, Kitchel Collection.

45. Shadegg, *Arizona Politics*, 156.

46. Interview with Ronald Crawford, September 11, 1990; "Barry Rides Again," *Newsweek*, October 4, 1968, 34–35; "Senator's Schedule," Box 13, Ruth Reinhold Papers, Arizona Historical Foundation.

47. Murphy, "Riding," 86–88; Tansik and Billings, "Current Impact," 11–12, 16; Himes, "New Phoenix Residents," 6–7; Hall, "1968 Election," 465, 467.

48. Quoted in Bamford, "Taking on the Mob," 11.

49. Interview with Roy Elson, December 14, 1991; Interview with Charles Pine, October 26, 1990; Interview with Orren Beaty, Jr., September 14, 1990; Elson interview by Ritchie, July 12, 1990.

50. Elson interview; Beaty interview; Elson interviews by Ritchie, June 20, 1990, July 12, 1990.

51. *New York Times*, March 8, 1968, p. 22.

52. Quoted in Wills, *Reagan's America*, 290.

53. Quoted in Hess and Broder, *Republican Establishment*, 176.

54. Telephone interview with William F. Buckley, Jr., August 10, 1990; Ambrose, *Nixon: Triumph of a Politician*, 118; Wills, *Nixon Agonistes*, 231, 244–46; Rusher, *Rise of the Right*, 209; Reinhard, *Republican Right*, 218.

55. Chester et al., *American Melodrama*, 190.

56. Rae, *Decline*, 93–95; Rusher, *Rise of the Right*, 204; White, *Making of the President 1968*, 40; White, *Why Reagan Won*, 66, 68, 80.

57. Interview with Barry Goldwater by Pat McMahon, KTAR Radio, March 25, 1993.

58. Buckley interview.

59. "Memo to the Files" from Hubert H. Humphrey, August 23, 1967, Box 23, W. Marvin Watson Papers, Lyndon Johnson Presidential Library.

60. Interview with Ronald Reagan, August 7, 1991; Interview with Barry Goldwater, August 30, 1990; *Arizona Republic*, January 1, 1989; Rusher, *Rise of the Right*, 207; Barry Goldwater to Lewis Strauss, July 22, 1968, Box 68, Strauss Papers; Barry Goldwater to Peggy Goldwater, January 18, 1976, Peggy Goldwater Papers.

61. The final count was: Nixon 692 votes, Rockefeller 277, and Reagan 182.

62. Barry Goldwater to Richard Nixon, March 26, 1969, Box 26, Rose Mary Woods File, Staff Member Office Files, White House Central Files, Richard M. Nixon Papers, Nixon Presidential Materials Project.

63. White, *Making of the President 1968*, 261–299; White, *Why Reagan Won*, 94, 100–101; Goldwater, *With No Apologies*, 207; Rae, *Decline*, 96; Wills, *Nixon*, 252; Wolfe, "Southern Strategy," 420–25; Chester et al., *American Melodrama*, 447–57;

New York Times, July 25, 1968, p. 21, August 6, 1968, p. 20; Quoted in Matusow, *Unraveling*, 403–4.

64. *Baltimore Sun*, October 4, 1968.

65. *Arizona Republic*, October 4, 1968.

66. Ibid., September 1, 1968.

67. Ibid., October 4, 1968.

68. Elson interview; *Arizona Republic*, September 5, 8, 12, and 22, 1968, October 4, 10, 12, 22, 23, and 25, 1968, November 1 and 3, 1968; Elson interview by Ritchie, August 16, 1990.

69. *Arizona Republic*, September 13, 1968.

70. Ibid., September 17, 19, and 25, 1968, October 10, 1968.

71. Ibid., October 4, 1968.

72. *Baltimore Sun*, October 4, 1968.

73. *Arizona Republic*, October 6, 1968.

74. Ibid., October 4, 1968.

75. Ibid.

76. Elson interview; *Arizona Republic*, September 12, 1968, October 2, 6, 9, 16, and 27 (quote), 1968.

77. Hall, "1968 Election," 462–65; *New York Times*, January 4, 1969, p. 17; *Arizona Republic*, November 6 and 7, 1968.

78. Barry Goldwater, "Don't Waste a Vote on Wallace," *National Review*, October 22, 1968, 1060–61.

79. "Memo to the Diary File" from Barry Goldwater, Alpha File, Goldwater Papers; Chester et al., *American Melodrama*, 626; Wolfe, "Southern Strategy," 511–15, 530; Phillips, *Emerging*, 207, 286.

80. Reichly, *Conservatives*, 28; Phillips, *Emerging*, 30, 38, 42, 44, 81, 83.

81. Judy Rooney Eisenhower interview; Interview with Ellen Thrasher, September 14, 1990; Reichly, *Conservatives*, 319–21, 422; Interview with George McGovern, September 12, 1990.

82. "May 17, 1969" and Barry Goldwater to Richard Kleindienst, June 9, 1972, Alpha File, Goldwater Papers; Interview with Barry Goldwater, Jr., July 29, 1991.

83. "February 8, 1969," Alpha File, Goldwater Papers.

84. Barry Goldwater to Richard Nixon, January 10, 1969, Box 9, Subject File, White House Central Files, Nixon Papers.

85. "February 8, 1969," Alpha File, Goldwater Papers.

86. Barry Goldwater to Bryce Harlow, July 2, 1969, Box 2, Subject File, White House Central Files, Nixon Papers.

87. Goldwater to Harlow, October 16, 1969, Box 3, Subject File, White House Central Files, Nixon Papers.

88. Goldwater to Nixon, December 18, 1969, Box 10, Subject File, White House Central Files, Nixon Papers.

89. Quoted in Kutler, *Wars of Watergate*, 112.

90. Ibid., 111–16.

91. Note to the file, April 9, 1969, Alpha File, Goldwater Papers.

92. Ibid., February 21, 1969, Alpha File, Goldwater Papers.

93. Harlow to Carl McMurray, January 19, 1969, Box 1, Harlow to Peter Flanigan, March 24, 1969, Box 1, Sally Studebaker to Flanigan, March 26, 1969, Box 1, Harlow to Dwight Chapin, February 24, 1969, Box 5, Subject File, White House Central Files, Nixon Papers; "First Meeting With President Nixon March 5, 1969," "March 24, 1970," "August 6, 1970," "My Visit With the President, December 14, 1970," Alpha File, Goldwater Papers.

94. Charles Colson to H. R. Haldeman, February 8, 1972, Box 71, Subject File, White House Central Files, Nixon Papers; Interview with Tom Korologos, September 11, 1990.

95. Colson to Haldeman, February 8, 1972, Box 71, Subject File, White House Central Files, Nixon Papers.

96. John D. Ehrlichman to Dwight Chapin, August 11, 1970, Box 11, Subject File, White House Central Files, Nixon Papers.

97. Colson to Haldeman, May 30, 1972, Box 96, Lamar Alexander to Harlow, April 14, 1969, Box 1, Helmut Sonnenfeldt to Henry Kissinger, August 24, 1971, Box 39, Subject File, White House Central Files, Nixon Papers.

98. "March 24, 1970," Alpha File, Goldwater Papers.

99. "January 27, 1971," Alpha File, Goldwater Papers.

100. "Additional Notes," February 15, 1969, Alpha File, Goldwater Papers.

101. Goldwater, *Conscience of a Majority,* 17.

102. "May 17, 1969," Alpha File, Goldwater Papers.

103. Goldwater, "Political Philosophy," 140.

104. Edsall and Edsall, *Chain Reaction,* 81, 85–87; Reichly, *Conservatives,* 154–58, 196–97; U.S. Senate, 91st Congress, 1st sess., December 19, 1969, *Congressional Record* 115: 34847–49, 91st Congress, 2nd sess., April 2, 1970, 116: 10166, 10187–89, April 7, 1970, 116: 10509–11, July 9, 1970, 116: 23395–99; Goldwater, *Conscience of a Majority,* 164–66, 170; Form letter from Barry Goldwater, September 29, 1970, Box 258, Rogers C. B. Morton Papers, University of Kentucky.

105. *Arizona Republic,* December 6, 1972.

106. "Statement on Conservative Complaints about the Nixon Administration," December 17, 1971, Box 94:50, Legislative Correspondence File, Goldwater Papers.

107. Reichly, *Conservatives,* 130–35, 213–25; Goldwater, *With No Apologies,* 272–73; Barry Goldwater to Milton Friedman, February 4, 1972, Friedman Papers.

108. U.S. Senate, 91st Cong., 2nd sess., December 2, 1970, *Congressional Record* 116: 39544.

109. McGovern interview.

110. *New York Times,* December 16, 1970, p. 47; Quoted in Dean, *Barry Goldwater,* 1.

111. U.S. Senate, 91st Cong., 1st sess., November 21, 1969, *Congressional Record* 115: 35343, 35345.

112. *Arizona Republic,* December 2, 1972.

113. Goldwater, *Conscience of a Majority,* 222.

114. Dean, *Barry Goldwater,* 4.

115. Goldwater, *Conscience of a Majority,* 226, 227–28.

116. *New York Times,* October 2, 1969, p. 23, February 20, 1970, p. 33, July 8, 1970, p. 15, September 2, 1970, p. 15, January 20, 1971, p. 14; U.S. Senate, 91st Cong., 2nd sess., August 25, 1970, *Congressional Record* 116: 29941–43, October 6, 1970, 116: 35120; Goldwater, *Conscience of a Majority,* 117–18.

117. Form letter from Barry Goldwater, 1969–1970, Box 91:17, Legislative Correspondence File, Goldwater Papers.

118. Barry Goldwater to Betty Simpson, July 14, 1971, Box 92:12, Legislative Correspondence File, Goldwater Papers.

119. Goldwater to Kay Doyon, May 5, 1972, Legislative Correspondence File, Goldwater Papers.

120. U.S. Senate, 91st Cong., 1st sess., June 9, 1969, *Congressional Record* 115: 15173; Form letter from Barry Goldwater, 1972, Goldwater to Lori Martin, April 7, 1972, to Bobbi Brownley, April 28, 1972, to Frank Appleton, May 5, 1972, to Mary Brown, June 8, 1972, Phyllis Schlafly to Goldwater, April 7, 1972, Box 92:12, Legislative Correspondence File, Goldwater Papers.

121. U.S. Senate, 91st Cong., 1st sess., November 21, 1969, *Congressional Record* 115: 35344.

122. Goldwater to Joanna Hines, March 13, 1970, Box 91:16, Legislative Correspondence File, Goldwater Papers.

123. Goldwater to Mrs. Thomas Loomis, December 18, 1969, to Thomas Hutton, October 15, 1970, to Mrs. James Brady, October 22, 1970, to Jim Durkee, October 28, 1970, to Dean Peyton, November 23, 1970, Box 91:16, to Nicholas Luca, January 29, 1971, to Mrs. Lester Ruffner, June 18, 1971, to Paula Moore, December 7, 1971, Box 92:9, Legislative Correspondence File, Goldwater Papers; Goldwater interview, August 30, 1990.

124. U.S. Senate, 91st Cong., 1st sess., July 23, 1969, *Congressional Record* 115:20515.

125. Ibid., May 1, 1969, *Congressional Record* 115: 11051.

126. Goldwater, *Conscience of a Majority,* 71–98.

127. Ibid., 101; *New York Times,* July 30, 1970, p. 9; Barry Goldwater, "An Adequate Defense Posture," *Vital Speeches* 37 (February 1, 1971): 230–32; "Is America Going Isolationist?" *U.S. News and World Report,* June 28, 1971, 26–27; U.S. Senate, 91st Cong., 2nd sess., August 5, 1970, *Congressional Record* 116: 27371–77, August 13, 1970, 116: 28725–27.

128. "February 21, 1969," Alpha File, Goldwater Papers.

129. Bernstein, "AuH$_2$O," 52.

130. Korologos interview.

131. Dean, *Barry Goldwater,* 15, 21; *New York Times,* June 10, 1971, p. 31; Thrasher interview.

132. Barry Goldwater to Melvin Laird, October 22, 1971, Box 3, Subject File, White House Central Files, Nixon Papers.

133. *Arizona Republic*, February 1, 1972.

134. Goldwater, *Conscience of a Majority*, 113.

135. Ibid., 95–96, 105–108; Tansik and Billings, "Rise," 4; McGovern interview.

136. Barry Goldwater to Charles Batarseh, May 2, 1969, Box 91:40, Legislative Correspondence File, Goldwater Papers. Batarseh, a combat medic with Company D, 1st Battalion, 1st Division had written Goldwater on March 15, 1969, asking "Why are we here?"

137. "July 4, 1969," Alpha File, Goldwater Papers.

138. *Los Angeles Times*, April 20, 1972.

139. "For Diary," no date, Alpha File, Goldwater Papers.

140. Barry Goldwater to Batarseh, March 15, 1969, to Jim Gerry, July 9, 1970, Box 91:40, Legislative Correspondence File, Goldwater Papers; *Los Angeles Times*, April 5, 1972; *New York Times*, April 5, 1972, p. 16, May 9, 1972, p. 19; "For Diary," Alpha File, Goldwater Papers.

141. "May 9, 1971," Alpha File, Goldwater Papers.

142. Goldwater, *With No Apologies*, 221, 222.

143. "May 9, 1971," Alpha File, Goldwater Papers.

144. *New York Times*, October 16, 1969, p. 18; Goldwater to John Augustine, September 28, 1970, Box 91:10, Legislative Correspondence File, Goldwater Papers; Goldwater, *With No Apologies*, 227; U.S. Senate, 92nd Cong., 2nd sess., May 11, 1972, *Congressional Record* 118: 16934.

145. Interview with Terry Emerson, September 13, 1990.

146. See Chapter 5. Goldwater believed that the War Powers Act was different from the Bricker Amendment because the latter was an attempt to amend the Constitution and involved states' rights issues while the former sought to alter the Constitution through "simple legislation." See Goldwater, "President's Constitutional Primacy," 474–75.

147. See Chapter 6.

148. *New York Times*, March 13, 1961, p. 16.

149. Interview with Barry Goldwater by William F. Buckley, Jr., *Firing Line*, PBS, March 13, 1990; Goldwater, "President's Ability," 443.

150. *New York Times*, February 11, 1972, 4.

151. Goldwater, "President's Ability," 439.

152. Goldwater, "President's Constitutional Primacy," 488.

153. U.S. Senate, 91st Cong., 2nd sess., June 15, 1970, *Congressional Record* 116: 19687.

154. Terry Emerson to the author, August 13, 1992; Emerson interview; *New York Times*, April 24, 1971, p. 4, August 25, 1971, p. 37; Goldwater, *Goldwater*, 24; Interview with Frank Moss, September 24, 1990; Interview with John Tower, September 14, 1990; "How Goldwater Sees it," *National Review*, September 24, 1971, 1045–46; Javits, *Autobiography*, 406–408; Wormuth and Firmage, *To Chain*, 29, 68,

143; Interview with Sandra Taylor, August 4, 1993; Barry Goldwater to the author, July 30, 1993.

155. Barry Goldwater to Richard Nixon, March 26, 1971, Subject File, White House Central Files, Nixon Papers.

156. *New York Times,* October 27, 1971, p. 16.

157. William Timmons to Barry Goldwater, April 30, 1971, Subject File, White House Central Files, Nixon Papers; *New York Times,* February 18, 1972, p. 14.

158. "The White House Report," February 29, 1972, Alpha File, Goldwater Papers.

159. Ibid.

160. Ibid.

161. William F. Buckley, Jr., "Senator Goldwater's Reassurance," *National Review,* March 31, 1972, 365.

162. Reinhard, *Republican Right,* 223–24; Rusher, *Rise of the Right,* 239–241.

163. Barry Goldwater to William Loeb, September 29, 1971, Box 93:30, Legislative Correspondence File, Goldwater Papers.

164. *New York Times,* July 24, 1971, p. 22, December 10, 1971, p. 35, September 3, 1971, p. 25, December 10, 1971, p. 35; "Statement on Conservative Complaints about the Nixon Administration."

165. "7–14–72," Alpha File, Goldwater Papers.

166. "August 28, 1972," Alpha File, Goldwater Papers.

167. *Arizona Republic,* October 19, 1972.

168. *Los Angeles Times,* October 15, 1972.

169. Judy Rooney Eisenhower interview; *Arizona Republic,* October 25, 1972; Barry Goldwater to Stephen Shadegg, July 18, 1977, Alpha File, Goldwater Papers.

170. See White, *Making of the President 1972.*

171. Phillips, *Post-Conservative,* 92; Phillips, *Emerging,* 436.

172. Rae, *Decline,* 48, 158–61; Bass and DeVries, *Transformation,* 33–35; 92; Reichly, *Conservatives,* 427.

173. "11–22–72," Alpha File, Goldwater Papers.

174. *New York Times,* January 19, 1973, pp. 1, 4; Ambrose, *Nixon: Ruin and Recovery,* 40 (quote), 51–52.

175. Goldwater, *With No Apologies,* 249.

176. Baritz, *Backfire,* 208–215; Clodfelter, *Limits,* ix–x, 125–27, 177, 183, 194, 201–8.

177. Barry Goldwater to Jack Williams, February 24, 1972, Alpha File, Goldwater Papers.

178. Ibid.

179. "11–22–72," Alpha File, Goldwater Papers.

180. Judy Rooney Eisenhower interview; "11–22–72," Barry Goldwater to Harry Rosenzweig, August 11, 1970, to Williams, February 24, 1972, to Richard Kleindienst, June 9, 1972, Alpha File, Goldwater Papers.

Chapter 11: Staying the Course

1. Goldwater, *Coming Breakpoint*, 175.

2. Reinhard, *Republican Right*, 226, 234–35; Goldwater, *With No Apologies*, 250; *Los Angeles Times*, August 4, 1973; *New York Times*, June 27, 1973, p. 7, August 3, 1973, p. 59; Quoted in White, *Breach*, 225.

3. Barry Goldwater to Richard Nixon, April 4, 1973, Box 8, President's Personal Files, Richard Nixon Papers, Nixon Presidential Materials Project.

4. Quoted in White, *Breach*, 218.

5. Note to the file, 1973, Alpha File, Barry Goldwater Papers, Arizona Historical Foundation.

6. Barry Goldwater to Peggy Goldwater, March 4, 1977, Peggy Goldwater Papers, private collection of Peggy Goldwater Clay.

7. Note to the file, 1973, Barry Goldwater to Harry Rosenzweig, July 23, 1973, Alpha File, Goldwater Papers; Barry Goldwater to Peggy Goldwater, January 14, 1975, Peggy Goldwater Papers; Interview with Judy Rooney Eisenhower, October 26, 1990; *New York Times*, December 25, 1975, p. 26.

8. Note to the file, 1973, Alpha File, Goldwater Papers; *Los Angeles Times*, March 2, 20, and 21, 1973; *New York Times*, June 23, 1973, p. 7; U.S. Senate, 93rd Cong., 1st sess., September 24, 1973, *Congressional Record* 119: 31014–15.

9. Goldwater, *Goldwater*, 261.

10. Note to the file, 1973, Alpha File, Goldwater Papers.

11. Interview with John Tower, September 14, 1990.

12. Goldwater, *Goldwater*, 256.

13. For detailed discussions of Watergate see Kutler, *Wars of Watergate*, White, *Breach*, Bernstein and Woodward, *All the President's Men*, and Woodward and Bernstein, *Final Days*.

14. Barry Goldwater to Chet Huntley, January 10, 1973, Alpha File, Goldwater Papers.

15. Goldwater, "President's Constitutional Primacy," 84.

16. Interview with Benjamin Bradlee, September 10, 1990.

17. Quoted in Bernstein, "AuH$_2$O," 65.

18. Interview with Barry Goldwater, August 30, 1990. Barry Goldwater to Denison Kitchel, September 6, 1979, Box 2, Denison Kitchel Collection, Hoover Institution Archives.

19. Barry Goldwater to Stephen Shadegg, July 18, 1977, Alpha File, Goldwater Papers.

20. Barry Goldwater to Richard Nixon, March 29, 1973, Box 8, President's Personal Files, Nixon Papers, Nixon Project; *Christian Science Monitor*, April 12, 1973. See also *New York Times*, April 12, 1973, p. 1.

21. *Arizona Republic*, May 1, 1973.

22. U.S. Senate, 93rd Cong., 1st sess., May 1, 1973 *Congressional Record* 119: 13721.

23. *Los Angeles Times,* April 18, 1973, May 1, 1973, May 20, 1973; *Arizona Republic,* May 1, 1973.

24. Press release, May 16, 1973, Alpha File, Goldwater Papers.

25. *New York Times,* May 17, 1973, pp. 1, 36; "May 17, 1973," Alpha File, Goldwater Papers.

26. Barry Goldwater to Richard Nixon, June 20, 1973, Alpha File, Goldwater Papers.

27. *New York Times,* June 21, 1973, p. 41.

28. Telephone interview with Barry Goldwater, Jr., September 17, 1991.

29. Quoted in Dean, *Blind Ambition,* 295.

30. *Arizona Republic,* July 3, 1973.

31. Interview with Barry Goldwater, September 24, 1992.

32. "September 9, 1973," Alpha File, Goldwater Papers.

33. *New York Times,* September 13, 1973, p. 21, September 19, 1973, p. 32; *Arizona Republic,* October 4, 8, and 11, 1973; "September 9, 1973," Alpha File, Goldwater Papers.

34. Barry Goldwater, "A Complete Clearing of the Air Is Long Overdue," September 11, 1973, p. 45, "Needed: Conservatives at the Top," September 12, 1973, p. 47, "Are There Any Leaders Left To Take Us To?" September 13, 1973, p. 47, *New York Times.*

35. *Los Angeles Times,* October 23, 1973.

36. *New York Times,* November 2, 1973, 24.

37. *Washington Post,* October 23, 1973; *Arizona Republic,* November 2, 1973.

38. *Los Angeles Times,* November 11, 1973.

39. *Christian Science Monitor,* December 17, 1973.

40. *Los Angeles Times,* November 14, 1973.

41. *Arizona Republic,* November 6, 1973.

42. Goldwater, *Goldwater,* 267–71. Belying his concerns, Goldwater wrote Nixon in a thank-you note following the dinner: "It's far and away the most enjoyable night I've had in a long, long time, and it was particularly so because you obviously were enjoying yourself." Goldwater to Nixon, December 18, 1973, Alpha File, Goldwater Papers.

43. Peter Steinfels, "The Goldwater Myth," *Commonweal,* February 1, 1974, 431.

44. Roy Reed, "The Rehabilitation of Barry Goldwater," *Los Angeles Times,* April 7, 1974.

45. Ibid.

46. Ibid.

47. "In His Heart, He Knows He's Right," *Newsweek,* October 1, 1973, 29; *New York Times,* September 25, 1973, p. 19, December 30, 1973, p. 14, March 24, 1974, p. 32; *Los Angeles Times,* December 29, 1974.

48. According to Stanley Kutler, more than seventy people were convicted of or pleaded guilty to crimes arising from Nixon administration scandals. *Wars of Watergate,* 620.

49. Nixon, *RN*, 978.

50. Quoted in Woodward and Bernstein, *Final Days*, 155.

51. White, *Breach*, 374, 378; *New York Times*, March 20, 1974, p. 29; Quoted in Ambrose, *Nixon: Ruin and Recovery*, 335.

52. *New York Times*, January 14, 1974, p. 13.

53. Ibid., January 16, 1974, p. 18.

54. *Los Angeles Times*, January 16, 1974.

55. Ibid., March 24, 1974.

56. Barry Goldwater to James Garrick, April 15, 1974, Legislative Correspondence File, Box 93:46, Goldwater Papers.

57. U.S. Senate, 93rd Cong., 2nd sess., April 30, 1974, *Congressional Record* 120: 12296.

58. Bradlee interview.

59. J. Terry Emerson to Garry Wills, April 19, 1974, Box 7, Tom C. Korologos Papers, Staff Member Office Files, White House Central Files, Nixon Papers, Nixon Project.

60. Korologos to Emerson, April 22, 1974, Box 7, Tom C. Korologos Papers, Staff Member Office Files, White House Central Files, Nixon Papers, Nixon Project.

61. "A Desperate Gamble for Survival," *Newsweek*, May 13, 1974, 23.

62. Woodward and Bernstein, *Final Days*, 147–49; Nixon, *RN*, 996.

63. No title, May 8, 1974, Alpha File, Goldwater Papers.

64. Woodward and Bernstein, *Final Days*, 159, 175–77; "How Barry Goldwater Sees It," *Newsweek*, May 27, 1974, 24.

65. "August 7, 1973," Alpha File, Goldwater Papers.

66. White, *Breach*, 32–34, 38; Woodward and Bernstein, *Final Days*, 300–302, 315–17, 333, 359, 367–74, 383–84; Goldwater, *With No Apologies*, 262–63; Goldwater, *Goldwater*, 274; Quoted in Ambrose, *Nixon: Ruin and Recovery*, 419.

67. Quoted in Woodward and Bernstein, *Final Days*, 406.

68. Goldwater, *With No Apologies*, 264–67; Woodward and Bernstein, *Final Days*, 360–62, 390–93, 396–99, 405–9; White, *Breach*, 38–40.

69. "August 8, 1974," Alpha File, Goldwater Papers.

70. Goldwater, *Goldwater*, 278. Although they are in substantial agreement, see other versions in White, *Breach*, 42–43, and Woodward and Bernstein, *Final Days*, 413–15.

71. Quoted in Woodward and Bernstein, *Final Days*, 421.

72. Interview with Wallace Bennett, September 7, 1990.

73. Quoted in White, *Breach*, 46–47.

74. *New York Times*, January 23, 1974, p. 1.

75. Quoted in Bernstein, "AuH$_2$O," 69–70.

76. "December 19, 1974," Alpha File, Goldwater Papers.

77. Ibid.

78. Ibid.; "November 5, 1976," Box 1207, Names File, White House Central Files, Gerald R. Ford Papers, Gerald R. Ford Presidential Library; William F.

Buckley, Jr., "Can Conservative Wing Recover from Nixonism?" *Arizona Republic,* September 5, 1974; *New York Times,* August 11, 1974, p. 44; Reichly, *Conservatives,* 299–300; "Was Justice Done?" *Newsweek,* September 16, 1974, 19; Goldwater to Paul Pennanen, December 17, 1974, Box 95:37, Legislative Correspondence File, Goldwater Papers.

79. Barry Goldwater to Richard Nixon, January 30, 1975, Alpha File, Goldwater Papers.

80. "August 7, 1974," Alpha File, Goldwater Papers.

81. *Arizona Republic,* September 9, 1974.

82. Ibid., September 9 and 30, 1974.

83. Ibid., October 28, 1974.

84. Ibid., October 11, 1974.

85. U.S. Senate, 93rd Cong., 2nd sess., September 16, 1974, *Congressional Record* 120: 31279.

86. *New York Times,* October 6, 1974, p. 28; *Arizona Republic,* September 12, 22, and 30, 1974.

87. U.S. Senate, 93rd Cong., 2nd sess., March 6, 1974, *Congressional Record* 120: 5564–67.

88. Form letters, February 16, 1973, Box 93:2, March 7, 1973, Box 93:3 Legislative Correspondence File, Goldwater Papers.

89. *Los Angeles Times,* October 18, 1974.

90. Interview with Michael Goldwater, August 29, 1990.

91. Interview with Jonathan Marshall, October 25, 1990.

92. "The Whistle-Stop," July 1974, Jonathan Marshall Papers, private collection.

93. Interview with Jonathan Marshall by Charles Colley, n.d.

94. *Arizona Republic,* October 10, 1974.

95. Position Papers on "Energy," "Congressional Reform," "Senior Citizens," "Foreign Policy," "The Economy," "Education," and "Conservation and Ecology," Jonathan Marshall Papers; Marshall interview; *Arizona Republic,* September 11 and 13, 1974, October 4, 6, 15, 18, 27, and 31, 1974, November 1 and 3, 1974; *New York Times,* December 12, 1975, p. 1.

96. *Arizona Republic,* October 11, 1974.

97. Ibid., October 20, 1974.

98. Ibid., October 14, 1974.

99. Ibid., November 7, 1974.

100. Interview with Gene Karp, September 11, 1990; Marshall interview; Interview with Orren Beaty, Jr., September 14, 1990; *Arizona Republic,* October 6, 10, and 20, 1974.

101. *Arizona Republic,* November 6 and 7, 1974; Reichly, *Conservatives,* 317.

102. *Phoenix Gazette,* April 1, 1993; *Arizona Republic,* August 30, 1992; Kammer, *Second Long Walk,* 5, 125–26.

103. Quoted in Kammer, *Second Long Walk,* 13.

104. U.S. House of Representatives, 93rd Congress, Testimony of Barry Gold-

water, *Partition of Navajo and Hopi 1882 Reservation,* Hearings Before the Sub-committee on Interior and Insular Affairs, May 14, 1973, Part 8, 42–43.

105. *Arizona Republic,* May 15, 1973, September 18, 1973; *New York Times,* July 24, 1974, p. 9; *Salt Lake Tribune,* May 23, 1994; Interview with Stephen Boyden, August 22, 1990; Interview with Paul Fannin, September 1, 1990; Beaty interview; Kammer, *Second Long Walk,* xiii–xiv, 3–5, 26–30, 46–48, 75–84; Benedek, *Wind,* 32–41; Billings and Shaw-Serdar, "Relocating," 43–45; Whitson, "Policy Review," 376–88.

106. In 1990 a tribal court sentenced Peter MacDonald to six years in prison for bribery and other ethical violations during his term as Navajo chair. Two years later, he was convicted of fraud and racketeering in charges stemming from a 1989 reservation riot. In 1993 he received a fourteen-year term, to run concurrently with his other sentences, for his part in the 1989 riot. *Arizona Republic,* October 26, 1990; *New York Times,* November 15, 1992, p. 14; *Salt Lake Tribune,* December 1, 1992, February 17, 1993, July 11, 1993.

107. Quoted in Benedek, *Wind,* 196.

108. *Arizona Republic,* February 24, 1974, February 18, 1977, August 30, 1992; Benedek, *Wind,* 196–99; Kammer, *Second Long Walk,* 97–99, 110, 164 (quote), 165–66.

109. Judy Rooney Eisenhower interview.

110. Barry Goldwater to Peggy Goldwater, November 23, 1974, Peggy Gold-water Papers.

111. Interview with Joanne Goldwater, September 1, 1990; Interview with Bette Quinn, September 13, 1990; Interview with Peggy Goldwater Clay, July 30, 1991; Barry Goldwater to Peggy Goldwater, January 14, 1975, October 18, 1975, Peggy Goldwater Papers; *New York Times,* December 25, 1975, p. 26.

112. "Excepts from Address on Detente with the Soviet Union," *Congressional Digest* 54 (October 1975): 235.

113. U.S. Senate, 94th Cong., 1st sess., March 21, 1975, *Congressional Record* 121: 15237.

114. *New York Times,* October 16, 1975, p. 10.

115. Transcript, "Face the Nation," CBS, April 27, 1975, Box 94:118, Legislative Correspondence File, Goldwater Papers.

116. U.S. Senate, 94th Cong., 1st sess., May 20, 1975, *Congressional Record* 121: 15237.

117. "Excerpts from Remarks on the B-1 Bomber Program," *Congressional Digest* 55 (December 1976): 296; *New York Times,* June 3, 1975, p. 11, June 4, 1975, pp. 1, 12; U.S. Senate, 94th Cong., 1st sess., March 21, 1975, *Congressional Record* 121: 8022–23; *Washington Post,* April 15, 1975, July 22, 1975.

118. U.S. Senate, 94th Cong., 2nd sess., "Individual Views of Senator Barry Goldwater," Final Report of the Select Committee to Study Government Operations with Respect to Intelligence Activities, Book 1, *Senate Report,* 94–755, April 26, 1976, 593.

119. Goldwater, "Congress and Intelligence Oversight," *Washington Quarterly* 6 (Summer 1983): 17.

120. *Washington Post,* November 3 and 5, 1975; *New York Times,* January 21, 1976, p. 3, April 27, 1976, p. 26, April 28, 1976, p. 35; Arnson, *Crossroads,* 13–15; Goldwater, "Individual Views," 586.

121. Goldwater, *Coming Breakpoint,* 43.

122. Ibid., 60.

123. Barry Goldwater to Milton Friedman, January 22, 1975, April 7, 1975, Milton Friedman Papers, private collection.

124. Denison Kitchel to Barry Goldwater, May 1, 1975, Box 2, Denison Kitchel Collection, Hoover Institution Archives.

125. Goldwater, *Coming Breakpoint,* 1, 3–4, 27–38, 61–63, 74, 78, 87–88, 98, 106–8, 139–46; *New York Times,* February 27, 1975, p. 49; Barry Goldwater to Paul De Falco, Jr., October 15, 1975, William Kendall to Goldwater, June 22, 1976, James Cannon to Goldwater, July 8, 1976, Box 1207, Name File, White House Central Files, Ford Papers; Milton Friedman to Barry Goldwater, May 19, 1975, Friedman Papers; Goldwater, "Why Gun-Control," 183–88.

126. "May 5, 1975," Alpha File, Goldwater Papers.

127. Barry Goldwater to Dean Burch, May 12, 1975, Note to the file, October 23, 1975, Alpha File, Goldwater Papers.

128. Goldwater, *With No Apologies,* 275.

129. Barry Goldwater to Peggy Goldwater, January 18, 1976, Peggy Goldwater Papers.

130. Goldwater, *With No Apologies,* 276.

131. Barry Goldwater to Peggy Goldwater, January 18, 1976, Peggy Goldwater Papers.

132. Tower interview.

133. Note to the file, October 23, 1975, Alpha File, Goldwater Papers.

134. Telephone interview with William F. Buckley, Jr., August 10, 1990; Fannin interview; Interview with Robert Goldwater, November 17, 1989; Note to the file, May 20, 1975, Alpha File, Goldwater Papers.

135. Interview with Ronald Reagan, August 7, 1991.

136. Rusher, "What Happened," 16.

137. Crawford, "Sunshine Boys," 9.

138. Viguerie and Edwards, "Goldwater," 10.

139. Goldwater was incensed by this piece. He consigned the Viguerie and Edwards article to a file labeled "SLANDER." Personal Files, Goldwater Papers.

140. Robert Goldwater interview; William F. Buckley, Jr., "Put Me Down for Reagan," *National Review,* August 6, 1976, 859; William F. Buckley, Jr., "Messrs Goldwater and Reagan," *National Review,* June 11, 1976, 640; Rusher, *Rise of the Right,* 155, 280–81; "Reaction to Goldwater," 2–3; Crawford, *Thunder,* 114–16.

141. Quoted in Reinhard, *Republican Right,* 233.

142. *Wall Street Journal,* November 13, 1975.

143. Quoted in Witcover, *Marathon*, 97.

144. LaFeber, *Panama Canal*, 140–48 (quote).

145. *Arizona Republic*, May 12, 1976.

146. Barry Goldwater to Robert L. Scott, Jr., May 11, 1976, Box 94:18, Legislative Correspondence File, Goldwater Papers.

147. *New York Times*, May 10, 1976, pp. 1, 20.

148. *Arizona Republic*, May 5, 1976.

149. Ibid., May 5, 7, 10, 13, 21, and 23, 1976; Barry Goldwater to Harold B. Green, Jr., February 13, 1976, Box 94:18, Legislative Correspondence File, Goldwater Papers; LaFeber, *Panama Canal*, 149; *New York Times*, May 3, 1976, pp. 1, 34.

150. Barry Goldwater to Gerald Ford, May 7, 1976, Box 393, Rogers C. B. Morton Papers, University of Kentucky.

151. *Phoenix Gazette*, December 3, 1986.

152. Goldwater, *With No Apologies*, 11.

153. Interview with Barry Goldwater by Harry Reasoner, "Sixty Minutes," CBS, 1980.

154. Quoted in Bowden, "Goldwater," 37.

155. Ambrose, *Nixon: Ruin and Recovery*, 489; *New York Times*, February 26, 1976, p. 3; Interview with Barry Goldwater, September 24, 1992.

156. *Arizona Republic*, August 17, 1976.

157. *New York Times*, August 17, 1976, p. 23.

158. Rae, *Decline*, 78, 114–17, 128, 131–33.

159. Barry Goldwater, letter to the editor, *New York Times*, November 1, 1976, p. 39.

160. Ibid.

161. White, *Why Reagan Won*, 194.

162. Barry Goldwater to David Bond, March 30, 1979, Box 96:47, Legislative Correspondence File, Goldwater Papers.

163. Barry Goldwater to Zbigniew Brzezinski, April 3, 1978, Subject File, White House Central Files, Jimmy Carter Papers, Jimmy Carter Presidential Library.

164. *Washington Post*, July 30, 1977.

165. Goldwater to Brzezinski, April 3, 1978, Subject File, White House Central Files, Carter Papers.

166. Barry Goldwater, letter to the editor, *Washington Post*, March 12, 1977.

167. Barry Goldwater to Jimmy Carter, April 28, 1980, Correspondence Tracking File, Carter Papers.

168. Barry Goldwater to Peggy Goldwater, July 28, 1977, Peggy Goldwater Papers; Goldwater, *With No Apologies*, 302; *New York Times*, February 2, 1978, p. 7, August 4, 1979, p. 3; Goldwater to Stephen Shadegg, April 20, 1978, Alpha File, Goldwater Papers; Barry Goldwater, "Mankind's Slow Painful Path," *Vital Speeches* 44 (May 15, 1978): 455–56; Barry Goldwater, "The Trouble with the War Powers Resolution," *Washington Post*, March 12, 1977; U.S. Senate, 95th Cong., 1st sess., September 12, 1977, *Congressional Record* 123: 28704–6; Barry Gold-

water to Jimmy Carter, April 28, 1980, Correspondence Tracking File, Carter Papers.

169. Barry Goldwater to Jimmy Carter, September 12, 1977, Subject File, White House Central Files, Carter Papers.

170. Barry Goldwater to Jimmy Carter, August 26, 1977, Name File, White House Central Files, Carter Papers.

171. "Panama Report," January 5, 1978, Alpha File, Goldwater Papers.

172. Jimmy Carter to Barry Goldwater, September 10, 1977, "September 12, 1977," "Panama Report," Alpha File, Goldwater Papers; *Los Angeles Times,* October 13, 1977; *New York Times,* February 3, 1978, p. 8, February 23, 1978, p. 9, March 1, 1978, p. 4; Goldwater interview, September 24, 1992; Interview with J. Terry Emerson, September 13, 1990; Kitchel, *Truth;* Moffett, *Limits,* 97, 176, 215. Operation Just Cause, the 1989 American invasion of Panama, has clouded the future of these treaties.

173. U.S. Senate, 96th Cong., 1st sess., February 8, 1979, *Congressional Record* 125: 2200.

174. *New York Times,* December 19, 1978, p. 1.

175. Ibid., December 24, 1978, p. 2.

176. Ibid., Barry Goldwater, letter to the editor, October 11, 1977, p. 37.

177. Quoted in Martin, "President's Power," 301.

178. U.S. Senate, 96th Cong., 1st sess., December 14, 1979, *Congressional Record* 125: 36141.

179. Barry Goldwater, letter to the editor, June 1, 1978, p. 20, February 8, 1979, p. 20, *New York Times;* Goldwater to Jimmy Carter, October 18, 1979, November 13, 1979, Correspondence Tracking File, Carter Papers; Goldwater, *China;* U.S. Senate, 96th Cong., 1st sess., November 15, 1979, 125: 32522–25, December 14, 1979, 125: 36141–43 *Congressional Record;* Barry Goldwater, "The Taiwan Termination Lawsuit," *Congressional Digest* 58 (June 1979): 166, 168, 192; Barry Goldwater, "Testimony Relating to the Treaty Process," *Congressional Digest* 58 (June 1979): 182, 184, 186, 188, 190; *Goldwater v. Carter,* Box 7, Robert Lipshutz Papers, Carter Library; Lawson, "Constitutional Twilight Zone," 147–49, 152, 159–65; Martin, "President's Power," 301–3, 310, 317, 319; Lawrence Tribe, "Goldwater v. Carter: A Constitutional Red Herring," *New Republic,* March 17, 1977, 14–15.

180. Goldwater, *With No Apologies,* 277–87.

181. U.S. Senate, 95th Cong., 2nd sess., February 21, 1978, *Congressional Record* 124: 3963.

182. Ibid., 123: 1698–1703, 2nd sess., February 21, 1978, 124: 3963–65; *Arizona Republic,* January 5, 1978, April 2, 1978.

183. *Phoenix Gazette,* March 15, 1977.

184. Barry Goldwater to Stephen Shadegg, March 22, 1977, Alpha File, Goldwater Papers.

185. Wendland, *Arizona Project;* Barry Goldwater to Mrs. Eugene Pulliam, June

24, 1976, William Saufley Papers, Arizona Historical Foundation; Goldwater interview, August 30, 1990.

186. Senator Barry Goldwater Voting Record, 95th Congress, Legislative File, M–Z, Goldwater Papers; Barry Goldwater to Stuart Eizenstat, June 27, 1977, Name File, White House Central Files, Carter Papers; *New York Times,* January 22, 1977, p. 10; *Phoenix Gazette,* September 13, 1978; *Yuma Daily Sun,* March 28, 1979; *Arizona Republic,* October 7, 1978, July 15, 1979.

187. Barry Goldwater to Jimmy Carter, February 22, 1977, Name File, White House Central Files, Carter Papers.

188. Fradkin, *River,* 5; Malone and Etulain, *American West,* 287–88.

189. Barry Goldwater to Peggy Goldwater, September 4, 1979, Peggy Goldwater Papers.

190. *Phoenix Gazette,* December 3, 1986; Barry Goldwater to Peggy Goldwater, September 4, 1979, Peggy Goldwater Papers; *Arizona Republic,* January 18, 1987; Notes to the file, April 25, 1979, May 9, 1979, July 19, 1979, Barry Goldwater to Michael Goldwater, July 21, 1979, Alpha File, Goldwater Papers.

191. For a more complete discussion of the New Right—its origins, personalities, and organizations—see Crawford, *Thunder;* Himmelstein, *To the Right;* Phillips, *Post-Conservative;* Gottfried and Fleming, *Conservative Movement;* Tyrrell, *Conservative Crack-Up;* Martin, *New Right;* Miles, *Odyssey;* Steinfels, *Neoconservatives;* Saloma, *Ominous Politics;* Peele, *Revival.*

192. Himmelstein, *To the Right,* 131–32, 141; Edsall, *New Politics,* 131.

193. Edsall, *New Politics,* 39–40, 73–75, 157, 161–64, 211–12, 231; Edsall and Edsall, *Chain Reaction,* 3–5, 17, 24, 103–9, 122–24, 127, 129, 135.

194. "A Pocket Guide to the Right," *Newsweek,* April 17, 1989, 25.

195. Barry Goldwater, "GOP Should Protect Gays from Job Discrimination," *Salt Lake Tribune,* July 15, 1994, reprinted from the *Washington Post.*

196. Quoted in Ribuffo, *Old Christian Right,* 263.

197. Goldwater, *Goldwater,* 110, 386–87.

Chapter 12: Conservatism Triumphant

Epigraphs: Copy of Ronald Reagan remarks in Michael Goldwater Papers, private collection; Interview with Barry Goldwater.

1. *Phoenix Gazette,* September 11, 1979.

2. Goldwater, *Goldwater,* 375.

3. Barry Goldwater to Peggy Goldwater, September 4, 1979, Peggy Goldwater Papers, private collection of Peggy Goldwater Clay; Note to the file, July 19, 1979, Alpha File, Barry Goldwater Papers, Arizona Historical Foundation.

4. Interview with Bette Quinn, September 13, 1990; Interview with Alice McGreavy, December 15, 1991; Barry Goldwater to Peggy Goldwater, September 4, 1979, Peggy Goldwater Papers; Interview with Peggy Goldwater Clay, July 30, 1991.

5. Clay interview.

6. Michael Goldwater to Barry Goldwater, September 20, 1979, Michael Goldwater Papers.

7. Interview with Joanne Goldwater, September 1, 1990; Interview with Barry Goldwater, Jr., July 29, 1991; Goldwater, *Goldwater,* 363, 374–75; Goldwater to Michael Goldwater, July 21, 1979, September 26, 1979, Michael Goldwater Papers.

8. Interview with Gene Karp, September 11, 1990.

9. Interview with Malcolm Straus, September 27, 1991.

10. Interview with Ronald Crawford, September 11, 1990; Weinstein et al., *Regional Growth,* 7; Note to the file, July 19, 1979, Richard Wirthlin to Barry Goldwater, July 14, 1981, Alpha File, Goldwater Papers; Interview with Earl Eisenhower, August 30, 1990; *Arizona Republic,* April 19, 1979.

11. Charles W. Pine, "Political Potpourri," November 24, 1979, Alpha File, Goldwater Papers; *Arizona Republic,* October 6 and 18 (quote), 1978.

12. Note to the file, July 19, 1979, Alpha File, Goldwater Papers.

13. Interview with Judy Rooney Eisenhower, October 26, 1990.

14. *Phoenix Gazette,* October 14, 1980.

15. Crawford interview.

16. Interview with Bill Schulz, August 29, 1990.

17. Karp interview.

18. *Arizona Republic,* September 10, 1980.

19. Ibid., September 30, 1980.

20. *Washington Post,* October 24, 1980.

21. *Arizona Republic,* September 10, 1980.

22. Karp interview; Schulz interview.

23. *Phoenix Gazette,* May 21, 1979.

24. Interview with Charles Pine, October 26, 1990; Schulz interview; *Scottsdale Progress,* October 17, 1980; *Arizona Republic,* October 17, 1980, January 18, 1987; Crawford interview.

25. *Arizona Republic,* May 25, 1980.

26. Goldwater, *Goldwater,* 376–78; *New York Times,* July 16, 1980, p. 18.

27. *Arizona Republic,* September 11, 1980.

28. Ibid., September 4, 1980.

29. Ibid., September 12, 1980.

30. Parker *Pioneer,* October 2, 1980.

31. *Arizona Republic,* September 12, 1980.

32. Ibid., September 17 and 23, 1980, October 27, 1980.

33. "1980 Campaign Seminar," M–Z Correspondence File, Goldwater Papers; *Arizona Republic,* September 17 and 29 (quote), 1980.

34. "November 7, 1980," Alpha File, Goldwater Papers.

35. *Arizona Republic,* September 27, 1980.

36. Ibid., September 29, 1980.

37. *Prescott Courier,* October 8, 1980; *Arizona Republic,* September 29 and 30, 1980, October 1, 1980.

38. *Arizona Republic,* September 26, 1980; Richard Wirthlin to Barry Goldwater, September 26, 1980, M-Z Correspondence File, Goldwater Papers; Wirthlin to Goldwater, July 14, 1981, Alpha File, Goldwater Papers.

39. Wirthlin to Goldwater, September 26, 1980, Alpha File, Goldwater Papers; Judy Rooney Eisenhower interview; Crawford interview; *Arizona Republic,* October 14, 1980; Earl Eisenhower interview.

40. Goldwater, *Goldwater,* 387.

41. *Arizona Republic,* October 22, 1980.

42. Ibid., October 31, 1992. He honored his pledge on January 22, 1981, by cosponsoring a Senate resolution that proposed a constitutional amendment to protect unborn children. U.S. Senate, 97th Cong., 1st sess., January 22, 1981, *Congressional Record* 127: 833.

43. *Arizona Republic,* October 31, 1992.

44. Form letter on abortion, 1975, Box 94:1, Goldwater to Terri Osborn, August 12, 1975, Goldwater to Dorothy Williamson, February 19, 1976, Goldwater to Nancy Roach, May 28, 1976, Box 94:6, Legislative Correspondence File, Goldwater Papers; *Arizona Republic,* October 22 and 24, 1080, November 1 (quote), 1980.

45. *Arizona Republic,* October 12, 1980.

46. Ibid., October 30, 1980.

47. Ibid., October 8, 1980.

48. Schulz interview; *Tempe Daily News,* October 8, 1980; *Arizona Republic,* October 8, 10, 12, 16, and 31, 1980.

49. *Arizona Republic,* November 2, 1980.

50. Ibid., October 16, 1980.

51. *Yuma Daily Sun,* October 1, 1980; *Arizona Daily Star,* October 2, 1980; *Prescott Courier,* October 8, 1980; *Phoenix Jewish News,* October 31, 1980; *Arizona Republic,* October 2, 6, 8, 9, 11, 13, 14, 16, 17, and 28, 1980, January 18, 1987.

52. *Arizona Republic,* September 11, 1980.

53. Ibid., September 8, 1980.

54. Ibid.

55. Ibid., October 15, 1980.

56. Ibid., October 19, 1980.

57. Ibid., October 28, 1980.

58. *Phoenix Gazette,* October 20, 1980.

59. *Arizona Republic,* September 12 and 19, 1980, November 2, 1980.

60. Ibid., November 5 and 6, 1980; Wirthlin to Goldwater, July 14, 1981, Alpha File, Goldwater Papers.

61. *Arizona Republic,* November 5, 6, and 9, 1980; Interview with Harry Rosenzweig, November 16, 1989; Judy Rooney Eisenhower interview; Crawford interview.

62. *Arizona Republic,* November 6, 1980.

63. Ibid.

64. Ibid.

65. Barry Goldwater to Howard Pyle, November 20, 1980, Box 76, Howard Pyle Papers, Arizona State University.

66. *Arizona Republic,* November 9, 1980.

67. *Phoenix Gazette,* November 11, 1980.

68. *Arizona Republic,* December 10, 1980.

69. Edsall and Edsall, *Chain Reaction,* 186.

70. Athearn, *Mythic West,* 205; Bernard and Rice, *Sunbelt Cities,* 1; Phillips, *Post-Conservative,* 91.

71. Edsall and Edsall, *Chain Reaction,* 143–45, 176; Edsall, *New Politics,* 208.

72. Phillips, *Post-Conservative,* 93; Sale, *Power Shift,* 148; Edsall, *New Politics,* 189; Peele, *Revival,* 2.

73. Barry Goldwater, Jr., interview.

74. *New York Times,* November 10, 1981, p. 23, March 12, 1982, p. 18; *Los Angeles Times,* November 4, 1982; Note to the file, July 26, 1982, Alpha File, Goldwater Papers.

75. Quoted in Johnson, *Sleepwalking,* 19.

76. Bette Quinn interview; Judy Rooney Eisenhower interview; Interview with William Quinn, September 11, 1990.

77. Phillips, *Politics,* 75, 78, 94; Edsall and Edsall, *Chain Reaction,* 166; Edsall, *New Politics,* 17–18, 227–28; Wills, *Reagan's America,* 364; Barrett, *Gambling,* 16–17, 130–33; Geoghegan, *Which Side,* 146, 278.

78. Edsall, *New Politics,* 22; Geoghegan, *Which Side,* 179; Phillips, *Politics,* 13, 70, 120, 126, 128; Judis, *Grand Illusion,* 247; Edsall and Edsall, *Chain Reaction,* 219.

79. Barry Goldwater to B. Lohmiller, October 21, 1982, Box C-8 (unprocessed), Legislative Correspondence File, Goldwater Papers.

80. Interview with Barry Goldwater, September 24, 1992.

81. *Wall Street Journal,* August 3, 1981.

82. "From Lawmakers, Words of Advice to Reagan," *U.S. News and World Report,* April 19, 1982, 39.

83. Goldwater interview, September 24, 1992.

84. Barry Goldwater, Jr., interview; Goldwater to Margaret Fitzpatrick, May 5, 1982, to Carl Worthy, Jr., October 28, 1982, Box C-8 (unprocessed), Legislative Correspondence File, Goldwater Papers; *Los Angeles Times,* March 25, 1981; "Congress's First Report Card on Reagan," *U.S. News and World Report,* April 6, 1981, 27.

85. Interview with Barry Goldwater by William F. Buckley, Jr., *Firing Line,* PBS, March 13, 1990.

86. Dotson Rader, "What Does Barry Goldwater say Today?" *Parade Magazine,* November 28, 1993, 5.

87. Goldwater interview, September 24, 1992.

88. *Arizona Republic,* March 28, 1982.

89. *New York Times,* March 12, 1982, p. 18.

90. Interview with Jake Garn, November 26, 1990; Barry Goldwater to William Saufley, September 13, 1983, William Saufley Papers, Arizona Historical Foundation; *Los Angeles Times,* December 6, 1984.

91. Quoted in Bernstein, "AuH$_2$O," 68.

92. Barry Goldwater, "The 'New Right' Has Nothing to Do With the 'Old Conservatism,'" *Los Angeles Times*, September 17, 1981.

93. *New York Times*, July 10, 1981, p. 11; "Barry Goldwater Tastes New Life," *Newsweek*, July 27, 1981, 24; Colman McCarthy, "Doth Mr. Conservative Protest Too Much?" *Los Angeles Times*, September 23, 1981; "Pulpit Bullies," *Time*, September 28, 1981, 27; *Wall Street Journal*, August 3, 1981.

94. *New York Times*, September 16, 1981, p. 1.

95. U.S. Senate, 97th Cong., 2nd sess., February 24, 1982, *Congressional Record* 128:2242–43. See also "Should Congress Curtail Jurisdiction of the Federal Courts?" *Congressional Digest* 61 (May 1982): 139, 141, 143.

96. *New York Times*, March 12, 1982, p. 18.

97. Ibid., October 4, 1988, p. 28.

98. Quoted in Karalekas, "Intelligence," 26.

99. Goldwater, *Goldwater*, 299.

100. *New York Times*, May 28, 1982, p. 14.

101. U.S. Senate, 96th Cong., 1st sess., August 2, 1979, *Congressional Record* 125: 22239; Persico, *Casey*, 230–31, 339; Woodward, *Veil*, 27; *New York Times*, November 12, 1980, p. 26.

102. Interview with John Tower, September 14, 1990.

103. Interview with J. Terry Emerson, September 13, 1990; Interview with George McGovern, September 12, 1990; Woodward, *Veil*, 28–30; Quoted in Persico, *Casey*, 205.

104. Garn interview.

105. Goldwater interview, September 24, 1992.

106. Quoted in Woodward, *Veil*, 155.

107. Tower interview.

108. Telephone interview with Patrick Leahy, February 22, 1991; Woodward, *Veil*, 154–59, 162–65; Persico, *Casey*, 232, 254, 260, 276; "Reagan's CIA Troubles," *Newsweek*, July 27, 1981, 18; "The CIA: Can Casey Survive?" *Newsweek*, August 3, 1981, 18; "As Pressure Built Against CIA's Casey," *U.S. News and World Report*, August 3, 1981, 7; "Behind the Casey Flap," *Newsweek*, August 10, 1981, 21; *New York Times*, July 22, 1981, pp. 1, 16, July 24, 1981, p. 9, July 29, 1981, p. 11, October 28, 1981, pp. 1, 23.

109. Goldwater interview, September 24, 1992.

110. Goldwater, *Goldwater*, 302.

111. Leahy interview.

112. Ibid.; Marshall et. al., *Iran-Contra Connection*, 204, 207, 214–15; Arnson, *Crossroads*, 14–16; *New York Times*, May 28, 1982, p. 14.

113. Quoted in Persico, *Casey*, 361.

114. U.S. Senate, 96th Cong., 1st sess., August 2, 1979, *Congressional Record* 125:22240.

115. Arnson, *Crossroads*, 71–72; Draper, *Very Thin Line*, 15–17.

116. Quoted in Persico, *Casey,* 296.

117. Quoted in Woodward, *Veil,* 227–28.

118. Arnson, *Crossroads,* 100–103.

119. Woodward, *Veil,* 257; Arnson, *Crossroads,* 65, 106–7, 118–21; "U.S. Aid to Nicaraguan Rebels—Lawmakers Speak Out," *U.S. News and World Report,* May 2, 1983, 29.

120. April 27, 1983, Alpha File, Goldwater Papers.

121. Telephone conversation between Ronald Reagan and Barry Goldwater, May 5, 1983, Alpha File, Goldwater Papers.

122. Draper, *Very Thin Line,* 18–19; Woodward, *Veil,* 279–80, 308–10; Arnson, *Crossroads,* 109, 118–20, 123–25, 137–38; *New York Times,* May 7, 1983, p. 1; "A Battle Over the Secret War," *Newsweek,* May 16, 1983, 46.

123. *New York Times,* April 17, 1984, p. 4.

124. *Wall Street Journal,* April 6, 1984; *Washington Post,* April 18, 1984; *New York Times,* April 8, 1984, p. 1; Arnson, *Crossroads,* 154; Persico, *Casey,* 373.

125. Quoted in Draper, *Very Thin Line,* 21.

126. *New York Times,* April 16, 1984, p. 1, April 17, 1984, pp. 1, 4; Draper, *Very Thin Line,* 18–19; Arnson, *Crossroads,* 156–57, 255; Interview with Daniel Moynihan, December 5, 1990; Leahy interview; Garn interview.

127. Persico, *Casey,* 373.

128. Interview with Barry Goldwater, August 30, 1990.

129. U.S. Senate, 98th Cong., 2nd sess., April 5, 1984, *Congressional Record* 130:8044–41; Goldwater, *Goldwater,* 301–2; Persico, *Casey,* 373–74; Woodward, *Veil,* 361–63; *New York Times,* April 16, 1984, p. 8.

130. Goldwater, *Goldwater,* 304.

131. Quoted in Persico, *Casey,* 375.

132. Goldwater, *Goldwater,* 306.

133. Leahy interview.

134. April 25, 1984, Alpha File, Goldwater papers.

135. Ibid.

136. Goldwater, *Goldwater,* 305.

137. U.S. Senate, 98th Cong., 2nd sess., April 10, 1984, *Congressional Record* 130: 8537.

138. Goldwater, *Goldwater,* 306–8; Woodward, *Veil,* 63–68; Barry Goldwater to Robert McFarlane, April 25, 1984, [CIA] "Employee Bulletin," April 12, 1984, Alpha File, Goldwater Papers.

139. Quoted in Persico, *Casey,* 378.

140. Quoted in Arnson, *Crossroads,* 157.

141. Garn interview.

142. *Washington Post,* April 18, 1984.

143. Interview with Benjamin Bradlee, September 10, 1990.

144. *New York Times,* April 18, 1984, p. 30.

145. Moynihan interview; Patrick J. Leahy, "What We're Doing in Nicaragua: A

Makeshift Policy Leading to War," *Washington Post,* April 15, 1984; William Safire, "Firestorm in a Teacup," *New York Times,* April 13, 1984, p. 35.

146. Bill Casey to Barry Goldwater, April 25, 1984, Alpha File, Goldwater Papers.

147. Johnson, *Sleepwalking,* 278.

148. Woodward, *Veil,* 381.

149. *Washington Post,* April 26, 1984; "The CIA Sues for Peace," *Newsweek,* May 7, 1984, 66; Barry Goldwater to Bill Casey, May 7, 1984, Barry Goldwater's "Opening Statement, Hearings on CIA Harbor Mining Program," April 26, 1984, Box C-20, Legislative File, Goldwater Papers; Woodward, *Veil,* 409, 481–83; Arnson, *Crossroads,* 162–63; Johnson, *Sleepwalking,* 278–79; Quoted in Persico, *Casey,* 380.

150. Persico, *Casey,* 379.

151. Barry Goldwater to Bill Casey, October 1, 1984, Box C-20, Legislative File, Goldwater Papers.

152. Arnson, *Crossroads,* 162, 164; "'Mr. Conservative' Sizes Up Challenges Reagan Faces," *U.S. News and World Report,* December 17, 1984, 54.

153. Barry Goldwater to Peggy Goldwater, May 11, 1984, Michael Goldwater Papers.

154. Barry Goldwater, "Freedom," *Vital Speeches* 50 (September 15, 1984): 714–15.

155. *New York Times,* August 23, 1984, pp. 1, 28; Edsall and Edsall, *Chain Reaction,* 169–72, 180.

156. "'Mr. Conservative,'" 53.

157. *New York Times,* December 6, 1984, p. 20, December 17, 1984, p. 12, January 28, 1985, p. 6; "Speaking His Mind," *Time,* December 17, 1984, 12; *Arizona Republic,* January 1, 1985; *Los Angeles Times,* February 13, 1985; *Wall Street Journal,* February 20, 1985.

158. Goldwater, *Goldwater,* 349.

159. "Can Civilians Run Our Wars? Goldwater Has His Say," *U.S. News and World Report,* March 19, 1984, 88; "Pull U.S. Marines Out of Lebanon?" *U.S. News and World Report,* September 19, 1983, 29; Goldwater, *Goldwater,* 341–42, 344, 348–50, 353–54; Hartmann and Wendzel, *Defending,* 176.

160. Goldwater, *Goldwater,* 351.

161. Ibid., 353.

162. "Pentagon Comes Under Fire from Its Friends," *U.S. News and World Report,* October 28, 1985, 28; Goldwater, *Goldwater,* 336–41, 351–52; Hartmann and Wendzel, *Defending,* 176–77, 181–82; "Drums," *Time,* October 27, 1985, 34–36.

163. Goldwater, *Goldwater,* 381.

164. Ibid., 80; *New York Times,* December 12, 1985, p. 31.

165. Some dissented from this consensus. The increased power given to the JCS chair drew the attention of critics who feared the creation of a "military czar" and "the first potential challenge to civilian control of the military in the history of the United States." Proponents of the different branches of the military also registered

concerns about the loss of service autonomy. Some believed that the act underestimated the power of ingrained service loyalty not only in the Pentagon but in Congress. See Previdi, *Civilian Control,* 9–10 (quotes), 29, 31, 131, 134, 140–41, 165.

166. U.S. Senate, 99th Cong., 2nd sess., May 7, 1986, *Congressional Record* 132: S5472.

167. Ibid., 132: S5463–5547; "Goldwater's Last Act," *National Review,* June 20, 1986, 18; Hartmann and Wendzel, *Defending,* 184–85, 362–65. For a thorough analysis of the Goldwater-Nichols Act see Blackwell and Blechman, *Making Defense Reform.*

168. Summers, *On Strategy II,* 241, 243; Goldwater, *Goldwater,* 354–57 (quote).

169. *Phoenix Gazette,* December 11, 1986; Goldwater, *Goldwater,* 359–61, 392; "Tributes to the Honorable Barry Goldwater in the United States Senate Upon the Occasion of His Retirement from the Senate," Reprinted from U.S. Senate, 99th Cong., 2nd sess., October 18, 1986, *Congressional Record.*

170. Quoted in Draper, *Very Thin Line,* 498. The final report of the special prosecutor declared that "President Reagan created the conditions which made possible the crimes committed by others by his secret deviations from announced national policy . . . and by his open determination to keep the contras together 'body and soul' despite a statutory ban on contra aid." *New York Times,* January 19, 1994, p. 6.

171. Buchanan, "Voice," xix–xx.

172. Tyrrell, *Conservative Crack-Up,* 171; *Phoenix Gazette,* December 1, 1986; Draper, *Very Thin Line,* 120, 136, 272, 474–75, 500, 505; Goldwater, *Goldwater,* 21, 26, 290; Interview with Barry Goldwater, August 30, 1990.

Chapter 13: Mr. Conservative

Epigraph: Interview with Barry Goldwater by Hugh Downs, "20//20," ABC, July 23, 1993.

1. *Arizona Republic,* January 18, 1987.

2. Bowden, "Goldwater," 36.

3. Goldwater, *Goldwater,* 33.

4. Barry Goldwater to Barry Goldwater, Jr., June 10, 1982, Personal File, Barry Goldwater, Jr., Papers, Arizona Historical Foundation.

5. *Women's Wear Daily,* January 9, 1989; *Phoenix Gazette,* January 7, 1989; Goldwater, *Goldwater,* 370–72; *Scottsdale Progress,* January 11, 1989; Interview with Ronald Crawford, September 11, 1990; Interview with Barry Goldwater, CBS "Morning News," November 20, 1986; *Arizona Republic,* April 10, 1988; Interview with Tim Sexson, August 30, 1990; Interview with Susan Goldwater, May 14, 1993.

6. *New York Times,* October 10, 1987, p. 12.

7. *New York Times,* February 24, 1988, p. 22.

8. Watkins, *High Crimes,* 9, 11, 58, 165, 248, 358; Interview with Jack Williams, December 16, 1991.

9. *New York Times,* February 16, 1988, p. 7.

10. Willie Horton was prominently featured during the 1988 campaign in Republican television commercials and literature to suggest that Massachusetts Governor Dukakis was soft on crime. Although convicted of second-degree murder, Horton was permitted to participate in a weekend furlough program. During one of these furloughs he disappeared, only to be arrested in Maryland for rape and assault.

11. *Scottsdale Progress*, September 22, 1988.

12. Edsall and Edsall, *Chain Reaction*, 216; Edsall, "Willie Horton," 7; *Arizona Republic*, August 16, 1988, October 16, 1988, November 6, 1992; Barry Goldwater to William Saufley, July 22, 1991, in the author's possession.

13. *Newsweek*, March 6, 1989, 57.

14. *Wall Street Journal*, February 4, 1991.

15. *Scottsdale Progress*, January 11, 1989.

16. Quoted in Watkins, *High Crimes*, 374.

17. Ibid., 379.

18. *Arizona Republic*, February 12, 1989.

19. Ibid., October 30 and 31, 1992, November 3 and 10, 1992, December 2, 1992, January 22, 1993, June 30, 1993, July 10, 1993, October 21, 1993; Pat Murphy, "Goldwater a Republican Party Pooper? Arizona Political Icon Is Kinder, Gentler to Demos," *Salt Lake Tribune*, December 6, 1992; Susan Goldwater interview.

20. "Barry's Choice," *U.S. News and World Report*, May 27, 1991, 23.

21. Murphy, "Visit," 128–29.

22. *Arizona Republic*, August 7, 1992.

23. Ibid., October 31, November 6, 1992.

24. *Arizona Republic*, November 6, 1992; Pat Murphy, "More Embarrassment May Be Brewing in Arizona," *Salt Lake Tribune*, January 2, 1994.

25. *Arizona Republic*, July 8, 1992.

26. Ibid., August 20, 1993.

27. Reprinted from the *Washington Post* in the *Salt Lake Tribune*, July 15, 1994.

28. Interview with Barry Goldwater, "Larry King Live," CNN, June 10, 1993.

29. *Washington Post*, June 10, 1993.

30. Goldwater interview with Downs; *Arizona Republic*, January 29, 1993, July 3 and 15, 1993, August 20, 1993; Bull, "Right Turn," 33.

31. Ty has also tested positive for the virus that causes AIDS.

32. Bull, "Right Turn," 35.

33. *Arizona Republic*, August 20, 1993.

34. Ibid., January 9, 1992, February 10, 1992, March 13, 1994; Bull, "Right Turn," 37; Susan Goldwater interview; Telephone conversation with Joanne Goldwater, June 17, 1992.

35. Goldwater interview by Downs.

36. Ibid.

37. Ibid.; Bull, "Right Turn," 37; *Arizona Republic*, October 21, 1993; *Phoenix Gazette*, November 21, 1993.

38. *New York Times*, April 12, 1992, p. 1.

39. Ibid., January 29, 1992, p. 14.

40. *Arizona Republic*, January 2, 1989, September 5, 1991; Summers, *On Strategy II*, 244; *Salt Lake Tribune*, November 4, 1992.

41. Quoted in Edsall, "Clinton's Revolution," 6.

42. *Salt Lake Tribune*, October 24, 1993.

43. *Arizona Republic*, March 17, 1994. The Whitewater affair concerns allegations that funds from Madison Guaranty, an Arkansas savings and loan run by a Clinton business partner, were illegally diverted to the Whitewater real estate venture, in which Bill and Hillary Clinton had an interest, and to a Clinton gubernatorial campaign. After Clinton was elected president the matter escalated; White House aides were charged with ethical violations in trying to keep apprised of the investigation, and Treasury Department officials were charged with covering up these breaches in testimony during U.S. Senate hearings.

44. Ibid., September 26, 1993, October 24, 1993, December 5, 1993; *New York Times*, October 18, 1993, p. 1, October 19, 1993, p. 1 (quote), October 31, 1993, p. 1.

45. *Salt Lake Tribune*, December 29, 1993; *Arizona Republic*, May 5, 1993; *Phoenix Gazette*, January 7, 1989.

46. Rader, "What," 6.

47. Judis, *Buckley*, 469–70; Himmelstein, *To the Right*, 199–201, 210.

48. *Salt Lake Tribune*, November 13, 1992.

49. Ibid., September 12, 1993.

50. Ibid., December 16, 1992, May 11, September 6 and 7, 1993; *New York Times*, June 3, 1994, p. 1, July 18, 1994, p. 6.

51. Tyrrell, *Conservative Crack-Up*, 208.

52. Ibid., 225, 278.

53. Dirk Johnson, "Far from an Arid Economy, Desert States Thrive," *New York Times*, May 13, 1991, p. 1.

54. Watkins, *High Crimes*, 41.

55. Reisner, *Cadillac Desert*, 312.

56. Wiley and Gottlieb, *Empires in the Sun*, 183, 188, 212; Reisner, *Cadillac Desert*, 305–6, 312–13.

57. *Arizona Republic*, September 27, 1991, December 7, 1992; *Wall Street Journal*, November 16, 1993; *Salt Lake Tribune*, December 23 1991, August 8, 1991, March 3, 1992, February 16, 1993, October 24, 1993; "A Fight Over Liquid Gold," *Time*, July 22, 1991, 20–26.

58. *Phoenix Gazette*, January 7, 1989.

59. Interview with Barry Goldwater, September 24, 1992.

60. Quoted in Leahy, "I'd Have Ended," 47.

61. Susan Goldwater interview.

62. Goldwater to Saufley, May 7, 1993, in the author's possession.

Bibliography

Manuscript Collections

Bastien, Joseph H., Papers. Arizona Historical Foundation, Arizona State University, Tempe.

Beaty, Orren, Jr., Papers. Private collection. Vienna, Virginia.

Bennett, Wallace F., Papers. Special Collections, Marriott Library, University of Utah, Salt Lake City.

Bricker, John, Papers. Ohio Historical Society, Columbus.

Bridges, Styles, Papers. New Hampshire State Archives, Concord.

Brown, Elizabeth Churchill, Collection. Hoover Institution Archives, Stanford University, Palo Alto, California.

Carter, Jimmy, Papers. Jimmy Carter Presidential Library, Atlanta.
  White House Central Files
    Correspondence Tracking File
    Diary Name Index
    Name File
    Subject File

Colegrove, Kenneth W., Papers. Herbert Hoover Presidential Library, West Branch, Iowa.

Cotton, Norris, Collection. University of New Hampshire, Durham.

Dewey, Thomas E., Papers. University of Rochester, New York.

Eisenhower, Dwight David, Papers. Dwight Eisenhower Presidential Library, Abilene, Kansas.
  Dwight D. Eisenhower Personal Files
    Administrative Series
    Ann Whitman Diary Series
    Campaign Series
    DDE Diary Series

   Legislative Meetings Series
   Name Series
  Post-Presidential Papers
   Appointment Book Series
   Convenience File
   Principal File
   Secondary File
   Signature File
   Special Names Series
  White House Central Files
   Alpha File
   Confidential File
   General File
   Official File
   Presidential Personal File

Emery, Carlos B., Papers. University of Kentucky, Lexington.

Fannin, Paul J., Papers. Arizona Historical Foundation, Arizona State University, Tempe.

Fireman, Bert, Papers. Arizona Historical Foundation, Arizona State University, Tempe.

Ford Gerald R., Papers. Gerald R. Ford Presidential Library, University of Michigan, Ann Arbor.
  White House Central Files
   Names File

Free Society Association Collection. Hoover Institution Archives, Stanford University, Palo Alto, California.

Friedman, Milton, Collection. Hoover Institution Archives, Stanford University, Palo Alto, California.

Friedman, Milton, Papers. Private collection. Hoover Institution, Stanford University, Palo Alto, California.

Goldberg, Robert A., Papers. Private collection. Salt Lake City.

Goldwater, Barry, Collection. Eugene C. Barker Texas History Center, University of Texas, Austin.

Goldwater, Barry, College Transcript. University of Arizona, Tucson.

Goldwater, Barry, High School Transcript. Staunton Military Academy, Staunton, Virginia.

Goldwater, Barry, Military Personnel Record. Department of the Air Force, Washington, D.C.

Goldwater, Barry, Papers. Arizona Historical Foundation, Arizona State University, Tempe.
  Alpha File
  Biographical File
  Correspondence File
  Legislative Correspondence File

Legislative File, A–L, M–Z

Personal File

Scrapbooks

Speeches

Goldwater, Barry, School Record. Phoenix School District.

Goldwater, Barry, Jr., Papers. Arizona Historical Foundation, Arizona State University, Tempe.

Goldwater, Joanne, Papers. Private collection. Scottsdale, Arizona.

Goldwater, Josephine, Biographical File, Arizona Historical Foundation, Arizona State University, Tempe.

Goldwater, Michael, Papers. Private collection. Phoenix.

Goldwater, Peggy, Papers. Private collection of Peggy Goldwater Clay, Newport Beach, California.

Goldwater, Peggy, School Records, Mount Vernon College, Washington, D.C.

Goldwater Family, Papers. Arizona Historical Foundation, Arizona State University, Tempe.

Hancock Family, Papers. Arizona Historical Foundation. Arizona State University, Tempe.

Hayden, Carl T., Collection. Arizona State University, Tempe.

Hickenlooper, Bourke B., Papers. Herbert Hoover Presidential Library, West Branch, Iowa.

Hill, Robert C., Collection. Hoover Institution Archives, Stanford University, Palo Alto, California.

Hoover, Herbert, Papers. Herbert Hoover Presidential Library, West Branch, Iowa. Post-Presidential Papers

Hruska, Roman L., Papers. Nebraska State Historical Society, Lincoln.

Humphreys, Robert, Papers. Dwight Eisenhower Presidential Library, Abilene, Kansas.

Javits, Jacob K., Collection. State University of New York at Stony Brook.

Johnson, Lyndon B., Papers. Lyndon B. Johnson Presidential Library, University of Texas, Austin.

Lyndon B. Johnson Personal Files

Congressional File

Famous Names File

Selected Names File

Senate Political File

Subject File

Vice Presidential Papers

White House Central Files

Appointment File

Famous Names File

Jonas, Frank H., Papers. Special Collections, Marriott Library, University of Utah, Salt Lake City.

Judd, Walter H., Collection. Hoover Institution Archives, Stanford University, Palo Alto, California.

Keating, Kenneth B., Papers. University of Rochester, New York.

Kennedy, John F., Papers. John F. Kennedy Presidential Library, Boston.
  White House Central Files
  White House Staff Files

Kirk, Russell, Papers. Central Michigan University, Mount Pleasant.

Kitchel, Denison, Collection. Hoover Institution Archives, Stanford University, Palo Alto, California.

Knowland, William F., Papers. University of California, Berkeley.

Kober, Margaret, Papers. Private collection, Phoenix.

Kohlberg, Alfred, Collection. Hoover Institution Archives, Stanford University, Palo Alto, California.

Lee, J. Bracken, Papers. Special Collections, Marriott Library, University of Utah, Salt Lake City.

Lewis, Orme, Papers. Arizona Historical Foundation, Arizona State University, Tempe.

Lipshutz, Robert, Papers. Jimmy Carter Presidential Library, Atlanta.

McFarland, Ernest, Papers. McFarland State Historical Park, Florence, Arizona.

MacArthur, Douglas, Papers. City of Norfolk, Virginia.

Manatos, Mike, Papers. Lyndon B. Johnson Presidential Library, University of Texas, Austin.

Marshall, Jonathan, Papers. Private collection, Scottsdale, Arizona.

Mitchell, James P., Papers. Dwight Eisenhower Presidential Library, Abilene, Kansas.

Moley, Raymond, Collection. Hoover Institution Archives, Stanford University, Palo Alto, California.

Morton, Rogers C. B., Papers. University of Kentucky, Lexington.

Morton, Thruston, Papers. University of Kentucky, Lexington.

Moyers, Bill, Papers. Lyndon B. Johnson Presidential Library, University of Texas, Austin.

Mundt, Karl E., Papers. Dakota State College, Madison, South Dakota.

Neville, Norman D., Papers. Special Collections, Marriott Library, University of Utah, Salt Lake City.

Nixon, Richard M., Papers. Nixon Presidential Materials Project, Washington, D.C.
  Richard M. Nixon Personal Files
  White House Central Files
    Special File
    Staff Member Office Files
      Patrick J. Buchanan
      J. Fred Buzhardt
      Dwight Chapin
      Charles Colson
      Harry S. Dent

John D. Ehrlichman
Peter Flanigan
Alexander M. Haig, Jr.
H. R. Haldeman
Tom C. Korologos
Hugh W. Sloan, Jr.
Rose Mary Woods
  Subject File
Nixon, Richard M., Vice Presidential Papers. National Archives, Pacific Southwest Region, Laguna Niguel.

O'Brien, Lawrence F., Papers. John F. Kennedy Presidential Library, Boston.

Panzer, Frederick, Papers. Lyndon B. Johnson Presidential Library, University of Texas, Austin.

Phleger, Herman, Papers. University of California, Berkeley.

Planned Parenthood, Central and Northern Arizona, Collection. Arizona Historical Foundation, Arizona State University, Tempe.

Pyle, Howard, Papers. Arizona State University, Tempe.

Pyle, Howard, Papers. Dwight Eisenhower Presidential Library, Abilene, Kansas.

Reedy, George E., Papers. Lyndon B. Johnson Presidential Library, University of Texas, Austin.

Reinhold, Ruth, Papers. Arizona Historical Foundation, Arizona State University, Tempe.

Republican National Committee, Office of the Chairman (Leonard Hall), Records. Dwight Eisenhower Presidential Library, Abilene, Kansas.

Rockefeller Brothers Fund Papers. Rockefeller Archive Center, Pocantico Hills, North Tarrytown, New York.
  Civic Interest Services
  Special Studies Project
Saufley, William, Papers. Arizona Historical Foundation, Arizona State University, Tempe.

Shouse, Jouett, Papers. University of Kentucky, Lexington.

Storke, Thomas M., Papers. University of California, Berkeley.

Strauss, Lewis L., Papers. Herbert Hoover Presidential Library, West Branch, Iowa.

de Toledano, Ralph, Collection. Hoover Institution Archives, Stanford University, Palo Alto, California.

Trohan, Walter, Papers. Herbert Hoover Presidential Library, West Branch, Iowa.

Watson, W. Marvin, Papers. Lyndon B. Johnson Presidential Library, University of Texas, Austin.

Wood, Robert E., Papers. Herbert Hoover Presidential Library, West Branch, Iowa.

Articles, Books, and Government Documents

Abbey, Edward. *Cactus Country*. New York: Time-Life Books, 1973.

Abbott, Carl. *The New Urban America: Growth and Politics in Sunbelt Cities*. Chapel Hill: University of North Carolina Press, 1982.

Adamic, Louis. *Laughing in the Jungle*. New York: Arno Press, 1969.

Albertson, Dean, ed. *Eisenhower as President*. New York: Hill and Wang, 1963.

Alexander, Charles C. *Holding the Line: The Eisenhower Era, 1952–1961*. Bloomington: Indiana University Press, 1975.

Alsberg, Henry G., ed. *Arizona, the Grand Canyon State: A State Guide*. New York: Hastings House, 1948.

Alsop, Stewart. *Nixon and Rockefeller: A Double Portrait*. Garden City, N.Y.: Doubleday, 1960.

Ambrose, Stephen E. *Eisenhower: The President*. Vol. 2. New York: Simon and Schuster, 1984.

———. *Nixon: Ruin and Recovery, 1973–1990*. New York: Simon and Schuster, 1991.

———. *Nixon: The Triumph of a Politician, 1962–1972*. New York: Simon and Schuster, 1989.

Andersen, Tolton J., and Lee, Eugene C. "The 1964 Election in California." *Western Political Quarterly* 18 (June 1965): 451–74.

Annunziata, Frank. "The Revolt Against the Welfare State." *Presidential Studies Quarterly* 10 (Spring 1980): 254–65.

Anthony, E. James, and Benedek, Therese, eds. *Parenthood: Its Psychology and Psychopathology*. Boston: Little, Brown, 1970.

Arnson, Cynthia J. *Crossroads: Congress, the Reagan Administration, and Central America*. New York: Pantheon, 1989.

Arrington, Leonard. "Arizona in the Great Depression Years." *Arizona Review* 17 (December 1968): 11–19.

Athearn, Robert G. *The Mythic West in Twentieth-Century America*. Lawrence: University Press of Kansas, 1986.

Augherton, T. G., Jr. "Arizona's Outspoken Insider." *Today's Business* 6 (March 25, 1981): 7–8.

Austin, Mary. *The Land of Journey's End*. New York: Century, 1924.

———. *The Land of Little Rain*. Boston: Houghton Mifflin, 1903.

"B. M. Goldwater." *Arizona Historical Review* 2 (April 1929): 9–10.

Balof, Eugene H. "A Rhetoric of Political Ideology." Ph.D. diss., University of Missouri-Columbia, 1975.

Bamford, James. "Taking on the Mob." *Los Angeles Magazine*, 9–14, 50–52.

Bancroft, Hubert Howe. *History of Arizona and New Mexico*. Albuquerque: Horn and Wallace, 1962.

Banfield, Edward C. *The Unheavenly City Revisited*. Boston: Little, Brown, 1974.

Baritz, Loren. *Backfire: A History of How American Culture Led the US into Vietnam and Made Us Fight the Way We Did*. New York: Ballantine, 1985.

Barnard, John. *Walter Reuther and the Rise of the Auto Workers*. Boston: Little, Brown, 1983.

Barney, James M. "Phoenix—A History of Its Pioneer Days and People." *Arizona Historical Review* 5 (January 1933): 264–85.

Baron, Salo. *The Russian Jew Under Tsars and Soviets*. New York: Macmillan, 1964.

Barone, Michael, and Ujifusa, Grant. *The Almanac of American Politics, 1986*. Washington, D.C.: National Journal Inc., 1985.

Barone, Michael; Ujifusa, Grant; and Matthews, Douglas. *The Almanac of American Politics, 1976*. New York: E. P. Dutton, 1975.

Barrett, Lawrence I. *Gambling With History: Ronald Reagan in the White House*. New York: Penguin, 1984.

Bass, Jack, and DeVries, Walter. *The Transformation of Southern Politics: Social Change and Political Consequences Since 1945*. New York: Basic Books, 1976.

Bates, Leslie Austin. "Race and the Republicans: The Goldwater Campaign for the Presidency in 1964." Seminar paper, University of Utah, 1993.

Baucom, Donald R. *The Origins of SDI, 1944–1983*. Lawrence: University Press of Kansas, 1992.

Beaty, Orren. "The Arizona Republic's First Hundred Years." Manuscript, 1990.

Bell, Daniel, ed. *The New American Right*. Garden City, N.Y.: Doubleday-Anchor, 1964.

Bell, Jack. *Mr. Conservative: Barry Goldwater*. New York: Macfadden-Bartell, 1962.

Bemis, M. E. "Agriculture in the Salt River Valley." *Progressive Arizona* 1 (November 1925): 17–23, 40.

Benson, Ezra Taft. *The Red Carpet*. Salt Lake City: Bookcraft, 1962.

Berman, David R. *Parties and Elections in Arizona: 1963–1984*. Tempe, Ariz.: Public Policy Series, 1985.

———. *Reformers, Corporations, and the Electorate: An Analysis of Arizona's Age of Reform*. Niwot: University Press of Colorado, 1992.

Bernard, Richard M., and Rice, Bradley R., eds. *Sunbelt Cities: Politics and Growth Since World War II*. Austin: University of Texas Press, 1983.

Bernstein, Burton. "AuH$_2$O." *New Yorker*, April 25, 1988, 43–44, 46, 49–50, 52–56, 61–73.

Bernstein, Carl, and Woodward, Bob. *All the President's Men*. New York: Simon and Schuster, 1974.

Bibby, John F. "The Goldwater Movement—Its Influence on the Republican Party in the 1970s." *American Behavioral Scientist* 17 (November–December 1973): 249–71.

Billings, R. Bruce, and Shaw-Serdar, David. "Relocating the Navajo and Hopi: History and Economic Impact." *Arizona Review* 37 (Spring 1989): 43–52.

Blackwell, James A., Jr., and Blechman, Barry M. *Making Defense Reform Work*. Washington, D.C.: Brassey's Inc., 1990.

Blumenthal, Sidney. *The Rise of the Counterestablishment: From Conservative Ideology to Political Power*. New York: Harper and Row, 1986.

Blunt, Barrie Edwin. "The Goldwater Candidacy: Its Effects on Racial Liberalism in the House of Representatives." *Presidential Studies Quarterly* 15 (Winter 1985): 119–27.

Boller, Paul F., Jr. *Presidential Campaigns*. New York: Oxford University Press, 1984.

Boorstin, Daniel J. *The Americans: The National Experience*. New York: Vintage, 1965.

Bowden, Charles. "Goldwater, Waiting for 16,000,000 Arizonans." *City Magazine*, November 1988, 36–37.

Bracken, Paul, and Kahn, Herman. *A Summary of Arizona Tomorrow, 1912–2012*. New York: Hudson Institute, 1979.

Broder, David S. *Changing of the Guard: Power and Leadership in America*. New York: Simon and Schuster, 1980.

Brooks, William. "A Field Study of the Johnson-Goldwater Campaign Speeches." *Southern Speech Communications Journal* 32 (1967): 273–81.

Browne, J. Ross. *Adventures in the Apache Country: A Tour Through Arizona and Sonora, 1864*. Edited by Donald M. Powell. Tucson: University of Arizona Press, 1974.

Broyles, J. Allen. *The John Birch Society: Anatomy of a Protest*. Boston: Beacon, 1966.

Buchanan, Patrick J. "The Voice in the Desert." Introduction to *The Conscience of a Conservative*. Washington, D.C.: Regnery Gateway, 1990.

———. *Right from the Beginning*. Boston: Little, Brown, 1988.

Buckley, William F., Jr., ed. *American Conservative Thought in the Twentieth Century*. Indianapolis: Bobbs-Merrill, 1970.

———. *The Jeweler's Eye*. New York: G. P. Putnam's Sons, 1968.

———. *Up from Liberalism*. New York: Bantam, 1959.

Buckley, William F., Jr., and Bozell, L. Brent. *McCarthy and His Enemies: The Record and Its Meaning*. Chicago: Henry Regnery, 1954.

Bull, Chris. "Right Turn." *The Advocate*, September 7 1993, 32–38.

Burnham, Walter Dean. "American Voting Behavior and the 1964 Election." *Midwest Journal of Political Science* 12 (February 1968): 1–40.

Burt, Larry W. *Tribalism in Crisis: Federal Indian Policy, 1953–1961*. Albuquerque: University of New Mexico Press, 1982.

Butler, Jay Q. "Construction Activity in Arizona: The First $2 Billion Year." *Arizona Business* 26 (March 1979): 3–9.

Carlson, Raymond. "Ernest W. McFarland." *Arizona Highways*, February 1955, 5–7.

———. "Goldwaters, Merchants Since 1862." *Arizona Highways*, May 1939, 6–7, 26–27.

Carney, Francis M., and Way, H. Frank, Jr., eds. *Politics, 1964*. Belmont, Calif.: Wadsworth, 1964.

Chafe, William H. *The Unfinished Journey: America Since World War II*. New York: Oxford University Press, 1986.

Chanin, Abraham S. "Arizona's Jewish Pioneers." *Arizona Highways*, November 1988, 30–32.

Chanin, Abraham, and Chanin, Mildred. *This Land, These Voices*. Tucson: Midbar Press, 1977.

Chester, Lewis; Hodgson, Godfrey; and Page, Bruce. *An American Melodrama: The Presidential Campaign of 1968*. New York: Viking, 1969.

Chilton, James K. "Goldwater vs. Elson, or Have's vs. Have Not's." Manuscript, 1969, Department of Archives and Manuscripts, Arizona State University.

Clark, Nancy Tisdale. "The Demise of Demon Rum in Arizona." *Journal of Arizona History* 18 (Spring 1977): 69–92.

Claunch, John M., ed. *The 1964 Presidential Election in the Southwest*. Dallas: SMU/Arnold Foundation, 1966.

Clayton, James L. "The Impact of the Cold War on the Economies of California and Utah." *Pacific Historical Review* 36 (November 1967): 449–73.

Clifford, Clark. *Counsel to the President: A Memoir*. New York: Random House, 1991.

Clodfelter, Mark. *The Limits of Air Power: The American Bombing of North Vietnam*. New York: Free Press, 1989.

Codevilla, Angelo. "The Substance and the Rules." *Washington Quarterly* 6 (Summer 1983): 32–39.

Cohen, William S., and Mitchell, George J. *Men of Zeal*. New York: Viking, 1988.

Congressional Quarterly Special Report. *The Public Records of Barry Goldwater and William Miller*. Washington, D.C.: Congressional Quarterly Service, 1964.

Congressional Record

Connelly, F. Martin, Jr., "Some Questions Concerning Lyndon Johnson's Rhetoric in the 1964 Presidential Campaign." *Southern Speech Communication Journal* 37 (1971): 11–20.

Conners, Jo. *Who's Who in Arizona*. Vol. 1. Tucson: Arizona Daily Star, 1913.

Connery, Robert H., and Benjamin, Gerald. *Rockefeller of New York: Executive Power in the Statehouse*. Ithaca, N.Y.: Cornell University Press, 1979.

Constantini, Edmond, and Craik, Kenneth H. "Competing Elites Within a Political Party: A Study of Republican Leadership." *Western Political Quarterly* 22 (December 1969): 879–903.

Converse, Philip E.; Clausen, Aage R.; and Miller, Warren E. "Electoral Myth and Reality: The 1964 Election." *American Political Science Quarterly* 59 (June 1965): 321–49.

Cook, Blanche. *The Declassified Eisenhower: A Divided Legacy of Peace and Political Warfare*. New York: Penguin, 1981.

Cook, Fred J. *Barry Goldwater: Extremist of the Right*. New York: Grove Press, 1964.

Cormier, Frank, and Eaton, William J. *Reuther*. Englewood Cliffs, N.J.: Prentice-Hall, 1970.

Cosman, Bernard. *Five States for Goldwater*. University: University of Alabama Press, 1966.

———. *The Case of the Goldwater Delegates*. University: University of Alabama Press, 1966.

Cosman, Bernard, and Huckshorn, Robert J. *Republican Politics: The 1964 Campaign and Its Aftermath for the Party*. New York: Praeger, 1968.

Council of the City of Phoenix. "Minutes." Vols. 26–31.

Craddock, John. "Barry Goldwater: Retired, Yes; Mellow, No." *Arizona Trend,* December 1986, 17–18.

Crawford, Alan. "The Sunshine Boys Bow Out: Goldwater and Tower, Stage Left." *New Guard* 16 (June 1976): 7–9.

———. *Thunder on the Right: The "New Right" and the Politics of Resentment.* New York: Pantheon, 1980.

Crespi, Irving. "The Structural Basis for Right-Wing Conservatism: The Goldwater Case." *Public Opinion Quarterly* 29 (Winter 1965): 523–43.

Cross, Jack L.; Shaw, Elizabeth H.; and Scheifele, Kathleen, eds. *Arizona: Its People and Resources.* Tucson: University of Arizona Press, 1960.

Crow, John. *Discrimination, Poverty, and the Negro: Arizona in the National Context.* Tucson: University of Arizona Press, 1968.

Cummings, Milton, Jr., ed. *The National Election of 1964.* Washington, D.C.: Brookings Institution, 1966.

Cunningham, Bob. "The Box that Broke the Barrier: The Swamp Cooler Comes to Southern Arizona." *Journal of Arizona History* 26 (Summer 1985): 163–74.

Dalleck, Robert. *Lone Star Rising: Lyndon Johnson and His Times, 1908–1960.* New York: Oxford University Press, 1991.

Dean, Elizabeth. *Barry Goldwater, Republican Senator from Arizona.* Washington, D.C.: Grossman, 1972.

Dean, John III. *Blind Ambition: The White House Years.* New York: Simon and Schuster, 1976.

———. *Lost Honor.* Los Angeles: Stratford, 1982.

Dell, George W. "The Republican Nominee: Barry Goldwater." *Quarterly Journal of Speech* 50 (December 1964): 399–404.

Desmond, James. *Nelson Rockefeller: A Political Biography.* New York: Macmillan, 1964.

Devine, Donald J. *Reagan Electionomics: How Reagan Ambushed the Pollsters.* Ottawa, Ill.: Greenhill, 1983.

Dobyns, Henry F. "How Goldwater Won in Arizona." *Frontier* 4 (January 1953): 17–18.

Donaldson, Sam. *"Hold On, Mr. President!"* New York: Fawcett Crest, 1987.

Donovan, Frank R. *The Americanism of Barry Goldwater.* New York: Macfadden-Bartell, 1964.

Doucette, Forrest E. *The Arizona Year Book, 1930–1931.* Phoenix: n.p., 1930.

Draper, Theodore. *A Very Thin Line: The Iran-Contra Affairs.* New York: Hill and Wang, 1991.

Drew, Elizabeth. *Barry Goldwater, Republican Senator from Arizona.* Washington, D.C.: Grossman, 1972.

Dubnow, S. M. *History of the Jews in Russia and Poland.* 2 vols. Philadelphia: Jewish Publication Society of America, 1916–1920.

Dudman, Richard. *Men of the Far Right.* New York: Pyramid, 1962.

Edsall, Thomas Byrne. "Clinton, So Far." *New York Review of Books,* October 7, 1993, 6–9.

————. Clinton's Revolution." *New York Review of Books,* November 5, 1992, 7–11.

————. *The New Politics of Inequality.* New York: Norton, 1984.

————. "Willie Horton's Message." *New York Review of Books,* February 13, 1992, 7–11.

Edsall, Thomas Byrne, and Edsall, Mary D. *Chain Reaction: The Impact of Race, Rights, and Taxes on American Politics.* New York: Norton, 1991.

Eggenhofer, Nick. *Wagons, Mules and Men.* New York: Hastings House, 1961.

Ehrlich, Karen Lynn. "Arizona's Territorial Capital Moves to Phoenix." *Arizona and the West* 23 (Autumn 1981): 231–42.

Ehrlichman, John. *Witness to Power: The Nixon Years.* New York: Simon and Schuster, 1982.

Emerson, J. Terry. "The War Powers Resolution Tested: The President's Independent Defense Power." *Notre Dame Lawyer* 51 (December 1975): 187–216.

Emery, Edwin. "Press Support for Johnson and Goldwater." *Journalism Quarterly* 41 (1964): 485–88.

Ensenberger, Peter. "Barry Goldwater on Photography." *Arizona Highways,* May 1988, 12–17.

Epstein, Benjamin R., and Forster, Arnold. *The Radical Right: Report on the John Birch Society and Its Allies.* New York: Vintage, 1967.

Epstein, Leon, and Ranney, Austin. "Who Voted for Goldwater." *Political Science Quarterly* 81 (March 1966): 82–94.

Ericson, Jon Louis. "The Reporting by the Prestige Press of Selected Speeches by Senator Goldwater in the 1964 Presidential Campaign." Ph.D. diss., University of Wisconsin-Madison, 1966.

Erikson, Robert. "The Influence of Newspaper Endorsements in Presidential Elections: The Case of 1964." *American Journal of Political Science* 20 (May 1976): 207–33.

Evans, M. Stanton. *The Future of Conservatism: From Taft to Reagan and Beyond.* New York: Holt, Rinehart and Winston, 1968.

————. *Revolt on the Campus.* Chicago: Henry Regnery, 1961.

Ewen, Stuart, and Ewen, Elizabeth. *Channels of Desire: Mass Images and the Shaping of American Consciousness.* New York: McGraw-Hill, 1982.

Faber, Harold, ed. *The Road to the White House.* New York: New York Times, 1965.

Farish, Thomas E. *History of Arizona.* 8 vols. Phoenix, n.p., 1915.

Ferguson, Thomas, and Rogers, Joel. *Right Turn: The Decline of the Democrats and the Future of American Politics.* New York: Hill and Wang, 1986.

Fergusson, Erna. *Our Southwest.* New York: Knopf, 1941.

Field, John, and Anderson, Ronald. "Ideology in the Public's Conceptualization of the 1964 Election." *Public Opinion Quarterly* 33 (Fall 1969): 380–98.

Fierman, Floyd. *Guts and Ruts: The Jewish Pioneer on the Trail in the American Southwest.* New York: KTAV, 1985.

————. "The Drachmans of Arizona." *American Jewish Archives* 16 (November 1964): 135–59.

————. "The Goldberg Brothers: Arizona Pioneers." *American Jewish Archives* 18 (April 1966): 3–19.

————. "Jewish Pioneering in the Southwest." *Arizona and the West* 2 (Spring 1960): 54–72.

Finn, Kris. "Leave Our Sacred Dances Alone!" *New Times* 14 (December 14–20, 1983): 7, 32, 34, 36–37.

Fireman, Bert M. "A Bar Mitzvah Message from Prescott, Arizona, in 1879." *Western States Jewish History* 12 (July 1980): 341–44.

————. *Arizona: Historic Land.* New York: Knopf, 1982.

————. "The Most Unforgettable Character I've Ever Met (Jo Goldwater)." Arizona Historical Foundation.

————. "Urbanization and Home Comfort." In *Progress in Arizona: The State's Crucial Issues,* William R. Noyes, ed. Tucson: University of Arizona Press, 1973.

Fixico, Donald L. *Termination and Relocation: Federal Indian Policy, 1945–1960.* Albuquerque: University of New Mexico Press, 1986.

Flemmer, Leslie. "The New York City Race Riot of 1964." Seminar paper, University of Utah, 1993.

Focht, Sandra. "An Analysis of Selected Speeches from the 1958 Senatorial Campaign of Barry Goldwater." Master's thesis, University of Arizona, 1961.

Forster, Arnold, and Epstein, Benjamin. *Danger on the Right.* New York: Random House, 1965.

Foster, James C. "1954: A CIO Victory?" *Labor History* 12 (Summer 1971): 392–408.

Fradkin, Philip L. *A River No More: The Colorado River and the West.* Tucson: University of Arizona Press, 1981.

Fraser, Steve, and Gerstle, Gary, eds. *The Rise and Fall of the New Deal Order, 1930–1980.* Princeton, N.J.: Princeton University Press, 1989.

Gall, Gilbert J. *The Politics of Right to Work: The Labor Federations as Special Interests, 1943–1979.* Westport, Conn.: Greenwood Press, 1988.

Genovese, J. Gen. *We Flew Without Guns.* Philadelphia: John C. Winston, 1945.

Geoghegan, Thomas. *Which Side Are You On?* New York: Farrar, Straus, and Giroux, 1991.

Gibson, James William. *The Perfect War: The War We Couldn't Lose and How We Did.* New York: Vintage, 1986.

Gilbert, Richard L., Jr. "Barry Goldwater: The Admonitions of an Older Man." *Esquire,* October 1962, 96, 170–73.

————. "Love, Dad." *Point West* 3 (July–August 1961): 18–23, 55, 56–57.

Gilder, George F., and Chapman, Bruce K. *The Party That Lost Its Head.* New York: Knopf, 1966.

Gill, Mary E., and Goff, John S. "Joseph H. Kibbey and School Segregation in Arizona." *Journal of Arizona History* 21 (Winter 1980): 411–22.

Ginzburg, Ralph, ed. "The Unconscious of a Conservative: A Special Issue on the Mind of Barry Goldwater. *Fact Magazine* 1 (September–October 1964).

Gitlin, Todd. *The Sixties: Years of Hope, Days of Rage.* Toronto: Bantam, 1987.

Glanz, Rudolf. "Notes on Early Jewish Peddling in America." *Jewish Social Studies* 7 (April 1945): 119–36.

———. "Notes on the Early Jews of Arizona." *Western States Jewish History* 5 (July 1973): 243–56.

Goetzmann, William. *Army Exploration in the American West, 1803–1863*. New Haven: Yale University Press, 1959.

Goldberg, Isaac. "Reminiscences of an Arizona Pioneer." *Western States Jewish History* 2 (April 1970): 172–81.

Goldberg, Robert A. *Grassroots Resistance: Social Movements in Twentieth Century America*. Belmont, Calif.: Wadsworth, 1991.

Goldman, Eric F. *The Crucial Decade and After: America, 1945–1960*. New York: Vintage, 1960.

———. *The Tragedy of Lyndon Johnson*. New York: Knopf, 1969.

Goldwater, Barry. "America's Best Hope for the Future Lies in Political Conservatism." In *The Great Ideas Today, 1962*, Robert Hutchins and Mortimer J. Adler, eds. Chicago: Encyclopedia Britannica, 1962.

———. *Arizona Portraits*. 2 vols. Phoenix: privately printed, 1940 and 1946.

———. "The Arrival of the 'Anglos.'" In *This Land, These Voices*, Abe and Mildred Chanin, eds. Tucson: Midbar Press, 1977.

———. *Barry Goldwater and the Southwest*. Phoenix: Troy's Publications, 1976.

———. "Bisbee Massacre." *Desert* 4 (August 1941): 5–9.

———. *China and the Abrogation of Treaties*. Washington, D.C.: Heritage Foundation, 1978.

———. *The Coming Breakpoint*. New York: Macmillan, 1976.

———. "Congress and Intelligence Oversight." *Washington Quarterly* 6 (Summer 1983): 16–21.

———. *The Conscience of a Conservative*. Shepherdsville, Ky.: Victor, 1960.

———. *The Conscience of a Majority*. Englewood Cliffs, N.J.: Prentice Hall, 1970.

———. "A Conservative Sets Out His Credo." *New York Times Magazine*, July 31, 1960, pp. 16, 18, 20–21.

———. "A Dream Come True." *McCall's*, March 1966, 64, 68, 185–86, 188.

———. "Economic and Political Tyranny." In *Anthology of Conservative Writing in the United States, 1932–1960*, A. G. Heinsohn, ed. Chicago: Henry Regnery, 1962.

———. Foreword. In Manual A. Machado, Jr. *Listen Chicano! An Informal History of the Mexican People*. Chicago: Nelson Hall, 1978.

———. *Goldwater*. With Jack Casserly. New York: Doubleday, 1988.

———. *The Goldwater Kachina Doll Collection*. With Byron Harvey. Tempe: Arizona Historical Foundation, 1969.

———. "Long Vistas and Stone Arches." *Explorer's Journal* 66 (September 1988): 114–19.

———. "Natural Bridge Discovery in Grand Canyon." *Arizona Highways*, February 1955, 8–13.

———. *An Odyssey of the Colorado and Green Rivers*. Phoenix: privately printed,

1940. Later reprinted as *Delightful Journey*. Tempe, Ariz.: Arizona Historical Foundation, 1970.

———. *People and Places*. New York: Random House, 1967.

———. "Political Philosophy and Supreme Court Justices." *American Bar Association Journal* 58 (February 1972): 135–40.

———. "The President's Ability to Protect." *Law and Social Order* 3 (1971): 423–49.

———. "The President's Constitutional Primacy in Foreign Relations and National Defense." *Virginia Journal of International Law* 13 (Summer 1973): 463–89.

———. "A Realistic Space Program for America." *Science and Mechanics* 34 (June 1964): 44–47, 109.

———. *Speeches of Henry Fountain Ashurst of Arizona*. Phoenix: Arizona-Messinger, 1954.

———. "Three Generations of Pants and Politics in Arizona." *Journal of Arizona History* 13 (Autumn 1972): 141–58.

———. *The West That Was*. Tucson: Western History Association, 1968.

———. *Where I Stand*. New York: McGraw-Hill, 1964.

———. "Why Gun-Control Laws Don't Work." *Reader's Digest*, December 1975, 183–88.

———. *Why Not Victory? A Fresh Look At American Foreign Policy*. New York: McGraw-Hill, 1962.

———. *With No Apologies: The Personal and Political Memoirs of Barry M. Goldwater*. New York: William Morrow, 1979.

"Goldwater Should be Removed from List of 'Favorite Conservatives' Readers Say." *Conservative Digest* 1 (December 1975): 2.

Golomb, Elan. *Trapped in the Mirror: Adult Children of Narcissists in Their Struggle for Self*. New York: William Morrow, 1992.

Goodall, Leonard E. "Phoenix: Reformers at Work." In *Urban Politics in the Southwest*, ed. Leonard E. Goodall. Tempe: Arizona State University Press, 1967.

Gordon, Linda. *Woman's Body, Woman's Right*. New York: Grossman, 1976.

Gordon-McCutchan, R. C. *The Taos Indians and the Battle for Blue Lake*. Santa Fe, N.M.: Red Crane Books, 1991.

Gottfried, Paul, and Fleming, Thomas. *The Conservative Movement*. Boston: Twayne, 1988.

Gould, Jean, and Hickok, Lorena. *Walter Reuther: Labor's Rugged Individualist*. New York: Dodd, Mead, 1972.

Graham, Mary W. "Margaret Chase Smith." *Quarterly Journal of Speech* 50 (December 1964): 390–94.

Gray, Charles H. "A Scale Analysis of the Voting Records of Senators Kennedy, Johnson, and Goldwater." *American Political Science Review* 49 (September 1965): 615–21.

Green, Mark. *Who Runs Congress?* New York: Dell, 1984.

Greenberg, Louis. *The Jews in Russia*. 2 vols. New Haven: Yale University Press, 1944–1951.

Greenstein, Fred I. *The Hidden-Hand Presidency: Eisenhower as Leader*. New York: Basic Books, 1982.

Griffith, Robert. *The Politics of Fear: Joseph R. McCarthy and the Senate*. Rochelle Park, N.J.: Hayden, 1976.

Grupp, Frederick W., Jr. "Social Correlates of Political Activists: The John Birch Society and the ADA." Ph.D. diss., University of Pennsylvania, 1968.

Hall, Donald R. "The 1968 Election in Arizona." *Western Political Quarterly* 22 (September 1969): 462–67.

Hamilton, Richard F. *Class and Politics in the United States*. New York: John Wiley and Sons, 1972.

Hammerback, John C. "Barry Goldwater's Rhetoric of Rugged Individualism." *Quarterly Journal of Speech* 58 (April 1972): 175–83.

Hargrave, Maria. "Overland by Ox-Train in 1870." *Southern California Quarterly* 26 (1944): 9–37.

Hartmann, Frederick H., and Wendzel, Robert L. *Defending America's Security*. Washington, D.C.: Brassey's Inc., 1990.

Harvill, Richard A. "Foundation Stones and Future Bulwarks of Arizona's Industrial Development." *Arizona Business and Economic Review* 5 (January 1956): 1–5.

Hayek, Friedrich von. *The Road to Serfdom*. Chicago: University of Chicago Press, 1944.

Headley, J. T. "The First Overland Trip to California." *Harper's New Monthly Magazine*, June 1860, 80–93.

Heale, M. J. *American Anticommunism: Combating the Enemy Within, 1830–1970*. Baltimore: Johns Hopkins University Press, 1990.

Hecht, Melvin E.; Reeves, Richard W.; and de Gennaro, Nat. "Agriculture: Its Historic and Contemporary Roles in Arizona's Economy." *Arizona Review* 27 (November 1978): 6–12.

Heinsohn, A. G., Jr., ed. *Anthology of Conservative Writing in the United States, 1932–1960*. Chicago: Henry Regnery, 1962.

Herzberg, Nathan. "Cornerstone Laying of the First Synagogue in Arizona." *Western States Jewish History* 19 (April 1987): 255–56.

Hess, Karl. *In a Cause That Will Triumph*. New York: Doubleday, 1967.

Hess, Stephen, and Broder, David S. *The Republican Establishment: The Present and Future of the G.O.P.* New York: Harper and Row, 1967.

Himes, Samuel H., Jr. "New Phoenix Residents: Implications for Local Business." *Arizona Business* 26 (May 1979): 3–10.

Himmelstein, Jerome L. *To the Right: The Transformation of American Conservatism*. Berkeley: University of California Press, 1990.

Hinton, Richard J. *The Hand-Book to Arizona*. San Francisco: Payot, Upham, 1878.

Hoeveler, J. David, Jr. *Watch on the Right: Conservative Intellectuals in the Reagan Era*. Madison: University of Wisconsin Press, 1991.

Hofstadter, Richard. *The Paranoid Style in American Politics and Other Essays*. New York: Vintage, 1967.

Hornaday, William T. *Camp Fires on Desert and Lava*. New York: Charles Scribner's Sons, 1908.

Horton, Arthur G. *An Economic, Political, and Social Survey of Phoenix and the Valley of the Sun*. Tempe, Ariz.: Southside Progress, 1941.

Houghton, N. D. "The 1950 Election in Arizona." *Western Political Quarterly* 4 (March 1951): 91.

―――. "The 1954 Election in Arizona." *Western Political Quarterly* 7 (December 1954): 594–96.

―――. "The 1956 Election in Arizona." *Western Political Quarterly* 10 (March 1957): 96–101.

Hughes, Emmet John. *The Ordeal of Power: A Political Memoir of the Eisenhower Years*. New York: Atheneum, 1963.

Hull, Christina. "Margaret Sanger and the Birth Control Movement." Term paper, University of Utah, 1992.

Humphrey, Hubert H. *Education of a Public Man*. New York: Doubleday, 1976.

Hundley, Norris, Jr. *Dividing the Waters: A Century of Controversy Between the United States and Mexico*. Berkeley: University of California Press, 1966.

―――. *Water and the West: The Colorado River Compact and the Politics of Water in the American West*. Berkeley: University of California Press, 1975.

Jamieson, Kathleen Hall. *Packaging the Presidency: A History and Criticism of Presidential Campaign Advertising*. New York: Oxford University Press, 1984.

Javits, Jacob. *The Autobiography of a Public Man*. Boston: Houghton Mifflin, 1981.

Jeffreys-Jones, Rhodri. *The CIA and American Democracy*. New Haven: Yale University Press, 1989.

Johnson, G. Wesley. "Generations of Elites and Social Change in Phoenix." In *Community Development in the American West*, Jessie Embry and Howard Christy, eds. Provo, Utah: Charles Redd Center for Western Studies, 1985.

Johnson, Haynes. *Sleepwalking Through History: America in the Reagan Years*. New York: Norton, 1991.

Johnson, Lyndon Baines. *The Vantage Point: Perspectives of the Presidency, 1963–1969*. New York: Holt, Rinehart and Winston, 1971.

Johnson, Rich. *The Central Arizona Project, 1918–1968*. Tucson: University of Arizona Press, 1977.

Jonas, Frank. "The 1964 Election in Utah." *Western Political Quarterly* 18 (June 1965): 509–13.

―――. "The Spirit of Contemporary Politics in the American West." *Western Political Quarterly* 18 (September 1965): 5–20.

Jonas, Frank, ed. *Political Dynamiting*. Salt Lake City: University of Utah Press, 1970.

―――. *Politics in the American West*. Salt Lake City: University of Utah Press, 1969.

―――. *Western Politics*. Salt Lake City: University of Utah Press, 1961.

Jones, Charles. "The 1964 Presidential Election." In *Public Opinion and Politics*, William Crotty, ed. New York: Holt Rinehart, 1970.

Jones, Kay F. "Ana Frohmiller: Watchdog of the Arizona Treasury." *Journal of Arizona History* 25 (Winter 1984): 349–68.

Joyner, Conrad. *The Republican Dilemma: Conservatism or Progressivism*. Tucson: University of Arizona Press, 1963.

Judis, John B. *Grand Illusion: Critics and Champions of the American Century*. New York: Farrar, Straus and Giroux, 1992.

———. *William F. Buckley, Jr.: Patron Saint of the Conservatives*. New York: Simon and Schuster, 1988.

Kahn, Herman. *Thinking About the Unthinkable*. New York: Horizon Press, 1962.

Kalman, Laura. *Abe Fortas: A Biography*. New Haven: Yale University Press, 1990.

Kammer, Jerry. *The Second Long Walk: The Navajo-Hopi Land Dispute*. Albuquerque: University of New Mexico Press, 1980.

Kammer, William. "Louisiana's Electoral Alignments and the Presidential Vote in 1964." *Southwestern Social Science Quarterly* 47 (September 1967): 127–35.

Karalekas, Anne. "Intelligence Oversight: Has Anything Changed?" *Washington Quarterly* 6 (Summer 1983): 22–31.

Karnow, Stanley. *Vietnam, A History*. New York: Viking Press, 1983.

Karsh, Audrey R. "Heyman Mannasse: An Arizona and San Diego Saga." *Western States Jewish History* 13 (October 1980): 37–42.

Kelley, Robert. "Ideology and Political Culture." *American Historical Review* 83 (June 1977): 531–62.

Kelso, Maurice M.; Martin, William E.; and Mack, Lawrence E. *Water Supplies in an Arid Environment: An Arizona Case Study*. Tucson: University of Arizona Press, 1973.

Kelso, Paul. *A Decade of Council-Manager Government in Phoenix, Arizona*. Phoenix: Council of the City of Phoenix, 1960.

———. "The 1952 Election in Arizona." *Western Political Quarterly* 6 (March 1953): 100–102.

———. "The 1948 Election in Arizona." *Western Political Quarterly* 2 (March 1949): 92–96.

Kennedy, David M. *Birth Control in America: The Career of Margaret Sanger*. New Haven: Yale University Press, 1970.

Kennedy, Robert F. *The Enemy Within*. New York: Harper Brothers, 1960.

Kessel, John H. *The Goldwater Coalition: Republican Strategies in 1964*. Indianapolis: Bobbs-Merrill, 1968.

Kirk, Russell. *The Conservative Mind: From Burke to Eliot*. 7th ed. Chicago: Henry Regnery, 1986.

———. *A Program for Conservatives*. Chicago: Henry Regnery, 1962.

———. "Sword of Imagination." Manuscript, 1992.

Kirk, Russell, and McClellan, James. *The Political Principles of Robert A. Taft*. New York: Fleet Press, 1967.

Kirkpatrick, Samuel. "Issue Orientation and Voter Choice." *Social Science Quarterly* 49 (June 1969): 87–102.

Kissinger, Henry. *The White House Years*. London: Weidenfeld, Nicolson and Michael Joseph, 1979.

Kitchel, Denison. *The Truth About the Panama Canal*. New Rochelle, N.Y.: Arlington House, 1978.

Kleindienst, Richard G. *Justice: The Memoirs of Attorney General Richard Kleindienst*. Ottawa, Ill.: Jameson, 1985.

Kohut, H. *The Analysis of Self*. New York: International Universities Press, 1971.

Kolkey, Jonathan Martin. *The New Right, 1960–1968: With Epilogue, 1969–1980*. Lanham, Md.: University Press of America, 1983.

Konig, Michael F. "Postwar Phoenix, Arizona: Banking and Boosterism." *Journal of the West* 23 (April 1984): 72–76.

———. "Toward Metropolis Status: Charter Government and the Rise of Phoenix, Arizona, 1945–1960." Ph.D. diss., Arizona State University, 1983.

Kotlanger, Michael, Jr. "Phoenix, Arizona, 1920–1940." Ph.D. diss., Arizona State University, 1984.

Kramer, Michael, and Roberts, Sam. *"I Never Wanted to be Vice-President of Anything!"* New York: Basic Books, 1976.

Kramer, William, and Stern, Norton B. "Early California Associations of Michel Goldwater and His Family." *Western States Jewish History* 4 (July 1972): 173–96.

Krutch, Joseph Wood. *The Desert Year*. New York: William Sloane Associates, 1952.

———. *The Voice of the Desert*. New York: William Morrow, 1955.

Kutler, Stanley I. *The Wars of Watergate: The Last Crisis of Richard Nixon*. New York: Norton, 1990.

LaFarge, Oliver. *The Eagle in the Egg*. New York: Houghton Mifflin, 1949.

LaFeber, Walter. *The Panama Canal: The Crisis in Historical Perspective*. New York: Oxford University Press, 1989.

Lamar, Howard Robert. *The Far Southwest, 1846–1912; A Territorial History*. New Haven: Yale University Press, 1966.

Lamb, Blaine P. "Fifty-Four Years on the Southwest Frontier: Nathan Benjamin Appel in New Mexico, Arizona, and Southern California." *Western States Jewish History* 16 (January 1984): 125–33.

———. "Jewish Pioneers in Arizona, 1850–1920." Ph.D. diss., Arizona State University, 1982.

———. "Jews in Early Phoenix, 1870–1920." *Journal of Arizona History* 18 (Autumn 1977): 299–318.

Lamb, Michael E., ed. *The Role of the Father in Child Development*. New York: John Wiley and Sons, 1976.

Larson, Arthur. *Eisenhower: The President Nobody Knew*. New York: Charles Scribner's Sons, 1968.

Lawson, Kari Lee. "The Constitutional Twilight Zone of Treaty Termination—Goldwater v. Carter." *Virginia Journal of International Law* 20 (Fall 1979): 147–69.

Lawson, Steven F. *Black Ballots: Voting Rights in the South, 1944–1969*. New York: Columbia University Press, 1976.

Leach, William R. "Transformations in a Culture of Consumption: Women and Department Stores." *Journal of American History* 71 (September 1984): 319–42.

Leahy, Michael. "I'd Have Ended the Vietnam War in a Week or Two." *New Choices* 32 (December 1992–January 1993): 42–47.

Lee, R. Afton. *Eisenhower and Landrum-Griffin: A Study in Labor Management Politics*. Lexington: University Press of Kentucky, 1990.

Leeper, Gertrude B., and House, Maude M. *Who's Who in Arizona in Business, Professions, and Arts*. Vol. 1, 1938–1940. Phoenix: Survey Publishing, 1938.

Leggett, Herbert A. "Arizona: The Nation's Fastest Growing State." *Arizona Highways*, February–March 1962, 43–57.

Levinson, Robert E. "American Jews in the West." *Western Historical Quarterly* 5 (July 1974): 285–94.

———. "Julius Basinski: Pioneer Merchant in Montana." *Montana, the Magazine of Western History* 22 (1972): 60–68.

Lingenfelter, Richard E. *Steamboats on the Colorado River, 1852–1916*. Tucson: University of Arizona Press, 1978.

Lipset, Seymour Martin, and Raab, Earl. *The Politics of Unreason: Right-Wing Extremism in America, 1790–1970*. New York: Harper and Row, 1970.

Lokos, Lionel. *Hysteria 1964: The Fear Campaign Against Barry Goldwater*. New Rochelle, N.Y.: Arlington House, 1967.

Lotchin, Roger, ed. *The Martial Metropolis: U.S. Cities in War and Peace*. New York: Praeger, 1984.

Luckingham, Bradford. *Phoenix: The History of a Southwestern Metropolis*. Tucson: University of Arizona Press, 1988.

———. *The Urban Southwest: A Profile History of Albuquerque—El Paso—Phoenix—Tucson*. El Paso: Texas Western Press, 1982.

Luey, Beth, and Stowe, Neil J., eds. *Arizona at Seventy-Five: The Next Twenty-Five Years*. Tucson: Arizona Historical Society, 1987.

Lynd, Robert S., and Lynd, Helen Merrell. *Middletown: A Study in Modern American Culture*. New York: Harcourt, Brace and World, 1929.

Lyon, William H. "The Corporate Frontier in Arizona." *Journal of Arizona History* 9 (Spring 1968): 1–17.

McAdam, Doug. *Political Process and the Development of Black Insurgency, 1930–1970*. Chicago: University of Chicago Press, 1982.

McClellan, John L. *Crime Without Punishment*. New York: Duell, Sloan, and Pearce, 1962.

McDowell, Charles, Jr. *Campaign Fever: The National Folk Festival from New Hampshire to November, 1964*. New York: William Morrow, 1965.

McDowell, Edwin. *Barry Goldwater: Portrait of an Arizonan*. Chicago: Henry Regnery, 1964.

McEvoy, James III. "Conservatism or Extremism: Goldwater Supporters in the 1964 Election." In *The American Right Wing: Readings in Political Behavior*, Robert A. Schoenberger, ed. New York: Holt, Rinehart and Winston, 1969.

―――. *Radicals or Conservatives: The Contemporary American Right*. Chicago: Rand McNally, 1971.

McFarland, Ernest W. *MAC: The Autobiography of Ernest W. McFarland*. Self-published, 1979.

McGerr, Michael E. "Is There a Twentieth-Century West?" In *Under an Open Sky: Rethinking America's Western Past*, William Cronon, George Miles, and Jay Gitlin, eds. New York: Norton, 1992.

McKitrick, Jeffery S. "The JCS: Evolutionary or Revolutionary Reform? *Parameters* 16 (Spring 1986): 63–75.

McMillan, James. "Ernest W. McFarland: Southwestern Progressive, the United States Senate Years, 1940–1952." Ph.D. diss., Arizona State University, 1990.

―――. "Style vs. Substance: The 1952 and 1958 Goldwater-McFarland Campaigns." Conference paper, Arizona and New Mexico State Historical Societies, 1990.

Magruder, Jeb Stuart. *An American Life: One Man's Road to Watergate*. New York: Atheneum, 1974.

Malone, Michael P., and Etulain, Richard W. *The American West: A Twentieth-Century History*. Lincoln: University of Nebraska Press, 1989.

Mann, Dean E. *The Politics of Water in Arizona*. Tucson: University of Arizona Press, 1963.

Marks, Barnett E. "An Arizona Visit to Phoenix, Miami, and Tucson in 1919." *Western States Jewish History* 15 (April 1983): 214–17.

Marshall, Jonathan; Scott, Peter Dale; and Hunter, Jane. *The Iran-Contra Connection: Secret Teams and Covert Operations in the Reagan Era*. Boston: South End Press, 1987.

Martin, Serge G. "The President's Power to Terminate Treaties—The Unanswered Question of Goldwater v. Carter." *Journal of International Law and Economics* 14 (1980): 301–19.

Mason, Bruce, ed. *Arizona General Election Results, 1911–1960*. Tempe, Ariz.: Bureau of Government Research, 1961.

Matusow, Allen J. *The Unraveling of America: A History of Liberalism in the 1960s*. New York: Harper and Row, 1986.

Mayer, George H. *The Republican Party, 1854–1964*. New York: Oxford University Press, 1964.

Mazo, Earl, and Hess, Stephen. *Nixon: A Political Portrait*. New York: Popular Library, 1968.

Meinig, D. W. *Southwest: Three People in Geographical Change: 1600–1970*. New York: Oxford University Press, 1971.

Melcher, Mary. "Blacks and Whites Together: Interracial Leadership in the Phoenix Civil Rights Movement." *Journal of Arizona History* 32 (Summer 1991): 195–216.

Meyer, Frank S. *The Conservative Mainstream*. New Rochelle, N.Y.: Arlington House, 1969.

Meyer, Louis S. "Federal Grants-in-Aid and States' Rights in Arizona." Ph.D. diss., University of Arizona, 1964.

Miles, Michael W. *The Odyssey of the American Right*. New York: Oxford University Press, 1980.

Miller, Alice. *The Drama of the Gifted Child*. New York: Basic Books, 1981.

———. *For Your Own Good: Hidden Cruelty in Child-Rearing and the Roots of Violence*. New York: Farrar, Straus and Giroux, 1990.

———. Miller, Darlis A. "Civilians and Military Supply in the Southwest." *Journal of Arizona History* 23 (Summer 1982): 115–38.

Miller, Merle. *Lyndon: An Oral Biography*. New York: Ballantine, 1980.

Miroff, Bruce. *Pragmatic Illusions: The Presidential Politics of John F. Kennedy*. New York: McKay, 1976.

Moffett, George D. III. *The Limits of Victory: The Ratification of the Panama Canal Treaties*. Ithaca, N.Y.: Cornell University Press, 1985.

Moore, Mark Paul. "Individuals Unite: Paradox as a Rhetorical Strategy in the Political Discourse of Barry Goldwater and the Resurgence of Conservatism in American Politics, 1950–1964." Ph.D. diss., Indiana University, 1984.

Moos, Malcolm. *The Republicans: A History of Their Party*. New York: Random House, 1956.

Morley, Jefferson. "Bush and the Blacks: An Unknown Story." *New York Review of Books*, January 16, 1992, 19–26.

Morris, Joe Alex. *Nelson Rockefeller: A Biography*. New York: Harper and Bros., 1960.

Moser, Don. *China-Burma-India*. Alexandria, Va.: Time-Life Books, 1978.

Mowry, Sylvester. *Memoir of the Proposed Territory of Arizona*. Washington, D.C.: Henry Polkinhorn Printer, 1857.

Mullen, James J. "Newspaper Advertising in the Johnson-Goldwater Campaign." *Journalism Quarterly* 45 (Summer 1968): 219–25.

Murphy, Pat. "A Visit with Barry." *Phoenix* 26 (November 1991): 126–31.

———. "Riding a Racehorse Named Growth." *Phoenix* 26 (November 1991): 86–89.

Nadeau, Remi A. *The Water Seekers*. Santa Barbara, Calif.: Peregrine Smith, 1974.

Nash, George H. *The Conservative Intellectual Movement in America Since 1945*. New York: Basic Books, 1976.

Nash, Gerald D. *The American West in the Twentieth Century: A Short History of an Urban Oasis*. Englewood Cliffs, N.J.: Prentice Hall, 1973.

———. *The American West Transformed: The Impact of the Second World War*. Lincoln: University of Nebraska Press, 1985.

———. *World War II and the West: Reshaping the Economy*. Lincoln: University of Nebraska Press, 1990.

Nash, Gerald D., and Etulain, Richard W., eds. *The Twentieth-Century West: Historical Interpretations*. Albuquerque: University of New Mexico Press, 1989.

Newhall, Richard. "Barry Goldwater." *Point West Magazine*, March 1966, 18–21.

Niebur, Jay Edward. "The Social and Economic Effect of the Great Depression on Phoenix, Arizona, 1929–1934." Master's thesis, Arizona State University, 1966.

Nisbet, Robert. *Conservatism: Dream and Reality*. Minneapolis: University of Minnesota Press, 1986.

Nixon, Richard M. *RN: The Memoirs of Richard Nixon*. New York: Grosset and Dunlap, 1978.

Noonan, Peggy. *What I Saw at the Revolution: A Political Life in the Reagan Era*. New York: Ballantine, 1990.

Norman's Who's Who for Arizona, 1951–1952. Portland, Ore.: R. O. Norman, 1952.

Novak, Robert D. *The Agony of the G.O.P.: 1964*. New York: Macmillan, 1965.

Nuechterlein, James. "Mr. Right." *Commentary* 86 (November 1988): 70–73.

O'Donnell, Kenneth P., and Powers, David F. *"Johnny, We Hardly Knew Ye:" Memories of John Fitzgerald Kennedy*. Boston: Little, Brown, 1970.

Ogden, Daniel M., Jr., and Peterson, Arthur. *Electing the President: 1964*. San Francisco: Chandler, 1968.

Osherson, Samuel. *Finding Our Fathers: The Unfinished Business of Manhood*. New York: Free Press, 1986.

Oshinsky, David M. *A Conspiracy So Immense: The World of Joe McCarthy*. New York: Free Press, 1983.

Parish, William J. "The German Jew and the Commercial Revolution in Territorial New Mexico." *New Mexico Quarterly* 29 (Fall 1959): 307–32.

Parker, Charles Franklin. *When the Smoki Dance*. Prescott, Ariz.: Peterson, Brooke, and Steiner, 1941.

Parker, Jeanette R. "*Dr. Strangelove*, Nuclear Annihilation, and Public Paranoia: Welcome to the War Room!" Seminar Paper, University of Utah, 1993.

Parmet, Herbert S. *JFK: The Presidency of John F. Kennedy*. New York: Dial, 1983.

Patterson, James T. *Mr. Republican: A Biography of Robert A. Taft*. Boston: Houghton Mifflin, 1972.

Peele, Gillian. *Revival and Reaction: The Right in Contemporary America*. New York: Oxford University Press, 1984.

Peplow, Edward, Jr. "The Goldwater Mystique." *Phoenix* 16 (September 1981): 102–10.

———. *The Taming of the Salt*. Phoenix: Salt River Project, 1979.

Perry, David C., and Watkins, Alfred J., eds. *The Rise of the Sunbelt Cities*. Beverly Hills, Calif.: Sage Publications, 1977.

Perry, James Moorhead. *Barry Goldwater: A New Look at a Presidential Candidate*. Silver Spring, Md.: National Observer, 1964.

Persico, Joseph E. *Casey: From the OSS to the CIA*. New York: Viking, 1990.

Pfister, A. J. *The Salt River Project: "Keeping the Spirit Strong."* New York: Newcomen Society of the United States, 1987.

Phillippi, Mary Jane. "Arizona, A Conservative Stronghold: Barry Goldwater Tells Why." *Arizona Today* 1 (October 1962): 6–8, 29, 31.

Phillips, Kevin P. *The Emerging Republican Majority*. New Rochelle, N.Y.: Arlington House, 1969.

———. *The Politics of Rich and Poor: Wealth and the American Electorate in the Reagan Aftermath*. New York: Random House, 1990.

———. *Post-Conservative America: People, Politics, and Ideology in a Time of Crisis.* New York: Vintage, 1982.

Pinart, Alphonse. *Journey to Arizona in 1876.* Los Angeles: Zamorano Club, 1962.

Pitt, Leonard. *The Decline of the Californios: A Social History of the Spanish-Speaking Californians, 1846–1890.* Berkeley: University of California Press, 1966.

Piven, Frances Fox, and Cloward, Richard A. *The New Class War: Reagan's Attack on the Welfare State and Its Consequences.* New York: Pantheon, 1982.

———. *Poor People's Movements: Why They Succeed, How They Fail.* New York: Pantheon, 1977.

Pollock, Paul W. *Arizona's Men of Achievement.* Vol. 1. Phoenix: self-published, 1958.

Porter, Sharon Bowers. "A Rhetorical Analysis of the Speaking of Barry Morris Goldwater, 1969–1974." Ph.D. diss., Louisiana State University, 1980.

Powell, John Wesley. *Report on the Land of the Arid Regions of the United States.* Cambridge: Harvard University Press, 1962.

Powell, Lawrence Clark. *Arizona: A History.* Albuquerque: University of New Mexico Press, 1990.

Previdi, Robert. *Civilian Control Versus Military Rule.* New York: Hippocrene, 1988.

Pry, Mark. "Uncertain Enterprise: Business Proprietorship and Proprietors in Phoenix, Arizona, 1880–1900." Conference paper, Pacific Coast Branch of the American Historical Association, 1990.

"The Public Record of Barry Goldwater." Special Report, *Congressional Quarterly* 21 (September 20, 1963): 1593–1625.

"The Question of Presidential Power." *Congressional Digest* 58 (June–July 1979): 161, 192.

Quinn, William. "Memoirs." Manuscript, 1991.

Rader, Dotson. "What Does Barry Goldwater Say Today?" *Parade Magazine,* November 28, 1993, 4–6.

Rae, Nicol C. *The Decline and Fall of the Liberal Republicans from 1952 to the Present.* New York: Oxford University Press, 1989.

Ragan, Sam. "Dixie Looked Away." *American Scholar* 34 (Spring 1965): 202–12.

Ranelagh, John. *The Agency: The Rise and Decline of the CIA.* New York: Simon and Schuster, 1986.

"Reaction to Goldwater: Leader or Legend?" *Conservative Digest* 1 (March 1976): 2–3.

Reagan, Ronald. *An American Life.* New York: Simon and Schuster, 1990.

———. *Speaking My Mind.* New York: Simon and Schuster, 1989.

Reagan, Ronald, with Hubler, Richard G. *"Where's the Rest of Me?"* New York: Duell, Sloan, and Pearce, 1965.

Reed, James. *From Private Vice to Public Virtue.* New York: Basic Books, 1987.

Reichly, James. *Conservatives in an Age of Change: The Nixon and Ford Administrations.* Washington, D.C.: Brookings Institution, 1981.

Reid, Ed, and Demaris, Ovid. *The Green Felt Jungle.* New York: Trident Press, 1963.

Reinhard, David W. *The Republican Right Since 1945.* Lexington: University Press of Kentucky, 1983.

Reisner, Marc. *Cadillac Desert: The American West and Its Disappearing Water*. New York: Penguin, 1986.

Reuther, Victor C. *The Brothers Reuther*. Boston: Houghton Mifflin, 1976.

Rex, Tom R. "Arizona Industrial Structure: Services and Trade Rank One and Two." *Arizona Business* 33 (November 1986): 1–5.

Ribuffo, Leo P. *The Old Christian Right: The Protestant Far Right from the Great Depression to the Cold War*. Philadelphia: Temple University Press, 1983.

Rice, Ross R. "The 1958 Election in Arizona." *Western Political Quarterly* 12 (March 1959): 166–76.

———. "The 1964 Election in the West." *Western Political Quarterly* 18 (June 1965): 431–38.

Richberg, Donald R. *Labor Union Monopoly: A Clear and Present Danger*. Chicago: Henry Regnery, 1957.

Ridenhour, Ron. "The Pentagon's Payroll in Arizona." *Today's Business* 6 (March 25, 1981): 12–16.

Rigby, Douglas. *Desert Happy*. Philadelphia: J. B. Lippincott, 1957.

Riordan, William L. *Plunkitt of Tammany Hall*. New York: E. P. Dutton, 1963.

Rischin, Moses, and Livingston, John. *Jews of the American West*. Detroit: Wayne State University, 1991.

Roberts, James C. *The Conservative Decade: Emerging Leaders of the 1980s*. Westport, Conn.: Arlington House, 1980.

Robinson, W. A. "Progress of Integration in Phoenix Schools." *Journal of Negro Education* 25 (Fall 1956): 371–79.

Rochlin, Harriet, and Rochlin, Fred. *Pioneer Jews: A New Life in the Far West*. Boston: Houghton Mifflin, 1984.

Rogin, Michael Paul. *The Intellectuals and McCarthy: The Radical Specter*. Cambridge: MIT Press, 1967.

Rohter, Ira. "Radical Rightists: An Empirical Study." Ph.D. diss., Michigan State University, 1967.

Romer, Margaret. "From Boulder to the Gulf." *Historical Society of Southern California* 5 (March 1953): 68–73.

Rose, Dick. "Barry, 1982." *Arizona*, July 4, 1982, 4–5, 14.

Rosenau, James N. *The Nomination of Chip Bohlen*. New York: Henry Holt, 1958.

Rosenthal, Paul I. "The Republican National Convention." *Quarterly Journal of Speech* 50 (December 1964): 394–99.

Rossiter, Clinton. *Conservatism in America: The Thankless Persuasion*. 2nd ed. New York: Vintage, 1962.

Rovere, Richard H. *The Goldwater Caper*. New York: Harcourt, Brace and World, 1965.

———. *Senator Joe McCarthy*. New York: Harper and Row, 1959.

Rusher, William A. *The Rise of the Right*. New York: William Morrow, 1984.

———. "What Happened to Barry?" *Conservative Digest* 1 (April 1976): 16.

Safer, Morley. *Flashbacks: On Returning to Vietnam*. New York: Random House, 1990.

Sale, Kirkpatrick. *Power Shift: The Rise of the Southern Rim and Its Challenge to the Eastern Establishment*. New York: Vintage, 1975.

Saloma, John S. III. *Ominous Politics: The New Conservative Labyrinth*. New York: Hill and Wang, 1984.

"Samuel Drachman—Arizona Pioneer." *Western States Jewish History* 20 (October 1987): 60–61.

Satir, Virginia. *Peoplemaking*. Palo Alto, Calif.: Science and Behavior Books, 1972.

Scammon, Richard. *America at the Polls*. Pittsburgh: Pittsburgh University Press, 1965.

Scammon, Richard, and Wattenberg, Ben J. *The Real Majority*. New York: Coward-McCann, 1970.

Schiller, Craig. *The (Guilty) Conscience of a Conservative*. New Rochelle, N.Y.: Arlington House, 1978.

Schlafly, Phyllis. *A Choice Not An Echo*. Alton, Ill.: Pere Marquette Press, 1964.

Schlereth, Thomas J. *Victorian America: Transformations in Everyday Life, 1876–1915*. New York: HarperCollins, 1991.

Schlesinger, Arthur M., Jr. *A Thousand Days: John F. Kennedy in the White House*. New York: Fawcett Crest, 1965.

———. *The Imperial Presidency*. New York: Houghton Mifflin, 1973.

Schlesinger, Arthur M., Jr., ed. *History of American Presidential Elections, 1789–1968*. 4 vols. New York: McGraw-Hill, 1971.

Schorr, Daniel. *Clearing the Air*. Boston: Houghton Mifflin, 1977.

Schuparra, Kurt. "Barry Goldwater and Southern California Conservatism: Ideology, Image and Myth in the 1964 Presidential Primary." *Southern California Quarterly* 74 (Fall 1992): 277–98.

Segal, David R. "Partisan Realignment in the United States: The Lessons of the 1964 Election." *Public Opinion Quarterly* 32 (Fall 1968): 441–44.

Sellers, William D., and Hill, Richard H., eds. *Arizona Climate, 1931–1972*. Tucson: University of Arizona Press, 1974.

Sevareid, Eric. "Over the Hump." In *World War II in the Air: The Pacific,* James F. Sunderman, ed. New York: Bramhall House, 1962.

———. "They're Closing on the Great Open Spaces." *Reader's Digest,* February 1963, 196–98.

Shadegg, Stephen C. *Arizona Politics: The Struggle to End One-Party Rule*. Tempe: Arizona State University Press, 1986.

———. *Barry Goldwater: Freedom Is His Flight Plan*. New York: Macfadden-Bartell, 1962.

———. *How to Win an Election: The Art of Political Victory*. New York: Taplinger, 1964.

———. *What Happened to Goldwater? The Inside Story of the 1964 Republican Campaign*. New York: Holt Rinehart and Winston, 1965.

Shahin, Jim. "Desert Patriarch." *American Way,* April 15, 1989, 61–69, 110.

Shalit, Gene, and Grossman, Lawrence K., eds. *Somehow It Works*. Garden City, N.Y.: Doubleday, 1965.

Shapley, Deborah. *Promise and Power: The Life and Times of Robert McNamara*. Boston: Little, Brown, 1993.

Sharfman, I. Harold. *Jews on the Frontier*. Chicago: Henry Regnery, 1977.

Sheehan, Neil; Smith, Hedrick; Kenworthy, E. W.; and Butterfield, Fox. *The Pentagon Papers*. New York: Bantam, 1971.

Shirer, John. "Business in Arizona, 1929–1951, As Reflected in Phoenix Department Store Sales." *Arizona Business and Economic Review* 1 (March 1952): 1–6.

Silvers, Arthur L., and Shelnutt, John. "Sectoral Bases of Economic Growth in Arizona: 1967–1986." *Arizona Review* 35 (Spring 1987): 19–35.

Sloan, Richard E., and Adams, Ward R. *History of Arizona*. 4 vols. Phoenix: Record Publishing, 1930.

Smith, Dean. *Conservatism: A Guide to Its Past, Present and Future in American Politics*. New York: Avon, 1963.

———. *The Goldwaters of Arizona*. Flagstaff, Ariz.: Northland Press, 1986.

Smith, Gaddis. *Morality, Reason, and Power: American Diplomacy in the Carter Years*. New York: Hill and Wang, 1986.

Snider, Don M. "DOD Reorganization: Part I, New Imperatives." *Parameters* 17 (September 1987): 88–100.

———. "DOD Reorganization: Part II, New Opportunities." *Parameters* 17 (December 1987): 49–58.

Sorensen, Theodore C. *Kennedy*. New York: Harper and Row, 1965.

Spencer, Otha C. *Flying the Hump: Memories of an Air War*. College Station: Texas A & M University Press, 1992.

Stans, Maurice H. *The Terrors of Justice: The Untold Side of Watergate*. New York: Everest House, 1978.

Steinfels, Peter. "The Goldwater Myth." *Commonwealth* 99 (February 1, 1974): 431.

———. *The Neoconservatives: The Men Who Are Changing America's Politics*. New York: Simon and Schuster, 1979.

Stempel, Guido H. III. "The Prestige Press in Two Presidential Elections." *Journalism Quarterly* 42 (Winter 1965): 15–21.

Stern, Norton B. "Herman Bendell: Superintendent of Indian Affairs, Arizona Territory, 1871–1873." *Western States Jewish History* 8 (April 1976): 265–82.

———. "The Tombstone, Arizona Jewish Saga." *Western States Jewish History* 19 (April 1987): 217–30.

Stern, Norton B., and Kramer, William M. "Arizona's Mining Wizard: Black Jack Newman." *Western States Jewish History* 11 (April 1979): 255–64.

———. "The Major Role of Polish Jews in the Pioneer West." *Western States Jewish History* 8 (July 1976): 326–44.

———. "Mayor Strauss of Tucson." *Western States Jewish History* 12 (July 1980): 347–69.

———. "Some Further Notes on Michel Goldwater." *Western States Jewish History* 5 (October 1972): 36–39.

———. "Who Was Isaacson, Arizona, Named For?" *Western States Jewish History* 19 (January 1987): 121–24.

Stilp, Peter. "Operation MARS." *Phoenix* 3 (April 1968): 20–21.

Stocker, Joseph. *Jewish Roots in Arizona*. Phoenix: Phoenix Jewish Community Council, 1954.

———. "The Pleasant Primitive." *Frontier* 5 (January 1954): 10–11.

———. "A Real Western Welcome." *Frontier* 1 (June 1, 1950): 7–9.

Stockman, David A. *The Triumph of Politics: Why the Reagan Revolution Failed.* New York: Harper and Row, 1986.

Stolley, Richard B. "The Senator's Pioneer Mother Talks About Barry and Herself." *Life*, July 12, 1963.

Stone, Barbara. "The John Birch Society of California." Ph.D. diss., University of Southern California, 1968.

Stone, Chuck. "An In-Depth Look at Senator Barry Goldwater's Senatorial Career from 1968 to 1974." Manuscript, 1984, Arizona Historical Foundation.

Stringfellow, William. "God, Guilt and Goldwater." *The Christian Century* 81 (September 2, 1964): 1079–83.

Summers, Harry G., Jr. *On Strategy II: A Critical Analysis of the Gulf War.* New York: Dell, 1992.

"The Taiwan Treaty Termination Lawsuit." *Congressional Digest* 58 (June–July 1979): 166, 168, 192.

Tansik, David A., and Billings, R. Bruce. "Current Impact of Military-Industrial Spending in Arizona." *Arizona Review* 20 (August–September 1971): 11–20.

———. "The Rise of Military-Industrial Spending in Arizona: 1970–1972." *Arizona Review* 22 (June–July 1973): 1–9.

Terman, Lewis. *The Measurement of Intelligence.* Boston: Houghton Mifflin, 1916.

Terrell, John. *War for the Colorado River: The California-Arizona Controversy.* 2 vols. Glendale, Calif.: Arthur Clark, 1965.

Thomas, Clive S., ed. *Politics and Public Policy in the Contemporary American West.* Albuquerque: University of New Mexico Press, 1991.

Thomas, Evan. *The Man to See: Edward Bennett Williams: Ultimate Insider; Legendary Trial Lawyer.* New York: Simon and Schuster, 1991.

Thompson, Steffney. "The Arizona Economy: A History to 1900." *Arizona Review* 33 (Winter 1985): 26–34.

———. "Arizona's Economic Development: The Middle Years, 1900–1970." *Arizona Review* 34 (Spring 1986): 22–32.

Thorne, Bliss K. *The Hump: The Great Military Airlift of World War II.* Philadelphia: J. B. Lippincott, 1965.

Tindall, George Brown. *America: A Narrative History.* 2 vols. New York: Norton, 1988.

———. *The Disruption of the Solid South.* Athens: University of Georgia Press, 1972.

Toffler, Alvin. "The Woman Behind Barry Goldwater." *Good Housekeeping*, May 1964, 58, 60, 62, 64–65.

de Toledano, Ralph. *The Winning Side: The Case for Goldwater Conservatism.* New York: G. P. Putnam's Sons, 1963.

Toy, Eckard V., Jr. "Ideology and Conflict in American Ultra Conservatism, 1945–1960." Ph.D. diss., University of Oregon, 1965.

Tunner, William H. *Over the Hump.* New York: Duell, Sloan, and Pearce, 1964.

Tyler, S. Lyman. *A History of Indian Policy.* Washington, D.C.: U.S. Department of Interior, 1973.

————. *Indian Affairs: A Work Paper on Termination with an Attempt to Show Its Antecedents.* Provo, Utah: Institute of American Indian Studies, 1964.

Tyrrell, R. Emmett, Jr. *The Conservative Crack-Up.* New York: Simon and Schuster, 1992.

U.S. Congress. House. Subcommitee on Indian Affairs. *Partition of Navajo and Hopi 1882 Reservation,* 93rd Cong., 1st sess., 1973.

————. House. Subcommittee on Irrigation and Reclamation. *The Central Arizona Project,* 81st Cong., 1st sess., 1949.

————. Senate. Committee on Armed Services. *Organization, Structure and Decisionmaking Procedures of the Department of Defense,* 98th Cong., 1st sess., 1983.

————. Senate. Committee on Banking and Currency. *Standby Economic Controls,* 83rd Cong., 1st sess., 1953.

————. Senate. Select Committee on Improper Activities in the Labor or Management Field. *Investigation of Improper Activities in the Labor or Management Field,* 85th Cong., 1st and 2nd sess., 1957–58.

————. Senate. Select Committee to Study Government Operations with Respect to Intelligence Activities. "Individual Views of Senator Barry Goldwater. *Senate Reports,* 94th Cong., 2nd sess., 1976.

————. Senate. Subcommittee on Indian Affairs. *Federal Indian Policy,* 85th Cong., 1st sess., 1957.

————. Senate. Subcommittee on Indian Affairs. *Termination of Federal Supervision over Certain Tribes of Indians.* 83rd Cong., 2nd sess., 1954.

————. Senate. Subcommittee on Indian Affairs. *Transfer of Indian Hospitals and Health Facilities to Public Health Service.* 83rd Cong., 2nd sess., 1954.

U.S. Department of Commerce, Bureau of the Census. *Census of Religious Bodies: 1916.*

————. *Census of Religious Bodies: 1926.*

————. *Eleventh Census of the Uni⌐ed States, 1890.* Reports on Population and Agriculture.

————. *Fifteenth Census of the United States, 1930.* Reports on Occupations, Population, Agriculture, and Manufactures.

————. *Fourteenth Census of the United States, 1920.* Reports on Occupations, Population, Agriculture, and Manufactures.

————. *Ninth Census of the United States, 1870.* Reports on Population and Industry and Wealth.

————. *Seventeenth Census of the United States, 1950.* Report on Population.

————. *Sixteenth Census of the United States, 1940.* Reports on Population, Agriculture, and Manufactures.

————. *Thirteenth Census of the United States, 1910.* Reports on Population, Occupations, Agriculture, and Manufactures.

————. *Twelfth Census of the United States, 1900.* Report on Population.

Uphoff, Walter H. *Kohler on Strike: Thirty Years of Conflict.* Boston: Beacon Press, 1966.

Van den Bosch, Govert W., ed. *Political Issues and Business in 1964.* Ann Arbor, Mich.: Foundation for Research on Human Behavior, 1964.

Van Dyke, John C. *The Desert.* New York: Scribner, 1901.

Vest, Marshall J. "Arizona's Economic Outlook." *Arizona Review* 28 (1st quarter, 1980): 11–22.

Viguerie, Richard. "Facts from Fiction: From the Publisher." *Conservative Digest* 1 (January 1976): 1.

————. *The New Right: We're Ready to Lead.* Falls Church, Va.: Viguerie, 1980.

Viguerie, Richard, and Edwards, Lee. "Goldwater: Leader or Legend?" *Conservative Digest* 1 (January 1976): 6–10.

Wade, Michael S. *The Bitter Issue: The Right to Work Law in Arizona.* Tucson: Arizona Historical Society, 1976.

Wagner, Ronnie Lynn. "The Conservative Vision of American Politics in the Campaign Biographies of Barry Goldwater." Ph.D. diss., University of Arizona, 1976.

Walker, Lawrence J., and Taylor, John H. "Family Interactions and the Development of Moral Reasoning." *Child Development* 62 (1991): 264–83.

Waltz, Waldo E. "Arizona: A State of New-Old Frontiers." In *Rocky Mountain Politics,* Thomas C. Donnelly, ed. Albuquerque: University of New Mexico Press, 1940.

Watkins, Ronald J. *High Crimes and Misdemeanors: The Term and Trials of Former Governor Evan Mecham.* New York: William Morrow, 1990.

Wegscheider-Cruse, Sharon. *Another Chance: Hope and Health for the Alcoholic Family.* Palo Alto, Calif.: Science and Behavior Books, 1989.

Weigley, Russell F. *Eisenhower's Lieutenants: The Campaign of France and Germany, 1944–1945.* Bloomington: Indiana University Press, 1981.

Weinstein, Bernard L.; Gross, Harold T.; and Rees, John. *Regional Growth and Decline in the United States.* New York: Praeger, 1985.

Weinstock, Robert. "Senator Barry Goldwater Traces Economic Development of Phoenix." *Phoenix Business Journal,* n.v. (November 30, 1981): 12–15.

Weisberg, Goldie. "Panorama: Phoenix, Arizona." *American Mercury* 4 (May 1929): 96–103.

Welch, Robert. *The Blue Book of the John Birch Society.* 9th printing. Belmont, Mass.: Western Islands, 1961.

————. *The Life of John Birch.* Boston: Henry Regnery, 1954.

————. *The New Americanism: And Other Speeches and Essays.* Belmont, Mass.: n.p., 1966.

———. *The Politician*. Belmont, Mass.: Western Islands, 1963.

Wells, A. J. "A Blossoming Desert." *Sunset*, August 1909, 209–14.

Wendland, Michael F. *The Arizona Project: How a Team of Investigative Reporters Got Revenge on Deadline*. Kansas City, Kan.: Sheed, Andrews and McMeel, 1977.

Wenzel, Joseph W. "The Moderate Republicans: Campaign for the Nomination, Rockefeller, Lodge, Scranton." *Quarterly Journal of Speech* 50 (December 1964): 385–90.

Whalen, Charles, and Whalen, Barbara. *The Longest Debate: A Legislative History of the 1964 Civil Rights Act*. Washington, D.C.: Seven Locks Press, 1985.

Whitaker, Robert W., ed. *The New Right Papers*. New York: St. Martin's Press, 1982.

White, F. Clifton. *Suite 3505: The Story of the Draft Goldwater Movement*. New Rochelle, N.Y.: Arlington House, 1967.

White, F. Clifton, and Gill, William J. *Why Reagan Won: A Narrative History of the Conservative Movement, 1964–1981*. Chicago: Regnery Gateway, 1981.

White, John P. "The 1964 Election in Arizona." *Western Political Quarterly* 18, part 2 (June 1965): 443–50.

White, Theodore H. *Breach of Faith: The Fall of Richard Nixon*. New York: Dell, 1975.

———. *The Making of the President 1960*. New York: Atheneum, 1961.

———. *The Making of the President 1964*. New York: Atheneum, 1965.

———. *The Making of the President 1968*. New York: Atheneum, 1969.

———. *The Making of the President 1972*. New York: Atheneum, 1973.

Whitson, Hollis A. "A Policy Review of the Federal Government's Relocation of Navajo Indians Under P.L. 93–531 and P.L. 96–305." *Arizona Law Review* 27 (1985): 371–414.

Who's Who in America, 1946–1947. Vol. 24. Chicago: A. N. Manquis, 1946.

Wildavsky, Adam. "The Goldwater Phenomenon: Purists, Politicians, and the Two-Party System." *Review of Politics* 27 (July 1965): 386–413.

Wiley, Peter, and Gottlieb, Robert. *Empires in the Sun: The Rise of the New American West*. Tucson: University of Arizona Press, 1982.

Wills, Garry. "The Hostage." *New York Review of Books*, August 13, 1992, 21–27.

———. *Nixon Agonistes: The Crisis of the Self-Made Man*. New York: New American Library, 1979.

———. *Reagan's America: Innocents at Home*. Garden City, N.Y.: Doubleday, 1987.

Wilson, Don W. "Pioneer Jews in California and Arizona, 1849–1875." *Journal of the West* 6 (April 1967): 226–36.

Winkelman, Richard D. "Arizona: A Quarter-Century of Economic Progress." *Arizona Business* 27 (February 1980): 3–8.

Witcover, Jules. *Marathon: The Pursuit of the Presidency, 1972–1976*. New York: Viking, 1977.

Wolfe, Donald Thomas. "Southern Strategy: Race, Region, and Republican Presidential Politics, 1964 and 1968." Ph.D. diss., Johns Hopkins University, 1974.

Wolfe, Gregory. *Right Minds: A Sourcebook of American Conservative Thought.* Chicago: Regnery Books, 1987.

Wollenberg, Charles M. "Recollections of Arizona, 1876–1891." *Western States Jewish History* 15 (October 1982): 31–39.

Wood, Rob, and Smith, Dean. *Barry Goldwater: The Biography of a Conservative.* New York: Avon, 1961.

Woodin, Ann. *Home Is the Desert.* New York: Macmillan, 1964.

Woodward, Bob. *Veil: The Secret Wars of the CIA, 1981–1987.* New York: Pocket Books, 1987.

Woodward, Bob, and Bernstein, Carl. *The Final Days.* New York: Simon and Schuster, 1976.

Wormuth, Francis D., and Firmage, Edwin B. *To Chain the Dog of War: The War Power of Congress in History and Law.* Dallas: Southern Methodist University Press, 1986.

Worster, Donald. *Rivers of Empire: Water, Aridity, and the Growth of the American West.* New York: Pantheon, 1985.

Wrage, Ernest J. "The Little World of Barry Goldwater." In *Methods of Rhetorical Criticism,* Robert Scott and Bernard Brock, eds. New York: Harper and Row, 1972.

Wright, Barton. *Kachinas: The Barry Goldwater Collection at the Heard Museum.* Phoenix: W. A. Krueger, 1975.

Wyllys, Rufus. *Arizona: The History of a Frontier State.* Phoenix: Hobson and Herr, 1950.

———. "The Historical Geography of Arizona." *Pacific Historical Review* 21 (June 1952): 121–28.

Yambert, Ralph F. "The Flying Clerks of Phoenix." *Flying* 39 (December 1946): 56–58, 128, 130.

Yenne, Bill. *The History of the Southern Pacific.* New York: Bison Books, 1985.

Index